P9-DHL-719

Vocational Guidance and Career Development

Vocational Guidance and Career Development

Selected Readings

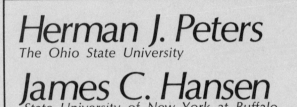

Herman J. Peters
The Ohio State University

James C. Hansen
State University of New York at Buffalo

Third Edition

Macmillan Publishing Co., Inc.
New York

Collier Macmillan Publishers
London

Copyright © 1977, Macmillan Publishing
Co., Inc.

Printed in the United States of America

All rights reserved. No part of this book
may be reproduced or transmitted in any
form or by any means, electronic or
mechanical, including photocopying,
recording, or any information storage
and retrieval system, without permission
in writing from the Publisher.

Earlier editions copyright © 1971 by
Macmillan Publishing Co., Inc., and
copyright © 1966 by Herman J. Peters and
James C. Hansen.

Macmillan Publishing Co., Inc.
866 Third Avenue, New York, New York
10022

Collier Macmillan Canada, Ltd.

Library of Congress Cataloging in Publication Data

Peters, Herman Jacob, (date)   ed.
    Vocational guidance and career development.

    Includes bibliographies.
    1. Vocational guidance—Addresses, essays, lec-
tures. I. Hansen, James C. II. Title.
HF5381.P46   1977   371.4′25′08
76-40475
ISBN 0-02-394670-9

Printing: 345678   Year: 890123

Preface to the Third Edition

As never before, career education and its complement, vocational guidance, are the top priorities in education. Guidance is a major factor in the full development of each educational movement, as the renaissance of the work ethic attests.

The impetus provided by technological advances to improved quality in the education profession is sustained in many ways, but it has especially sharpened interest in the individual, his job, and his life style. It is this increased concern that has given career education and vocational guidance a new respectability and renewed effectiveness. We believe such guidance will result in optimal career development.

This book of readings provides access to articles that complement standard informational sources. The process of selection, however, was made difficult by an imbalance between information-oriented articles and articles stressing assistance in vocational choice (through means other than the usual general counseling procedure) and placement. Many articles on vocational guidance disseminate occupational information. Few discuss the use of this information. In the first edition we stated that the close relationships between industry and education and between education and leisure made it seem the wiser course to stress materials for the counselor and to concentrate on guidance for the average individual, rather than to emphasize special aspects of guidance; hence the development of most individuals is encompassed by the included articles. However, the emphasis is on work not welfare for all, and some special articles are included.

Our decision to divide this anthology into eleven sections was dictated largely by the materials available. Part 1 explores various concepts and issues of work, Part 2 focuses on society's dimensions of work (with consequent implications for career guidance), and Part 3 emphasizes career education and career development. As discussed by an article in Part 1 we have omitted a section on theories because they seem to be going nowhere. They reflect the obvious: once you have basic skills, the economy, who you know, and your personality become the critical differences. We wonder why there are so few articles on these topics. Parts 4, 5, 6, and 7 take up information procedures, general guidance procedures, counseling procedures, and placement. Caution is advised in the use of interests inventories—most are useless or are improperly applied. In Part 8 the articles reflect the continuing process of vocational development from the elementary through the college level. Part 9 discusses vocational guidance and career development for the adult. Part 10 discusses the continuing needs in adult vocational guidance and career development for the disadvantaged. Part 11 discusses vocational guidance and career development of women.

It is expected that the primary reader of this collection will be the counselor in a school, college, or community agency working with youth. Because of its coverage and direct relevance for counselors in a number of settings—in school, college, vocational education, and employment service work—we believe that this book should be used as a text in courses variously labeled occupational information, vocational development theories, vocational guidance, school resources, and the information services.

The compilation of material represents the fruitful thinking of many people. It is impractical to give specific acknowledgment to all of them, but we do appreciate the kindness of those colleagues who gave permission to reprint their articles here.

H. J. P.

J. C. H.

Contents

part 9 Career Development: Adulthood

*part 10 Vocational Guidance and Career
Development of the Disadvantaged*

part 11   *Vocational Guidance and Career Development of Women*

part 1
Work

Our life style is central to whatever else we do. Today this is often referred to as career education. A major part of career education—which is developmental in nature—is work, particularly a specific job with its tasks, processes, and goals. Work is a central activity of human existence and continues to be so despite threats of automation, overpopulation, underemployment, affluence, lethargy, confusion over appropriate and inappropriate welfare approaches, and relationships of the United States' work market with the world—in particular, third-force or the new emerging nations.

The nature of vocational guidance and career development reflects the place of work in society. Most people take work for granted; it is a necessity. This does not mean that people can fully realize what work means to them. Although leisure, better home living, and social participation are emphasized in the United States, work continues to be the central demand of modern living. The other activities of daily living depend in large measure on the nature and conditions of one's work and on whether it is enjoyed.

Our society considers it only natural that each member enter the labor force. From childhood on, we are often asked, "What do you want to be?" We are always aware that it is necessary to focus on at least an occupational field, if not a specific job area within it. Work is the means of meeting needs in other areas of life; awareness of it must begin in childhood.

Work has not always been universally considered dignified.[1] To the ancient Greeks, work was a curse; the Romans thought much of work was vulgar; and the ancient Hebrews thought it was a form of drudgery. The modern attitude toward work evolved slowly after the beginning of Christianity. Now work is emerging as more than a method for earning a living and is becoming a means of achieving satisfaction for one's self, family, and community.

It is interesting to note that the vocational guidance movement is just giving proper attention to work as a philosophical-sociological

[1] Adriano Tilgher, *Work: What It Has Meant Through the Ages*, trans. by Dorothy C. Fisher (Chicago: Henry Regnery Company, 1964).

dimension. *Scattered articles offer some excellent starts, but there is a need to examine some of the conceptual constructs relating to work.*

The following articles illustrate a variety of approaches to the nature of work. These (and others [2]) are the substance of vocational guidance. In this section the reader will find provocative articles ranging from work as a realistic ethic to work as a developmental model for one full life. The development of early occupational attainment and vocational education work is considered an economic force and can also provide the basis for manpower programs for human (personal) and social means and goals. The counselor must necessarily consider this background to counsel well, especially with the dilemmas we face as we emerge from the late 1970s.

[2] Additional references on the nature and meaning of work are given at the end of Part 1.

Is There a New Work Ethic?

Alan Gartner
and
Frank Riessman

During the last few years, the media, academics, industrialists, and some labor union officials, notably Leonard Woodcock[7] of the UAW, have brought considerable attention to the development of a "new work ethic," which is said to to be characterized by the desire of blue- and white-collar workers to humanize work. Efforts toward this end would include reducing the boredom, routinization, and fragmentation of the work process; modifying the traditional industrial discipline with its hierarchical organization and lack of autonomy for individual workers; and making work more meaningful in general. A number of major publications, including *Work in America*, the report of a special DHEW task force,[6] and *Where Have All the Robots Gone?*, by Sheppard and Herrick,[5] have supported this new ethic whose main thrust is that work should be more than a means of acquiring expendable income—it should enhance the quality of life.

However, the existence of a "new work ethic" has been challenged by many who say that it is an enormous exaggeration; those who take this view argue that the great majority of workers in the main sectors of industry remain relatively satisfied, and that those workers who have demonstrated dissatisfaction point to traditional "bread and butter" concerns (wages, hours, fringe benefits) as its cause.

Let us turn now to an investigation of actual experiences that have been reported, to see, first, if there is in fact a new work configuration, and, if so, whether its dimensions match those of the "new work ethic"—that is, whether they are appropriately interpreted by this formulation.

1. Beginning in the antipoverty period of the sixties, blacks, minorities, and poor workers began to reject various types of "dead-end" jobs, "dirty" work, domestic work, etc., and demanded jobs that were "meaningful," served the community, provided training and education, respect, and the possibility for advancement.

2. Teachers, government workers, social workers, counselors, and other professionals evidenced discontent with their lack of autonomy

Reprinted from the *American Journal of Orthopsychiatry*, **44**:563–567 (July 1974), by permission of the publisher and the authors.

on the job, and with the bureaucratization that prevents them from using and improving their skills and knowledge. The rapid growth of unionization of these workers is perhaps, in part, a reflection of this discontent.

3. Quite a number of women began to reject their traditional work roles—e.g., housework, child care, etc.—and demanded much more access to, and equality in, paid work outside of the home. This is evidenced, in part, by the tremendous increase of the number of women in the labor force—they now make up more than 40 per cent of the work force—and is reflected in the Women's Movement.

4. There seems to be considerable desire on the part of at least a portion of workers to resist compulsory overtime. The heart of the 1973 settlement at the Big 3 automobile companies involved reduction in the work demands upon both the present labor force with the restrictions upon compulsory overtime work, and those close to retirement with the instituting of a full "30-and-out" retirement plan.

5. There is also evidence reported by the American Management Association that some managers have expressed dissatisfaction with their work and the fact that they are being "robbed by computers" of their decision-making roles. Moreover, career change by professionals, managers, and executives in their forties and fifties is now a common occurrence.

6. Public opinion poll data indicate that the higher the educational level attained by workers, the more they express dissatisfaction with their jobs. It is clear that the level of education of those in the work force continues to rise.

In sum, professionals, white- and blue-collar workers, women, managers and executives, youth, blacks and Third World minorities have all expressed dissatisfaction with their work. That their complaints and demands have taken varying forms and relate to numerous aspects of the work process demonstrates that for different people the good work life means something different. Expressed work objectives include: equal pay for equal work and equal opportunities for advancement; jobs that are worthy of respect and lead to careers; better-paying jobs that provide more interesting work, greater autonomy, and more schooling; jobs that are minimally involving in terms of work and hours, which allow for more leisure time; and many other combinations. Corresponding to these different objectives, various proposals have been made: higher wages, shorter or rearranged hours, more amenities, rigorous enforcement of equal employment opportunities, a national full employment program, reorganization of work, reallocation of work place control, job enrichment, and worker control and ownership.

Thus, while we cannot subscribe to the notion of a "new work ethic" in which all forms of discontent are focused on the quest for increased participation, greater autonomy, etc., we note a wide range of dissatisfactions, including those that have led to the formulation of a new ethic. However, we do believe that the demand for a humanization of the work process, which is a relatively recent phenomenon in the industrial sector that has caught the attention of the media, will become increasingly popular due to shifts in the kind of work being done and in those who do it.

In recent years there has been an enormous increase in the proportion of service workers in the labor force. They are employed in such interpersonal occupations as sales and advertising, personal services, and government-provided services going far beyond health, education, and welfare to day care, family planning, mental health, and new services concerned with the dying, the handicapped, etc. Predictions indicate that this trend will continue.

While service work has been routinized and bureaucratized, the intrinsic nature of the work itself and preparation for it, particularly in the human service areas, have traditionally required more autonomy, relational skills, and self-expression. Moreover, historically, service work has been less hierarchically organized than work in the goods-producing sector. As Bell[1] has written, the latter is a world "in which men are treated as 'things' because one can more easily coordinate things than men." But, as Fuchs[2] has pointed out, the service industries have traditionally operated on a smaller scale with more self-employment, and we would argue that work in this sector, where there is greater emphasis on serving and on relations between people, lends itself less readily to bureaucratization.

However, as the services have come to be organized on a larger scale, such as in school, health, and mental health systems, a conflict has arisen between the new hierarchical practices and the old tradition of humanized relationships. One of the rallying cries in the human service professions is that emerging bureaucracies are stifling the creativity that professional workers have been trained to bring to the job and expect once on it. To some extent, it is the traditional model of human service work that is implicitly affecting the new expectations about work in general.

In addition to the expansion in the service sector in general, there has been a change in the composition of the work force; it is increasingly younger, more educated, and includes considerably more women and minority group members. These groups are not only being employed in greater proportion in the old industrial sector, but their numbers are disproportionately great in the expanding service sector. The discontent that they expressed in national life in the 1960s, largely around consumer issues, seems to be reflected more and more in the work force itself. Consumer-oriented demands—focused in the sixties on the quality of life, the environment, community control, welfare rights, student participation, personal liberation, consumer boycotts, and alternative life-styles—now seem to be focused on the work place, and are reflected in concern about health and working conditions in the factory and greater participation and autonomy on the job in both the goods-producing and service sectors.

An additional source of the consumer orientation may be found in the role of leisure or nonwork time in our society. By all measures leisure time has increased. Johnson [4] has reported that the percentage of his life the average twenty-year-old workingman spends in the work force decreased from 93 per cent in 1900 to 84 per cent in 1968. While this has resulted in part from a greater life expectancy and longer retirement, there is also indication that increasing numbers of people are working part-time simply because they want to work less. More leisure time is also acquired by the increasing number of college students and others who choose to continue their education, by the affluent and near-affluent, and also by the unemployed whose leisure time is imposed.

The character of leisure time in our consumer-oriented society is quite different from the highly structured, repetitive character of much work. Such unbounded time allows for more autonomous decision making, is less subject to hierarchical supervisory relationships, promises the possibility of self-development, makes possible participation in self-selected volunteer activities that are not characterized by the usual work norms, and call for less direct pressure and competition (although naturally there is some spillover from the competitive work world). Many of these consumer-oriented, nonwork values have been brought into the work place, particularly by women, youth, blacks and other minority groups.

Implications for Mental Health Workers

Social workers, counselors, and a variety of other mental health professionals and paraprofessionals have been deeply concerned by the bureaucratizing, routinizing features that have come to characterize their work structures. André Gorz [3] has noted that these workers experience the possibility of putting their creative abilities to work; they feel overtrained, and underused. Their training, skills, and personality have been stifled on the job by overcontrol and top-down directives that leave little room for discretion, autonomy, and the use of an authentic serving, caring orientation. They are alienated from their work and of course from the consumers, their clientele. The servers and the served both suffer. If their mental health and their services are to be improved, the work process clearly must allow for much more decentralization, local autonomy, individualization, involvement, opportunities for growth and for responding to the consumer rather than to the bureaucrat.

In the industrial field, it is also becoming increasingly clear that the mental health hazards of alienating work include a great increase in drug use, alcoholism, absenteeism, accidents on the job, as well as depression, withdrawal, and all forms of mental disturbance.

Thus we are arguing that the reorganization of work to provide greater choice, autonomy, and decision making should lead to the decrease of mental disturbances and to the increase of mental health as people become less alienated.

This is true for all kinds of work in our society—white collar, blue collar, managerial, professional, industrial, and service—and for all groups—women, men, blacks, young people, students, professors, teachers, paraprofessionals, and so on. The problems of alienated work are not new to our day, but they are more pronounced due to the far greater expectations of large groups in the population. The mental health profession consequently has to give greater attention to the issues and problems around the nature of work, and the disturbances arising from it.

Conclusion

We have seen a shift in the kind of work done and in those who do it. It is not surprising, then, that there are new feelings about work. They derive from the great expansion of the service sector, with its people-serving, relational ethos; the entry of women, youths, and minority groups into the service work sector and to a lesser extent into industry, and from the consumer-oriented values they bring with them into the work place; and from the increasing leisure time that Americans have at their disposal, which has led to new and different expectations about work roles. That something new is going on in the work place seems to be clear. Surely it is more than one group of social scientists stumbling over another.

References

1. BELL, D. 1972. Labor in the post-industrial society. Dissent 19(1):166.
2. FUCHS, 1. 1968. The Service Economy. Columbia University Press, New York.
3. GORZ, A. Strategy for Labor. Beacon Press, Boston.
4. JOHNSON, D. 1972. The future of work: three possible alternatives. Monthly Labor Review 95(5):4.
5. SHEPPARD, H. and HERRICK, N. 1972. Where Have All the Robots Gone? Worker Dissatisfaction in the 70s. The Free Press, Glencoe, Ill.
6. SPECIAL TASK FORCE TO THE SECRETARY OF HEALTH, EDUCATION AND WELFARE. 1973. Work in America. MIT Press, Cambridge, Mass.
7. WOODCOCK, L. 1973. The New York Times, September 23.

What's Wrong with Work in America?—A Review Essay

Harold Wool

The rash of rank-and-file union contract rejections and wildcat strikes during the late 1960s and early 1970s, particularly the well-publicized strike by workers at the General Motors facility in Lordstown, Ohio, highlight what some are interpreting as a sort of gut revolt against work as it is organized in the American economy.

Reports of apathy, absenteeism, and even industrial sabotage among blue-collar workers, of poor morale among some white-collar workers (particularly those in repetitive dead-end jobs), of college youths' disdain of bureaucratic jobs in government or industry, and even of executives forsaking promising careers to head out to fields unknown—all these have caused some observers, notably commentators from the print and broadcast media, to question the future of work in American society. Is our commitment to the work ethic fading?

Since all of these symptoms appeared to imply some weakening of this commitment, it is not surprising that the search for a culprit has turned its spotlight on the institution of work itself—the way it is organized, its adequacy in meeting human needs, and the effects of work upon other dimensions of human welfare. A special focus of concern has been the "blue-collar worker" with the automobile assembly-line worker as the inevitable archetype. The "blue-collar blues" has become part of the media lexicon, together with knowing references to more esoteric psychological terms such as "work satisfiers and dissatisfiers," "alienation," and "anomie."

The media, moreover, have simply reflected a growing concern on the part of key officials in industry, labor, and the Government—a concern that "all is not well" among important segments of our nation's work force. An initial official effort to place these concerns in broader perspective was contained in a paper on the "Problems of the Blue-Collar Worker," prepared in early 1970 by U.S. Department of Labor staff for an ad hoc White House Task Group. The paper pointed to symptoms of growing disaffection among lower-middle-income work-

Reprinted from *The Vocational Guidance Quarterly,* **24**:155–164 (Dec. 1975) by permission of the publisher and author. Copyright 1975 American Personnel and Guidance Association. Reprinted with permission.

ers (those in the $5,000–10,000 family income range), and suggested that this was due to a combination of pressures: an "economic squeeze," resulting from inflationary pressures and limited advancement opportunities; a "social squeeze," reflected especially in deterioration of their communities and in racial ethnic conflicts; and a "workplace squeeze" associated with a variety of depressing working conditions, ranging from grinding monotony to unpleasant or unsafe work environments.

Against this backdrop, Elliot Richardson, then Secretary of Health, Education, and Welfare, approved initiation in December 1971 of a broadgaged study of the "institution of work" and of its implications for health, education, and welfare.

The study was conducted by a 10-member Task Force, chaired by James O'Toole, a social anthropologist serving as a staff assistant in Secretary Richardson's office. Patterned after an earlier HEW study group on higher education policies, the members of the task force were apparently given full rein to develop their own thinking on the issues, independent of the usual bureaucratic constraints. The resulting report, Work in America, was released in December 1972, together with a cautious foreword by Secretary Richardson, which praised the report for "the breadth of its perspectives and its freshness of outlook," but clearly disassociated himself and the Administration from many of its recommendations.

The Task Force View

The study takes as its point of departure the premise that "work"—broadly defined as socially useful activity—is central to the lives of most adults. In addition to the obvious economic functions of work, work performs an essential psychological and social role in providing individuals with a status, a sense of identity, and an opportunity for social interaction. Referring to recent surveys as evidence, it concludes that individuals on welfare and the poor generally have the same needs and compulsions for work as do those in the economic mainstream.

But, though the work ethic is still "alive" in America, the report finds that it is not "well"—and it ascribes this condition to the institution of work itself. Citing a variety of psychological studies and survey findings, the task force concludes that large numbers of American workers at all occupational levels are pervasively dissatisfied with the quality of their working lives. Significant numbers of employed workers are locked in to "dull, repetitive seemingly meaningless tasks, offering little challenge or autonomy." And many others, including large numbers of older workers, "suffer the ultimate in job dissatisfaction" in being completely deprived of an opportunity to work at "meaningful" jobs.

The principal sources of worker discontent as seen by the authors are to be found in the confines of the individual workplace itself. The central villains of the piece are (1) the process of work breakdown and specialization associated with the pernicious influence of Frederick W. Taylor and his industrial engineer disciples, and (2) the diminished opportunities for work autonomy, resulting from the shift in locus of jobs from self-employment or small scale enterprises to large impersonal corporate and government bureaucracies. Although these trends are recognized as having been underway for many decades, what is new in the current climate, the study contends, is a revolutionary change in attitudes and values among many members of the work force—youth, minority members, and women. With higher expectations generated by increased educational achievement, these groups in particular are placing greater emphasis on the intrinsic aspects of work, its inherent challenge and interest, and less on strictly material rewards. In the case of minority workers, the study recognizes that large numbers are still concerned with the elemental needs for a job—any job—that pays a living wage, but it notes relatively high rates of discontent among black workers in many better paying jobs as well. The relegation of women to poor paying, low status jobs, and the plight of older workers, both in and out of the labor force, are also discussed.

This complex of discontents is, in turn, identified as the root cause of various ills besetting the American economy—"reduced productivity," "the doubling of man-days per year lost through strikes," and increases in absenteeism, sabotage, and turnover rates. In addition, a variety of other ills are attributed to work-related problems, including problems of physical and mental health, family instability, and drug and alcohol addiction.

Since the central diagnosis for this wide array of economic and social problems is found in the faulty organization of work, the principal remedy presented by the task force is the reorganization of work. Although "work redesign" is never explicitly defined by the authors, a number of recent experiments are cited—both here and abroad—which have had in common an extensive restructuring of jobs designed to broaden and vary the scope of workers' duties and to provide increased worker autonomy and participation in work-related decisions, often accompanied by some form of profit sharing. Collaborative efforts by labor, management and government in Norway and Sweden, resulting in a number of pilot job redesign projects, are cited as a model for emulation.

Although work redesign is identified as the "keystone" of the report, the authors concede that this is not a sufficient solution to the problems of work—and of workers—in America. The final two chapters therefore address themselves, more generally, to a range of other work-related problems and possible solutions. Since some jobs can "never be made satisfying," an alternative approach is to facilitate movement of workers out of these jobs, through a massive midcareer retraining option or "self-renewal program" for workers.

In a concluding chapter, the report addresses itself broadly to a variety of other manpower and welfare policy issues. It endorses a "total employment" strategy, designed to produce "reasonable satisfying" jobs not only for the 5 million workers currently reported as unemployed but for an estimated 10 to 30 million additional persons who are underemployed, on welfare, or out of the labor market but who—the authors contend—would take meaningful jobs, if available. This is to be accomplished through a combination of large-scale manpower training and public employment programs and through appropriate fiscal and monetary policies. With respect to welfare reform, it is strongly critical of mandatory work provisions, as applied to welfare mothers, as reflecting a lack of appreciation of the social value of the mother's role in housekeeping and childrearing activities. The report suggests that policy emphasis be shifted to obtaining suitable employment for the fathers, while upgrading the status of housework—in part, by including housewives in the statistical count of the labor force.

Evaluating the Report

From this summary, the coolness of official response to this study will not be difficult to understand.

For somewhat different reasons, this reviewer also has mixed feelings about the value of this study as a basis for broad social policy. Its strength—and its weaknesses—lie in its advocacy of a humanistic approach to assessment of work as a social institution. Its perspective is primarily that of the behavioral scientist, who appraises the "value" of work in terms of its total impact upon the individual—in contradistinction to the market-oriented perspective of many economists, who view work primarily as another factor contributing to the GNP and measure its "value" solely in terms of financial rewards. The task force offers insightful—if still fragmentary—documentation concerning the ways in which many jobs (both blue collar and white collar) are proving "dissatisfying" particularly to some members of the new generation. And scattered through its chapters are a number of provocative recommendations which deserve further study and follow-through. However, in its zeal to advance the cause of "humanization of work" the report suffers from overgeneralization concerning the extent and nature of work dissatisfaction and from overstatement of the potentials of work redesign as a primary solution to work related ills.

A central theme of this study is that "a general increase in their educational and economic status has placed many American workers in a position where having an interesting job is now as important as having a job that pays well" and that the organization of work "has not changed fast enough to keep up with rapid and widescale changes in worker attitudes, aspirations and values." From this premise it is reasonable to infer that the level of worker discontent has significantly increased in recent years.

A Look at Available Data

Yet a review of available research and statistical evidence offers very limited support for this hypothesis. For this purpose we have explored two types of data: (1) job satisfaction survey findings, and (2) those statistical indicators which have frequently been cited as manifestations of worker discontent, such as quit rates, strikes, absenteeism, and productivity.

Job Satisfaction Surveys. In a recent review of the extensive literature on job satisfaction, Robert Kahn reports that some 2,000 surveys of "job satisfaction" were conducted in the United States over a period of several decades. These surveys have varied greatly in scope and design, from intensive studies of workers in a particular plant, occupation, or industry to much more general polls covering a national cross-section of the work force. In spite of these differences, Kahn—as well as earlier observers—has noted a certain consistency in the response patterns. "Few people call themselves extremely satisfied with their jobs, but still fewer report extreme dissatisfaction. The modal response is on the positive side of neutrality—'pretty satisfied.' The proportion dissatisfied ranges from 10 to 21 per cent . . . Commercial polls, especially those of the Roper organization, asked direct questions about job satisfaction in hundreds of samples and seldom found the proportion of dissatisfied response exceeding 20 per cent." Neither Kahn nor other scholars could detect a consistent trend in job satisfaction from the available data.

Statistical Indicators. It is not unreasonable to infer, as does the task force report, that job dissatisfaction will be reflected in a variety of cost-increasing worker behaviors, such as low productivity, high voluntary turnover, high absenteeism, and increased strike activity. Research evidence based mainly on specific plant or industry studies is available to support at least some of these direct relationships, notably in the case of turnover and absenteeism. If worker discontent has been significantly increasing, some indication of this might be reflected in the overall trends of the relevant statistical indicators. Yet the evidence in this respect is inconclusive:

1. *Labor turnover.* A detailed multivariate analysis of quit rates of manufacturing workers recently completed by the Bureau of Labor Statistics indicates that year-to-year fluctuations in these rates over a 20-year period are largely explained by cyclical variations in job opportunities, as measured by the rate of new hires, and that there has been *no* discernible trend in the quit rate over this period.

2. *Absenteeism.* In the absence of any direct program for statistical reporting of absenteeism trends, the Bureau of Labor Statistics has analyzed data from the Current Population Survey on trends in the

proportion of workers who have been absent from their jobs for all or part of a week due to illness or other personal reasons. This initial analysis does point to a small increase in worker absence rates since 1966. The average daily rate of unscheduled absences rose from 3.3 per cent in 1967 to 3.6 per cent in 1972, an increase of about 10 per cent. The data are, however, far from conclusive, and do not provide a basis for generalization longer-term trends or their causes.

3. *Strikes.* A sharp increase in the level of strike activity was recorded in the second half of the 1960s and in the early 1970s. Mandays of idleness due to strikes rose from 0.13 per cent of estimated working time in 1961–65 to 0.26 per cent in 1966–71. However, the incidence of strikes normally tends to increase during inflationary periods. Strike idleness, as a percentage of working time, was actually considerably higher during the years immediately following the end of World War II (1946–50) and following the outbreak of the Korean War (1952–53) than during the more recent period of rapid price increases. Moreover, "bread and butter" issues, such as pay, benefits, job security, and union organization or security issues, have continued to account for all but a modest percentage of all strikes. In 1971, only 5.5 percent of strike idleness was attributed to plant administration or other working condition issues.

4. *Productivity.* Productivity growth, as measured by output per man-hour in the private economy, which had experienced a longer-term growth trend of about 3–3½ per cent a year, slackened appreciably following the mid-1960s and dropped to less than 1 per cent a year in 1969 and 1970. Declines in productivity growth have occurred in the past during or immediately after periods of high economic activity. The productivity growth rate rebounded sharply, moreover, in 1971–72, thus suggesting that cyclical factors, rather than any deepseated worker unrest, were mainly responsible for the previous decline.

5. *Labor force participation.* Abstention from work or work-seeking activity is the ultimate form of rejection of work as an institution. Yet there has been no evidence of a downtrend in the overall proportion of the population, 16 years and over, reported as in the labor force. In fact, this percentage has increased over the past two decades, from 59.9 per cent in 1950 to 61.3 per cent in 1970.

From this necessarily brief review, it will be evident that there is little objective evidence to support an inference of a rising wave of discontent among workers, associated directly with the nature of their jobs. Fluctuations in some of the indicators, which appeared at first blush to support this hypothesis (such as labor turnover rates, strike activity and productivity growth rates) can, on closer inspection, be attributed to quite different causes, notably to the tight labor market and inflationary trends prevailing in the late 1960s and to associated labor market forces. The overall labor force participation trends—such as the sharp and sustained inflow of married women into gainful employment—simply cannot be reconciled with any hypothesis of an extensive rejection of "low quality" work. The available absenteeism data, which suggest some increase since the mid-1960s, are still too incomplete to support any broad generalizations—although they do tend to reinforce more specific reports concerning the special frustrations of the automobile industry assembly-line workers. Even the mass of survey data designed to elicit direct measures of job dissatisfaction have failed to show any consistent trend.

Why Are Supposed Trends Not Visible?

If this trend has not in fact developed in visible and measurable dimensions, we may well ask "Why not?" Is it because the statistical barometers for measuring emerging social trends are two incomplete, too gross, and too insensitive for this purpose? Or is it because the theoretical constructs which lead to certain expectations as to worker behaviors and attitudes simply do not conform to reality?

Most of the available statistical indicators are clearly much too aggregative to serve as reliable indexes of worker discontent. Statistical series such as productivity and labor turnover were designed for quite different purposes. Much more disaggregation of the data, and supplementary research, is needed before we can reliably isolate the influence of specific causal factors. And we are still in the early stages of development of meaningful indexes of job satisfaction and of absenteeism. It is quite possible, therefore, that the available measures—separately and in combination—are too crude and insensitive to detect any new emerging social force.

In part, however, the explanation lies in the model of worker aspirations and behavior postulated by the social psychologists. Their point of departure is a hierarchical ordering of human needs, which, as outlined by Abraham Maslow, begins with satisfaction of basic material wants, such as food and shelter, and ascends to higher order needs, such as "self esteem" and "self actualization." An alternative formulation by Herzberg is couched in terms of "extrinsic" and "intrinsic" job factors. Extrinsic factors, such as poor pay, inadequate benefits, or poor physical working conditions may lead to job dissatisfaction, while true satisfaction depends upon the intrinsic nature of the job, its work content, and its inherent challenge and interest. But both models lead to the inference that, as the general wage level increases and physical working conditions improve, the emphasis shifts from strictly economic issues to demands for improvement in the nature of work itself.

It is difficult to challenge this scale of aspirations in the abstract. In fact, numerous surveys indicate that when workers are asked what aspects of work are most important to them, "interesting work" often heads the list, particularly among the more educated or more affluent segments of the population. Given this apparent scale of values and the rising "affluence" of American workers, why—then—have most workers not overtly attempted to change the contents of their work? For example, has the continued concentration of organized labor on "bread and butter" issues, rather than "quality of work," simply reflected a lack of sensitivity on the part of union leaders to the real needs of their members—or has it in fact reflected the priorities of their rank-and-file members?

As a broad generalization, we believe that the latter assumption corresponds much closer to reality. One fallacy in the Maslow-Herzberg model of worker aspirations, as a guide to behavior, lies in its inherently static premises. Even though individual earnings and family incomes have increased steadily over the decades, the great majority of American workers certainly do not consider themselves as "affluent," when they relate their spendable income to their spending needs, for what they now consider an acceptable standard of living. As Christopher Jencks has recently pointed out, this escalation of living standards "is not just a matter of 'rising expectations' or of people's needing to 'keep up with the Joneses' " but is due in part to the fact that with changes in our mode of life, such goods as an automobile, a telephone, or packaged foods have become an integral part of our cost of living—of participating in our social system. Thus, when hard choices have to be made between a monotonous job in a regimented environment, which pays relatively well and which offers job security, and a poorer paying, less secure but more "satisfying" job, most workers—particularly those with family commitments—are still not in a position to make the trade-off in favor of meeting their "intrinsic" needs.

Moreover, most workers and most union leaders tend to be highly skeptical of the real potential of "job enrichment'" as a practicable means of improving their work environment. This skepticism results from earlier experiences when worker participation, profit sharing, and similar approaches were instituted by some firms as an alternative to pay increases or as a means of staving off unionization. This point of view has recently been colorfully expressed by William W. Winpisinger, general vice-president of the International Association of Machinists:

> If you want to enrich the job, enrich the pay check. The better the wage, the greater the job satisfaction. There is no better cure for the blue-collar blues.

Prestige rankings of various civilian occupations, based on a number of surveys, have failed to reveal any consistent preference for autonomous, self-directed employment, in comparison with more regimented, but better paying and more secure occupations. Office machine operators and bookkeepers rate higher than small independent farmers in these rankings. Assembly-line workers outrank taxi-drivers, in popular esteem. And as we have previously noted, many millions of married women have moved from household work, which—though unpaid—has the virtue of being self-directed, into the more regimented world of gainful employment.

The foregoing comments are clearly not designed to imply that "all is well" with the quality of work in America or that, as a nation, we can afford to be complacent about some of the danger signals which have been brought to our attention. The fact that over 10 per cent of employed workers express general dissatisfaction with their jobs, that many more are dissatisfied with specific aspects of their work situation, and that these proportions are much higher for youth, for women, and for minorities, is a challenge to management, unions, and the government to pursue corrective actions.

However, if our interpretation of the recent labor market behavior and attitudes of American workers is valid, it does imply a different set of criteria for measuring quality of jobs and a different set of priorities for improvement of the quality of work. Our premise is that workers have no difficulty in distinguishing between the "good" and the "bad" jobs in our economy. The least desirable jobs, typically, are inferior *both* in terms of pay and related benefits and in terms of the intrinsic nature of the work itself. Included in this category are most domestic service and hired farm labor jobs and a large proportion of the 20 million jobs occupied by workers in the private nonfarm economy which, according to a recent BLS survey, paid less than $2.50 per hour in April 1970. Numerous unskilled or semiskilled jobs paying somewhat higher wages can also be included in this category because of the oppressive nature of the work and lack of advancement opportunities.

It has been possible for employers to recruit an adequate supply of workers for most of these low-level jobs because of the continued existence of a large pool of workers who have had no effective labor market choices. Included in this pool are a disproportionate number of minority members, teen-aged youth, women, and recent immigrants —who share common handicaps of limited skill, limited work experience, restricted mobility, and various forms of institutionalized discrimination. These categories of workers constitute a relatively large share of the 5 million "visibly" unemployed workers and probably represent an even larger proportion of the "invisible" unemployed not included in our statistics of active job-seekers. So long as this reservoir of low-wage labor is available, employers have little incentive to increase the pay or to enhance the quality of these jobs.

The most potent strategy for improving the quality of these jobs and/or reducing their relative numbers is by reducing the size of this reserve pool of workers. It is no coincidence that the most significant progress in improving the relative status of low-range workers in this country has been made during periods of acute wartime labor shortage, such as during World War II. It is no coincidence, either, that employer initiatives for experimentation with work redesign abroad have been most evident in countries such as Sweden and West Germany, which have managed their economies with much lower ratios of peacetime unemployment than in the United States— and have been initiated in precisely those industries, such as the automobile industry, which have most acutely felt a labor shortage situation.

The most important single set of measures which can contribute to improvements of *quality* of work in America are, thus, those designed to increase the *quantity* of work in America. This requires a much more positive national commitment to a maximum employment policy —even, if need be, at the cost of a somewhat higher level of acceptable inflation. In turn, a climate of sustained high employment can make possible more effective implementation of specific manpower and labor market policies designed to upgrade the status of workers in low level jobs and to promote equality of employment opportunity. It may, in fact, bring us closer to the era of the "post-subsistence" economy when those jobs which do not meet minimum economic *and* psychological standards will be effectively ruled out from the labor market competition.

Vocational Theories: Direction to Nowhere

Charles F. Warnath

The perceptions of the world of work presented by a variety of writers who appear infrequently in the vocational psychology literature confront those in counseling with the possible unreality of current vocational theories—theories based on propositions and assumptions relevant for an ever-decreasing proportion of the American work force. These perceptions also confront some fundamental issues raised by those inside and outside the profession who view counselors in their

Reprinted from *Personnel and Guidance Journal,* **53**:422–428 (Feb. 1975), by permission of the publisher and author. Copyright 1975 American Personnel and Guidance Association. Reprinted with permission.

social context as primary supporters of the status quo (Bond 1972; Halleck 1971; Stubbins 1970; Torrey 1974).

One basic assumption underlying the current vocational theories is populist in nature: that each individual, with adequate motivation, information, and guidance, can move through the educational process to satisfying job goals that allow him or her to express personality characteristics or implement self-concept. This assumption cannot be made unless one holds a prior assumption that every job is capable of engaging the human qualities of an individual and that, in the Protestant tradition, each job has the potential of being a "calling." The vocational theorists have reinforced the concept that the job is the primary focus of a person's life. This may have been true during the years of the small farmer and the independent entrepreneur; but under present conditions, where almost all people work for organizations whose survival is dependent on generating profit and operating efficiently, the needs of the individual are subordinated to the goals of the organization.

Working Conditions: Implications for Self-fulfillment

The implementation of automation throughout the American work world raises questions about the logic of continuing to encourage people to believe that their jobs should be the central focus of their lives. The arguments over whether automation increases or decreases the number of jobs do not address themselves to the critical issue of whether the jobs created can carry the weight of importance consigned to work by vocational psychologists. A recent HEW report (U.S. Department of Health, Education and Welfare 1973) has stated unequivocally: "It is illusory to believe that technology is opening new high-level jobs that are replacing low-level jobs. Most new jobs offer little in the way of 'career' mobility—lab technicians do not advance along a path and become doctors" (p. 20). And earlier in the report: "Many workers at all occupational levels feel locked-in, their job mobility blocked, the opportunity to grow lacking in their jobs, challenge missing from their tasks. . . . For some workers, their jobs can never be made satisfying, but only bearable at best" (pp. xvi–xvii). The findings of the HEW Special Task Force have been given added weight through interviews conducted by Terkel (1972) and Lasson (1972) with workers in a wide range of jobs.

Career development is an abstract construct. It permits vocational theorists to hypothesize about factors that appear to affect vocational decision making without regard for the quality of jobs in which people eventually find themselves. Although career development research may result in more efficient means of sorting people into vocational slots, the assumptions about personality expression and self-concept implementation in work on which this research is based may encourage workers to expect self-fulfillment in jobs that the modern industrial-bureaucratic work structure is not designed to meet. As Green (1968) has indicated: "Under the conditions of a society in which automation is fully exploited . . . such an understanding of work would constitute a cruel hoax" (p. 85).

Trends toward a reduced work week and part-time work also pose serious questions regarding the assumption that jobs can serve as a major focus of personal fulfillment, as do the pressure toward early retirement and the shifting of middle-aged people out of jobs with which they have identified to jobs in which age is considered less damaging to the efficiency or public image of the organization. Older workers are becoming victims of the youth image and economic demands of a work system that has little sympathy for the needs of the individual.

The Changing Nature of Work

The world of work in America has changed significantly over the past few decades. The proportion of people working on small, privately owned farms, working in rural areas, and working in small businesses is now relatively small in comparison to those working for administrators and managers in the bureaucracies of the large metropolitan centers. Job activities have been reduced to ever-smaller units of specialization. White-collar and professional workers have been organized into pools or teams, decisions about their work being made at some higher level of management. Academic credentials have been given added importance for entrance into jobs, while the complexity of those jobs has remained the same or actually been reduced. As Berg (1971) has stated: "The use of educational credentials as a screening device effectively consigns large numbers of people, especially young people, to a social limbo defined by low-skill, no-opportunity jobs in the 'peripheral labor market' " (p. 186). Berg's evaluation is echoed by the HEW report, which notes: "While new industries have appeared in recent decades that need a well-educated work force, most employers simply raised educational requirements without changing the nature of the jobs. . . . For a large number of jobs, education and job performance appear to be inversely related" (p. 135).

Holland (1973), in a recent book, has indicated: "The goal of vocational guidance—matching men and jobs—remains the same despite much talk, research, and speculation. Our devices, techniques, classifications and theories are more comprehensive than in the days of Parsons, the founder of vocational guidance, but the goal is still one of helping people find jobs that they can do well and that are fulfilling" (p. 85). There is no doubt that vocational guidance has remained steadfast in its goal of matching people and jobs, but it is problematic whether vocational counselors can claim that their matches have resulted in placing people in jobs that are "fulfilling." Observations from the field seem to indicate that personal fulfillment in jobs is more mythical than real for the great mass of workers. One would have to assume that Holland's reference to "fulfillment" is connected to the fact that counselors administer and interpret tests that presumably permit some "fit" with the characteristics of persons already on the job. This appears to be a rather flimsy rack on which to hang a person's self-fulfillment.

Neither vocational theorists nor counselors have confronted the issue raised by writers such as Jenkins (1973), who has stated: "There is no question that work, and the image of work, has sunk badly—for blue-collar workers, for organization men, for contemptuous young people, for almost everyone. . . . One can almost conclude that the only force keeping anyone at it is the mythology of the nobility of the thing, however distasteful it may be" (p. 16). The vocational theorists have ignored the growing number of writers who seriously question the myth of the meaningfulness of work in our industrial society. Those who write for a readership of counselors, as a matter of fact, appear to be the principal supporters of the myth, speaking for the status quo no matter how oppressive the working world may be to most individuals. "Even as adults, only a small percentage of Americans have the privilege of feeling that their work is essential or important" (Benet 1971 cited in Jenkins 1973, p. 54). That is the central issue, which vocational theorists and counselors have avoided. The world of work as they view it no longer exists.

Decision Making for What?

Although holding a liberal attitude toward the development of human potential, vocational counselors and theorists have been conservative in their assumptions about the world of work. Their perspective has been fixed within a nineteenth-century model. Their efforts are devoted primarily to increasing the efficiency of matching people and jobs, which they humanistically translate as improving vocational decision making. Few ask the question, "Decision making for what?" despite the fact that, for an increasing number of workers, "Work comes to be less and less defined as a personal contribution and more and more as a role within a system of communication and social relations" (Touraine 1974, p. 185). The counseling literature, seemingly unrelated to the new realities of work for the great majority, reflects obsolete assumptions about work as a "calling," stripped of its religious connotations but nevertheless related to the internal imperatives of self-concept fulfillment, personality expression, and the like.

Responsibility and Powerlessness

Our society has become characterized by individuals' struggle for personal meaning and by their feelings of increasing powerlessness. If those who have studied the world of work are to be believed, the sense of meaninglessness and powerlessness is probably most intense on the job. As Green (1968) has put it: "We have learned to view work as the way in which a man defines for himself who he is and what he shall do with his life. The difficulty is, however, that today men must do this increasingly in a society that lists among its primary purposes the efficient production of goods and services rather than the celebration of human dignity. They have to undertake their self-definition in an environment that has purposes of its own and for that reason does not necessarily have room for individuals to express their own purposes" (p. 35).

Vocational psychologists have centered their theories of vocational decision making on the individual. They have assumed an open market, the dignity of all work, and, as Stubbins (1973) has put it, the person's "ability to operate free of environmental constraints. . . . The vocational psychologist operates in a world that economics and political science have long since discarded—a perspective that ignores the fact that the [person's] world has already taught him that socioeconomic status, racial origin, and power are more determinative than aptitude or interests" (p. 24). As leading advocates of populism and romantic individualism, vocational theorists have concentrated their attention almost exclusively on those characteristics of the individual that can be exploited in the individual's search for self-realization. This perspective has blinded them to the realities of the social forces swirling through the society in general and the world of work in particular. Vocational theorists and counselors ignore the fact that, in the American work world, "What is wanted is not the person but the fulfillment of a function, not the human capacity for work but the human potential for labor" (Green 1968, p. 39).

With their attention focused on improving the efficiency of input to the work force, counselors appear to those outside the profession as not only the major supporters of the status quo but also the key to the entire educational credentialing system, which depends for its effectiveness on the counselor's assigned functions of guiding, selecting, and sorting. "In short, the role of the guidance counselor is strategic because of its importance in reinforcing the tendency to couch the language of teaching, schools and schooling increasingly in terms of output and product. . . . The fundamental work metaphor is strong: the school is a productive institution, its productive work is in the hands of teachers, its quality control in the hands of the guidance staff" (Green 1968, p. 164).

Personal Needs Versus Organizational Needs

Vocational theories are almost uniformly grounded on the proposition that jobs are intrinsically satisfying. The person need only find that job which offers an outlet for personal abilities, interests, values, and personality traits (Holland 1973; Super et al. 1957; Tiedeman and Schmidt 1970). That jobs within the American economy are designed to meet the needs of production and profit or bureaucratic relationships and not to meet the personal needs of the people who fill those jobs has not been included as a contingency factor in the theoretical structures. Little attention has been paid to the fact that over the past few decades the power of individual workers in their work situations and their control over their work activities have been significantly diminished, although these are critical factors in the worker's ability to express personal characteristics.

This reduction of human expression in work is not restricted to the poorly trained or poorly educated; Denitch (1974) has commented, in regard to college graduates: "Whole generations trained to think in terms of societal issues are offered roles as powerless, if well-paid employees. Those with specific skills find their work compartmentalized and routinized. The shift in the authority of engineers and skilled scientists in industry also reduces them to a *new* highly-trained working class" (p. 176). But nowhere in the vocational theories is there even an allusion to the steady reduction of power and control in jobs at all levels of the American economy. "What dominates our type of society is not the internal contradictions of the various social systems but the contradictions between the needs of these social systems and the needs of individuals. This can be interpreted in moral terms, which has aroused scant sociological interest because there is nothing more confused than the defense of individualism against the social machinery" (Touraine 1974, p. 185).

Vocational theorists too have avoided the moral issues related to the individual's struggle with the social system of work. "There is considerable interest among the theorists in classifying, stratifying, compartmentalizing and, more recently, computerizing. While purporting to have as its major purpose the facilitation of a person's educational-vocational planning, its effect is to stabilize the economic system by offering hope that there are reasonable logical paths through the maze of the occupational structure to the one best job that can make each individual happy and satisfied" (Warnath 1973, p. 16). Ostensibly, vocational counseling is a humanistic enterprise. Its theories, however, are designed to explain principles concerning the process of occupational decision making and vocational adjustment to the end that the individual's behavior might be predicted and controlled (Super 1957). These goals are softened by the humanistic affirmation of human potentials, which the theories—through their application by counselors

—will presumably assist individuals to discover and exploit. Counselors have defined themselves as humanists on the basis of their stated purpose of helping clients make maximum use of their potentials through a process in which the counselor expresses personal qualities of warmth, empathy, and authenticity.

But neither theorists nor counselors come to grips with conflict between the needs of the people who are the objects of their attention and the needs of the economic system—which are the needs that determine the operations of the world of work. On the contrary, the romantic individualism inherent in both theory and practice leaves the individual isolated and exposed by its proposition that the person alone is responsible for his or her fate, that only an unwillingness to be sufficiently motivated or to discover and use some unique talent stands in the way of the individual's finding a self-fulfilling work situation. Neither theorists nor counselors address themselves to the world of work as experienced by most workers—or, for that matter, to the contradiction pointed out by Aronowitz (1974) between the rising level of education of larger numbers of workers and the increasingly restricted scope of their labor.

Both vocational theorists and counselors are engaged in a basically amoral activity, operating on the premise that the working world is just and is guided by rational principles in regard to those employed in work—despite the fact that the system within which those workers are engaged responds to factors quite unrelated to the welfare of the individual worker and can fulfill the needs of individuals only insofar as those needs support the needs of the organization.

Needed: A New Perspective

Touraine (1974) has pointed out that a new kind of society is being born; it can be called the programmed, or technocratic, society. This new society is served by vocational theorists and counselors whose perspectives of work are drawn from the past, causing their efforts at increasing the effectiveness of moving people into jobs to negate their professed humanistic concern for people.

The counselor continues to assume that vocational counseling can result in a match of the person with a satisfying job, but as Ferkiss (1970) has noted: "The myth of 'the happy worker' is still just that. Where the old centralized rigid processes have been automated with machines taking over routine tasks, working conditions, especially psychological ones, have not improved. Such evidence as exists indicates that the watchers of dials—the checkers and maintainers—are likely to be lonely, bored, and alienated, often feeling less the machine's master than its servant" (p. 123). And these feelings are not restricted to specific job categories or classifications. They are pervasive throughout the working world, not only among the lower level of jobs but extending up through the white-collar and managerial ranks. Their effects generalize, leading workers "to become 'stupid and ignorant' not only on the job, but off as well" (Jenkins 1973, p. 40).

Braginsky and Braginsky (1974) have argued convincingly that psychologists, either unwittingly or as a means of self-preservation, operate within a framework of generally accepted cultural values that are encouraged and supported by those in power to ensure societal stability and their own dominant positions. In accordance with this concept, the prediction and control models used by psychologists are more for the benefit of those with power than for the benefit of the individual whose behavior is being predicted.

Counselors are positioned at the service delivery end of a chain of information, data, and how-to-do-it prescriptions generated by vocational psychologists. They have a direct involvement with the clients who come to them for assistance, and they carry the burden of responsibility for ensuring that their promises about the improvement of human welfare through counseling can be kept. With the values of society in flux, counselors must not only evaluate their own attitudes toward the concept of work as the major source of self-fulfillment; they must also test their attitudes against the experiences of workers in a variety of occupations. They need not be passive consumers of the products of academia. They can, through direct communication with the writers and theorists and through discussions within their professional groups, begin to raise questions about the assumptions on which vocational theorizing is based as well as about the perspectives through which conclusions and interpretations of research data are filtered.

Six years ago, Osipow (1969) suggested that perhaps vocational psychologists were not asking the "right" questions, that concern with vocational preference and selection might be of relevance for only a minority of the population, and that we should be placing more emphasis on questions related to those factors in the work situation which encourage satisfaction and permit feelings of worth and human dignity. But beyond these considerations, counselors might begin considering a theoretical model or framework broader than the vocational choice or vocational development models, a theoretical model that is based on general human effectiveness and that does not require a fulfilling job as its core concept.

The connection between work and the confirmation of one's worth as a human being has been severed for the great majority of our population. Other disciplines are already engaging in a search for alternative means by which people can express their individuality and gain a sense of control over some significant parts of their lives. Counselors should be no less involved in this search. Because they are central to the life planning of millions of people, their responsibility for assisting in the search for means other than paid employment through which people can gain meaning from life is all the greater.

References

ARONOWITZ, S. Does the United States have a new working class? In B. Silverman and M. Yanowitch (Eds.), *The worker in "post-industrial" capitalism.* New York: The Free Press, 1974.

BENET, S. Why they live to be 100 or even older in Abkhasia. *New York Times Magazine,* December 26, 1971. (Cited in D. Jenkins, *Job power.* Garden City, N.Y.: Doubleday, 1973).

BERG, I. *Education and jobs: The great training robbery.* Boston: Beacon Press, 1971.

BOND, J. Address to the Annual Conference of University and College Counseling Center Directors, Vail, Colorado, November 1972. *Proceedings,* Colorado State University, 1972.

BRAGINSKY, B., and BRAGINSKY, D. *Mainstream psychology.* New York: Holt, Rinehart and Winston, 1974.

DENITCH, B. Is there a new "working class"? In B. Silverman and M. Yanowitch (Eds.), *The worker in "post-industrial" capitalism.* New York: The Free Press, 1974.

FERKISS, V. C. *Technological man.* New York: Mentor Books, 1970.

GREEN, T. *Work, leisure and the American schools.* New York: Random House, 1968.

HALLECK, S. *The politics of therapy.* New York: Science House, 1971.

HOLLAND, J. *Making vocational choices: A theory of careers.* Englewood Cliffs, N.J.: Prentice-Hall, 1973.

JENKINS, D. *Job power.* Garden City, N.Y.: Doubleday, 1973.

LASSON, K. *The workers: Portraits of nine American jobholders.* New York: Bantam Books, 1972.

OSIPOW, S. H. Some revised questions for vocational psychology. *Counseling Psychologist,* 1969, *1,* 17–19.

STUBBINS, J. The politics of counseling. *Personnel and Guidance Journal,* 1970, *18,* 611–618.

STUBBINS, J. Social context of college counseling. In C. Warnath (Ed.), *New directions for college counselors.* San Francisco: Jossey-Bass, 1973.

SUPER, D. E.; CRITES, J.; HUMMEL, R.; MOSER, H.; OVERSTREET, P.; and WARNATH, C. F. *Vocational development: A framework for research.* New York: Teachers College, Columbia University, 1957.

TERKEL, S. *Working.* New York: Pantheon Books, 1972.

TIEDEMAN, D. V., and SCHMIDT, I., D. Technology and guidance: A balance. *Personnel and Guidance Journal,* 1970, *49,* 234–241.

TORREY, E. *The death of psychiatry.* Radnor, Pa.: Chilton, 1974.

TOURAINE, A. New classes, new conflicts. In B. Silverman and M. Yanowitch (Eds.), *The worker in "post-industrial" capitalism.* New York: The Free Press, 1974.

U.S. DEPARTMENT OF HEALTH, EDUCATION AND WELFARE, SPECIAL TASK FORCE. *Work in America.* Cambridge, Mass.: MIT Press, 1973.

WARNATH, C. F. *New myths and old realities: College counseling in transition.* San Francisco: Jossey-Bass, 1971.

WARNATH, C. F. Whom does the college counselor serve? In C. Warnath (Ed.), *New directions for college counselors.* San Francisco: Jossey-Bass, 1973.

Toward an Understanding of Work-Leisure Relationships

R. Arthur Winters
and
James C. Hansen

The major theories of vocational development and adjustment assume that work is the central force in the lives of most Americans; leisure is not recognized as a significant aspect of the individual's life. Theorists who do give consideration to leisure [17] view it as an inferior partner to work, as directly determined by the individual's work situation. Even so, there is little doubt that leisure is becoming an increasingly significant factor in the lives of many people. The advent of the four-day work week, the rise in the numbers of early retirements, and the increasing life span of the individual indicate the need to come to grips with the concept of leisure. That the counseling profession is beginning to recognize the importance of this aspect of the individual's life is evident in the NVGA-AVA position paper on career development and career guidance [12], and in Wrenn's [18] recent comments on the future of counseling. Wrenn [18] stated that "there must be counseling for leisure. . . . Can the counselors of the future . . . help clients plan for leisure as well as for work?" (p. 261).

In spite of this concern, there is disagreement over the meaning of the term *leisure* and the relationship between leisure and work. For example, the NVGA-AVA position paper [12] viewed work as an "expenditure of effort designed to effect some change, however slight, in some province of civilization" (p. 2). Thus, leisure may be work under certain circumstances but not under others—and confusion reigns. The following review of literature and research is an attempt to define leisure more clearly and to examine work-leisure relationships.

Definition of Leisure

The literature on leisure, most of which is based on little or no research, offers a confusing array of definitions of the term. However, Parker [13] has offered the following categories, which represent an

Reprinted from *The Vocational Guidance Quarterly*, **24**:238–243 (March 1976), by permission of the publisher and the authors.

adequate attempt to bring order out of confusion: (1) definitions that concentrate on the dimension of time, (2) definitions concerned with quality of activity or being, and (3) definitions that attempt to combine the two.

Time definitions of leisure have been offered by Soule [16], Gross [6], and Lundberg [10], among others. The major concern of this group is the determination of what is to be taken out of total time in order that leisure alone remains. There is by no means a consensus with regard to this problem. Soule [16], for example, defined leisure as unsold time (one's own time) regardless of what is done with it. Within this framework, *sold time* refers simply to one's job. Gross [6], on the other hand, suggested that leisure consists of time left over after work and maintenance activities have b?en carried out. Maintenance may include a number of activities that are entirely out of the realm of work (eating, sleeping, hygiene). Lundberg [10], however, viewed leisure in terms of the time one is free from the "more obvious and formal duties" imposed by one's job or other obligations.

Representative of definitions that stress the quality of leisure are those offered by Peiper [14] and deGrazia [2]. For example, deGrazia [2] noted the difference between "free time" and leisure:

> Leisure and free time live in two different worlds. We have got in the habit of thinking them the same. Anybody can have free time. Free time is a realizable idea of democracy. Leisure is not fully realizable. . . . Free time refers to a special way of calculating a special kind of time. Leisure refers to a state of being, a condition of man, which few desire and fewer achieve (p. 78).

According to deGrazia, it is free time that individuals have at their disposal in American society. His view corresponds with the classical Greek concept of leisure (still prevalent to some degree in European cultures), which emphasizes the aspects of being and contemplation. Such a definition offers nothing to the study of leisure, however, as it treats the concept as an immeasurable variable. The extensive research of deGrazia in the area of free time has, to some degree, aided in conceptualizing that elusive term; however, according to his own pseudoaristocratic definition, this is, at best, the leisure of industrial society.

Between the time and quality definitions of leisure are those which include the concept of leisure as residual time but go further by adding a "positive description of its content or function, usually a prescriptive element" [13, p. 21]. Definitions of this type are offered by Gist and Fava [5] and Dumazedier [4]. Gist and Fava [5] stated that leisure is "the time which an individual has free from work or other duties and which may be utilized for purposes of relaxation, diversion, social achievement or personal development" (p. 411). According to Dumazedier [4], the individual may use leisure time "to rest, to amuse himself to add to his knowledge, or improve his skills . . . or to increase his voluntary participation in the life of the community after discharging his professional, family and social duties" (p. 382).

In most of the above definitions, but not in those that stress the quality of leisure exclusively, it is assumed that leisure and work are at opposite extremes of a time continuum. That is, it is assumed that leisure time and work time do not overlap. However, there is little agreement as to what actually constitutes leisure time. Thus, Parker [13] has drawn on the contributions of a number of writers in an effort to devise an orderly time scheme for analyzing individual life space. It includes work time and nonwork time, with work time divided into work and work obligations, and nonwork time divided into physiological needs, nonwork obligations, and leisure. *Work time,* of course, refers to time spent earning a living—job time. *Work obligations* may include the time spent traveling to and from work, preparing to work, and attending work-related meetings or conferences. Time spent meeting physiological needs includes sleeping, eating, washing, and so forth. *Nonwork* obligations refer to those activities that usually involve obligations to other people but may include "non-human objects" [13, p. 26] such as the home, pets, garden. *Leisure* is viewed as time left over after other commitments and obligations have been met.

Parker [13], however, felt that a time scheme alone does not adequately define leisure; it presents a static picture of that phenomenon without taking into account the individual leisure participant. Thus, he has added another critical variable: "the extent to which the activity is constrained or freely chosen" (p. 28).

Constraint ←		→ Freedom	
work	work (employment)	work obligations	"leisure in work"
non-work	physiological needs	nonwork obligations	leisure

This appears more flexible than a time scheme alone. For example, it allows for leisure-type activities within the work setting. Thus, an individual may engage in some freely chosen activities while at the work site (e.g., a lunch-hour card game). Parker [13] pointed out, however, that such activities do not constitute true leisure, because the individual remains constrained by the requirements of the work environment and, ultimately, by the necessity of earning a living.

Parker's [13] scheme also allows for a wide range of individual differences in the conceptualization and use of nonwork time. For example, visiting relatives on a Sunday afternoon may be viewed as a nonwork obligation by one individual because of the external pressure from family members of the feeling that it is "the right thing to do."

Some degree of constraint accompanies the activity. For another individual, however, visiting relatives may be viewed as leisure, freely chosen with "no strings attached." Similarly, one individual may feel the pressure from neighbors or family to maintain the yard, whereas another may feel none of this pressure and may view such activities as true leisure.

Parker [13], by devising this two-dimensional scheme, has avoided the pitfalls of many of the authors mentioned earlier: prescribing the kinds of activities that should be engaged in during one's leisure time. To assume that specific activities—whether deGrazia's [2] contemplation or Dumazedier's [4] community participation—constitute the only genuine use of leisure time is, to say the least, presumptuous. Parker [13], possibly in defense of beer drinking and TV watching, has placed the responsibility for determining what activities constitute leisure on the individual, where it belongs.

The recognition of individual freedom and choice in the pursuit of leisure activities, as well as the definite break between work and leisure, included in Parker's [13] conceptualization is important for counselors who are concerned with assisting people with their leisure development as well as their vocational development. Perhaps, just perhaps, it helps to point the way out of the morass created by the work-leisure literature over the years.

Relationships Between Work and Leisure

It is generally assumed in the literature that work and leisure are directly related. There is little agreement, however, about the nature of this relationship. Most theorizing in this area can be separated into opposing positions: polarity or fusion.

Studies of industrial workers by Dubin [3], Kornhauser [8], and Lafitte [9] appear to provide evidence for the polarity of the work-leisure relationship. Work (the job) is imbued with so many negative characteristics, particularly for semiskilled or unskilled workers, that they use their leisure to escape, often participating in activities that are the complete antithesis of their work.

The polarity view of leisure has been advanced by a number of other writers, particularly the professional recreationists who advocate planned leisure programs for the public from cradle to grave. Meyer [11], for example, stated, "Adults need to establish a definite rhythm between work and recreation, to balance vocational and avocational interests" (p. 58). In other words, leisure is a therapeutic mechanism in the life of the individual; one "gets away from it all" to "recreate" for a while.

Blum [1], who also studied the leisure pursuits of industrial workers, proposed an entirely different concept: a fusion between work and leisure. He found that most workers, although desiring to get away from work and everything it stands for, participate mainly in leisure activities similar to the work process. Such activity requires little initiative or attention and "makes it possible to carry an essential attitude growing out of the work process into the leisure time . . . it eliminates the necessity of a basic change in attitude, of effort, and attention" (pp. 109–110).

Riesman [15] explained the work-leisure fusion in terms of the changing American character from "inner-directedness" to "other-directedness." "The other-directed person has no clear core of self to escape from; no clear line between production and consumption; between adjusting to the group and serving private interests; between work and play" (p. 185). According to Howe [7], however, other-directedness is a mode of adjustment to industrial civilization. It is through mass culture that the fusion between work and leisure occurs in the highly industrial system:

> Whatever its manifest content, mass culture must . . . not subvent the basic patterns of industrial life. Leisure time must be so organized as to bear a factitious relationship to working time: apparently different, actually the same. It must provide relief from work monotony without making the return to work unbearable (p. 45).

On one side are those who claim that (at least for some groups within American society) work and leisure are consciously separated into two distinct spheres, with the latter sometimes providing individuals' major satisfactions in life. On the other side are those who maintain that the two spheres cannot be separated either by choice or by subconscious psychological processes. Parker's [13] conceptualization allows for the incorporation of both fusion and polarity in work-leisure relationships. Leisure, for some individuals, may represent an attempt to flee the pressures or boredom of work; others may consciously choose to participate in leisure activities similar to the work process. Thus, the polarity-fusion argument is eliminated. This refreshingly different view of leisure and work-leisure relationships should be given careful consideration by those in the counseling profession seriously concerned about the leisure life of the individual.

References

1. BLUM, F. H. *Toward a democratic work process.* New York: Harper, 1953.
2. DEGRAZIA, S. *Of time, work, and leisure.* New York: Doubleday, 1964.
3. DUBIN, R. Industrial workers' worlds: A study of the "central life interests" of industrial workers. *Social Problems,* 1956, 4, 131–142.
4. DUMAZEDIER, J. *Toward a society of leisure.* New York: Free Press, 1967.
5. GIST, N. P., and FAVA, S. F. *Urban society.* New York: Crowell, 1961.
6. GROSS, E. A functional approach to leisure analysis. *Social Problems,* 1961, 9, 3–16.
7. HOWE, I. Notes on class culture. *Politics,* 1948, 6, 44–57.

8. KORNHAUSER, A. *Mental health of the industrial worker.* New York: Wiley, 1965.
9. LAFITTE, P. *Social structure and personality in the factory.* London: Routledge, 1958.
10. LUNDBERG, G. A.; KOMAROVSKY, M.; and McILLNERY, M. A. *Leisure: A suburban study.* New York: Columbia University Press, 1934.
11. MEYER, H. D. The adult cycle. *Annals of the American Academy of Political and Social Science,* 1957, *63,* 58–67.
12. NATIONAL VOCATIONAL GUIDANCE ASSOCIATION AND AMERICAN VOCATIONAL ASSOCIATION. Career development and career guidance. *NVGA Newsletter,* 1973, *22,* 5–8.
13. PARKER, S. *The future of work and leisure.* London: MacGibbon & Lee, 1971.
14. PEIPER, J. *Leisure: The basis of culture.* London: Faber, 1952.
15. REISMAN, D. *The lonely crowd.* New York: Doubleday, 1953.
16. SOULE, G. The economics of leisure. *Annals of the American Academy of Political and Social Science,* 1957, *63,* 16–24.
17. SUPER, D. E. Avocation and vocational adjustment. *Character and Personality,* 1941, *10,* 51–61.
18. WRENN, C. G. Hopes and realizations, past and present. *Vocational Guidance Quarterly,* 1974, *22,* 256–262.

UNIT BIBLIOGRAPHY

DEUTSCH, H. *Selected Problems of Adolescence.* New York: International Universities Press, 1967.
ERIKSON, E. *Childhood and Society.* New York: W. W. Norton & Company, Inc., (Chap. 7).
———. *Young Man Luther.* New York: W. W. Norton & Company, Inc., 1958.
FENICHEL, O. *The Psychoanalytic Theory of Neurosis.* New York: W. W. Norton & Company, Inc., 1945.
FREUD, A. *Normality and Pathology in Childhood.* New York: International Universities Press, 1965.
FREUD, S. *The Future of an Illusion.* London: Hogarth Press, 1927. (Std. ed., 1961).
———. *Civilization and Its Discontents.* London: Hogarth Press, 1930. (Std. ed., 1961).
FROMM, E. *The Sane Society* New York: Holt, Rinehart and Winston, 1941.
———. *Escape from Freedom.* New York: Holt, Rinehart and Winston, 1941.
GINSBURG, S. "Work and Its Satisfactions." *J. of Hillside Hosp.* **5** (1956), 301–311.
HORNEY, K. *Neurosis and Human Growth.* New York: W. W. Norton & Company, Inc., 1950 (Chap. 13).
JAHODA, M. "Notes on Work in Psychoanalysis." In *A General Psychology: Essays in Honor of Heinz Hartman.* New York: International Universities Press, 1966.
MENNINGER, K. *Love Against Hate.* New York: Harcourt Brace Jovanovich, Inc., 1942, (Chap. 6).
MILLS, C. W. *White Collar.* New York: Oxford University Press, Inc., 1951 (Chap. 10).
NEFF, W. "Psychoanalytic Conceptions of the Meaning of Work." *Psychiat.,* **28** (1965), 324–333.
ORWELL, G. *Coming Up for Air.* New York: Harcourt Brace Jovanovich, Inc., 1950.
OVESEY, L. "Fear of vocational success." *Arch. Gen Psychiat.* (1962).

REICH, W. *Character Analysis.* New York: Orgone Institute Press, 1949.

REISMAN, D. "The themes of Work and Play in the Structure of Freud's Thought" *Psychiat.,* **13** (1950), 1–17.

ROE, A. *The Making of a Scientist.* New York: Dodd, Mead & Company, 1953.

WHITE, R. "Competence and the Psychosexual Stages of Development." In *Nebraska Symposium on Motivation.* Lincoln: University of Nebraska Press, 1960.

WHEELER, S. "The Structure of Formally Organized Socialization Settings." *In Socialization After Childhood.* New York: John Wiley & Sons, Inc., 1966.

part 2
Society and Career
Development

Our society is characterized by change. Social change refers to broad and basic transmutations in the nature of a society, as in, for example, the technology employed, the organization of the family, the arrangements for earning a living, and the growth and character of the population. The United States developed rapidly into a highly industrial organization. Complex patterns and pressures generated by industrial innovations have had far-reaching effects on our society and have crystallized in our highly urbanized way of life. Family patterns are also changing. During the last century the family has forfeited many of its traditional functions to the school, including much of its responsibility for the educational and vocational guidance of the young. One clear result has been the steady rise in the importance of education per se in the direction of and preparation for individual vocational goals.

Planning the development of a career in a rapidly changing society can be a complicated process, for numerous social factors affecting attitudes toward career development demand consideration. To understand vocational development and adjustment a counselor must consider social influences on the individual. The individual will certainly be influenced by the family, social class variables, the school, community, pressure groups, and role perceptions. The references at the conclusion of Part 2 focus on these specific factors; the articles selected cover broad social factors affecting career development.

S. David Hoffman and Stephen A. Rollin profile the factors of speeded social change and the impact of future shock on the world of work. They examine the impact of rapid change on the worker's life style and draw implications for vocational counselors.

Leona Tyler asks questions regarding work and poverty populations that affect vocational psychology. She believes we must become more aware of the social limitations on vocational development and suggests that studies on poverty groups will enhance our knowledge. She proposes that the variables of "alternatives," "limits," "plans," and "concepts about time" can broaden our understanding of career development.

Edward Gross focuses on the socialization that occurs when an individual begins working in an organization. He considers the place of new skills, self-image, involvements, and values as an adult becomes socialized in a work environment.

Although the last article is titled "Aging and the Nature of Work," it concentrates on broad social variables that affect career choice and change. The article examines the attitudes and values of college-aged youth as they make educational and vocational plans.

Implications of Future Shock for Vocational Guidance

S. David Hoffman
and
Stephen A. Rollin

This article focuses on how a few of the ideas of Alvin Toffler [5] may be applied to the theory of vocational development. The purpose is not to argue that Toffler has a theory of vocational development or that his thinking replaces the work that has been done in this field. He does, however, generate some observations about the nature of our changing society, the pace of change, and implications for personality and vocational development that are worth discussion and incorporation into the field.

Most vocational theories seem to agree that vocational choice is developmental, a process. Further, most agree that personality factors both affect and are affected by vocational or career processes. Super's conceptualization of the vocational process, simply stated, is that an individual's occupation provides a role that is appropriate to his self-concept [4]. Vocational choice is the translation of self-concept into occupational terms.

Roe's theory sought to relate Maslow's need hierarchy to vocational development by examining the relationships between parent and child that generate needs, attitudes, and interests influencing vocational choice [6]. Holland set up personality conditions that sought satisfaction and matched them to corresponding occupational environments that provided satisfaction [6]. The reality of the rapidly changing environment as it affects the individual and the occupational world is not adequately dealt with in most vocational theory. This issue is, as Barry and Wolf [1] point out, merely a corollary included in most theories and does not occupy the position of prominence that Toffler demands. Toffler adds a new dimension to the concept of developmental process—speed of transience:

> Much of our theorizing about social and psychological change presents a valid picture of man in relatively static societies—but a distorted and

Copyright 1972 American Personnel and Guidance Association. Reprinted with permission.

incomplete picture of the truly contemporary man. It misses a critical difference between the men of the past or present and the men of the future. This difference is summed up in the word *transience* [6, p. 44].

What is future shock? It is the dizzying disorientation brought on by the premature arrival of the future. It is culture shock in one's own society. Toffler demonstrates the accelerated thrust of change. A profile of some of the factors reflecting this speeded change with its radical impact on man and society has been constructed (from Toffler's writings) by Joseph Luft [3, p. 68], as follows:

1. *Population*. The time required to double the world's population has dropped from 1,000,000,000 years to 1,000 years, to 200 years, to 80 years, until now. At present accelerated rate of population growth, the earth's population will double in 35 years.
2. *Production*. The GNP of goods and services in the 21 advanced nations of the world is doubling every decade and a half.
3. *Scientists*. Between 85 and 95 percent of all scientists who ever lived are alive in 1970.
4. *Energy*. Approximately half of all the energy consumed in the last 2,000 years was consumed in the last 100 years.
5. *Speed*. The top speeds of transportation never exceeded 20 MPH until the mid-nineteenth century. Rockets now take man at over 20,000 MPH and commuter speed for many exceeds the speed of sound.
6. *Innovative*. The innovative cycle between a new idea and its application has shortened from as much as a millennium to a few years. Combinations of inventions, including those using computers, have drastically speeded up new inventions.
7. *Moving*. Approximately 36,000,000 people move from one place to another each year in the United States.
8. *Books*. In four and a half centuries the publication of new books has increased from 1,000 a year to 1,000 a day.
9. *Scientific literature*. The number of journals and articles appears to be doubling every 15 years, with current output of some 20,000,000 pages per year.
10. *Information*. The number of words and ideas taken in daily by the average adult from newspapers, magazines, radios, and television has risen sharply, and new technologies to increase the speed of information flow proliferate at a rapid rate.

Things are changing so fast that our expectancies for duration of relationships have decreased and we are a society in transcience. At present, there is evidence of "temporariness" in the world of work. An example is problem oriented task forces—experts gathered to solve a problem, complete a project, and move on. Toffler predicts more of this kind of "work" and calls it "the coming ad-hocracy." Speeded change and transience have an impact. The coming consultant model in counseling is one of working to change organizational patterns rather than the static in-office relationship. Herein lies one of the important features of future shock vis-à-vis vocational theory.

Life Style

Life style is a major component in vocational development. In the rapidly accelerating, kaleidoscopic world of tomorrow/today, Toffler posits that life style is no longer tied to class position. Rather, it is one's ties to subcults that determine life style. Moreover, the multiplicity of subcults in society has brought an explosive multiplicity of life styles. This is further complicated by the rather free movement between subcults, of which the drop-out and drop-back-in syndrome is an example. This movement and identification with groups condition the choices an individual makes in his daily life.

Being bombarded by information and lured by multiple subcults and life styles in the mass media and through transient relationships results in more and more people adopting and discarding life styles at a rate that would have staggered the members of any previous generation. The life style itself has become a throw-away item. Essentially, this is a theory that takes into account discontinuity. If people are shopping around for life styles, how much investment of self are they willing to make in their temporary "selves"?

This way of thinking about life style and self-concept poses relevant questions for counselors and vocational theorists. We must, says Toffler, confront the agonizing problems of individual integration. Stability of self-concept is threatened by constant reality testing and by coping strategies that call for multiple identifications and less investment of self in the throw-away life style. As Toffler uses the term *future shock,* he is precisely talking about adaptive breakdown, sequential, serial selves, a rush for variety, choice, and freedom converging head-on with transience and diversity in time and space. Occupational choice, if we are in agreement with Super [4], would seemingly require consistency or stability of awareness of both self and reality. The bases of choice become indistinct in so ephemeral and temporal an environment as Toffler projects will be the case in the future.

Decision Stress

Novelty upsets the balance between programmed and nonprogrammed decisions. Programmed decisions are routine, easy decisions such as how to get to work, or school, where to have lunch, etc. Not much information is processed and decisions are of "low psychic cost." Nonprogrammed decisions are high in "psychic cost" and require more information processing. They are typified by such questions as, What do I want as an occupation? What am I as a person suited to do? Should I go to college? What skills do I have? These require non-routine answers and result in decision stress, which occurs when new, nonprogrammed decisions are required. Novelty tips the balance toward the most difficult and costly form of decision making. Acceleration of the life pace forces us to make these harder decisions faster, sometimes faster than we can process the new information required. This results in what Toffler calls cognitive overload and may be thought of as the ever increasing amounts of occupational information that need to be processed in order to make vocational choices.

Decision stress and cognitive overload lead to coping strategies, which Toffler notes are familiar to information scientists. These strategies may also be observed in counseling:

1. *Denial*. Denying—blocking out unwelcomed reality.
2. *Specialization*. Specializing—not blocking out all novelty and information, but attempting to keep pace in a specific narrow sector.
3. *Reversion*. Going backward to previously successful routines, now irrelevant and inappropriate.
4. *Super-simplification*. Seeking a simple, neat equation to solve everything. This may explain dropping out or drugging out to substitute one big problem for all the overwhelming little ones.

We are already faced with overchoice and our clients are already bombarded with decisions to make for which they may be poorly prepared and loaded with information they cannot effectively process.

Implications

Realizing that occupational choice is not an end point is saying that the process of living is as important as the product of life. [2] If counseling effective, the client begins to act in more self-supporting, independent, realistic ways. Then the problems of ability, expectations of others, motivation to explore, and attitudes toward the world of work are seen in a different light by the client. The primary function of the counselor—to help the client by any means available to find himself —inherently includes vocational development. Counselors need to be aware of societal patterns and social forces which are shaping the lives of clients. Toffler's message is clear: Transience, discontinuity, and novelty are affecting the decision making processes now and will increasingly continue to do so in the future.

A rational choice process, as it is seen in vocational development theory, depends on continuity, order, and regularity in the environment. Toffler says this choice process is based "on some correlation between pace and complexity of change, and man's decision capacities [5, p. 367]." We can incorporate Toffler's thinking into practical application in counseling, if not directly into the body of theory. Transience needs to be reckoned with in any process of self-evaluation and decision making. Vocational counseling, as we see it, needs to be concerned with freeing the individual from personal limitations that interfere with the development/choice process. The direction this may take is toward teaching the process method. Toffler recommends teaching for adaptation, and counselors are now exploring methods of teaching vocational theory to their clients.

Ivey and Morrill [2] see clients "not as individuals hunting for a place in a stable society, but as changing organisms engaging in a series of career related developmental tasks that enable them to adapt themselves to a changing society [p. 645]." Counselors can incorporate theories and notions of developmental process in their counseling practice. What is important about wrestling with self-knowledge, self-assessment, and life styles is both the process and the outcome—observing *how* one gets where he gets is a valuable learning experience. The old test-and-tell model of vocational counseling may not allow the client to learn appropriate decision behavior for the future. Toffler is saying that the rapid acceleration of our society makes it increasingly difficult for people to use developmental tasks for growth or survival.

The next step for vocational counselors may be to define developmental tasks appropriate to the conditions Toffler describes and predicts. An interesting suggestion from Toffler is situational groups. Situational groups, unlike human potential or encounter groups, are set up around particular issues such as people who are moving soon, or new arrivals in a community, or people who are about to lose their jobs (or already have). Why not set up situational groups for potential problems rather than after the fact? Why not develop preventive vocational and personal counseling? Such groups could meet to examine developmental strategies with the goal of deciding upon some developmental tasks to try out.

Simulation and gaming might be a good way to encourage people to look at what they do and to examine new strategies for growth. An example of this type of program is currently being tried at the Florida State University Counseling Center by means of "future groups." In these groups gestalt and fantasy exercises are used to aid the client in understanding his own fears, hopes, and expectations of what the future holds in store for him—especially as it relates to his vocational outlook. This awareness training helps the client to focus on the decision making processes and the self-in-time continuum.

References

1. BARRY, R., and WOLF, B. *Epitaph for vocational guidance.* New York: Teachers College, Columbia University, 1962.
2. IVEY, A., and MORRILL, W. Concept for vocational behavior. *Personnel and Guidance Journal,* 1968, *46,* 644–649.
3. LUFT, J. *Group process: An introduction to group dynamics.* Palo Alto, Calif: National Press, 1970.
4. SUPER, D. E., *Career development: Self-concept theory.* New York: College Entrance Examinations Board, 1963.
5. TOFFLER, A. *Future shock.* New York: Bantam Books, 1970.
6. ZYTOWSKI, D. G. (Ed.) *Vocational behavior: Readings in theory and research.* New York: Holt, Rinehart & Winston, 1968.

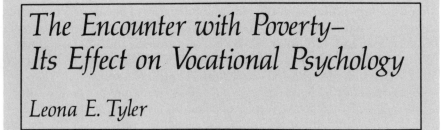

The Encounter with Poverty— Its Effect on Vocational Psychology

Leona E. Tyler

Much of what we know about the stages through which an individual passes as he prepares to find his place in the world of work might appropriately be labeled "The Vocational Development of Middle Class Males." How much of the knowledge is peculiar to this one particular group and how much can be generalized to large fractions of the human population constitutes a theoretical and practical problem of considerable importance.

Enough forays into the unknown territory have been made to suggest that different groups in the population may indeed differ considerably in their vocational development. Interest testing of girls and women has shown, for example, that the concept of a "career" is a much less important factor in the organization of their choices and rejections than it is for their brothers and male classmates. A comprehensive theory of vocational development in females parallel to that being evolved by Super and his associates at Columbia (1963) for males has yet to be presented. McArthur's studies (1954) of upper class boys have shown

Reprinted from *Rehabilitation Counseling Bulletin,* Vol. XI. Special, Fall 1967, pp. 61–70. Copyright 1967 American Personnel and Guidance Association. Reprinted with permission.

that in the relationship between interests and career the upper class differs markedly from the middle class. Clark (1961) has demonstrated that differentiated interest patterns do develop in men who work at the skilled and semi-skilled level—plumbers, electricians, mechanics, and the like—but we know little as yet about the career patterns characterizing persons in these occupations over long periods of time. About the occupational thinking of the groups below such workers in the class status pyramid, the traditional "hewers of wood and drawers of water" as well as the chronically unemployed, we as yet know very little.

The various anti-poverty programs are now making it possible for psychologists and vocational educators to gain some of this much needed knowledge. Progress here does not depend entirely on formal research undertakings, although these are to be encouraged wherever possible. Just the kind of familiarity with the way other people think, that comes from interviewing them, working on group projects together, and participating in the happenings of their everyday lives, can generate new concepts, new research approaches, new theoretical ideas. The involvement of thousands of intelligent young persons in the life of the poor as VISTA volunteers, community youth leaders, or Job Corps counselors can hardly fail to affect profoundly the research and theoretical formulations of the next decade or two.

Important Research Questions

Certain questions can be singled out for special mention, questions to which research of the past has never given satisfactory answers. One of these is the motivational question: Why do people work? In the middle class society most thoroughly explored, it is clear that income alone is not the answer. While we glibly say, "A person has to eat!" when anyone asks us about our motives, we know that it is not actually hunger or the threat of hunger that is driving us, and some understanding of the full complexity of the motivational fabric into which the work we do is woven has been obtained—for selected occupational groups. But how general are such motives? To what extent are they developed through circumstances peculiar to a minority of human beings in a single period of history?

Psychologists have tended to assume that there is something pathological about non-work, that a healthy, normal person would not be "lazy." Thus we look for personality conflicts and difficulties to explain underachievement in school, "goldbricking" on the job, and willingness to live indefinitely on welfare checks. It may well be that our basic assumption is wrong. It may be that not to work at tasks set up by somebody else is a natural human reaction, and that only persons conditioned to it through appropriate course of training from early childhood on find holding down a job really congenial. At this juncture in history we need perhaps to consider this alternative hypothesis. Will a belief in the sanctity of work be of any use to us when technological progress has released mankind from the necessity of unremitting toil? This is an example of the kind of basic question that involvement in anti-poverty programs may stimulate us to ask. A thorough study of non-workers may point the way to a deeper understanding than we have heretofore achieved of what it is that an individual human being is basically motivated to do and to seek in a situation where work is not required of him.

Another set of research questions revolves around the concept of identity. How does a person develop a clear sense of *who he is?* What kinds of experience must he undergo to achieve identity? In the middle class males we have studied most extensively, career development is a fundamental component of identity development. When a man can say, "I am an architect," or even, "I am studying to be an architect," he indicates that his thinking about himself and his place in life is now organized around a strong central core, one that exercises an integrating influence on all the other aspects of life that surround it.

But how general is this phenomenon of identity formation through career choice? Are there other processes that can be substituted for this one, other organizing concepts that may serve the same purpose the concept of a professional role serves for middle class boys? Does a worker in a low-prestige occupation define his identity in occupational terms? Does inability to break into the labor force at all leave a young person handicapped in identity development, or does he find some other core concept around which to organize his perceptions and ideas about himself? When technological progress eliminates an occupation suddenly and completely, how is the identity of a worker in this occupation affected? If, with or without help, he shifts to an entirely different sort of work, does his identity then change? Things that are happening to people in this period of rapid change furnish us with many kinds of natural experiments to be utilized in furthering our knowledge of personality development.

A third variety of questions stimulated by association with the poor has to do with the ways in which work and human relationships are linked together. In this research domain, work can be either the dependent or the independent variable. If we are interested in work variables as *effects,* we can inquire into the ways in which family instability affects work motivation or occupational choice. Or we may ask how mothers' attitudes are related to sons' aspirations. Does the son of a family deserted by the father identify with some other male figure or does identification fail to occur in such cases? If, on the other hand, we view work variables as *causes,* we might ask such questions as: How does prolonged unemployment affect husband-wife relationships? When a ghetto youth gets a job and moves to another area, how are his relationships to family members and former friends changed?

It is evident as we consider all these kinds of research questions brought to the fore by experience in anti-poverty programs that such questions are important for both theoretical and practical reasons. Theories of vocational development, as well as more general theories of personality development, would be broadened and enriched by knowledge of these kinds. At the same time, practical efforts to deal with school dropouts, slums, unwanted leisure, family disintegration, and a host of other social problems really require that we have such knowledge to build on. Perhaps it is not possible on the basis of what we now know to design a "great society." But if we can in this first round of attempts to do so find out some essential things about personal development and social institutions, the next round may be far more efficacious than this one has been.

A New Theoretical Formulation

As is suggested in the previous section, if we are to make the most of our expanded opportunities for research we need to elaborate a set of theoretical concepts broad enough to include, along with vocational behavior and attitudes, other kinds of behavior and attitudes that may serve the same psychological purposes. One such theoretical structure rests on the central proposition that a developed human personality is only one of a larger number of *possible* personalities that could have developed from the same beginning. Nature is lavish in its provision of alternative possibilities. An intelligent, newborn infant is a creature capable of learning any one of thousands of languages, mastering any one of hundreds of special skills or crafts. In the course of his development a few of these possibilities are selected, a far larger number permanently ruled out. The choice of an occupation is one of these major acts of selection. We can use vocational development as a prototype of the developmental selective process as a whole, or we can study other kinds of choices crucial for later development and use our increased knowledge of the ongoing choice process to deepen our understanding of occupational choices.

Four important variables in this theoretical formulation are *alternatives, limits, plans* and *concepts about time.* We can start with any one of these variables to explore the system as a whole. If we start with *alternatives,* we might seek information about the ways in which a limited number of possibilities become differentiated from the vast matrix of biologically possible lines of development. It would be interesting to know what the effects are—on immediate behavior and on long-range development—of generating different numbers of alternatives from which choices must be made. If we start with questions about *limits,* we might wish to compare the effects—on immediate behavior and on long-range development—of *external* as compared with *internal* limiting factors. If we choose to ask questions about *plans,* we might compare the effects of detailed and specific plans for one's future with the effects of vague and undifferentiated plans. If we focus our research on *time concepts,* we might compare the developmental effects of short time perspectives with those of long time perspectives, or seek to find out how the development of highly "time-conscious" individuals differs from that of persons who pay little or no attention to the flight of time.

The results of longitudinal studies, continued through several decades in some instances, have thrown some light on questions like the foregoing, but mainly for middle class subjects. The crystallization of the alternative courses of action from which career choices and other important life choices are made seems to come about as a child masters the organized bodies of knowledge presented to him in school, and as he practices in his out-of-school hours those skills upon which his family and his age-mates place a high value—athletic, musical, mechanical, and many others. At the same time, probably mainly through identification with adults or peers who are important to him, he develops complex and subtle concepts about what life should or should not include, concepts that guide him in his choices and rejections among the available alternatives.

Whether or not this same process typically occurs in the children of the poor is a debatable (and researchable) question. It seems likely that the alternative courses of action available to a middle class adolescent are often not available to a slum youth because he has not mastered the knowledge presented to him in school and has not participated in out-of-school activities through which the skills valued by society are developed. It seems likely also that his concept of the nature of the good life may be much less clear than that of the middle class youth, or quite different in its outlines. Thus the life choices he makes and the plans based on such choices are likely to be very different from those of persons from wealthier families.

The fundamental nature of the limits that mark the channels within which development can occur also seems to be different for poor and for affluent families. For the poor youth the limiting factors are mainly *external.* He must take whatever job he can get rather than one that he wants. He must live where he can afford to rather than where he wishes to. For the reasonably wealthy youth, on the other hand, the limiting factors are mainly *internal.* It is required of him that he make conscious choices of what he will do, whether he wishes to choose or not. As suggested in the paragraph above, the value concepts he has internalized offer some guidelines for such choices. But often they do not suffice to narrow the range of alternatives sufficiently so that choices can be made easily or automatically. Any college counselor who has tried to help a talented student decide whether to major in law or architecture for example, knows how demanding this requirement that a person impose his own limits and definitely close out further development in certain directions can be. Research comparing the long-range effects of externally imposed limits and self-chosen limits would be of great interest and utility.

Preliminary research efforts suggest that time concepts of poor persons may be markedly different from those of middle class persons. The habit of looking far into the future and making plans for years to come seems to be much less common in poor than in affluent groups. This difference is of course related to all the other kinds of difference we have been considering. Whether a short time perspective is the cause or the effect of a lack of clearly delineated alternatives, vagueness in concepts about the good life, or externally imposed limits on choices, is probably less important than are questions about whether and how short time perspectives can be lengthened, and what the consequences of such modifications are. The important practical challenge research faces is to determine which of the variables in this interrelated system it is most feasible to change in order to bring about changes in the others. We have agreed that the kind of development that typically occurs in slum children does not lead to a desirable adaptation to the kind of world in which their adult lives must be lived. But we are by no means clear what should be done to change the course of this development.

It is to be hoped that through our efforts to modify the process of vocational development in children from poor families we shall be able to learn something about general developmental processes. Thinking about these efforts in terms of the theoretical concepts just presented, two overall comments about such attempts would seem to be in order. In the first place, we should aim for the *optimum* rather than the *maximum* level of the variables with which we are dealing. Much of the current discussion of human potentialities suggests that it would be desirable for each individual to actualize *all* of his potential. A proper appraisal of the finiteness of the time at an individual's disposal leads to a re-definition of this purpose. Nobody, regardless of how gifted or how successful he is, actualizes *all* of his potential. Limits are essential to development. To actualize some potentialities we must rule out any hope of actualizing others. While it may be better for a person to have several tentative courses of action than to be limited to a single one, to have too many alternatives may be as crippling a handicap as to have too few. Thus not all of the constriction in outlook that tends to characterize the lives of the poor is necessarily disadvantageous in the making of choices and plans, if enough room for freedom of movement is still present in the area that does remain open to the individual.

The other general thought it would be well to keep in mind, in all the anti-poverty efforts, is that advances in techniques of education and behavior modification now make it feasible to *produce* alternative courses of action if no reasonably attractive ones have been generated in the natural course of an individual's development. Because of new technological developments, the concept of a vocational counselor as in part a coordinator of available services makes more sense that it often has in the past. A counselor helps his client choose and plan, but one of the things that may be chosen and planned for is a learning experience that will open up one or more new alternative paths. When, for example, an illiterate slum dweller achieves literacy, several jobs may be open to him and he is now in a position to choose. Similarly, when a bright but rebellious dropout masters enough of the high school curriculum to pass an equivalency test for a high school diploma, he greatly enlarges the scope of his alternatives.

In order to learn as much as possible from the war on poverty, well-designed evaluation studies must be conducted. They need not be elaborate or complex, but they should be provided for at the time a program begins. It is not just a matter of "What *works?*" or "What does not work?" but also a matter of what *happens?* What *changes* occur in certain kinds of people under certain circumstances? Many of the programs now in progress or planned for the future constitute natural experiments, potentially far more rewarding than any we might set up in a laboratory.

Some Related Ideas

We can conclude, then, that what the various poverty programs have contributed so far to research on vocational development has been challenges rather than conclusions, questions rather than answers, new directions for research rather than research results. But even before these programs were launched, some new ideas related to those we have been considering had been proposed. The idea of subsuming occupational concepts under some broader class of concepts was proposed in a thoughtful and comprehensive analysis by Wrenn (1964) of the social and cultural milieu in which American youth are growing up. Wrenn revives the concept of *vocation* in its original sense of a *calling.* A person's decision about what he will do with his life may lead to a career, but it may not. The wealthy woman who devotes herself wholeheartedly to the improvement of conditions for the mentally ill or the development of a community art museum may have a clearer sense of vocation than most salaried office workers. If the time comes when shelter and sustenance are freely made available to all, this kind of decision about one's life may become essential for productive and rewarding living. The broader concept of *vocation* forms a more solid foundation for theories about the place of work in personality integration than the narrower concept of *occupation* does.

Another main type of modification that has been occurring in theoretical thinking about vocational development is the introduction of more flexibility into the concept of *stages.* The idea that successive periods of life are qualitatively different from one another has figured largely in what Freud, Piaget, Erikson, and several other prominent writers have had to say about development in general, and in what Ginzberg, Super, and others have had to say about vocational development in particular. It has become more and more clear that the sequences are not linked to particular ages and that the pattern that emerges under one set of circumstances may turn out to be very different from the pattern emerging under another set. In some individuals, for example, Ginzberg's fantasy choices may persist for a much longer time than in others. Some persons prolong Erikson's search for identity far beyond adolescence. While these developmental theorists probably never intended that their concepts be used in a rigid, all-or-none way, the habit of thinking flexibly about developmental stages has not been easy to inculcate and we are only now beginning to master it.

A third sort of change in the structure of our thinking that has been occurring is the coalesence of the two main varieties of psychological inquiry, experimental and correlational, first called for in Cronbach's presidential address (1957). The need for such a synthesis was especially acute in occupational research. For decades, applied psychologists schooled in manipulative experimental techniques worked on problems of industrial training and performance, while applied psychologists schooled in psychometric techniques worked on problems of selection. The goal of the first group was to *change* behavior, and the more change that could be brought about the better satisfied they were with their experimental techniques. The goal of the second group was to *measure* aptitudes, and the more unchanging such measurements were from test to retest the better satisfied they were with the reliability of their psychometric techniques. Cronbach and Gleser (1965) succeeded in constructing new models for research designed to investigate selection and training simultaneously. Decision theory ties the two together.

The implications of a shift of this sort for vocational counseling have not yet been fully explored. It is clear that counselors must become creators as well as assessors of aptitudes. It has become very clear that the measured aptitudes on which a person's occupational decisions are based have developed to their present level through learning processes and that, even though individuals differ in hereditary endowments on which talents are based, what a person is able to do depends to a considerable extent on what he has learned and practiced. But, at any given period of his life, the individual has only a finite amount of time and energy to devote to the cultivation of new talents. Thus a person with several options will usually find it advantageous to capitalize on some aptitude he has already developed. But a person who has very few possibilities open to him may be wise to devote a large amount of time and energy to bring at least one usable aptitude into existence. To do this requires skill in both assessment and experimental manipulation.

Other Areas of Application

Occupational thinking along the lines we have been following can be brought to bear on problems having nothing to do with poverty. One example is the problem of technologically displaced workers. The first matter on which the efforts of counselor and counselee must be focused in such cases is a determination of the valid alternative courses of action open to the client. If we interpret "courses of action" broadly enough to include other productive efforts besides work for salary or wages, it will sometimes turn out, especially in the cases of workers not far from retirement age, that such "vocations" as the cultivation of a craft, or wholehearted participation in some project for civic improvement, may constitute a sounder decision than retraining for a new occupation, provided that financial pressures are not too compelling. For an individual who must continue to earn his living, an educational program designed to develop an aptitude for a whole new field of work may be preferable to a briefer training program designed to develop a particular skill that may be rendered obsolete by the next round of technological change.

Another kind of problem that may benefit from consideration in terms of possibilities, limits, and choices is the problem of workers in underdeveloped countries. What sense of "vocation" does the individual in, for example, a poor Latin American country now have? Is he investing time and energy in something important to him, even if he is not doing what we consider to be productive work? If not, what alternatives does he have, or does he see? If they are non-existent or unappealing, how can the person develop psychological resources he does not now possess, and what economic changes in his country would need to occur concurrently in order for such resources to be utilized?

A third kind of problem that would be more readily solved if counselors were to think in terms of the concepts proposed here is the case of the handicapped person whose disability was incurred at such an early age that he has been unable to make any sort of vocational choice at any stage of his development. It is more meaningful to analyze such a person in his life situation in terms of possibility structures than in terms of stages of vocational development. How has he dealt with the arbitrary and fixed limits imposed on him by his handicap? Has he been active or passive in his response? Has he thought about his own future, immediate or remote, or has the time span he encompasses in his thinking become unusually restricted? Some assessment of such factors can help the counselor decide what must be done first. It is useless to try to stimulate a client to choose an occupation and formulate plans for training and entry into the occupation if he does not already possess some awareness of the future and some concepts about what is and is not possible for him. This awareness may need to be brought into existence through actual and vicarious experience before occupational planning is feasible. While rehabilitation counselors are the professional workers to whom such cases are ordinarily assigned, they have often noted that the process involved in helping such persons is not really rehabilitation at all. *Habilitation* would be a more descriptive term. The important thing is that they do need help and counselors must learn to help them.

A Final Word

Psychologists who have in the past designated their special fields as vocational development, counseling, or rehabilitation, along with many educational, clinical, and social psychologists, are now in the process of creating a new specialty focusing on the conservation of human resources. Just what the new specialization will be called or what its detailed structure will be like is not really the important consideration right now. What we can do is to set our course in this direction and to invest our energies in the tasks of elaborating ideas and inventing techniques for the new undertaking. If the psychologists' encounter with poverty accomplishes nothing more than to turn their efforts in this direction, it will have been well worthwhile.

References

CLARK, K. E. *Vocational interests of nonprofessional men*. Minneapolis: Univ. Minnesota Press, 1961.

CRONBACH, L. J. The two disciplines of scientific psychology. *American Psychologist*, 1957, *12*, 671–684.

CRONBACH, L. J. and GLESER, C. G. *Psychological tests and personnel decisions*. (2nd ed.) Urbana: Univ. Illinois Press, 1965.

McARTHUR, C. Long term validity of the Strong Interest Test in two subcultures. *Journal of Applied Psychology*, 1954, *38*, 346–353.

SUPER, D. E., STARISHEVSKY, R., MATLIN, N., and JORDAAN. J. P. *Career development: self-concept theory*. Princeton, N.J.: College Examination Board, 1963.

WRENN, C. G. Human values and work in American life. In H. Borow (Ed.), *Man in a world at work*. Boston: Houghton Mifflin, 1964.

Patterns of Organizational and Occupational Socialization

Edward Gross

Although traditional studies of socialization have focused on infancy and childhood, recent research has turned to adult socialization [4; 5; 15; 33]. Such research suggests that socialization is far from complete in childhood; it goes on throughout persons' lives, involving adjustment to and becoming members of schools, universities, occupations, and organizations. In later life persons disengage from such organizations to become socialized to appropriate roles in old age. Our focus in this article is on the socialization that occurs when persons begin working in organizations, a process that may involve socialization not only to the organization and its particular demands but also to occupations practiced within an organization. In the present day organizational world [8], the overwhelming majority of occupations are practiced within larger scale organizations.

In its basic sense the word *socialization* refers to making the individual into a member of society. In considerations of adult socialization, however, the term has been generalized to refer to the process by which individuals become members of any organization. Caplow [6] has grouped the changes that occur in organizational socialization into four categories: skills, self-image, involvements, and values. I shall use those categories in my analysis of what happens to persons in organizations.

New Skills or Accomplishments

The new member of any organization is expected to learn and is assisted in learning new kinds of skills that will enable him or her to accomplish desired organizational ends. That much is obvious and, indeed, many persons assume that that is all there is to organizational or occupational socialization. One must learn to operate a machine, how to wait on tables, how to command a military platoon. Such learning may be didactic or may take the form of an apprenticeship. Whatever the case, one ends up learning skills. Such a view, in my

Reprinted from *Vocational Guidance Quarterly*. Copyright 1975 American Personnel and Guidance Association. Reprinted with permission.

opinion, is simplistic and hardly catches the enormous complexity of the processes involved.

We may first call attention to the fact that there are a great many kinds of skills and some are so complex that the word *skill* is hardly adequate. Nor is the word *learning* especially helpful since it is a fuzzy description of involved articulated social processes. To disentangle some of the processes, it is profitable to distinguish between technical skills, tricks of the trade, and social skills.

Technical skills are the most obvious: The waitress learns to carry trays or to make out slips, the accountant learns the organizational routines for payment, students learn to do addition or multiplication, the safecracker learns how to make nitroglycerin [20]. Some such skills admit of didactic instruction or machine-paced learning; many do not but must instead be picked up in childhood. This is especially true of occupations socially inherited such as farming, and, indeed, becoming a farmer really means taking on a parental role. Hence, it is hardly surprising that it is in agriculture that child labor is found most frequently all over the world in spite of governmental attempts in some places to stamp it out. The situation is somewhat similar in other rural occupations such as fishing, lumbering, and, to some extent, mining.

Then there is a small group of occupations that seems to be strictly hereditary and in which an assortment of very special skills are passed down from generation to generation as family secrets. Some examples are bell casters, circus performers, croupiers, and often chefs. Learning such technical skills is not the only problem; how do persons get access to situations in which these technical skills are taught? One cannot arrange somehow to be born into a circus performer's family. In medicine, the key skills are not taught to any great extent in medical school but in the internship, during which students experience their first work with live patients [2]. Therefore the key problem is getting a good internship, and this is a major way that medicine restricts the entry of minority groups [17]. Such also would be the case for learning crime; Letkemann entitled one of his chapters "The Prison as School" [20].

Tricks of the trade are devices to save persons from their own mistakes. The most important tricks are those that save time, save energy, or prevent a person's being hurt. All occupations have shortcuts and a part of the efficiency of an experienced worker is attributable to them. A new teacher, for example, marks each examination paper in its entirety; the old hand marks one question at a time. In some occupations one must learn to lift heavy weights without strain. In others one learns how to avoid cutting oneself or hitting one's thumb with a hammer.

Matthews [22] has described the tricks of the trade in fighting fires. Rookie firefighters learn never to look up when scaling a ladder lest burning material fall on the face. They are told to put on their helmets before buttoning the firecoat so that, should they fall off the truck, the head at least will be protected. Most ingenious is the trick of the "smoke-eaters," who can stay in a smoky room for long periods. They develop the knack of getting breaths of fresh air through the nozzle of the hose before the water is pumped through, and, by listening, to know when to remove the mouth from the nozzle before the water comes roaring out.

Professional criminals run the continued risk of being "hurt" (caught) so they use tricks of the trade in great profusion. For example, professional pickpockets station themselves in a public place directly under a sign that reads "Beware of Pickpockets." Most men with money, after reading the sign, will reach for their wallets and women will clutch their purses a little more tightly, hence signaling to the thief who it is with significant amounts of money and where the money is. In organizations perhaps the most obvious trick is learning to cheat and get away with it [27].

Social skills refer to learning to get along with other workers or with clients and customers. One learns what is considered a day's work, what it is safe to talk about, and what one must keep secret. One discovers to whom one can talk, whom one must avoid, and how to protect fellow workers from criticism. One reason farming is inherited is that success depends heavily on the acquisition of entrepreneurial skills such as how to buy and sell, how to drive a bargain and with whom, and on whose word one can depend. Factory workers check one another's work and share in emergencies. In restaurants, the key social skill is handling customers. Whyte [35] has traced the problem of the "crying waitress" to her being in the middle of pressure from the customer on the one hand and the chef on the other. In crime, an important social skill revolves about the assessment of risk [20].

In many professions there is a heritage to acquire—folklore, persons of notoriety, famous events. There is also professional etiquette; knowledge of special titles, insignia, and dress; and marketplace information such as salaries and job information. Finally, there is the occupational argot. Examples include the familiar soldier's language, the language of the professional criminal, and the language of jazz and rock music players. The phenomenon seems to be universal for all well-established occupations and may be a sign that an occupation is well-established. The functions of such language seem to be only partly communicative; they seem also to have important social functions such as providing a means for identifying the experienced person and the person one can trust [16]. It is clear that such skills can hardly be learned outside actual work situations.

A final question is: Who does the teaching? This seems obvious and one would assume the answer would be a teacher, a foreman, or a trainer, but the situation is by no means clear. Thus, Geer and others [10] described the socialization process in a business machines school, a barber college, a school for nursing assistants, and a hospital for medical interns. In the case of the business machines school, the teacher was clearly indicated, although students learn some things from other students. By contrast, in the barber college the "teacher" turns out to be other students almost completely. In the cases of both the nursing assistants' school and medical interns' hospital, still another "teacher" turns out to be the patient.

New Self-image

Besides acquiring the skills and accomplishments described above, organizational or occupational recruits must learn new ways of seeing themselves. Becker and Carper [3] have described the way beginning students in physiology are at first unexcited but later come to see themselves as budding scientists. On the other hand, engineers in their sample see engineering as primarily a way to enter industry and move up the organizational ladder. In this process there may be age contingencies. Persons may see themselves as destined for a high position but later in their careers will settle for a lower one.

Westby [31] studied 70 members of a major U.S. symphony orchestra. He found a large difference in self-conceptions according to the age of the musician. The young tended to be enthusiastic and hopeful of becoming soloists someday; they often played in chamber music groups. The older members (often in their 40s) were more likely to settle down and to decide that such ambitions were not so rewarding in any case. These different values led to splits between the two groups in the orchestra. Clark [7] has described the way the junior college may function to shift the ambition pattern of persons who discover they do not have the motivation or perhaps the ability to succeed in a university.

Shifts in age bring up the whole question of demotion, about which there has grown a considerable body of literature [12]. Organizations must emphasize upward mobility opportunities in order to encourage motivation on the part of their employees, but not everyone has the ability. Nor will there necessarily be a place for everyone. Inevitably some will have to settle for lesser positions or, at some point, will have to be demoted because of changes in organizational demand or need. Such processes may require changes in self-attitudes that can be destructive; More [24] has noted that some persons may then become alientated. Further, demoting persons reflects on their sponsors and such demotions are not encouraging to younger persons, who speculate that the same sort of thing could happen to them in twenty or thirty years. Consequently, organizations adopt many devices such as creating the position of "assistant to" or making ambiguous moves [14] to avoid the appearance of demotion.

New Involvements

The new person begins to associate with new persons. University freshmen find themselves surrounded by persons just as capable as they, and, since many freshmen were among the top performers in their high schools, that experience is likely to be upsetting. Further, the university may become increasingly competitive (partly because of dropouts) as one moves through the system. Caplow [6] pointed out that socialization involves not simply the development of new relationships but the abandonment of old ones:

> For the recruit, the convert, the newly elected, adopted, or graduated, there is always the awareness that becoming what one is now means forgetting what one was before. The bride is no longer a maiden; the new chief is expelled from the peer group. The extent and importance of the old relationships that are to be abandoned usually determine what kind of socialization process is necessary. In those cases in which socialization takes a drastic form, the severity of the new experience is explained not so much by the difficulty of learning a new part as by the difficulty of forgetting the old (p. 171).

Perhaps the outstanding description of the problem of forgetting or eliminating prior statuses is provided by Goffman [13] in his vivid description of the process of mortification in mental hospitals. In occupations and organizations this is often accompanied by sequestration. Such sequestration may be ecological, in which persons are sent off to retreats, or may be temporal, in which the whole of the day and the night or longer periods may be given over to training. In some cases one lives in separate communities, as Lipset, Trow, and Coleman [21] have described for the case of printers.

New Values

One is expected to accept the values of some organizations wholeheartedly. Such may be the case in ideological parties, those committed to the election of certain persons, or convents. In other organizations one is not necessarily expected to absorb the organization's values but one is expected at least to be indifferent to them. For example, private businesses do not necessarily insist that the recruit become identified with the organization's goals but they assume that at least he or she will not resist them. This is likely to become less true as one moves up in the organization and, indeed, the top executives may be wholeheartedly identified with the organization and with what it stands for. Finally, in some organizations one must assume that persons reject the values of the organization, as in prisons or other organizations in which persons experience involuntary servitude. But even there inmates may find they have to accept the norms of the organization just to get out, or at least to minimize the pains of imprisonment. In turn, they may accept fellow-inmate values.

The acceptance of values is especially important where socialization takes the form of an apprenticeship and, where the learning takes place on the job, in association with the experienced members of the organization or the occupation. Examples include graduate schools, artist schools, and executive suites. Here it is assumed that you must do more than simply learn; you must take a special view of the world.

A number of researchers have reported a shift among nurse trainees from a lay conception of the job to a more technical conception [26]. The matter is described vividly by Simpson [28]:

Know This

Without exception our student nurses said that their main reason for choosing nursing as a career had been the wish to be of service to suffering people. When their freshman year began, they were disappointed upon finding that the entire first semester was devoted to academic classroom work: they had expected to learn things that were immediately useful in helping the sick. When basic nursing training began in the hospital during the second freshman semester, the students mainly wanted to develop nurturant relationships with patients. They found, however, that sometimes the faculty's training requirements thwarted this wish.

The purpose of the hospital experience, as this was defined by the nursing faculty, was not so much to serve individual patients as it was to impart certain specialized skills as well as proficiency in following routines and procedures. This technical orientation was evident in the teaching of simple basic nursing tasks, which were defined as standardized procedures to be performed in precise sequences of steps. Making a bed, for instance, called for 21 consecutive steps. In both teaching and grading the faculty emphasized the accuracy with which these routines were mastered, not the welfare of the patients on whom the students practiced their nursing skills. . . .

During the two semesters of basic nursing, the gradual shift of interest from a humanistic concern with patients as individuals to a concern with mastery of technical repertoires was evident in off-duty conversations among student nurses. At first they talked mainly about patients as persons: what a sad life Mrs. Jones had led, or how much better Mr. Brown felt this morning. Later, however, technical considerations were found to predominate in conversations. Mrs. Jones was now a "challenging patient," and Mr. Brown was taking his medicine more willingly. Instead of discussing the suffering of a patient, they were more likely to talk about the severity of his illness or the rarity of his disease.

Thus a definite transformation was visible during the first year and a half of nursing school. The entering freshman wanted to serve others, and she wanted to be a nurse as a means to this end. A year and a half later she wanted above all to be a nurse; and she had learned that to be regarded as a nurse by others, she had to know the specific skills which are the mark of the nurse. Service values were transformed, not displaced, by technical interests. . . . Throughout the training experiences of basic nursing the primary concern of the student shifted from helping a patient to playing the role of a nurse. During this shift, the service value started to be generalized to the nurse role; its expression was no longer dependent on developing a nurturant relationship with a patient (pp. 48–49).

Westley [32] has called attention to the fact that the police operate in a world often hostile to the police function itself. As a result, the police have been pushed into isolation and secrecy in their work. This leads to a pervasive secretiveness and to a willingness to condone violence. One result of this is that the police often see themselves as being concerned with defending each other from society as much as defending society from criminals.

Generally speaking it seems clear that teaching or learning such values is difficult and probably can be learned only on the job, where persons associate with already committed workers or their models. This has led to an emphasis in research on what has been called "anticipatory socialization" [3; 23]. In addition, it is usually necessary that such values be communicated subtly. For example, Olesen and Whittaker [25] show how laughter and silences are used by nursing instructors as teaching devices.

Socialization or Selection?

It is worth emphasizing that one way by which organizations make it easy for themselves to socialize new recruits is careful screening or selection. Not much is known about this process, however, it must be recognized that all organizations try to select their membership and, in that sense, organizations are almost never random samples of the population. Selection is difficult and even when successful may produce problems, as when persons who have been selected because of certain traits turn out to be ill-adapted to the requirements of the organization once they are promoted to new positions [1]. The schools try to control this process by selection according to qualifications. If forced to take all students, then they are likely to select within the schools for special programs. There will be ability groupings within grade schools and in universities there are special requirements for entry into professional schools.

The phenomenon of selection raises an important issue. If organizations try to select persons according to certain ideal characteristics, then perhaps they do not socialize their members at all. Or, to put the matter in another way, how does one study socialization if the members of organizations have been preselected? What one attributes to socialization may in fact be due to the process of selection, assisted by dropouts.

Studies by Wheeler [34] in Scandinavian prisons, Massachusetts institutions for juvenile delinquents, and California prisons concluded that selection is more important than socialization in accounting for the values and behavior of prison inmates. This conclusion tends to be supported by studies of women's prisons [11; 19; 30]. However, other studies tend to support a deprivation theory that suggests that it is the prison itself which accounts for prisoner behavior. Street, Vinter, and Perrow [29], for example, showed that when prisoners in therapeutic prisons were compared with those in more orthodox custodial prisons, there was less deprivation in the former, a situation that may account for the finding that the values and behavior of the prisoners were different. The trouble is that, as prisoners are not randomly assigned to such prisons, there is a confounding effect of selection and deprivation.

Studies in universities [18] tend to show that socialization is much more important in accounting for student behavior than is selection. It is probably important to note that the difference between the two kinds of organizations, prisons and universities, includes the degree of voluntariness. It is perhaps not surprising that socialization is less successful where persons do not want to be socialized (prisons) than where they are presumably more willing, as in the case of universities.

A Four-Process Model

Any model of organizational socialization will have to consider the effects of selection both at entry (in-selection) and at departure (dropouts or persons being selected out in other ways—a process we may call "out-selection"). It is also possible that the members of the organization themselves may affect the goals or values of the organization, thus producing a kind of "counter-socialization."

All four processes (in-selection, out-selection, socialization, and counter-socialization) operate in all organizations but probably differ depending on the kind of organization. In-selection is probably most common when an organization has an excess of applicants, as in the case of elite colleges, medical schools, elite military academies, or Wall Street law firms. Out-selection is also present in such elite institutions, but those institutions rarely select out very many because it is too embarrassing for them to confess failure and it may interfere with their ability to attract others. However, it does take place, as in the case of religious excommunication and, occasionally, of deviant labor unions. Those examples illustrate a danger. An excommunicated cleric may found a new sect; the United Mine Workers, if thrown out of the AF of L, may go ahead and form the CIO.

Socialization is most common and most effective where the organization expects to make major changes in the personality or attitudes of its members and where the members willingly lend themselves to such changes. Examples include schools, convents, monasteries, certain kinds of therapeutic prisons, and certain kinds of mental hospitals, especially those to which persons voluntarily commit themselves. Garnier [9] has described this process for the case of the Sandhurst Military Academy in England.

Finally, although counter-socialization does go on, we have few research examples. It seems to occur when there is a considerable change in the makeup of the members of an organization, as, for example, when an organization hires a considerable number of women or blacks. After World War II there was a large influx of veterans many of whom rejected traditional college fraternity values as being frivolous, a process that helped to bring about a decline in those values and a lessening of interest in joining fraternities. It also seems highly likely that it was the sheer increase in the number of students who came of college age in the 1960s that led to some of the troubles of that period.

The emphasis of this paper on organizational and occupational socialization has naturally placed the organization or occupation in an active role. However, it must be recognized that a good deal of organizational and occupational socialization takes place at a young age. In one sense the whole culture tends to socialize persons for organizational and occupational performance at an early age through media and organizational exposure. Perhaps the most important influence is school itself—certainly a large organization. Students at a tender age are exposed to hierarchy every time they are asked to report to the principal's office, and to specialization when they are exposed to different teachers or when they meet the counselor. The emotional disciplining that is felt to be so characteristic of organizations is taught when students must wait in line to get into the cafeteria or when the fire drill occurs. Class scheduling introduces young students to the importance of time. The study of the way childhood socialization articulates with adult socialization is an important area of inquiry that has hardly begun. Similarly, organizational and occupational socialization have obvious important implications for job satisfaction and this relationship should be investigated.

References

1. ARGYRIS, C. Organization of a bank. New Haven, Conn.: Labor and Management Center, Yale University, 1954.
2. BECKER, H. S.; GEER, B.; HUGHES, E.; and STRAUSS, A. L. Boys in white. Chicago: University of Chicago Press, 1961.
3. BECKER, H. S., and CARPER, J. W. The development of identification with an occupation. American Journal of Sociology, 1956, 61, 289–298.
4. BRIM, O. G., JR. Socialization through the life cycle. In O. G. Brim, Jr., & S. Wheeler, Socialization after childhood: Two essays. New York: Wiley, 1966.
5. BRIM, O. G., JR. Adult socialization. In J. A. Clausen (Ed.), Socialization and society, Boston: Little, Brown, 1968.

6. CAPLOW, T. *Principles of organization*. New York: Harcourt Brace & World, 1964.
7. CLARK, B. *The open door college*. New York: McGraw-Hill, 1960.
8. ETZIONI, A. *Modern organizations*. Englewood Cliffs, N.J.: Prentice-Hall, 1964.
9. GARNIER, M. Changing recruitment patterns and organizational ideology: The case of a British military academy. *Administrative Science Quarterly*, 1972, *17*, 499–507.
10. GEER, B., et al. Learning the ropes: Situational learning in four occupational training programs. In I. Deutscher and E. J. Thompson (Eds.). *Among the people: Encounters with the poor*. New York: Basic Books, 1968.
11. GIALLOMBARDO, R. *Society of women*. New York: Wiley, 1966.
12. GLASER, B. G. (Ed.) *Organizational careers*. Chicago: Aldine, 1968.
13. GOFFMAN, E., *Asylums*. Garden City, N.Y.: Doubleday, 1961.
14. GOLDNER, F. H. Demotion in industrial management. *American Sociological Review*, 1965, *30*, 714–724.
15. GOSLIN, D. (Ed.) *Handbook of socialization theory and research*. Chicago: Rand-McNally, 1969.
16. GROSS, E. *Work and society*. New York: Crowell, 1958.
17. HALL, O. The stages of a medical career. *American Journal of Sociology*, 1948, *53*, 327–336.
18. HARGENS, L. L., and HAGSTROM, W. O. Sponsored and contest mobility of American academic scientists. *Sociology of Education*, 1967, *40*, 24–38.
19. HEFFERNAN, M. E. Inmate social systems and subsystems: The "square," the "cool" and the "life." Doctoral dissertation, Catholic University of America, 1964.
20. LETKEMANN, P. *Crime as work*. Englewood Cliffs, N.J.: Prentice Hall, 1973.
21. LIPSET, S. M.; TROW, M.; and COLEMAN, J. S. *Union democracy*. Garden City, N.Y.: Doubleday, 1962.
22. MATTHEWS, T. J. *The urban fire station*. Unpublished masters thesis, Department of Sociology, Washington State University, 1950.
23. MERTON, R. K., and KITT, A. S. Contributions to the theory of reference group behavior. In R. K. Merton and P. F. Lazarsfeld (Eds.), *Studies in the scope and method of "The American Soldier."* Glencoe, Ill.: Free Press, 1950.
24. MORE, D. M. Demotion. *Social Problems*, 1962, *9*, 213–221.
25. OLESEN, V. L., and WHITTAKER, E. W. Adjudication of student awareness in professional socialization: The language of laughter and silences. *Sociological Quarterly*, 1966, *7*, 381–396.
26. PSATHAS, G. The fate of idealism in nursing school. *Journal of Health and Social Behavior*, 1968, *9*, 52–64.
27. ROY, D. Efficiency and "the fix": Informal intergroup relations in a piecework machine shop. *American Journal of Sociology*, 1954, *60*, 255–266.
28. SIMPSON, I. H. Patterns of socialization into professions: The case of student nurses. *Sociological Inquiry*, 1967, *37*, 47–53.
29. STREET, D.; VINTER, R. D.; and PERROW, C. *Organization for treatment*. New York: Free Press, 1966.
30. WARD, D., and KASSEBAUM, G. *Women's prison*. Chicago: Aldine, 1965.
31. WESTBY, D. L. The career experience of the symphony musician. *Social Forces*, 1960, *38*, 223–230.
32. WESTLEY, W. A. *Violence and the police*. Cambridge, Mass.: MIT Press, 1970.
33. WHEELER, S. The structure of formally organized socialization settings. In O. G. Brim, Jr. and S. Wheeler, *Socialization after childhood: Two essays*. New York: Wiley, 1966.

34. WHEELER, S. Socialization in correctional institutions. In D. Goslin (Ed.), *Handbook of socialization theory and research.* Chicago: Rand-McNally, 1969.
35. WHYTE, W. F. *Human relations in the restaurant industry.* New York: McGraw-Hill, 1948.

Aging and the Nature of Work

Seymour B. Sarason,
Esther K. Sarason,
and
Peter Cowden

In Western society, at least, the view that the nature of work poses serious personal and social problems is not new. The age of the machine, nurtured by the science, technology, and invention ushered in by the Renaissance and growing rapidly as a result of the industrial revolution, was early on seen as a mixed blessing. One part of the blessing was wrapped up in the concept of progress: man's capacity through reason (impersonal, objective, and implacable) to understand and use the laws of nature so as to lead, slowly but surely, to an earthly heaven. The other part was in the nature of a curse: the means whereby this earthly heaven was to be achieved would come to dominate man, alienating him from himself (his "true" nature) and others (the "natural" order of social living). Whatever criticisms can be directed at Marx's heroic intellectual effort to conceptualize the past in order to factor out the harbingers of an inevitable future, no one has seriously contested his analysis of how the age of the machine has adversely transformed the nature of work and, therefore, man's consciousness. Just as in the 1954 desegregation decision when the Supreme Court contended that segregation had adverse effects both on the segregatee and the segregator, almost a century earlier Marx was making the identical point about capitalists and workers. It is beyond the scope of this article to examine the history of the changing

Reprinted from *American Psychologist,* **30:**584–592 (May 1975). Copyright 1975 by the American Psychological Association. Reprinted by permission.

nature of work. The interested reader should consult the writings of Lewis Mumford, and also Thomas Green's (1968) illuminating *Work, Leisure, and the American Schools*. We allude to history not only as a caution against the parochialism that is a consequence of the ahistorical stance but, as we hope to make clear shortly, because history ill prepared us to recognize that work has become a problem for many *professionals* who heretofore were viewed as the chosen few exempt from feelings of boredom, lack of challenge, and sense of worth. Professionals have long sold themselves and others the view that it was the factory worker who was victimized by the nature of his work.[1] In Green's terms, the man in the factory *labored;* the professional *worked.* And the difference between laboring and working (in Green's terms) is no different than that between Marx's industrial slave and capitalist exploiter. One was stamped or branded *by* his work; the other put his stamp or brand *on* his work.

A brief comment is in order about the title of this article, if only to note and explain why we will have relatively little to say about aging. A basic hypothesis in our approach is that one's relationship to work is one of the important determinants of how present and future time is experienced, that is, one's sense of the passage of time. This sense of the passage of time inevitably shapes and becomes one's psychological sense of aging. It follows that there should be no significant correlation between the psychological sense of aging and biological processes, although at some point they become intertwined. When we use such words as *aging* or the *aged,* we usually implicitly assume that the awareness of aging begins at or after midlife. When we see in ourselves or others the visible signs of biological aging, it takes no particular psychological wisdom to assume that they have psychological correlates. In our culture, at least, we do not think of people as aging or aged until we literally see the visible signs of biological aging. We are not accustomed to thinking of the psychological sense of aging in developmental terms, as an internal set of attitudes shaped by experiences of various kinds in a culture suffused with reminders of the passage of time—reminders that almost always are wittingly or unwittingly calculated to make us view that passage in dysphoric terms. But once it becomes obvious that the psychological sense of aging has its developmental roots in our experience of the

[1] There is a serious problem in interpreting findings about job satisfaction from available studies, especially because almost all of the studies are based on questionnaire data. To express dissatisfaction or boredom with, or a waning interest in, one's work—*particularly if one's work is judged by society as fascinating and important as in the case of many professions*—is no easy matter. To face up to such dissatisfaction is literally to question what one *is* and to have to justify continuing as one has. It is no less difficult, upsetting, and propelling than to come to the realization that one no longer wishes to live with one's spouse. Our experience suggests that to talk candidly about one's relationship to one's work is as difficult as talking about one's sex life. We define ourselves, and are defined by others, by what we do: our work. To question this definition produces internal conflict, in part precisely because we know that we have come to see ourselves quite differently than others do.

passage of time—once we unlearn the habit of thinking in terms of a high correlation between the psychological sense of aging and chronological age—we can direct our attention to those things that influence the content and vicissitudes of the experience of the passage of time and, therefore, the emerging sense of aging. And one of these important factors is one's experiences in the world of work: how one plans for, enters, and experiences work. This is one factor, but it is very complicated, related as it is to the major dimensions by which our society is organized, for example, economic, class, sex, education, the family unit, religion, race, etc. In this article, therefore, we restrict ourselves to some of the considerations directing our exploratory studies.

Policy and Populations

When this project began to be developed in 1972, our sole focus was on the problems of older people. As we read the literature, talked with numerous professionals, and drew upon a variety of personal experiences, several things became apparent or started to emerge. The literature was overwhelmingly clinical and, not surprisingly, so were and are the myriads of public programs to which it gave rise. Stated most simply: Old people had a lot of serious personal, social, financial, housing, and medical problems, and society had an obligation to alleviate their plight. There was, of course, a secondary preventive thrust to these programs in that they aimed to avoid having existing problems worsen and create new problems. It is fair to say that a primary preventive approach was conspicuous by its absence, although on the level of rhetoric it was given lip service. A second factor, related to the first, was the enormous and morally upsetting discrepancy between defined needs and available resources, a characteristic endemic to the clinical endeavor. Frankly, as we became more involved with aged individuals and their families, with settings we euphemistically call *convalescent* or *nursing homes,* as well as with a medical profession whose knowledge of and attitudes toward the elderly quintessentially illustrate the pernicious aspects of the self-fulfilling prophecy, we had inordinate difficulty maintaining our own stability. For the first year we found ourselves deeply focused on examination of policies and programs (retirement, age discrimination, housing, transportation, public education): their underlying assumptions, the cultural attitudes which powered them, implementation, and effectiveness.

Our disquietude had another source: our bias in favor of a preventive–developmental approach to human problems. We were aware that, despite our bias, we were being drawn more and more into a remedial framework which, given our project resources, seemed inefficient if not ludicrous. It should go without saying that anyone whose efforts are directed to clinical work—be it with the elderly, children, or any other group in need—does not have to justify his activities (their effectiveness is another issue). When you are in need and seek help, you are (or should be) grateful that clinicians exist. But when these needs are staggering in their frequency, and in varying ways and degrees reflect characteristics of our society, the limitations of an exclusively clinical approach are obvious (Sarason, 1974). This is especially true when the nature of and the rationale for the clinical approach hardly reflects a sensitivity to the larger social context.

It was both our bias and disquietude that opened our eyes and ears to "messages" to which we had been responding in terms as far removed from aging as one could imagine. Embedded as we were in a university, interacting constantly with students of widely differing backgrounds and interests, trying hard to comprehend their articulated dissatisfactions with society's past, present, and future, puzzled by their bleak projections of themselves over their life span, fascinated by the different life-styles they were trying—at some point we attached several significances to these observations that gave expression to our bias and allowed us to think differently about aging.

A sizable fraction of students feared being *trapped* in life. This was phrased and fantasied in different ways by students, but there was the common theme that their postcollege future would be a downhill experience. This did not mean (for most, at least) that they did not wish it would be otherwise or that they would not strive to make it otherwise, but rather that they feared the probabilities were high that they would become mired in an "establishment" existence tantamount to a slow death. They spoke about the future with a depressive and oppressive anxiety similar to that which one hears in the elderly. What we are trying to say is captured in the title of a book written by an undergraduate, *Growing Up Old in the Sixties* (Maynard, 1973). When we would ask students to write about "How young or old do you feel?" a surprising number said that they did not feel young but, rather (surprising *to them*), old. When we would interrogate them, sometimes in long no-holds-barred discussion, about how they would account for such a feeling—why they viewed the future so bleakly—they were not very articulate until they forced us (the interrogators) to face the fact that we grew up in very different times; that is, we grew up when it was possible to believe that society could be significantly reformed, whereas they were growing up when such a possibility was virtually nonexistent.

In light of the above, it was not surprising that so many students thought about and planned for a career with reluctance, anxiety, and even anger. As one student put it: "Why blame us for trying to postpone dying?" Or as another student put it: "Why should it be puzzling to you that we have serious doubts about striving for something that may kill us?" We make no claims about the generality of these feelings and attitudes except to say that we obtained them from undergraduate and graduate students in different universities. Obviously, there are many students who do not share these feelings and attitudes. Although it is important, it is not crucial for our purposes here to estimate the percentage of students who do have these reactions. Of the countless colleagues, at Yale and elsewhere, with whom we have discussed these matters, not one doubted that these attitudes were frequent. And, let us not overlook another obvious fact: the number of students who have dropped out of school and society not available to us for questioning.

When we put our experiences with college students together with our knowledge of public policy and programming for the elderly, we were struck by something we consider of enormous significance. *Theory and practice in regard to the elderly are almost totally determined by the perceived characteristics of those who are now elderly. In three or more decades we will have the most formally educated aged population any society has ever had. There is good reason to believe that becoming aged will pose for them and society problems radically different and potentially more personally and socially disruptive than is the case with today's elderly population.*[2] Once the "obvious" dawned on us it reinforced our determination to pursue a developmental course of investigation. It also gave substantive direction to the kinds of studies we had to undertake. These studies are in their initial phases. Their thrust is best communicated by the considerations underlying them.

Considerations

Our studies, for a while at least, will concentrate on people who have had or are now obtaining a higher education. This focus, as we have suggested, is dictated not only by the relative narrowness in the literature on work but also by the knowledge that over the next few decades an increasing segment of our society will have had some degree of college experience.

1. *The process of making a career choice is the first significant confrontation with the sense of aging, involving as it does the knowledge or belief that such a decision is fateful because it determines how the rest of one's life will be "filled in."* It is a "moment of truth" kind of problem which makes for varying degrees of vacillation, postponement, and anxiety because the choice involves numerous factors: strength of interests, familial relationships and pressures, economic factors (personal and national), love and peer relationships, time per-

[2] In April 1974, after this article was prepared, the Federal Administration on Aging circulated guidelines and priorities for support of model projects of national scope. There is no doubt from these documents that policy and programs are being viewed only in terms of those who are currently elderly. One should be thankful, of course, for this concern, but in terms of national programs and policies it is amazingly shortsighted.

spective, and how one reads and structures the future. The need for independence and autonomy comes face-to-face with societal pressure to conform, not the least of which is that one feels one *has* to make a decision at a particular point in time. One can no longer sample from the smorgasbord of opportunity; one *must* choose and live with the choice. There are, of course, individuals, probably small in number, who long have known what they were going to do; they are viewed by some with envy, by others with derision, and by still others with an effete attitude that seems to be saying "anyone who willingly and joyously enters this real world with the expectation of happiness has postponed his moment of truth." However one conceptualizes the process of career choice, one cannot ignore that at this particular time in our society the process is for many suffused with dysphoric anticipations about what may be symbolically called *dying*. It is not only a matter of "am I making the right or wrong choice" but, for many, "will society allow me to be the kind of person I want to be, regardless of choice?" The locus of control is perceived as external rather than internal. This has probably been the case for past decades, but it was accompanied by the belief that by striving, diligence, and maneuvering one could lick the odds. This accompaniment is much less in evidence today.

2. Since World War II, and in no small measure because of it, the number of new fields and career possibilities has escalated. Just as during this same period it has become possible to easily travel and vacation any place on this earth, a young person today is aware of a much greater array of career possibilities than was true in his parents' generation. *Both within and among fields the choices are many. Students are aware of this as they are of the stubborn fact that they must make a choice. They are also aware that at the same time that society tells them that there are numerous directions available to them, the educational system (beginning in high school) is organized increasingly to pressure the student to narrow his choices.* In college they must choose a major, and in graduate and professional school they are also forced to declare their choice. For example, a student does not apply to graduate school because he is interested in the field of psychology but rather because he has been required, formally or informally, to declare his special interest, e.g., clinical, physiological, social, personality, child, cognitive, industrial, educational, learning. Theoretically the options are many; in practice they are few. The discrepancy, for some students, arouses a strange mixture of sense of loss, the need to justify choice by eliminating dissonance, and a passive acceptance of fate's workings. For others the discrepancy is far less of a problem. By the time a student of either type has been in graduate or professional school for a year or more he already knows how narrow his horizons have become. This is especially true for that ever-increasing number of students who choose medicine or law because each of

these fields was perceived as containing many more career options than other fields.

3. *For many reasons, chiefly demographic and economic, our society will increasingly contain individuals who will go through life knowing that they never were able to enter the career of their first choice.* There has always been a discrepancy between the number of graduate and professional school applications and openings. In recent years this discrepancy has become nothing short of scandalous. Not having the opportunity to enter the career of first choice need not be a tragedy, and undoubtedly there are some individuals who enter other careers that give them satisfactions. But for many the disappointment will be a festering irritant interacting with later frustrations to cloud present and future with the deprivations of the past. To go through life knowing that one's work is one's second or third choice must affect one's sense of the passage of time, how one justifies existence and looks to an ever-shortening future. The sense of worth has diverse sources, but few are as potent as how one regards one's work. It could be argued that the market place of life finds ways of compensating for disappointments; that is, an unsatisfied demand will be made up for by some substitute supply of compensation. But markets, economic and psychological, break down, sometimes with convulsive consequences. When we consider that our society will have an increasing number of educated people as well as an increasing number who will not have been "allowed" to pursue a primary interest, it is difficult to adopt an indifferent or positive stance. Rising expectations together with rising frustrations have a revolutionary potential which, when and if it becomes manifest, can take a retrograde rather than a progressive form.

4. *There has been an increase in the number of people who seek a career change, be that change within or between fields of work.* There are no data on the frequency of such changes, but our observations, interviews, and some exploratory studies lead us to the conclusion that it is far from an infrequent phenomenon. The dynamics powering such changes are complicated and varied. The sought-for change can take place at any time after one has begun a career. Indeed, it is our impression that whereas it used to be a "midcareer crisis," it now can occur much earlier. Several factors have contributed to both the increased frequency and earlier timing of career changes. One of these factors is the emphasis placed on the social worth of one's work. It has always been the case that professionals were expected to experience their work as personally satisfying, its social worthiness being taken for granted. It is precisely the social worth of much professional work that has been called into question in recent years. The atomic bombing of Hiroshima, the generalized consequences of the turbulent sixties, the turmoil surrounding the Vietnam war—this train of events instigated in many professionals profound questioning about the significance of their work. If the questioning was not strong enough to

produce wholesale career changes, it nevertheless placed the significance of work high on the social agenda. When individuals no longer believe in the inevitability of progress, when they see themselves and their work as perhaps contributing to the moral confusion, it is small wonder that some will seek to make radical changes in their work and life style. Another factor, no less important than the first, is that recent generations have expected more from their work, that is, that their work will and should always be challenging and novelty producing. That is to say, work should be intrinsically stimulating and productive of "self-actualization" or "personal growth." And can anyone doubt that the past few decades has seen a fantastic rise in the number of people who spend their time helping others to "grow," to recognize their "true selves," to be unafraid of change and novelty, and "to do their thing"? Ours is a time of conflicting and even contradictory tendencies: a new form of rugged individualism and a heightened sense of social responsibility. It was inevitable that these tendencies would have repercussions in the world of work in the form of an increase in career changes. The dynamics and their consequences are similar to those with respect to marriage and divorce. On the level of rhetoric, at least, it used to be that when one got married it was supposed to be forever, a view of the future supported by religion and law. And if one did not believe that marriages were made in heaven, there was no doubt that they could not easily be undone on earth. One was expected to make the best of the marriage. One life, one marriage partner. That, of course, has changed as it is changing in the world of work. It is true that our society has made it far easier to change marriage partners than to change careers, but that difference may well be in the process of being eroded. What is involved here is not only a changing set of attitudes toward work but to the experience of the passage of time in which dying and "imprisonment" are symbolically or literally somewhere in the background. To see one's self as remaining "unfulfilled" or "bored" or "locked in" in what is perceived as a world of endless possibilities in a finite, shortening life raises the conflict between activity and passivity to a very heightened level, higher, we think, than it has ever been before in our society.

Each of the above four statements could be elaborated into a book and, in fact, each has received extended comment and analysis from different perspectives in hundreds of books written in the past two decades. Despite these different perspectives there is agreement on one thing: Although their sources and dynamics have roots in the distant past and there have been and probably will be a waxing and waning in their surface manifestations, there has been a significant alteration in people's attitudes and values in regard to self, work, and social living. To some this alteration is prologue to social decay; to others it is prodromal to a better world in the making; to still others it is only confusion compounded of mystery and meaninglessness leading nowhere in particular. Without question, it is the younger generations who tend to pessimism, cynicism, and even nihilism. Their view of themselves in the future bears some startling similarities to what one frequently finds among the aged. Whereas many of the aged (or not so aged) look back and ask: *"Was it worth it?"* many younger people look forward and ask: *"Will it be worth it?"* And although these two questions have a complex of referents, the experience of work is among the most important.

The four statements have given and will give direction to a variety of initial studies on the process and phenomenology of career choice among college students: changes in attitudes toward the career and the future that take place in the course of graduate and professional education, the timing and frequency of career changes, and the ever developing awareness of the sense of the passage of time and its merging into the sense of aging. We do not doubt that our studies will cause us to change our conceptions in certain respects. Our initial data, however, confirm what we suspected in two very important respects. First, the years devoted to professional education are experienced as an ever-narrowing of horizons and options in which personal choice and style are compromised by the need to conform to externally set criteria of "success." For example, when one interviews students headed for law, medical, or graduate school, they have two major expectations: Either they see themselves as having boundless opportunities to absorb new knowledge and experience which will subsequently open all sorts of career possibilities to them in the near and distant future, or they recognize that there will or may be a conflict between what they hope and what they will be required to do, but somehow their internal compass for maintaining integrity will protect them (a subsegment of this group are those who truly view professional education with foreboding and no compass). When one interviews students near the end of their professional training, one is struck by their feeling that they have been "molded," have been forced to become "realistic," and that the options they once expected to be available to them have been reduced drastically. There is in many of them a quiet desperation, a knowledge that the status, capabilities, and satisfactions that society projects onto them, far from being balm, create in them a guilty unease. And when we find, as we have, that at least 20 per cent of a sample of physicians explicitly express dissatisfaction with their careers, the forebodings of our younger interviewees cannot be viewed as without some merit.[3]

The second way in which our exploratory studies support what we

---

[3] These data were obtained by Victor Lieberman in a study not designed to get at job satisfaction, but three questions relevant to job satisfaction were added. These data are not reported in his write-up (Lieberman, 1974). The interviews were of necessity brief and there was a marked age discrepancy between the interviewer and the physicians. It was surprising, therefore, that 20 per cent unambiguously expressed dissatisfaction with their work. Informal interviews with physicians we knew well—enabling us to ask direct and unambiguous questions—lead us to believe that 20 per cent is an underestimate.

and others have intuited is that the number of people who seek a career change is not small. Based on an analysis of graduate school applicants, and depending on how one defines career change, we found between 10 and 20 per cent who were 25 years or older and sought a change. We have also become aware (by reading the advertising section for professional personnel in the *New York Times*) that within the past few years agencies have come into existence with the exclusive purpose of counselling professional individuals seeking a career change. We interviewed the director of one agency who told us that he could not keep up with requests for service, and his fee was not small. He was also in the process of setting up satellite offices in several other big cities. What the figures would be nationally or by the different professions we cannot say. We have been discussing individuals who are actively seeking a career change. We have no good basis for hazarding a guess as to how many people would like to change careers but take no active step to do so. In any event, we can no longer afford to reinforce the view that work dissatisfaction is peculiar to blue or white collar workers. Terkel's (1974) book *Working* deservedly received a good deal of acclaim, but we fear that one of its unintended consequences will be to reinforce the belief that work is a major problem only for certain segments of the population.

Our discussions with diverse professionals have brought out a consideration deserving of special comment. It is what might be called the "How many times do you climb Mt. Everest?" phenomenon. Most simply put, it is the experience that one has successfully mastered one's "trade" but that is not sufficient reason to continue doing the same thing, albeit successfully, for the rest of one's life. It is not that the work is not intrinsically interesting but that it has lost some if not most of its novelty or challenging features. They enjoy the status and financial rewards that success has brought them but there is the nagging thought that there are other things they would like to try to be; and if, as they thought quite likely, they would not make a change (because in each instance of great loss in income) they may find their remaining years somewhat disappointing or empty. As has been pointed out elsewhere (Sarason, 1972), in the context of the nature of leadership, the consequences of success *because* one has mastered the job can have untoward consequences. There is a prepotent tendency to view job dissatisfaction as in part reflecting intrinsically negative features of the work *qua* work. But as a surgeon said to us: "Surgery *is* interesting. For a period of years it did fascinate me. I *am* a good surgeon. In fact, I'm a damned good one. So I'm good, so what? What I really want to do is to get into the history of medicine." This individual was in his middle years, but he, like others with whom we have talked, was voicing something similar to what younger interviewees were saying; that is, they did not want to feel that they were going to do one thing in life, to be walled in by narrow specialization.

Thus far in this article we have emphasized several major points, but chief among them has been that work is a problem for many highly educated, professional people and that many of today's would-be professionals view the world of work with critical questioning, doubts, and negative affect. The significance of these points, it should be remembered, lies in the indisputable fact that policy and programs in aging have been based almost entirely on the perceived characteristics of those who are currently elderly. If, as we have maintained, our society will increasingly consist of educated, professional people (with longer life spans), then it is necessary to begin to think about what possible futures might look like from the perspective of our view (undoubtedly wrong in certain respects) of the characteristics of today's younger people. This is a tall and risky order but needs to be attempted if only, as we shall do, with respect to some of its educational implications.

Educational Implications [4]

It is not because we are optimists, or believers in progress and the inevitability of "good" winning out over "bad," or because we have any sense of security in weighing the significances of diverse social trends that we shall note and discuss some recent suggestions and developments. Within several months of each other there appeared two publications. One was *Youth: Transition to Adulthood,* a report of the Panel on Youth of the President's Science Advisory Committee (1973). A major recommendation in this report is that in the high school years work and school should be coequal experiences, that is, that work should not be an after-school or summer experience. During these years the world of work can be as productive of knowledge, factual and conceptual, as sitting in a classroom. What is noteworthy about this recommendation is that it is meant to apply to all students and not only, as in the past, to those destined to be blue or white collar workers. This recommendation, of course, makes no sense unless it reflects the fact that high school students are massively indifferent to their school experiences—a conclusion well documented by Buxton (1973)—as well as the conclusion that work has become problematic for *all* segments of society. The second publication was *Scholarship in Society, a Report on Emerging Roles and Responsibilities of Graduate Education in America* (1973). One of its recommendations for graduate education is no different than what was recommended for high school students, with the additional suggestion that graduate education be made far easier than it now is for those able only to go part-time. And then Boyer (1974), as Chancellor of the State University of New York,

[4] It is our impression that what we have to say in this article about the problematic nature of work for professional people has first been said by social critics, novelists, and artists rather than by social scientists. If there is any question about priority, there can be none about sensitivity and description of the issues. See, for example, DeMott's (1971) slender but powerful book of social comments *Surviving the 70's,* amazingly similar in theme and thrust to what we have earlier presented in this article.

has vigorously supported lifelong education and flexibility in educational programming.

What is significant about all these recommendations is not their newness (they are not all that new) but who is presenting them. In each instance they are either policy makers or people in positions of influencing educational policy. When these kinds of people are calling for a realignment between the world of work and school, it is safe to assume that they are reflecting widespread dissatisfaction with both worlds for *all* segments of society.

We have no quarrel with these suggestions except in one respect. *The major thrust of these suggestions implicitly assumes or does not explicitly question that people should choose a single career or that people are and in the future will continue to be satisfied with one career.* The problem these suggestions attack is how to help people make this choice on grounds of more varied experiences in the world of work. One must applaud any suggestion that would make it easier for people of all ages to avail themselves of more education, be it for sheer intellectual pleasure or refinement of existing skills. But if, as we think it increasingly to be the case, people will seek career changes both small and great in degree, then the suggestions above do not get to the heart of the matter.[5] And the heart of the matter, like the structure of the atom, is fantastically complex. After all, we are dealing with attitudes and practices deeply ingrained in our culture and reflected in the substance and structure of education, of our economic system, and of the family. We have said that important changes may be taking place in regards to the concept of the single career and we are now emphasizing the obstacles such changes must encounter. For example, if one looks at children's books—those used in or out of schools—it quickly becomes obvious how directly or indirectly we instill in children the idea of a single career. And if one looks at the "career messages" students receive in high school, it is also obvious that students are asked to think in terms of a single career. It used to be that the college-bound student was expected to choose a single college in which, *of course,* he would spend four years. This is no longer true. Unlike the past when the student who wanted to transfer was made to feel atypical and it was extraordinarily difficult for him to be admitted elsewhere, we now view it more positively and indeed encourage it. It also used to be that the college student who wanted to take a year off, almost regardless of reason, would encounter administrative rules, regulations, and attitudes that seemed based on

---

[5] The reader should consult a book *Essays on Career Education* (McClure & Buan, 1973). The first paper is by an anthropologist, J. P. Spradley, who raises and discusses the necessity of thinking through the educational and cultural implications of the concept of multiple careers. Twenty-one of the remaining 22 papers (Thomas F. Green, not surprisingly, being the exception) never take up the questions Spradley addresses. When one considers that this book has the imprimatur of the Office of Education, one cannot be enthusiastic about what to expect from renewed interest and funding in career education.

two assumptions: It should be made difficult for the student, and his motivations should be suspect unless he clearly could prove otherwise. Despite these and similar changes and their implications, the thrust and structure of the college years are to help the student make a life-enduring choice. That this "help" is increasingly experienced by the student as untimely and unreasoned pressure, stemming from the fear of making *the* wrong decision among a welter of possibilities, either goes unrecognized or is interpreted as a reluctance to face up to the realities of life. "They are afraid to grow up"—and indeed many are—but it would be the most ludicrous form of psychologizing to explain the fear exclusively in intrapsychic terms.

If we are correct in our assessment, the concept of lifelong education must deal directly with two questions: How do we prepare children of all ages for thinking about and planning for more than one career? [6] How do we begin to make it more possible for people to change careers without indulging dilettantism and requiring a self-defeating degree of sacrifice? The second question is the more thorny of the two because it so obviously brings to the fore the economic structure of marriage, business, industry, professional work, and education itself. It would be inappropriate for us in this article either to anticipate the many problems that would arise or to attempt to outline schemes by which they could be dealt with. The immediate task has been to suggest that the change process has already begun because the nature of work in our society has made many people dissatisfied and has forced some to actively seek a change. We are not talking about something that may happen but about something that is happening, and we have chosen to emphasize the potential significances of it among the highly educated who will represent an increasing segment of our population.

Ours is a society that prides itself on the ever-expanding opportunities that education provides to more and more segments of the population. These opportunities create and reinforce risking expectations about what to expect over the life span, not only in a material sense but also in terms of level of personal satisfaction. It is our belief that for some time the highly educated, professional person has been aware of a discrepancy between what he expected and what he experiences in his work, and that the younger people of today anxiously sense that this is what is in store for them and they have difficulty thinking about a future that will deny expression to their

[6] One of our studies by Fountain (1975) focused on job satisfaction of teachers, who in comparison to other professionals tend to report significantly lower levels of satisfaction. She interviewed most of the teachers in one high school and found a level of job satisfaction higher than was reported in other studies. But she also found that for a surprising number of interviewees teaching was a second or third career, in which respect this school was probably atypical. Their satisfaction was as much a reaction to previously unsatisfying work as it was to what they perceived to be worthy work. We would be very surprised if the students knew the work histories of their teachers.

needs, talents, and interests. Young people ordinarily do not worry about aging in its conventional sense, and they do not have a long future perspective. But what many of them do have is a heightened sensitivity to the worthwhileness of how they are "filling in" and will fill in time, and it is our suggestion that how that sensitivity continues to develop is fateful for when and how they become aware of aging in its more conventional sense. Intuitively and inchoately they know that their relationship to their work will be a major factor in their experience of worthwhileness. Their intuitions have a basis in a reality that justifies a dysphoric wariness.

References

BOYER, E. Higher education for all, through old age. *New York Times,* April 8, 1974.

BUXTON, C. E. *Adolescents in school.* New Haven, Conn.: Yale University Press, 1973.

DEMOTT, B. *Surviving the 70's.* New York: Dutton, 1971.

FOUNTAIN, P. *What teaching does to teachers.* Unpublished doctoral dissertation, Yale University, 1975.

GREEN, T. *Work, leisure, and the American schools.* New York: Random House, 1968.

LIEBERMAN, V. *Sexual problems in family practice: Why don't physicians refer?* Unpublished master's thesis, Department of Epidemiology and Public Health, Yale University, 1974.

MAYNARD, J. *Growing up old in the sixties.* New York: Doubleday, 1973.

MCCLURE, L., and BUAN, C. (Eds.). *Essays on career education.* Washington, D.C.: U.S. Government Printing Office, 1973.

PRESIDENT'S SCIENCE ADVISORY COMMITTEE. *Youth: Transition to adulthood.* Washington, D.C.: U.S. Government Printing Office, 1973.

SARASON, S. B. *The creation of settings and the future societies.* San Francisco: Jossey-Bass, 1972.

SARASON, S. B. *The psychological sense of community. Prospects for a community psychology.* San Francisco: Jossey-Bass, 1974.

Scholarship in society, a report on emerging roles and responsibilities of graduate education in America. Princeton, N.J.: Educational Testing Service, 1973.

SPRADLEY, J. P. Career education in cultural perspective. In L. McClure and C. Buan (Eds.), *Essays on career education.* Washington, D.C.: U.S. Government Printing Office, 1973.

TERKEL, S. *Working.* New York: Pantheon, 1974.

UNIT BIBLIOGRAPHY

BURCH, WILLIAM R., JR. "Resources and Social Structure: Some Conditions of Stability and Change." *The Annals of American Academy of Political and Social Science,* **389** (1971), pp. 27–34.

CLACK, RONALD J. "Occupational Prestige and Vocational Choice." *Vocational Guidance Quarterly,* **16** (1968), 282–286.

CUTRIGHT, PHILLIPS. "Income and Family Events: Family Income, Family Size, and Consumption." *Journal of Marriage and the Family,* **33** (1971), 161–173.

GROSS, EDWARD. "Patterns of Organizational and Occupational Socialization." *The Vocational Guidance Quarterly,* **24** (Dec. 1975), 140–149.

HAUSER, ROBERT M., and PETER J. DICKINSON. "Inequality on Occupational Status and Income." *American Educational Research Journal,* **11** (1974), 161–168.

HUBER, BETTINA J., and WENDELL BELL. "Sociology and the Emergent Study of the Future." *The American Sociologist,* **6** (1971), 287–295.

JOCOBSEN, R. BROOKE. "An Exploration of Parental Encouragement as an Intervening Variable in Occupational-Educational Learning of Children." *Journal of Marriage and the Family,* **33** (1971), 174–182.

KOHN, MELVIN L. "Bureaucratic Man: A Portrait and an Interpretation." *American Sociological Review,* **36** (1971) 461–474.

MICHAEL, DONALD N. "Social Engineering and the Future Environment." *American Psychologist,* **26** (1971), 888–892.

MEAD, MARGARET. "Working Mothers and Their Children." *Manpower,* **2** (1970), 3–6.

PARKER, GERALD E. "Is the Changing Work Ethic Evolutionary or Revolutionary?" *Hospital Progress,* **55** (1974), 56–59.

STANDLEY, NANCY V. "Kierkegaard and Man's Vocation." *Vocational Guidance Quarterly,* **20** (1971), 119–122.

SUPER, DONALD E. "Vocational Development Theory in 1988: How Will It Come About?" *Counseling Psychologist,* **1** (1969), 9–14.

SUSSMAN, MARVIN B. "Family Systems in the 1970s: Analysis, Policies, and Programs." *The Annals of the American Academy of Political and Social Science,* **396** (1971), 40–56.

SZYMANSKI, ALBERT. "Race, Sex, and the U. S. Working Class." *Social Problems,* **21** (1974), 706–725.

WERTS, CHARLES E. "Paternal Influence on Career Choice." *Journal of Counseling Psychology,* **15** (1968), 48–52.

WILKINSON, KAREN. "The Broken Family and Juvenile Delinquency: Scientific Explanation or Ideology?" *Social Problems,* **21** (1974), 726–739.

ZAFIRAU, S. JAMES. "A Developmental Model for the Occupational Socioeconomic Status of American Men." *Journal of Vocational Behavior,* **5** (1974), 293–305.

ZUZANEK, JIRI. "Society of Leisure or the Harried Leisure Class? Leisure Trends in Industrial Societies." *Journal of Leisure Research,* **6** (1974), 293–304.

part 3
Career Education

Career education is a pivotal experience in contemporary society. It is a blending of one's occupational field, job in particular, and style of living. Career education includes awareness, exploration, decision-making preparation entry, advancement, and retirement. It includes all other forms of education. Therefore, most any topic is related—for example, job attractiveness, career development strategies, counselor education methods, follow-up elementary schools, middle schools, high schools, and vocational technical education.

The real key is to have this material permeate teacher education in classrooms throughout the country. This means that staff development and a revision of curriculum materials should be blended with career education into the singular subject matter under consideration, for example, English literature. Career education can be incorporated as the literature to read.

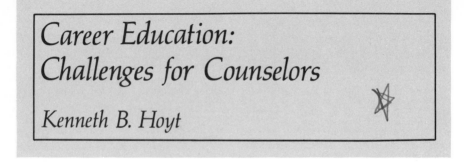

Career Education: Challenges for Counselors

Kenneth B. Hoyt

The counselor is a key person in the career education concept, thus the future of career education will obviously be affected by the counseling and guidance movement. The degree to which counseling and guidance will be affected by career education is neither clear nor obvious. It is the purpose of this paper to provide one view of possible challenges for counselor change posed by career education. It will, of course, be up to each counselor to decide whether to accept or reject these challenges; I pose them here because, in my opinion, they can no longer be ignored.

As background for this contention, I will refer to two facts that became clear during the summer of 1974, when I conducted 20 miniconferences for leading career education practitioners from school districts throughout the United States. Each miniconference consisted of 10 to 15 persons nominated by their state coordinator of career education as representing the best K–12 career education programs in their state. In all, approximately 275 persons attended these miniconferences. Two facts pertinent to this discussion became apparent: (1) of persons nominated to attend these conferences, more came from a guidance background than from any other single professional specialty in education, and (2) when conference participants were asked to name factors currently impeding career education in senior high schools they most frequently mentioned counselors. Both of these facts have implications that form the basis for the challenges I present here. That the facts may appear contradictory simply adds to the challenge.

Before I proceed, let me state my own personal biases as clearly and as forcefully as possible. I believe that career education is a vehicle that can be used to strengthen greatly the status of counselors, the effectiveness with which counselors function, and the personal satisfactions that can accrue to practicing school counselors throughout the nation.

Reprinted from *The Vocational Guidance Quarterly*, **23**:303–310 (June 1975), by permission of the publisher and the author. Copyright 1975 American Personnel and Guidance Association. Reprinted with permission.

As I have worked in career education, various positive potentials for change in counselor role and function have become more and more obvious to me. By relating them here, I hope to present a basis each counselor can use for deciding whether or not to become involved in career education.

The Significance of Work in Career Education

In my opinion, the concept of work is central to conceptualization of the entire career education movement, and this concept holds several key implications for change in counselor role and function. I am well aware of the negative connotations of the word *work* in today's society; thus, my first task must be to present a definition of work that may foster more positive attitudes.

Thanks to my many critics, I have frequently revised the specific definition of work that I want to use in career education. My current definition: *Work is conscious effort, other than activities whose primary purpose is related to either coping or relaxation, aimed at producing socially acceptable benefits for oneself or for oneself and others.* The key words in that definition are: *conscious*—chosen by the individual, not forced on him or her involuntarily; *effort*—some necessary degree of difficulty is involved; *produce*—some clear outcome is sought as a result of the effort being expended; and *socially acceptable benefits*— the outcome is one aimed at helping, rather than hurting, those who receive the results of the effort being expended.

Several basic concepts are implied in this definition. First, this definition of work is not limited to the world of paid employment; it includes work done as part of leisure time, the work of the volunteer, of the full-time homemaker, and of the student. Second, this definition of work allows economic, sociological, and psychological reasons for working to exist singly or in combinations. Third, while in no way denying economic reasons for working, this definition extends beyond those reasons to include the basic human need to accomplish—to do— to achieve something. To feel that one is needed for something. To know that, because one is alive, the world is, in some way to some degree, benefited.

The concept of work implied in this definition is a very humanistic one indeed. As such, it is applicable to all persons, of all ages, in all settings—both within and outside the formal educational system. Because the concept extends from preschool through retirement it is truly developmental in nature. This leads logically to defining *career*: *Career is the totality of work one does in his or her lifetime.* That, to me, is what the word *career* means in the term career education. You can see why I must insist that the word *work* is central to the basic meaning of career education. It must also be obvious why I reject a view of career education as being concerned with all of life.

Several direct implications for change in counselor role and function are immediately apparent to those who recognize the centrality of work in the conceptualization of career education. Perhaps the most obvious is the degree to which the concept of work focuses on accomplishment—on performance. The research literature of guidance has, for years, clearly demonstrated that the best prediction of future performance is past performance, but in typical student appraisal programs we often seem to have overlooked the operational significance of this common research finding. For example, we know the best single predictor of future grades is the record of past grades, yet we continue to value various scholastic aptitude tests more than we do grades. John Holland has demonstrated that the best way to predict future vocational activities is to ask students about their vocational interests, not to measure them with interest inventories. This, too, has had little apparent effect on practices.

One of career education's tenets is that a person is, to a very large degree, a product of his or her past accomplishments and experiences. When we ask individuals who they are, the individuals, if responding honestly and completely, tell us primarily about their past accomplishments. True, they often begin answering the question by describing their characteristics—name, age, physical appearance, interests, and values. Such descriptions help us differentiate one person from another, i.e., they serve as "identifiers." They do not help us greatly in our attempts to understand the person. We predict a person's behavior, to a limited degree, by the way in which we combine data concerning that person's characteristics; we understand another person only through behavioral expressions. The emphasis on accomplishments that the word work brings to career education can assist counselors in better understanding those persons they seek to serve. In the past, we have put undue emphasis on describing students by their characteristics and not enough emphasis on understanding students through their behavioral accomplishments. Career education holds great potential for helping counselors correct this imbalance.

Further, an emphasis on accomplishment, if carried out in a positive fashion, holds great potential for increasing meaningful student self-understanding. We have spent too much time telling students they are worthwhile and too little time letting students discover their own worth through their successful accomplishments. The key word there, of course, is success. Our guidance literature is heavily burdened with normative approaches to increasing student self-understanding, with attempts to help students understand themselves through comparisons with others on some set of norms. The prime approach to self-understanding used in career education is one of helping students see what they have accomplished, not in showing them what they have failed to accomplish. Career education challenges all counselors to correct this imbalance.

Finally, the emphasis on work found in career education holds great potential for helping individuals discover the personal meaning and meaningfulness of work in their total life style. Too often counselors have spoken to students about work only in terms of paid employment. Broader lifestyle implications, when discussed in conjunction with occupational decisions, have failed to account for either the desirability of, or, in many instances, the necessity for work during part of leisure time. This is particularly tragic for the many individuals who find their roles in the world of paid employment so dehumanizing that it could not possibly be called work. Instead, it must surely be regarded as labor, as primarily an involuntary set of activities individuals endure to gain enough economic benefits to find some happiness when away from their place of paid employment.

Those who find themselves in such dehumanizing roles in the world of paid employment have no less a human need for work than do any other human beings. A discussion of occupational goals devoid of discussion of the meaning and meaningfulness of work in the total lifestyle of the individual results in many individuals finding both their paid jobs and their total lifestyles largely lacking in significant personal meaning. That, I am afraid, is what has happened much too often. This, then, is a third imbalance that career education challenges counselors to correct.

The Significance of Action in Career Education

Career education is action centered and experience oriented. If you have read the career education literature, you must be impressed by the emphasis on such expressions as "hands on," "work experience," "field trips," and "work study." The emphasis on the project approach and general learning-by-doing is reminiscent of the philosophy and the recommendations of John Dewey. Insofar as this portion of career education is concerned, the analogy is justified.

This approach seems to have great appeal for the present generation of students. Rather than talking about the future in abstract terms, they are experiencing what it would be like if, as adults, they were to engage in various forms of work. Because of the implications such activities hold both for increasing student self-understanding and for decision making, it would seem worthwhile for counselors to consider becoming actively involved in helping students gain such experiences. Perhaps it is time, as one student expressed, for counselors to "spend less time giving me sympathy and more time giving me help."

If counselors were to accept this challenge, they would be spending less time collecting and filing standardized test score data and more time helping to design and use performance evaluation measures. They would spend less time talking with students about their need for part-time work and more time helping students find it. They would spend less time helping students gain admission to college and more time helping students decide what they plan to do after college, so that going to college would not be a way of avoiding work but rather a way of preparing for it. It would give college attendance a purpose that is largely nonexistent for many of our college bound students today.

The action orientation of career education calls for more action-oriented counselors. Further, if counselors were to change in this direction, they would be perceived by students in a more positive light. In asking counselors to consider this kind of change, I am simply asking that we reflect on Maslow's needs structure and consider its implications for change in counselor behavior. We may discover that we have spent too much time attempting to meet student self-actualization needs and too little time meeting their prior needs for survival and for security.

The Significance of Collaboration in Career Education

A third basic emphasis in career education is one of collaboration of efforts within the formal educational system, outside that system, (including the business-labor-industry-professional-government community) and the home and family structure. Much of the rationale and organizational structure of career education is based on this basic principle of collaborative, not merely cooperative, effort. It is an emphasis that places a high value on the total amount of help made available to any given individual and a low value on assigning specific persons or organizations credit for such help.

This emphasis asks those teachers we call academic and those we call vocational to join together in making education as preparation for work a prominent and a permanent goal for all who teach and all who learn. It encourages an approach to teaching that allows several teachers to be involved in a single project. It encourages the use of resource persons from the business-labor-industry-professional-government community in the classroom. It encourages the active involvement of parents in exposing youth to work values, to teaching good work habits, and in assisting youth in career decision making. It urges the classroom teacher to discuss the career implications of subject matter and to help students explore the nature of various kinds of work and student aptitude for such work as regular classroom activities. In short, the career education movement has proclaimed that career guidance, in its fullest sense, is the proper business and concern of the entire school staff, of the business-labor-industry-professional-government community, and of the home and family. By so doing, career education has denied that career guidance is the exclusive responsibility of the counselor.

Counselors can, of course, choose to react to this emphasis in a variety of ways. Some may react negatively by asserting that career guidance is one of the unique roles of the professional counselor; others may react by pointing to the obvious lack of skill in and understanding of career guidance on the part of many who work in career education. Still other counselors may, when faced with a career education program, profess to be uninterested in career guidance, and busy themselves with other kinds of activities that they consider more proper for their role.

The most appropriate and productive role counselors could play is to endorse enthusiastically and enter into the collaborative efforts of the career education movement. Counselors should be actively seeking to help teachers discover and infuse career implications of their subject matter into the teaching-learning process. Counselors should be active participants in establishing and engaging in collaborative relationships with persons from the business-labor-industry-professional-government community. Counselors should seek to involve parents actively in the career decision-making process. In short, counselors will gain most if, instead of proclaiming career guidance as their unique role, they share their expertise in career guidance with all others involved in the career education program. Counselors will, in my opinion, gain more status and acceptance by sharing their expertise than by hoarding it.

This would demand that counselors give a higher priority to career guidance than many now do. If this happens, both students and parents will be happier with counselors than many now are. It would demand that counselors spend less time in their offices and more time working directly with teachers. If this happens, counselors will be better accepted as members of the school staff. It would demand that counselors spend more time outside the school building interacting with parents and with members of the business-labor-industry-professional-government community. If this happens, students will, in the long run, receive more and better career guidance than they will if the counselor tries to be the primary person helping them in this area. Finally, the need for elementary school counselors will become clearer to school boards everywhere and the number of such counselors will increase.

In short, I view career education's call for a collaborative emphasis as one holding high potential for increasing both the acceptability and the effectiveness of the professional counselor. I do not see negative results for the guidance movement if it follows this direction.

Conclusion

This paper has been purposely limited to challenges for future change that the career education movement poses for counselors. It seems mandatory to conclude by concentrating briefly on the appropriateness of such a limitation at this time.

To those who would prefer to wait to discuss counselor roles until we know for sure whether or not the career education movement is going to survive, I say that, by the time we find that answer it will be too late. I do not know if the career education movement can survive without the active involvement and commitment of the counseling and guidance profession. I do know that, if it survives without that involvement, it will be because it has been forced to find other personnel to do what we are now asking counselors to do. The long-run implications here are obvious.

To those who would try to proclaim that career guidance is part of the unique role and function of the counselors, I say that they are living in the past and, professionally, are already dead. The days of educational isolationism are, in my opinion, gone forever; relationships between education and the larger society become closer each year. We have reached a point at which we must abandon the false assumption that the best way to prepare students for the real world is to lock them up inside a school building and keep them away from that world. It is, to me, not a question of whether or not the counselor must become involved in activities outside the school, but rather, the kinds of activities in which the counselor will be involved. In my opinion, career education is the most viable option now available to school counselors.

To those counselors who may be inclined to claim the career education movement as their own, I say that they have missed the basic point of collaboration inherent in the career education concept. True, if viewed as a process consisting of career awareness; exploration; decision making; preparation; entry; and progression, career education and career guidance have much in common. When viewed as a collaborative, program effort they do not. Career development, like vocational education, is properly viewed as one programmatic component of career education. Career education is no more a simple extension of what has been known as career development than it is of what has been known as vocational education.

To those who profess no interest in either career guidance or career education, I say that they should study carefully the reactions of students, parents, and the general public to recent public opinion polls concerned with both counselors and career education. In my opinion, these polls clearly support both the career education movement and the counselor's deep involvement in that movement. While such polls are no suitable substitute for professional decisions made by counselors, it seems unwise to ignore them.

The career education movement and the guidance movement are both faced with crucial decisions regarding future directions. It seems to me that both have much to gain by joining forces.

Career Guidance in the Elementary School

Column Editor
George E. Leonard,

Column Contributors
Doris Jefferies
and
Sally Spedding

In 1967, James Coleman directed a national research study for the U.S. Office of Education. The results of this study, entitled *Equality of Educational Opportunity* (Washington, D.C.: Government Printing Office, 1967), discussed many important findings. Perhaps the most important conclusion was that "a pupil attitude factor which appears to have a stronger relationship to achievement than do all the 'school' factors together is the extent to which an individual feels that he has some control over his destiny" (p. 23).

This conclusion has great meaning for the counselor of disadvantaged youth. A number of research studies indicate that disadvantaged youth have little feeling of control over their destiny. In other words, disadvantaged youth have little faith that the world has a place for them and do not believe that school will aid them in making progress in our occupational-educational world. What more appropriate way can be found to help a child to gain a feeling of control over his future than to provide him with appropriate career development experiences? Children cannot, of course, project themselves into their adult future, but they *do* fantasize about occupations and do have an interest in what they can or cannot become. Consequently, it is crucial for the counselor of disadvantaged youth to constantly be aiding them to increase their level of aspiration and to believe that they can become what they wish to become. It is important to recognize that reality factors such as aptitude and ability have little meaning for children before the ages of eleven or twelve. Therefore, the words "you can't" have no place in elementary school career development and guidance

Reprinted from *Elementary School Guidance and Counseling*, **9**:48–51 (Oct. 1974), by permission of the publisher and authors. Copyright 1974 American Personnel and Guidance Association. Reprinted with permission.

activities. This does not mean that requirements for success in particular occupations cannot or should not be discussed. Quite the contrary. Following are several suggestions taken from the Developmental Career Guidance Project's *Career Guidance Manual for Elementary Teachers* (Detroit: Wayne State University, 1971) that illustrate how this can be accomplished.

Education and the World of Work

The elementary school child must be assisted in his awareness of the relationship between education and the world of work. One way this can be accomplished is through discussion of various categories of occupations. The teacher can first discuss with the class the following questions:

"Why do you need a good education?" (to get a good job)

"What is a good job?" (enjoy the work, money, etc.)

"There are thousands of different kinds of jobs. You tell me the names of some jobs that you know. I will write the jobs on the blackboard." Divide the blackboard into four parts. Label the parts *unskilled, skilled, semiprofessional,* and *professional*. As the jobs are being named, list them under the proper category. For example:

UNSKILLED	SKILLED	SEMIPROFESSIONAL	PROFESSIONAL
Car washer	Plumber	Store manager	Teacher
Assembly line	Electrician	Car salesman	Engineer
Janitor	Secretary	Computer programmer	Doctor

Compare the jobs listed in the four categories, discussing such factors as education or training needed, salary to be expected, and job satisfaction. Then have the students complete the following assignment:

"We have listed many jobs. Now I would like you to draw a picture of what you would like to be when you grow up. While you are drawing your picture, think about *why* you want the job. What is it about the work that you think you would like? What is it about the work that you might not like? Is it a daytime job or a nighttime job? Is it a quiet job or a noisy job? Will you work with other people or work alone? How much education or training do you think you will need to do the job?"

Invite the children to talk about the jobs they have illustrated in relation to these questions. After the discussion, take each child's paper and categorize it according to the four levels of skills. Encourage the children to talk about the level most frequently selected and the one least selected. Guide the children in evaluating the reasons certain jobs are more chosen than others.

Invite a speaker from the Employment Security Commission to talk to the children about jobs with bright future outlooks and those that will be disappearing by the time the second graders will be ready for the world of work. Remind the speaker that visual aids are more useful in working with young children. Encourage the children to question the speaker. This technique helps the speaker address himself to the children's level of concern.

Take the children on a tour to a business to observe workers. When possible, let them ask questions about job activity, qualifications, rewards, and failures.

Have the children talk about their trip into the world of work. Guide the children in listing the kinds of jobs they saw. Let the children try to categorize the jobs according to the skill.

A Look at My Education

"So far we have talked about the amount of education people need to get certain jobs. Now, we are going to take a look at *your education.* You have learned many things. In some subjects you may do very well, but in other subjects you may not do as well as you would like. For example, Jesse may get Bs in arithmetic but get Ds in gym. Or, Sally may get As in science and Cs in writing.

"Who would like to tell us about the subject you are good in and the ones you are not so good in and why?"

Direct the children to evaluate their education thus far by filling out a form, "A Look at My Second-Grade Education." Glance at the children's papers to see if they have realistically evaluated themselves from your own knowledge of the class. *At this grade level it is not necessary to challenge unrealistic self-concepts.* Often pupils still are primarily fantasizing. Later on, at about 12 to 14 years of age, they are ready to begin understanding and coping with reality factors.

Adult Workers on Our Street

Young children (first or second graders) can be assisted in their career development through studying the adults on their street who are participants in the world of work. Following are some introductory discussion questions. "Every day you see grown-ups leaving their homes to go to work. Who leaves your house to go to work? Where or to what place do your parents go to work? What kind of work do your parents do? What kind of clothing do they wear to work?" (Some children will describe uniforms. Point out that different types of jobs require different forms of dress.)

"Henry, what do your father and mother *like* about their jobs? What do your father and mother *dislike* or *not like* about their jobs? When you get big, would you like to have your father's or mother's job? Why? Why not?"

Following this, students may be asked to draw a picture of how they think their parents look when they are at work. Are they happy? Why or why not? Then invite several parents to talk to the class about their work. Encourage the children to ask questions.

Filling Out Job Applications in the Classroom

Children should become acquainted with the need for language arts skills in applying for the future job of their choice.

"We have talked a lot about the kind of work that people you know can do. We have heard about many jobs. Now, we are going to pretend that you need a job and that I have the jobs you want. In order to get the jobs, you must fill out a job application paper. This job application paper will tell me something about you. Listen carefully so that you can follow my directions." Direct the children in filling out the job application paper.

The teacher should evaluate the aspirational levels of the children on the job application form (unskilled, skilled, semiprofessional, professional) to determine as nearly as possible those areas that need greater understanding and emphasis for the children's future employment outlook. Those jobs that will be extinct should be pointed out. Those with bright future outlooks should be emphasized.

Display the application forms and have the children discuss filling out job applications correctly. Assign classroom jobs. Repeat the job application process at intervals during the semester in order to provide all children with the chance for job success.

Career Exploration in Middle/Junior High Schools

Merrill L. Meehan

Educators typically differentiate among levels of contemporary career education programs on the basis of labels derived from common practice and sage; for example, awareness, exploration, and preparation. However, such distinctions appear to be more artificial than real due to

Reprinted from *Man/Society/Technology*, **34**:44–116 (Jan. 1975), by permission of the publisher and author.

the developmental nature of career-oriented behaviors. It appears that, although helpful to educators in communicating about their programs, distinctions between career awareness, career exploration, and career preparation as specific age/grade designations suffers when subjected to theoretical analysis. But theory and practice do not always complement each other, and the utility of the terms should probably allow their continuance.

The term *career exploration* also suffers from varying definitions and interpretations. At different times and by different authors and projects, career exploration can mean a life stage, a process, a program, outcomes of processes and programs, or a goal. The purpose of this paper is to discuss several definitions and offer a viable interpretation of career exploration for the middle/junior high school level.

Various Meanings

Career exploration has often been defined as a life stage in vocational development literature. The importance of exploration in career development theory was first stated by Ginzberg et al. (1951), when they discuss it as a substage of their realistic stage of vocational development. Super (1957) gives credit to Buehler for his formulation of the developmental life stages of career development and indicates that the exploration stage involves the years of fifteen to about twenty-four.

> Adolescence is, clearly, a period of exploration. It is a period in which boys and girls explore the society in which they live, the subculture into which they are about to move, the roles they may be called upon to play, and the opportunities to play roles which are congenial to their personalities, interests, and aptitudes (p. 81).

When career exploration is considered as process, emphasis is on the dynamics involved and the evolving nature of exploration. Writers holding this view feel that it is important at the early and mid-adolescent years to pursue occupational and educational information in a process of vocational exploration. Evans et al. (1973) assert that: "It (career education) is a process through which this exploration can occur so far as productive achievement, career choice, and career performance are concerned (p. 30)." Jordaan views career exploration as being essentially problem-solving behavior. The nature of the process by which the learner arrives at new knowledge and discovery determines whether or not it is exploratory. This position will be discussed later.

Career exploration can be considered a program when the emphasis is on the features—that is, personnel, strategies, learning activities, or evaluation procedures—involved. Budke (1971) provides such a definition:

Occupational (career) exploration broadly defined will generally describe organized educational efforts directed at exposing students to a wide spectrum of career occupations through discussion, films, resource persons, and field trips, as well as exploration of their interests and abilities through manipulative skills and simulations in a laboratory or a work setting (p. 4).

Career exploration can be considered outcomes when emphasis is placed on observable behaviors resulting from conscious or unconscious acts by the learner. Here, significance may be on changed behaviors regarding the developmental tasks associated with vocational development. These outcomes may be the results of a planned program as advocated above. Concern is not so much with the dynamics of the processes as with particular outcomes being observed and studied.

Finally, career exploration may be a goal statement for a teacher, administrator, school system, state or regional system, or an organization. Such an influence is expressed by Kapes (1971): "Exploration, then, is the appropriate emphasis for education in the middle schools and junior high schools (p. 9)."

Middle School Role

Recent interest in career exploration experiences by educators is due, in part, to knowledge of the developmental nature of vocationally relevant decisions and behaviors. In fact, the school has been described as the single most important exploratory institution. After an extensive review of career education programs reported in the literature, Evans et al., 1973, concluded an "almost universal agreement exists on viewing the middle/junior high school years as concentrating on career exploration activities (p. 100)." Budke (1971, p. 69) determined that career exploration programs at the junior high school level are both the most numerous and highly developed.

Expertise in providing career exploratory programs by middle/junior high schools is understandable since this was one of the original tenets for the formation of junior high schools in America. More recently, the middle school concept is postulating that this is the proper time when student responsibilities can be related directly to consequences of the decisions they made. According to Evans et al., social and sexual roles and skills are the only middle/junior high school concerns outranking career considerations, and these same authors declare that omission of the elements of career education at this level means the institution is neglecting its duty. Career exploration programs in middle/junior high schools answer the need for systematic strategies for occupational information and exploration permitting preadolescent learners to gradually and methodically assess and evaluate their interests, aptitudes, values, and abilities in relation to the world of work.

Career education programs in schools vary considerably in nature.

Over-all, present career education programs at the middle/junior high school level stress occupational exploration at the expense of self-exploration in relation to work roles. Of primary concern at this level is the integration of vocational values and information into the school curriculum along with the relationship between subject matter content and careers. Career development literature is providing educators with propositions and principles for the organization and structuring of career exploration learning activities. Career exploration learning activities, thus designed, will purposely utilize various stimuli and information regarding work and work roles in order "to perpetuate a continuing clarification of self, including one's needs, interests, attitudes, values, and work role perceptions and competencies (Tennyson, 1973, p. 104)."

Exploration as Problem Solving

Jordaan (1963, pp. 42–78) provides the most extensive presentation of exploratory behaviors in relation to self and career-oriented behaviors. He claims that exploratory behaviors not only modify but play a crucial role in shaping the way in which a person thinks about himself and about the world of work. Exploratory behavior is not only physical; it can be purely mental activity. Similarly, a person may or may not realize that he is exploring. According to Jordaan, such exploration is multidimensional; any given behavior could be placed in several continua. He provides ten such continua.

The most important contribution of Jordaan is his criteria for assessing when learner behaviors are exploratory or not. To differentiate exploration from orientation, he concluded that such behaviors must be problem solving in nature. Behaviors can be considered exploratory only when they involve the qualities of search, investigation, trial, experimentation, and hypothesis testing. Thus, exploration need not take place in a vocational setting to be vocationally relevant; for example, exploration could easily involve library research about a personally meaningful career topic. In summarizing his thoughts, Jordaan says:

> Vocational exploratory behavior refers to activities, mental or physical, undertaken with the more or less conscious purpose or hope of eliciting information about oneself or one's environment, or of verifying or arriving at a basis for a conclusion or hypothesis which will aid one in choosing, preparing for, entering, adjusting to, or progressing in an occupation (p. 59).

Summary

In sum, we can say that career exploration is a term used to describe any one or combination of the following: a life stage, processes, programs, outcomes, or goals. The middle/junior high school years are widely accepted for providing careful exploration activities aimed at allowing preadolescent learners to systematically assess their interests, aptitudes, and skills relative to the work world. Student exploratory behaviors in regard to self and occupational concepts are best denoted by their inclusion of problem solving of hypothesis testing.

References

BUDKE, W. E. *Review and synthesis of information on occupational exploration* (Information Series No. 34). Columbus: The center for vocational and technical education, 1971, VT 912 730.

EVANS, R. N., HOYT, K. C., and MANGUM, G. L. *Career education in the middle/junior high school.* Salt Lake City: Olympus, 1973.

GINZBERG, E., GINZBERG, S. W., AXELRAD, S., and HERMA, J. L. *Occupational choice: An approach to a general theory.* New York: Columbia University Press, 1951.

JORDAAN, J. P. "Exploratory behavior: The formation of self and occupational concepts," in Super, D. E., Starishevsky, R., Matlin, N., and Jordaan, J. P. *Career development: Self-concept theory.* New York: College Entrance Examination Board, 1963.

KAPES, J. T. The relationship between selected characteristics of ninth grade boys and curriculum selection and success in tenth grade. *Vocational development study series, VDS Monograph Number 2.* University Park, Pennsylvania: The Pennsylvania State University, August 1971.

SUPER, D. E. *The psychology of careers.* New York: Harper and Row, 1957.

TENNYSON, W. W. "Career exploration," in Magisos, J. H. (Ed.) *Career education.* Washington, D.C.: American Vocational Association, 1973.

Vocational Education in the Secondary School

Robert B. Bradley

In the early years of this century, Ontario's economy was beginning to show signs of a slight swing away from agriculture and towards manufacturing. Against this background of growing industrial activity,

Reprinted from *Education Canada*, **15**:53–58 (Winter 1975), by permission of the author and publisher.

Dr. John Seath, Superintendent of Education for Ontario, presented in 1909 his now famous report on "Education for Industrial Purposes," which was to form the basis for the introduction of technical education into the school system of the province. Adoption of this report by the legislature paved the way for the establishment of Central Technical School and other similar institutions across the province.

By 1961, Ontario had acquired 66 schools which offered technical courses at the secondary level of education. With the signing of a federal provincial agreement for providing financial support for the building of vocational facilities, the number of schools offering technical education grew dramatically. By 1969 a total of 400 were involved with the program.

In 1962, the Ontario Departmen⁺ of Education, unhappy with an increasing "drop-out rate" among high school students and an 80 per cent enrolment of students in the general course, which was university oriented, introduced the Re-organized Program of Studies to the school boards of the province. The timing could not have been better. School boards were able to take immediate advantage of the federal provincial agreement which was just beginning to function.

The Re-organized Program of Studies implied a shift in philosophy for technical education. Early courses placed great emphasis upon the development of skill learning. Upwards of 75 per cent of classroom time was devoted to practical work assignments which included a high proportion of repetitive operations. This approach was taken so that a grade 12 graduate would be able to qualify for a one or two-year credit against his total time as an apprentice.

During the past few years, increasing emphasis has been placed upon the student's understanding of basic scientific principles and supporting mathematical concepts. The improvement of language skills as they relate to technical subjects is also being stressed.

In 1917, Alfred North Whitehead called for a fundamental change in attitude by educators toward education:

> I lay it down as an educational axiom that in teaching you will come to grief as soon as you forget that your pupils have bodies. The connection between intellectual activity and the body, though diffused in every bodily feeling, is focused in the eyes, the ears, the voice and the hands. There is a co-ordination of senses and thought, and also a reciprocal influence between brain activity and material creative activity. In this reaction, the hands are peculiarly important.

He denied that there was a fundamental opposition between technical education and academic education. He believed that there could be no education at all which did not include both.

H. B. Dean, while assistant general secretary of the OSSTE, gave an address which included the following statement:

I discriminate between education and training. Training is the development of a specific skill so that it may be accomplished with ease and precision. Education is concerned with the much broader development of the individual in mind and character. The vehicle for development is not of paramount importance. The basic principles of high frequency alternating currents are as sound today as when I learned them some 40 years ago. The applications have changed with the advent of radio, radar, television and micro-wave communications. New elements such as semi-conductors have altered the technology but the basic principles remain.

Last week when I spent some time in one of our offset lithography shops, I found the students applying the principles of colour separation and using solutions with different PH values, both old ideas applied to a technology. Both of these so called "practical" subjects can make a real contribution in the field of education for the individual, provided the emphasis is on the basic ideas of why things happen as they do, rather than on the development of a specific skill which may have a relatively short term value. I have known many secondary school pupils whose difficulties in the field of mathematics disappeared when the use of the micrometer solved the mystery of decimals or experience with a sine bar made trigonometry a living subject. I feel sure that many pupils who would have been "drop-outs" are in the school today because of the imaginative revised program of studies and the widespread introduction of vocational education through the province.

Technical courses in today's typical non-graded composite school vary in difficulty, in time allotments, and in objectives. These courses may be vocational in nature, exploratory, or narrow in scope, or pre-engineering in content. The introduction of the "technologies" to the senior division in 1968 was a method of moulding two or three complementary technical subjects into one united whole.

These courses tend to bring into clear focus the interdependence of various technical disciplines. Teachers are required to work as a team in planning course content. Classroom work must also be co-ordinated on a daily and weekly basis. These courses meet three basic objectives of technical programs.

1. They stress the interdependence of several disciplines such as English, mathematics and science.
2. They provide a core of knowledge that is fundamental to further study of technology at the post secondary level.
3. Graduates of these courses are finding ready acceptance by employers seeking grade 13 graduates with some technical competence.

The introduction in Ontario of Circular H.S.1 1969–70 has laid the groundwork for radical changes in the organization of high schools in the province. The adoption of the credit system means that students are no longer designated by branch or program. The number and variety of courses is increasing rapidly in all departments. The "Elements of Technology Courses" present a wealth of content designed for 600 hours of instruction or three credits in each of the two years in the senior division technical departments. However, the material in the curriculum guide may be arranged so that several double or single credit courses may be offered.

Technical education teachers are convinced that the technical curriculum constitutes an essential element in the education of every child. They endorse without reservation Whitehead's claim that there are three main roads along which we can proceed, with good hope of advancing towards the best balance of intellect and character; these are the way of literary culture, the way of scientific culture, and the way of technical culture. No one of these methods can be exclusively followed without grave loss of intellectual activity and of character. (D. E. Loney, McArthur College, Kingston)

Dwight Allen said that "our major priority is to confront the myths of education." If there ever was a myth of education, it is the 18th century philosophy that using the hands excludes the use of the mind, or at least is unworthy of the mind. According to all the evidence, nothing could be further from the truth.

Most people entertain a gross misconception of technical education in the secondary schools. They assume that technical subjects have only one purpose—to teach and develop craft and trade skills. In the minds of many, the connotations of technical education are manual training, shop work, manipulative expertise and preparation for a specific job. This is just not so. The technical curriculum is versatile and vital. What makes it that way is technology, which may be defined as "the scientific use of energy and materials to create produce required by society."

Technology embraces technical skills as part of a broad educational base. There are many arguments for the study of technology in the secondary schools. They are not apologies in defense of, but positive reasons for, technical education. They range from "soft" cultural considerations to the "hard" immediacy of occupational competence. In other words, the study of technical subjects may be for a vocational reason, or for skill training leading to university, colleges of applied arts and technology or apprenticeship.

First, a vocational technical literacy has many aspects. It involves having sufficient technical information and intelligence to avoid being victimized by those who understand technology. It is an essential component in the education of the city dweller. He has little or no understanding of the hardware about him, with which he lives, works, and is frequently entertained. Moreover, he is likely to grossly misuse it.

Secondly, vocational or occupational, many students still leave secondary school and go directly into the work force. A study of secondary school technical graduates indicated that approximately half the number went on to some form of post-secondary school education, or grade 13, and the other half went to work. Of the 50 per cent who went directly to work 20 entered apprenticeships. It is the 30 who went directly into a job without further training that we should be concerned about, because without any kind of skill they would have little to offer to an employer. The Work-Study Department has proven many times that it is much more difficult to place students from the academic stream into positions than it is from any others.

One of the prime virtues of the study of technical subjects at the secondary level is that they tend to clarify abstract concepts. Abstracts like force, modules of elasticity, rate of flow, accuracy and precision, energy transfer and dozens of others are given reality because machines and materials that embody these concepts are operated or handled by the student. Not only does this "hands-on" approach clarify the abstractions, it also tends to fix them in the mind by virtue of the active involvement with material objects. The operational skills may be limited to the specific machine, but the concepts are likely to serve a lifetime of understanding and adaptation to new machines and circumstances.

Technical education can be as interdisciplinary as you would like to make it. Where else can you reinforce the concept of ratio and proportion any better than in a machine shop or auto shop? The need to express oneself is fundamental. Perhaps it is not too much to claim that nothing is more helpful in self identification than the production of an object in which one has laboured creatively. We often hear it said that secondary school students are being taught obsolete ideas with obsolete equipment. It is true that changes have taken place in the automotive field, in the technology of production, in electricity and electronics and other technical areas, but for the most part, the secondary schools have been able to keep up. Some examples of this—transistors have replaced tubes, disc brakes have replaced drum brakes, aluminum wire has replaced copper wire, but in every case, the technology has remained the same as it was before.

One may argue that technical education is expensive, but it can be justified. First, there are many students who would never have received a secondary school graduation diploma without it. This is not only because nearly half of the 27 credits can be technical, but also because it reinforces concepts in mathematics, science and other academic subjects. Secondly, we are living in a technological age when everyone should acquire some technical skills. This latter applies to university bound students as well. It is easy to relate technical skills to medical doctors, surgeons, dentists and engineers.

There are good numbers of female students acquiring technical skills, as many as 80 in one school in North York. This may be the only chance for a girl to learn the basic servicing of an automobile and what to look for in purchasing a new or used car. Girls are very successful in drafting courses and electrical courses.

Statistics show that half of all the students enrolled in grade 9, or year 1 through to grade 12 or year 4, in Ontario, are in technical or business education courses of some kind. At a time when we are hearing about declining enrollments, it is interesting to note that in North York the number of technical credits has risen from 7,567 in 1971 to 10,153 in 1974, and they are still increasing. In 1972 there were 8,312 and in 1973, 9,779 credits.

There are now approximately 50 special vocational schools in Ontario. These are secondary schools offering courses for students who lack academic ability. The courses are of the service variety, such as auto servicing, electrical appliance repair, horticulture, tailoring, oil burner servicing, etc. Graduates of these schools, for the most part, go directly to work so that the skills learned in a special vocational school are very important to them. This kind of vocational education is the difference between working and not working for many of these students.

Business Education

The educational objectives of business education courses may be vocational or academic. As vocational, they will prepare students for a career in business or further specialized training. As academic, they will form part of their general education—to develop their thinking processes, to provide supplementary skills for further learning, to create an awareness of the business community and to prepare the individual to cope with the economic world.

Vocational education has undergone dramatic changes particularly since the mid 1960s. No longer are we "turning out" from our packaged programs highly skilled graduates trained for specific jobs. Rather, we are providing a variety of programs at different levels of difficulty to meet the needs and interests of individual students. It is possible for a student to *choose* a combination of courses that will make it possible to graduate with a higher concentration of specialization than ever before. But it is more likely that the student of today will wish to broaden his or her educational base to better prepare for life, leisure and appreciation as well as for employment.

As a result, we have a higher proportion of students enrolled in some business education courses than ever before and a smaller proportion who are majoring in any given specialty area.

Those who have majored are ready for employment or for a short employer-sponsored specialized training program, while those who have not specialized in any area may make reasonably knowledgeable career choices for further education at the secondary school, community college or university.

Further, those who do not specialize in the vocational program but who "sample" courses from various areas obtain a much better insight and appreciation of the role and function of those who do follow a career in some aspect of business.

The curriculum of business education has changed—it is reflecting the changing needs and interests of our students. It is still vocationally oriented, but many courses have taken on new thrusts and emphases. Typewriting, for example, is now offered as a personal communications skill for all students and is carried on for those wishing vocational competence. Accountancy is now more than a course in bookkeeping; it is a vehicle for students to learn the concepts of business and the implications for the private individual.

New courses have been added to the curriculum reflecting student interest in some aspects of business and economic life. These would include consumer studies, law and personal note taking.

On the cost of vocational education compared to a straight academic program, while there may be a small increase in the per pupil cost to provide basic equipment and supplies, this is offset by the benefits: (1) Students who specialize in business education courses are "ready for employment." Within a very short time they will be productive workers contributing to the economy; (2) Students who have not majored in business are in a position to accept part-time employment or summer employment to supplement their further education. In addition, courses such as typewriting, accountancy, and applied business machines will always give them "some marketable skills" should their primary career goals not materialize; (3) In most schools business education facilities are used for both day school and evening programs; and (4) The equipment provided for the instructional areas of our schools is rarely an expensive "specialized piece of machinery." It is understood that on-the-job training is the best learning environment for unique equipment. We provide those basic skills that are common to most equipment.

The job market has been rapidly changing because of technological advances and this has had an impact on vocational training in schools. Schools only provide vocational competence in basic skills and concepts. Specialization and "job training" have only limited places in secondary schools. Rather, the very nature of secondary school today is to prepare our young people for change and adaptability. The reason for choice and the emphasis on individual selection is in part to let students know that change is a fact of life. Vocational education, both technical and business, is involved directly in this accelerating change and is prepared to meet the challenge.

In conclusion—and to quote Whitehead again—"the law is inexorable that education to be living and effective must be directed to informing pupils with those ideas, and to creating for them those capacities which will enable them to appreciate the current thought of their epoch." We live in a technological society in which also the world of commerce is at once complex and vital to the survival of our civilization in its diverse societies. With all the recent talk of a compulsory core in the secondary school curriculum I would pose for the consideration that fundamental literacy in technology and commerce is as essential for our young people as is an understanding of Canadian history or improved reading and writing skills. The real issue is not "can we afford vocational education?" but rather can we, in societal terms, afford not to provide it to every single student while he or she is in our secondary schools?

Implementing Change in Vocational-Technical Education: The Research Coordinating Unit in Tennessee

Garry R. Bice

The establishment of Research Coordinating United for Vocational Education was, essentially, a result of concern voiced in Congressional hearings on Public Law 88-210 (The Vocational Education Act of 1963). Concerns expressed during those hearings indicated that research in vocational education was intermittent, uncoordinated, and primarily directed toward the administration and operation of programs (Huber, 1973). Recognizing the need to stimulate, encourage and coordinate research activities among state departments of education, universities, local school districts, and others with an interest in vocational-technical education, P.L. 88-210 carried special provisions to meet the need of developing a conscientious and systematic thrust for research in vocational-technical education. USOE personnel encouraged the establishment of Research Coordinating Units as one strategy for meeting that need.

By 1968, Research Coordinating Units were functioning in 46 of the

Reprinted from *Journal of Research and Development in Education,* 7:101–109 (Spr. 74).

states. These units were funded, primarily, with monies made available through P.L. 88-210.

In an evaluation of Research Coordinating Unit Programs, Gold-hammer, et al., (1969) identified 16 varied objective of the units, with no consensus among the various states as to which objectives were of the highest priority.

In 1968, the Amendments to the Vocational Education Act of 1963 (P.O. 90-576), better known as the 1968 Amendments, a new thrust was provided the Research Coordinating Units. In addition to the additional funding and better identification of objectives for RCUs being included in the Amendments, further direction and coordination of research efforts in vocational-technical education was provided by the National Center for Vocational Education at the Ohio State University and the Center for Occupational Education, North Carolina State University at Raleigh. Among other activities, the Centers assisted with the development of guidelines for Statewide Information dissemination systems and cooperatively sponsored national meetings of research coordinating unit directors.

With the renewed support and coordination efforts, Research Coordinating Units began to formulate well-designed programmatic efforts and develop specific objectives. Four of the major objectives that have become trademarks of the RCUs are:

1. To collect and disseminate information on the progress and application of research in vocational education.
2. To stimulate and encourage vocational education research and development activities in State Departments of Education, colleges and universities, local school districts, and nonprofit educational organizations.
3. To coordinate vocational education research activities within states.
4. To conduct vocational education research and development projects.

Objectives of the Tennessee RCU

The Tennessee Research Coordinating Unit (TRCU) was established in 1966. Original objectives of the TRCU were focused upon dissemination activities, research and development activities related to disadvantaged persons, and the development of programs to improve the literary research of vocational-technical clientele within the state. Recognizing the changing needs of personnel within the state, the basic needs and objectives of the Tennessee RCU were redefined in 1970. The resulting efforts developed into a systematic research and development program for vocational-technical education, aimed at implementing changes in local school vocational-technical programs with the changes based upon sound research findings.

In concert with objectives developed at the national level, the Tennessee RCU strategy for effecting change included four programmatic efforts. Initial development of an information dissemination program began in 1970. A management information system programmatic effort was initiated in 1971. Development of an occupational information system for students was begun in 1972 and a product utilization programmatic effort was initiated in 1973.

The Information Retrieval and Dissemination System

The information retrieval and dissemination system is essentially a document based system. The prime source of input to the system is the nationwide ERIC system. Components of that system include complete microfiche collections, computer search capabilities (using the "Query" program), and supporting publications such as "Research in Education" (RIE), "Abstracts of Research and Related Materials in Vocational Education" (ARM), "Abstracts of Instructional Materials in Vocational Education" (AIM), "Current Index to Journals in Education" (CIJE), and related indexes.

Regional Resource Center Component

Thirteen strategically located institutions serve as Regional Resource Centers (RRCs) where individuals have access to necessary indexes, view microfiche on a reader or reader-printer, and print out pages as necessary. Two RRCs are located in secondary schools, three in State Technical Institutes, seven in Area Vocational Schools, and one in a Community College. Workshops for Regional Resource Center personnel are held regularly in November and May as a means of keeping the individuals up-to-date on both RCU activities and current trends in information needs throughout the state. RRC personnel serve voluntarily as a liaison between their institution and local schools, and are supplied with 1500 free microfiche and a reader-printer. Additional microfiche may be requested from the central RCU.

Information Retrieval

To facilitate retrieval, dissemination, and consumption of research and research-related information at the local level, three Regional Research and Development Offices were established. These offices, staffed with professional and clerical personnel are located in east, middle and west Tennessee. In addition to operating as strategic contact points for referrals and requests, the Regional Research and Development Coordinators provide valuable technical assistance in the writing of research proposals, conducting small research projects, and analyzing and utilizing packaged information such as manual and computer searches.

With the central data base located in the College of Education at the University of Tennessee in Knoxville, retrieval and dissemination of library materials is supported and facilitated by both Regional Resource Center Representatives, where files are individually organized and maintained, and Regional Research and Development Offices (Jackson, Murfreesboro, Knoxville), which have been linked by a teletype system to the central RCU.

The "Query" computerized retrieval system is used to access ERIC files at the University of Tennessee Computing Center. Increased emphasis has been placed on maximum utilization of already completed computer searches by the printing and dissemination of an "Index to Query Computer Searches," with updates added to it every three months.

A monthly awareness paper is published by the RCU to focus attention on key research and development results. The "RCU Circulator" has proven to be a valuable feedback mechanism from readers and is mailed to approximately 4,500 persons bimonthly from September through May. The mailing list has expanded from the original total of 2,600 in 1970 to the above mentioned total by individual and group requests.

Selective Dissemination of Information

The Tennessee Selective Dissemination of Information (SDI) Sub-System for Area Vocational Schools, State Technical Institutes, Community Colleges, and Secondary Schools was initiated in September of 1972. Using the "Directory of Personnel in Vocational Education in Tennessee," a faculty profile was constructed for each school, listing the total number of teachers in each vocational instructional area. The profile serves as a key for assembling the SDI package for each school. The package provides individual teachers with listings of available materials in specific instructional areas on a regular basis.

In many cases, documents from the AIM and ARM indexes on topics such as cosmetology and cooperative education were limited. The Tennessee RCU SDI sub-system has, therefore, proven to be a valuable checkpoint for the types of documents that are scarce in the Vocational-Technical ERIC Clearinghouse files and has put the RCU in a position to be able to make recommendations to ERIC Clearinghouses to put greater emphasis in the instructional areas for which there is both a demand and little supply throughout the State.

Management Information System

The Management Information System is a data based information system consisting of files of student enrollment, instructional personnel, census data, program cost, and student placement.

The total system is a computerized data bank with the primary goal of providing comprehensive, current and accurate data to educators and administrators at all levels. Approximately twenty items of information are collected on each secondary and contract adult vocational-technical student and teacher in the state. From the initial input, basic demographic, attitudinal and enrollment accounting data are generated on units varying in size from the entire state to a single class. After initial data collection in the fall, output is sent to contributors in January and April for up-dating. The following fall, follow-up information is collected on each student in the previous year's records.

Profiles and analyses are regularly disseminated to teachers, superintendents, and regional and state offices of the state Division of Vocational-Technical Education. Appropriate data is generated for required state reports to the U.S. Office of Education. Additionally, all data are stored for specialized analysis in the future by these groups and other individuals or organizations involved in educational economic research. The single most important use for the data generated is for evaluating the adequacy and effectiveness of existing programs so that better planning of future educational programs can be achieved.

The Occupational Information System for Students

Project INFOE (Information Needed for Occupational Entry) was developed and implemented to disseminate career information to students in grades 7 through 14.

An INFOEscript format which provided for general career information on three pages and for specific information, pertinent to local communities, on the fourth page was developed. In localizing information for the fourth page, data were obtained from local offices of the Tennessee State Employment Service, regional vocational education supervisors, state area vocational-technical schools, state technical institutes, state community colleges, and businesses and industries. Content for the first three pages of general information was adapted from existing guidance materials. After being validated for use in Tennessee, the four pages were photographed and reproduced on aperture cards.

Elementary INFOE

In cooperation with the Tennessee Valley Authority the RCU developed a career information system for students in grades 4, 5, and 6. The system, called Elementary INFOE (Information Needed for Occupational Exploration) was designed to provide students with basic information on career clusters as well as general information on specific job titles. The key to INFOE is an INFOEscript reproduced on a microfilm aperture card. Twenty INFOEscripts have been developed for each of the fifteen career clusters identified by U.S. Office of Education.

One INFOEscript for each cluster consists of an introduction and an overview of the careers contained in the cluster. In addition, nineteen scripts for each cluster contain general information on specific job titles.

The Product Utilization System

As the three primary programmatic areas and enabling systems developed, it became evident that not enough change and progress was occurring at the local classroom level. Since all systems had been carefully designed and tested (empirical evidence was gathered on each system and sub-system), it was decided that the weak point was still the linking agent between researcher and practitioner. Analysis of change strategies and models as developed by Rogers (1962), and Havelock (1970) led to the development of a product utilization system that included five different components, each with a somewhat similar function, but each playing a different role in the system. In addition, some of the components have functions to be completed in other programmatic areas within the RCU.

The first component of the system is an obvious but most often overlooked one. The central administration of the RCU is the point at which the whole product utilization system begins. The very fact that educational research and development activities are often viewed from a jaundiced perspective by local administrators and instructional staff, necessitates the development of a system that will meet the needs of local clientele. The administrator of the unit that is change oriented, must make possible all the activities, in appropriate sequential order, at strategic points and they must be made available to all clientele from the innovator to the late adopter. The unit must commit time, personnel and other resources needed to accomplish the task of change; and the administrator must provide appropriate publicity to the program in order that it might diffuse via the social interaction process.

The second component is the resource base. The resource base consists of:

1. Hard copy and microfiche from Central ERIC and selected clearinghouses;
2. Selected curriculum materials and publications produced by local educational agencies from within a limited geographical area (in this case the State of Tennessee):
3. A data bank of census statistics, economic information, educational statistics and educational program enrollments, program cost information and program evaluation (accountability) information;
4. Experts representing various disciplines that are skilled in problem solving processes and able to interpret research reports, statistics, legislation and the writings of theoreticians and research writers; and

5. A source of funds (known as the mini-grant program in Tennessee) that can be used to assist local educational agencies experiment with or simply try something new or different from what they had been doing.

The third component of the system is an extension-change agent, strategically located and capable of effectively communicating with research oriented clientele, state and local supervisors and administrators, and classroom instructional personnel. The role of the extension-change agent in Tennessee has been developing over the last three years. The extension-change agent, with clerical support, is located in the regional office of vocational-technical education. That arrangement permits immediate contact with up to 12 supervisors, each of whom has many contacts and daily working relationships with local instructional personnel. (A regional office is centrally located in each of the east, middle and west Tennessee areas.) The agent actually serves as an *extension* of the main RCU office, which houses most of the data, information, and resource bases. In addition to having direct access to the total resource system at the main office, the agent has mini-collections of materials and resources in his own office. The nature and extent of these collections are determined by the nature of the problems confronting the educators in that particular region.

The agent serves both as a *solution giver* and a *process helper* so actually he is a change agent according to Havelock (1970).

The fourth component of the system is a coordinator of product utilization, located at the central office. That coordinator has the prime responsibility of packaging the results of research and development activities. Various types of packages are developed, dependent on the product, but are aimed at serving two primary groups, namely the extension-change agent or the regional resource center person.

The resultant system has, then, developed into a *paired change process* and can best be summarized as follows:

NATIONAL POLICY AND TRENDS IN EDUCATION

National Centers, Basic Research, Etc.	⟷	Central RCU Office
Central RCU Office (Resource Bases)	⟷	Product Utilization Coordinator
Produce Utilization Coordinator	⟷	Extension-Change Agent
Extension-Change Agent	⟷	Regional Resource Center
Regional Resource Center	⟷	Local Instructional Personnel

The system was designed to try to focus the efforts of national research centers and laboratories, the State Department of Education, and the University upon the problems of the local school system and its instructional personnel. With the information explosion resulting from technological developments and massive numbers of researchers and agencies exploring alternative systems, methods, techniques, etc., it has become necessary to establish a series of screens through which information and related products flow, with key results being sifted out and packaged for the various users of those efforts.

The objective of the organizational structure as described, is to provide *something for everyone*. More specifically, the researcher has access to rather complete document and data based information from the information systems housed at the Central RCU; the teacher educator and in-service education coordinator have access to packages of information, designed to acquaint teachers, administrators, and supervisors with new concepts and current developments, from the system's coordinator of product utilization; the local administrator or supervisor has access to information related to practical applications of research and development results from the extension-change agent; and the local teacher has access to similar information from the regional resource center. In addition, since any educator can access the system at any point, all types of people from the innovator to the laggard (Rogers, 1962) can be accommodated. For example, an innovative teacher in a local education agency may access information, about a new instructional technique, from one of the regional resource centers located near him geographically to see who is using the technique or how it is being used, or the teacher may access more detailed information and results of research on the instructional technique directly from the Central RCU. Further, a less-innovative teacher may be less interested in technically written research reports and go to the extension-change agent who provides interpretation of research results to the teacher.

At this point the information dissemination system must be re-emphasized. In order for clientele to make changes, they must be aware of and have knowledge about improved concepts, techniques, methods and processes. The information dissemination system is designed to assist with this critical area.

In the adoption (of change) process, individuals usually progress through the awareness, interest, evaluation, trial and adoption or rejection phases (Rogers, 1962). Various products and activities of the RCU are targeted to most of these phases. Specifically, the "RCU Circulator" contains short notes related to research and development results—and is disseminated bimonthly to clientele throughout the State. The objective of the "Circulator" is to assist with making clientele aware of various developments. Selective dissemination of information (SDI) sheets are disseminated in alternate months to specific audiences and contain information related to how the previous development or concept is applied to their specific instructional area. The SDI sheet may include abstracts of projects utilizing the concept, lists of selected curriculum guides or sources of additional information. This technique helps to develop the interest of various clientele. To assist clientele with the evaluation phase, the information dissemination system has the responsibility of developing and disseminating such products as annotated bibliographies, popularized (condensed) versions of technically written research and development reports and indexes to additional sources of information.

Assuming that, after sufficient evaluation, the individual wants to move to the trial phase, he may find a human resource and development coordinator at the Central RCU and financial resources through the Mini-grant program (usually $1000 limit) from the RCU's small grant program. Depending upon results of the mini-grant project, the individual may decide to adopt or reject all or part of his product. Results of mini-grant projects are also incorporated into the information dissemination system and utilized at the awareness, interest and evaluation phases for other clientele.

Does It Work?

One way of judging the value or effectiveness of the total system is to examine how many people are making use of the system and how much and what kinds of information is being requested. A study by Kelly (1973) revealed that after 2 years, approximately 30 per cent of the vocational-technical teachers in local schools throughout Tennessee had some knowledge of the role and function of the RCU. That study also revealed that all segments of the system were being utilized to some degree.

Analysis of requests for information have been most encouraging. In 1971, an average of twenty-one people per month made on-site use of the document and data based systems at the Central RCU. In 1973 that number had increased to 96 on-site user per month. In 1971, requests for copies of microfiche titles averaged approximately 10 per month. In 1973, monthly requests for 520 titles were received. And in 1971, requests for complete (computer and manual) searches of the ERIC system for specific information averaged five per month. In 1973, 32 requests for new searches were received each month. An analysis of RCU funded mini-grant projects in Tennessee (Sutton, 1973) revealed that 98 per cent of the mini-grant project directors felt that local school students had benefited as a direct result of mini-grant projects. Project directors listed 23 different ways in which students had benefited from the mini-grant program. In addition to yielding benefits to students, there is evidence (Sutton, 1973) that other teachers, administrators, parents and other community leaders derived benefits from the mini-grant program. Examples of changes, based upon the results of research, directly affecting students include individualizing selected units of some courses in a school, revising the content of selected courses, updating the total curriculum of a school and the implementation of a pupil placement program. In addition, approximately 200 schools are making more and better occupational information available to their students through the use of the INFOE (Information Need For Occupational Entry) system.

Summary

The primary purpose of the Research Coordinating Unit in the State of Tennessee is to bring about change in the vocational-technical education system in the State. Utilizing strategies suggested by Rogers and Havelock, a system consisting of data and information bases, human resources, product utilization coordinators, extension-change agents, and regional resource centers was developed. Pairing various components of the system, it has become possible to work with all levels of clientele, from the local school teacher to the researcher, and all types of individuals from the innovator to the laggard. In this way it is possible to move nearly anyone from the awareness stage through the adoption stage in the long process of change.

References

ALDRIDGE, BILL and GOLDHAMMER, KEITH. *Research Coordinating Unit Program Evaluation.* Center for Educational Research and Service, Oregon State University, Corvallis, Oregon, March, 1969.

BICE, GARRY R. *The Relationship of Group Structural Properties and Communication Behavior Patterns to Opinion Leadership Among Teachers.* The Center for Vocational and Technical Education, The Ohio State University, Columbus, Ohio, August, 1970.

BICE, GARRY R. *Working with Opinion Leaders to Accelerate Change in Vocational-Technical Education.* ERIC Clearinghouse on Vocational and Technical Education, The Center for Vocational and Technical Education, The Ohio State University, Columbus, Ohio, November, 1970.

HAVELOCK, RONALD G. *A Guide to Innovation in Education.* Center for Research on Utilization of Scientific Knowledge, The University of Michigan, Ann Arbor, Michigan, 1970.

KELLY, MARVIN D. *An Evaluation of Regional Research and Development Units. Unpublished doctoral dissertation.* The University of Tennessee, Knoxville, December, 1973 (offset printing).

MCCRAKEN, J. DAVID and GILLESPIE, WILMA B. *Information Needs of Local Administrators of Vocational Education.* The Center for Vocational and Technical Education, The Ohio State University, Columbus, Ohio, March, 1973.

PRATZNER, FRANK C. and WALKER, JERRY P. *Programmatic Research and Development in Education: Positions, Problems, Propositions.* The Center for Vocational and Technical Education, The Ohio State University, Columbus, Ohio, June, 1972.

ROGERS, E. M. *Diffusion of Innovations.* The Free Press, New York, 1964.

SUTTON, SUE. *An Analysis of RCU-Funded Mini-Grant Projects.* Tennessee Research Coordinating Unit for Vocational Education. The University of Tennessee, Knoxville, May, 1973.

UNIT BIBLIOGRAPHY

ANTHOLZ, MARY BEE. "Illustrative Resources and Programs for Implementing Career Development Curricula in the Elementary Grades." *Social Education,* **39** (May 1975), 316–319.

BERKEY, ARTHUR L. "Building Valid Occupational Images." *American Vocational Journal,* **49** (December 1974), 37.

FLAKE, MURIEL, et al. "Effects of Short-Term Counseling on Career Maturity of Tenth-Grade Students." *Journal of Vocational Behavior,* **6** (February 1975), 73–80.

GYSBER, NORMAN C., and EARL T. MOORE. "Beyond Career Development— Life Career Development." *Personnel and Guidance Journal,* **53** (May 1975), 647–652.

HOYT, KENNETH B. "Evaluation of Career Education: Implications for Instruction at the Elementary School Level." *Journal of Career Education,* **1** (Spring 1975), 69–79.

HUMES, CHARLES W. "Elementary Counselor Role Can be Helped by Career Education." *Journal of the International Association of Pupil Personnel Workers,* **19** (March 1975), 68–70.

LOGACZ, GREGORY, et al. "Career Development: Applications to the Elementary Classroom." *Social Education,* **39** (May 1975), 313–315.

NOETH, RICHARD J. "Student Career Development: Where Do We Stand?" *Vocational Guidance Quarterly,* **23** (March 1975), 210–218.

RANDOLPH, JAMES R. "Computer-Based Occupational Exploration: A Study of Ninth Grade Students." *Journal of Industrial Teacher Education,* **12** (Winter 1975), 79–86.

SILBERMAN, HARRY F. "Involving the Young." *Phi Delta Kappan,* **56** (May 1975), 596–600.

part 4
Vocational Guidance: Information

Vocational guidance is implemented in the schools through the use of appropriate career, job, and life-style information along with curricular programs. The school may be vocational, technical, trade, comprehensive, continuing, community, or the general school in the community. The National Vocational Guidance Association (NVGA) has established criteria for evaluating occupational information publications.[1] The Guidance Information Review Service Committee of the NVGA evaluates current publications. The results are published in the Vocational Guidance Quarterly.

The articles in this section examine the nature of occupational information and some procedures for promoting career information, including some personality correlates that have an impact on the information one obtains.

The reader is alerted to the conflict inherent in the essence of occupational information, the activities necessary to getting that information across to pupils, and its meaning in directing the behaviors of students for career development. Perhaps the focus should be put on the possible misuse of procedures to alert pupils to the view that career education and vocational guidance are composed of a fusion of several events that are integral parts of a process of exploring, choosing, and developing in a career.

[1] "Guidelines for Preparing and Evaluating Occupational Materials, 1964," National Vocational Guidance Association, 1607 New Hampshire Avenue, N.W., Washington, D.C.

An Index of Vocational Awareness

Lawrence E. Currie

This research concerns an attempt to make operational the construct of vocational awareness. In general, the term, or its common companion, occupational awareness, has been given little empirical exposure in the literature. The investigation has conceptualized vocational awareness as the extent to which persons perceive their relationship to the world of work. More specifically, vocational awareness has two essential elements: (1) conscious recognition of a life experience or set of experiences as being vocationally relevant and, therefore, important; and (2) a behavioral response or several responses involving the selection of what one believes to be a positive vocational activity.

An example of vocational awareness that includes these elements comes from my own experience. Social parties were, and still are, considered very important in the predominantly black neighborhoods of Chicago's South Side. The big party nights are Fridays and Saturdays, so most people from this community who seek employment attempt to choose a job that will keep their weekends completely free or let them off before midnight. Hence, an environmental situation, such as social parties, is a vocationally relevant experience and an individual recognizes its importance when selecting a job (a good job, in part, then provides working hours compatible with one's cultural life style).

Relevant Literature

The term *awareness* has appeared frequently in psychological literature; unfortunately, most writers use the term without providing the reader a clear definition. One notable exception is Angyal [1], who stated that awareness is the symbolic representation of some portion of our experience. Rogers [11] incorporated Angyal's conception of awareness into his writing and used the term synonymously with consciousness. Beier [2] concluded that reportability is the only operational definition of awareness.

The concept of vocational awareness is more completely described

Reprinted from *The Vocational Guidance Quarterly*, **23**:347–353 (June 1975), by permission of the publisher and author. Copyright 1975 American Personnel and Guidance Association. Reprinted with permission.

by Super [13]. If, in Super's terms, work is the implementation of the self-concept, vocational awareness is believed to be the directional component of that implementation process. A person could choose any number of jobs from the world of work, however, most people choose a particular job. Their vocational awareness has provided them with that specificity. Super [14] also emphasized that the adolescent is bringing his self, likes, dislikes, and abilities to the vocational exploration process.

Although Super believed that adolescent exploration of the self and work begins at home with the family, then continues in school, and part-time employment, Ginzberg's [8] restatement of his theory of occupational choice pointed to other equally important experiences such as race, sex, neighborhood influences, socioeconomic status factors, and physical capability. Ginzberg described most of these experiential dimensions as constraints on occupational choice. One of the first attempts to integrate Super's description of the self-concept, vocational self-awareness, and vocational behavior was an investigation by Geist [7], who developed a Picture Interest Inventory to measure vocational self-awareness.

The Vocational Development Project, headed by John O. Crites, was designed to fill the theoretical and psychometric gaps in previous vocational development research [3]. The project attempted to provide a measurement model for vocational maturity, and resulted in the construction of the Vocational Development Inventory (VDI). Among the dispositional response tendencies that the attitude scale of the VDI was constructed to assess were: (1) involvement in the choice process, (2) orientation toward work, (3) independence in decision-making, (4) preference for vocational choice factors, and (5) conceptions of the choice process. The competence test of the VDI focused on comprehension and vocational problem-solving [4]; the attitude scale was used throughout the project as the prime measure of vocational maturity. Recently, the VDI has been renamed the Career Maturity Inventory (CMI), to accentuate the developmental variable of maturity [5].

Vocational maturity is the construct closest to vocational awareness. They are distinguished by the current investigator in three major ways:

1. Vocational maturity implies a value of correctness in attitude, while vocational awareness implies the ability to express experiential data.
2. Hypothetically, the attribute of vocational awareness precedes vocational maturity. An individual must recognize the importance of vocationally relevant experiences before his attitude toward the world of work can be judged mature or immature.
3. Vocational maturity reflects a normative view of attitudes toward the world of work, while vocational awareness reflects only the recognition of the importance of vocationally relevant experi-

ences (even though these experiences may differ across demographically divergent groups).

The construct of vocational awareness is the end product of an attempt to integrate awareness theory, self-concept theory, and vocational development theory from a phenomenological perspective. That perspective dictates that, if given a strong enough set, people (and particularly adolescents) will be able to draw on their own experiences to provide a focus for vocational choice. An emphasis is placed on the value of individual experiences, which may include references to race, family, education, community, socioeconomic status, sex, or physical capability.

Operationalizing the Construct

Method

The Vocational Awareness Index (VAI) was developed to measure the construct of vocational awareness and to focus on seven experiential dimensions: socio-economic, familial, environmental-community, educational, ethnic, sex, and physical-capacity. These dimensions reflect the respective seven scales of the VAI. Scale items represented a particular aspect of an experiential dimension in reference to the world of work, and each item was divided into the two response categories of agreement and relevance. The items for the seven scales were rationally derived and constructed to depict situation-specific, vocationally related experiences. An example of an item in each scale is presented in Figure 1. Respondents are asked to express agreement or disagreement with item content, as well as determine whether the situation depicted is relevant to them. Items of the VAI appeared in random order without reference to scale designation.

Persons are assessed as vocationally aware if they recognize the reality of the world of work activity expressed by items in the 7 experiential categories and also recognize the relevance of item content to them personally. There is nearly an equal number of agree and disagree items. Each item can receive a total of 2 points (1 point per response category). There are 10 items in each scale and 70 points overall. The maximum score for each scale is 20 points and the maximum score for the entire VAI is 140 points.

The VAI item judges were a Ph.D. level rehabilitation counselor educator, a Ph.D. level city school district special program coordinator, and the vocational education director of a city school district. They unanimously agreed on all items in each scale except the sex scale, where there was 90 per cent agreement. Care was taken to construct items that represented succinct and descriptive situational statements. By employing a formula developed by Fry [6], the readability of the VAI was found to be at the 7.5 grade level.

FIGURE 1. Examples of VAI Scale Items and Response Categories

		RESPONSE	CATEGORIES		
					NOT
			DIS-	RELE-	RELE-
VAI SCALE	ITEM	AGREE	AGREE	VANT	VANT
1. Socio-economic	A good job does not help you plan for the future.	___	___	___	___
2. Familial	A good job can be found by knowing what members of your family do.	___	___	___	___
3. Environmental-community	There are people in your neighborhood that can help you find a good job.	___	___	___	___
4. Educational	Most people you read about in school had some type of job.	___	___	___	___
5. Ethnic	After getting a good job, most people wind up working for whites.	___	___	___	___
6. Sex	Women don't need specific education and training to get a good job.	___	___	___	___
7. Physical-capacity	You can't *do* a good job if you don't have a good sight, hearing, or are without an arm or leg.	___	___	___	___

The VAI was administered to 35 randomly selected Onondaga County, New York, rural high school adolescents for the purpose of establishing the reliability of the index. Retesting occurred 2 weeks later with a net test-retest sample of 30. For concurrent validation, the VAI was administered, along with the attitude scale of the CMI, to 370 out-of-school Neighborhood Youth Corps intake clientele, beginning out-of-school students of a Syracuse occupational learning center program, and students from various selected high schools in urban and rural areas of Onondaga County, New York and 1 suburban high school in adjacent Madison County, New York. The clustered sampling approach [12] was used, which resulted in a sample of adolescents of divergent ethnic, educational, and socioeconomic backgrounds.

Results

The VAI was subjected to the Kuder-Richardson Formula 21 (K-R$_{21}$) to determine the reliability (internal consistency) of each of the seven VAI scales and of the entire index. These correlations constitute moderate to high reliability for the VAI scales and total index. The test-retest reliability of the VAI was ascertained through Pearson product-moment correlations and intraclass correlations [10]. The familial and ethnic scales have modest test-retest reliability, while the

TABLE 1. Kuder-Richardson Reliability and Test-Retest Reliability Correlations of the VAI and Correlations Between the VAI and CMI Attitude Scale

VAI SCALES	K-R$_{21}$	R^a	R^b	R^c
Socioeconomic	.78	.77	.77	.03
Familial	.84	.40	.37	.20*
Environmental-community	.59	.88	.87	.20*
Educational	.91	.63	.63	.24*
Ethnic	.82	.34	.33	—.01
Sex	.84	.72	.72	.08*
Physical-capacity	.87	.75	.72	.06*
Total Index	.81	.64	.63	.08*

^{a} Pearsonian correlation.
^{b} Intraclass correlation.
^{c} Pearsonian correlation for the VAI scales and total index versus the CMI attitude scale.
* $p < .05$.

other scales have moderate to high test-retest reliability. The total index demonstrates moderate test-retest reliability.

VAI scale and total score data and CMI attitude scale data were correlated to determine the concurrent validity of the VAI. Low correlations (no higher than .30) were desired to establish that the VAI measures an overlapping but distinctly different psychological construct than does the CMI attitude scale. The VAI socioeconomic and ethnic scales do not correlate with the CMI attitude scale; the VAI familial, environmental-community, educational, sex, and physical-capacity scales and total VAI scores have positive and significant correlations with the CMI attitude scale. All correlations are presented in Table 1.

Discussion

It appears that the rational approach to the delineation of the seven vocational awareness domains (VAI scales) and the item content employed in this study resulted in consistent subject responses to the VAI. The modest test-retest reliabilities of the familial and ethnic VAI scales indicate the need for further item refinement in these scales, however, it is believed the preliminary establishment of the VAI would not have been possible without the construction of items based on an integrated, theoretical foundation. It is further suggested that this rational approach contributed to the sufficient reliabilities reported.

In reference to concurrent validity, positive and significant correlations were desired between the VAI scales and CMI attitude scale. However, it was hoped that these correlations would have two characteristics: (1) the correlations should be $r = .30$ or below, and (2) the correlations for those VAI scales least emphasizing formal educational experiences should be lowest. The highest correlation was between the VAI educational scale and CMI attitude scale ($r = .24$). Since the attitude scale was constructed on an age-grade linear model, a scale that depicts vocational situations in an educational context (the VAI educational scale) would have the highest positive and significant relationship to vocational maturity as measured by the CMI attitude scale. All other VAI scales represent a departure from this educational framework, with the ethnic scale, as expected, demonstrating the greatest distinction.

In general, the correlations between the VAI scales and CMI attitude scale followed the pattern sought by the investigator. Except for the VAI educational, familial, and environmental-community scales, correlations were somewhat lower than anticipated. The overall positive and significant VAI-CMI attitude scale correlation is explained by the integration of different vocational awareness situational sets embodied in the VAI that are similar to those vocational areas depicted in the CMI attitude scale not solely dependent on educational development. Thus, the two instruments are similar in their emphasis on vocational functioning. Future research with the VAI should concern the factorial composition of the measure [9] and greater scoring efficiency.

The career counselor will find his job increasingly complex in the coming decades. Rapidly changing technology and life styles will require him to be a highly knowledgeable as well as a personal resource. His knowledge will be increased by the flood of materials and texts pertaining to the occupational information and systems of his times. However, the career counselor may lose his most productive asset, if he is not careful; his ability to relate personally to an individual should be highly protected. He should choose vocational materials and instruments that augment his ability to relate to varying individuals in varying situations. The VAI was conceived as a preliminary step in exploring the area of instrument-assisted career counseling facilitation. It is believed, at the present time, that VAI items may be used to stimulate important areas of discussion without scoring them as an index. Future research may determine the utility in plotting VAI scale patterning to assist in counseling intervention (dealing with potential vocationally related trouble areas). The ability to be personal and preventive rather than impersonal and reactive is greatly needed in all areas of human service.

References

1. ANGYAL, A. *Foundations for a science of personality.* New York: Commonwealth Funds, 1941.
2. BEIER, E. G. *The silent language of psychotherapy.* Chicago: Aldine, 1966.
3. CRITES, J. O. A model for the measurement of vocational maturity. *Journal of Counseling Psychology,* 1961, *8,* 255–259.
4. CRITES, J. O. Proposals for a new criterion measure and research design.

In H. Borow (Ed.), *Man in a world at work*. Boston: Houghton Mifflin, 1964. Pp. 324–340.

5. CRITES, J. O. *Career Maturity Inventory: Theory and research handbook.* Monterey, Calif.: McGraw-Hill, 1973.
6. FRY, E. A readability formula that saves time. *Journal of Reading,* 1968 (April), 513–517.
7. GEIST, H. *The Geist Picture Interest Inventory, General Male.* Missoula, Mont.: Psychological Test Specialists, 1959.
8. GINZBERG, E. Toward a theory of occupational choice: A restatement. *Vocational Guidance Quarterly,* 1972, 20(3), 169–176.
9. NUNNALLY, J. C. *Psychometric theory.* New York: McGraw-Hill, 1967.
10. ROBINSON, W. S. The statistical measure of agreement. *American Sociological Review,* 1957, 22, 17–25.
11. ROGERS, C. R. A theory of therapy, personality, and interpersonal relationships in the client-centered framework. In S. Koch (Ed.), *Psychology: A study of science.* New York: McGraw-Hill, 1959.
12. SCOTT, W. A., and WERTHEIMER, M. *Introduction to psychological research.* New York: Wiley, 1962.
13. SUPER, D. E. Vocational adjustment: Implementing a self-concept. *Occupations,* 1951, 30, 88–92.
14. SUPER, D. E. *The psychology of careers.* New York: Harper, 1957.

Some Correlates of Work Values

Ramon J. Aldag
and
Arthur P. Brief

Work values have been considered both as determinants of employee affective responses and as moderators of task-dimension–affective-response relationships. For instance, Blood (1969) developed an eight-item scale gauging "pro-Protestant Ethic" and "non-Protestant Ethic" attitudes. Administration of that scale to two groups of airmen, both students and individuals in permanent assignments, yielded results suggesting that adherence to pro-Protestant Ethic ideals was positively

Reprinted from *Journal of Applied Psychology,* **60:**757–760 (1975). Copyright 1975 by the American Psychological Association. Reprinted by permission. Portions of this paper were presented at the 7th Annual Convention of the American Institute for Decision Sciences, Cincinnati, November, 1975.

related to job satisfaction, while agreement with non-Protestant Ethic ideals was inversely related to job satisfaction.

Hulin and Blood (1968) suggested that conflicting findings relating to reactions to job enrichment could be reconciled if alienation from middle-class work norms was considered as a moderator. Wanous (1974), using the pro-Protestant Ethic items of the Blood (1969) scale, found adherence to Protestant Ethic ideals to moderate task characteristic-satisfaction relationships as expected, though the moderating effects were not as strong as those evidenced by higher order need strength. Relationships between job behaviors and task characteristics were not, however, moderated by adherence to Protestant Ethic ideals. Merrens and Garrett (1975) administered the Protestant Ethic Scale developed by Mirels and Garrett (1971) to introductory psychology students and formed subgroups on the basis of those scores. The high Protestant Ethic group was found to spend more time on a subsequent task and to produce greater output.

Given the apparently key role played by work values in influencing employee affective responses to work in general and to specific task characteristics, this study attempted to replicate the Blood (1969) findings using a markedly different sample and different measures of affective responses. Furthermore, while correlations of scores on the Protestant Ethic Scale with such variables as sex guilt, conscience guilt, authoritarianism, locus of control, and social desirability have been reported (Mirels and Garrett, 1971), relatively little is known about the relationships of adherence to Protestant Ethic ideals with task and leader dimensions. Consequently, correlations between work-value indices and employee perceptions of task dimensions and of leader behavior were examined. Information concerning these latter correlations is important if work-value indices are to be viewed as moderators of task-dimension–employee-response or leader-behavior–employee-response relationships. Finally, in an exploratory vein, this study examined whether work values were associated with biographical measures or with particular individual needs, traits, or abilities.

Method

Subjects of the study were hourly employees of a manufacturing firm in a midwestern state. A large number of position titles were represented (for example, crane operator, furnace tender, die caster, material handler, mechanical finisher, heat treater, welder). Questionnaires and a follow-up letter were mailed to all hourly employees. Of 415 questionnaires mailed, 131 were returned by the time of the analysis. Completed questionnaires were sent directly to the researchers and were anonymous.

To gauge work values, the Blood (1969) scale was used. That scale includes four items intended to be in agreement with Protestant Ethic

TABLE 1. Rotated Factor Loadings

ITEM [a]	FACTOR 1	FACTOR 2
1. When the workday is finished, a person should forget his job and enjoy himself.	—.233	.436
2. Hard work makes a man a better person.	.641	—.097
3. The principle purpose of a man's job is to provide him with the means for enjoying his free time.	.032	.691
4. Wasting time is as bad as wasting money.	.726	.048
5. Whenever possible a person should relax and accept life as it is, rather than always striving for unreachable goals.	—.078	.710
6. A good indication of a man's worth is how well he does his job.	.672	.096
7. If all other things are equal, it is better to have a job with a lot of responsibility than one with little responsibility.	.486	—.232
8. People who "do things the easy way" are the smart ones.	.060	.539

[a] Items 2, 4, 6, and 7 are "pro-Protestant Ethic" items. Others are "non-Protestant Ethic" items.

ideals (pro-Protestant Ethic) and four not agreeing with those ideals (non-Protestant Ethic). For the data of the current study, principal components analysis of the eight items with varimax rotation of two components yielded the loadings presented in Table 1, which are very similar to those reported by Blood. The two factors accounted for 21.1 per cent and 19.2 per cent of the common variance, respectively.

The questionnaire included a slightly revised version of the Yale Job Inventory used by Hackman and Lawler (1971). This version has been used by Lawler, Hackman, and Kaufman (1973), and by Brief and Aldag (1975), and is reported on by Hackman (1973). Eight affective response measures were taken from the Yale Job Inventory (job involvement, internal work motivation, general satisfaction, hygiene satisfaction, existence satisfaction, supervisory satisfaction, growth satisfaction, and peer satisfaction).

Five core task dimensions were also gauged by the Yale Job Inventory (skill variety, task identity, task significance, autonomy, and feedback from the job itself). Evidence relating to reliability and validity of the task dimension measures is provided by Hackman and Lawler (1971) and by Brief and Aldag (1975).

The leader Behavior Description Questionnaire (LBDQ) was used to gauge leader consideration and initiating structure. Evidence is available to support the reliability and validity of some forms of the LBDQ (cf. Schriesheim and Kerr, 1974; Stogdill, 1969).

Individual abilities, traits, and needs were measured by the Ghiselli Self-Description Inventory, a 64-item forced-choice inventory (Ghiselli,

TABLE 2. Correlates of Work-Value Indices

VARIABLE	PRO-PROTESTANT ETHIC	NON-PROTESTANT ETHIC
Affective response		
General satisfaction	.117	—.203*
Job involvement	.167	—.098
Internal work motivation	.176*	—.213*
Hygiene satisfaction	.095	—.081
Existence satisfaction	.169	—.111
Peer satisfaction	.027	—.111
Supervisory satisfaction	—.043	—.304***
Growth satisfaction	.184*	—.230**
Perceived task dimension		
Skill variety	.039	—.288***
Task identity	.046	—.219*
Task significance	.068	—.279***
Autonomy	—.048	—.185*
Feedback from job	.094	—.179*
Perceived leader behavior		
Consideration	.085	—.298***
Initiating structure	.113	.003
Higher order need strength		
Measure A	.179*	—.183*
Measure B	.233**	—.343***

* $p < .05$, two-tailed.
** $p < .01$, two-tailed.
*** $p < .001$, two-tailed.

1971). That scale gauges 13 individual characteristics (for example, initiative, maturity, and need for job security). Also, two measures (Measures A and B) of higher order need strength were taken from the Yale Job Inventory. While Measure A is an absolute gauge of higher order need strength, Measure B is a gauge of higher order need strength relative to lower order need strength.

Employee age, educational level, tenure in organization, time on current job, and urbanization of area of socialization and of current home location were also measured. The latter pair of measures were scored as urban, suburban, or rural.

Results

Table 2 presents correlations of work-value indices with affective responses, perceptions of task dimensions and of leader behavior, and higher order need strength.[1]

[1] Tables presenting means, variances, and potential ranges of all variables are available from the first author.

Most correlations of the pro-Protestant Ethic score with affective responses are positive, with two reaching significance. Negative relationships are evident between the non-Protestant Ethic score and all affective response measures, with four of the correlations being significant. Thus, the Blood (1969) findings are generally replicated.

While perceptions of task dimensions are essentially independent of the pro-Protestant Ethic score, the non-Protestant Ethic score is significantly negatively related to *all* perceptions of task dimensions.

Somewhat similar findings are evident in relation to consideration. That is, perceptions of leader's consideration are significantly negatively related to the non-Protestant Ethic score.

The only significant biographical correlate of the pro-Protestant Ethic score was age ($r = .305$, $p < .001$).[2] No relationships of the non-Protestant Ethic score to biographical indices were significant.

Only 2 of 26 correlations of work-value indices with the characteristics measured by the Ghiselli Self-description Inventory were significant. Those two significant correlations were between the non-Protestant Ethic score and masculinity–femininity ($r = -.207$, $p < .05$) and maturity ($r = -.230$, $p < .05$).

As shown in Table 2, both of the Yale Job Inventory higher order need strength measures are significantly positively related to the pro-Protestant Ethic score and significantly negatively related to the non-Protestant Ethic score.

Summary and Discussion

The findings of Blood (1969) regarding relationships of work-value indices to employee affective responses were replicated using a different sample and different affective response measures. Further, numerous, significant relationships of the indices to perceptions of task dimensions and of leader behavior were evident. While correlations of the work-value indices with higher order need strength measures were significant, relationships with other individual difference measures were generally weak.

The significantly positive correlation of the pro-Protestant Ethic score with age is consistent with popular conceptions of that relationship. Similarly, the findings relating to correlations of work values with higher order need strength agree with the arguments and findings of Wanous (1974). However, the suggestion of Hulin and Blood (1968) and of Wanous (1974), that urbanization of area of socialization may be related to adherence to Protestant Ethic ideals, was not supported by this study. It should be noted that while Wanous argued in terms of a developmental sequence from socializing experiences, to work

[2] Tables presenting correlations of work value indices with biographical measures and individual abilities, traits, and needs are available from the first author.

values, to higher order need strength, his own data revealed no significant relationship between the pro-Protestant Ethic score and the degree of urbanization of the area of socialization.

Despite the fact that work-value–affective-response relationships were found in this study to closely approximate those presented by Blood (1969), the overall set of results does little to enhance confidence in the existence of a causal relationship between those variables. In particular, the relationships found between work-value indices and perceptions of task dimensions and of leader behavior are disquieting and potentially important. For example, if an employee's perceptions of the dimensions of his task color his work values and also influence affective responses, spurious work-value–affective-response relationships may result. On the other hand, if as Blood (1969) suggests, "It seems more logical . . . to assume that work values precede and influence job satisfaction than the opposite" (p. 458), and if those work values also influence perceptions of task dimensions, findings of task-dimension–affective-response relationships may be spurious. Similar potential dangers of spurious results are suggested by the findings relating to consideration.

Thus, while the findings indicate that previously neglected relationships may be relevant, further investigations of causal mechanisms are required. Such investigations must include either longitudinal analysis or objective measures of such variables as task dimensions and leader behaviors. Also, relationships of perceptions of task characteristics and leader behaviors to other work-value measures, such as those of Wollack, Goodale, Wijting, and Smith (1971), should be considered. Finally, since it could be argued that correlations in the current study may have been inflated because of method variance, future studies should be structured so as to minimize such a possibility. Until studies such as those outlined above are completed, adequate determination of the roles of work values is precluded. Consequently, caution should be exercised in the use of such indices and in the interpretation of findings from studies in which work values may be relevant.

References

BLOOD, M. R. Work values and job satisfaction. *Journal of Applied Psychology*, 1969, *53*, 456–459.

BRIEF, A. P., and ALDAG, R. J. Employee reactions to task characteristics: A constructive replication. *Journal of Applied Psychology*, 1975, *60*, 182–186.

GHISELLI, E. E. *Explorations in managerial talent.* Pacific Palisades, Calif.: Goodyear, 1971.

HACKMAN, J. R. *Scoring key for the Yale Job Inventory.* New Haven: Yale University Department of Administrative Sciences, 1973.

HACKMAN, J. R., and LAWLER, E. E. Employee reactions to job characteristics. *Journal of Applied Psychology*, 1971, *55*, 259–286. (Monograph)

HULIN, C. L., and BLOOD, M. R. Job enlargement, individual differences, and worker responses. *Psychological Bulletin*, 1968, *69*, 41–55.

LAWLER, E. E., HACKMAN, J. R., and KAUFMAN, S. Effects of job redesign: A field experiment. *Journal of Applied Social Psychology*, 1973, *3*, 49–62.

MERRENS, M. R., and GARRETT, J. B. The Protestant Ethic Scale as a predictor of repetitive work performance. *Journal of Applied Psychology*, 1975, *60*, 125–127.

MIRELS, H. L., and GARRETT, J. B. The Protestant ethic as a personality variable. *Journal of Consulting and Clinical Psychology*, 1971, *36*, 40–44.

SCHRIESHEIM, C., and KERR, S. Psychometric properties of the Ohio State Leadership Scales. *Psychological Bulletin*, 1974, *81*, 756–765.

STOGDILL, R. M. Validity of leader behavior descriptions. *Personnel Psychology*, 1969, *22*, 153–188.

WANOUS, J. P. The role of individual differences in human reactions to job characteristics. *Journal of Applied Psychology*, 1974, *59*, 616–622.

WOLLACK, S., GOODALE, J. G., WIJTING, J. P., and SMITH, P. C. Development of the Survey of Work Values. *Journal of Applied Psychology*, 1971, *55*, 331–333.

Career Information Days— When, Where, and How Much?

Cordelia M. Esry Hamilton

Career information, career days, career preparation, career placement! When, where, how and how much? This is a relevant area which now is being encountered by local, state and federal agencies.

Many vocational counselors, classroom teachers and professional people have been involved with career education for many years through informal interviews, lectures and conversations. Efforts to formalize the opportunities that are available in career areas are now coming to the fore.

At a recent career information day in our junior high, we learned that few schools have a program such as ours. The philosophy behind our career information days is to present a career information educational process. Even if a student has no expressed interest in an occupation, he can increase his general education by knowing about its

Reprinted from *School and Community* **62**:37 (Oct. 1975), by permission of the author and publisher.

opportunities, advantages and disadvantages. He also can better understand his neighbor, who might be employed in a job other than his.

Our junior high has about 215 students, grades six through eight.

Our building can accommodate 12 areas of participation, with a maximum of 35 students in the larger rooms and 20 in the smaller rooms. Screens must be provided for slides, films or overhead projectors, and display areas should be available for presenters.

Before our career information day, vocational areas are selected. Students have input, because after each career day they fill out questionnaires, asking for other areas of interest and suggestions for improvement. We select about 15 vocational areas, contact representatives of these areas and wait for replies. If as many as 12 representatives can and will participate, we have our day filled.

Participants have included representatives from the armed forces, conservationists, law enforcement officials, beauticians, restaurant managers, waiters and waitresses, nurses, mechanics, farmers, teachers, coaches, retailers, insurance agents, real estate agents, secretaries, truck drivers, lawyers, home economists, ministers, bankers, and college professors.

These people present the pros and cons of their vocational area. Whenever possible, we use local people who are successful in their vocations. This is good for the students, the school and the community, as it involves local professional people in the school system.

To avoid confusion, students register in five areas they wish to visit. Registration forms are collected and not returned to students until the day of the program. Sixth, seventh and eighth graders are often forgetful, and it is very tempting for friends to fill out identical schedules.

As physical facilities dictate the optimum size of a group, sections are changed when necessary so that all may comfortably attend the presentations of their choice. It has never been necessary to move students into areas they did not choose. Occasionally, times have had to be changed, however. By evening out sections, presenters have five groups of more equal size, which encourages student participation.

We allow two and one-half hours for the presentations—five sessions of about 30 minutes each. Bells ring only to signal that a session is over. Teachers, who rotate with the students, are free to attend any session they like. After the day is over, they evaluate the presenters and make suggestions.

Discipline has never been a problem with this program. But it has been our experience that the amount of time we allot is long enough. Another day is better than more than two and one-half hours in one day.

Both students and teachers enjoy career information days. With organization and the cooperation of faculty and administration, I have found this an excellent way to involve both community and school in a rewarding experience.

Knowledge of Occupations–Is It Important in Occupational Choice?

Troy E. Nuckols
and
Raymond Banducci

Most individuals in our society express an on-going and active concern with occupations. For most of these people, a major portion of their life is spent in a job or profession of their choice. They therefore may experience considerable anxiety if they have difficulty in making an appropriate choice, a choice they may perceive as being final and unalterable. In most instances, individuals respond to potential occupations on the basis of the perceptions they hold of a particular occupation or cluster of occupations. These perceptions may be sketchy or incomplete, accurate or inaccurate, and broad or narrow; yet vital decisions which may potentially affect an entire lifetime are predicated upon the occupational images to which one subscribes. That significant relationships exist between occupational stereotypes and other variables has been demonstrated using variables such as academic achievement (Krasnow, 1968; Nunnally and Kittross, 1958) and social status (Grunes, 1957; O'Dowd and Beardslee, 1960, 1967). In 1970, Banducci studied the accuracy of occupational stereotypes of male youth. In the present study, the knowledge that male high school students had of certain jobs was examined in relation to their academic achievement, social status, personal experiences, and formulation of future plans.

The rate of technological change and the isolation of young people from the majority of places of employment have created problems in occupational choice. Most students are not able to obtain informal exposure to a variety of occupations, nor can they easily obtain relevant data about occupations. If students are to make well-informed and carefully considered educational and vocational decisions, they must be assisted in critically examining the social and psychological aspects of work as they relate to personal assets. Additionally, these individuals must be provided with early occupational experiences which will allow them to expand their knowledge and widen their view of the range of

Reprinted from *Journal of Counseling Psychology*, **21**:191–195 (1974), by permission.

alternatives available to them. During this process, attention should be given to providing students with information about requirements within specific occupations. This should enable them to become more aware of the essential elements necessary for successful performance in the occupations they have examined. This process should assist students to discriminate more among the alternatives to which they have been exposed in depth and to determine which occupational alternatives would be socially and psychologically satisfying.

The research question studied was, "Do male high school seniors who differ in academic achievement, social status, formulation of future plans, and personal experiences also differ in the knowledge they have of selected occupations?"

Method

Sample
The sample consisted of 648 twelfth-grade boys in three public high schools in Cedar Rapids, Iowa. The subjects represented a range from high- to low-level social status groups.

Source of Data
The Worker Traits Inventory and a Personal Data Sheet (Banducci, 1970) and the Range of Experience Inventory (Abe, Holland, Lutz, and Richards, 1965) were administered in the boys' physical education classes. Twelfth-grade composite standard scores of the Iowa Tests of Educational Development were obtained from recorded information available from the Iowa Educational Information Center of the University of Iowa. Students were rated on social status on the basis of their fathers' occupations by utilizing the Hieronymus Scale Values (Hieronymus, 1948) for 140 male occupations and the North and Hatt National Opinion Research Center Occupational Prestige Scale (Bendix and Lipset, 1966). Scale values ranged from .4 to 10.8 and were divided so that score values .4 to 3.69, 3.70 to 6.69, and 6.70 to 10.8 represented low, middle, and high social status, respectively.

On the Worker Traits Inventory students were asked to rate 12 occupations on selected worker traits as indicated in the Dictionary of Occupational Titles (United States Department of Labor, 1965), namely interests, temperaments, general educational development, and specific vocational preparation. These ratings were used to assess the knowledge that students had with regard to worker traits for each of the 12 occupations. Students were asked to identify the traits they felt were necessary for the occupation being considered or to indicate that they did not know the required worker traits. For example, if a student did not know the temperaments a civil engineer should possess to perform

* Italics supplied.

his job adequately, he was instructed to indicate this by a "don't know" response. Presumably, not knowing the required traits indicated a constriction in the student's knowledge of the occupation. A summation of all "don't know" responses, subtracted from a constant, represented the degree to which a student's knowledge was considered to be constricted.

Students were asked to respond to six high-level and six low-level occupations selected for this study. The occupations corresponded identically with those used in Banducci's (1970) study when he investigated the accuracy of occupational stereotypes. They represented Holland's Vocational Preference Inventory types, namely, Realistic, Investigative, Social, Conventional, Enterprising, and Artistic jobs. The high-level occupations were civil engineer, physicist, psychiatrist, accountant, college president, and actor. The low-level occupations were electrician, medical technologist, playground supervisor, credit investigator, insurance salesman, and window decorator. Care was taken to choose occupations to which young people would realistically aspire, yet which would represent jobs within the Holland typology.

Hypotheses and Statistical Analyses
Hypotheses tested were: *

1. Students with high academic achievement have a greater knowledge of high-level occupations than of low-level occupations.
2. Students with low academic achievement have a greater knowledge of low-level occupations than of high-level occupations.
3. Students with high social status have a greater knowledge of high-level occupations than of low-level occupations.
4. Students with low social status have a greater knowledge of low-level occupations than of high-level occupations.
5. Students who have formulated future plans have a greater knowledge of occupations than students who have not formulated future plans.
6. Controlling for academic achievement and social status, personal experiences of students and their knowledge of occupations are related positively.

Prior to testing specific hypotheses, a multiple regression analysis determined the relative contribution of the independent variables of academic achievement, social status, and personal experiences to the prediction of the total knowledge of occupations of students, summed across the occupational levels. Results of this analysis led to treating academic achievement (Iowa Tests of Educational Development composite standard score) as the control variable in the Type I analyses of covariance (Lindquist, 1953) used in this study.

* Italics supplied.

TABLE 1. Analysis of Variance for Academic Achievement Levels

SOURCE	DF	MS	F
Academic achievement levels (A)	3	672.33	26.97*
Error between	644	24.93	
Occupational levels (B)	1	470.00	86.18*
A × B	3	26.33	4.83*
Error within	644	5.45	

* $p < .05$.

Hypotheses 1 and 2 were subjected to a Type I analysis of variance (ANOVA) since covariance procedures were unnecessary and to one- and two-tailed t tests to test differences between high- and low-level occupation means. A Type I analysis of covariance was used to test Hypotheses 3 and 4, which pertained to social status, and Hypothesis 5, which pertained to formulation of future plans. One-tailed t tests followed the Type I covariance analyses to test differences between high- and low-level occupation means for the top and bottom social status groups, while a two-tailed t test was applied to the middle social status group. A two-tailed t test was used to test differences between the mean high- and low-level occupation scores of the students in the plan and no-plan groups of Hypothesis 5. All hypotheses were tested at the .05 level of significance.

Results

The results of a Type I ANOVA at different levels of academic achievement appear in Table 1.

Students differed significantly in their total knowledge of occupations and in the way they viewed high- and low-level occupations, as

TABLE 2. t Ratios for Academic Achievement Levels

ACADEMIC ACHIEVEMENT LEVEL	N	OCCUPATIONAL LEVEL—MEANS		TOTAL	CONTRIBUTION TO INTERACTION (HIGH MINUS LOW)	T
		HIGH	LOW			
Top quarter	217	47.41	48.05	47.73	—.64	—4.93*
Second quarter	142	45.95	47.07	46.41	—1.12	—8.63*
Third quarter	135	45.24	46.59	45.91	—1.35	—10.41*
Bottom quarter	154	43.45	45.40	44.13	—1.95	—15.03*
Total	648	45.69	46.90	46.30		

* $p < .05$.

TABLE 3. Analysis of Covariance for Social Status Levels

SOURCE	DF	MS	F
Social status levels (A)	2	1.96[a]	.08
Error between	644	24.83[a]	
Occupational levels (B)	1	470.00	85.20*
A × B	2	19.00	3.44*
Error within	645	5.52	

[a] Adjusted for covariance with academic achievement.
* $p < .05$.

indicated by the F ratios for academic achievement levels and occupational levels, respectively.

*Hypothesis 1 was rejected, while Hypothesis 2 was supported.** One-tailed t tests (see Table 2) between the mean knowledge of occupation scores of high- and low-level occupations indicated that students with high- and low-level academic achievement (top and bottom quarters) had greater knowledge of low-level occupations than of high-level occupations.

The results of applying a Type I covariance analysis to students of high, middle, and low social status levels appear in Table 3.

The difference was significant in the knowledge students had of high- and low-level occupations when controlling for academic achievement, as indicated by the F ratio for occupational levels.

*Hypothesis 3 was rejected, while Hypothesis 4 was accepted.** One-tailed t tests (See Table 4) between the mean knowledge of occupation scores of high- and low-level occupations indicated that students with high and low social status had a greater knowledge of low-level occupations than of high-level occupations.

TABLE 4. t Ratios for Social Status Levels

SOCIAL STATUS LEVEL	N	OCCUPATIONAL LEVEL—MEANS		TOTAL	CONTRIBU- TION TO INTERACTION (HIGH MINUS LOW)	T
		HIGH	LOW			
High	157	44.88	46.60	45.74	—1.72	—7.47*
Middle	292	45.82	46.80	46.31	—.98	—7.53*
Low	199	46.48	47.46	46.47	—.98	—13.13*
Total	648	45.69	46.90	46.30		

* $p < .05$.

* Italics supplied.

TABLE 5. Analysis of Covariance for Formulation of Future Plans

SOURCE	DF	MS	F
Plan–no plan (A)	1	94.64[a]	3.72
Error between	644	5.45[a]	
Occupational Levels (B)	1	500.00	91.55*
A × B	1	2.00	0.37
Error within	645	5.46	

[a] Adjusted for covariance with academic achievement.
* $p < .05$.

Table 5 illustrates the results of applying a Type I covariance analysis to students in the plan and no-plan groups.

As noted in the F test for occupational levels, students differed significantly in their perception of high and low-level occupations. The main effect for plans, however, indicated no significant difference in the knowledge students had of occupations with regard to whether or not they had formulated future plans. Hypothesis 5 was rejected. Two-tailed t tests (see Table 6) between mean high- and low-level occupation scores revealed that the knowldege students had of occupations from both the plan and no-plan groups was significantly different for high- and low-level occupations. Both groups had a greater knowledge of low-level occupations than of high-level occupations.

Hypothesis 6 was supported. The relationship between personal experiences and total knowledge of occupations was .14. This correlation is significant at the .05 level and indicates that independently of academic achievement and social status, personal experiences of students are positively related to the total knowledge they hold of the occupations considered in this study.*

TABLE 6. t Ratios for Formulation of Future Plans

FORMULATION FUTURE PLAN	N	OCCUPATIONAL LEVEL—MEANS		TOTAL	CONTRIBUTION TO INTERACTION (HIGH MINUS LOW)	T
		HIGH	LOW			
Plan	426	46.00	47.17	46.59	—1.17	—9.01*
No plan	222	45.16	46.46	45.81	—1.30	—10.05*
Total	648	45.69	46.90	46.30		

* $p < .05$.

* Italics supplied.

Discussion and Implications

Banducci (1970) found that academic development was related to accuracy of stereotypic perceptions of occupations. Krasnow (1968) also found that knowledge of general occupational information was significantly related to academic development. *Findings of this study, however, indicate that the academic achievement of students did not exert an influence on how knowledgeable they were of occupations. Students of all academic levels had greater knowledge of low-level than of high-level occupations.** In the past, it has been presumed that students with high academic achievement had a more firm basis for making occupational decisions than did students with low academic achievement. Presumably, high academic achievement students had more knowledge about occupations than low academic achievement students and could organize this knowledge in a more meaningful way. This belief would imply that high academic achievement students would be more likely to have knowledge about high-level occupations. Banducci's study (1970) revealed that high academic development students had a more accurate perception of high-level jobs than of low-level jobs. The results of this study, however, indicate that all students, regardless of academic achievement, know more about low-level occupations than of high-level occupations. *When information regarding occupations is disseminated in the educational system, perhaps specific emphasis should be given to familiariizing students of all achievement levels with high-level occupations that are less visible in the environment.** In this manner, all students would have the opportunity to gather occupational information which may not now be readily available to them.

Banducci (1970) reported that students of low social status had more accurate perceptions of low-level jobs than of high-level jobs. In this investigation, however, *social status had no effect on the knowledge students had of the twelve occupations considered in this study.** Students of high, middle, and low social status had greater knowledge of low-level occupations than of high-level occupations. One might expect students of high social status because of the environment in which they live, to have greater knowledge of high- rather than low-level occupations. These data reveal, however, that this was not the case. Moreover, students often make educational and vocational decisions with limited information or knowledge. *These data indicate that students of all levels lack information and knowledge about high-level occupations.* Efforts should be made to provide students with information and to expose them to a variety of experiences that will broaden their knowledge of occupations. In this way, students may become more aware of the wide range of educational and vocational oppor-

---

* Italics supplied.

tunities that may be realistic alternatives for them to consider.

Banducci (1970) found that students who had formulated future plans had more accurate occupational stereotypes than those without formulated plans and that students without plans viewed low-level jobs more accurately than high-level jobs. *In this study, students who had formulated future plans had no more knowledge of the 12 occupations considered in this study than students who had not formulated future plans. Both plan and no-plan students had greater knowledge of low-level occupations than of high-level occupations.** However, young people are often expected to determine the occupation they wish to pursue, even though they may not possess the knowledge required to make reasonable decisions. Additionally, the community or geographical area in which students live may require that plans be formulated early because of limited opportunities available. Counselors need to be aware of this phenomenon and should be prepared to provide assistance to their counselees which will help them in formulating and achieving realistically attainable goals.

Personal experiences were positively related to the knowledge students held of the occupations considered in this study.* Although the relationship between personal experiences and knowledge of occupations was statistically significant, the correlation of .14 indicates that conclusions drawn about this relationship should be guarded. This finding may suggest, however, that a wide range of personal experiences can serve to increase the occupational knowledge of a student. *Therefore, consideration should be given in the educational process and in personal life to exposing students to as wide a range of experiences as possible.** This may be of valuable assistance to them in helping to choose educational goals and may ultimately be significant in the formulation of future plans and the broadening of occupational choices.

References

ABE, C., HOLLAND, J. L., LUTZ, S. W., and RICHARDS, J. M., JR. *A description of American College freshmen.* (ACT Research Report No. 1) Iowa City, Iowa: American College Testing Program, 1965.

BANDUCCI, R. Accuracy of occupational stereotypes of grade-twelve boys. *Journal of Counseling Psychology,* 1970, **17,** 534–539.

BENDIX, R., and LIPSET, S. M. (Eds.) *Class, status and power: social stratification in comparative perspective.* New York: The Free Press, 1966.

GRUNES, W. F. Looking at occupations. *Journal of Abnormal and Social Psychology,* 1957, **54,** 86–92.

HIERONYMUS, A. N. *Relationship between anxiety for education and certain socio-economic variables.* Unpublished doctoral dissertation, University of Iowa, 1948.

KRASNOW, B. S. Occupational information as a factor in the high school

* Italics supplied.

curriculum chosen by ninth grade boys. *The School Counselor,* 1968, **15,** 275–280.

LINDQUIST, E. F. *Design and analysis of experiments in psychology and education.* Boston: Houghton Mifflin, 1953.

NUNNALLY, J., and KITTROSS, J. M. Public attitudes toward mental health professions. *American Psychologist,* 1958, **13,** 589–594.

O'DOWD, D. D., and BEARDSLEE, D. C. *College student images of a selected group of professions and occupations.* (Final Report, Cooperative Research Project No. 562, United States Office of Education) Middletown, Conn.: Wesleyan University, 1960.

UNITED STATES DEPARTMENT OF LABOR. *Dictionary of occupational titles.* (3rd ed.) Washington, D.C.: United States Government Printing Office, 1965.

UNIT BIBLIOGRAPHY

BROWN, STEPHEN J. "Career Planning Inventories: 'Do-It-Yourself' Won't Do." *Personnel and Guidance Journal,* **53** (March 1975), 512–519.

CHRISTENSEN, KATHLEEN C. "The Career Motivation Process Program." *Catalyst for Change,* **4** (Spring 1975), 26–28.

CURRIE, LAWRENCE E. "An Index of Vocational Awareness." *Vocational Guidance Quarterly,* **23** (June 1975), 347–352.

HEALY, CHARLES. "Interrelationships Among Indexes of Vocational Maturity." *Vocational Guidance Quarterly,* **23** (Dec. 1974), 146–151.

KEHER, ANDREW. "Knowledge of the World of Work: A Test of Occupational Information for Young Men." *Journal of Vocational Behavior,* **6** (Feb. 1975), 133–144.

STERN, BARRY E. "The Occupational Information Systems Grants Program of the U.S. Department of Labor." *Vocational Guidance Quarterly,* **23** (March 1975), 202–209.

———. "Assessment of Career Awareness of Elementary School Children." *Journal of Career Education,* **1** (Spring 1975), 80–86.

part 5
Vocational Guidance: Assessment

Assessment is an important, yet often misused, source of information for the counselor and client. The use of an appropriate test may provide the client with information not previously available. One often hears that tests are used to label and place individuals; however, a properly trained counselor will understand what test to select and how to administer and interpret it. Tests are helpful only when they are used appropriately and ethically.

Information from tests can play an important role in the process of career development and guidance. Dale J. Prediger of the American College Testing Company, formerly professor of testing at the University of Toledo, Ohio, discusses and illustrates objective procedures for converting test data into counseling information. It is such procedures that can make test data useful to the client.

Assessment in vocational guidance may involve many types of instruments. Interest inventories and career development tests are frequently used to assess individuals and program development. Two articles are included here that compare several tests in these areas. Nancy S. Cole and Gary R. Hanson analyze the internal structural relationships of scales from the major interest instruments. They have found that the configurations of scales for all the inventories are similar and they discuss some of the implications for counselors. Bert W. Westbrook presents a content analysis of career development tests. His analysis shows which behaviors are assessed by the tests and can assist the counselor in test selection.

The final article in this part is a national survey of secondary school students' knowledge and attitudes about career development. The findings show a contrast between students' need for help with career planning and the help they have received. This article was selected to encourage counselors to use surveys in local assessment programs both for evaluation and program development.

Data-Information Conversion in Test Interpretation

Dale J. Prediger

This article is concerned with objective procedures for converting test scores and other data into information that is relevant to a counselee's educational and vocational plans, decisions, or problems. Validity studies are crucial to data-information conversion procedures. However, the scattered, nonlocalized validity studies often reported in support of an instrument are seldom of direct help to the counselor who has Fred and a set of test scores before him. While it is true that an accumulation of studies performed within a theoretical framework may support various uses of a particular test, the task of converting a counselee's test scores into usable information is left undone. Typically, the counselor can find the standing of a counselee in some norm group; after that he is on his own. Professional knowledge, clinical judgment, and personal sensitivity always will play crucial roles in test interpretation. However, objective data-information conversion procedures can make the counselor's job easier. Just what does a percentile rank of 63 on the XYZ Mechanical Aptitude Test say to Fred and his counselor?

Local Validity Data and Decision Making

Almost 15 years have passed since Dyer (1957) made a convincing case for local studies of test validity. Dyer was only one of a host of measurement specialists that cautioned test users about accepting tests on the basis of face validity or assuming that one or two validity studies conducted in some other setting provided sufficient evidence that a test would be useful in their setting and for their purposes. Recent reviews of validation research (Ghiselli, 1966; Prediger, Waple, and Nusbaum, 1968) have reinforced this caution. Dyer saw little help with development of local validity data coming from the statisticians and professional researchers. Instead, he felt the job must fall to the local practitioner.

The same thought was reflected 8 years later by Clarke, Gelatt, and

Reprinted from *Journal of Counseling Psychology*, **12**:306–313 (1971). Copyright 1971 by the American Psychological Association. Reprinted by permission.

Levine (1965) who placed the need for local validity data in the context of decision theory and presented a decision-making paradigm for local guidance research. Attention was focused on the process of decision making, with information on the possible outcomes of various courses of action being seen as a necessary if not sufficient condition for wise decisions. Examples of local validity studies conducted in the Palo Alta, California, schools were given to illustrate the development of objective probabilities useful in educational planning. As with Dyer, use of experience (expectancy) tables was emphasized. Subsequent articles (Gelatt and Clarke, 1967; Katz, 1966, 1969; Thoresen and Mehrens, 1967) elaborated on the role of objective probabilities in decision making, the influence of these probabilities on subjective probabilities, and the interaction between subjective probabilities, choice option utilities, and personal values.

Katz (1963, 1966), in particular, showed how the decision-making process is related to the broader process of vocational development. Results from the massive Project TALENT validation studies also have been placed firmly within the context of vocational development theory and decision theory (Cooley and Lohnes, 1968). The era in which the Parsonian concept of test interpretation could be viewed as the epitome of educational and vocational guidance is past. However, the above studies and formulations leave little doubt about the continued importance of test information in the vocational development process.

Bridges between Data and Information

Goldman (1961) described three objective bridges between test scores and their meaning for the counselee: the norm bridge, the regression bridge, and the discriminant bridge. Most of our current data-information conversion procedures consist of some form of the norm bridge. As Goldman notes, the norm bridge is an incomplete bridge since test norms simply permit one to estimate tending in some group and do not, per se, indicate the implications of this standing. The regression bridge, however, is a complete bridge from test scores to their implications and, as such, readily lends itself to data-information conversion. Usually, the implications are in the form of success predictions obtained via experience tables or regression equations.

The third bridge noted by Goldman, the discriminant bridge, provides an objective measure of a counselee's *similarity* to various criterion groups. Discriminant analysis techniques, when combined with the centour score procedures developed by Tiedeman, Bryan, and Rulon (1951), permit the comparison of counselee's test results with those of various criterion groups along the major dimensions of test data that differentiate the groups. The complementary nature of similarity and success estimates was first discussed some 20 years ago

(Rulon, 1951; Tiedeman et al., 1951). Many counselors, however, are unfamiliar with the characteristics of similarity (centour) scores or their potential role in test interpretation since these topics have received little attention in testing texts or test interpretation manuals.

Data-Information Conversion via Similarity Scores

Consider the information needs of Fred, a high school senior who is thinking about enrolling in a post–high school vocational–technical program. Centour score procedures applied to Fred's high school grade record and test scores could result in a report indicating Fred's similarity to successful and satisfied students in various vocational programs. In the example that follows, the similarity scores shown in parentheses after each of the vocational programs are on a scale running from 0 to 100 with 100 representing the highest degree of similarity. The closer Fred's scores on the relevant tests are to the test scores of the *typical* successful and satisfied student in a vocational program, the higher his similarity score will be for that program. Fred's similarity score report might look like this: vocational horticulture (87), carpentry (41), commercial art (28), auto body (26), distributive education (25), auto mechanics (14), radio–TV repair (3), and data processing (1).

Thus, on the basis of the measures used, Fred's aptitudes and interests are most similar to students in vocational horticulture. Carpentry ranks second and three other programs are in an approximate tie for third. Fred is least similar to students in data processing and radio–TV repair.

In this example, test data have been transformed into information that is directly relevant to one of the major functions of tests in educational and vocational guidance—*facilitating exploratory behavior*. Fred's counselor might use the similarity scores quite advantageously in stimulating Fred to explore the options available to him. Of course, the similarity scores should not be used alone. Their potential value lies in suggesting vocational program possibilities that might not have been recognized otherwise. The degree to which Fred explores these possibilities will be a function of his value system and his opportunities.

Secondary Role of Success Estimates

Success estimates obtained from regression analysis or expectancy tables also can be used to facilitate exploratory behavior. For example, Fred might be encouraged to explore the vocational programs for which he is predicted to receive the highest grades. However, estimates of success might be more appropriately incorporated into the actual exploration process where they could take their place along with a host of other relevant considerations. After all, Fred may not place much value on making high grades. His similarity scores could identify areas in which he would have a reasonable chance for success. His probable level of success could then be determined upon further exploration. Thus, a two-stage strategy is suggested with similarity scores being used to stimulate and facilitate exploration and success estimates being one of the many things to be considered during the process of exploration.

Other considerations also indicate the need for caution in the use of success estimates as the primary basis for facilitating exploration. Consider, for example, an experience table showing the relationship between the scores on some test and grades in carpentry. Could this table be used appropriately with Sally, Fred's sister? Can Sally be considered to be similar to the group from which the experience table data were obtained? To what degree would the trends shown in the results apply to her? Similarly, to what degree would success predictions in radio–TV repair apply to Fred (similarity score = 3)? Can Fred's test scores legitimately be used to predict lab grades in cosmetology? Or, in another context, is one justified in comparing a high school senior's college freshman GPA predictions in engineering, humanities, education, physical science, or business? These questions, recently discussed by Roulon, Tiedeman, Tatsuoka, and Langmuir (1967), need further investigation. A "reasonable" degree of similarity between counselees and the validation sample might well be an appropriate prerequisite for the use of success estimates in counseling.

A second difficulty with success predictions results from the well-known "criterion problem." Obtaining a suitable criterion of success in education and training is difficult enough. When one moves into the world of work, the definition and measurement of success become infinitely more complex (Thorndike, 1963; Thorndike and Hagen, 1969). Members of various occupations or occupational clusters can be readily identified, however. (Gross selective standards for determining criterion group eligibility could also be applied.) This is all that is needed to permit use of discriminant analysis and centour score procedures. Thus, data-information conversion would be possible.

Overcoming the Profile Problem

Judgment of a counselee's similarity to various criterion groups is not new in counseling. Certain commercially available inventories, for instance, the Strong Vocational Interest Blank and the Kuder Occupational Interest Survey, provide indices of similarity. However, special test construction and criterion group requirements present formidable barriers to the development of such inventories. In addition, existing inventories cover only one area of measurement, usually interests. Simultaneous coverage of other areas (for example, aptitudes, aspirations, biographical data) is not practical.

Profiles showing the typical performance of various criterion groups often have been provided for other tests and inventories. Counselors are expected to use these profiles by noting the similarity of a counselee's profile to the profiles of the criterion groups. Anyone who has engaged in this process needs no description of what has long been known as the profile problem (Tiedeman, 1954).

Similarity scores take the guesswork out of profile comparison but, unless they are used in conjunction with discriminant analysis procedures, they fail to deal directly with important aspects of the profile problem; for instance, do the criterion groups actually look different on the measures involved? If so, what are the important measures and how should they be weighted? Unfortunately, a set of similarity scores can be obtained from purely irrelevant variables.

For the above reasons, discriminant analysis procedures often are used in conjunction with similarity scores. These procedures enable one to determine whether the criterion groups are, in fact, differentiated by the measures. If so, the measures can be weighted and combined into independent factors (discriminant functions) that maximize criterion group differentiation. Furthermore, the number of factors needed for criterion group differentiation can be determined. Thus, one may, and usually will, find that two factors account for most of the discriminatory power of a set of measures when applied to criterion groups relevant to educational and vocational counseling. Finally, the nature of the factors can be identified by noting the measures that correlate highly with them.

Equations resulting from discriminant analysis can be used to calculate criterion group positions on the discriminating factors. These positions, in turn, can be plotted on a coordinate grid with the vertical and horizontal axes representing the two major factors. In the same manner, the factor scores of a given student may be calculated and plotted. The student's position on the coordinate grid then may be compared visually with the criterion group positions.

This technique for graphically depicting a student's similarities and dissimilarities was implicit in early work on the profile problem (Tiedeman, 1954) and was specifically suggested more than 10 years ago (Dunn, 1959; Whitla, 1957). However, it has been mentioned only occasionally in the professional literature since then (for example, Baggaley and Campbell, 1967; Cooley and Lohnes, 1968) and has received little attention in testing texts. Rulon et al. (1967) have provided a detailed discussion of the rationale underlying discriminant analysis and similarity score procedures along with ample illustrations of the resulting graphical solution to the profile problem. However, in presenting the illustrations, emphasis was placed on representing the geometry of the statistical procedures. Little attention was given to test interpretation applications of the illustrations.

Data-Information Conversion via Similarity Score Profiles

The graphical procedures described above can serve several important functions in data-information conversion. Application of these procedures to the problem faced by Fred and his counselor—consideration of vocational program options—is illustrated by the similarity score profile presented in Figure 1. Note that the two dimensions or factors that best differentiate the vocational programs are represented by the axes of the coordinate grid. Each factor is scaled with a mean of 50 and a standard deviation of 10 for students in all vocational pro-

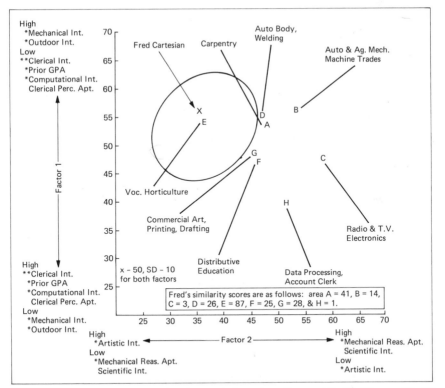

FIGURE 1. Similarity Score Profile for Fred Cartesian. (* r = .50–.59, ** r = .60–.69, *** r > .69; correlations of .40–.49 are unmarked.)

grams combined. Of the 10 aptitude and interest measures used in the analysis on which the profile is based, those having factor correlations with an absolute value of .40 or more are listed as factor anchors.

Fred's factor scores of 56 and 36 for Factors 1 and 2, respectively, have been plotted on the coordinate grid along with the mean scores of the eight vocational programs. (In several instances—for example auto body and welding—related vocational programs have been combined into one group). The ellipse surrounding the vocational horticulture group encloses the factor scores of approximately 50 per cent of the students in the group and is analogous to the scatter diagrams often seen in discussions of correlation. Similar but not identical ellipses could be used to represent the scatter of factor scores for the other vocational programs. One ellipse should be sufficient, however, to obtain a good estimate of program overlap.

Fred's similarity scores have been inserted for ready reference in a box in the lower right-hand section of the coordinate grid. Notice that they are reflected in the relative positions of Fred and the vocational programs on the profile. For example, Fred's position is quite close to that of the vocational horticulture group, the group for which he received his highest similarity score, that is, 83. On the other hand, programs for which he has low similarity scores are further away.

By comparing Fred's position on the profile with the positions of the various vocational programs, one can obtain valuable insights into the reasons underlying Fred's similarity scores. Field trials with potential vocational school students (Prediger, 1970) have shown that this is important, since use of similarity scores by themselves often leaves the counselee with the question, "But why did the scores come out like that?" In Fred's case it can be seen that both he and the typical horticulture student score only slightly above average on Factor 1, while Factor 2 scores suggest relatively strong artistic interests and relatively low mechanical reasoning aptitude and scientific interests. Fred may wonder why his similarity score for area H was so low. From the profile it can be seen that the Factor 2 scores for Fred and area H students are relatively far apart. In addition, the position of area H students on Factor 1 suggests that they have stronger clerical skills and interests than Fred. Similar reasoning can be followed in comparisons with the other groups represented on the profile.

In helping Fred understand the possible reasons underlying his similarities and dissimilarities, one is, in a sense, helping him to project certain aspects of his *self* into the choice options. This might be viewed as a vicarious exploration that tells Fred what persons who have exercised various choice options are like in terms of the characteristics that have been measured. The considerable variation in these characteristics among students who have made a specific choice will be clearly evident from the ellipse shown on the profile. If ellipses are shown for all of the vocational programs, overlap *among* the various groups also will be evident. Criticisms of counseling applications of trait and factor research sometimes are based on the fact that divergencies within criterion groups and similarities among criterion groups are concealed. Similarity score profiles reveal these facts of life. At the same time, useful differences among criterion groups, if present in the data, are presented in a manner that permits the counselee to "try the various groups on for size."

Once the reasons underlying Fred's similarity scores have been determined, Fred and his counselor may be able to develop a program of activities and study that would increase his similarity score for a given criterion group. The feasibility of doing this would, of course, depend on the variables involved. However, the suggested strategy represents one of the few counseling applications of test data that facilitates change in the status quo rather than merely being a representation of it. Other strategies for computing the status quo have been presented by Prediger (1970) and Rulon et al. (1967). Since these strategies are institution oriented rather than counselee oriented, they will not be discussed here.

Some Technical Considerations

One obvious limitation of similarity score profiles is the difficulty in representing more than two test or factor dimensions at one time. Discriminant analysis, fortunately, results in a reduction in the number of dimensions needed to represent criterion group differentiation. Usually two dimensions are sufficient. Nevertheless, similarity score profile techniques can be used with three factors by developing a series of profiles representing group positions on the first two factors for successive values of the third (Prediger, 1970). Instances in which more than three factors would be required to represent criterion group discrimination are rare, judging from the results of discriminant analyses reported in the literature.

The discussion, so far, has involved only one of two general approaches that have been used to develop similarity scores. The centour score approach, which has been illustrated above, gives an *independent* estimate of a counselee's similarity to each of the criterion groups under consideration. The second approach, which is based on the maximum likelihood principle, provides probabilities that take into account the *relative* degree of a counselee's similarity to each of the criterion groups (Cooley and Lohnes, 1962). The resulting similarity scores are given as decimal probabilities that total 1.00. Thus, if five criterion groups of equal size were involved and a counselee were equally similar to all five, his similarity scores via the second approach would be .20 for each group. This would be true whether his similarity scores obtained via the centour method were all 99 or all 1. That is, relative degree of similarity rather than absolute amount is determined.

As another example, suppose that a counselee had factor scores of 70 and 25 on Factors 1 and 2, respectively, in Figure 1. Through use of the maximum likelihood approach, he would receive a very high similarity score for area E, possibly even higher than Fred Cartesian's score. This would occur because the counselee's relative similarity to students in area E is much greater than his similarity to students in the other areas. However, his *actual* degree of similarity is quite low. Since a counselor (and counselee) undoubtedly would want to know this, educational–vocational counseling applications of the maximum likelihood approach are limited.

Implications

All of this is likely to be of little comfort to the conscientious counselor or personnel worker who has neither the time, training, or inclination to become involved in data-related duties as versus people-related responsibilities. Few test users would argue about the need to strengthen the bridges between test scores and their meaning for the counselee; but how is the job to be done?

Two of the major stumbling blocks to conducting validity studies are data collection and analysis, fields in which great strides have been made in the last 10 years through the use of computers. In addition to providing help with record-keeping functions, computers have made time-consuming and/or highly sophisticated data analyses economically and psychologically feasible. Approaches to data-information conversion that have been available for some time are now possible on a large scale. This is nowhere better illustrated than in the work of Project TALENT staff members, in particular, Cooley and Lohnes (1968). However, practical applications of Project TALENT findings are limited because of the multitude of measures involved and their unavailability to practitioners. Unless the test equating studies proposed by Colley and Lohnes (1968) eventually are undertaken, counseling use of Project TALENT data will be restricted to special programs such as Project PLAN (Flanagan, 1969).

The computer-based *system* illustrated by the Cooley-Lohnes studies is generalizable to other settings, however. Development of such systems, either by educational institutions or private enterprise, and provision for wide access to them is essential to any major improvements in test interpretation procedures. If systems for data-information conversion were available at the local level, the need for the do-it-yourself validation research described by Dyer could be met with little sacrifice of counselor time and mental equanimity. Much of the work required in data preparation could be completed by clerical help or one of the several types of guidance technicians proposed by Hoyt (1970). The counselor's only tasks would be to ask important questions of his data and to help his counselees use the resulting information. While data-information conversion systems will never replace professional knowledge, judgment, and experience, they can go a long way toward moving test interpretation beyond the era of squint and tell.

References

BAGGALEY, A. R., and CAMPBELL, J. P. Multiple-discriminant analysis of academic curricula by interest and aptitude variables. *Journal of Educational Measurement,* 1967, **4,** 143–150.

CLARKE, R., GELATT, H. B., and LEVINE, L. A decision-making paradigm for local guidance research. *Personnel and Guidance Journal,* 1965, **44,** 40–51.

COOLEY, W. W., and LOHNES, P. R. *Multivariate procedures for the behavioral sciences.* New York: Wiley, 1962.

COOLEY, W. W., and LOHNES, P. R. *Predicting development of young adults.* Pittsburgh, Pa.: University of Pittsburgh, American Institutes for Research and School of Education, 1968.

DUNN, F. E. Two methods for predicting the selection of a college major. *Journal of Counseling Psychology,* 1959, **16,** 15–26.

DYER, H. S. The need for do-it-yourself prediction research in high school guidance. *Personnel and Guidance Journal,* 1957, **36,** 162–167.

FLANAGAN, J. C. The implications of Project TALENT and related research for guidance. *Measurement and Evaluation in Guidance,* 1969, **2,** 116–123.

GELATT, H. B., and CLARKE, R. B. Role of subjective probabilities in the decision process. *Journal of Counseling Psychology,* 1967, **14,** 332–341.

GHISELLI, E. E. *Validity of occupational aptitude tests.* New York, Wiley, 1966.

GOLDMAN, L. *Using tests in counseling.* New York: Appleton-Century-Crofts, 1961.

HOYT, K. B. Vocational guidance for all: New kind of personnel needed. *American Vocational Journal,* 1970, **45,** 62–65.

KATZ, M. *Decisions and values: A rationale for secondary school guidance.* Princeton, N.J.: College Entrance Examination Board, 1963.

KATZ, M. A model of guidance for career decision making. *Vocational Guidance Quarterly,* 1966, **15,** 2–10.

KATZ, M. R. Can computers make guidance decisions for students? *College Board Review,* 1969, **12** (Summer), 13–17.

PREDIGER, D. J. Validation of counseling-selection data for vocational school students. (Grant No. OEG-3-6-551169-0379, Bureau of Research, United States Office of Education) Toledo, Ohio: University of Toledo, 1970.

PREDIGER, D. J., WAPLE, C. C., and NUSBAUM, G. I. Predictors of success in high school level vocational education programs: A review, 1954–60. *Personnel and Guidance Journal,* 1968, **47,** 143–145.

RULON, P. J. Distinctions between discriminant and regression analysis and a geometric interpretation of the discriminant function. *Harvard Educational Review,* 1951, **21,** 80–90.

RULON, P. J., TIEDEMAN, D. V., TATSUOKA, M. M., and LANGMUIR, C. R. *Multivariate statistics for personnel classification.* New York: Wiley, 1967.

THORESEN, C. E., and MEHRENS, W. A. Decision theory and vocational counseling: Important concepts and questions. *Personnel and Guidance Journal,* 1967, **46,** 165–172.

THORNDIKE, R. L. Prediction of vocational success. *Vocational Guidance Quarterly,* 1963, **11,** 179–187.

THORNDIKE, R. L., and HAGEN, E. *Measurement and evaluation in psychology and education.* (3rd ed.) New York: 1969.

TIEDEMAN, D. V. A model for the profile problem. In *Proceedings, 1953 In-*

vitational Conference on Testing Problems. Princeton, N.J.: Educational Testing Service, 1954.

TIEDEMAN, D. V., BRYAN, J. G., and RULON, P. J. *The utility of the Airman Classification Battery for assignment of airmen to eight Air Force specialties.* Cambridge, Mass.: Educational Research Corporation, 1951.

WHITLA, D. K. *An evaluation of differential prediction for counseling and guidance.* (Doctoral dissertation, University of Nebraska) Ann Arbor, Michigan: University Microfilms, 1957. No. 20–991.

An Analysis of the Structure of Vocational Interests

Nancy S. Cole
and
Gary R. Hanson

The several inventories of vocational interest used in this country were constructed in different ways, scored by different methods, and report scores on different numbers of scales with different names. However, the similarity of scale names across instruments raises the question of the degree to which the different inventories measure the same or similar interests.

The degree of correspondence between various inventories has been investigated by directly comparing an individual's interests as measured by various instruments. Several such studies yield apparently contradictory results. Triggs (1943, 1944) and Wittenborn, Triggs, and Feder (1943) reported similarities in the Strong Vocational Interest Blank (SVIB) and the Kuder Preference Record by considering overall profiles and correlational configurations. In more recent studies, King, Norrell, and Powers (1963), O'Shea and Harrington (1971), Wilson and Kaiser (1968), and Zytowski (1968) reported low correlations between corresponding scales of the Strong and various Kuder forms, and Kuder (1969) discussed methodological differences in construction of the in-

Reprinted from *Journal of Counseling Psychology*, **18**:478–486 (1971). Copyright 1971 by the American Psychological Association. Reprinted by permission.

strument which could lead to low correlations. In still other comparisons, Rose and Elton (1970) and Wall, Osipow, and Ashby (1967) used intermediate variables (such as vocational choice or major field) to demonstrate the relationship between two inventories—this time the Strong, and Holland's Vocational Preference Inventory (VPI).

Although the direct approaches have produced different conclusions, many writers have proposed categories of vocational interest which indirectly suggest correspondence between inventories. Super and Crites (1962) compared the factors of interests reported in several factor analytic studies, including those of Turstone (1931), Strong (1943), and Guilford, Christensen, Bond, and Sutton (1954). The following factors were commonly found: scientific, social, language-literary, mechanical, business, and artistic factors. Cottle (1950) and Harrington (1970) also reported correspondence of many factors of the Strong and different Kuder forms.

Many classifications of occupations have used categories which resemble the factors listed. Roe (1956) proposed eight groups (Technology, Outdoor, Science, General Cultural, Arts and Entertainment, Service, Business Contact, and Organization) in her two-way classification of occupations. Super (1957) named similar groups: Technical or Material, Scientific, Musical or Artistic, Literary, Humanistic or Social Welfare, Business Contact, and Business Detail. Further similarities are found in the families of scales of the Strong (Darley and Hagenah, 1955; Strong, 1943). Holland (1966b) described six major occupational and personality types (Realistic, Intellectual, Artistic, Social, Enterprising, and Conventional) and used the types to classify occupations (Holland, 1966a).

These classes of occupations and interests have been used primarily as discrete and independent categories. However, recent considerations of the relationships among the categories suggest a basis for the comparison of interest inventories which may help to unify previous results. Roe (Roe, 1956; Roe and Klos, 1969) suggested that her interest categories were related to each other in a circular ordering in which classes adjacent in the circle were most closely related while those most widely separated were the least related. Several studies supported the proposed continuum of interests (Jones, 1965; Roe, Hubbard, Hutchinson, and Bateman, 1966). Holland examined the relationships of the six scales of the Vocational Preference Inventory and empirically demonstrated a circular arrangement of the scales (Holland, Whitney, Cole, and Richards, 1969) from Realistic to Intellectual to Artistic to Social to Enterprising to Conventional and back to Realistic. Cole, Whitney, and Holland (1971) used a statistical analysis of spatial configuration to relate occupational groups to the six Holland scales. The results also demonstrated that the circle of Holland scales can be considered as a continuum of interests with each location in the circle representing a different mix of the six Holland interests.

The similarities of the many proposed categories of occupational interests and the recent demonstrations of relations among the categories suggest that a simple configuration or structure (such as that demonstrated by Holland) may underlie the vocational interests assessed by various inventories. If such a configuration does exist, the inventories may be sampling interests from a common underlying interest domain, and the configuration thus may provide a useful perspective for research and interpretation.

The purpose of this paper is to determine whether the circular configuration of interests proposed and demonstrated by Roe and Holland (as previously discussed) is common to other interest inventories. Since Holland's six interest categories represent one of the simplest skeletal versions of the interest categorizations, it is the basis of comparison. The following inventories were studied: the Strong Vocational Interest Blank (SVIB), the Kuder Occupational Interest Survey (Kuder OIS), Holland's Vocational Preference Inventory (VPI), the Minnesota Vocational Interest Inventory (MVII), and a new instrument, the American College Testing Program's Vocational Interest Profile (ACT VIP). If the circular arrangement is common to the internal structure of several instruments, the arrangement would provide a basis for comparisons of the instruments that might resolve the conflicting results of previous research and provide a basis for counselor interpretation.

Method

The Analysis of Spatial Configuration

Cole and Cole (1970) described an analysis of spatial configuration which used the method of principal components to examine variable relationships. This analysis, when performed on Holland's Inventory, yielded a circular configuration of the six Holland scales (Cole et al., 1971). The same analysis was applied to the Strong, the Kuder OIS, the Minnesota Inventory, and the ACT instrument to determine if the scales on each of these inventories are also arranged in a corresponding circle.

The analysis of spatial configuration uses the correlation matrix as the source of information about relationships among the variables. The geometric configuration of vectors (or points) representing variables (in this case scales of an inventory) is then reduced by fitting a smaller space to the vector points. If the variables lie predominately in a smaller space, then the relationships among the variables may be more easily understood. Often, in practice, the smaller space is two dimensional (a plane) and the variables may be plotted and visually represented as in the analysis of Holland's instrument.

Two results of the configural analysis are of special importance to our considerations. The first is the degree to which the relations among the scales on an interest inventory may be represented by a plane and the second is the particular arrangement of the scales in that plane. The percentage of the trace for the first two components of the second stage analysis (Cole and Cole, 1970, p. 3) can be interpreted as indicating the percentage of the variance of the scale points accounted for by the fit of the plane. The projection of the interest scales onto the plane (Cole and Cole, 1970, p. 4) provides the particular scale configuration.

Comparisons of Configurations

In order to compare the planar configuration of one instrument with that of another, differences in types and numbers of scales used in the instruments must be accommodated. Holland's simple system of six categories, which is similar in many ways to other categorizations and has the circular configuration under consideration, is used as the basis of comparison. Scales of the Strong and the Kuder were classified into Holland's system on the basis of a classification of 400 occupations reported in Holland, Viernstein, Kuo, Karweit, and Blum (1970). (Scales without a corresponding classification in that report were left unclassified.) Then the positions in the configural analysis for all the scales in each Holland class were averaged, resulting in mean planar locations representing the six Holland categories. These mean planar points could then be examined for indication of the circular configuration in the Holland ordering.

Data

Separate correlation matrices of the scales in each of the interest inventories were submitted to the analysis described. The intercorrelations of 50 SVIB occupational scales for 301 men were reported in Campbell (1966, pp. 37–39); those for the 22 SVIB basic scales for 647 men were found in Campbell, Borgen, Eastes, Johansson, and Peterson (1967, p. 49). *The Kuder Occupational Interest Survey Manual* (Kuder, 1966, pp. 58–59) gave the intercorrelations of the 23 core scales for 276 men. Intercorrelations of the nine homogeneous keys of the Minnesota Inventory for 400 men were obtained from Clark (1961, p. 65). The intercorrelations of the 12 scales of the ACT instrument for 311 male students are given in the *Handbook for the ACT Career Planning Profile* (American College Testing Program, 1970). The analysis of a correlation matrix for men on Holland's inventory was adapted from Cole et al. (1971) in order to facilitate comparisons with the other inventories.

Results

Goodness of Fit of the Planes

The goodness of fit of a planar surface to the points representing the scales of an inventory was measured by the percentage of the trace given by the first two dimensions. Table 1 gives the results for the fit of

TABLE 1. Goodness of Fit of the Planes

NUMBER OF SCALES	INSTRUMENT	PERCENTAGE TRACE ACCOUNTED FOR BY THE PLANE
6	Holland's VPI Scales	63.7
50	SVIB Occupational Scales	56.4
22	SVIB Basic Scales	37.8
23	Kuder OIS Core Scales	60.7
9	MVII Homogeneous Keys	58.2
12	ACT VIP Scales	47.3

the plane for each of the inventories considered. The percentage of the trace may be interpreted as the proportion of variance of the scale points accounted for by the two dimensions.

The planar configuration accounted for over half (between 56 and 64 per cent) of the variance in the scale points for four of the inventories while the SVIB basic scales gave the poorest fit. Since the basic scales were constructed to be as nearly independent as possible, this poorer planar fit is not surprising. Two dimensions do not offer a complete representation of the internal structure of any of the inventories. However, the percentages near 50 per cent and higher are substantial for instruments having many factors and, supposedly, great complexity.

The Planar Configurations

The scale points were projected onto the best-fitting planar surface for each of the inventories. Since the location of the principal component axes is of no special interest in this configural analysis, the planar configurations have been oriented in the same general way for each inventory to simplify visual comparisons.

Figure 1 gives the configuration of Holland's six scales as reported in Cole et al. (1971). The circular configuration in the Realistic–Intellectual–Artistic–Social–Enterprising–Conventional ordering is apparent.

The Strong occupational scales, the Strong basic scales, and the Kuder scales are given in Figures 2, 3, and 4. Those configurations invite comparison not only with Holland's categories but also with the configuration of occupations derived on the basis of the means on Holland's inventory for occupational groups and reported in Cole et al. (1971). The locations of corresponding scales (of the Strong and the Kuder) and occupational groups (based on Holland's instrument) are, in general, comparable. For example, Farmer, Forest Service Man, and Engineer scales on the Strong are located close to each other in Fig-

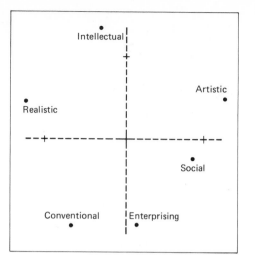

FIGURE 1. Spatial configuration of Holland's six Vocational Preference Inventory scales.

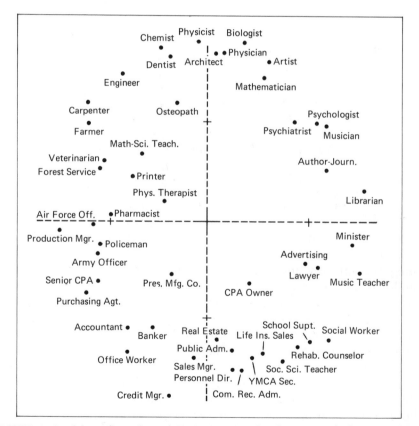

FIGURE 2. Spatial configuration of 50 Strong Vocational Interest Blank occupational scales.

FIGURE 3. Spatial configuration of the 22 Strong Vocational Interest Blank basic scales.

ure 2 as are Agriculture, Mechanical, and Technical Supervision in Figure 3, Electrical Engineer and Engineering: Heating/Air Conditioning of the Kuder in Figure 4, and Farming, Forestry, and Engineering in the Cole configuration. Other similar groupings correspond to the other Holland categories just as those mentioned correspond to the Realistic category. Not only are there similar clusters of occupations, but also similar relationships of the clusters to each other which correspond basically to the Holland circular ordering.

The configuration of the Minnesota Inventory is given in Figure 5 and that of the ACT Vocational Interest Profile in Figure 6. Both inventories are oriented to technical occupations and therefore the technical side of the circle is expanded. In both cases, Carpentry, Mechanical, and Electronics for the Minnesota Inventory, and Carpentry, Mechanical, and Electrical for the ACT instrument maintain the same ordering, the ordering also reported by Cole et al. (1971) for Construction, Mechanical Engineering, and Electrical Engineering. Similarly, Health Service of the Minnesota Inventory and Health of the ACT instrument fall in the same general area of each configuration as do the Business

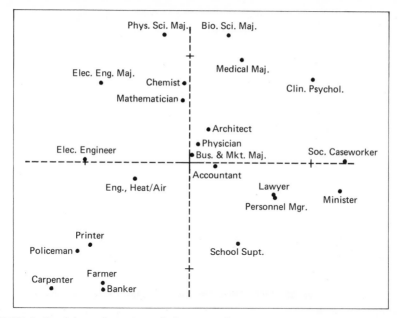

FIGURE 4. Spatial configuration of the 23 Kuder Occupational Interest Survey core scales.

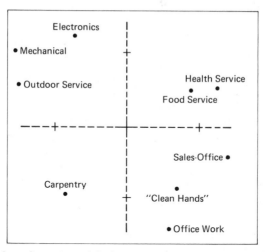

FIGURE 5. Spatial configuration of the Minnesota Vocational Interest Inventory homogeneous keys.

scales (Sales–Office, "Clean Hands," and Office Work) of the MVII and the Business scales of the ACT VIP.

Comparison of Configurations

Only the Strong and the Kuder have enough scales corresponding to occupations classified by Holland et al. (1970) to group the scales into the six Holland categories. Figure 7 gives the mean planar location

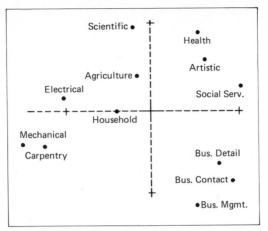

FIGURE 6. Spatial configuration of the 12 American College Testing Program Vocational Interest Profile scales.

for each category. The mean locations are connected by lines in the order under investigation. If lines were drawn from the center of the configuration to each mean location, in each case the ordering of these lines would duplicate the Realistic–Intellectual–Artistic–Social–Enterprising–Conventional ordering. Thus, the results in Figure 7 confirm the circular ordering already reported in connection with the individual scales.

Discussion

The purpose of this study was to examine the degree to which Holland's circular configuration of interests is common to various inventories. The results of the analysis of spatial configuration provide answers to two basic questions. The first question is: To what extent can the relationships among the scales be described in a plane (in two dimensions)? The answer, provided by the goodness of fit of the planes, is that the interrelations among the scales can be described to a large and important degree by two dimensions. The second question is: To what extent are the particular planar configurations of scales common from one instrument to another? Investigation of the configurations demonstrates that Holland's (and Roe's) configuration is, to a large degree, common to all the instruments investigated. This second result would have been an important finding even if present only on less dominant dimensions. That the circular configuration always appeared on the first two dimensions of variation among the scale points and that these two dimensions accounted for a large part of variation provide even stronger evidence for the practical importance of the circular ordering of interests.

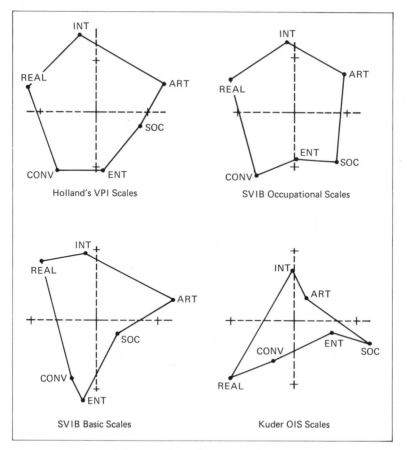

FIGURE 7. Comparison of the spatial configuration of the Strong Vocational Interest Blank (SVIB) and the Kuder Occupational Interest Survey (OIS) with Holland's Vocational Preference Inventory (VPI) using scales categorized by Holland's classification. (Abbreviations: REAL = realistic, INT = intellectual, ART = artistic, SOC = social, ENT = enterprising, CONV = conventional.)

Relation to Previous Research

A related purpose of the study was to use the results about the configuration of the scales to help reconcile the conflicting results of previous research. The demonstration of a common, underlying, circular ordering of vocational interest scales for several instruments provides a new basis for comparison of different inventories which may make the results of previous studies more understandable.

In one group of previous studies low correlations on same-named or similarly named scales were reported and it was concluded that the inventories measured very different things. However, a new look at the results of these studies using the common configuration of interest provides evidence of great similarities between instruments. Table 3 of King et al. (1963, pp. 398–399) presented a list of Strong scales with which a particular Kuder, Form D, scale correlated more highly than it did with a similarily named Strong scale (and vice versa). For example, the Kuder-D Physician scale correlated more highly with the SVIB Psychologist scale than it did with the SVIB Physician. The SVIB Physician scale correlated more highly with the Kuder-D Meteorologist, Pediatrician, High School Science Teacher, and Chemist scales than with the Kuder-D Physician scale. If each scale in Table 3 of King et al. is categorized into one of the Holland et al. (1970) categories, then in almost every case the listed scales conform to the same Holland category or an adjacent one. Similar results are found in the few examples given by O'Shea and Harrington (1971). Thus, by reinterpreting results on the basis of the circular configuration, the overall correspondence of the Strong and Kuder scales is clear even though the correspondence of particular individual scales may be small.

In a second group of studies (Triggs, 1943, 1944; and Wittenborn et al., 1943) a general correspondence between inventories was reported. In those studies the use of patterns of profiles or patterns of correlations as the bases for comparison meant that many aspects of the circular configuration were being implicitly used. Thus the results provided evidence for similarities between the inventories. Similarly the factor analytic studies, using correlational configurations, usually demonstrated in similarities.

Although the comparisons of the present study were indirect in the sense that correlation matrices for different groups were used, reconsideration of the results of studies making direct comparisons provides confirmation of the direct relation of one instrument's circular configuration to that of another. That is, those scales of Interest Inventory A that fall into one of Holland's categories, as a whole, tend to correlate most highly with the scales of Inventory B that fall into the same category. Furthermore, the scales in an adjacent category (in the circular ordering) tend to provide the next highest correlations.

Implications for Counseling

Since much research on comparing interest inventories has been motivated by counselors who were frustrated and confused by contradictory results, consideration of the relevance of these findings to counseling practice is appropriate. The results of this study have implications for the interpretation of scores from a single inventory as well as for comparison of scores from more than one inventory. By using the circular structure, a counselor may determine patterns of interest by observing scores on groups of scales rather than considering scales individually. For example, a person's high scores on scales such as Farmer, Carpenter, Forester, and Engineer together indicate Realistic interests which may be applicable to many other occupations. These results also suggest that correspondence of the scores on two or more interest inventories can best be determined by considering patterns of scales rather than individual scales. If a person scores high on several Intellectual scales on one instrument, he will likely score high on Intellectual scales on another. However, he may be highest on Chemist on one instrument and on Physicist on the other.

The discrepancies that occur in the comparison of scores on similarly named scales of different instruments deserve further consideration. This study suggests some reasons for the discrepancies which may be helpful to counselors. Most occupational titles, such as engineer, physician, lawyer, and salesman, do not represent narrowly defined occupations. Instead many different types of activity occur under the same occupational title. The activities of an engineer may range from building bridges to teaching electrical engineering. While the activities have common aspects and reflect many common interests, in the Holland scheme the bridge builder represents almost typical Realistic interests while the electrical engineering professor combines Intellectual interests with the Realistic ones. Similarly, the physician may be a pediatrician or a surgeon. Both share the Intellectual interests common to all physicians but the pediatrician likely reflects strong Social interests as well as Intellectual interests and the surgeon, Realistic interests. If we consider the circular structure of interests we can better understand why a scale based on one physician group (composed of pediatricians) would correlate more highly with a teacher scale, say, than with another physician scale (based on surgeons). Thus, the circular configuration of interests provides a possible explanation for differences in performance on scales having the same name but possibly based on groups reflecting somewhat different vocational interests.

References

THE AMERICAN COLLEGE TESTING PROGRAM. *Handbook for the ACT Career Planning Profile.* Iowa City: Author, 1970.

CAMPBELL, D. P. *Manual for the Strong Vocational Interest Blank for men and women.* Stanford: Stanford University Press, 1966.

CAMPBELL, D. P., BORGEN, F. H., EASTES, S. H., JOHANSSON, C. B., and PETERSON, R. A. *A set of basic interest scales for the Strong Vocational Interest Blank for men.* Minneapolis: University of Minnesota Press, 1967.

CLARK, K. E. *The vocational interests of nonprofessional men.* Minneapolis: University of Minnesota Press, 1961.

COLE, N. S., and COLE, J. W. L. *An analysis of spatial configuration and its application to research in higher education.* ACT Research Report No. 35. Iowa City: The American College Testing Program, 1970.

COLE, N. S., WHITNEY, D. R., and HOLLAND, J. L. A spatial configuration of occupations. *Journal of Vocational Behavior,* 1971, **1,** 1–9.

COTTLE, W. E. A factorial study of the Multiphasic, Strong, Kuder, and Bell inventories using a population of adult males. *Psychometrika,* 1950, **15,** 25–47.

DARLEY, J. G., and HAGENAH, T. *Vocational interest measurement.* Minneapolis: University of Minnesota Press, 1955.

GUILFORD, J. P., CHRISTENSEN, P. R., BOND, N. A., and SUTTON, M. A. A factor analysis study of human interests. *Psychological Monographs,* 1954, **68** (4, Whole No. 375).

HARRINGTON, T. F. A factor analysis of 27 similar named scales of the SVIB and the Kuder OIS, Form DD. Paper presented at the meeting of the American Psychological Association, Miami Beach, September 1970.

HOLLAND, J. L. A psychological classification scheme for vocations and major fields. *Journal of Counseling Psychology,* 1966, **13,** 278–288. (a)

HOLLAND, J. L. *The psychology of vocational choice.* Waltham, Mass.: Blaisdell, 1966. (b)

HOLLAND, J. L., VIERNSTEIN, M. C., KUO, H., KARWEIT, N. L., and BLUM, Z. D. A psychological classification of occupations. (Research Report No. 90.) Center for Social Organization of Schools, Johns Hopkins University, 1970.

HOLLAND, J. L., WHITNEY, D. R., COLE, N. S., and RICHARDS, J. M., JR. *An empirical occupational classification derived from a theory of personality and intended for practice and research.* (ACT Research Report No. 29.) Iowa City: The American College Testing Program, 1969.

JONES, K. J. Occupational preference and social orientation. *Personnel and Guidance Journal,* 1965, **43,** 574–579.

KING, P., NORRELL, G., and POWERS, G. P. Relationships between twin scales on the SVIB and the Kuder. *Journal of Counseling Psychology,* 1963, **10,** 395–401.

KUDER, F. G. *Kuder Occupational Interest Survey general manual.* Chicago: Science Research Associates, 1966.

KUDER, F. G. A note on the comparability of occupational scores from different interest inventories. *Measurement and Evaluation in Guidance,* 1969, **2,** 94–100.

O'SHEA, A. J. and HARRINGTON, T. F. Using the SVIB and Kuder, Form DD, with the same clients. *Journal of Counseling Psychology,* 1971, **18,** 44–50.

ROE, A. *The psychology of occupations.* New York: John Wiley, 1956.

ROE, A., HUBBARD, W. D., HUTCHINSON, T., and BATEMAN, T. Studies of occupational history Part I: Job changes and the classification of occupations. *Journal of Counseling Psychology,* 1966, **13,** 387–393.

ROE, A., and KLOS, D. Occupational classification. *The Counseling Psychologist,* 1969, **1,** 84–89.

ROSE, H. A., and ELTON, C. F. Ask him or test him? *Vocational Guidance Quarterly,* 1970, **19,** 28–32.

STRONG, E. K., JR. *Vocational interests of men and women.* Stanford: Stanford University Press, 1943.

SUPER, D. E. *The psychology of careers.* New York: Harper & Row, 1957.

SUPER, D. E., and CRITES, J. O. *Appraising vocational fitness.* New York: Harper & Row, 1962.

THURSTONE, L. L. A multiple factor study of vocational interests. *Personnel Journal,* 1931, **10,** 198–205.

TRIGGS, F. O. A study of the relation of Kuder Preference Record scores to various other measures. *Educational and Psychological Measurement,* 1943, **3,** 341–354.

TRIGGS, F. O. A further comparison of interest measurement by the Kuder Preference Record and the Strong Vocational Interest Blank for men. *Journal of Educational Research,* 1944, **37,** 538–544.

WALL, H. W., OSIPOW, S. H., and ASHBY, J. D. SVIB scores, occupational choices, and Holland's personality types. *Vocational Guidance Quarterly,* 1967, **15,** 201–205.

WILSON, R. N., and KAISER, H. E. A comparison of similar scales on the SVIB and Kuder, Form DD. *Journal of Counseling Psychology,* 1968, **15,** 468–470.

WITTENBORN, J. R., TRIGGS, F. O., and FEDER, D. D. A comparison of interest measurement by the Kuder Preference Record and the Strong Vocational Interest Blank for men and women. *Educational and Psychological Measurement,* 1943, **3,** 239–257.

ZYTOWSKI, D. G. Relationships of equivalent scales on three interest inventories. *Personnel and Guidance Journal,* 1968, **47,** 44–49.

Content Analysis of Six Career Development Tests

Bert W. Westbrook

Several tests are now available for measuring various aspects of career development. About 15 years ago, the ETS Guidance Inquiry (Educational Testing Service 1958) was published. Within the past six years the following five tests have been published: the Readiness for Vocational Planning (Gribbons and Lohnes, 1968), the Cognitive Vocational Maturity Test (Westbrook 1970), the Career Development Inventory (Super et al. 1971), the Assessment of Career Development (American College Testing Program 1972), and the Career Maturity Inventory (Crites 1973). A persistent question has been raised about these instruments: What are they measuring? This article seeks to shed light on this question by identifying the learner behaviors which are assessed by the six tests.

Method

Each of the 609 items on the six career development tests was examined to determine the behavior required of the learner. Behavioral statements were written for each item to describe the behavior required of the learner and the situation in which the behavior occurs. An example of one of the 609 behavioral statements is as follows: "Given a brief description of a job performed by an individual and a

Reprinted from *Measurement and Evaluation in Guidance,* 7:172–180 (Oct. 1974). Copyright 1974 American Personnel and Guidance Association. Reprinted with permission.

TABLE 1. ANALYSIS OF TESTS ACCORDING TO COVERAGE OF CAREER DEVELOPMENT BEHAVIORS

	CATEGORY OF OBJECTIVES											
	COGNITIVE DOMAIN						PSYCHOMOTOR DOMAIN			AFFECTIVE DOMAIN		
TEST	IA	IB	IC	ID	IE	IF	IIA	IIB	IIC	IIIA	IIIB	IIIC
Assessment of Career Development	1a,1b,1c	1a,1b,2a(1), 2b(1),2b(2), 2c(2),2d,2e, 2f(1),2f(2), 2f(3),2f(4), 2f(5),2f(7), 2h(1),2h(2), 2i(1),2i(2), 2i(3),2i(4), 2i(5),2i(6), 2j	1	1c(1), 1c(2)	2	1,2	1,2,3, 4,5,6, 7,8,9, 10,11, 12	1,2,3, 4,5,6	1,2,3, 4,5,6, 7,8,9, 10	1	1,2,3, 4	1,3
Career Maturity Inventory	2a	2h(2)	1		1,2	1,2	2			1,2		3
Career Development Inventory	2a	1a,1b, 2c(1),2f(3), 2g,2k(2)	1			2	2		7,8,10, 11,12, 13,14, 15,16, 17,18			2

Cognitive Vocational
Maturity Test

	2a(1),2b(1),	1
	2d,2f(1),	
	2f(2),2f(3),	
	2f(4),2f(5),	
	2g,2h(1),	
	2h(2),2i(1),	
	2i(2),2i(3),	
	2i(4),2i(5),	
	2i(7),2i(8),	
	2i(9),2i(10),	
	2k(1)	

ETS Guidance
Inquiry

1a,1b,	1a,1b,		1a,1b(1),	2
1c,2a,	2b(2),		1C(1),	
2b(2)	2f(3)		2a,2b	

Readiness for
Vocational Planning

2b(1),2b(2),	2a(2),2b(3),	2,3	1b(2),1C(3),	3	1,2,5
2b(3),2b(4),	2c(3),2f(6),		1d,1e,1f,2c,		
2b(5),2b(6),	2h(3)		2d,2e,2f		
2b(7),2b(8)					

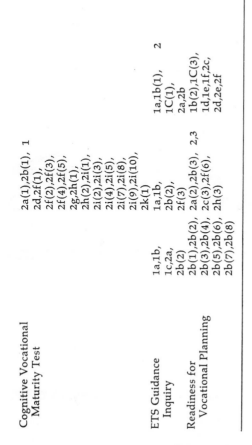

list of occupational titles, the learner will be able to identify the correct occupational title for the given job description." Inasmuch as a large number of items was found to provide a measure of many of the same behaviors, the total number of *different* descriptive behavioral statements was 117.

To reduce the length of the descriptive behavioral statements, an abbreviated behavioral statement was written for each of the 117 behavioral statements. For example, the abbreviated behavioral statement for the behavior described in the paragraph above is as follows: "Identify occupational titles of job descriptions." All of the 117 abbreviated behavioral statements were organized into an outline shown in Appendix 1. The outline contains a total of 12 major components. Six of the components are classified under the cognitive domain (IA, IB, IC, ID, IE, IF); three components fall within the psychomotor domain (IIA, IIB, IIC); and three components are included within the affective domain (IIIA, IIIB, IIIC).

Each of the six tests was examined to determine which of the specific behaviors can be appraised by using that test. Table 1 shows how the data were organized for comparing the behaviors appraised by the different tests. The columns in the table marked IA, IB, etc. represent the major categories of behaviors from Appendix 1. The entries in each of the columns under a major component are the number or letter and number of a specific behavior falling in the major component. Thus, in the category of individual attributes (IA) the Assessment of Career Development test has been judged by this author to have items that assess the learner's ability to identify statements describing an individual's abilities (1a), interests (1b), and values (1c).

Results and Discussion

What does an analysis such as that in Table 1 reveal? First, it shows that only the Assessment of Career Development provides for assessing the learner's involvement in a wide range of worker activities (IIB). In other words, measurement of these behaviors is included in only one of the six tests.

Second, it shows the difference among the tests in their coverage of cognitive (IA through IF), psychomotor (IIA through IIC), and affective (IIIA through IIIC) behaviors. For example, the Assessment of Career Development, Career Maturity Inventory, and Career Development Inventory provide for an assessment of behaviors in all three domains (cognitive, psychomotor, and affective), whereas the Cognitive Vocational Maturity Test and the ETS Guidance Inquiry cover only cognitive behaviors. The Readiness for Vocational Planning test includes behaviors in the cognitive and affective domain but not in the psychomotor domain.

Third, the analysis shows the difference among the tests in the range of cognitive behaviors (IA through IF) appraised. The range of coverage varies from the Assessment of Career Development, which includes behaviors in all six cognitive components (IA through IF), to the Cognitive Vocational Maturity Test, which covers only two of the cognitive components (IB and IC). The Career Maturity Inventory has items in all but one of the six cognitive components. The remaining three tests provide for an appraisal of four of the six cognitive components.

Fourth, Table 1 shows that the tests vary enormously in their coverage of specific behaviors within a given component. Although all of the tests provide for some measure of occupational information (IB), the Career Maturity Inventory measures only the ability to identify occupational titles of job descriptions. On the other hand, the Assessment of Career Development measures 22 additional behaviors within the occupational information component.

Fifth, the table shows the difference among the tests in the range of psychomotor behaviors (IIA through IIC). Only the Assessment of Career Development and the Career Development Inventory assess the learner's involvement in activities related to preferred occupation (IIC), and only these two tests and the Career Maturity Inventory assess the learner's involvement in career planning activities (IIA).

Finally, the analysis shows the difference among the tests in their coverage of behaviors within the affective domain (IIIA through IIIC). Only the Assessment of Career Development and the Career Maturity Inventory include items that were judged to provide an assessment of all three components in the affective domain. However, the Readiness for Vocational Planning does include items dealing with two of the three affective components, attitudes (IIIA) and preferences (IIIB); the Career Development Inventory provides for an appraisal of the learner's perception of help received from various sources of information (IIIC2).

Table 1 shows whether a particular career development test has at least one item appraising a specific career development behavior; it does not show how adequately each behavior is measured. Thus, for example, both the Assessment of Career Development and the Career Maturity Inventory appraise the ability to identify appropriate jobs for given individuals (IC1). The Assessment of Career Development uses only 7 items to assess this behavior, whereas, in a separate subtest, the Career Maturity Inventory uses 20 items. Since the reliability of the appraisal of a particular skill depends in part upon the number of items calling for the use of that skill, judgments as to the extent to which the learner can identify appropriate jobs for given individuals can probably be made with more confidence on the basis of the score from the Career Maturity Inventory than from the Assessment of Career Development.

Table 2 shows the number and per cent of items in each major component. Although the table does not present the number of items

TABLE 2. ITEMS IN EACH CATEGORY OF BEHAVIORS ON CAREER DEVELOPMENT TESTS

CATEGORY OF OBJECTIVES

TEST	COGNITIVE DOMAIN						PSYCHOMOTOR DOMAIN			AFFECTIVE DOMAIN			TOTAL ITEMS
	IA	IB	IC	ID	IE	IF	IIA	IIB	IIC	IIIA	IIIB	IIIC	
Assessment of Career Development													
Number	4	78	7	5	13	14	25	90	12	1	10	8	267
Per cent	1	29	3	2	5	5	9	34	4	0	4	3	
Career Maturity Inventory													
Number	20	20	20	0	45	28	6	0	0	5	5	1	150
Per cent	13	13	13	0	30	19	4	0	0	3	3	1	
Career Development Inventory													
Number	1	33	2	0	5	3	22	0	11	0	0	14	91
Per cent	1	36	2	0	5	3	24	0	12	0	0	15	
Cognitive Vocational Maturity Test													
Number	0	105	15	0	0	0	0	0	0	0	0	0	120
Per cent	0	87	13	0	0	0	0	0	0	0	0	0	
ETS Guidance Inquiry													
Number	13	10	0	10	1	0	0	0	0	0	0	0	34
Per cent	39	29	0	29	3	0	0	0	0	0	0	0	
Readiness for Vocational Planning													
Number	9	10	4	18	0	0	0	0	0	3	3	0	47
Per cent	19	21	9	39	0	0	0	0	0	6	6	0	

covering each specific behavior, it does show that the tests vary considerably in the proportion of items measuring each of the major career development components. The point being made here is that, in evaluating a particular test, one should give consideration to the adequacy of the appraisal of each behavior as well as to the variety of behaviors appraised.

Although the analysis presented here can be very useful in determining the learner behaviors assessed by the six tests reviewed, the development of the outline of career development behaviors and the classification of items by the behavior being measured is a subjective procedure. The career development outline in the appendix and the classification in Table 1 represent the author's judgment; another person classifying the same items might arrive at a somewhat different result. However, some of the subjectivity seems to have been reduced by writing behavioral statements for each item. Perhaps the reader can determine how much judgment is involved by classifying the same items according to the outline presented here.

References

AMERICAN COLLEGE TESTING PROGRAM. *Assessment of Career Development.* Iowa City, Iowa: American College Testing Program, 1972.

CRITES, J. O. *Career Maturity Inventory.* Monterey, Calif.: California Test Bureau/McGraw-Hill, 1973.

EDUCATIONAL TESTING SERVICE. *ETS Guidance Inquiry.* Princeton, N.J.: Educational Testing Service, 1958.

GRIBBONS, W. D., and LOHNES, P. R. *Emerging careers.* New York: Columbia University, Teachers College Press, 1968.

SUPER, D. E.; BOHN, M. J., JR.; FORREST, D. J.; JORDAAN, J. P.; LINDEMAN, R. H.; and THOMPSON, A. S. *Career Development Inventory.* New York: Columbia University, Teachers College, 1971.

WESTBROOK, B. W. *Cognitive Vocational Maturity Test.* Raleigh, N. C.: North Carolina State University, 1970.

Appendix 1

Outline of Career Development Behaviors Derived from Six Career Development Tests

   I. *Cognitive Domain* (What the learner knows)
      A. Individual attributes
         1. Individual attribute concepts
            a. Identify statements describing an individual's abilities.
            b. Identify statements describing an individual's interests.
            c. Identify statements describing an individual's values.
         2. Individual attribute appraisal skills
            a. Identify conclusions from description of individual's attributes.
            b. Appraise one's own attributes.
               (1) Describe one's own scholastic abilities accurately.
               (2) Name a valid basis for estimating one's own scholastic ability.

(3) Identify one's own level of verbal ability.

(4) Name a valid basis for estimating one's own verbal ability.

(5) Identify one's own level of quantitative ability.

(6) Name a valid basis for estimating own quantitative ability.

(7) Name one's own interests.

(8) Name one's own values.

B. Occupational information

  1. General occupational information

    a. Identify job market trends and characteristics.

    b. Identify dependable sources of information about jobs.

  2. Characteristics and requirements of occupations

    a. Relationship between abilities and occupations.

      (1) Identify occupations requiring given abilities.

      (2) Name own abilities helpful in own preferred occupation.

    b. Relationship between interests and occupations.

      (1) Identify occupations associated with specific interests.

      (2) Identify workers having similar interests.

      (3) Name own interests which preferred job would satisfy.

    c. Relationship between values and occupations.

      (1) Identify values likely to be important in given jobs.

      (2) Identify jobs that would satisfy specified values.

      (3) Name own values which preferred job would satisfy.

    d. Identify occupations associated with worker experiences.

    e. Identify jobs associated with personality characteristics.

    f. Relationship between education and occupations.

      (1) Identify occupations requiring least amount of education.

      (2) Identify occupations requiring most amount of education.

      (3) Identify education level required of given occupations.

      (4) Identify occupations matching given education levels.

      (5) Identify occupations requiring an apprenticeship.

      (6) Name education level required of one's preferred job.

      (7) Identify accurate statements about postsecondary education.

    g. Classify occupations into fields of work.

    h. Job duties and responsibilities.

      (1) Identify job descriptions for occupational titles.

      (2) Identify occupational titles of job descriptions.

      (3) Name duties performed in own preferred occupation.

    i. Work conditions associated with occupations.

      (1) Identify occupations requiring irregular hours.

      (2) Identify occupations involving physical danger.

      (3) Identity occupations requiring the worker to stand.

      (4) Identify indoor and outdoor occupations.

      (5) Distinguish between data, people, and things occupations.

      (6) Identify occupations involving mental stress.

      (7) Identify occupations performed in one's home.

      (8) Identify workers with highest income level.

      (9) Identify occupations requiring much walking.

    (10) Identify jobs requiring workers to be away from home.

    j. Identify occupations associated with organizations.

    k. Tools and occupations.

  (1) Identify occupations requiring use of tools.

  (2) Identify names of tools used in given occupations.

C. Job selection

 1. Identify appropriate jobs for given individuals.

 2. Name valid reasons for choosing own occupation.

 3. Name facts needed about self before selecting a job.

D. Course and curriculum section

 1. Course selection

  a. Identify valid course selection principles.

  b. Courses and abilities.

   (1) Identify abilities associated with school courses.

   (2) Name own abilities helpful in own school courses.

  c. Courses and occuptions.

   (1) Identify occupations related to given school courses.

   (2) Identify courses providing training for given occupations.

   (3) Describe relationship between own courses and preferred job.

  d. Name school courses required in chosen curriculum.

  e. Name valid reasons for choosing one's own courses.

  f. Name facts needed to select own school courses.

 2. Curriculum selection

  a. Identify characteristics of different school curricula.

  b. Identify appropriate curricula for given individuals.

  c. Name curricula available at one's own school.

  d. Name valid reasons for choosing one's own curriculum.

  e. Name facts needed to make one's own curriculum choice.

  f. Name valid sources of information used to choose own curriculum.

E. School and career planning

 1. Identify sequence of steps required to enter given occupations.

 2. Identify valid principles of career planning.

F. School and career problem solving

 1. Identify solutions to own school and career problems.

 2. Identify solutions to school and career problems of given individuals.

II. *Psychomotor Domain* (What the learner says he has done)

A. Involvement in career planning activities

 1. Talked to others about school and career planning.

 2. Thought about and planned for school and career decisions.

 3. Read material about educational and career planning.

 4. Received instruction about careers and career planning.

 5. Visited business and industries to learn about careers.

 6. Attended career day programs.

 7. Engaged in hobbies and out-of-school activities.

 8. Engaged in career-simulated activities.

 9. Engaged in part-time and/or summer employment.

 10. Engaged in actual or practice job interviews.

 11. Filled out job application forms.

 12. Prepared resumé describing one's own qualifications.

B. Involvement in wide range of worker activities

 1. Engaged in worker activities dealing with personal-social jobs.

 2. Engaged in worker activities dealing with sales and promotion jobs.

3. Engaged in worker activities dealing with business operations jobs.
4. Engaged in worker activities dealing with industrial and trades jobs.
5. Engaged in worker activities dealing with science and medicine jobs.
6. Engaged in worker activities dealing with creative and applied arts jobs.

C. Involvement in activities related to preferred occupation(s)
   1. Talked to workers employed in one's preferred occupation.
   2. Received instruction in one's preferred occupation.
   3. Thought about one's preferred occupation.
   4. Discussed preferred occupation with parents.
   5. Discussed preferred occupation with counselor.
   6. Identified values to be realized in preferred occupation.
   7. Identified school courses helpful in preferred occupation.
   8. Identified amount of education required of preferred occupation.
   9. Identified values associated with one's preferred occupation.
   10. Identified steps needed to enter preferred occupation.
   11. Identified the duties performed in preferred occupation.
   12. Identified the abilities required in preferred occupation.
   13. Identified places of employment of workers in preferred occupation.
   14. Identified specialities in one's preferred occupation.
   15. Identified physical working conditions of one's preferred occupation.
   16. Determined the need for workers in one's preferred occupation.
   17. Identified the income level of workers in preferred occupation.
   18. Determined the chances for advancement in preferred occupation.

III. *Affective Domain* (Attitudes, preferences, and perceptions of learner)
   A. Attitudes
      1. Endorse positive statements about oneself.
      2. Endorse positive statements about work.
      3. Accept responsibility for one's own career decisions.
   B. Preferences
      1. Educational aspiration level preferred by learner.
      2. Occupational preference(s) of learner.
      3. Job values preferred by learner.
      4. Working conditions preferences of learner.
      5. Curriculum preferences of learner.
   C. Perceptions
      1. Perceived value of help provided by school in career planning.
      2. Perception of help received from various sources of information.
      3. Perception of certainty of one's own vocational choice.

Career Development of Youth: A Nationwide Study

Dale J. Prediger,
John D. Roth,
and
Richard J. Noeth

Career education and career guidance are currently high-priority items on the national agenda. Many believe student career development to be the unifying theme and primary goal of career education efforts. It was in the context of this national interest and the new developments in career education and career guidance that the Nationwide Study of Student Career Development (Prediger, Roth and Noeth 1973) was conducted. The primary purpose of the study was to assess and summarize core aspects of the career development of American youth enrolled in grades 8, 9, and 11. This is a particularly crucial period in the career development of students, one in which many experiences and decisions related to the post-high-school transition occur. Information on students' preparation for these decisions is certainly desirable as a basis for determining what is being done now and what needs to be done in the future.

The purpose of this article is to present some of the more significant findings of the study, findings that have implications for all counselors, but especially for those in school guidance programs. The article focuses primarily on what students *say* about their career development and about their current guidance needs. In addition, what students have *done* about career planning and what they *know* about career development are covered briefly.

Because the large amount of data obtained in the study precludes a complete discussion, we have attempted to identify some of the more salient findings and to draw some implications from them. Admittedly, this is a subjective process. Readers are therefore reminded that judgments concerning the implications of the findings are the authors' and that detailed study results are available for readers who wish to draw their own conclusions after inspecting the data.

Reprinted from *Personnel and Guidance Quarterly*, Sept. 1975, pp. 12–19. Copyright 1975 American Personnel and Guidance Association. Reprinted with permission.

Sample and Assessment Procedures

The target population for the study was defined as all full-time 8th, 9th, and 11th grade students enrolled in public or Catholic schools in the United States in the spring of 1973. The sample, which consisted of approximately 32,000 students in 200 schools located in 33 states, was selected by Research Triangle Institute using sampling frame data developed for the National Assessment of Educational Progress. Stratification variables included region of country and size and socioeconomic status of community. When it was not possible to test all students, students in the specified grade within each selected school were randomly chosen. Weights were applied to sample data to insure that study results would be nationally representative. A detailed description of sampling procedures has been provided by Bayless, Bergsten, Lewis, and Noeth (1974).

Under the supervision of local school personnel, students in the sample completed the Assessment of Career Development (ACD), a 267-item paper-and-pencil inventory/test. The ACD, which was developed from detailed content specifications drawn from career development theory and guidance practice (American College Testing Program 1974), covers the following core components of career development: (1) occupational awareness, including occupational knowledge and exploratory experiences; (2) self-awareness, including career plans and perceived needs for help with career planning; and (3) career planning and decision making, including career planning knowledge and involvement in career planning activities. The ACD also elicits student reactions to career guidance experiences, provides scores for 11 scales, and summarizes student responses to 42 specific questions.

Results and Discussion

Student-Perceived Needs for Help

One of the most striking findings of this study is students' apparent receptivity to receiving help with career planning. As shown in Table 1, more than three-fourths of the nation's high school juniors would like such help; the proportion is almost as high for 8th graders. In both grades, more girls than boys are looking for career planning help. If recognition of the need for help with career planning is interpreted as an indicator of readiness, then American teenagers appear to be anxious to get on with career development.

Help with "making career plans" is by far the major area of need indicated by 11th graders; "finding after-school or summer work" is in second place. Far down on the list is "discussing personal concerns," the primary task for which many school counselors have been trained.

TABLE 1. Student-Perceived Needs for Help

AREA OF STUDENT CONCERN [a]	GRADE 8 "YES" RESPONSES			GRADE 11 "YES" RESPONSES		
	% M	% F	% TOT.	% M	% F	% TOT.
Improving study skills	74	72	73	68	61	65
Improving reading skills	65	60	63	61	56	58
Improving math skills	71	74	73	63	58	60
Choosing courses	62	66	64	57	58	58
Discussing personal concerns	38	40	39	29	32	30
Discussing health problems	31	26	29	17	13	15
Making career plans	71	75	73	76	80	78
Obtaining money to continue education after high school	57	57	57	56	55	56
Finding afer-school or summer work	72	73	73	64	70	67

[a] Directions to students were as follows: "The list below covers several things with which students sometimes would like help. If you would like help with any of these things, mark A for YES. Otherwise mark B for NO."

Reactions to School Guidance Services

The incidence of student-expressed need for help with career planning is in sharp contrast to the amount of help students say they receive. Item 1 in Table 2 shows that only 13 per cent of the 11th graders feel that they receive "a lot" of help with career planning from their school. Another 37 per cent feel that they receive "some" help. However, half of the 11th graders and slightly more 8th graders state that they receive little or no help with career planning. Yet, in a separate item not shown in the table, 85 per cent of the 11th graders indicate that they recognize that career planning must begin before the final year of high school. It would appear, then, that a need exists that remains for the most part unfulfilled.

One explanation for the large number of students who feel they receive little or no career planning help might be the unavailability of school counselors. However, item 2 in Table 2 shows that only 3 per cent of the 11th graders do not have a guidance counselor. An overwhelming 84 per cent say that they can usually or almost always see a counselor when they want to. The implication, then, is that many counselors are simply not providing help with career planning, either on a one-to-one basis or through group guidance activities. Perhaps time constraints and conflicting responsibilities are the chief cause. We believe, however, that many counselors and administrators have failed to accept and communicate career planning as an appropriate respon-

TABLE 2. General Reactions to School Guidance Services

PARAPHRASED QUESTIONS AND SUMMARY OF STUDENT RESPONSES

1. Over all, how much help with career (educational and job) planning has your school (teachers, counselors, principal, librarian, etc.) given you?

	GRADE 8			GRADE 11		
	% M	% F	% TOT.	% M	% F	% TOT.
A. None	25	24	24	20	15	17
B. Little	31	30	31	33	32	32
C. Some	33	34	33	36	39	37
D. A lot	12	12	12	11	15	13

2. Do you feel you can see a guidance counselor when you want to or need to?

	GRADE 8			GRADE 11		
	% M	% F	% TOT.	% M	% F	% TOT.
A. Hardly ever	17	14	16	13	14	13
B. Usually	35	34	34	41	41	41
C. Almost always	31	31	31	43	44	43
D. We don't have a guidance counselor	17	20	19	4	2	3

sibility of the school and that, as a result, students do not expect or request help with career planning.

Table 3 summarizes student reactions to some of the career guidance activities commonly described in textbooks and implemented in schools. Item 1 supports the notion that many counselors—for whatever reasons—are not providing career guidance help. Over half of the 11th graders (56 per cent) indicate that they receive little or no help with career planning in discussions with counselors. As would be expected, the percentage is substantially higher for 8th graders. The number of 11th graders indicating that they receive some or a lot of help from counselors (43 per cent) is somewhat lower than the number indicating that they receive some help or a lot of help from their school (50 per cent; see Table 2). It appears that counselors provide most, but not all, of the career planning help received by 11th graders. In the 8th grade, the relative contribution of the school as a whole is substantially higher.

For many years teachers have been urged to make their subjects relevant to the "real world." More recently, and particularly in career education programs, attention has shifted to "the world of work."

TABLE 3. Reactions to Typical Career Guidance Activities

PARAPHRASED QUESTIONS AND SUMMARY OF STUDENT RESPONSES

General directions: "Some of the ways schools help students with career planning are listed below. For each, show how you feel about the help provided at your school."

1. Discussion with a counselor about education and job plans for after high school.

	GRADE 8			GRADE 11		
	% M	% F	% TOT.	% M	% F	% TOT.
A. Help not provided/used	56	56	56	38	32	35
B. Of little help	19	17	18	21	21	21
C. Of some help	17	16	17	29	28	28
D. A lot of help	8	11	10	12	18	15

2. Class discussion by teachers of jobs related to their subjects.

	GRADE 8			GRADE 11		
	% M	% F	% TOT.	% M	% F	% TOT.
A. Help not provided	38	40	39	37	34	35
B. Of little help	28	27	27	27	23	25
C. Of some help	24	23	24	27	28	27
D. A lot of help	10	10	10	10	15	12

3. Films on jobs, talks by workers (in person or on tape), "career days," tours.

	GRADE 8			GRADE 11		
	% M	% F	% TOT.	% M	% F	% TOT.
A. Help not provided/used	46	51	48	44	43	44
B. Of little help	21	20	20	22	18	20
C. Of some help	23	20	21	24	25	24
D. A lot of help	11	11	11	11	14	12

4. File of job descriptions, pamphlets, or books on jobs.

	GRADE 8			GRADE 11		
	% M	% F	% TOT.	% M	% F	% TOT.
A. Help not provided/used	46	48	47	38	30	34
B. Of little help	25	21	23	24	20	22
C. Of some help	21	22	21	30	37	33
D. A lot of help	9	10	9	9	13	11

While the emphasis of these efforts is on instructional effectiveness and career awareness rather than on career planning, certainly help with the latter would be a reasonable concomitant to expect. Item 2 in Table 3 shows that about 35 per cent of the 11th graders and 8th graders do indeed say that class discussions of jobs related to the subjects they are studying provide some help or a lot of help with career planning. However, a similar proportion of students indicate that help is "not provided" in class discussions of this type—possibly because a large number of teachers have yet to accept the career-relevance approach to instruction.

Items 3 and 4 in Table 3 summarize student reactions to other types of common career guidance practices. Tables 2 and 3 indicate that somewhat less than one-fifth of the 11th graders feel that they receive a lot of help with career planning through the various educational programs and guidance services offered by schools.

Career Plans

One of the questions in the study asked students to indicate their first occupational preference and then to select, from a list of 25 job families, the job family appropriate to this preference. While several discrepancies with U.S. Department of Labor employment projections are evident in the distributions of student preferences, the most striking feature of the data is the evidence of differences in responses of the two sexes. The nature of these differences is not surprising, but their extent is quite dramatic. For example, over half of the 11th grade girls choose occupations falling in only 3 of the 25 job families: clerical and secretarial work, education and social services, nursing and human care. By contrast, 7 per cent of the boys prefer occupations in these areas. Nearly half of the boys' choices fall in the technologies and trades cluster of job families, in contrast to only 7 per cent of the girls' choices. Results for 8th, 9th, and 11th graders are essentially the same. It is obvious that efforts to broaden the career options and choices of both males and females must overcome the pervasive influence of work role stereotypes related to sex.

Table 4 provides evidence of the amount of thought students give to their occupational preferences and career plans. Slight trends in favor of 11th graders appear for the first two questions but not for the third question, which taps the certainty of the students' first occupational preference. Only 13 per cent of the 8th graders answer "not sure at all" to the question, whereas 22 per cent of the 11th graders choose that response—a substantial proportionate increase. Perhaps, with the approach of major career decisions, 11th graders take the task of career choice more seriously and begin to weigh more heavily the reality factors involved.

Whether more 11th graders should be "very sure" of their first occu-

TABLE 4. Self-evaluation of Career Planning

1. Have you given much thought as to why your first two job choices are right for you?

	GRADE 8			GRADE 11		
	% M	% F	% TOT.	% M	% F	% TOT.
A. A little	16	13	15	13	8	10
B. Some	36	37	36	38	32	35
C. A lot	49	50	49	50	60	55

2. Is the amount of education you are planning in line with what is needed for the jobs?

	GRADE 8			GRADE 11		
	% M	% F	% TOT.	% M	% F	% TOT.
A. Yes	52	52	52	58	60	59
B. Not sure	39	42	41	34	34	34
C. Probably not	9	6	7	7	6	7

3. Students often change their minds about job choices. How sure are you that your "First Job Choice" will be the *same* in a year?

	GRADE 8			GRADE 11		
	% M	% F	% TOT.	% M	% F	% TOT.
A. Very sure	41	39	40	31	33	32
B. Fairly sure	46	48	47	45	47	46
C. Not sure at all	13	13	13	24	20	22

Note.—Directions for items 1 and 2 were as follows: "A few minutes ago, you were asked to print the names of your first two job choices on the answer folder. The rest of the questions on this page all refer to these two jobs. THINK ONLY OF THESE TWO JOBS as you answer each of the following items."

pational preference depends on one's views about the career development process. Certainly there is ample testimony in the professional literature and labor market projections that youth should "stay loose" occupationally and keep doors open as long as possible. However, if vocational choice is the zeroing-in process that some believe it to be (Super 1963), one might expect that students finishing the 11th grade would be "fairly sure" of their occupational preferences. This would imply that they have at least given them a lot of thought; 55 per cent of the 11th graders say they have (Table 4, item 1).

What Students Do and Know
About Career Development

The following are capsule highlights of conclusions based on a large amount of additional information gathered in the study.

1. As indicated by a 32-item self-report inventory, 20 per cent of the nation's 11th graders exhibit what can only be called a very low level of involvement in career planning activities. Another 50 per cent barely approach a minimally desirable level. Responses to specific items indicate that a substantial number of 11th graders have had very little involvement in frequently recommended career guidance practices (for example, field trips, worker interviews, role-play job interviews).

2. As indicated by six scales covering job-related activities and experiences organized by occupational cluster, the exploratory occupational experiences of most students appear to be quite limited. Although many of these experiences occur outside of the school, none require actual employment. Rather, they represent a component of career awareness that schools can do much to develop.

3. When the exploratory occupational experiences of males and females are compared, the results suggest distinct patterns related to sex roles endemic to American society. Again, schools can do much to broaden these experiences through the career awareness and career exploration programs now being developed.

4. Results obtained from a 40-item career planning knowledge scale show both a lack of knowledge and a substantial amount of misinformation. For example, 53 per cent of the 11th graders believe that *more* than one-third of all job openings require a college degree; 41 per cent of the 8th graders believe that *few* women work outside of the home after marriage; and 61 per cent of the 11th graders believe that *most* persons remain in the same jobs throughout their adult lives.

Implications

What, then, can be said about the career development of the nation's youth? First and foremost, student-expressed need for help with career planning is in sharp contrast to the amount of help students feel they receive. This discrepancy is reflected in what students have (and more often, have not) done to prepare for the difficult career decisions they face. Their lack of knowledge about the world of work and about the career planning process also testifies to their need for help. We believe that, considered together, these vantage points for viewing student career development—what students say, do, and know—provide a consistent and dismal picture. If we were speaking of physical development rather than career development, we would describe American youth as hungry, undernourished, and physically retarded.

Does this mean that 11th graders will be unable to cope with the career development tasks posed by society at the difficult high school to post-high-school transition point? Certainly youth in the past have been able to muddle through. However, we believe study results presage unfortunate amounts of floundering and prolonged states of indecision that are costly both to the individual and to society. Perhaps society can continue to absorb these costs while it avoids the costs inherent in the remedy. This is the course of least resistance, and its acceptance may involve the least controversy, especially since the remedies currently receiving attention are largely untested. However, thoroughly researched and proven effectiveness is seldom a prerequisite for programs designed to meet demonstrated human need. If it were, most of what is provided in the name of education (both lower and higher) would be recalled for further research and development. While efforts to facilitate student career development should not proceed haphazardly, it would appear from the results of this study that current attempts to implement new approaches to career guidance and career education are amply justified.

We firmly believe that the traditional one-to-one counseling model for helping youngsters "choose their life's work" can no longer be justified. This model must be reoriented to encompass what is known about how careers develop and must be broadened to include the resources of the classroom and the community. As counselors and counselor educators come to recognize work as one of the central experiences of men and women, as the making of a life as well as a living (Super 1957), we are hopeful that they will accept the challenge posed by the career development needs of American youth.

References

AMERICAN COLLEGE TESTING PROGRAM. *Handbook for the assessment of career development.* Iowa City: Author, 1974.
BAYLESS, D. L.; BERGSTEN, J. W.; LEWIS, L. H.; and NOETH, R. J. *Considerations and procedures in national norming: An illustration using the ACT assessment of career development and the ACT career planning program, grades 8–11* (ACT Research Report No. 65). Iowa City: American College Testing Program, 1974.
PREDIGER, D. J.; ROTH, J. D.; and NOETH, R. J. *A nationwide study of student career development: Summary of results* (ACT Research Report No. 61). Iowa City: American College Testing Program, 1973.
SUPER, D. E. *The psychology of careers.* New York: Harper & Row, 1957.
SUPER, D. E. The definition and measurement of early career behavior: A first formulation. *Personnel and Guidance Journal,* 1963, *41*(9), 775–780.

UNIT BIBLIOGRAPHY

ARVEY, RICHARD D., and STEPHEN J. MUSSIO. "Test Discrimination, Job Performance and Age." *Industrial Gerontology,* **16** (1973), 22–29.
CRITES, JOHN O. "Methodological Issues in the Measurement of Career Maturity." *Measurement and Evaluation in Guidance,* **6** (1974), 200–209.
———. "Problems in the Measurement of Vocational Maturity." *Journal of Vocational Behavior,* **4** (1974), 25–31.

FISHBURNE, FRANCIS J., JR., and W. BRUCE WALSH. "Concurrent Validity of Holland's Theory for Non-College-Degreed Workers." *Journal of Vocational Behavior,* **8** (1976), 77–84.

GOLDMAN, LEO. "It's Time to Put Up or Shut Up." *Measurement and Evaluation in Guidance,* **5** (1972), 420–429.

GOLDMAN, LEO. "Test and Counseling: The Marriage That Failed." *Measurement and Evaluation in Guidance,* **4** (1972), 213–220.

JENKINS, MERCILEE M. "Age Discrimination in Employment Testing." *Vocational Guidance Quarterly,* **21** (1972), 139–143.

KROGER, ROLF O. "Faking in Interest Measurement: A Social-Psychological Perspective." *Measurement and Evaluation in Guidance,* **7** (1974), 130–134.

MINER, J. B. "Psychological Testing and Fair Employment Practices: A Testing Program That Does Not Discriminate." *Personnel Psychology,* **27** (1974), 49–62.

O'CONNELL, EDWARD J., JEROME B. DUSEK, and RICHARD J. WHEELER. "A Follow-up Study of Teacher Expectancy Effects." *Journal of Educational Psychology,* **66** (1974), 325–328.

OTTO, LUTHER, B., ARCHIBALD O. HALLER, ROBERT F. MEIER, and GEORGE W. OHLENDORF. "An Empirical Evaluation of a Scale to Measure Occutional Aspiration Level." *Journal of Vocational Behavior,* **5** (1974), 1–11.

PETTY, M. M. "Relative Effectiveness of Four Combinations of Oral and Written Presentations of Job Related Information to Disadvantaged Trainees." *Journal of Applied Psychology,* **59** (1974), 105–106.

SEILER, JOSEPH. "Preparing the Disadvantaged for Tests." *Vocational Guidance Quarterly,* **19** (1971), 201–205.

WESTBROOK, BERT W., and MARJORIE M. MASTIE. "Three Measures of Vocational Maturity: A Beginning to Know About." *Measurement and Evaluation in Guidance,* **6** (1973), 8–16.

WESTBROOK, BERT W., JOSEPH W. PARRY-HILL, JR., and ROGER W. WOODBURY. "The Development of a Measure of Vocational Maturity." *Educational and Psychological Measurement,* **31** (1971), 541–543.

WHITE, WILLO P. "Testing and Equal Opportunity." *Civil Rights Digest,* **7** (1975), 42–51.

part 6
Vocational Guidance:
Counseling

Vocational counseling began in the United States with Frank Parsons' (founder of the guidance movement in 1909 in Boston) "scientific" approach. He recommended a counseling procedure in which the individual studied himself, studied the occupational world, and then by "true reasoning" made a choice based on the facts. Even though some of these activities are still involved, many advances have been made in vocational guidance and counseling. The counseling relationship conditions of counselor congruence, acceptance, and empathy are as important in vocational counseling as in any counseling relationship. This relationship permits a counseling climate in which the individual may express his or her hopes and fears about self and the occupational world.

To assist the individual in integrating the information about himself and the occupational world and to evolve a plan for career development is the encompassing objective of vocational counseling. Robert H. Dolliver and Richard E. Nelson, Professor of Guidance, Purdue University, present some assumptions about vocational counseling. They point out common false assumptions held by the general public, test makers, counselors, and clients. They conclude by proposing some working assumptions. Weston H. Morrill and David J. Forrest suggest that counseling practice has not reflected the current thinking about career development and go on to describe four type of vocational counseling.

John O. Crites compares and contrasts major approaches to career counseling. He analyzes them across common dimensions of theory and technique to identify their relative strengths and weaknesses Crites examines the trait-and-factor, client-centered, psychodynamic, developmental, and behavioral approaches to counseling in terms of diagnosis, the process, outcomes, interview techniques, test interpretation, and the use of information.

Assumptions Regarding Vocational Counseling

Robert H. Dolliver
and
Richard E. Nelson

Vocational counseling interviews involve the client and counselor in viewing each other, as the term *inter-view* indicates. As counseling begins, counselor and client view each other's assumptions about the nature of counseling processes and outcomes. Clients have assumptions about the kind of help they need to make occupational choices, what they can expect of counselors, what they can expect from any tests used, what they may be asked to do, and what will occur in the total process. Counselors need to understand the kinds of results clients expect from vocational counseling. Many assumptions, when held by either clients or counselors, lead to client (and possibly counselor) dissatisfaction with counseling because the assumptions build false anticipations for the client. Essentially, both clients and counselors often expect more definite outcomes and less effort from each party than is reasonable. This paper is written to promote counselors' reflections on their own and their clients' vocational counseling assumptions.

Common False Assumptions

A number of assumptions about vocational counseling originate from the general public, test makers, counselors, and clients. These assumptions interact with and overlap one another; assumptions from one source reinforce those from another source. Most of the assumptions contain an element of truth but they have been overused and overextended until they are treated as truths.

From the General Public
There is a single right occupation for everyone. Much of the vocational counseling movement has been based on this premise. Although it is undoubtedly true that there are appropriate and inappropriate occupations for almost everyone, it seems futile to attempt to find the

Reprinted from *The Vocational Guidance Quarterly,* **24**:12–19 (Sept. 1975). Copyright 1975 American Personnel and Guidance Association. Reprinted with permission.

job that exactly fits the client. Given the uncertainties of today's job market, finding the right job seems especially doubtful. Clients may view finding the right academic major or job idealistically as holding the promise of drastically improving the quality of their lives. Everyone knows people who floundered and then became highly successful; clients sometimes believe that they can duplicate this experience through identifying the occupational interest that exactly fits them. Occasionally it is possible through such means for a client to transform apathy into interest and become motivated but such hopes are largely illusory.

Vocational diagnosis can achieve pinpoint accuracy in a relatively short time without making demands on the client. The general public would like vocational counseling to be like their ideal concept of medicine: the physician asks a few questions, pokes around, runs some laboratory tests, and is then able to pinpoint the problem in a quick, definite, and painless manner. What the general public does not realize is that medicine rarely works this way and that vocational counseling doesn't either.

Everyone can find inherent satisfactions in his or her occupation. Although it is pleasant to idealize work as fulfilling and meaningful, this is simply not the case for many workers. Large numbers of people do not have any particular pride in the work that they do, nor do they derive much satisfaction from it other than their pay check. Work itself seems to many people simply a means of enabling them to enjoy themselves during their nonworking hours. If satisfactions are available at all they may be the result of enjoyable work associates, status, or the ability to structure one's work rather than the result of the job function.

From Vocational Test Makers

Occupational groups are sufficiently homogeneous to be clearly differentiated from other occupational groups. Certainly there are some differences among groups of occupations but differences within occupations have often been disregarded. Many occupations include a wide variety of work tasks in addition to important personality differences among people with the same occupational title. Nurses and physicians each serve roles of patient care, administration, research, teaching, laboratory work, and operative care. The extent to which all members of a given occupation are alike has been oversimplified in order to conceptualize occupational groups.

One ought to choose an occupation in which one resembles members of that occupation. This assumption is particularly evident in the Strong Vocational Interest Blank (SVIB), the Strong-Campbell Interest Inventory, and the Kuder form DD. Someone characterized the theory behind SVIB as being that birds of a feather flock together. Certain similarities are necessary between an aspirant and members of the aspired-to occupational group, other similarities are only convenient, others are simply comfortable. A number of vocational test antagonists have questioned the extent to which interest inventories such as the SVIB have narrowed the range of personality differences within an occupational group. Such narrowing may restrict the kind of changes and growth that can occur within the occupations and the people in them.

The more generalized the occupational interest, the greater is the likelihood that one of the occupations in the category will be entered. This is the assumption behind primary patterns on the SVIB. This is also the assumption behind the Holland Vocational Preference Inventory, on which the number of occupations selected within a personality type are tallied. One of the occupations in the type with the highest number of selected occupations is assumed to be appropriate for the test taker. It is quite conceivable (although this happens infrequently) that someone could have a high degree of interest in a particular occupation without necessarily having interests in related occupations.

From Vocational Counselors

Vocational tests predict the specific occupation that a person will enter. The SVIB looks as though it is based on this assumption. However, the makers of the SVIB have urged that such use is not feasible. Rather, they ask that the results be used to get a general sense of vocational interests and possible direction. Vocational interest inventories are accurate in that high scores often predict occupational entry. The SVIB is accurate approximately 50 per cent of the time in the sense that one of several high scores will relate to the occupation entered [2].

Vocational interest test results are more accurate than the expression of vocational interests. Dolliver [7] reviewed comparative studies with the SVIB and reported that the expression of interest was more frequently accurate in predicting future occupation than was the SVIB. Whitney [23] reported a similar finding for other vocational interest inventories.

It is not only possible but also sensible to do vocational counseling apart from educational and personal counseling. When vocational counseling is carried out in this manner, it is easy for clients to believe that their choice of an occupation does not involve their total personality and does not involve the consideration of educational ability and opportunity. Separating vocational counseling from other kinds of counseling, so that the counselor deals only with certain aspects of the client, has helped to make vocational counseling seem rather dull and unappealing to many counselors. The term *career counseling* has been used by some counselors to designate a wider range of counseling activities than is sometimes indicated with the term *vocational counseling.*

From Vocational Clients

Doubts, confusion, uncertainties, lack of information, lack of commitment, and lack of decision regarding one's occupational future are usually superficial. Clients may assume that the counselor, with the aid of vocational tests, will be able to identify a heretofore unknown but readily acceptable pattern of interests, abilities, and personality traits that will solve their vocational choice problem. Some clients do not manifest this belief but many hope that significant portions of this assumption are true.

Vocational counseling will be a rather impersonal process demanding little of the client in discomfort, commitment, or effort. The client may assume that various standardized tests will carry the major burden for both the client and counselor. Vocational inventories certainly have a moderate place in vocational counseling but their place easily becomes exaggerated by clients and counselors who do not understand the limitations of such inventories. The willingness, even desire, to rely on tests and inventories is puzzling, given the importance that such decisions may have in the clients' lives. Presumably, counselors have played a part in perpetuating the assumption that good vocational decisions can be made with such little effort from the client.

Good vocational counseling can reduce to almost zero the client's risk in heading for an occupation. Vocational counselors ought to reduce the amount of uncertainty and risk engendered in heading toward an occupation but a number of uncertainties will remain. Selection for training programs is often made from an oversupply of qualified applicants. Sometimes counselors can help clients by providing them with a view of the degree of risk involved, for example, in applying to law school. Sometimes when training has been completed there are no appropriate jobs available. Many unknowns remain in the best occupational plans and the client inevitably carries the risk.

A whole subset of assumptions involves sexist vocational roles; they are beyond the scope of this paper. Both women and men today resist being pushed toward or denied an occupation solely because of sex-role stereotypes. Assumptions about working women are described by Guttman [10], Matthews [14], the U.S. Department of Labor [21], and Zytowski [26].

Proposed Working Assumptions

We have hinted at some dimensions of our proposed assumptions by identifying some common false assumptions. The following assumptions may be used to help counselors structure their work; some are appropriate to discuss with clients.

Different clients need or want different things to help them make occupational decisions. A variety of available services is important to serve a range of clientele. Sometimes seeing a counselor is helpful, sometimes it is not. The same is true of vocational exploration groups, vocational tests, or discussion with someone who has experience in an occupation of interest to the client. In college counseling centers students often seem to want the opportunity to use occupational information files without seeing a counselor. The Strong-Campbell Interest Inventory [2] (with extensive explanation on the back of the report form) and the Self-Directed Search (with programmed instructions) are clearly oriented for use without a counselor to interpret the results. Vocational counseling agencies should, appropriately, offer a variety of services from which to find help with a vocational decision.

The vocational counseling outcome is often enhanced by the active involvement of the client. Clients can engage in a variety of services whether or not they wish for the kind of active involvement counselors may promote. Counselors, though, would properly encourage the client's active involvement on the basis that such involvement leads to better counseling outcomes. If clients perceive that counselors consider vocational counseling to be important, they are more likely to devote additional time and energy.

We believe that clients' involvement is enhanced when the counselor recognizes the predictive value of the clients' ideas [7]. We have used the Tyler Vocational Card Sort [20; 6; 4] and the Dole Vocational Incomplete Sentences Blank [5] to promote clients' use of those data as an important consideration in making occupational choices. Vocational fantasies can be used [18] in this same manner. Counselors are usually perceived as experts, which promotes clients' paying attention to counselors' opinions. Clients need to be perceived as experts also regarding their vocational decisions, so that counselors will pay greater attention to clients' opinions.

Difficulty making occupational decisions often stems from a number of circumstances within clients' lives. In our experience, three major approaches are available to meet clients' needs:

1. Occupational information. We believe that clients frequently need help to envision themselves functioning in an occupation. The book *Working* [19] can be useful because it contains the personal statements of people in occupations. Clients also benefit from being able to talk with someone in an occupation that seems attractive to them. This allows clients to learn about the day-to-day demands, the rewards, and frustrations not usually covered in written occupational information.
2. Values clarification. Satisfaction in an occupation often stems

from belief in the worth of the occupation. Values clarification is identifying what individuals consider worthwhile in their lives. Value clarification exercises [17] are often carried out in groups. In this setting, clients can be aided by hearing about the values of others.

3. Decision-making skills. Specific steps in decision making can be taught [9; 13] either in a group or individually, perhaps as part of a sequential process in a vocational exploration group [8]. Various writers have developed models of decision making, which are reviewed by Herr [11] and Miller [15].

Counselors need to perceive clearly the importance of clients' personalities in occupational performance and success. Counselors can promote clients' willingness to learn about, talk over, and consider the ways in which personality characteristics enter into occupational selection. Counselors often give insufficient consideration to client characteristics such as preference for certain kinds of relationships with other people and for certain processes (for example, creativeness with materials, interpersonal problem solving). Clients in career exploration groups [8] consistently indicate that clarifying the way they feel about themselves is of primary importance to them before they can make occupational decisions. The field of vocational counseling has not gone very far in relating personality to occupational choice, and the usual vocational counseling methods only consider client personality superficially.

Vocational counseling is rarely a matter of clients' making a final occupational choice, but rather a matter of several occupational possibilities being defined for further exploration. Successful vocational counseling is a focusing process in which clients discard some alternatives and select others. Clients after the termination of formal vocational counseling are often involved in the process of getting more information about how a particular occupational area fits their abilities, interests, personality, and opportunities.

We are impressed by the number of others who have identified assumptions in counseling or vocational counseling [1; 3; 12; 15, pp. 238–239; 16; 22, p. 78; 24, pp. 200–214; 25].

Conclusion

When clients come for vocational counseling, they have assumptions about what will occur and what the outcomes will be. For instance, some clients believe that there is a single right occupation for them and expect the counselor to help them find it. Vocational counselors also have their view of probable counseling processes and outcomes. For instance, counselors may assume that occupational selection is a process of narrowing, trying out, weighing potential benefits, and selecting the direction that leaves the most desirable alternatives open.

Sometimes counselors fail to identify the clients' views. When counselor and client do not reach agreement at the beginning of counseling, the client may harbor resentment, or perhaps drop out before the counseling series is completed, or be disappointed with the outcome. Counselors could be pleased with an outcome that is disappointing to clients, but if the counselor has said during one of the first interviews that the client is not likely to identify a specific occupation, the client can reorient expectations about the outcome of the counseling. When clients and counselors hold reasonable assumptions, satisfaction for both parties is more likely to occur.

References

1. BARRY, R., and WOLF, B. *Epitaph for vocational guidance.* New York: Bureau of Publications, Teachers College, Columbia University, 1962.
2. CAMPBELL, D. *Manual for the Strong-Campbell Interest Inventory.* Stanford, Calif.: Stanford University Press, 1974.
3. DAWIS, R. V.; ENGLAND, G. W.; and LOFQUIST, L. H. A theory of vocational behavior. Minneapolis: University of Minnesota, Industrial Relations Center, Project no. 422, 1963. Cited in E. G. Williamson, *Vocational counseling.* New York: McGraw-Hill, 1965.
4. DEWEY, C. R. Exploring interests: A non-sexist method. *Personnel and Guidance Journal,* 1974 52(5), 311–315.
5. DOLE, A. The Vocational Sentence Completion Blank in counseling. *Journal of Counseling Psychology,* 1958, 5(3), 200–205.
6. DOLLIVER, R. H. An adaptation of the Tyler Vocational Card Sort. *Personnel and Guidance Journal,* 1967 45(9), 916–920.
7. DOLLIVER, R. H. The SVIB vs. expressed vocational interests: A review. *Psychological Bulletin,* 1969, 72(2), 95–107.
8. GARFIELD, N., and NELSON, R. *Vocational exploration groups.* Columbia: University of Missouri, Career Information Center, Counseling Services, 1974.
9. GELATT, H. B.; VARENHORST, B.; and CAREY, R. *Deciding: A leader's guide.* New York: College Entrance Examination Board, 1972.
10. GUTTMAN, M. A. J. Counselor biases and practices in counseling females, implications for training the nonsexist counselor. In M. A. J. Guttman and P. A. Donn (Eds.) *Women and ACES: Perspectives and issues.* Association for Counselor Education and Supervision Monograph, 1974.
11. HERR, E. L. *Decision-making and vocational development.* Boston, Houghton Mifflin, 1970.
12. HOLLAND, J. L. Vocational guidance for everyone. *Educational Researcher,* 1974, 3(1), 9–15.
13. IOVINE, J. W., and ABBOTT, D. W. A series of activities to aid career decision making. Unpublished paper, Salem, New Hampshire, undated.
14. MATTHEWS, E. (Ed.) *Counseling girls and women over the life span.* Washington, D.C.: National Vocational Guidance Association, 1972.
15. MILLER, C. H. Career development theory in perspective. In E. L. Herr (Ed.), *Vocational guidance and human development.* Boston: Houghton Mifflin, 1974. Pp. 235–262.
16. PRITCHARD, D. H. The occupational exploration process: Some operational implications. *Personnel and Guidance Journal,* 1962, 04(8), 674–680.

17. SIMON, S. B.; HOWE, L. W.; and KIRSCHENBAUM, H. *Values clarification: A handbook of practical strategies for teachers and students*. New York: Hart, 1972.
18. SKOVHOLT, T. M., and HOENNINGER, R. W. Guided fantasy in career counseling. *Personnel and Guidance Journal*, 1974, *52*(10), 693–696.
19. TERKEL, S. *Working: People talk about what they do all day and how they feel about what they do*. New York: Pantheon Books, 1974.
20. TYLER, L. Research explorations in the realm of choice. *Journal of Counseling Psychology*, 1961, *8*(3), 195–201.
21. U.S. DEPARTMENT OF LABOR. *Female workers: The myth and the reality*. Washington, D.C.: The Women's Bureau, April 1971.
22. WARNATH, C. F. *New myths and old realities*. San Francisco: Jossey Bass, 1971.
23. WHITNEY, D. R. Predicting from expressed vocational choice: A review. *Personnel and Guidance Journal*, 1969, *48*(4), 279–286.
24. WILLIAMSON, E. G. *Vocational counseling*. New York: McGraw-Hill, 1965.
25. WRENN, C. G. What has happened to vocational counseling in our schools? *School Counselor*, 1963, *10*(3), 101–107.
26. ZYTOWSKI, D. G. Toward a theory of career development for women. *Personnel and Guidance Journal*, 1969, *47*(7), 660–664.

Dimensions of Counseling for Career Development

Weston H. Morrill
and
David J. Forrest

Since Parsons originally proposed a systematic approach to matching men and jobs, much has been written about vocational counseling. Different theorists have postulated that a certain factor—unconscious motivation, needs, self-concept, sociological and economic influences, chance factors—is most important in the consideration of career development and career counseling. Although there has been considerable theorizing and some research in the area of vocational or career counseling, there has been little change in the actual practice of vo-

Reprinted from *Personnel and Guidance Journal*, **49**:299–305 (Dec., 1970).

cational counselors. Generally, vocational counseling involves some combination of interest, aptitude, and personality testing and the presentation of occupational and educational information. Today, however, there is a need for descriptions of counseling practice which reflect more adequately current developmental thinking about career counseling.

The purpose of this article is to describe vocational counseling in terms of dimensions. Clients who seek vocational counseling do so for a variety of reasons and therefore their expectations of counseling are different. Yet too often vocational counselors are like the one-tool counselor which Callis (1962) describes, who applies the same assumptions and methods to all cases. Vocational counseling can be described in terms of steps along a continuum in which the focus of the counseling effort changes at each step. Counseling events which have relevance for only one situation and which do not generalize to later events represent one end of the continuum, while events which generalize to future behavior represent the opposite end. Thus, several types of vocational counseling events can be defined in terms of the width of focus and might be as follows:

Type 1. Counseling which aids the client with a specific decision by providing information and clarification of issues.

Type 2. Counseling which aids the client with a specific decision by focusing on decision-making skills rather than only on the decision at hand. This has application for the specific situation as well as later choice-points.

Type 3. Counseling which views career as a process rather than an end-point toward which all decisions lead. Thus, the focus changes from the objective of making the correct ultimate choice and once-and-for-all pronouncement of identity to the process of making a continual series of choices.

Type 4. Career process counseling which focuses on creating in the individual the ability to utilize his personal attributes to achieve self-determined objectives and to *influence* the nature of future choices rather than merely adapt to external pressures.

The continuum, then, is from focus on a specific decision at a given time to focus on career as a process in which the individual is a potent force.

Figure 1 presents a graphic illustration of the various vocational counseling approaches. An individual seeks counseling when he feels some discrepancy between his development and a theoretical occupational development curve (his felt potential). Counseling is an effort to reduce the distance between the individual's development and this theoretical curve.

Type 1

Much of the vocational counseling being done is geared to the first type—aiding a client with a specific decision. The client is provided information about his interests and abilities with the use of tests, as well as information about the world of work from the counselor's experience and occupational information sources; then the decision is made by matching man and job. This type of counseling is most often the focus of our present training programs which stress courses in testing and occupational information. The client is helped with his decision, but he may need to return to the counselor when he is again confronted by a difficult choice situation. This focus, while appropriate where short-term crisis counseling of a vocational nature is needed, may be of value only in the short-run situation. The following example is illustrative of Type 1 counseling.

Steve, a college freshman, came to the counseling center because he was not sure whether he was "in the right field." Since all freshmen were required to declare a major, he had chosen history because this had been one of his best courses in high school. The counselor administered and interpreted interest tests to Steve, and encouraged him to seek information from the occupational information files and to talk with faculty members in the areas of his highest interest. In addition, the counselor provided Steve with information about the results of his entrance examination scores. On the basis of the interest test and the information he obtained about specific areas, Steve decided to change his major to business.

Type 2

Counseling of the second type focuses on teaching the skills needed for making a decision, with the objective of providing the client with the ability to make the decision at hand as well as future decisions. It is evident that a decision involves much more than merely having relevant and accurate educational and occupational information; such an approach focuses on factors external to the individual and ignores the processes within the individual. As Thoresen and Mehrens (1967) point out, the individual needs much more than the facts to make a wise decision; he needs assistance in acquiring an effective way to approach decision-making problems. They propose that some of the key concepts from decision theory provide an excellent framework for analyzing, organizing, and synthesizing information in order to make good decisions. Two such concepts are (1) the *utility* value or desirability of the outcome of the alternatives and (2) the *probabilities* of these outcomes.

Thus, Type 2 counseling should focus on helping the client understand the factors involved in making a choice or decision. Before the

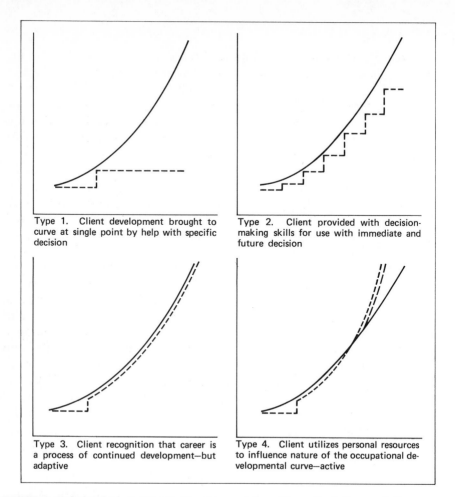

Type 1.   Client development brought to curve at single point by help with specific decision

Type 2.   Client provided with decision-making skills for use with immediate and future decision

Type 3.   Client recognition that career is a process of continued development—but adaptive

Type 4.   Client utilizes personal resources to influence nature of the occupational developmental curve—active

FIGURE 1. Relationship of Client's Development to a Theoretical Curve of Occupational Development in Four Counseling Approaches.

individual can approach a decision, he must first clearly understand the range of alternatives available to him. He must then think through and understand what each of the various alternatives would offer him. He must also make some judgments about the utility value or the desirability of these outcomes for him. In addition, he must be concerned about his chances of success if he chooses a particular direction. This may be further complicated by possible discrepancies between what the individual himself thinks and feels his chances of success are (subjective probabilities) and the predictions of success which emanate from tests and expectancy tables (objective probabilities). Thus, vocational counseling of Type 2 will focus on much more than merely providing information. It will focus on important variables in the decision-making process with the objective of teaching decision-making skills.

The case of Dorothy provides an example of Type 2 counseling. She was a college junior who was one of a few women admitted to a difficult medical program. She came for counseling because she was not sure she wanted to continue. She valued the profession toward which the program led, had publicly committed herself to it, and felt that she could complete the program. All objective information available (tests, grades, etc.) indicated that it was most likely that she could successfully complete the required coursework. Yet, she felt that the work demanded so much of her that she was becoming defeminized and deprived of a social life.

The focus of counseling was to help Dorothy understand the variables involved in her decision and to consider the alternatives open to her and the desirability of the prospective outcomes. She had to struggle with her personal interest and public commitment to the program versus the negative effects she felt it was having on some important areas of her life and development. She was able to deal with her personal feelings about the program and decided to leave the medical program and take up an academic major in an allied field. The counseling helped her work through this specific decision while teaching her how to focus on the important variables in making any such decision that may arise in the future.

Type 3

Type 3 counseling recognizes the tentativeness of any decision and views the process of career development as a *series* of choices, not a single vocational choice. Thus, the focus changes from the objective of making *the* correct choice to the process of making a continual series of choices. The individual is viewed as a growing, changing, developing person who must continually evaluate old choices and make new ones. A decision is not an end in itself, but must be viewed in relationship to the alternatives it makes possible or eliminates for the future. This focus differs from Type 2 counseling in that the emphasis is on the developmental attitude or outlook required to make decisions throughout life, rather than simply on the decision-making process itself. This following case is an example.

Ron, about to finish his freshman year, could not decide whether to change his major or drop out of school and go into the service; he was dissatisfied with his school experience to date. An aggressive person and an athlete, he did not normally have difficulty making decisions. But he did view his choices as irrevocable decisions which would fix his life course. The counseling effort focused first on the factors in his decision—what seemed to be really important to him then, and what the probabilities were of getting what he wanted. Then the focus shifted to examining this choice point in the perspective of his educational and vocational career. He quickly understood that what he was deciding need not be the last word in setting a direction. He later changed majors from mathematics to chemical engineering with the thought that he might go into the service a year later if he were still dissatisfied with school. He could finish his education afterward.

Type 4

The term *career process* has been suggested as a more adequate concept than vocational choice. Career process is defined as the continuing process through which a person engages in the developmental tasks necessary for personal growth in occupational life (Ivey and Morrill, 1968).

In career process counseling, the psychologist or counselor is concerned with identifying the individual's developmental competencies and inadequacies and helping him select and work through appropriate tasks leading to greater self-direction. The focus of career process counseling thus becomes not only making the individual capable of a series of choices but also creating in the individual the ability to utilize his own strengths to achieve self-determined objectives and to profit and grow personally from vocational experience. Type 3 counseling recognizes that the individual is engaged in a developing process, but there the focus is on adjustive or adaptive responses through intelligent decision-making. Type 4, however, focuses on the individual as an *active agent* engaged in developmental tasks and having an impact on, as well as reaction to, his vocational experience. Many people approach life with a view of themselves as pawns, powerless to effect their future and the nature of the choices and alternatives open to them. Their efforts are to adjust and accommodate rather than to effect and influence. They see themselves as being acted upon by their environment rather than acting upon it.

Recent work (Tiedeman and Dudly, 1967) on an innovative approach to vocational counseling places emphasis on personal responsibility in the individual's mediation of occupational facts or data. A related concept which is important in career development is that of commitment. Segal (1967), in developing a broad definition of work, defines commitment as an ability or attitude that allows a person to utilize his personal attributes toward self-determined objectives. It is related to Erikson's (1963) developmental tasks of autonomy, initiative, industry, and identity. Traditional vocational counseling deals with the concept of commitment by exploring the attributes of the individual which are utilized in commitment, such as capabilities, needs, and interests, and then relating these to a *specific goal*. However, commitment is not something that is achieved or completed. As Tiedeman (1967) points out, development requires commitment with tentativeness. Career process counseling recognizes both commitment and change as being central for the individual who is to profit and grow personally from vocational experience, and who is to be the key force in determining his future. The focus is to provide the individual with the view of himself as having the "power" to make a commitment and to influence and create his future.

The case of Mark provides an example of Type 4 counseling. The counseling consisted of participating as a group member in a day-long Life Planning Workshop. Sponsored by the Student Development faculty, it provided students with laboratory experiences designed to foster self-direction and awareness of career process. The workshop consisted of a series of semi-structured individual and group tasks which deals with the individual and his relationship to his future life.[1]

Mark, an 18-year-old college freshman majoring in psychology, arrived at the workshop as a rather "lost" individual, unsure of his own identity and unclear about why he was in college. His being in college seemed to be more the result of parental and societal expectations than of his own decision. In answering the question "Who am I?" his main emphasis was on being "an objective person." Through the process of discussion and through the workshop method of stripping and reassuming roles, he decided that he had been limiting himself through his own definition of being "objective." He had created limitations by negating the whole area of feelings and emotions from his life.

During the workshop he changed his most important desired role identity to being an "experiencing person." He felt that this gave him much more freedom and that new areas of life had been opened up to him. By the end of the workshop day, he could clearly see that what he did in the future was up to him, that he would have to be the one to make the decisions. This was quite a reversal from his original statements about going off in all directions and not knowing what to do about it. At the end of the workshop, he recognized that being in college needed to be for his own reasons. He reported that he felt more in control of his own life and more able to begin some constructive and realistic planning, and he could accept this responsibility.

In a follow-up contact six months later, Mark reported that he was feeling much more comfortable about himself and his future direction. He was taking courses in a number of areas both to find out about himself and to locate opportunities available for him. He had formulated some tentative goals, which included at least two alternative directions. The following quote is indicative of his reaction to the workshop:

It helped me stabilize myself and my direction. It really improved my general outlook on how to take the rest of my college experience and how to go about solving some problems.

[1] A more complete description of the workshop can be obtained by writing to Student Life Planning Team, Office of Student Development, Colorado State University, Fort Collins 80521.

Discussion and Implications

A characteristic of good theory is that it should stimulate research and provide a basis for improvement in practice. Although there has been considerable theorizing and some research in the area of vocational counseling, there has been little change in the actual practice of vocational counselors since Parsons's original proposition that the characteristics of man and job should be matched. This article proposes that counseling for vocational development should parallel the developmental process; that is, the focus should be narrow when only a point—a specific decision—in the developmental process is being considered, and broad when the concern is the whole person in relation to his career process.

There are a number of factors to consider in determining the level or focus of counseling to be used. The expectations of the client are a major consideration in selecting an appropriate course of counseling. A client seeking help with a specific decision may not appreciate or need an effort designed to confront him with his life's direction and commitment. Conversely, a client seeking a general direction in which to move would be chagrined at being urged to consider work as a YMCA secretary or a mortician. Along with client expectations, client needs and level of development must be considered. Super's (1967) description of life stages suggests that the same counseling approach at all life stages would be highly inappropriate. Considering the levels of career counseling can better clarify the alternative approaches available.

Other factors which influence the counseling approach include the training, competence, and theoretical bias of the counselor. Career process counseling requires that the counselor (1) be more involved with the client as a developing person and (2) use greater skill in dealing with the client's internal processes.

Counselor education needs to stress the developmental nature of vocational counseling. There needs to be an emphasis on keeping the "person" in counseling about careers and an effort to avoid the compartmentalization of personal and vocational counseling. There has been a tendency to view vocational counseling as relatively dull and routine, while personal counseling is interesting and dynamic. In many cases vocational counseling is delegated to the less able, less trained counselor, while personal counseling is the domain of the better qualified professional. Career process counseling recognizes the developmental nature of vocational counseling and places it in perspective as an aspect of the growth of the whole person.

The major part of an individual's life is spent in activity related to his vocation and avocation. His ability to function in and profit from these experiences is a major indication of positive mental health. If counseling provides the individual with only the information and self-knowledge to select a single vocational direction or job or even just to make a series of decisions, thus barely keeping up with a constantly changing environment, it has done little to provide the client with the developmental skills and abilities necessary to make him able to progress continually and shape his own destiny.

References

CALLIS, R. Toward an integrated theory of counseling. In J. F. McGowan and L. D. Schmidt (Eds.), *Counseling: Readings in theory and practice.* New York: Holt, Rinehart, & Winston, 1962. Pp. 208–215.

ERIKSON, E. H. *Childhood and society.* (2nd ed.) New York: W. W. Norton, 1963.

IVEY, A. E., and MORRILL, W. H. Career process: A new concept for vocational behavior. *Personnel and Guidance Journal,* 1968, *46,* 644–649.

SEGAL, S. J. Work leisure: The psychology of time utilization. In *Implications of career development theory and research for counselor education,* Workshop report, June 11–23, 1967. New York: Teachers College, Columbia University, 1967. Pp. 112–125.

SUPER, D. E. Recent finding from the career pattern study. In *Implications of career development theory and research for counselor education,* Workshop report, June 11–23, 1967. New York: Teachers College, Columbia University, 1967. Pp. 17–33.

THORESEN, C. E., and MEHRENS, W. A. Decision theory and vocational counseling: Important concepts and questions. *Personnel and Guidance Journal,* 1967, *46,* 165–172.

TIEDEMAN, D. V. Predicament, problem, and psychology: The case for paradox in life and counseling psychology. *Journal of Counseling Psychology,* 1967, *14,* 1–8.

TIEDEMAN, D. V., and DUDLY, G. A. Recent developments and current prospects in occupational facts mediation. In *Implications of career development theory and research for counselor education,* Workshop report, June 11–23, 1967. New York: Teachers College, Columbia University, 1967. Pp. 34–67.

┌───┐
│   │
│ *Career Counseling: A Review of*   │
│ *Major Approaches¹*   │
│   │
│ *John O. Crites*   │
│   │
└───┘

Concurrent with the development of vocational psychology as a scientific discipline (Crites, 1969), there has emerged during the past half century the related yet distinct practice earlier known as vocational guidance and more widely called *career counseling*. More precisely, a historical survey of vocational guidance and career counseling reveals not one but several different approaches to assisting individuals with their choice of a life's work.[2] Dating from Parson's (1909) tripartite model for "choosing a vocation," the trait-and-factor approach to career counseling dominated the field during the 1930s and 1940s. In the latter decade, however, its tenets were seriously questioned by Rogers' (1942) system of nondirective or client-centered counseling as applied to career decision making (Covner, 1947; Combs, 1947). By the fifties, still another orientation to career counseling was being articulated within the conceptual framework of psychoanalytic theory (Bordin, 1955) and exemplified by case studies (Cautela, 1959). Embracing elements from each of these but embellishing them with concepts and principles drawn from developmental psychology, Super (1957b) proposed a broadly based developmental approach to career counseling in which decision making is viewed as an on-going, life-long process. Most recently in the history of career counseling, the focus has been upon the application of behavioral principles to the analysis and modification of information-seeking and other decisional behaviors (Krumboltz and Thoreson, 1969).

Substantive statements of each of these approaches are available to the career counselor but nowhere are they collectively compared and contrasted. Nor have they been critically analyzed across common dimensions of theory and technique to identify their relative strengths and weaknesses, so that their strengths might be synthesized to provide a conceptual and experiential basis for formulating a compre-

---

Reprinted from *The Counseling Psychologist*, Vol. IV, 1974, pp. 3–23.

[1] Condensed from a book in process entitled *Career Counseling: Models, Methods, and Materials*.

[2] Only the major approaches are discussed here. Others, such as the sociological (Sanderson, 1954), rehabilitative (Lofquist, 1957), and computer-assisted (Super, 1970), are more specialized in applicability.

hensive approach to career counseling. Indeed it would appear that now, possibly more than ever before, there is a need for comprehensive counseling maximally applicable to idiosyncratic combinations of counselors and clients in a great variety of settings. Given the contemporary emphasis upon career education, with one of its principal objectives being the facilitation of career development, career counseling appropriate to students at any and all grade levels in the elementary and secondary schools assumes critical proportions. At the same time, in many colleges and universities across the nation, recent surveys have established that, in this period of job scarcity and hard money, the psychological service students request more than any other is career counseling. The Army and Air Force, too, have felt the need to institute transitional career counseling programs for returning and retiring servicemen to aid them in readjustment to civilian life, and the Veterans' Administration continues to offer career counseling through many of its hospitals and other services. Industry also has found a new role for career counseling with the hard-core unemployed, the work-alienated and the executive in mid-career crisis.

That any one approach to career counseling is applicable to these diverse populations and situations is unlikely, just as there appears to be no one type of psychotherapy which is universally effective (Kiesler, 1966). What is needed is a system of career counseling sufficiently comprehensive so that it approximates as closely as possible the uniqueness of each client-counselor dyad. To facilitate such a formulation the taxonomy shown in Figure 1 was conceived. Along the horizontal axis are listed the major approaches to career counseling which have evolved over the years, in their approximate order of historical development from left to right. On the vertical axis are ennumerated the principal dimensions of theory and technique which the various approaches have in common and which provide a framework for comparing and contrasting their *models* and *methods*. These dimensions are neither exclusive nor exhaustive, but they *are* central to all kinds of career counseling. In this paper, each approach will be descriptively reviewed on each dimension (proceeding down columns). Then in a later paper, the several approaches will be critically analyzed dimension by dimension (reading across rows), and an attempt will be made to synthesize them into a comprehensive approach to career counseling which is maximally applicable to various combinations of client/counselor parameters.

Approaches to Career Counseling

The term *approach* as applied to career counseling refers to a relatively well-articulated model and method of assisting individuals in making decisions about their lifelong roles in the world of work and in solving problems which arise in the course of the choice process

FIGURE 1. Taxonomy of Approaches to Career Counseling.

	Trait-and-Factor	Client-Centered	Psychodynamic	Developmental	Behavioral
MODELS					
Diagnosis					
Process					
Outcomes					
METHODS					
Interview techniques					
Test interpretation					
Use of occupational information					

(Crites, 1969). The *model* of an approach is defined along the temporal continuum which career counseling spans, beginning with the *diagnosis* of a client's problem, proceeding through the *process* of client-counselor interviews or interactions, and culminating in certain *outcomes*. The model, then, is a theoretical explication of the assumptions and propositions which are made about the principal components of any approach to career counseling. In contrast, the *methods* of an approach are the specific procedures used to implement the model of career counseling and include *interview techniques, test interpretations* and *use of occupational information*. The models and methods of career counseling vary widely from one approach to another, as an analysis of each on these dimensions makes clear. Following the schema outlined in Figure 1, the various approaches to career counseling are briefly reviewed in this order: (1) Trait-and-Factor; (2) Client-Centered; (3) Psychodynamic; (4) Developmental; and (5) Behavioral. Limitations of space preclude an extensive discussion of the models and methods; therefore, only the central concepts and practices have been selected for the summary which follows.

Trait-and-Factor Career Counseling

The *model* of this approach was fashioned from the pragmatics of assisting men and women dislocated from their jobs during the era of the Great Depression to retrain and find new employment (Paterson and Darley, 1936). Stemming from the interdisciplinary work of the Twin Cities Occupational Analysis Clinic, early trait-and-factor career counseling reflected the rudiments of Parson's (1909) "matching men-and-jobs" conceptualization but it went beyond his pioneer paradigm to incorporate the sophistication of the newly developing psychometrics, which produced the fabled "Minnesota" tests of clerical aptitude, manual dexterity, spatial perception, etc., and the fund of occupational information compiled by the U.S. Employment Service for the first edition (1939) of the Dictionary of Occupational Titles (DOT). Philosophically, trait-and-factor career counseling has always had a strong commitment to the uniqueness of the individual; psychologically this value has meant a long-time predilection for the tenets of differential psychology. As a consequence, there have been two significant implications for the model upon which this approach is based: First, it is largely *atheoretical,* other than that it subscribes to the proposition that individuals differ. It does not posit organizing concepts or hypothetical constructs, such as are characteristic of the client-centered and psychodynamic approaches. Second, it is analytical and atomistic in its orientation. It adheres closely to the schemata of scientific problem solving, as exemplified by a nosological concept of diagnosis, a rationalistic process of counseling and a specific set of decisional outcomes:

1. *Diagnosis* is the hallmark of trait-and-factor career counseling. Williamson (1939a) defines it as:

> a process in logical thinking or the 'teasing out', from a mass of relevant and irrelevant facts, of a consistent pattern of meaning and an understanding of the [client's] assets and liabilities together with a prognosis or judgment of significance of this pattern for future adjustments to be made by the [client] (pp. 102–103).

To aid in diagnosing problems in career decision-making, Williamson (1939b) has proposed these four categories: (1) no choice; (2) uncertain choice; (3) unwise choice; and (4) discrepancy between interests and aptitudes. Contingent upon which problem a client is judged to have, an appropriate process of career counseling would be formulated. Thus, the role of diagnosis in trait-and-factor career counseling is much like it is in the "medical model": differential courses of treatment stem from a determination of what is "wrong" with the client.

2. *Process.* Williamson (1939b) delineates six steps which comprise trait-and-factor career counseling:

> Analysis—collecting data from many sources about attitudes, interests, family background, knowledge, educational progress, aptitudes, etc., by means of both subjective and objective technics.
> Synthesis—collating and summarizing the data by means of case-study techniques and test profiles to 'highlight' the [client's] uniqueness or individuality.
> Diagnosis—describing the outstanding characteristics and problems of the [client], comparing the individual's profile with educational and occupational ability profiles, and ferreting out the causes of the problems.
> Prognosis—judging the probable consequences of problems, the probabilities for adjustments, and thereby indicating the alternative actions and adjustments for the [client's] consideration.
> Counseling, or treatment—cooperatively advising with the client concerning what to do to effect a desired adjustment now or in the future.
> Follow-up—repeating the above steps as new problems arise and further assisting the [client] to carry out a desirable program of action (p. 214).

The first four steps of this process are exclusively engaged in by the counselor; only in the last two does the client actively participate. Most of the process, then, involves the mental activity of the counselor in gathering, processing and interpreting data on the client.

3. *Outcomes.* The immediate goal of trait-and-factor career counseling is to resolve the presenting problem of the client. If his/her choice was unwise, for example, then counseling should eventuate in a more realistic career decision. The longer term objective has been stated by Williamson (1965) as follows:

"The task of the trait-factor type of counseling is to aid the individual in successive approximations of self-understanding and self-management by means of helping him to assess his assets and liabilities in relation to the requirements of progressively changing life goals and his vocational career (p. 198)." Stated somewhat differently, Thompson (1954) has pointed out that this approach should not only assist the client to make a specific decision but it should also "result in the individual's being better able to solve future problems" (p. 535).

The *methods* used by trait-and-factor career counselors reflect the rationalistic, cognitive model of this approach. Interview techniques, test interpretation procedures, uses of occupational information: taken together, they constitute a logical "attack" upon the client's decision-making problem. They are what the "thinking man" would do when confronted with a choice among alternative courses of action. They are largely action-oriented, and the counselor is highly active in using these methods. Not only is most of the processing of data on the client a counselor activity, as outlined in the process of trait-and-factor career counseling, but the lead in the interviews is typically taken by the counselor. This role should not be construed to mean, however, that the counselor is insensitive or unresponsive to the client's feelings and emotions and attitudes. Quite the contrary, as Darley (1950) notes in discussing acceptance of the client: "The interviewer must indicate to the client that he has accepted but not passed judgment on these [the client's] feelings and attitudes (p. 268)." Whether dealing with feeling or content, the trait-and-factor career counselor nevertheless appears to be "in charge." The counselor role in this approach is probably best characterized as assertive, dominant and participative (as contrasted with reactive and reflective), all of which earned the trait-and-factor counselor the appellation of "directive" during the heyday of Rogerian "nondirective" counseling in the 1950's. To use these methods effectively presumes that they are compatible with the counselor's personality:

1. *Interview techniques.* Williamson (1939a) has identified five general techniques which he recommends for trait-and-factor career counseling: "(1) establishing rapport, (2) cultivating self-understanding, (3) advising or planning a program of action, (4) carrying out the plan, and (5) referring the [client] to another personnel worker for additional assistance (p. 130)." More specifically, Darley (1950) ennunciates four principles of interviewing which the counselor should follow:

1. Do not lecture or talk down to the client.
2. Use simple words and confine the information that you give the client to a relatively few ideas.
3. Make very sure that you know what it is he really wants to talk about before giving any information or answers.
4. Make very sure that you sense or feel the attitudes that he holds, because these will either block the discussion or keep the main problems out of it (p. 266).

He then discusses several different aspects of the interview which are too numerous to recount here but which cover such functions as opening the interview, phrasing questions, handling silences and maintaining control of the interaction. If these methods were to be described and summarized by one rubric, it would be *pragmatic*. Their essence is technological, not teleological.

2. *Test interpretation.* This phase of trait-and-factor career counseling is subsumed by those interview techniques which Williamson (1939a) calls "advising or planning a program of action" (p. 139), and they include the following:

a. *Direct advising,* in which the counselor frankly states his opinion as to what the client should do.

b. *Persuasion,* in which the counselor "marshals the evidence in such a reasonable and logical manner that the [client] is able to anticipate clearly the probable outcomes of alternative actions."

c. *Explanation,* in which the counselor extrapolates "the implications of the diagnoses and the probable outcome of each choice considered by the [client] (p. 139)."

In Williamson's (1939a) opinion, the last method is "by all odds the most complete and satisfactory method of counseling" (p. 139). He illustrates this type of test interpretation in this excerpt from a counselor explanation:

> As far as I can tell from this evidence of aptitude, your chances of getting into medical school are poor; but your possibilities in business seem to be much more promising. These are the reasons for my conclusions: You do not have the pattern of interests characteristic of successful doctors which probably indicates you would not find the practice of medicine congenial. On the other hand you do have an excellent grasp of mathematics, good general ability, and the interests of an accountant. These facts seem to me to argue for your selection of accountancy as an occupation (p. 139).

Thus, the counselor relies upon his/her expertise to make authoritative interpretations of the test results and to draw conclusions and recommendations from them for the client's deliberation.

3. *Occupational information.* Probably the most widely cited statement of the use of occupational information in trait-and-factor career counseling is that of Brayfield (1950), who has distinguished among three different functions of this material:

a. *Informational:* the counselor provides a client with information about occupations in order to confirm a choice which has already been made, to resolve indecision between two equally attractive and appropriate options, or to simply increase the client's knowledge about a choice which otherwise is realistic.

b. *Readjustive:* the counselor introduces occupational information, so that the client has a basis for reality testing an inappropriate choice, the process unfolding something like this:

the counselor first uses leading questions regarding the nature of the occupation or field which the counselee has chosen. In turn, the counselor provides accurate information which may enable the client to gain insight into the illusory nature of his thinking when he finds that his conception of the occupation or field does not fit the objective facts. At this point the counselor usually is able to turn the interview to a consideration of the realistic bases upon which sound occupational choices are founded (Brayfield, 1950, p. 218).

c. *Motivational:* the counselor uses occupational information to involve the client actively in the decision-making process, to "hold" or maintain contact with dependent clients until they assume greater responsibility for their choice, and to maintain motivation for choice when a client's current activities seem irrelevant to long-term career goals. Other delineations of essentially the same strategies in presenting occupational information to clients have been made by Baer and Roeber (1951), and Christensen (1949). If there is any significant difference among them, it is Brayfield's (1950) insistence that "Any use of occupational information should be preceded by individual diagnosis (p. 220)," which stems directly from the process sequence in the model of trait-and-factor career counseling.

Comment. For many years, trait-and-factor career counseling held sway as the only approach to assisting clients engaged in the process of deciding upon their life's work, and in the hands of its highly competent and enlightened originators it is probably as viable today as it was in the past (Willimson, 1972). But as practiced by too many journeyman trait-and-factor counselors who have not updated the model (Super and Bachrach, 1957) and methods (Williamson, 1972), this approach has gone into an incipient decline. It has devolved into what has been caricatured as "three interviews and a cloud of dust." The first interview is typically conducted to gather some background data on the client and for the counselor to assign tests. The client takes the tests, usually a lengthy battery administered in "shotgun" style (Super, 1950), and then returns for the second interview at which time the results are interpreted. Not atypically, this session amounts to the counselor "teaching" the client certain necessary psychometric concepts, for example, the meaning of percentile ranks or standard scores, in order to engage in a lengthy discussion of the tests—one by one, scale by scale. The third interview is usually devoted to reviewing the client's career choice in light of the test results and to briefing the client on the use of the occupational information file for possible further exploration of the world of work. And then the client leaves ("cloud of dust"), often without using these materials on his own, due to the lack of initiative which produced the problems that brought him to career counseling in the first place. At best, this widespread over-simplification of trait-and-factor career counseling provides the client with a mass of test information, which is frequently forgotten or distorted (Froehlich and Moser, 1954). At worst, it completely ignores the psychological realities of decision making which lead to indecision and unrealism in career choice (Crites, 1969), and it fails to foster those more general competencies, for example, self-management, which are the essence of true trait-and-factor career counseling (Williamson, 1972).

Client-Centered Career Counseling

The *model* for this approach to career counseling stems only indirectly and by inference from the more general system of psychotherapy proposed by Rogers (1942; 1951). In the latter, Rogers had little to say about career decision-making processes, his concern being primarily with the emotional-social adjustment and functioning of the person. Some client-centered counselors (for example, Arbuckle, 1961; Doleys, 1961) have contended that, if a client becomes well-adjusted psychologically, then he/she will be able to solve whatever career problems are encountered without specifically attending to them in career counseling. Other counselors of a client-centered bent, however, have recognized that, although general and vocational adjustment are related, the correlation is less than perfect (Crites, 1969), and thus a separate focus upon career choices can be justified. During the early years of client-centered counseling (the 1940s), when trait-and-factor counselors were attempting to reconcile and synthesize its principles and procedures with established techniques, several extrapolations from the newer approach to traditional career counseling were made (for example, Bixler and Bixler, 1945; Covner, 1947; Combs, 1947; Bown, 1947; Seeman, 1948). There ensued a heated controversy in which the relative merits of the "directive" and "non-directive" orientations were debated loud and long, with seemingly no immediate resolution other than a contrived and tenuous eclecticism awkwardly known as "non-directive" career counseling (Hahn and Kendall, 1947). Not until almost two decades later was an articulate and comprehensive statement of client-centered career counseling formulated by Patterson (1964), although it had been presaged by Super's (1950; 1951, 1957) writings on the self-concept and career development. It is primarily Patterson's conceptualization which is drawn upon in explicating the client-centered position on diagnosis, process and outcomes:

1. *Diagnosis.* Of all the concepts on which directive and nondirective counselors differed, the divergence in their viewpoints was probably greatest on diagnosis. Whereas diagnosis was the fulcrum of the trait-and-factor approach, it was eschewed by Rogers (1942) as potentially disruptive of the client-counselor relationship:

"When the counselor assumes the information-getting attitude which is necessary for the assembling of a good case history, the client cannot help feeling that the responsibility for the solution of his problems is being taken over by the counselor (p. 81)."

Similarly, although he does not discuss diagnosis directly, Patterson (1964) subscribes to this point-of-view when he states that "the client-centered counselor does not deal differently with a client who has a vocational problem and one who has any other kind of problem (p. 435)." Yet, he argues that career counseling can be distinguished from other types of counseling because it focuses "upon a particular area—or problem—in an individual's life" (Patterson, 1964, p. 435) and facilitates the "handling" of it. Thus, he implies that some determination is made whether a client has a "vocational" problem, but he does not consider this a diagnosis.

2. *Process.* Patterson (1964) refers generally to the "process" of client-centered career counseling but neglects to analyze it into distinct stages or phases as does Rogers (1961) for psychotherapy. Extrapolating from the latter, however, as well as from empirical research, it can be inferred that vocational clients enter career counseling at a stage of "experiencing" roughly equivalent to that at which personal clients leave psychotherapy. This is the sixth stage in experiencing, during which a higher level of congruence is achieved by the client, so that he/she "owns" feelings and problems rather than externalizing them: "The client is living, subjectively, a phase of his problem. It is not an object" (Rogers, 1961, p. 150). Clinical impressions of vocational clients, in addition to findings on their general adjustment status (Gaudet and Kulick, 1954; Goodstein, Crites, Heilbrun and Rempel, 1961), suggest that they have reached this stage, on the average, before they start career counseling. Corroboration also comes from a study by Williams (1962), in which he obtained Q-adjustment scores on vocational-educational clients and compared them with [personal] clients from Dymond's (1954) research on client-centered psychotherapy, the *pre*counseling mean of the former being 50.53 and the *post*counseling mean of the latter being 49.30. From these findings, Williams (1962) concluded that "the adjustment level of personal clients *following* counseling is approximately that of [vocational-educational] clients *before* counseling . . . (p. 26)." Since the vocational-educational clients' *post*counseling mean was 58.76, indicating a still higher level of adjustment, it would appear that career counseling largely encompasses the seventh (and highest) stage in Rogers' (1961) schema of counseling process. Patterson (1973) describes this stage thusly: "The client experiences new feelings with immediacy and richness and uses them as referrents for knowing who he is, what he wants, and what his attitudes are. . . . Since all the elements of experience are available to awareness, there is the experiencing of real and effective choice (p. 394)."

3. *Outcomes.* Implicit in this conceptualization of process are the assumed outcomes of client-centered career counseling. Grummon (1972) notes that:

> It is difficult to distinguish clearly between process and outcomes. When we study outcomes directly, we examine the differences between two sets of observations made at the beginning and end of the interview series. Many process studies make successive observations over a series of counseling interviews and, in a sense, are miniature outcome measures which establish a trend line for the case (p. 110).

At each point along this line and as the overall outcome, the goal in client-centered psychotherapy is *reorganization of the self:* the client is more congruent, more open to his experience, less defensive (Rogers, 1959). In client-centered career counseling, however, the "successful resolution of many educational and vocational problems (as well as other presenting problems) does not require a reorganization of self" (Grummon, 1972, p. 119). Rather, the goal is to facilitate the clarification and implementation of the self-concept in a compatible occupational role, at whatever point on the continuum of career development the client is. Patterson (1964) cites Super's (1957) revision of the NVGA definition of "vocational guidance" as delineating the desired outcomes of client-centered career counseling:

> [It] is the process of helping a person to develop and accept an integrated picture of himself and of his role in the world of work, to test this concept against reality, and to convert it into reality, with satisfaction to himself and benefit to society (p. 442).

The *methods* by which these outcomes are attained presume certain basic attitudes on the part of the counselor. Much as Rogers (1957) emphasized such conative dispositions as necessary for successful client-centered psychotherapy, so Patterson (1964) has observed that the client-centered approach to career counseling is "essentially an *attitude* rather than a technique (p. 442)." More specifically, there are three attitudes which characterize the ideally functioning client-centered counselor (Rogers, 1957; 1961):

1. *Congruence:* being genuine and open; not playing a role or presenting a facade; the counselor "is aware of and accepts his own feelings, with a willingness to be and express these feelings and attitudes, in words or behavior" (Patterson, 1973, p. 396).

2. *Understanding:* perceiving the client's phenomenal field; sensing the client's inner world "as if" it is the counselor's; not diagnostic or evaluative; empathy.

3. *Acceptance:* "unconditional positive regard"; the counselor accepts the client "as an individual, as he is, with his conflicts and inconsistencies, his good and bad points" (Patterson, 1973, p. 396).

Given these counselor attitudes and their communication to a client, who must be experiencing at least a minimal degree of incongruence as a source of motivation for treatment, there results a relationship in which change, that is, increased client congruence, can occur. These counselor attitudes are communicated in client-centered career counseling via distinctive techniques of interviewing, test interpretation, and use of occupational information:

1. *Interview techniques.* Once stereotyped as "unhuh" counseling in its early days of development, due to Rogers' (1942) emphasis upon nondirective interview techniques, the client-centered approach has evolved into a much more sophisticated repertoire of counselor interview behaviors in recent years. In tracing this evolution, Hart and Tomlinson (1970) have delineated three periods during which different interview techniques predominated:

a. *Nondirective period* (1940–1950). [The] counselor used verbal responses with a minimal degree of "lead" (Robinson, 1950), such as simple acceptance, clarification and restatement, to achieve client insight.

b. *Reflective period* (1950–1957). [The] counselor concentrated almost exclusively upon reflection of feelings, which was substituted for clarification from the preceding period, the goal being to "mirror the client's phenomenological world to him" (Hart and Tomlinson, 1970, p. 8).

c. *Experiential period* (1957–present). [The] counselor engages in a wide range of interview behaviors to express basic attitudes and, in contrast to previous roles, relates relevant personal experiences to the client, in order to facilitate the latter's experiencing.

Thus, in contemporary client-centered psychotherapy, the counselor is much more active than ever before, as indexed, for example, by client/counselor "talk ratios." Presumably the same would be true of client-centered career counseling, although neither Patterson nor others have made this application as yet. Assuming that the extrapolation is justified, it would mean that the client-centered career counselor would make responses during the interview with a higher degree of "lead," such as approval, open-ended questions and tentative interpretations, the purpose of which would be to foster and enrich client experiencing as it relates to implementing the self-concept in an occupational role.

2. *Test interpretation.* One of the central issues with which client-centered career counselors have had to contend has been how to reconcile the use of tests with the tenets of the Rogerian approach. To resolve what appears to be a basic incompatibility between the nonevaluative counselor attitudes of acceptance, congruence and understanding on the one hand, and the evaluative information derived from tests on the other, client-centered career counselors have proposed that tests be used primarily for the *client's* edification, not the coun-

selor's. Patterson (1964) argues that "The essential basis for the use of tests in [client-centered] career counseling is that *they provide information which the client needs and wants,* information concerning questions raised by the client in counseling" . . . (p. 449). Similarly, Grummon (1972) concludes that "Tests can be useful in [client-centered career counseling], provided that the information they supply is integrated into the self-concept" (p. 126). To achieve this "client-centeredness" in using tests, several innovative procedures have been proposed: First, tests are introduced as *needed* and *requested* by the client—what Super (1950) has termed "precision" testing as opposed to "saturation" testing. In other words, the client can take tests whenever appropriate throughout the course of career counseling, rather than as a battery before it starts. Second, the client participates in the test selection process (Bordin and Bixler, 1946). The counselor describes the kind of information the client can gain from the various tests available, and the client decides which behaviors he/she wants to assess. The counselor then usually designates the most appropriate measures with respect to their psychometric characteristics (applicability, norms, reliability, validity). Finally, when the tests have been taken and scored, the counselor reports the results to the client in as objective, nonjudgmental a way as possible and responds to the latter's reactions within a client-centered atmosphere (see Bixler and Bixler, 1946, for interview excerpts which illustrate this type of test interpretation).

3. *Occupational information.* The principles underlying the use of occupational information in client-centered career counseling are much the same as those governing test interpretation. Patterson (1964) enumerates four of them:

1. Occupational information is introduced into the counseling process when there is a recognized need for it on the part of the client . . .
2. Occupational information is not used to influence or manipulate the client . . .
3. The most objective way to provide occupational information and a way which maximizes client initiative and responsibility, is to encourage the client to obtain the information from original sources, that is, publications, employers, and persons engaged in occupations . . .
4. The client's attitudes and feelings about occupations and jobs must be allowed expression and be dealt with therapeutically (pp. 453–455).

Grummon (1972) adds the observation that, in the process of presenting occupational information, the career counselor should not lose sight of the Rogerian dictum, stemming from phenomenological theory, that "reality for the individual is his perception of that reality (p. 122)." Thus, Rusalem (1954) proposes that "the presentation of occupational information must assume that for the client it becomes a process of selective perception (pp. 85–86)." Likewise, Samler (1964) states that "The process of occupational exploration is psychological in the sense that the client's perceptions are taken into account (p. 426)." The client-centered career counselor recognizes, then, that occupational information has personal meanings to the client which must be understood and explored within the context of needs and values as well as objective reality.

Comment. The model and methods of client-centered career counseling represent not only an application of Rogerian principles to decision making, they also synthesize this approach with core concepts from trait-and-factor and developmental theory. Patterson (1964) incorporates a refined "matching men and jobs" concept of career choice when he states that it "may still be broadly conceived as the matching of the individual and a career, but in a manner much more complex than was originally thought (p. 441)," and he draws heavily upon Super's (1957) self-theory of career development to introduce this dimension into the otherwise historical, "right now" focus of client-centered psychotherapy. It is problematical, however, whether even this comprehensive a synthesis, which might also include the contemporary client-centered emphasis upon greater counselor activity, meets some of the criticisms which have been levelled at client-centered career counseling. Theoretically, Grummon (1972) has expressed concern over the almost exclusively phenomenological orientation of the client-centered approach, which ignores the effect of stimulus variables upon the acquisition and processing of information about self and the world of work. He observes that: The theory's failure to elaborate how the environment influences perception and behavior is for the writer [Grummon] a significant omission which has special relevance for many counseling situations (p. 123)." Pragmatically, the principal pitfall also concerns the potential disjunction and disruption that the introduction of information into the interview process by the counselor often creates. It is still not clear from Patterson's formulation how the counselor informs the client about occupations without shifting from a client-centered role to a didactic one and thereby compromising the very attitudes which supposedly promote self-clarification and actualization. His suggestion that the counselor *read* occupational information aloud to the client does not appear to be the panacea.

Psychodynamic Career Counseling
The *model* underlying this approach to career counseling has been constructed primarily by Bordin (1968) and his associates, although others (for example, King and Bennington, 1972) have also applied the principles of psychoanalytic theory and therapy to counseling phenomena. It has been Bordin, however, who has had an enduring in-

terest and involvement in conceptualizing career counseling, as well as career development (Bordin, Nachmann and Segal, 1963), within the psychonanalytic tradition. The term *psychodynamic* has been chosen to characterize his orientation, not only because it more accurately portrays the broader scope of Bordin's model than does the scholastic meaning of psychoanalytic, but also because it more precisely connotes the essence of his theoretical commitment, which is twofold: career choice involves the client's needs, and it is a developmental process. Bordin (1968) asserts that:

> Our pivotal assumption is that insofar as he has freedom of choice an individual tends to gravitate toward those occupations whose activities permit him to express his preferred ways of seeking gratification and of protecting himself from anxiety . . . Psychoanalytic theory suggests that a developmental approach to vocation should examine the full sweep of influences shaping personality from birth, even from conception (p. 427).

To "prevent crippling psychological conflicts" in the course of personality-vocational development, the psychodynamically oriented career counselor intervenes at the "transitional points in the life cycle," utilizing these concepts of diagnosis, process, and outcomes:

1. *Diagnosis.* On the issue of whether to diagnose or not, Bordin (1968) is unequivocal: "we are convinced that counselors should not undertake counseling responsibility without at least a rudimentary knowledge of diagnosis and diagnostic techniques (p. 296)." But, his view of diagnosis is not the traditional, nosological one of trait-and-factor career counseling. In fact, Bordin (1946) was the first to seriously question such non-dynamic taxonomies of client problems and proposed instead more psychologically based constructs, such as choice anxiety, dependence and self-conflict. Just recently, he (Bordin and Kopplin, 1973) has reiterated the value of dynamic diagnosis in asserting: "we must reject a false dichotomy between classification and dynamic understanding. It is true that classifications have been used in static ways; neither as tools in an ongoing process of understanding nor as guides in an interaction process (p. 155)." Analyzing the sources of motivational conflict experienced by college students seeking career counseling, Bordin and Kopplin (1973) have proposed a new diagnostic system consisting of several major categories with some further subdivisions into more specific problems. These categories are as follows:

> A: Synthetic difficulties—A limiting case of minimum pathology and conflict in which the major problem is to be found in the difficulty of synthetizing or achieving cognitive clarity. The client is able to work productively in counseling.
> B: Identity problems—These are assumed to be associated with the

formation of a viable self and self-percept (not necessarily fully conscious).

C: Gratification conflicts—This classification takes its inspiration from the point of view that examines occupations in terms of the opportunities each offers for finding particular forms of psychosocial gratification in the work activities.

D: Change orientation—the client is dissatisfied with himself and struggles via vocational choice to change himself.

E: Overt pathology—Even though the contact was initiated around vocational choice, it becomes evident that the disturbance makes it impossible for the student to do any kind of work on this question.

F: Unclassifiable—Except that it is a problem-involving [sic] motivational conflict.

G: Unclassifiable—Except that it is a problem involving no motivational conflict (pp. 156–159).

To assess the reliability of this system, two judges classified the career motivational conflicts of 82 former clients. On the first 47 cases, they reconciled disagreements through consultation, but still attained only 51 per cent exact agreement, with partial agreement in a remaining 28 per cent. From these results, Bordin and Kopplin (1973) concluded that:

> In general, was must concede that, though tolerable, our level of agreement was not satisfying. However, we do not find it discouraging because we take into account the sparseness of the case notes in so many instances that forced us into the guessing situation that the reliability figures document. A further factor in unreliability is that the counselors were not oriented to the issues raised by our categories (p. 159).

Even granting that the reliability of this new system might be increased to a satisfactory level, however, of what use is it to the career counselor? It is wholly *post hoc:* the diagnosis is made from reading the notes and summaries of cases which have already been closed out! Such a procedure may have some value for research purposes, but it does not provide the career counselor with the requisite data for diagnosis *before* a course of career counseling is formulated. As Bordin (1946) stipulated many years ago: "the most vital characteristic of a set of diagnostic classifications is that they form the basis for the choice of treatment" (p. 172).

2. *Process.* Bordin (1968) breaks the process of career counseling down into three stages, which are a microcosm for the overall process of career development. In the first stage, *exploration and contract setting,* the critical task of the psychodynamic career counselor is to avoid a superficial rationalistic examination of the client's choice problem as well as a seductive attempt to engage him/her in nonvocationally oriented therapy. Rather, as the name of this approach implies, the focus should be upon the *psychodynamics* of career decision mak-

ing, the interface between the personal and the vocational in the client's life. The counselor strives to articulate the relationship between these two—to extrapolate the implications, for example, of a fearful, defensive identification of a failing engineering student, who wants to change majors, with an overdemanding and stern father. The second stage is that of *critical decision,* not necessarily of career but between the alternatives of counseling limited to choice or broadened to encompass personality change. In other words, the psychodynamic counselor offers the client the option of becoming engaged in counseling focused upon facets of personal development other than just the vocational. The last stage in the process of psychodynamic career counseling is *working for change.* It is presumed that the client will opt for at least some change in personality, even if it is circumscribed to vocational identity—hence the thrust of this final stage toward increased awareness and understanding of self.

3. *Outcomes.* Although not explicitly stated, the expected outcomes of psychodynamic career counseling are apparent from an analysis of the stages in the process. One objective is to assist the client in career decision making. The problems which clients may present run the gamut of those enumerated previously in the discussion of "diagnosis," for example, synthetic difficulties, gratification conflicts, etc. A broader goal is to effect some positive change in the client's personality, which can be accomplished in two principal ways. Even though the client may choose more narrowly defined career counseling, it may well have salubrious effects upon personal development. Thus, a juxtaposition of a pervasive indecisiveness in decision making with submission to an authoritarian father may motivate a dependent client to assume greater personal responsibility without the counselor directly dealing with the latter. If the client is willing to undertake personal counseling relatively distinct from a career emphasis, then the avowed outcome is some kind of personality change, albeit only symptomatic anxiety reduction. Both career decision and personality change, achieved through whatever modes, are the desired end states of the client following successful psychodynamic career counseling.

The *methods* of psychodynamic career counseling, as espoused primarily by Bordin (1968), are an amalgam of techniques derived not only from psychoanalytic practices but also from the trait-and-factor and client-centered approaches. More than a mere eclectic, gathering together of disparate counseling procedures, they are a true synthesis of theories and methods, leavened by Bordin's many years of experience as an active counselor. As the ensuing descriptions of psychodynamic interview techniques, test interpretation processes, and uses of occupational information bring out, they constitute sophisticated and refined methods for assisting clients in career decision making:

1. *Interview techniques.* Drawing upon the work of Colby (1951), a psychoanalytically disposed psychotherapist, Bordin (1968) enumer-

ates three "interpretive" counselor response categories which can be used to conduct the interview. The first of these, *clarifications,* are intended to focus the client's thinking and verbalization upon material relevant to the presenting problem. They also serve to open up new areas of discourse and summarize others. Typically, clarifications take the grammatical form of questions, mild imperatives or simplified restatements—what Colby calls "interpositions"—and, because of their form and content, their highest incidence is usually during the beginning stage of counseling. A second type of counselor response is *comparison,* in which two or more topics are juxtaposed to present in sharper relief the similarities or differences among dynamic phenomena. This technique is central to explicating the inter-relationship of personal and career development. To illustrate, a counselor might respond to an indecisive client's unconscious rebellion against imposed parental occupational aspirations by saying: "On the one hand, your parents want you to be something you don't want to be, yet on the other you cannot decide what you want to be. Do you see any connection between the two?" Comparisons are probably most characteristic of the middle stage of counseling. The third technique, which is more pointedly therapeutic in purpose than the other two, is the interpretation of *wish-defense* systems, as exemplified in a case study cited by Cautela (1959). A client who was well-suited for medicine by virtue of both abilities and interests, and who was doing well in his pre-med course, expressed a desire in career counseling to change his major to architecture, for which he had no apparent talent. In subsequent interviews, he reported that shortly before his decision to consider architecture, his mother was almost completely paralyzed due to a cerebral hemorrhage and that his father had intimated he was partially responsible because she waited on him continually. On the psychodynamic hypothesis that "buildings symbolically represent the female figure," the counselor interpreted the client's contemplated shift to architecture as a way of "rebuilding his mother" and hence reducing his guilt over having originally precipitated her paralysis. Pursuing the implications of this wish-defense interpretation over a span of twenty interviews, which psychodynamic career counseling not infrequently runs, the client finally decided that architecture was an unrealistic, reactive choice, and that he would pursue his studies in pre-med.

2. *Test interpretation.* Bordin has made three major contributions to using tests in psychodynamic career counseling: First, in collaboration with a colleague (Bordin and Bixler, 1946), he proposed, in the spirit of the client-centered approach, that the client be an active participant in selecting the tests which he/she would take. A description of different types of tests (for example, aptitude, interest, personality) is given to the client, who then determines which kind of self-appraisal information might be most useful in terms of the career problem. But

the counselor selects the specific tests (for example, the Strong Vocational Interest Blank) to be administered, since he/she knows what their psychometric characteristics are.

Second, once the client has taken the tests, Bordin (1968) delineates four ways in which they may be used: (1) to provide diagnostic information for the counselor; (2) to aid the client in developing more realistic expectations about counseling; (3) to make appraisal data available to the client; and (4) to stimulate the client in self-exploration. In communicating test results to clients, Bordin subscribes to the procedure developed by Bixler and Bixler (1946), in which scores are reported in as nonevaluative a way as possible. The counselor simply gives the client a statistical prediction, such as "The chances are about 3½ to 1 that if you go into this occupation you will stay in it for 20 years or more," and then discusses the client's reaction to the factual statement.

Third, Bordin (1968) has suggested that this method of test interpretation not only lends itself but is enhanced by the counselor *verbally* relating the client's scores rather than presenting them visually on profile sheets or psychographs. Several advantages accrue from this approach: (1) the counselor can maintain a consistent role as a "collaborator" with the client, rather than shifting to one of "expert" or teacher who explains the psychometric meaning of test scores; (2) the test results can be introduced into the client-counselor interaction as needed, rather than all at once as is routinely done in trait-and-factor career counseling; and (3) the client has a greater likelihood of remembering the implications of the testing, because they have been expressed and integrated into his/her vernacular and thinking about career choice. There is compelling research evidence that clients either forget or distort test information disseminated by the traditional method (Froehlich and Moser, 1954; Kamm and Wrenn, 1950), a problem which can be largely circumvented by the counselor's verbal presentation of test results as part of the ongoing dialogue with the client.

3. *Occupational information.* The type of information about occupations which is integral to psychodynamic career counseling is that which might best be described as based upon "need analysis" of job duties and tasks. A series of such studies has been conducted under Bordin's general sponsorship at the University of Michigan on accountants and creative writers (Segal, 1961); dentists, lawyers, and social workers (Nachmann, 1960); clinical psychologists and physicists (Galinsky, 1962); and engineers (Beall and Bordin, 1964). In addition, Bordin, Nachmann and Segal (1963) have delineated several dimensions of psychosexual development along which occupational groups can be characterized in terms of need-gratifying activities and instrumental modes of adjustment to work. Knowledge of how and why

members of specific occupations engage psychodynamically in their jobs as they do can be used to assist clients in choosing careers in which they may have the greatest probability of satisfying their needs. Thus, although this is clearly the trait-and-factor paradigm of "matching men and jobs," the variables are personality dynamics (needs) and gratifying work conditions (satisfiers), rather than the static characteristics of the individual and occupation.

Comment. As has been true of psychoanalytic theory in general, the model of psychodynamic career counseling suffers from the limitation that it disproportionately emphasizes "internal" factors as the most salient ones in career choice and minimizes external ones (Ginzberg, Ginsburg, Axelrad and Herman, 1951). The assumption is that "insofar as the client has freedom of choice," career choice is a function of individual psychodynamics, but scant attention is given to the conditions and variables which impose constraints upon the decision-making process (Crites, 1969, Ch. 3). Moreover, from a behavioristic point of view, the excessive concern of the psychodynamic career counselor with motivational (nonobservable) constructs introduces unnecessary complexity into the conceptualization of career determination, and rests upon the tenuous assumption that overt decision-making behaviors are somehow mediated by internal "needs." This criticism might be less telling were it not that Bordin has not yet devised an *a priori* diagnostic system which is linked to differentially effective career counseling methods. He is acutely aware, however, of the need for such a conceptualization when he and Kopplin (1973) observe that "it would be useful to make more explicit the differential treatment implications of this classification of motivational conflicts related to vocational development (p. 160)." They then propose some general considerations which the psychodynamic career counselor should make in treating clients with different problems, but these recommendations, for example, "the counselor must explore the family constellation and client's experience of it so as to understand how identity formation is influencing his learning" (Bordin and Kopplin, 1973, p. 160), are hardly specific enough to guide interview behavior. Their value lies not on this tactical level but on the strategic one of fashioning career counseling to the psychodynamics of each client, a flexibility and perspicacity in approach which is too often missing from the pedestrian practice of trait-and-factor and client-centered career counseling.

Developmental Career Counseling

A confluence of several streams of conceptualization in career counseling has contributed the theoretical foundation upon which the developmental approach to assisting clients engaged in decision-making has been built. Foremost among the architects of this frame of reference, and its recognized progenitor is Donald E. Super, who has articulated the precepts and principles of developmental career counseling since the early 1940's. At that time, when the trait-and-factor orientation was predominant, he adapted Buehler's (1933) life stage schema to the analysis of career behavior in his book, *The Dynamics of Vocational Adjustment* (Super, 1942). However, he did not neglect the demonstrated value of the "actuarial method," as he referred to it later (Super, 1954), which he considered to be the "cornerstone of vocational guidance." Indeed his monumental volume on *Appraising Vocational Fitness* (Super, 1949) represents the traditional approach at its best, but throughout his treatment of vocational appraisal by means of psychological tests there is interwoven his long-standing commitment to developmental psychology and his nascent self-concept theory, as evidenced particularly in his summary of "The Nature of Interests" (Super, 1949). His synthesis of these diverse, and often manifestly contradictory, substantive areas evolved through a series of landmark papers (Super, 1951, 1954, 1955, 1957a, 1960), a book on the *Psychology of Careers* (Super, 1957b), and a Career Pattern Study monograph (Super and Overstreet, 1960) during the 1950s and early 1960s. Implicit in these writings is a model of developmental career counseling based upon distinctive concepts of diagnosis, process and outcomes:

1. *Diagnosis.* Super (1957a) uses the term *appraisal* instead of diagnosis but considers them to be essentially synonymous, although it is apparent from his discussion of appraisal that this concept is not only broader in scope than diagnosis but that it has a more positive connotation and portent. He delineates three kinds of appraisal, which focus upon the client's potentialities as well as problems (cf., Witryol and Boly, 1954):

a. *Problem appraisal:* the client's experienced difficulty and expectations of career counseling are assessed, much as in the psychodynamic approach, presumably using some classification system such as Bordin's (1946), although Super (1957a) does not discuss the diagnostic constructs he would use.

b. *Personal appraisal:* a psychological "picture" of the client is obtained from a variety of demographic, psychometric and social data, the analogue being the clinical case study (Darley, 1940); both vocational assets and liabilities are assessed and expressed in normative terms (for example, "The client is above average in fine finger dexterity but below average in clerical speed and accuracy.").

c. *Prognostic appraisal:* based largely upon the personal appraisal, predictions of the client's probable success and satisfaction—the two principal components of career adjustment (Crites, 1969)—are made. More specifically, appraisal data can be collected and organized according to the format shown in Table 1, which has been devised by the writer from Super's (1957a) formulation. (See next page.)

TABLE 1. Outline for a Vocational Appraisal

This outline is applicable to either a counseling or a personnel situation. Also, it might be used for research purposes. It is designed to summarize background, interview, and test data on an individual in a systematic fashion. Changes in the outline may be necessary, however, to adapt it to special problems or situations.

Title ("Vocational Appraisal of _____")

Person Appraisal
(Description of the individual in terms of his status on psychological, sociological and physical dimensions.)

Present Status and Functioning. (1) How does the individual "stand" on the various pertinent dimensions? What are his general and special attitudes? Interests? Personality characteristics? Attitudes? Educational background and achievement? Socioeconomic status? (2) How is the individual adjusting to the various aspects or areas of his physical and psychological environment, including himself? What is his "self-concept?" Daily pattern of living (sleeping, eating, personal hygiene, study, work and recreational habits)? What are the nature and quality of his relationships with peers? Family? Teachers? Superiors and subordinates? General authorities (administrative officers, police)? What is his general level of adjustment? Personality integration? What are his predominant adjustment mechanisms?

Developmental History. (1) Has the individual had any significant physical illness which either affected his psychosocial development or left him with special disabilities and handicaps? (2) What is the family background of the individual? Intact or broken home? Number and order of siblings? Parents? Parental attitudes (acceptance, concentration, avoidance)? Parental identification? What were the individual's relationships to peers (accepted as equal, leader, follower, isolate, etc.)? (3) Early interests and abilities (hobbies, sports, organizations, etc.)? (4) Early vocational choices and plans (preferred occupations, age of first choice, motives for choices, indecision, etc.)? (5) School achievement and adjustment (grades, attitudes toward school, best and least liked subjects, favorite teachers, etc.)?

Problem Appraisal
(Identification of the individual's problem; assessment of his strengths as well as his weaknesses, e.g., motivation to change self or assume responsibility for problem solution, adaptability and flexibility, equanimity and sense of humor, constructive and integrative behavior.)

Vocational Problem. (1) Classify according to one of the currently available diagnostic systems. (2) Assess the individual's vocational thinking. How involved is he in the decision-making process? How does he perceive occupations—as ends in themselves or means to other ends? Does he think in "either-or" terms about occupations? How does he "reason through" the problem of vocational choice? Is his thinking logical or does it have "Psychological" fallacies in it, e.g., parataxic distortions? (3) Evaluate whether the individual's vocational problem arises because of immaturity or maladjustment. Does he simply not know how to choose an occupation, or is he conflicted to the extent that he cannot make the appropriate response?

Factors Related to Vocational Problem. (1) What part is played by the individual's family in his choice problem? (2) What is the relationship of his personality to his choice problem? (3) What other factors, such as financial resources, military obligations, marriage plans, academic achievement, etc., are relevant?

Prognostic Appraisal
(Predictions about the individual's future behavior in counseling or on the job.)

Vocational Counseling. (1) Motivation: How well will the individual respond to counseling? Will he "work" on his problem, or will he want the counselor to solve it for him? Why did he apply for counseling? What are his expectations? (2) Interview behavior: How will the client respond verbally? Will he talk readily or not? Will he be verbally hostile or not? How will he relate to the counselor? Will he be dependent, aggressive, aloof, etc.? (3) Counseling goals and plans: What can be achieved with this individual? Should the counselor simply give him test and occupational information, or should he try to "think through" the vocational problem with the individual? Should the counselor focus only upon the specific choice problem of the individual, or should he help him learn how to solve other vocational problems which he may encounter in the future? Can the counseling be primarily vocational in nature, or should personal adjustment counseling precede a consideration of the individual's vocational problem? How can the counseling best be implemented? What techniques should be used?

Vocational Adjustment. (1) Success: Which occupations are within the limits of the individual's capabilities? (2) Satisfaction: In which occupation is the client most likely to find satisfaction? What problems might his personality create for him on the job with respect to doing the work itself, getting along with others, adjusting to the physical conditions of the work, and in realizing his aspirations and goals (material rewards, recognition, prestige, etc.)? (3) Contingencies: What factors which are known might either facilitate or adversely affect the individual's future vocational adjustment if they should occur (for example, military service, marriage, change of job duties, transfer to another region of the country, slow or fast promotion, incompatible social life and obligations, etc.)?

Summary
(A "thumb-nail" sketch of the individual which pulls together the various parts of the vocational appraisal.)

This outline (Table 1) can be used for both cross-sectional and developmental appraisals, although Super (1942; 1954) clearly opts for the latter if the appropriate data are available. What he terms the "thematic-expolative" method of appraisal, as contrasted with a more narrowly conceived actuarial model, strives to provide an impression of the client's behavior within a developmental context. "The assumption underlying this approach is that one way to understand what an individual will do in the future is to understand what he did in the past. It postulates that one way to understand what he did in the past is to analyze the sequence of events and the development of characteristics in order to ascertain the recurring themes and underlying trends" (Super, 1954, p. 13). From data on the patterning of the client's educational and vocational experiences, from knowledge of the subsequent careers of others like the client at the same life stage, and from assessment of the client's personal resources and competence to use them (Super, 1957b), the counselor derives what Pepinsky and

Pepinsky (1954) have called a "hypothetical client," which serves as a basis for making predictions about future career development. That is, from this personal appraisal, and with cognizance of the problem appraisal, extrapolations are made as to the client's future career behavior and the effect which interventive career counseling may have upon it.

Throughout this process of accumulating data and making appraisals, the client is an active participant in extrapolating thema concerning his/her career choice and development. Super (1957b) states that "the best appraisals are made collectively" (p. 307) and that the counselor's "sharing the results of his appraisal with the client" constitutes a safeguard against faulty inferences (Super, 1957a, p. 158). He has further stated that "The client's reactions to the data and to the counselor's tentative interpretations (often put in the form of a question beginning with 'could that mean . . .') 'provide a healthy corrective for the counselor's own possible biases'" (Super, 1959, pp. 536–540). By including the client in the appraisal process, Super largely resolves the dilemma, posed by the opposition of client-centered theory to the counselor's assuming an evaluative attitude, of whether to diagnose or not. No longer is the counselor solely responsible for the appraisal process. Endorsing and elaborating upon a similar viewpoint proposed by Tyler (1953), Super (1957a) observes that: "It will be instead a course of action for which the client is completely willing to take the consequences, *leading to a goal which is based on a cooperative realistic appraisal of the factors involved*" (italics are Super's addendum to Tyler) (p. 156). Thus, in developmental career counseling, as formulated primarily by Super but widely received and refined by others, appraisal (or diagnosis) plays a central role in "getting to know" the client, both hypothetically from life history data and personally from his/her active engagement in the appraisal process.

2. *Process.* The course of developmental career counseling follows closely the broader spectrum of career development. What takes place in the contacts between client and counselor depends upon the point the client has reached on the continuum of career development. The counselor must first determine the career life stage of the client and assess his/her degree of career maturity (Super, 1955). If the client is relatively immature in career behavior, as compared with his/her age or peers (Super and Overstreet, 1960), then developmental career counseling concentrates upon orientation and exploration, which precede decision making and reality testing in the macrocosm of career development. With the career immature client, Super and Overstreet (1960) observe that: "It is not so much counseling concerning choice, as counseling to develop readiness for choice, to develop planfulness. It involves helping [the client] to understand the personal, social, and other factors which have a bearing on the making of educational and vocational decisions, and how they may operate in his own vocational

development" (p. 157). In contrast, if the client is more career mature, that is, has a more fully developed awareness of the need to
choose a career, then the counselor proceeds differently: "Working
with a client who is vocationally mature is essentially the familiar
process of vocational counseling. It involves helping him to assemble,
review, and assimilate relevant information about himself and about
his situation, which will enable him to draw immediately called-for
conclusions as to the implications of these choices for future decisions" (Super and Overstreet, 1960, p. 150). In sum, the overall
process of career development progresses from orientation and readiness for career choice to decision making and reality testing, and the
developmental career counselor initiates counseling at that point in
the process which the client has reached.

3. *Outcomes.* The immediate, and more circumscribed, objective
of developmental career counseling is to facilitate and enhance the
client's career development, whether this means fostering increased
awareness of the world of work or mastering the career developmental
tasks of choosing and implementing a career goal. The maturation of
the client toward these desiderata of career development can be
charted on a career maturity profile, which encompasses several dimensions of career behavior (Super, 1955; Crites, 1973). The latter include Consistency of Career Choice, Realism of Career Choice, Career
Choice Competencies and Career Choice Attitudes (Crites, in press).
The more a client develops ("gains") along these dimensions, the more
efficacious the career counseling is. But, there is a broader, more inclusive goal of developmental career counseling which Super (1955)
would propose:

> One underlying hypothesis has been that, by relieving tensions, clarify-
> ing feelings, giving insight, helping attain success, and developing a
> feeling of competence in one important area of adjustment, it is possible
> to release the individual's ability to cope more adequately with other
> aspects of living, thus bringing about improvements in his general adjust-
> ment. A second hypothesis underlying the approach used is that this is
> best done by building on the individual's assets, by working with his
> strengths rather than with his weaknesses (p. 217).

That these hypotheses are viable ones is evidenced not only by the
demonstrated empirical relationship (moderate positive) between general and career adjustment (Super, 1957; Crites, 1969), but also by the
studies of Williams (1962) and Williams and Hills (1962), in which it
was found that self-ideal congruence, as an index of personal adjustment status, significantly increases as a by-product of career counseling
without direct treatment of the client's personality functioning. In
short, career counseling can further both career *and* personal development.

Much as the model of developmental career counseling reflects an integration of different conceptual and substantive emphases, so too the *methods* of this approach constitute a synthesis of diverse counseling procedures. They have been drawn by Super and others primarily from the trait-and-factor and client-centered orientations, although the influence of developmental principles is also apparent. That the synthesis is more than a superficial eclecticism follows from Super's (1951) imaginative and meaningful interweaving of career counseling conceived as information-giving and as personal therapy. His basic premise is that people are both rational *and* emotional and that, therefore, "the best vocational counseling is a combination of the two, somewhere between the theoretical extremes" (Super, 1951, p. 91). He (Super, 1951) then describes such a *via media* in terms of the kinds of questions the counselor may assist the client in answering:

"What sort of person do I *think* I am? How do I feel about myself as I think I am? What sort of person would I *like* to be? What are my values and needs? What are my aptitudes and interests? What can I do to reconcile my self-ideal with my real self? What outlets are there for me with my needs, values, interests and aptitudes? How can I make use of these outlets?" (p. 91). Consonant with the foci of these questions, upon both the objective and subjective facets of the client's personality and environment, are the *modus operandi* of developmental career counseling: its interview techniques, test interpretation procedures, and uses of occupational information:

1. *Interview techniques.* Because Super (1957) sees career counseling as dealing with both the rational and emotional aspects of self-exploration, decision-making, and reality-testing, he contends that, if the techniques of interviewing are appropriate and consistent, they should occur in approximately the following cycle:

1. Nondirective problem exploration and self-concept portrayal.
2. Directive topic setting, for further exploration.
3. Nondirective reflection and clarification of feeling for self-acceptance and insight.
4. Directive exploration of factual data from tests, occupational pamphlets, extracurricular experiences, grades, etc., for reality testing.
5. Nondirective exploration and working through of attitudes and feelings aroused by reality testing.
6. Nondirective consideration of possible lines of action, for help in decision making (p. 308).

Similarly, Kilby (1949) has outlined a similar sequence of the cyclical use of directive and nondirective interviewing techniques in career counseling, and both he and Super give examples of how they can be used by the counselor to interact with the client which are too extensive to cite here. Suffice it to say that the essence of the "cyclical" approach is to respond directively to content statements by the client and nondirectively to expressions of feeling. Thus, the counselor ranges back and forth among such response categories as restatement, reflection, clarification, summary, interpretation and confrontation.

2. *Test interpretation.* The philosophy and pragmatics of using tests in developmental career counseling which Super has evolved, as is true of his entire approach, synthesizes the best of other orientations into a coherent method for disseminating psychometrics to the client, so that they will be maximally useful. The rationale for his use of tests stems from the distinction between *saturation* and *precision* testing, the former referring to a battery of tests administered to the client usually after a short, preliminary interview (as in trait-and-factor career counseling), and the latter designating individual test administration throughout the course of career counseling. With reference to precision testing, Super (1950) describes it as: "testing which is done as part of the counseling process, to get needed facts as these facts are needed and as the individual is ready to use them. It is *testing-in-counseling*" (p. 96). As such the client is intimately involved in selecting, taking and interpreting the tests, and, as a consequence, the likelihood increases that "the test results will be accepted and used intelligently by the client" (p. 96). This is particularly the case if the counselor orients the client with respect to the precision use of tests in career counseling. Structuring how the process will unfold, both verbally and nonverbally, gives the client an explicit expectation of what is going to happen and counteracts the stereotype of saturation testing which many clients bring to the initial interview (Super and Crites, 1962, pp. 613-620). The thrust of using tests in developmental career counseling, then, is to maximize their value in decision making (1) by administering them in a discriminating way, and (2) by involving the client in every phase of the process.

3. *Occupational information.* To inform the client about the structure of the world of work, occupational trends and forecasts, job duties and tasks, and employment opportunities, traditional types of occupational information can be presented by brochures, pamphlets or volumes like the *Occupational Outlook Handbook*. The most appropriate information for developmental career counseling, however, is the description of career patterns in different occupational pursuits. There have been some studies of career patterns, notably those of Davidson and Anderson (1937) and Miller and Fromm (1951), but they are out of date and dealt only with occupational level, not field. Super (1954) observes that there are at least six kinds of descriptive data on career patterns which are needed for developmental career counseling:

1. What are the typical entry, intermediate, and regular adult occupations of persons from different socio-economic levels?
2. To what extent do 'regular adult occupations' exist, and what is the relationship between parental socio-economic level and having a regular adult occupation?

3. What are the lines and rates of movement from entry toward regular adult occupation?
4. What factors are related to the direction and rate of movement from one job or occupation to another?
5. What is the relationship between occupational field and factors such as accessibility of the occupation or industry, and the possession of various aptitudes, values, and personality characteristics?
6. What is the relationship of differences between actual and parental occupational levels to possible causal factors such as accessibility of the occupation or industry, and the possession of aptitudes, interests, values, personality characteristics? (pp. 17–18).

Unfortunately, both private publishers and governmental agencies, as well as professional organizations, continue to proliferate occupational information which is largely irrelevant for developmental career counseling. In lieu of career pattern data, the career counselor must rely upon his/her knowledge of career psychology, leavened with astute observation and personal experience.

Comments. The hallmark of developmental career counseling is its synthesis of several theoretical and procedural strains, particularly the trait-and-factor and client-centered. But it goes beyond these and casts them into the context of the client's ongoing career development, which Super (1957b) aptly characterizes as "coterminal" with career counseling. Some may contend, however, that even as comprehensive an approach as this suffers from conceptual lacunae which make it less than optimally effective. Psychodynamically-oriented career counselors might question the basically descriptive or normative, rather than explanatory, nature of developmental concepts and principles, whereas certain behavioristically-inclined career counselors might contend that the historical focus of developmental career counseling is unnecessary, since career behavior is largely conditioned by its consequences, not its antecedents. Perhaps these are less shortcomings of commission than they are of omission. Only recently have measures of career maturity (Super, 1970) been constructed and related to other aspects of personality functioning (Crites, 1973). Likewise, conceptualization of learning models of career development has just begun (Crites, 1971), but research designed to test them has been initiated (Oliver, 1973). All of which leads to the conclusion that, although developmental career counseling may still be incomplete in certain respects, it is the most comprehensive and coherent system of assisting clients with career problems which has as yet been formulated, and it may be refined even further by articulating its relationship to learning phenomena and processes.

Behavioral Career Counseling

It is more accurate to refer to the *model* for this approach in the plural than the singular. Goodstein (1972) observes that, although they share common antecedents in the experimental psychology of learning, there are two distinct orientations in behavioral counseling: one which he terms the *indirect,* which focuses upon the linguistic mediational variables which precede and elicit overt responses, and the other the *direct,* which concentrates upon the consequences of responses—whether they are followed by a rewarding or punishing state of affairs. A further differentiation might also be made between two emphases within direct behavioral counseling, which might be labelled behavioral-*theoretic* and behavioral-*pragmatic.* As these designations connote, the former draws upon concepts and principles from learning theory to explain career behaviors and to deduce counseling methods for changing them, whereas the latter proceeds more inductively and empirically to identify those techniques which "work" in bringing about behavioral changes. The recognized spokesmen of the two viewpoints are Goodstein (1972) for the theoretic and Krumboltz and Thoresen (1969) for the pragmatic. These relative theoretical dispositions are juxtaposed to each other, when they differ pointedly, in the discussion of diagnosis, process, and outcome which follows as well as with indirect behavioral counseling:

1. *Diagnosis.* Goodstein (1972) attributes a central role to anxiety in the etiology of behavioral problems in general, and career choice problems in particular. He makes a detailed analysis of the part which anxiety can play, both as an antecedent and a consequent, in career indecision. He distinguishes between what might be called simple *indecision* and pervasive *indecisiveness* (Tyler, 1961). These two types of client choice problems can be conceptualized as shown in Figure 2 (Crites, 1969), where it can be seen that they develop sequentially from different origins. The principal etiological factors in simple indecision, according to Goodstein, is lack of information about self and work due to a limitation of experience, much as is assumed in the classical trait-and-factor approach. The client cannot make a choice, or possibly makes an unrealistic one, and as a consequence feels anxious about not having mastered the career developmental task (often expressed socially as "What are you going to do when you grow up?") of declaring an appropriate vocation. Note that in this process the anxiety is a *consequent,* not an antecedent, of the indecision. In contrast, indecisiveness arises from long-standing anxiety associated with decision making which precedes the task of career choice. It is not infrequently attributed by clients to domineering or over-demanding parents. For this individual, who is often paralyzed in making *any* kind of choice, anxiety also follows failure to decide upon a career, i.e., it is both an antecedent *and* a consequent, thereby compounding the client's feelings of discomfort and inadequacy. Goodstein (1972) concludes that: "One of the goals of diagnosis in counseling and therapy with such cases is the identification of the cues that arouse this anxiety so that the anxiety can be eliminated or reduced, permitting the client to now learn appropriate skills" (p. 261).

FIGURE 2. The Role of Anxiety in Indecision and Indecisiveness (After Goodstein, 1972, et passim).

(INDECISION)	*Limitation of Experience* (Insufficient opportunity to acquire or learn adaptive or adequate responses)	*Inadequate or Non-Adaptive Behavior* (No vocational choice; unrealistic vocational choice)	*Failure* (Unable to solve choice problem)	*Anxiety (Consequent)* (Conflict between inability to solve choice problem and social pressure to do so)
(INDECISIVENESS)	*Availability of Experience* (Sufficient opportunity to acquire or learn adaptive or adequate responses)	*Anxiety (Antecedent)* (Making a choice is anxiety arousing, because it may mean defying parents, becoming independent, etc., all of which "cue" anxiety)	*Nonuse of Learning Opportunities* (May have appropriate information for making a choice but anxiety prevents him from utilizing it, or anxiety may interfere with acquisition of information, even though opportunity to learn it is available)	*Inadequate or Non-Adaptive Behavior* (No vocational choice or in-realistic choice)

223

Krumboltz and Thoresen (1969) and their associates seldom mention either anxiety or diagnosis in their pragmatically-oriented version of behavioral career counseling. Rather, they prefer the rubrics *behavioral analysis* or *problem identification,* and they closely relate these to the specification of goals for counseling. That is, the client's difficulties are complementary to the goals ("outcomes") which client and counselor strive to achieve through their interactions with each other. Thus, if the client's presenting problem is that he/she has "no career choice," then the goal of the career counseling is to make a career choice. Krumboltz and Thoresen (1969) enumerate seven general categories of problems ("difficulties in formulating goals") which may beset clients in counseling:

1. The problem is someone else's behavior.
2. The problem is expressed as a feeling.
3. The problem is the absence of a goal.
4. The problem is that the desired behavior is undesirable.
5. The problem is that the client does not know his behavior is inappropriate.
6. The problem is a choice conflict.
7. The problem is a vested interest in not identifying any problem (pp. 9–18).

Of these problems, those which bear upon career counseling are indecision ("absence of a goal"), unrealism ("expressed feeling" about overly high aspirations), and multipotentiality ("choice conflict" among equally desirable alternatives). Within each of these problem types, specific behaviors can be delineated as the goals of career counseling (see "Outcomes").

2. *Process.* In the behavioral-*theoretic* view of career counseling, if it is determined diagnostically that a client's decision-making problems are a function of antecedent anxiety, then it is assumed that this anxiety must be eliminated *before* effective cognitive consideration of career choice can be undertaken. In other words, the elimination of anxiety is a *sine qua non* for subsequent career decision making. In this case, then, the process of career counseling has two stages, much as Shoben (1949) has proposed for psychotherapy: during the first, the counselor attempts to eliminate the anxiety associated with decision making, whether career or otherwise, primarily through counterconditioning it; and in the second, after the client has been freed of the interfering effects of anxiety, instrumental learning can occur, in which the client can acquire those responses, for example, information seeking, needed to choose a career. If the client's problem is one of simple indecision, however, with no evidence of debilitating previous anxiety, then career counseling would begin with stage two, instrumental learning. What this client needs to learn is *how* to make a career choice, *which* options are available to him/her, *what* the consequences

of each are, etc.—in short, to be exposed to the experiences which have not been available in his/her prior career development. Thus, the process of career counseling, as deduced from behavior theory primarily by Goodstein (1972), varies with the etiology of the client's problem: if it involves antecedent anxiety there are the two stages of counterconditioning and instrumental learning, but if it stems from limited decision-making experiences, it consists only of instrumental learning.

Juxtaposed to this model is that of Krumboltz, Thoresen and others, the most recent exposition of which has been summarized by Krumboltz and Baker (1973), who outline eight steps taken by the counselor and client in the course of career counseling:

1. Defining the problem and the client's goals.
2. Agreeing mutually to achieve counseling goals.
3. Generating alternative problem solutions.
4. Collecting information about the alternatives.
5. Examining the consequences of the alternatives.
6. Revaluing goals, alternatives and consequences.
7. Making the decision or tentatively selecting an alternative contingent upon new developments and new opportunities.
8. Generalizing the decision-making process to new problems (p. 240).

This series of mutual actions on the part of the counselor and client generally follows informed opinion on how career decisions can best be made (Gelatt, 1962; Yabroff, 1969), but it is not necessarily invariant: "The sequence may vary, but the priorities remain" (Krumboltz and Baker, 1973, p. 240). Conspicuous by its absence in this process is any mention of anxiety or its reduction. Rather, the focus is upon "the external environment" (Krumboltz and Baker, 1973, p. 262). Behavioral-pragmatic career counseling, therefore, appears to be closely aligned with the view expressed by Eysenck (1960) and others that "anxiety elimination should not be the counselor's primary concern but rather that therapy should be directed at the elimination of nonadjustive behavior pattern (sic) and/or providing conditions for learning more adjustive responses" (Goodstein, 1972, p. 274).

3. *Outcomes.* The two hypothesized outcomes of behavioral-*theoretic* career counseling are (1) elimination or reduction of both antecedent and consequent anxiety, and/or (2) acquisition of decision-making skills. Whether both outcomes are expected depends upon the extent to which anxiety preceded the emergence of the client's problem, as mentioned previously. An experimental paradigm for evaluating the effectiveness of this variety of behavioral counseling has been designed (Crites, 1969) but not yet utilized in research. The goals of behavioral-*pragmatic* career counseling are akin to the general one of skill acquisition but are more idiosyncratic. Krumboltz (1966) states that any set of goals for counseling should satisfy three criteria:

1. *The goals of counseling should be capable of being stated differently for each individual client.* . . .
2. *The goals of counseling for each client should be compatible with, though not necessarily identical to, the values of the counselor.* . . .
3. *The degree to which the goals of counseling are attained by each client should be observable.* . . . (italics in original) (pp. 154–155).

Given these constraints, he then identifies three counseling goals which are consistent with them: (1) altering maladaptive behavior, (2) learning the decision-making process, and (3) preventing problems. Ultimately, however, Krumboltz (1966) contends that any "type of behavior change desired by a client and agreed to by his counselor" (p. 155) regardless of the above criteria, is an acceptable goal (outcome) of counseling, whether it deals with career or some other aspect of functioning.

The methods of behavioral career counseling, of whichever subspecies, sometimes strike counselors of other persuasions as "cookbookish" and unduly specific, and they question their expediency in terms of broader goals and values (Patterson, 1964), for example, the "self-actualization" of the client. The behaviorists are quick to reply that they subscribe fully to such ideals as "self-actualization," but "as a counseling goal, the abstract and ambiguous terminology makes it difficult for clients or counselors to know what they are trying to do and when they have succeeded" (Krumboltz and Thoresen, 1969, p. 2). Hence the emphasis upon, and commitment to, whatever counseling technique "works." What may seem like blatant pragmatism to some, however, is tempered by the behavioral career counselor's recognition of his/her relationship to the client as a basic dimension of their interaction, along with communication. Goodstein (1972) notes that:

> Several writers in this area, especially Wolpe (1958, 1969), point out the need for establishing a good interpersonal relationship as an integral part of the treatment process. Indeed, it has been noted that an essential role for the counselor to play is that of a reinforcing agent, a role that depends upon the developing counseling relationship (p. 281).

It should be understood, therefore, that the interview techniques, methods and test interpretation and uses of occupational information described below are sketched in relief against a background of the relationship which develops between counselor and client:

1. *Interview techniques.* For the alleviation of anxiety, particularly that which is etiologically significant in aberrant career decision-making processes, Goodstein (1972) proposed three procedures which are widely used in behaviorally-oriented psychotherapy and which are applicable to career counseling: (1) desensitization, (2) inhibitory conditioning, and (3) counterconditioning. He notes that these techniques are theoretically distinguishable, but that most "real-life attempts to

eliminate or reduce anxiety would seem to involve some combination of these methods, and it is difficult to find pure procedures" (p. 264). The most general, and hence most potent, of them is counterconditioning, which involves desensitization as well. For the acquisition of skills, for example, information-seeking, deliberation and decision behaviors, Goodstein recommends (1) counselor reinforcement of desired client responses, (2) social modeling and vicarious learning, and (3) discrimination learning. He discusses these techniques generally, and cites some examples, but he does not explicate them in nearly the detail provided by Krumboltz and Thoresen (1969) in their "casebook" for behavioral counseling. No attempt will be made here to review and summarize these procedures, except to note that none of them which are designed to reduce "self-defeating fears and anxiety" are also suggested by Krumboltz and Thoresen (1969) for improving "deficient decision-making skills." Again the fundamental variance between the behavioral-*theoretic* and behavioral-*pragmatic* conceptualizations of career counseling is highlighted, the role of anxiety in career problems being the differentium.

2. *Test interpretation.* Allusions to the use of tests in career counseling, much less extended discussions, by either those of a theoretical or pragmatic behavioral bent are difficult to find. The reason is, of course, that they subscribe to an S-R model of behavior, with or without intervening variables like anxiety, whereas most tests are constructed within an R-R model, with S (items) standardized across individuals (Underwood, 1957; Crites, 1961). In other words, test scores measure individual differences in behavior, but they seldom reflect individual-environment interactions, which are of primary concern to the behavioral career counselor. Consequently, traditional tests (aptitude, interest, personality) are typically eschewed and objective indices of behavior *in situ* are gathered, although some effort is being expended to assess S-R situations with paper-and-pencil instruments (Goldfried and D'Zurilla, 1969). Krumboltz and Baker (1973) do allow that "Objective empirical data can be useful to counselor and client in their study of outcome probabilities" (p. 255) as part of "examining the consequences of alternatives" (see "Process" above). In addition, they present a counselor-client dialogue, in which the counselor reports entrance test scores as expectancy data much as a client-centered career counselor would, viz., as simple statistical predictions. But they otherwise ignore tests, although they conclude from Thorndike's (1935) early study that interests "are assumed to be learned; they are acquired by experience" (p. 274). They reason further that "If interests are learned, then it should be possible to alter, shape, promote, or diminish them by means of experimental intervention" (p. 274), and they cite studies by Krumboltz, Sheppard, Jones, Johnson and Baker (1967) and by Krumboltz, Baker and Johnson (1968) which they interpret as confirmatory of this hypothesis.

3. *Occupational information.* Some of the most creative and imaginative contributions which have been made by behavioral career counselors are in the area of occupational information. Krumboltz and his associates (Krumboltz and Bergland, 1969; Bergland and Krumboltz, 1969; Hamilton and Krumboltz, 1969; Krumboltz and Sheppard, 1969) have systematically devised a set of problem-solving career kits which simulate selected activities from 20 different occupations, including accountant, electronics technician, police officer, X-ray technologist, etc. The specifications for these kits were as follows:

> (1) the problem should be realistic and representative of the type of problems faced by members of the occupation; (2) 95 per cent of the target population (high school students) should have no difficulty in reading the problem; (3) the problem should be considered intrinsically interesting by the majority of the target population; (4) at least 75 per cent of the target population should be able to read the material and solve the problem successfully within 50 minutes; (5) the problem should be completely self-contained and self-administered (Krumboltz and Sheppard, 1969).

Evidence from try-outs and evaluations by experts indicates that the kits largely fulfill these criteria. Results are also available from several studies (Krumboltz, Sheppard, Jones, Johnson and Baker, 1967; Krumboltz, Baker and Johnson, 1968) which establish that the kits are useful in stimulating further career exploration and decision making. Career counselors can use them with the expectation that clients will learn at least as much, if not considerably more, about different careers than they will from printed occupational information.

Comment. Krumboltz (1966b) has heralded the behavioral approach as no less than a "revolution in counseling," and the temptation to agree unreservedly would be great, were it not that several disquieting issues are yet to be resolved. Foremost among these concerns the role of anxiety in the etiology of problems in career decision making. If a counselor follows the current formulation of behavioral-*pragmatic* career counseling, he/she would take the client's presenting problem of "no choice," for example, at face value and most likely agree to work toward the goal of "deciding upon a career," using reinforcement and modeling and simulation in the process. For insufficient prior learning experiences, this would probably be effective career counseling, but for the client with pervasive indecisiveness the outcome would be problematical. How many of these clients have career counselors expended their best information-giving and decision-making efforts on, only to have them terminate counseling with the epitaph "Well, I still don't really know what I want to do." It is not long before the mounting frustration of the counselor prompts him/her to wonder whether there is some competing response tendency which inhibits the client from making a career decision, given the relevant information about self and work or not. The behavioral-*theoretic* point of view would posit that it is the anxiety associated with decision making, occasioned by punishing past experiences, which prevents the indecisive client from declaring a career choice. Once this anxiety has been sufficiently reduced, information-seeking and decisional responses can be learned, or made if they were already in the client's behavioral repertoire, and the instrumental phase of career counseling can proceed. A resolution of this issue, both theoretically and pragmatically, appears critical, if a coherent system of behavioral career counseling is to be formulated.

Summary

Each of the approaches to career counseling which has been reviewed makes a unique contribution to the ways in which clients can be assisted in their career decision making. From the trait-and-factor orientation, the model of "matching men and jobs" is as viable today as it was in yesteryear, and it finds expression, in one form or another, in most of the other approaches. The client-centered point of view has heightened the career counselor's sensitivity to the role which the client should play throughout the decision-making process and has highlighted the implementation of the self-concept in an occupational role. The psychodynamic framework broadens even more the scope of career counseling to encompass motivational constructs and conflicts within the context of interacting aspects of personal and career development, incorporating procedures from both the trait-and-factor and client-centered approaches for its implementation. Equally systematic, but with greater emphasis upon maturational than motivational factors in decision making, developmental career counseling accepts the client at whatever vocational life stage he/she has reached and attempts to increase the career maturity of the client by providing relevant conative and cognitive learning experiences. And, behavioral career counseling, whether direct or indirect, theoretic or pragmatic, has made counselors aware, as they have never been before, of the actual behaviors which they and their clients are striving to change. The task is now to synthesize these several theoretical and procedural contributions, each of which has its unique value but none of which is sufficient, into a comprehensive approach to career counseling that has both generality and specificity in its applicability. In a later paper, a "provisional try" will be made to accomplish this task.

References

ARBUCKLE, D. S. *Counseling: An introduction.* Boston: Allyn & Bacon, 1961.
BAER, M. F., and ROEBER, E. C. *Occupational information: Its nature and use.* Chicago: Science Research Associates, 1951.

BEALL, L., and BORDIN, E. S. The development and personality of engineers. *Personnel and Guidance Journal,* 1964, 43, 23–32.

BERGLAND, B. W., and KRUMBOLTZ, J. D. An optimal grade level for career exploration. *Vocational Guidance Quarterly,* 1969, 18, 29–33.

BIXLER, R. H., and BIXLER, V. H. Clinical counseling in vocational guidance. *Journal of Clinical Psychology,* 1945, 1, 186–190.

BIXLER, R. H., and BIXLER, V. H. Test interpretation in vocational counseling. *Educational and Psychological Measurement,* 1946, 6, 145–156.

BORDIN, E. S. Diagnosis in counseling and psychotherapy. *Educational and Psychological Measurement,* 1946, 6, 169–184.

BORDIN, E. S. *Psychological counseling.* New York: Appleton-Century-Crofts, 1955.

BORDIN, E. S. *Psychological counseling.* (2nd ed.) New York: Appleton-Century-Crofts, 1968.

BORDIN, E. S., and BIXLER, R. H. Test selection: A process of counseling. *Educational and Psychological Measurement,* 1946, 6, 361–373.

BORDIN, E. S., and KOPPLIN, D. A. Motivational conflict and vocational development. *Journal of Counseling Psychology,* 1973, 20, 154–161.

BORDIN, E. S., NACHMANN, B., and SEGAL, S. J. An articulated framework for vocational development. *Journal of Counseling Psychology,* 1963, 10, 107–116.

BRAYFIELD, A. H. Putting occupational information across. In A. H. Brayfield (Ed.), *Readings in modern methods of counseling.* New York: Appleton-Century-Crofts, 1950, 212–220.

BUEHLER, C. *Der menschliche Lebensauf als psychologisches Problem.* Leipzig: Hirzel, 1933.

BROWN, O. H. The client-centered approach to educational and vocational guidance. *The Personal Counselor,* 1947, 2, 1–5.

CAUTELA, J. R. The factor of psychological need in occupational choice. *Personnel and Guidance Journal,* 1959, 38, 46–48.

CHRISTENSEN, T. E. Functions of occupational information in counseling. *Occupations,* 1949, 28, 11–14.

COLBY, K. M. *A primer for psychotherapists.* New York: Ronald, 1951.

COMBS, A. Nondirective techniques and vocational counseling. *Occupations,* 1947, 25, 261–267.

COVNER, B. J. Nondirective interviewing techniques in vocational counseling. *Journal of Consulting Psychology,* 1947, 11, 70–73.

CRITES, J. O. A model for the measurement of vocational maturity. *Journal of Counseling Psychology,* 1961, 8, 255–259.

CRITES, J. O. *Vocational psychology.* New York: McGraw-Hill, 1969.

CRITES, J. O. The maturity of vocational attitudes and learning processes in adolescence. Paper presented at the 17th Annual Convention of the International Congress of Applied Psychology, Liege, Belgium, 1971.

CRITES, J. O. *Theory and research handbook for the Career Maturity Inventory.* Monterey, Calif.: CTB/McGraw-Hill, 1973.

CRITES, J. O. Career development processes: A model of vocational maturity. In E. L. Herr (Ed.), *Vocational guidance and human development.* Boston: Houghton Mifflin, in press.

DARLEY, J. G. The structure of the systematic case study in individual diagnosis and counseling. *Journal of Consulting Psychology,* 1940, 4, 215–220.

DARLEY, J. G. Conduct of the interview. In A. H. Brayfield (Ed.), *Readings in modern methods of counseling.* New York: Appleton-Century-Crofts, 1950. Pp. 265–272.

DAVIDSON, P. E., and ANDERSON, H. B. *Occupational mobility in an American community.* Palo Alto: Stanford Unversity Press, 1937.

DOLEYS, E. J. Are there "kinds" of counselors? *Counseling News and Views,* 1961, 13, 5–9.

DYMOND, R. F. Adjustment changes over therapy from self-sorts. In C. R. Rogers and R. F. Dymond (Eds.), *Psychotherapy and personality change.* Chicago: University of Chicago Press, 1954. Pp. 76–84.

EYSENCK, J. H. (Ed.) *Behavioral therapy and the neuroses.* New York: Macmillan, 1960.

FROEHLICH, C. P., and MOSER, W. E. Do counselees remember test scores? *Journal of Counseling Psychology,* 1954, 1, 149–152.

GALINSKY, M. D. Personality development and vocational choice of clinical psychologists and physicists. *Journal of Counseling Psychology,* 1962, 9, 299–305.

GAUDET, F. J., and KULICK, W. Who comes to a vocational guidance center? *Personnel and Guidance Journal,* 1954, 33, 211–215.

GELATT, A. B. Decision-making: A conceptual frame of reference for counseling. *Journal of Counseling Psychology,* 1962, 9, 240–245.

GINZBERG, E., GINSBURG, S. W., AXELRAD, S., and HERMAN, J. L. *Occupational choice.* New York: Columbia University Press, 1951.

GOLDFRIED, M. R., and D'ZURILLA, T. J. A behavioral-analytic model for assessing competence: In C. D. Spielberger (Ed.), *Current topics in clinical and community psychology.* Vol. 1. New York: Academic Press, 1969. Pp. 151–196.

GOODSTEIN, L. D. Behavioral views of counseling. In B. Stefflre and W. H. Grant (Eds.), *Theories of counseling.* New York: McGraw-Hill, 1972. Pp. 243–286.

GOODSTEIN, L. D., CRITES, J. O., HEILBRUN, A. B., JR., and REMPEL, P. P. The use of the California Psychological Inventory in a university counseling service. *Journal of Counseling Psychology,* 1961, 8, 147–153.

GRUMMON, D. L. Client-centered theory. In B. Stefflre and W. H. Grant (Eds.), *Theories of counseling.* (2nd ed.) New York: McGraw-Hill, 1972. Pp. 73–135.

HAHN, M. E., and KENDALL, W. E. Some comments in defense of non-directive counseling. *Journal of Consulting Psychology,* 1947, 11, 74–81.

HAMILTON, J. A., and KRUMBOLTZ, J. D. Simulated work experience: How realistic should it be? *Personnel and Guidance Journal,* 1969, 48, 39–44.

HART, J. T., and TOMLINSON, T. M. (Eds.) *New directions in client-centered therapy.* Boston: Houghton Mifflin, 1970.

KAMM, R. B., and WRENN, C. G. Client acceptance of self-information in counseling. *Educational and Psychological Measurement,* 1950, 10, 32–42.

KIESLER, D. J. Some myths of psychotherapy research and the search for a paradigm. *Psychological Bulletin,* 1966, 65, 110–136.

KILBY, R. W. Some vocational counseling methods. *Educational and Psychological Measurement,* 1949, 19, 173–192.

KING, P. T., and BENNINGTON, K. F. Psychoanalysis and counseling. In B. Stefflre and W. H. Grant (Eds.), *Theories of counseling.* New York: McGraw-Hill, 1972. Pp. 177–242.

KRUMBOLTZ, J. D. Behavioral goals for counseling. *Journal of Counseling Psychology,* 1966, 13, 153–159. (a)

KRUMBOLTZ, J. D. (Ed.) *Revolution in counseling: Implications of behavioral science.* Boston: Houghton Mifflin, 1966. (b)

KRUMBOLTZ, J. D., and BAKER, R. D. Behavioral counseling for vocational decision. In H. Borow (Ed.), *Career guidance for a new age.* Boston: Houghton Mifflin, 1973. Pp. 235–283.

KRUMBOLTZ, J. D., BAKER, R. D., and JOHNSON, R. G. Vocational problem-solving experiences for stimulating career exploration and interest: Phase II.

Final Report, Office of Education Grant 4-7-070111-2890. School of Education, Stanford University, 1968.

KRUMBOLTZ, J. D., and BERGLAND, B. W. Experiencing work almost like it is. *Educational Technology,* 1969, 9, 47–49.

KRUMBOLTZ, J. D., SHEPPARD, L. E., JONES, G. B., JOHNSON, R. G., and BAKER, R. D. Vocational problem-solving experiences for stimulating career exploration and interest. Final Report, Office of Education, Stanford University, 1967.

KRUMBOLTZ, J. D., and SHEPPARD, L. E. Vocational problem-solving experiences. In J. D. Krumboltz and C. E. Thoresen (Eds.), *Behavioral counseling: Cases and techniques.* New York: Holt, Rinehart & Winston, 1969. Pp. 293–306.

KRUMBOLTZ, J. D., and THORESEN, C. E. (Eds.), *Behavioral counseling: Cases and techniques.* New York: Holt, Rinehart & Winston, 1969.

LOFQUIST, L. H. *Vocational counseling with the physically handicapped.* New York: Appleton-Century-Crofts, 1957.

MILLER, D. C., and FORM, W. H. *Industrial sociology.* New York: Harper & Row, 1951.

NACHMANN, B. Childhood experience and vocational choice in law, dentistry, and social work. *Journal of Counseling Psychology,* 1960, 7, 243–250.

OLIVER, L. Verbal reinforcement of career choice realism in relation to career attitude maturity. Unpublished manuscript, Department of Psychology, University of Maryland, 1973.

PARSONS, F. *Choosing a vocation.* Boston: Houghton Mifflin, 1909.

PATERSON, D. G., and DARLEY, J. G. *Men, women, and jobs.* Minneapolis: University of Minnesota Press, 1936.

PATTERSON, C. H. Counseling: Self-clarification and the helping relationship. In H. Borow (Ed.), *Man in a world at work.* Boston: Houghton Mifflin, 1964, 434–459.

PATTERSON, C. H. *Theories of counseling and psychotherapy.* (2nd ed.) New York: Harper & Row, 1973.

PEPINSKY, H. B., and PEPINSKY, P. N. *Counseling theory and practice.* New York: Ronald, 1954.

ROBINSON, F. P. *Principles and procedures in student counseling.* New York: Harper, 1950.

ROGERS, C. R. *Counseling and psychotherapy.* Boston: Houghton Mifflin, 1942.

ROGERS, C. R. *Client centered therapy.* Boston: Houghton Mifflin, 1951.

ROGERS, C. R. The necessary and sufficient conditions of therapeutic personality change. *Journal of Consulting Psychology,* 1957, 21, 95–103.

ROGERS, C. R. A theory of therapy, personality, and interpersonal relationships, as developed in the client-centered framework. In S. Koch (Ed.), *Psychology: A study of a science.* Study I. *Conceptual and systematic.* Vol. 3. *Formulations of the person and the social context.* New York: McGraw-Hill, 1959. Pp. 184–256.

ROGERS, C. R. *On becoming a person.* Boston: Houghton Mifflin, 1961.

RUSALEM, H. New insights on the role of occupational information in counseling. *Journal of Counseling Psychology,* 1954, 1, 84–88.

SAMLER, J. Occupational exploration in counseling: A proposed reorientation. In H. Borow (Ed.), *Man in a world at work.* Boston: Houghton Mifflin, 1964. Pp. 411–433.

SANDERSON, H. *Basic concepts in vocational guidance.* New York: McGraw-Hill, 1954.

SEEMAN, J. A study of client self-selection of tests in vocational counseling. *Educational and Psychological Measurement,* 1948, 8, 327–346.

SEGAL, S. J. A psychoanalytic analysis of personality factors in vocational choice. *Journal of Counseling Psychology,* 1961, 8, 202–210.

SHOBEN, E. J., JR. Psychotherapy as a problem in learning theory. *Psychological Bulletin,* 1949, 46, 366–392.

SUPER, D. E. *The dynamics of vocational adjustment.* New York: Harper, 1942.

SUPER, D. E. *Appraising vocational fitness.* New York: Harper, 1949.

SUPER, D. E. Testing and using test results in counseling. *Occupations,* 1950, 29, 95–97.

SUPER, D. E. Vocational adjustment: Implementing a self-concept. *Occupations,* 1951, 30, 88–92.

SUPER, D. E. Career patterns as a basis for vocational counseling. *Journal of Counseling Psychology,* 1954, 1, 12–20.

SUPER, D. E. The dimensions and measurement of vocational maturity. *Teachers College Record,* 1955, 57, 151–163.

SUPER, D. E. The preliminary appraisal in vocational counseling. *Personnel and Guidance Journal,* 1957, 36, 154–161. (a)

SUPER, D. E. *The psychology of careers.* New York: Harper, 1957. (b)

SUPER, D. E. The critical ninth grade: Vocational choice or vocational exploration? *Personnel and Guidance Journal,* 1960, 39, 106–109.

SUPER, D. E. (Ed.) *Computer-assisted counseling.* New York: Teachers College Press, 1970.

SUPER, D. E. (Ed.) *Measuring vocational maturity for counseling and evaluation.* Washington, D. C.: National Vocational Guidance Association, in press.

SUPER, D. E., and BACHRACH, P. B. *Scientific careers and vocational development theory.* New York: Teachers College Bureau of Publications, 1957.

SUPER, D. E., and OVERSTREET, P. L. *The vocational maturity of ninth grade boys.* New York: Teachers College Bureau of Publications, 1960.

SUPER, D. E., and CRITES, J. O. *Appraising vocational fitness.* (Rev. ed.) New York: Harper & Row, 1962.

THOMPSON, A. S. A rationale for vocational guidance. *Personnel and Guidance Journal,* 1954, 32, 533–535.

THORNDIKE, E. L. *Adult interests.* New York: Macmillan, 1935.

TYLER, L. E. *The work of the counselor.* (2nd ed.) New York: Appleton-Century-Crofts, 1961.

UNDERWOOD, B. J. *Psychological research.* New York: Appleton-Century-Crofts, 1957.

WILLIAMS, J. E. Changes in self and other perceptions following brief educational-vocational counseling. *Journal of Counseling Psychology,* 1962, 9, 18–30.

WILLIAMS, J. E., and HILLS, D. A. More on brief educational-vocational counseling. *Journal of Counseling Psychology,* 1962, 9, 366–368.

WILLIAMSON, E. G. *How to counsel students.* New York: McGraw-Hill, 1939. (a)

WILLIAMSON, E. G. The clinical method of guidance. *Review of Educational Research,* 1939, 9, 214-217. (b)

WILLIAMSON, E. G. Vocational counseling: Trait-factor theory. In B. Stefflre (Ed.), *Theories of counseling.* New York: McGraw-Hill, 1965. Pp. 193-214.

WILLIAMSON, E. G. Trait-factor theory and individual differences. In B. Stefflre and W. H. Grant (Eds.), *Theories of counseling.* (2d ed.) New York: McGraw-Hill, 1972. Pp. 136-176.

WITRYOL, S. L., and BOLY, L. F. Positive diagnosis in personality counseling of college students. *Journal of Counseling Psychology,* 1954, 1, 63-69.

WOLPE, J. *Psychotherapy by reciprocal inhibition.* Stanford, Calif.: Stanford University Press, 1958.

WOLPE, J. *The practice of behavior therapy.* New York: Pergamon, 1969.

YABROFF, W. Learning decision making. In J. D. Krumboltz, and C. E. Thoresen (Eds.), *Behavioral counseling: Cases and techniques.* New York: Holt, Rinehart, & Winston, 1969. Pp. 329-343.

UNIT BIBLIOGRAPHY

BERDIE, RALPH F. "The 1980 Counselor: Applied Behavioral Scientist." *Personnel and Guidance Journal,* **50** (1972), 451–456.

BIGGERS, JULIAN L. "The Use of Information in Vocational Decision-Making." *Vocational Guidance Quarterly,* **19** (1971), 171–176.

COCHRAN, DONALD J., MICHAEL H. VINITSKY, and PENELOPE M. WARREN. "Career Counseling: Beyond 'Test and Tell.'" *Personnel and Guidance Journal* **52** (1974) 659–664.

COCHRAN, LESLIE H. "Counselors and the Noncollege-bound Student." *Personnel and Guidance Journal,* **52** (1974), 582–585.

CRITES, JOHN O. "Career Counseling: A Review of Major Approaches." *The Counseling Psychologist,* **10** (1974), 3–23.

DOLLIVER, ROBERT H., and RICHARD E. NELSON. "Assumptions Regarding Vocational Counseling." *The Vocational Guidance Quarterly,* **24** (1975), 12–19.

EHRLE, RAYMOND A. "Vocational Maturity, Vocational Evaluation, and Occupational Information." *Vocational Guidance Quarterly,* **19** (1970), 41–45.

FORER, BERTRAM R. "Framework for the Use of Clinical Techniques in Vocational Counseling." *Personnel and Guidance Journal,* **43** (1965), 868–872.

GRAFF, ROBERT W., DAVID RAQUE, and STEVEN DANISH. "Vocational-Educational Counseling Practices: A Survey of University Counseling Centers." *Journal of Counseling Psychology,* **21** (1974), 579–580.

HAMILTON, JACK A., and G. BRIAN JONES. "Individualizing Educational and Vocational Guidance Designing a Prototype Program." *Vocational Guidance Quarterly,* **79** (1971), 293–299.

HEALY, CHARLES C. "Toward a Replicable Method of Group Career Counseling." *Vocational Guidance Quarterly,* **21** (1973), 214–221.

HERSHENSON, DAVID B. "Techniques for Assisting Life-Stage Vocational Development." *Personnel and Guidance Journal,* **8** (1969), 776–780.

HOPPOCK, ROBERT, and BERNARD NOVICK. "The Occupational Information Consultant: A New Profession?" *Personnel and Guidance Journal,* **49** (1971), 555–558.

JAQUES, MARCELINE, and DAVID HERSHENSON. "Culture, Work, and Deviance Implications for Rehabilitation Counseling." *Rehabilitation Counseling Bulletin,* **13** (1970), 49–56.

JENSEN, VERN H. "A Model for Extending Career Concepts." *Vocational Guidance Quarterly,* **21** (1972), 115–119.

JEPSEN, DAVID A. "Vocational Decision-Making Strategy-Types: An Exploratory Study." *The Vocational Guidance Quarterly,* **23** (1974), 17–22.

LARAMORE, DARRYL. "Counselors Make Occupational Information Packages." *Vocational Guidance Quarterly,* **19** (1971), 220–224.

MAC KAY, WILLIAM R. "The Decision Fallacy: Is It If or When?" *The Vocational Guidance Quarterly,* **23** (1975), 227–231.

MARSHALL, PATRICIA. "Career Guidance Through Group Dynamics." *Manpower Magazine,* **6** (1974), 14–18.

MENCKE, REED A., and DONALD J. COCHRAN. "Impact of a Counseling Outreach Workshop on Vocational Development." *Journal of Counseling Psychology,* **21** (1974), 185–190.

MORRILL, WESTON H., and DAVID J. FORREST. "Dimensions of Counseling

For Career Development." *Personnel and Guidance Journal,* **49** (1970) 299–305.

NATIONAL EMPLOYMENT COUNSELORS ASSOCIATION. "Role of the Employment Counselor." *Journal of Employment Counseling,* **4** (1975) 148–153.

NATIONAL ADVISORY COUNCIL ON VOCATIONAL EDUCATION. "Counseling and Guidance: A Call for Change." *Vocational Guidance Quarterly,* **21** (1972), 97–101.

PARKER, CAROL, STEVEN BUNCH, and RICHARD HAGBERG. "Group Vocational Guidance with College Students." *The Vocational Guidance Quarterly,* **23** (1974) 168–172.

PETTY, M. M. "Relative Effectiveness of Four Combinations of Oral and Written Presentations of Job Related Information to Disadvantaged Trainees." *Journal of Applied Psychology,* **59** (1974), 105–106.

WESTBROOK, FRANKLIN D. "A Comparison of Three Methods of Group Vocational Counseling." *Journal of Counseling Psychology,* **21** (1974), 502–506.

part 7
Placement Process

Because schools and colleges are more concerned about job placement than they were, there is a growing demand for such services. This demand evolved out of a two-fold recognition: of the needs of students who are not college bound and of the responsibility of the schools to give them attention and concrete help.

The problem of who is responsible for job placement has long plagued vocational guidance programs. It is now being worked out, and employment services, schools, and social agencies are integrating their programs. Placement involves more than just getting jobs for students. It means preparing them to be successful in a job seeking program and in their roles as employees.

An important part of the placement process is the follow-up procedure, which offers support and guidance to students. Placement is not a dumping ground for students who do not achieve academically, as it has been viewed in the past; rather, it is a viable resource for change and growth in the schools, as well as for individual students who once would have been labeled losers.

Counseling—A Friend to Placement

Robert E. Philbrick

Many counselors in the federal/state employment system have watched with interest and some pain the changing attitudes of the agency planners toward employment counseling during the last few years. In 1964 when the Manpower Development Training Act (MDTA) became a standard for action, counseling gained new status. Recognition of wasted or undeveloped manpower resources became popular. Programs such as Youth Opportunity Centers, Community Action, Job Corps, and Neighborhood Youth Corps were designed to reach out to poor, disadvantaged, minority groups—the non–job-ready people having severe barriers to successful employment. Budget and staff resources were marshalled to find innovative ways to serve people needing special help, people that the employment service rarely served. To assist these individuals the role of counseling took on a new meaning and depth.

Professional development and training of counselors for the employment service was encouraged and became a priority activity. Studies were made concerning community need for services. Materials and resources were developed. Social agencies united their strength and expertise. Skills and techniques for helping to change behavior were sharpened. As a result many people were helped in their employability development.

The negative outcomes were that the employment service neglected to maintain close relations with the employer community and to keep up sufficient placement strength. In effect there was a deemphasis of job referral and placement. An imbalance of services occurred favoring counseling—a supportive activity—at the expense of weakening the resources most needed in helping the applicant become self-sufficient.

For the last two years members of Congress, the Department of Labor, and the Manpower Administration have changed their attitudes and, thus, their priorities and program emphasis. Referring people to jobs resulting in placement is now the top priority activity in the employment service. The change has been so compelling, pulling budget and staff resources in that direction, that counseling is struggling to remain viable. The conflict arises when a set budget is available and

Reprinted from *Journal of Employment Counseling*, **12**:18–25 (March 1975). Copyright 1975 American Personnel and Guidance Association. Reprinted with permission.

decisions need to be made concerning allocation of funds. An increased outlay in one area necessarily decreases expenditures in another. The question of allocation need not be dichotomous, that is, placement or counseling. Rather, how can a balanced program be reached to help the people in the communities in solving their employment problems?

A New Opportunity

With the change in emphasis by the policy makers, a new challenge and opportunity stand before state employment service planners. The implementation of the Comprehensive Employment and Training Act (CETA) of 1973 provides for prime sponsors, usually a local government unit, to contract with the employment service for services, especially counseling. Nearly every piece of manpower legislation includes the delivery of employment counseling. The employment service should be prepared to fulfill this obligation.

Another innovation is the introduction of the Balanced Placement Formula. Briefly, this is a plan whereby state budget allocations are made by considering (1) state employment agency plan of service—how well employment and manpower services were planned and accomplished; (2) productivity—the number of placements per staff member, planned and accomplished; (3) the types of jobs filled; (4) the pay rates of the jobs filled; (5) the duration of jobs; and (6) the types of applicants placed. These factors are weighted and compared with a national standard. From this, two-thirds of a state's budget is computed. Two other factors considered are services to employers (for example, penetration rate—rate of jobs registered compared to those available—and job cancellation rate) and service to applicants (for example, per cent of counselees taking the General Aptitude Test Battery, number of Scholastic Aptitude Test Batteries given, etc.). From this orientation a state budget is calculated. Seven per cent of the total state employment service budget is allocated for counseling.

Within the framework of these concepts and other proposed legislation, counseling is an important component to be integrated into a meaningful perspective for serving the employment needs of the community. With the resources available, the employment service faces the challenge of developing a balanced program to serve the applicant and the employer effectively.

The Problem

Most people contact the employment service as applicants seeking suitable employment or as employers seeking qualified workers. Rarely does a person come in for counseling only. The primary goal of the agency is to help satisfy the individual employment needs of workers and employers. Several services are available for these purposes, for example, employer relations, labor market information, test development, occupational analysis, placement, and counseling.

Since the established priority for the employment service is placement, the position of counseling in the fulfillment of that goal becomes an issue when the balance of services is considered and a plan of action for budget and staff use is designed. An accounting of the contributions of counseling services is needed. To illustrate and emphasize the effect of counseling on placement, studies of individuals placed were conducted in the Utah State Department of Employment Security for the fiscal years 1973 and 1974.

Data Collection

The Utah agency is operated on a computerized job match system. All applications and all job orders received by the agency are stored in a computer so that applicants can be matched with jobs. Whenever an individual receives service or a job order is acted on, the interviewer initiates a transaction ledger which informs the computer of the action and is subsequently recorded in the proper place in the computer. Thus, the Employment Service Automated Recording System (ESARS) keeps a record of all transactions for each applicant and each job order.

A sampling technique has been devised where the computer is queried for the necessary information. This sampling technique randomly selects a 40 per cent sample with a very low error factor (i.e., the sample varies only slightly from the total population recorded in the computer). The study used the following questions: (1) How many applicants were available for work? (2) How many people were placed? (3) How many people were counseled? (4) How many counseled applicants were placed? Placement rates were computed on each of the following variables: sex, age, marital status, disadvantaged, veteran, handicapped, and minority.

Two sets of data have been gathered for fiscal year (FY) 1974 and FY 1973. Even though the total applicant intake of FY 1974 increased by 16 per cent over FY 1973, the percentages of total available applicants, applicants placed, applicants counseled, and counseled applicants placed remained similar for the two years. The major part of this discussion is based on the 1974 figures, which are supported by the study of the previous year.

Applicant Data

Description of Applicants
During FY 1974, 154,096 individuals contacted the Utah employment service local offices and filed applications for employment. The following are some of the characteristics of the population studied: 57 per

cent were male; 50 per cent were in the age range of 22–24 years; 13 per cent were 45 years and older; 43 per cent were married; 20 per cent were separated, divorced, or widowed; 90 per cent were Caucasian; 10 per cent were from minority groups; 17 per cent were classified as disadvantaged; and 16 per cent were handicapped.

Applicant Placement Rate

The placement rate of applicants looking for work who contacted the Utah local offices is important. Table 1 indicates that of the total applicant intake in FY 1974, 27.5 per cent were placed with an employer in the community. This varied one percentage point from the preceding year. With the increase in intake there was also an increase in placement; however, the increase in intake (16.2 per cent) was higher than the increase in placement (12 per cent). Other variables may have been operating to keep the percentage of Utah placement somewhat constant.

Another observation, although not reflected in Table 1, was that people possessing certain characteristics often thought of as barriers to employment, such as being handicapped, a minority group member, or separated, divorced, or widowed, were placed in jobs at a higher rate than other applicants when processed through regular channels. The following are the percentages of applicants with these characteristics who were placed in jobs: minority, 39 per cent; veteran handicapped, 46 per cent; handicapped, 33 per cent; and separated, divorced, or widowed, 34 per cent. The key seems to be characteristics that make a person different or require special attention from the interviewer. Perhaps interviewers conducted more thorough appraisals and worked harder to place these people. In some cases legislation mandates the services certain groups are to receive.

Undoubtedly there were many others who found employment on their own as a result of the local office contact. These may be people who needed job information, some direction and encouragement, or the experience of being interviewed or counseled, from which they learned what kinds of information they needed when presenting themselves to a potential employer. Since we have no statistics to show the number of people who found jobs on their own as a result of help received from the employment service, we can only speculate about them. Further study is needed on this group.

Placement of Counseled Applicants

From the total of available applicants, 6.2 per cent were referred for counseling. This is a small portion of the total intake that received counseling services. There is reason to believe that many applicants who needed or could have benefited from the additional service of counseling were not recognized or referred by the Utah agency interviewers. Part of this may be the result of less emphasis on coun-

TABLE 1. CHANGES IN UTAH DEPARTMENT OF EMPLOYMENT SECURITY APPLICANT INTAKE AND PLACEMENT FOR FY 1973 AND FY 1974

APPLICANTS	APPLICANTS INTAKE			APPLICANTS PLACED			% APPLICANTS PLACED		
	FY 1974	FY 1973	% CHANGE	FY 1974	FY 1973	% CHANGE	FY 1974	FY 1973	% CHANGE
Total number of applicants	154,096	132,572	16.2	42,388	37,804	12.1	27.5	28.5	—1.0
Applicants counseled	9,515	8,789	8.3	5,458	4,548	20.0	57.4	51.7	5.7
Times counseled									
1	5,345	4,809	11.1	2,400	1,982	21.1	44.9	41.2	3.7
2	1,741	1,650	5.5	1,038	928	11.9	59.6	56.2	3.4
3	798	880	—9.3	618	555	11.4	77.4	63.1	14.3
4	578	435	32.9	455	307	48.2	78.7	70.6	8.1
5–9	838	672	24.7	743	523	42.1	88.7	77.8	10.9
Over 10	218	344	—36.6	206	257	—19.8	94.5	75.0	19.5

seling which reduces the available staff. The people most often referred for counseling were disadvantaged, veterans, minorities, separated, divorced, or widowed, handicapped, and in the age range of 22 to 44 years. Men were referred to counseling at about the same percentage rate of intake as women. However, since men came to the employment office more often than women, they comprised about 59 per cent of the counseling cases.

How many of the people sent to counseling were placed in jobs? Does counseling improve placement chances? The answers to these questions are significant for the administrative planner.

As noted in Table 1, 57.4 per cent of the counseled applicants were placed in jobs. The chances of an applicant's finding work more than doubles with the added advantage of counseling. The percentage of applicants placed increased from 27.5 per cent to nearly 45 per cent with one counseling interview. Of the counseled applicants 63 per cent had only one or two counseling interviews. It appears that the number of counseling interviews significantly improves an applicant's chances of placement. Eleven per cent of the applicants had five or more interviews and of these only 2 per cent had more than ten. A question arises as to the value of time expended beyond 5 to 10 interviews. Counselors may be dealing with problems that should be handled by some other agency. They should increase their skills in being effective sooner or discerning more readily when to refer the applicant for special assistance. The employment counselors in Utah significantly cut down the number of long-term counseling contacts during FY 1974, as compared to FY 1973. This appears to be the counselors' response to the priority goal of replacement by helping applicants to start working sooner.

Conclusions

The information in this study demonstrates that counseling services make a positive contribution to job placement in the Utah employment service. Surely there is no magic in counseling, but one may wonder what happens in that setting which improves the applicant's chances of finding work. Several factors may contribute to a positive outcome:

1. Because of the time frame and the counselor's skill and orientation toward people, counseling gives identity to the applicant, for whom the staff serves as an agent. A strong commitment for a job search is made by both the applicant and the counselor.
2. Humanizing the job seeking experience may alter the attitudes of the applicant. Personalized service may stimulate more cooperation in sharing information, more willingness to take time for assessment and modification of employment barriers, and the

establishment of greater receptiveness to employment services.

3. During the interviews, a counselor-applicant relationship develops in which the counselor becomes a significant influence on the applicant. Thus, success in carrying out an employability plan can be partly attributed to the applicant's desire to please the counselor or to justify the faith felt toward someone who is offering help.

4. Counselor services help applicants to meet, define, and subsesequently alleviate barriers to their employability.

5. Through counseling the applicant becomes more actively involved, serving as a resource and a functioning component of the placement effort.

Recommendations

To channel all applicants through the counseling process is neither reasonable nor desirable. National, regional, and local estimates suggested that approximately 25 per cent of the population contacting the employment service for work needed or would have benefited from counseling. On-site evaluations at several Utah local offices indicated that 35 per cent of the applicants contacting the offices needed counseling. Many of these individuals would not have been placed by the service or have found suitable employment on their own without some counseling intervention. In Utah, where only 6 per cent of the applicants were referred to this basic service, the counseling needs of many are being overlooked. A more thorough analysis describing the nature of the intervention (counseling) and identifying the factors contributing to successful placement is needed.

It is not desirable to make every interviewer a counselor; however, some of the components of counseling could be assimilated in the placement process to improve effectiveness. For the employment service to carry out its mission a variety of services, including employer services, placement, counseling, testing, and recording, must be available. Success depends on the balance and interrelationship of these services in meeting the needs of the community.

Rather than increase the volume of applicants to improve the placement rate the agency should improve its service to current applicants. Of course, a good job market is necessary for the greatest success. Other considerations in attaining priority goals might include:

1. Improving the assessment tool—the basic employment service applicant record does not lend itself to effective service. This is particularly true in Utah where the application is designed to meet ESARS requirements and the computerized job matching system. (This will take some imagination to improve.)

2. Creating a better balance between placement and counseling, which will require management to consider counseling as an integral

part of placement. (This is easy to say—but how to do it is a challenging problem.)

3. Establishing a one-week service for applicants in keeping with the one-day service for employers. Placement interviewers and counselors should exert a concentrated effort to place the applicant as soon as possible. Each placement should be in response to some vocational plan or a comprehensive employability development plan.

4. Continuing to refine the means whereby job-ready applicants could have faster and easier access to available jobs, minimizing staff intervention in placement. Initially this may be for selected groups where some categories of individuals can initiate a self-referral process. Perhaps this group could have query access to the computer.

5. Updating interviewing skills for placement interviewers and counselors to improve applicant assessment. Assimilating into daily activities the kinds of skills and attitudes that were demonstrated in the recently prepared "Experimental Approach to the Interview Process" training in addition to a refresher session on "Recognizing Counseling Need" may help in this area. Training in assessment and appraisal techniques must also be considered. There is an assessment and appraisal training package now available.

6. Comparing the value of the time spent by interviewers with applicants who were placed and the value of the time spent with the 70 per cent who were not placed.

The initial assessment of an applicant's needs is a vital key in serving both the employer and the applicant. This may call for a more extensive appraisal in the application process and may be a bit more costly than present methods. Meaningful appraisal interviews take a little longer than the normal process of rushing individuals through inadequate and often worthless applications. The outcome of this approach may be far more impressive when compared to the practice of no service beyond registration which appears to be so prevalent in services now.

The data included in this study show that counseling services are a positive support to employment service placement activities. These services should be an integrated part of the overall employment service program. The counselors should be well trained and skilled in giving professional assistance to those needing help. Their competence will be quickly noted by colleagues and the applicants they serve. The objectives of counseling should continue to be within the framework of employability development leading to the successful employment or placement of the applicant. Individualizing service to job seekers and employers will greatly enhance the value and success of employment services to the community.

A Strategy for Establishing a School-Based Job Placement Program

Jimmy G. Cheek

Most vocational teachers agree that one of the primary goals of vocational education is training students for employment. Many school districts, however, do not provide a formally organized job placement program for vocational students leaving school and seeking employment. What if you, the vocational agriculture teacher, assumed the role of change agent and sought to introduce the innovation of a school-based job placement program into your school district? How could you accomplish this change? What would be your strategy? The following is a step-by-step description of a strategy that you could use in bringing about this change in your school district.

Step 1: Contacting the School Administrators

The initial phase of the change strategy involves contacting the school administrators to present a rationale for a job placement program for vocational education students and to seek approval to investigate the need for a job placement program in the school district. Using this approach, school administrators would be informed from the very beginning of the program. Doing so also gives the administrators a stake in the outcome.

It would not be appropriate to have all of the data establishing a need for a job placement program gathered at this time because the change process should be collaborative in nature, with you the change agent forming a partnership with the school system and the community in planning the change.

Step 2: Creating Awareness

Next, create an awareness of the potential benefits of a school-based job placement program among the faculty and the community. One method of creating awareness involves scheduling a person, already directly involved with a school-based job placement program, to

Reprinted from *The Agricultural Education Magazine*, **47**:63–64 (Sept. 1974), by permission.

speak on the topic of job placement for vocational education students at a faculty meeting, in-service training program, or similar event. This technique would produce a general awareness of the job placement concept and would stimulate thought concerning the implications of such a program in the school district.

A special effort should be made to allow all vocational education teachers in the district and the speaker an opportunity to visit together informally. This technique would provide the vocational teachers additional information and clarification concerning this innovation. Additionally, it should aid in convincing the vocational teachers that a school-based job placement program for vocational education students would help each of their programs.

Further support for this kind of program can be developed by having representatives of the local mass media interview this speaker and other persons already involved in job placement programs concerning the concept of job placement. This technique could create an awareness of the innovation among businesses, employers, industries, parents, and students. The mass media coverage should also reinforce the concept in the minds of the school district's personnel.

Step 3: Determining the Impact of the Innovation

This may be done by organizing a committee to determine the potential impact of such a job placement program on vocational education students and the community. Committee membership should include vocational teachers, school counselors, school administrators, representatives of the vocational education advisory committees, state employment agency personnel, businessmen, vocational education students and others. Bice [1] cautioned that involving only opinion leaders in the change process should be practiced with caution. Therefore, this committee should be composed of opinion leaders as well as non-opinion leaders.

This committee should study the potential impact of a school-based job placement program by

1. Studying vocational education follow-up reports to determine the percentage of students placed in employment commensurate with their vocational training.
2. Interviewing former vocational education students concerning their reactions to the job placement program concept and to determine if such a program would have been beneficial to them.
3. Interviewing present vocational education students concerning their reactions to a job placement program.
4. Interviewing state employment commission personnel and employers concerning their willingness to participate in a job placement program.
5. Collecting other data deemed necessary.

At the conclusion of the committee's work, arrange a formal meeting for vocational education personnel, school counselors, and school administrators. The committee should present its findings and recommendations at this meeting.

Real-life examples, using local persons, should be used to dramatize the need for a school-based job placement program and to help persuade the school personnel that the need is real. Another technique to illustrate the potential impact of a job placement program would involve describing the discrepancies between the present situation and what it could be.

The committee's work could also serve further to convince the vocational teachers, counselors, and administrators of their capability of implementing this change. One way of doing this would involve describing the experiences of a similar school district that has successfully adopted a school-based job placement program.

Step 4: Developing a School-Based Job Placement Program and Gaining Its Acceptance

A committee, similar in composition to the one described in step three, can be the vehicle by which a model for the school-based job placement program can be developed. Using this approach, a program oriented toward the needs of the school, the vocational education students, and the community would result. This local orientation is vital when we consider that Rogers and Shoemaker [2] concluded that the success of a change agent in introducing an innovation is positively related to the degree to which the innovation is client oriented and compatible with the client's needs.

Various models for school-based job placement programs are available in the literature, such as the ones described by Allen [3], Gingerich [4], and Buckingham [5]. This latter article describes a school-based job placement program in the Baltimore Public Schools which began as an outgrowth of guidance and counseling in 1928. These models and others are guides around which the school-based job placement program could be developed.

After the tentative job placement program has been developed it should then be presented to all vocational teachers, school counselors, and school administrators for their comments and suggestions. Considering these recommendations, then develop and present the final model to the superintendent and board of education for final action. If board action is favorable, the task still remains of insuring school and community acceptance of the job placement program.

The major emphasis at this stage of the change strategy is persuading vocational teachers, vocational students, and the community that the job placement program is workable. Strategies to be employed by the change agent and the job placement coordinator to help persuade the client system to adopt the innovation would include

1. Contacting each vocational teacher to provide clarification and additional information concerning the job placement program.
2. Persuading each vocational teacher to discuss the potential benefits of the job placement program with his classes.
3. Contacting the state employment commission to solicit assistance with the job placement program.
4. Contacting employers concerning the job placement program and securing assurances of their willingness to participate in the program.
5. Contacting each vocational education advisory committee concerning the job placement program and securing their active participation.

Do not be surprised if everyone does not participate in the program initially because different adoptor categories, ranging from innovator and early adoptor to laggard, will probably exist in the school district. However, it may be your responsibility or that of the person given responsibility for the job placement program to attempt to get people in the adoptor categories to accept the program as rapidly as possible in order to achieve its adoption.

Step 5: Continuing the Job Placement Program Once Initiated

The person responsible for the program's operation needs to provide evidence concerning the effectiveness of the job placement program to the vocational teachers, school administration, employers, and the community. Evidence concerning the number of students placed on jobs, type of employment received, and present job openings should provide reinforcement to those who have adopted the innovation and would stimulate continued participation. Similar information should be provided to non-adoptors to aid in persuading them to adopt the innovation.

For example, one activity prior to the close of school might be to arrange a meeting of vocational teachers, school administrators, representatives of the vocational education advisory committees, state employment agency personnel, businessmen, and others. The purposes of this meeting would be to present an interim report concerning the success of the job placement program and to receive recommendations for improving and modifying the program. After this meeting, you should become less involved in the job placement program and the job placement coordinator should assume the major role for the program.

In the subsequent years the job placement coordinator should continually seek information concerning changes needed in the job placement program and change the program to meet these needs. Also he should continue to provide evidence indicating the effectiveness of the program.

Footnotes

[1] G. R. Bice, *Working With Opinion Leaders to Accelerate Change in Vocational-Technical Education,* (Columbus, Ohio: The Center for Vocational-Technical Education, The Ohio State University, 1970).

[2] E. M. Rogers and F. F. Shoemaker, *Communication of Innovations,* (New York: The Free Press, 1971).

[3] T. R. Allen, Jr., *Job Placement Coordinator's Handbook,* (Huntington, West Virginia: Department of Vocational Technical Education, 1972).

[4] G. E. Gingerich, *School-Based Job Placement Service Model: Phase I Planning,* (Harrisburg, Pennsylvania Research Coordination Unit for Vocational Education).

[5] L. Buckingham, "Job Placement as a School Program," *American Vocational Journal,* XLVII, (March, 1972), 63–64.

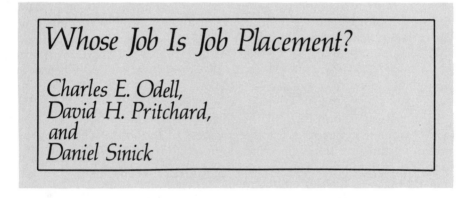

Whose Job Is Job Placement?

Charles E. Odell,
David H. Pritchard,
and
Daniel Sinick

The locus of responsibility, the role of societal agencies, and placement as part of career development are among dimensions discussed in a dialogue between Charles E. Odell, Assistant to Executive Director, Bureau of Employment Security, Harrisburg, Pennsylvania, and David H. Pritchard, Education Program Specialist (Research), U.S. Office of Education, Washington, D.C., moderated by Daniel Sinick, Professor of Education, George Washington University, Washington, D.C., and editor of *The Vocational Guidance Quarterly.* (Note: The views expressed herein are those of the authors and not necessarily those of their employing institutions.)

Reprinted from *Vocational Guidance Quarterly,* 23:138–145 (Dec. 1974), by permission. Copyright 1974 American Personnel and Guidance Association. Reprinted with permission.

SINICK: Placement is a problem that has long plagued vocational guidance. Which societal institutions and professional personnel should be responsible for placement? How does placement relate to other aspects of vocational guidance? These questions and their ramifications can properly be discussed by you, Chuck and Dave, because of your pertinent experience and professional concern. As moderator, I have kicked off; now who wants to pick up the ball?

PRITCHARD: Well, certainly the schools and colleges are much more concerned about job placement today than probably they've ever been. This relates directly to the recognition, now, that the so-called non–college-bound student needs just as much attention and concrete specific help from the educational institution as does the so-called college-bound. The arrangements between colleges and agencies of various kinds to aid the transition of the student from secondary school to college developed immensely over many years. We have no equivalent arrangements in terms of transition of students from the secondary school directly to work, and so it is a matter of equally effective attention being needed.

ODELL: I disagree a bit with Dave's view on that. We started a very long time ago. In fact I really started my career in the Employment Service in a demonstration project on school-Employment Service relations and the transition from school to work in Baltimore in 1939, out of which came a book called *Matching Youth and Jobs*, by Howard Bell. I sometimes wish people would read the book because a lot of its message is as valid today as it was then.

Beyond that, by 1950 with the help and understanding of Harry Jager, who was then head of the Occupational Information and Guidance Service of the U.S. Office of Education, the Employment Service and OIGS had formal agreements and working relationships to improve the transition from school to work. By about 1960, of the 26-odd thousand secondary schools in the country, more than half of them were involved in formal working relationships with the Employment Service.

Historically, there has been a lot of interest in this subject. What has happened to us is that in the '60s the Employment Service got diverted into a preoccupation and concern with the really hard-to-place, the hard core, the disadvantaged, the inner-city school systems, and began to taper off its outreach to the schools on a universal basis. The U.S. Office was, in my judgment, more preoccupied with the pursuit of excellence than what now seems to be its concern with career education. I agree with Dave that we are now coming full circle on the issue of what we will do for the student who is not going on to college. I think that's a healthy development and one which justifies our sitting here talking about what can be done to strengthen the placement impact of existing institutions and institutional arrangements.

SINICK: Perhaps the source of whatever disagreement there is stems from disparities between policies and practices, the failure of written agreements to be implemented.

ODELL: Well, I think part of that problem is that the U.S. Office has a very tangential impact on the day-to-day operation of local school systems. The Employment Service likes to think it has a profound impact on the day-to-day operations of local employment offices because of its 100 per cent funding of state and local operations, but there is a tremendous problem of communication and implementation in a proliferated bureaucracy like the Employment Service and an even more difficult problem of proliferation in the schools. That only suggests the importance of the institutional representation of these programs at the national level, sitting down as we're sitting down here, to have some dialogue about how we can do something about this problem. I quite agree that there is a big gap between expressed policy and implementation.

PRITCHARD: Well, we in the Office of Education are thinking in a much broader sense than just the relationship between a particular school and a particular office of the Employment Service; we are thinking of more than relationships with the public Employment Service at large. I made my opening comments in a very global sense, comparing the arrangements for transition between secondary school and college and the arrangements for transition from secondary school directly to work. Even in its heyday, the cooperative Employment Service program, in terms of placing all the students who wanted placement and actually getting them suitable jobs, was never very effective. There are many reasons for that, and that's why we need to take a global picture here—there are more than two kinds of institutions involved in this whole matter. You have, for example, the employers and the worker group organizations involved, their needs, their policies, and so on.

Moving from the global, I'm trying to get down to something more specific—that is, what we have to do within institutions and across institutions, internally and in linkages among them, to help with this whole large process we call transition from school to work.

ODELL: I think that's the right attack on the problem, and it's one that we need to explore in depth because my concern has been that each of the institutional bureaucracies we're talking about tends to think of itself as a self-contained delivery system for all the things that ought to be done. Yet we know that the schools' resources are limited for doing the total job. I am assuming that schools have a responsibility for seeing to it that their students are placed—not only that they're placed but that there is some learning and feedback from that placement as it relates to curriculum, as it relates to guidance and counseling services, and so on.

Certainly, the Employment Service is never going to be in the position to monopolize or pre-empt the placement business. Its principal function, not particularly in relation to schools or colleges but in its relationship to the community at large, is properly one of facilitating movement, intelligent movement, guided or choice-oriented movement, into the market on the basis of sharing, interpreting, and using more intelligently the informational resources and potentials that exist within the system.

For example, I would be much happier if I felt that counselors or placement officials in schools were using intelligently information about the job market. I find an abysmal lack of information and of basic occupational information resources within the schools. We have a large responsibility for seeing to it that the information flow is improved and that the tools available are improved. For that to happen, schools have to make greater demands on the Employment Service, on the employer community, and on the labor movement for the kinds of information that can be used in planning curricula, developing curriculum content, and in helping students and parents to make meaningful choices and decisions about work and the world of work.

PRITCHARD: Serious program development needs to be done with respect to placement, the same as other program components are worked out. One needs to survey the student body to begin with, in terms of their needs for placement assistance of various kinds and for other kinds of help contributing to placement. Then one needs a community survey of employers and of other community resources that are involved with placement, such as the Employment Service, the state and local Vocational Rehabilitation offices, minority group organizations, churches, the whole gamut of community agencies that have some relationship to what we're talking about here.

Phase 2 of this kind of development is establishing broad goals and process and outcome objectives. District-wise—speaking now of educational agencies, the local educational agency district, and the particular school buildings within it—one of the patterns evolving within the last few years is that of a centralized director at the district level who deals with the employers to develop job opportunities and so on plus a placement team headed by a coordinator in the local school building. The local board of education has to make a commitment to this; superintendents have to make a commitment to this; principals and the whole line of authority of management and administration have to be committed to this.

ODELL: My concern is that most administrative officials from the superintendent of schools in the district on down tend to play down this aspect of their responsibilities. I am wondering if it will ever come off as a self-generated, internalized function of the educational system or whether we don't really have to build a much greater awareness and concern on the part of the community, employers, labor, and the parents themselves to get this job done.

PRITCHARD: What you have said helps to explain why more has not been done within and by educational institutions. Needed implementation has to stem from a commitment to the role of the school, the very concept of the school, as preparing and aiding people to make the transition from school to work, not just from school to further education.

ODELL: In that regard, Dave, what is your current perception of where career education is? Is it really a banner we can march under or is it largely rhetoric?

PRITCHARD: Rather than comment directly, Chuck, on where career education is or where it's headed, I would like to say that we do have a commitment underway to try to explore what would be effective in the way of placement in educational settings.

One thing the Office of Education recently did, as part of a larger study contracted with the American Institutes for Research in Palo Alto, was to test the hypothesis that placement services operated within the school improve school accountability and promote and enhance the relationship of the school to business, industry, and other agencies providing jobs for students. From a review of literature of the last five years or so, AIR found the hypothesis to be only partially true, although at least 90 per cent of the documents reviewed supported the assumption that narrowly defined school-based placement and follow-up services should exist. By "narrowly defined" they mean placement concerned with just education and job. Those writers who did not agree with the hypothesis believe that maintaining placement programs in both schools and state employment agencies is uneconomical.

The literature indicates that placement services get youths employed and that some self-enlightened businesses and industries cooperate with schools. None of the literature covers the accountability that such cooperation achieves within the schools. There are no explicit studies of the process, products, and cost benefits of such services in the direct terms of the hypothesis. In addition, few data exist on the availability of placement services in schools or the quality of the placement services offered.

ODELL: A task force in the Department of Labor, under the auspices of the Assistant Secretary for Planning, Evaluation, and Research in the last days of James Hodgson's tenure as Secretary of Labor, made recommendations for more effective bridging arrangements and relationships between schools and employment services and other community agencies. Their basic recommendation, which was supported by studies done by the Urban Institute on the transition from school to work, was that there ought to be an arrangement for the out-stationing of Employment Service counseling-trained personnel in school systems. That is, there ought to be at least one full- or part-time Employment Service counselor identified with and working on behalf of the school guidance program as a placement and occupational information and vocational guidance officer. Such a counselor could take full advantage of the potentials in the Employment Service job bank system, which provides updated information on a daily basis on microfiche or computer printout hard copy for use by schools in identifying job opportunities currently available to which students can be referred.

Unfortunately, after Secretary Hodgson's departure, it was decided that this was not a high enough priority in terms of the use of Employment Service and manpower funds to justify the effort.

I happen to think this is a very critical matter. I'm less concerned about whether it is an Employment Service counselor stationed in the schools than I am that there is someone in each school who has this responsibility and who has the available information.

PRITCHARD: The view that is emerging today, in principle anyway, is that, in both the planning and the operation of programs, the school and its personnel and the community and its personnel need to be involved so that programs become school-based *and* community-linked. The team within the school can well include a representative from the Employment Service where that seems useful and feasible. It can have representatives from other community organizations also, both for planning and for operation.

ODELL: I'm concerned about the word "accountability" you raised earlier in staking out the hypothesis. It seems significant that for 50 years follow-up has presumably been an integral part of the total vocational guidance process. What a vocational counselor does, or is supposed to do, not only includes placement but it also includes follow-up and presumably feedback from follow-up. What does it all mean to the individual as well as to the institution preparing the individual for work or for life? One way to approach accountability is to say we are concerned with constructive criticism, evaluation, and feedback on what guidance accomplishes and then open our doors to our severest critics.

SINICK: With respect to accountability, you both have emphasized a need for a meshing of operational mechanics and underlying philosophies. A philosophy of long standing—rugged individualism—might function in such a way among school superintendents and others to place the onus for job placement upon the students or graduates or other people who are to be placed.

ODELL: Well, we clearly are a nation of people who like to believe that, in the best of all possible worlds, we all make our own decisions about work and life with a minimum of social intervention. And I think there is nothing basically wrong with that. The difficulty is that individuals in an increasingly complex society need at least information, if not guidance and direction, so that they can make reasonably adequate choices.

Some feel that what we deplore as an inordinately high rate of youth unemployment in this country is a good thing because in milling around in the job market individual young people have an opportunity to try things out, to make judgments and decisions, and ultimately to make choices. That's a very comfortable sort of laissez-faire, rugged individualistic approach, but when you see how many students get crunched by that process, by repeated failure, by the revolving-door approach to young people in the job market, you begin to wonder whether it isn't terribly wasteful, terribly frustrating, and ultimately self-defeating. Young people—and older ones, too—need information; they need assistance, and I would hope the assistance would be in the direction of facilitating their decision-making processes, not directing them in the interest of the state.

PRITCHARD: I want to stress that we need to build in capabilities and competencies within the individuals themselves. Many people are talking about placement in terms of *job* development, but they are not talking about placement in terms of *student* development. Both terms of the equation are involved here. Individuals cannot be left just shopping around in the labor market; they ought to know what that market's like; they ought to know what's on the "shelves"; they ought to have built-in capabilities and competencies that have to do not only with job *getting* but also with job *holding*.

Too many people are thinking of follow-up just in the sense of program evaluation—getting data to revise the curricula and the guidance programs. I see follow-up in terms of follow *through*, which is more the guidance idea of it—follow through with individuals, not only into the job, but on the job, at least for a period of adjustment, and be available to them when they consider significant job change, further education or training, or other important career redirections.

ODELL: I would certainly agree that when follow-up leaves substantial numbers of individuals hanging in a very unsatisfactory situation and simply records the fact that they're there, it certainly is not a professionally well-conceived approach to either career development or personal growth and development. Many adults went to work at an early age, stayed in one line of work, with one organization, with one employer, for almost the duration of their working lives, and then suddenly there's a reorganization, a merger, a technological shift, a geographic move, and they're dumped. They've never looked for a job in any real sense; they don't know about anything else that's available in the market; and they sit there wondering what to do next.

When you get into the problems of special groups among adults, such as the physically and emotionally handicapped, the people coming out of penal institutions, the people confronted with problems in mental health, there is a tremendous unmet need for this kind of service and the need for continuing relationships between educational institutions and other community agencies.

PRITCHARD: We must be concerned not only with transition from school to work, but also with transition from *work to school*, or other education or training setting, through the life span of individuals and groups. Adults may want to move from employment status back to some educational or training situation or to some mix of employment and education. As to the oncoming stream of students, they ought to be afforded experiences not only in the academic setting and in the vocational programs and shops within the school, but also out in actual work situations—sometimes on a paid basis, sometimes nonpaid.

ODELL: Programs with labels like "distributive education" and "cooperative education" and "work-study" offer tremendous opportunities, since most people learn most effectively on the job, doing something in a hands-on discovery method way. . . . W. Willard Wirtz had an interesting idea when he was Secretary of Labor—we ought to identify the points of entry or reentry where substantial numbers of people move into the job market, whether from secondary school or college, rehabilitation agency or Veterans Administration, or the separation centers from the military, and assist in bringing the people entering or reentering the market together with suitable jobs. If we really worked at it, we could demonstrate tremendous cost benefits to the society through this kind of organized approach.

PRITCHARD: If the career development concept is to guide us in education and in other institutions, placement has to be regarded as a process which puts people in situations for further growth. Placement in the old limited sense—now you're ready to leave school, you have to get a job, you're referred to the Employment Service or something—simply is not an adequate conception of either need or response to need.

ODELL: I certainly agree on that. It's interesting that some European countries operate on the principle that workers who migrate are to be supported in the new work location with social workers, psychologists, and counselors to ensure that they're not simply exploited in the work setting to which they go. We've almost lost sight of, and interest in, that whole concept of personal growth and freedom of vocational choice in our approach to these problems in this country.

There should be greater concern than I now perceive among top policy makers and legislators, as well as front-line counselors and placement personnel, with the basic issue of whose interest we represent. Are we representing the client's interest or the interests of the state? That's a terribly important issue and one that we ought not to overlook when we talk about placement—whose responsibility and where should the responsibility lie?

Mt. Ararat Finds the Keystone

Ken Gray

Fred is a National Merit semifinalist; he has decided to pursue his part-time radio announcer job full time after graduation, maybe go on to school later. Judy has enrolled in vocational courses in her senior year; she has decided to go to work. The reasons are numerous, the summation conclusive. More and more seniors are turning to full-time employment upon graduation.

In the State of Maine the percentage of high school graduates going on to college has declined 13 per cent in four years. Our graduates at Mt. Ararat School are no exception. From primarily rural, coastal "down east" communities, they are quick to point out that the belief that college means good jobs is "not necessarily so." At the same time, it has been clear to us on the faculty that without help, these students will be ill-equipped to seek or keep jobs. They need help and have the right to expect it.

(Mt. Ararat, incidentally, is Maine's largest consolidated school. It serves four rural communities in central coastal Maine, grades 7–12, 1,360 students.)

Two Models

In an effort to meet the placement needs of undergraduates as well as graduating seniors, the Mt. Ararat Guidance Department has developed two alternate plans for job placement at the high school level. One is a guidance-based model in which the guidance department conducts the job placement effort as part of its on-going program. The second is a team approach involving interested faculty members who organize a team placement effort.

The models were developed on the following guidelines: Neither would require additional personnel; each would be viewed as an extension of existing services rather than an addition to them; both would reflect the needs of rural youth, and both would take a comprehensive view of placement.

Taking a "comprehensive view" means that job placement is more than getting kids jobs. It means preparing students to be successful employees as well as preparing them to wage a successful job-seeking campaign. At Mt. Ararat, we use a five-segment program which in-

Reprinted from *American Vocational Journal*, **29**:33–36 (Dec. 1974), by permission.

cludes (1) needs assessment, (2) job development, (3) student development, (4) placement, and (5) follow-up.

Trite But True

"Look before you leap," is the way the saying goes. Needs assessment is exactly that. What is the student demand for placement services? Is the greater demand for full-time or part-time employment? Where are the students working now? Who are the major employers? What is the average wage? All are questions that must be answered.

It may sound a bit hollow, but needs assessment is important. The demand for job placement services can be awesome. Before starting a program, the school staff should determine realistically how many students can be served. In many circumstances, it may be possible to provide a true placement service to graduating seniors only. This should be decided before the program starts.

Needs assessment is not complicated, by the way. In most instances, a simple paper-and-pencil questionnaire filled out by an advisory group is sufficient.

Personal Visits Pay Off

Job development is broadly defined as an effort that results in job orders—specifically, that which is done to get information on employment opportunities to which students can be referred. The major effort in this vein is contacting businessmen to inform them of the service. The hope is that in the future they will turn to the placement office when they have openings.

Some job development techiques we have used are:

Personal contact with individual employers at their business.
Mailings—a good preliminary to the above.
Speaking engagements to civic groups.
Newspapers and radio spots.

It is significant to note that of the companies visited personally, 79 per cent have supplied job orders and 44 per cent have hired students. Clearly, getting out to visit employers pays off. It is crucial to any placement effort.

One last word on job development: A first step is to organize a system of job order management. Specifically this means keeping track of who is looking for employees, and equally important, finding out exactly what they are looking for. The more information you can get about an employer and the job, the better equipped you are to prepare a student for successfully applying for that job.

"Kids today can't even fill out an application." "The way they come in for an interview, they couldn't get hired if their father owned the company." Sound familiar?

"You have to keep telling them every minute what to do." "They think you owe them something." Anyone dealing with employers has heard it all. Doing something about this state of affairs is the primary objective of student development.

How does a student get a job? Better still, how does he keep one? Teaching these skills is student development. It can be the most challenging, creative, important, and frustrating aspect of job placement.

The prime vehicle of student development at Mt. Ararat is a job-seeking/job-keeping seminar. A one-day intensive format is used, as it tends to interfere least with class scheduling and other activities. The seminar covers sources of jobs, resumes, letters of introduction, interviews, job keeping, and labor laws. Each participant is given a job packet containing relevant materials for review. Only the packet binder is purchased; thus the seminar involves no great expense. Of all aspects of this seminar, students seem to enjoy hearing from local businessmen the most.

Currently being developed are activities that take place within the classroom. Seniors are being asked to report on a troublesome work situation as a writing assignment. Teams of students use these reports to write short, work-related role-playing scripts for videotaping. It is the author's belief that such activities included in the ongoing curriculum will be the most effective type of student development.

Mutual Trust Essential

Placement is the payoff of the program. It is a process of matching a potential employee with an employer—of providing students with information and support to ensure that they are hired.

At Mt. Ararat, we are committed to the premise that effective placement depends on a personal, trusting relationship between placement counselor and student. If you don't know the kids, you can't do the job. Fancy cybernetics, roving placement counselors, satellite trailers are not, in our opinion, "where it's at." The key to good job placement is that the effort be handled within the school by people the students know and trust, and vice versa.

Several others points are worth considering:

In placement, the employer bears the responsibility to hire or not to hire.
Don't get trapped into recommending hiring; it will backfire.
If a student isn't hired, find out why and use this as a learning experience for the student.
Provide some method to identify students being referred by your service as opposed to those applying off the street.

Most Prefer to Wait It Out

Unfortunately, unlike institutions of higher learning, employers cannot wait until graduation day. Any secondary school committed to job placement must develop a procedure to allow seniors the opportunity to take full-time jobs prior to graduation.

The process at Mt. Ararat is facilitated by a graduation contract. Briefly, students and teachers make arrangements whereby the student will finish required courses and any other course he may want. The student agrees to return to school if full-time employment ends, and the contract spells out these additional stipulations: the exact tasks that must be completed to finish courses, when they are due, how work will be submitted, and the time the student will report for his weekly meeting with the counselor.

The last point calls for explanation: We at Mt. Ararat view the program as a transition effort. We still consider the student to be in fact a full-time student involved in a final educational project—working full time. Under these circumstances, we require that participants meet weekly or biweekly with the placement counselor to review the work project. In short, we don't cut them loose. We attempt to support them in those crucial first weeks in the world of work.

One finding may be helpful: At first glance one might anticipate that the opportunity to cut education short would result in half the senior class vanishing after Christmas. Not so. The fact is that the end of the senior year is a time that few want to miss. We have found that only the most seriously job-oriented seniors are tempted. Most prefer to take a chance and wait for whatever opens up after graduation.

Kids who lose jobs seldom take long in doing so. Those first weeks on a job are critical and, as we all know, the most trying. Thus follow-up is, first of all, support.

At Mt. Ararat, students who register with the placement office agree that if placed, they will attend two follow-up group sessions. In these sessions, job-seeking skills are stressed and potential conflicts explored.

A second form of follow-up concerns graduates. In this follow-up, two types of data are looked for: Who needs placement and help? and how are employed graduates faring?

Getting graduates back to school to meet with the faculty is both fun and rewarding; it is also excellent public relations. Parents are amazed and pleased that the school is still interested.

Logical Extension

Guidance departments have long provided placement services to students pursuing higher education. The guidance-based model recognizes this precedent, and sees its job placement effort as a logical extension of these services. The model revolves around one counselor identified as placement coordinator.

This counselor becomes solely responsible for job development and is given the mobility to spend considerable time outside the school in the business community. He also handles placement counseling whenever possible. The remaining activities—needs assessment, student development, and follow-up—are shared by the other members of the guidance staff.

This model is feasible in any guidance department of three or more counselors. Job placement offers the coordinating counselor a unique opportunity to demonstrate to kids and their parents that the guidance department serves all students.

Alternative for Small Schools

In the placement team approach, an ad hoc committee of school staff—turned on by helping kids get jobs—organizes to run a placement program. Team members can include parents, businessmen, and other interested laymen. Job development is also part of this group effort. Everyone has some contacts in the business community which can be pooled by the group.

At Mt. Ararat, the placement team's responsibility is restricted to seniors planning on full-time work after graduation. The team takes this group as a "case load." A team approach to placing seniors has several advantages over other types of organization. First, a student's instructor can supply accurate information about his skills. We found early that placing a student in a job he is undertrained for can be a great disservice. Secondly, placement often involves motivation, support, and personal concern. A number of adults providing this type of support is dynamic.

The team approach is particularly promising for small schools. It is an excellent alternative for rural schools that have no guidance services. In Maine we are currently exploring the possibility of providing a placement facilitator in each regional vocational center to organize placement teams in the rural member schools.

Dividends—Selfish and Otherwise

We are excited about job placement at Mt. Ararat—for some very selfish reasons. It has paid dividends. Here are a few of them:

We have demonstrated to students, to parents, and to the community that we care about all students.
We have gone to the business community offering a service instead of asking for a handout.
We have met the real needs of a lot of kids.

Job placement is fun. Get into it. If we can help you get started, let's hear from you. We're in Topsham, Maine, 04086.

UNIT BIBLIOGRAPHY

BREBNER, R. A. "Career Planning and Placement Strategies for Women." *Journal of College Placement,* **36** (Winter 1976), 19–20.

DYE, G. R. "Pre-Professionals: A New Source of Help." *Journal of College Placement,* **35** (Summer 1975), 36–38.

ELLIS, E. "Charting New Ideas in the Profession." *Journal of College Placement,* **35** (Summer 1975), 57–59.

HOPF, J. "Self-direction and a Placement Service That Instructs." *Journal of College Placement,* **36** (Winter 1976), 65–67.

MENKE, R. F., and D. REGNER. "Placement: The Neglected Resource for Career and Curriculum Planning." *Journal of College Placement,* **35** (Winter 1975), 62–65.

MEYERS, S. L., "Placements 7th Dimension." *Journal of College Placement,* **35** (Summer 1975), 36–38.

PARKER, V. "Placement Programs: A New Philosophy." *Community and Junior College Journal,* **45** (Autumn 1975), 30–31.

SHIER, D. W. "Job Opportunities Bulletin for Sale." *Journal of College Placement,* **36** (Winter 1976), 21.

STEWART, W. C. "From Shoebox to Computer." *Journal of College Placement,* **35** (Summer 1975), 57–59.

WASIL, R. A. "Job Placement: Keystone of Career Development." *American Vocational Journal,* **49** (Dec. 1974), 32.

———. "Placement Services: The Common Denominator for Educational Fragmentation." *American Vocational Journal,* **51** (1976), 49–52.

YENAWINE, G. "Placement Counselor to Educator." *Journal of College Placement,* **35** (Winter 1975), 34–38.

part 8
Vocational Guidance: A Variety of Different Kinds of School Preparation

There has been an awakening regarding the career developmental needs of the elementary school child. The mature person is not an event; he develops from infancy to life's end. Thus, it is now seen that the foundation for his later years is laid in the elementary school. Although one cannot be sure of the specific methods with which to guide children vocationally, it is known that attitudes toward work are formed during the elementary school years. Those years, then, are foundational ones for attitudinal development; the junior high school grades are exploring years; and the senior high school and college years blend discovery and decision, especially in regard to a life career.

Vocational Decision-Making Models: A Review and Comparative Analysis

David A. Jepsen
and
Josiah S. Dilley

Vocational development has been described as the processes of preparation for and entry into a series of education and work roles over a lifetime. During the 1960s, a number of vocational theorists speculated that these processes could be understood better by employing concepts suggested by psychological decision theory. Indeed the promise that fundamental decision concepts have for enriching our understanding of vocational development received early acclaim (Blau, Gustad, Jesser, Parnes, and Wilcock, 1956; Brayfield, 1963, 1964; Super, 1961; Tyler, 1961). Recent reviews of vocational development theories have concluded that this promise remains largely unfulfilled (Crites, 1969; Kroll, Dinklage, Lee, Morley, and Wilson, 1970; Osipow, 1968).

One major problem in integrating this literature is that various theorists have not employed either the framework or the language of their predecessors. Several questions can be raised: Among the various theories, are there similarities in the basic concepts that are observed by the differences in language? Do the theories fit the same population of decision situations? Do certain theories better describe certain types of decisions? How do the theories vary in terms of assumptions about characteristics of decision-makers and their resources?

The authors believe that psychological decision theory provides a useful framework for clarifying the relationships among various vocational decision-making theories and between these theories and the population of decision situations with which people are faced. This paper outlines psychological decision theory; summarizes eight promi-

Reprinted from *Review of Educational Research,* **44**:331–344 (July 1974), by permission. Copyright 1974, American Educational Research Association, Washington, D.C.

nent vocational decision-making (VDM) models; compares and contrasts VDM models on basic assumptions and fundamental concepts; and suggests applications of theory to theoretical decision types. Implications for research, theory, and practice are discussed.

Psychological Decision Theory

Psychological decision theory seeks to "describe in an orderly way what variables influence choices [Edwards and Tversky, 1967, p. 7]." A set of concepts common to a wide-ranging literature were described in an early review by Edwards (1954), and more recently by Edwards (1961), Taylor (1963), Becker and McClintock (1967), and Lee (1971). Feather (1959) compared the central constructs used in "utility-expectancy theories" (that is, theories by Atkinson, 1957; Edwards, 1954; Lewin, 1951; Rotter, 1954; Tolman, 1959) and found that the given meanings were similar but the labels differed. (For example, what Edwards named as "subjective probability" serves the same function as the concept Atkinson called "expectancy.") Cellura (1969) extended the comparison and showed that, although constructs have similar meanings, their theoretical interrelationships differed in important ways (for example, relationship between expectancy and utility). Despite these differences, it is clear that decision theory stems from markedly different traditions and assumptions than do "behavior theories" (for example those of C. Hull and K. Spence), psychoanalytic theories, or developmental theories.

The form of theory construction reviewed in this paper is the model —a conceptual analogue chosen (or erected) for its heuristic value in organizing the ideas and/or observed phenomena it represents (Marx, 1963). Decision theory provides "an orderly way" to describe conceptualizations of vocational behavior in sequence and juxtaposition. Theoretical models serve as conceptual frameworks or "schematic maps" that often result from efforts to identify and to clarify the major concepts in an area of study. It is assumed that the decision-maker processes information relevant to his goals. Bross (1953) helped to clarify the conceptual framework by describing the functional categories into which the information is sorted. Edwards, Lindman, and Phillips (1965) attempted to list all functions necessary for designing future decision-making systems. What follows is primarily a synthesis of the two.

A decision-making conceptual framework assumes the presence of a *decision maker*, a *decision situation* (social expectation), and relevant *information* both from within and outside the person. The information is arranged into decision-making concepts according to the functions it serves. Two or more *alternative actions* are considered, and several *outcomes* or consequences are anticipated from each action. Each outcome has two characteristics: *probability,* or likelihood of occurrence in the future, and *value* or relative importance to the decision maker. The information is arranged according to a strategy so that the decision maker can readily recognize an advantageous course of action and make a *commitment* to this action. Strategies, also called rules or criteria, guide the assembling of the above concepts into an array so that straightforward judgments can reveal the commitment. Strategies are not concepts but structures; that is, they are aspects of the personality acquired prior to initiating the decision process and, as such, function as properties of the organism (for example, the disposition called "risk taking").

Vocational Decision-Making (VDM) Models

The eight VDM models reviewed here were selected because each employs concepts that appear to be similar to concepts in psychological decision theory and because each attempts to provide a picture of the entire VDM process. Each model will be labelled by the authors' names, for example, the Tiedeman-O'Hara model.

Since this review is limited to models related to decision theory, several important vocational development theories are not discussed. For example, Super's treatment of career development (for example, Super, Starishevsky, Matlin and Jordaan, 1963) does not lend itself to analysis as a decision theory. The same can be said for Holland's work (1966). By making this distinction, we have focussed on one of four major types of vocational choice theory according to Crites' (1969) descriptions. Osipow (1968), Crites (1969), and Zaccaria (1970) have reviewed the other types thoroughly.

Decision theory has been applied to human situations as both a prescriptive model to be emulated and a description of actual decision-making behavior (Becker and McClintock, 1967; Taylor, 1963). In order to facilitate comparisons, the eight VDM models are divided into two groups. *Descriptive VDM models* purport to represent the ways people generally make vocational decisions, that is, the "natural" phenomena. This classification includes models by Tiedeman and O'Hara (1963), Hilton (1962), Vroom (1964), Hsu (1970), and Fletcher (1966). *Prescriptive models* represent attempts to help people make better decisions—rules people should use—to reduce decision errors. Models in this group were written by Katz (1963, 1966), Gelatt (1962), and Kaldor and Zytowski (1969).

The distinction between prescriptive and descriptive approaches is slippery and depends on the conditions of a decision situation. For example, as the "stakes" are increased, the decision maker tries harder to approximate the prescriptive model in order to maximize returns (Edwards et al., 1965).

Descriptive VDM Models

Tiedeman-O'Hara Model. Tiedeman (1961), and Tiedeman and O'Hara (1963) developed a VDM model which they named a "paradigm of differentiation and integration in attempting rational solutions to the problems of one's vocational situation [1963, p. 37]." The problem-solving process is initiated by the experiencing of a vocational problem and by the recognition that a decision must be made. In later writings, Tiedeman refers to vocational problems as "discontinuities" (Tiedeman, 1964, 1965; Tiedeman and Field, 1961).

Tiedeman and O'Hara divide the process into two periods, called Anticipation and Implementation-Adjustment, that distinguish between behavior prior to and following instrumental action on the decision. (Only the Anticipation period will be discussed here.) The Anticipation period is subdivided into four stages, representing discrete changes in the condition of the decision. The decision maker may reverse himself in the order of stages, but advancement predomiates over time. Since decisions interconnect, a person may be at an advanced stage on one particular decision, yet at an earlier stage with regard to another decision.

The first stage, called Exploration, accounts for trial-and-error efforts to differentiate among alternate goals. Activity is principally imaginary as the decision maker attempts to give order and meaning to several possible goals and to the context (Tiedeman calls it "field") of each goal. During exploration, fields are relatively transitory, highly imaginary ideas about what the self might be like in later situations—situations specifically associated with a possible goal. In short, the decision maker attempts to take the measure of himself in relation to each alternative goal as he senses it.

The next three stages, Crystallization, Choice, and Clarification, are relatively inseparable. Crystallization describes attempts to clarify the order and pattern of goals and their fields. Assessment of personal values and their bases is a primary activity. Goals are compared on the basis of competing demands, costs and returns, advantages and disadvantages, and take on the qualities of definiteness, clarity, complexity, and rationality. Thought about the problem becomes more stable (less random), durable, reliable. The Choice stage involves commitment to one goal and its field, which, in turn, orients the person to act. The particular commitment is probably a function of qualities of the alternatives such as complexity, clarity, and "degrees of freedom." The certainty of a choice orientation (its "motive power") is probably the product of the complexity and antagonism of alternatives. The Clarification stage, brought on by doubt experienced during the waiting period between choice and action, involves attempts to perfect the image of self in the later situation.

Hilton's Model. A career decision-making model based on complex information-processing mechanisms was outlined by Hilton (1962). Although clearly influenced by Herbert Simon's work in human problem solving (Newell, Shaw and Simon, 1958; Simon, 1955, 1958), Hilton borrowed the concept of "plans" from Miller, Galanter and Pribram (1960) and the concept of "cognitive dissonance" from Festinger (1957). The key elements in the model are premises, plans, and cognitive dissonance. Premises are beliefs and expectations about self and the world, for example, self-perceptions, attributes of occupational roles, needs, perceptions of social structure, and things important to the decision maker. Plans are not explicitly defined, but apparently they denote an image of sequential actions associated with entering an occupational role. Cognitive dissonance accounts for a method of testing out plans against current premises.

Hilton's decision-making process is initiated by an input from the environment that alters the decision maker's present plans. The decision maker "tests" to see if the input has raised dissonance sufficiently above the satisfactory threshold—that is, whether an imbalance or inconsistency among plans and premises has been created. If dissonance has been raised above threshold, the decision maker examines his premises, and if there is no imbalance, he continues acting on the present plan for action. If the premises can be revised, they are, and then submitted (with the plans) for a dissonance test, and the cycle is complete. If, on the other hand, premises cannot be revised, the person searches his stored knowledge or his surroundings for another behavioral plan. Future work roles, not previously tested as plans, are scanned to find one that may now "pass the test." The new plan is tested and, if dissonance is below threshold, it becomes the controlling plan for future action.

Hilton's mechanism for testing cognitive dissonance determines whether the outcomes of tentative plans and/or premises remain acceptable or not, that is, whether dissonance is below or above the threshold level. The operation of the mechanism assumes that people classify outcomes dichotomously as satisfactory or unsatisfactory. The basis for such an assumption rests on Simon's (1955) critique of classical economic models. He suggests substituting "satisficing" for maximizing in problem-solving models where imperfect knowledge is available. Simon argues that the decision maker does not have enough information to order the value of all possible outcomes at one time, therefore the decision maker simply determines whether each is satisfactory or not as he considers them one at a time.

Vroom's Model. Vroom (1964) outlined a cognitive decision-making model that included algebraic equations to define principal concepts: the concept of Valence, the concept of Expectancy, and the concept of Force. Vroom drew upon psychological theories where similar concepts had been employed, for example, Lewin (1951), Rotter (1955), Peak (1955), Davidson, Suppes, and Siegel (1957), Atkinson (1957), and Tolman (1959).

Valence refers to the decision maker's preferences among outcomes (future states of nature) or, more specifically, to the affective orientations toward particular outcomes. It is the anticipated satisfaction from an outcome, as contrasted with the actual satisfaction. An outcome acquires Valence from the decision maker's conception of its instrumentality for attaining more distant and prized goals. Instrumentality is a belief about the association between immediate and eventual outcomes. The mathematical definition of Valence says that Outcome A's Valence is a function of the summed products of affect associated with prized, distant goals and the cognized instrumentality of A for attaining each goal.

Expectancy refers to the degree to which a decision maker believes outcomes are probable. It is defined as "the momentary belief concerning the likelihood that a particular act will be followed by a particular outcome [Vroom, 1964, p. 17]." Expectancies range from subjective certainty that an outcome will follow an act to subjective certainty that it will not. Expectancy is differentiated from Valence in that the former is an action-outcome association and the latter is an outcome-outcome association.

Behavior, or the decision commitment, is controlled by the direction and magnitude of forces to perform particular and competing acts. Force is the hypothetical cognitive factor that controls behavior—it is the product of Valence and Expectancy, and consequently controls which alternative is acted upon. It is a function of the sum of the products of Valences and Expectancies over all outcomes.

Hsu's Model. Hsu (1970) presented a VDM model based on familiar concepts—largely those used by Vroom—but included major variations in the relationships among concepts. The concept of Force (as defined by Vroom) is employed by Hsu to describe all alternative occupations considered and is assumed to have maximum value for the decision-maker's unique vocational goal. The vocational goal is defined as the algebraic sum of Valence-Expectancy products of all outcomes for an occupation where the Expectancy of each outcome is unity. The essential difference between Vroom and Hsu is that the Hsu model suggests a final step in the VDM process where the Force for vocational choices is subtracted from the Force for the vocational goal. Hsu assumes that the decision maker is attempting to minimize the disparity between a choice and a goal.

Hsu assumes that the decision-maker can be represented as a "sytem" where information in the form of occupational values, occupational information, and evaluative information about the self serves as the environmental "input" and occupational choice is the "output."

Fletcher's Model. Although his purpose was not to explain decision, Fletcher (1966) "roughs out" a VDM paradigm based on conceptual learning ideas. He assumes that decision processes are not wholly rational and that commitment is as much a function of timing as it is of the data available to the decision-maker. Motivation for VDM is, initially, to satisfy basic human needs but later may derive from curiosity or conceptual conflict.

Fletcher hypothesized that the formulations for career decisions are concepts about the future. These concepts are based on experiences associated with one or more basic human needs (for example, Maslow's hierarchy). A career concept system is the composite of several concepts, such as self-concept, interests, attitudes, and values—all derived from experiences that the decision-maker associates with a given career alternative. Each career concept has an affect charge defined as the particular feeling or emotional tone associated with, or actually a part of, the concept. Affect charges for a complex career concept system may be the summed resultant of several affect charges related to several experiences both positive and negative. The career chosen is that one for which the career concept's affect charge is the highest at the time of decision.

Career concepts have two additional dimensions, with the opposite poles being degree of specificity contrasted with degree of generalization and degree of concreteness vs. degree of abstractness. Specific concepts are directly related to particular experiences but become generalized as they interact with other concepts. The movement from concrete to abstract concepts follows an inferential process toward higher levels of classification identity.

Other Descriptive Models. Loughary (1965), Dolliver (1967), and Simons (1966) have each described aspects of the VDM process but have not proposed complete models.

Prescriptive VDM Models

Katz Model. Katz (1963) sketched a "general model for career decision making" and later added detail in his "model of guidance for decision making (1966)." The model emphasizes a structure to be used in the practical art of helping people. Indeed Katz (1969c) suggested that career development theory contributes the content and outcome for guidance theory. In this sense, it prescribes preferred VDM behavior. The major difference from other models is that the entry point into the VDM process is the identification and definition of values (rather than the listing of alternatives).

Values are regarded as the satisfying goals or desired states that are sought but not in terms of motivating drive or specific instrumental action (Katz, 1963, 1969a). The decision maker develops his own list of dominant values and scales them according to their relative "magnitude of value." For each value a "threshold level" that meets his personal requirements is identified. For each option (or alternative) the decision maker estimates the "strength of return" it offers in respect to each value's threshold level. This refers to probabilities inherent in the option itself (for example, the proportion of people earning the desired "threshold level" income in an occupational option). The sum of products of "strength of return" and "magnitude of values" provides a "value return" for each option.

Objective probabilities regarding success or entry for each option are multiplied by the value return to obtain an "expected value." The strategy is to select that option for which the expected value is greatest.

Gelatt Model. Assuming that one important purpose of counseling is to help students make "good" decisions, Gelatt (1962) suggested that a decision be evaluated by the process it follows rather than the outcome alone. He described a "proposed decision-making framework" derived from Bross' (1953) design for statistical decisions and Cronbach and Gleser's (1957) description of decision sequences. The model assumes a decision-maker who requires information as "fuel" and who produces a recommended course of action which may be terminal (that is, final) or investigatory (that is, calling for more information) depending upon how it relates to his purposes. Information is organized into three systems: (1) *predictive system,* information about alternatives actions, possible outcomes, and probabilities linking actions to outcomes; (2) *value system,* relative preferences among outcomes; and (3) *decision criterion,* or rules for evaluation.

A "good" decision includes adequate and relevant information in each system (Clarke, Gelatt, and Levine, 1965; Gelatt, 1962). Clarke et al. argued that, since the content of prediction and value systems is more readily observable and far less complex than the decision criterion, improving information services would increase the likelihood of good decisions. Gelatt and Clarke (1967) emphasize the importance of subjective probabilities, the place of objective probability data in modifying subjective estimates, and the indeterminable, but significant effect of subjective probability estimates on preferences. In effect, the Gelatt model prescribes characteristics of adequate informational inputs and suggests an organization to be imposed on it. No specific rules are offered for proceeding from information to commitment.

Kaldor-Zytowski Model. A model of occupational choice derived from the tenets of economic decision making was developed by Kaldor and Zytowski (1969) to specify classes of determinants and to describe their interrelationships in producing a final choice.

The occupational choice process is assumed to approximate maximizing behavior and, as such, can be described in terms of inputs and outputs. The inputs include personal resources, e.g., intellectual and physical characteristics. When applied to a given occupational alternative (in imagination), certain outputs, or consequences, follow as a function of the inputs and the alternative. Likewise, the inputs are priced in terms of what the decision maker foregoes in using them in a particular occupational alternative. The chosen alternative is the one offering the greatest net value—the highest value when input costs are balanced against output gains.

Kaldor and Zytowski present detailed forms for assessing the values of outcomes and inputs. "Occupational utility functions," the extent to which a person obtains the outcomes he wants in the proportion he wants them, are computed for successive pairs of values. An aggregate occupational utility function can be derived from each alternative. This method assumes that a decision maker can rank order relevant values for each available alternative and that he can assign a value to the sacrifices made to attain each alternative. Once these assumptions are accepted, the authors provide elaborate graphic techniques (for example, indifference curves) to plot the information and determine the maximal occupational alternative.

Other Prescriptive Models. Prescriptive models dealing specifically with college choice decisions have been offered by Hills (1964) and Hammond (1965). Thoresen and Mehrens (1967) describe variables relevant to vocational decisions and suggest research questions about the influence of information on decisions.

Comparisons of VDM Models: Assumptions

Decision theorists make assumptions about the decision-maker or his surroundings. In this section VDM models are examined in terms of five of these assumptions.

1. *Assumptions about the amount of information available to decision makers.* Specifically, how much does the decision maker know about possible alternatives, how much is known about a given alternative, what is known about the projected outcomes and the probabilities connecting alternatives to outcomes?

The most apparent contrast is between the Hilton and Kaldor-Zytowski models. On the basis of his research on the careers of teachers (Hilton, 1960; Hilton, Levin, and Leiderman, 1957) and business administration graduate students (Hilton, Baenninger, and Korn, 1962), Hilton assumed decision makers have limited knowledge about alternatives. Kaldor and Zytowski, on the other hand, assume that the decision maker has relatively unlimited knowledge about alternatives, outcomes, resources, and values. They recognize the difficulties in accepting this assumption but report that hypotheses derived from their model are consistent with the occupational plans of farm boys (Kaldor, Eldridge, Burchinal, and Arthur, 1962).

The other models apparently assume that more moderate but unspecified amounts of information are available to the decision maker. For example, the Gelatt model encourages a thorough information search, but in the absence of "stop" rules, we can only guess at how much information is considered sufficient. As long as only one model (Kaldor-Zytowski) suggests that values be assigned to each new "bit" of information received, this assumption is argued at a very general level.

At least two models have been implemented through computer-assisted information systems. The Tiedeman-O'Hara model was applied through the Information System for Vocational Decisions (ISVD) (Tiedeman et al., 1967, 1968), and the Katz model has been translated to the System of Interactive Guidance Information (SIGI) (Katz, 1969a). Both systems supply considerable information to the decision-maker.

2. *Assumption of conditions of risk or uncertainty in VDM processes.* The models can be roughly divided into two groups on this issue. The *risk* group sees vocational decisions as among those where probabilities about future events are assigned. The *uncertainty* group sees vocational decisions as among those to which no generally accepted probabilities of future events can be attached. Put another way, the difference refers to the amount of so-called "objective" data directly applied to the VDM process.

The risk models utilize "objective" probability statements based on other persons' experiences (for example, expectancy tables or regression equations), where available, in the VDM process. This procedure was suggested in the Katz and Kaldor-Zytowski models and implied in the Gelatt model. Perhaps the extreme risk advocates are Gelatt and Clarke (1967) who assume that "objective data" is the base-line against which subjective probabilities are compared for "distortions."

The uncertainty models suggest that the probability statements about future events are filtered through the decision maker's subjective judgments before fitting into the array of information used to make a final commitment. Tiedeman's (1967) distinction between data (facts) and information (interpreted facts) seems to capture the essence of the different assumptions. Hilton, Vroom, and Hsu appear to incorporate information rather than facts into their VDM models.

The arguments probably boil down to choosing between beliefs about the differences between the contemporary experiences of the decision maker and the experiences of several past decision makers. Those who prefer the risk assumption find this difference insignificant for decision purposes, whereas those preferring the uncertainty assumption attach considerable importance to these differences.

3. *Assumptions about the decision strategy being implemented by*

the decision maker. Decision strategies in VDM models can be considered of two general sorts: the *classical models* that attempt to select the alternatives with maximum subjective expected utilities, and the *satisficing models* that attempt to minimize the difference between an alternative and some preconceived standard (for example, level of aspiration). The former group includes Vroom, Gelatt, and Kaldor-Zytowski. All see the decision maker as comparing several alternative actions and selecting the one that is "best"—usually the one with the greatest multiplicative products of values and subject probabilities summed over all outcomes. Kaldor-Zytowski add the concept of net value which is the aggregate value less the aggregate costs for a given occupation. From the satisficing group, Hilton and Hsu assume that the decision-maker has a standard in mind that must be met. This standard is usually not fixed and fluctuates as a result of the decision-maker's experiences. The alternative selected is the one that first meets the standard (Hilton) or the one that comes closest to meeting the standard (Hsu).

Katz uses strategies from both classical and satisficing models. The latter approach is used when the decision-maker is asked to estimate the "threshold level" of a value dimension. The former applies to comparisons of expected value sums across options.

Fletcher does not develop a complete strategy but rather suggests that people decide upon the alternative with the greatest "affect change" at the time a commitment is required.

4. *Assumptions about the level of precision in combining information to make a commitment.* The pivotal concern here usually has to do with assumed performance by the decision-maker in ordering his value preferences. Hilton assumed a simply binary grouping of "yes" or "no" on all outcomes. Others discussed means for ordering value preferences that increase in complexity from Katz and Hsu's constant-sum method to Kaldor-Zytowski's indifference curves.

Perhaps the models break down into those that include mathematical computations as necessary to descriptions of the process of combining information and those that do not. Vroom, Kaldor-Zytowski, Hsu, and Katz use algebraic formulas to define concepts. Gelatt strongly suggests it would be included in a more specific statement of his model.

5. *Assumptions regarding the relationship between two conceptualizations about anticipated future states (outcomes).* The relationship between the subjective probability that the state will obtain and the value attached to it constitutes another issue upon which there are basic differences among VDM models. Two aspects of the relationships are involved: (a) how much distinction a model assumes between the two concepts; and (b) the direction of influence, if any, between them. Kaldor-Zytowski, Vroom, Hsu, Fletcher, Gelatt, and Katz assume that the two concepts are distinctive, whereas Tiedeman-O'Hara and Hilton

blend the two together into one nearly inseparable concept. Gelatt and Clarke (1967) gather evidence to show interrelated effects between the concepts, but most of the models avoided the knotty problems of isolating values and subjective probabilities.

Comparison of VDM Models: Concepts

Table 1 shows a comparison of VDM models on the decision concepts presented earlier. VDM concepts appear to be quite similar although their labels are different. For example, alternative actions are labelled as "goals," "plans," "actions," "options," "career concepts," and "occupational alternatives." Generally speaking, the definitions describe cognitions of anticipated behaviors relevant to vocational goals. A notable exception occurs where the function of alternatives is applied to roles rather than actions, for example, occupational roles. If we assume that the roles designation applies to role entry behavior, the differences fade into insignificance. If, on the other hand, the roles designate relatively stable future *situations* rather than behavior, then they serve different functions: roles as more distant ends, and actions as more immediate means. Indeed roles would be more properly considered as outcomes.

Not all VDM models fit comfortably into the decision theory array of concepts. Models proposed by Hilton, Fletcher, and Katz are particularly difficult. None have a concept that clearly fulfills the "outcomes" function. Hilton's "plans," though not explicitly defined, apparently refer to rather complex actions lasting over a long period of time. Katz starts with personal values and works towards actions— a reversal of the order used to explain behavior in other models. Consequently Katz' "options" may fulfill the functions of both alternative actions and outcomes. Fletcher's "career concepts" may be comfortably viewed as spanning the decision theory function for both alternative actions and outcomes.

Key differences among models appear to be related to notions about time. Some models combine outcomes (thoughts about somewhat distant events) with actions (thoughts about more immediate events), and others separate the two at some point on the conceptalized timeline. This difference (which may constitute a sixth set of separate assumptions) may account for the variation in conceptualizations of "alternative actions." "Situations" or roles may be more temporally distant descriptions of actions.

There are concepts important to some VDM models that can not be neatly placed into Table 1. For example, Hilton's "dissonance test" and "premises," Kaldor-Zytowski's "costs," and Katz' "expected values" are not included. In addition, varied emphasis is placed on concepts from model to model. Emphases on values by Katz and plans by Hilton have already been reviewed. Tiedeman-O'Hara emphasize

TABLE 1. A COMPARISON OF MAJOR DECISION CONCEPTS ACROSS SELECTED VDM MODELS

DECISION CONCEPTS	VOCATIONAL DECISION-MAKING MODELS			
	TIEDEMAN-O'HARA (1963)	HILTON (1962)	VROOM (1964)	HSU (1970)
A. Awareness of decision situation	Awareness that present situation is or will become unsatisfactory	Input that alters present vocational status		
B. Alternative actions	Goals which can possibly be attained from opportunities	Plans	Actions—behavior within repertoire of the person	Alternatives—behavior associated with vocational choice
C. Outcomes	Psychological field—imagined situations including attitudes	Premises about attributes of vocational roles	Outcomes—more distant and less controlled events (than actions)	Outcomes—anticipated rewards from an occupation
C1. Subjective probability	Commitment or orientation		Expectancy—an action-outcome association	Expectancy—probability of chosen behavior leading to particular outcome
C2. Value	Personal values	Satisfactoriness	Valence—anticipated satisfaction	Valence—attractiveness or desirability
D. Commitment	Choice	Plan accepted	Force	Force

VOCATIONAL DECISION-MAKING MODELS

DECISION CONCEPTS	FLETCHER (1966)	KATZ (1963, 1966, 1969A, 1973)	GELATT (1962)	KALDOR-ZYTOWSKI (1969)
A. Awareness of decision situation	Need satisfaction	Disequilibrium—motivated by needs and anticipation of societal pressures	(Statement of) Purpose or objective	
B. Alternative actions	Career concepts—composite of concept system associated with a career	Options	Possible alternative actions	Occupational alternatives
C. Outcomes			Possible outcomes	Outputs
C1. Subjective probability		Strength of return—probabilities that an option will satisfy value dimension. (Objective) probability of entry	Subjective probabilities—estimates of how likely that certain actions will lead to certain outcomes	Subjective probabilities
C2. Value	Affect charge	Values—goals or satisfactions sought	Desirability of outcomes	Occupational utility—extent of obtaining outputs in the proportion desired
D. Commitment			Investigatory decision or terminal decision	Occupational choice

the psychological field, Fletcher the career concept, Kaldor-Zytowski the occupational utilities, and Gelatt the information about probabilities.

VDM Models and Decision Types

By utilizing an analytic model introduced by Braybrooke and Lindblom (1963), a clearer picture emerges of the purposes VDM models serve. Earlier it was proposed that VDM models differed on assumptions about (1) the amount of understanding—information and computational skill—assumed to be available to the decision maker, and (2) the distance in time from the present situation to the imagined futures under consideration (for example, the choice of an occupational role has long-range effects, but selection of a part-time job has short-range consequences). By imagining these two assumptions on continua and describing the extremes, four recognizable decision types appear:

1. Decisions that effect long-range changes and are guided by considerable information and understanding.
2. Decisions that effect long-range changes but are based on limited information.
3. Decisions that effect short-range changes and are based on minimal information.
4. Decisions that effect short-range changes and are based on considerable information and high understanding.

In Figure 1 these types appear as quadrants 1, 2, 3, and 4 respectively.

The four decision types generally refer to vocational behaviors described in the VDM models. Type 1 vocational decisions occur where decision makers have rich informational and computational resources and are ready to make long-range commitments. These decisions are rarely observed. Perhaps the closest approximations are those decisions faced by upper-class, bright males, such as the Harvard undergraduates studied by McArthur (1954), who were found to be highly predictable occupational decision makers. At least one VDM model, Kaldor-Zytowski, describes Type 1 decisions. In order to apply such a model, a considerable amount of computation is required which necessitates "intelligent" resources such as brilliant thinkers, computers, or both. With the full operation of computer information systems, such as ISVB and SIGI referred to previously, the Tiedeman-O'Hara and Katz models can be applied to Type 1 decisions.

Type 2 decisions apply to long-range commitments rather than commitments to immediate action, but require lesser amounts of information and computational skill. There are several "unknowns," but situations often hold out the prospect of some highly-prized rewards.

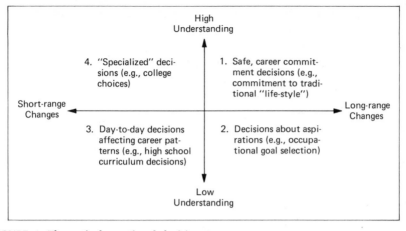

FIGURE 1. Theoretical vocational decision types.

Such decision processes may precede setting career goals that function as "levels of aspiration" in shorter-term decisions. Braybrooke and Lindblom included under Type 2 decisions those that led to "grand opportunities" on the one hand, or crises on the other.

Fletcher's model appears to operate under the condition of Type 2 decisions—selection of an occupational goal where less-than-complete information is necessary. Perhaps the "career concepts" that Fletcher describes are functioning as "aspirations."

Type 3 decisions assume short-range changes and relatively low understanding—the day-to-day decisions that make up a career. Osipow (1968) refers to these decisions as links in a complex decision network. Type 3 decisions lead to incremental moves that often make headway but sometimes retrogress. They are characteristically exploratory and serial; that is, they effect gradual changes on short-range goals as decisions are made in sequence.

Among the VDM models reviewed, those by Tiedeman-O'Hara, Hilton, and the investigatory portion of the Gelatt model come closest to describing Type 3 vocational decisions. They assumed relatively low levels of knowledge and computational skill. Most of the decision situations for which these models were intended cover shorter periods of time than the usual "occupational choice." Tiedeman-O'Hara have assumed that their model would be applied to several vocational decision situations simultaneously. Hilton's model was intended to deal with decisions in sequences.

Type 4 vocational decisions are those for which many VDM models have been adopted. Such decisions involve elaborate and detailed information utilized by exacting processes to accomplish a more immediate change. Consequently, Type 4 decisions are referred to as "technical" decisions such as college choices where sufficient data are sometimes available. Hills (1964), Hammond (1965), and Gelatt

(1967) describe models especially for college selection. Vroom, Gelatt, and Katz appear to offer the most applicable VDM models. Each requires considerable and detailed information, and each is intended to apply to short-range decisions. Machine and mathematical technologies have been developed to assist the decision maker with Type 4 decisions. Ehling (1966) developed an elaborate computer model describing high school students' decision processes when considering whether or not to enroll in a college. Marshall (1967) has described applications of "Bayesian decision" to vocational problems. Novick and Jackson (1970) discussed a mathematically sophisticated "Bayesian guidance technology" that would increase the accuracy of prediction about two or more career opportunities. The authors note that the time is ripe to use this technology. Perhaps the precise thought behind the Novick-Jackson "technology" can be wedded to hardware in computer-assisted vocational decision programs (for example, those described in Super, 1970, and United States Dept. of Health, Education and Welfare, 1969) to yield meaningful assistance in making vocational decisions of this type.

Conclusions

We have shown that the VDM models are similar in many ways to decision theory and to each other but certainly not to the point where parts of one can be interchanged for parts of another.

We have shown that VDM models vary substantially on their assumptions about the decision maker and the conditions under which the decision is made.

We have shown that VDM models are applicable to different types of decisions.

The models are not clearly enough defined nor is there sufficient research evidence to consider discussions about which might be the better explainer or predictor. As a matter of fact, the models appear to be more complementary than competitive. For example, Fletcher's model explains the derivation of "career concepts" that, in turn, may function as "goals" in the Tiedeman-O'Hara model. Thus, they may connect. Likewise the Katz model may suggest strategies suitable for "technical decisions," whereas Hilton's model would apply to decisions where less information is available.

Although we have not been able to make evaluative conclusions about the various VDM models, we think we have been able to sift through the semantic jungle and isolate some of the fundamental issues with which future theorists and researchers must come to grips if VDM models are ever to achieve their promise in describing vocational development over a lifetime.

References

ATKINSON, J. W. Motivational determinants of risk-taking behavior. *Psychological Review*, 1957, **64,** 359–372.

BECKER, G. M., and MC CLINTOCK, C. Value: Behavioral decision theory. *Annual Review of Psychology*, 1967, **18,** 239–286.

BLAU, P. M., GUSTAD, J. S., JESSER, R., PARNES, H. S., and WILCOCK, R. C. Occupational choice: A conceptual framework. *Industrial Labor Relations Review*, 1956, **9,** 531–543.

BRAYBROOKE, D., and LINDBLOM, C. E. *A strategy of decision: Policy evaluation as a social process.* New York: The Free Press, 1963.

BRAYFIELD, A. H. Counseling psychology. *Annual Review of Psychology*, 1963, **14,** 319–350.

BRAYFIELD, A. H. Research on vocational guidance: Status and prospect. Part I: A critical examination of research issues. In H. Borow (Ed.), *Man in a world at work.* Boston: Houghton Mifflin Co., 1964.

BROSS, I. *Design for decision: An introduction to statistical decision-making.* New York: The Free Press, 1953.

CELLURA, A. R. The application of psychological theory in educational settings: An overview. *American Educational Research Journal*, 1969, **6,** 349–382.

CLARKE, R., GELATT, H. B., and LEVINE, L. A decision-making paradigm for local guidance research. *Personnel and Guidance Journal*, 1965, **44,** 40–51.

CRITES, J. O. *Vocational psychology.* New York: McGraw-Hill, 1969.

CRONBACH, L. J., and GLESER, G. C. *Psychological tests and personnel decisions.* Urbana, Ill.: University of Illinois Press, 1957.

DAVIDSON, D., SUPPES, P., and SIEGEL, S. *Decision-making: An experimental approach.* Stanford, Calif.: Stanford University Press, 1957.

DOLLIVER, R. H. An adaptation of the Tyler Vocational Card Sort. *Personnel and Guidance Journal*, 1967, **45,** 916–920.

EDWARDS, W. H. The theory of decision-making. *Psychological Bulletin,* 1954, **51,** 380–417.

EDWARDS, W. H. Behavioral decision theory. *Annual Review of Psychology*, 1961, **12,** 473–498.

EDWARDS, W. H., LINDMAN, P., and PHILLIPS, L. Emerging technologies for making decisions. In *New directions in psychology, II.* New York: Holt, Rinehart & Winston, 1965.

EDWARDS, W. H., and TVERSKY, A. *Decision-making.* Baltimore: Penguin Books, Inc., 1967.

EHLING, W. P. *Development of a computer model of the factors which influence school students to continue or discontinue their education.* Syracuse University, 1966.

FEATHER, N. T. Subjective probability and decision under uncertainty. *Psychological Review*, 1959, **66,** 150–164.

FESTINGER, L. *A theory of cognitive dissonance.* Stanford, Calif.: Stanford University Press, 1957.

FLETCHER, F. M. Concepts, curiosity and careers. *Journal of Counseling Psychology*, 1966, **13,** 131–138.

GELATT, H. B. Decision-making: A conceptual frame of reference for counseling. *Journal of Counseling Psychology*, 1962, **9,** 240–245.

GELATT, H. B. Information and decision theories applied to college choice and planning. In *Preparing school counselors in educational guidance.* New York: College Entrance Examination Board, 1967.

GELATT, H. B., and CLARKE, R. B. Role of subjective probabilities in the decision process. *Journal of Counseling Psychology,* 1967, **14,** 332–341.

HAMMOND, J. S. Bringing order into the selection of a college. *Personnel and Guidance Journal*, 1965, **43**, 654–660.

HILLS, J. R. Decision theory and college choice. *Personnel and Guidance Journal*, 1964, **43**, 17–22.

HILTON, T. L. Alleged acceptance of the occupational role of teaching. *Journal of Applied Psychology*, 1960, **44**, 210–215.

HILTON, T. L. Career decision-making. *Journal of Counseling Psychology*, 1962, **19**, 291–298.

HILTON, T. L., BAENNINGER, R., and KORN, J. H. Cognitive studies in career decision-making. Cooperative Research Project No. 1046. Pittsburgh: Carnegie Institute of Technology, 1962.

HILTON, T. L., LEVIN, H., and LEIDERMAN, G. L. Studies of teacher behavior. *Journal of Experimental Education*, 1957, **26**, 81–91.

HOLLAND, J. L. *The psychology of vocational choice*. Waltham, Mass.: Blaisdell, 1966.

HSU, C. C. A conceptual model of vocational decision-making. *Experimental Publication System*, 1970, **8,** Ms. #270–276.

KALDOR, D. R., ELDRIDGE, E., BURCHINAL, L. G., and ARTHUR, I. W. *Occupational plans of Iowa farm boys*. Research Bulletin 508. Ames, Iowa: Iowa State University, 1962.

KALDOR, D. R., and ZYTOWSKI, D. G. A maximizing model of occupational decision-making. *Personnel and Guidance Journal*, 1969, **47**, 781–788.

KATZ, M. R. *Decisions and values: A rationale for secondary school guidance*. New York: College Entrance Examination Board, 1963.

KATZ, M. R. A model of guidance for career decision-making. *Vocational Guidance Quarterly*, 1966, **15**, 2–10.

KATZ, M. R. Can computers make guidance decisions for students? *College Board Review,* Summer, 1969, **12,** 13–17. (a)

KATZ, M. R. Interests and values: A comment. *Journal of Counseling Psychology*, 1969, **16**, 460–461. (b)

KATZ, M. R. Theoretical formulations of guidance. *Review of Educational Research*, 1969, **39,** 127–140. (c)

KATZ, M. R. The name and nature of vocational guidance. In H. Borow (Ed.), *Career guidance for a new age*. Boston: Houghton Mifflin, 1973.

KROLL, A., DINKLAGE, L. B., LEE, J., MORLEY, E. D., and WILSON, E. H. *Career development: Growth and crisis*. New York: Wiley, 1970.

LEE, W. *Decision theory and human behavior*. New York: Wiley, 1971.

LEWIN, K. *Field theory in social science*. New York: Harper & Row, 1951.

LOUGHARY, J. W. Some proposed new developments in vocational aspects of counselor education. In C. McDaniels (Ed.), *Conference on vocational aspects of counselor education*, 1965.

MARSHALL, J. C. Bayesian decision. *Journal of Counseling Psychology*, 1967, **14**, 342–345.

MARX, M. H. The general nature of theory construction. In M. H. Marx (Ed.), *Theories in contemporary psychology*. New York: Macmillan, 1963.

MC ARTHUR, C. Long term validity of the Strong Interest Test in two subcultures. *Journal of Applied Psychology*, 1954, **38**, 346–353.

MILLER, G. A., GALANTER, E., and PRIBRAM, K. *Plans and the structure of behavior*. New York: Holt, Rinehart and Winston, 1960.

NEWELL, A., SHAW, J. C., and SIMON. H. A. Elements of a theory of human problem-solving. *Psychological Review*, 1958, **65**, 151–166.

NOVICK, M. R., and JACKSON, P. H. Bayesian guidance technology. *Review of Educational Research*, 1970, **40**, 459–494.

OSIPOW, S. H. *Theories of career development*. New York: Appleton-Century-Crofts, 1968.

PEAK, H. Attitude and motivation. In M. R. Jones (Ed.), *Nebraska Symposium on Motivation*. Lincoln, Neb.: University of Nebraska Press, 1955.

ROTTER, J. B. *Social learning and clinical psychology*. Englewood Cliffs, N.J.: Prentice-Hall, 1954.

ROTTER, J. B. The role of psychological situation in determining the direction of human behavior. In M. R. Jones (Ed.), *Nebraska Symposium on Motivation*. Lincoln, Neb.: University of Nebraska Press, 1955.

SIMON, H. A. A behavioral model of rational choice. *Quarterly Journal of Economics*, 1955, **49,** 99–118.

SIMON, H. A. *Administrative behavior*. New York: The Macmillan Co., 1958.

SIMONS, J. B. An existential view of vocational development. *Personnel and Guidance Journal*, 1966, **44,** 604–610.

SUPER, D. E. Book reviews. *Journal of Counseling Psychology*, 1961, **8,** 190.

SUPER, D. E. (Ed.) *Computer-assisted counseling*. New York: Teachers College Press, Columbia University, 1970.

SUPER, D. E., STARISHEVSKY, R., MATLIN, N., and JORDAAN, J. P. *Career development: Self-concept theory*. New York: College Entrance Examination Board, 1963.

TAYLOR, D. W. *Decision-making and problem-solving*. New Haven: Dept. of Psychology and Dept. of Industrial Administration, Yale University, 1963.

THORESEN, C. E., and MEHRENS, W. A. Decision theory and vocational counseling: Important concepts and questions. *Personnel and Guidance Journal*, 1967, **46,** 165–172.

TIEDEMAN, D. V. Decision and vocational development: A paradigm and its implications. *Personnel and Guidance Journal*, 1961, **40,** 15–21.

TIEDEMAN, D. V. Purposing through education: The further delineation of goal and program for guidance. In E. Landy and P. A. Perry (Eds.), *Guidance in American education: Backgrounds and perspectives*. Cambridge: Harvard Graduate School of Education, 1964.

TIEDEMAN, D. V. Career development through liberal arts and work. *Vocational Guidance Quarterly*, 1965, **14,** 1–7.

TIEDEMAN, D. V. Predicament, problem, and psychology: The case for paradox in life and counseling psychology. *Journal of Counseling Psychology*, 1967, **14,** 1–8.

TIEDEMAN, D. V., and FIELD, F. L. Guidance: The science of purposeful action applied through education. *Harvard Educational Review*, 1961, **32,** 483–501.

TIEDEMAN, D. V., and O'HARA, R. P. *Career development: Choice and adjustment*. New York: College Entrance Examination Board, 1963.

TIEDEMAN, D. V. et al. *Information system for vocational decisions: Annual report, 1966–67*. Cambridge, Mass.: Harvard Graduate School of Education, 1967.

TIEDEMAN, D. V. et al. *Information system for vocational decisions: Annual report 1967–68*. Cambridge, Mass.: Harvard Graduate School of Education, 1968.

TOLMAN, E. C. Principles of purposive behavior. In S. Koch (Ed.), *Psychology: A study of a science*. Vol. 2. New York: McGraw-Hill, 1959.

TYLER, L. E. Research exploration in the realm of choice. *Journal of Counseling Psychology*, 1961, **8,** 195–201.

UNITED STATES DEPT. OF HEALTH, EDUCATION AND WELFARE. *Computer-based vocational guidance systems*. Washington, D.C.: U. S. Govt. Printing Office, 1969.

VROOM, V. H. *Work and motivation*. New York: Wiley, 1964.

ZACCARIA, J. S. *Theories of occupational choice and vocational development*. Boston: Houghton Mifflin, 1970.

Relationship of Self-Concept and Vocational Maturity to Vocational Preferences of Adolescents

Octavia M. Jones,
James C. Hansen,
and
Barbara A. Putnam

Research on theories of vocational development and choice has typically been conducted separately with little or no attempt to combine concepts from different theories. This paper investigated the relationships among Super's vocational theory involving the variables of self-concept and vocational maturity and Holland's variables of personality and environmental vocational categories.

Super's (1963) theory emphasizes the process of vocational development. Vocational development is an extended process that has as its key construct the self-concept. A recurring theme is that an individual chooses an occupation which permits the individual to function in a role consistent with his or her self-concept. As the individual matures vocationally, he or she passes through a series of developmental stages which afford him or her opportunities to deal with specific tasks. The ability to cope with the attitude and behavioral tasks is a measure of an individual's level of vocational maturity. Vocational maturity attitudes include orientation toward future work, independence in decision making, preferences for various vocational choice factors, and perceptions of the vocational choice process.

Whereas Super focuses on the developmental process, Holland concentrates more on vocational choice. Holland's (1966, 1973) theory states that a career choice is an extension of personality as an individual attempts to implement broad personal and behavior styles into the context of work. An individual's vocational choice is a preference for a certain sterotyped work environment and that environment will be consistent with the individual's personal orientation. Holland has de-

Reprinted from the *Journal of Vocational Behavior*, **8**:31–40 (1976). Copyright © 1976 by Academic Press, Inc. Reproduced by permission.

fined six work environments into which all vocational preferences can be categorized.

Super and Holland's theories have been researched as distinct and separate theories. Making a distinction between a theory of vocational development and a theory of vocational choice is an artificial distinction. Any theory of vocational choice is founded upon a theory of an individual's vocational development. It is not a separate entity but part of the life cycle of an individual's career pattern. Further, an integration of the variables of self-concept (Super) and personality types (Holland) provides the foundation for integrating the two theories. The self-concept is a function of the developmental life history of the individual which leads to the incremental building of Holland's topology of personality types. Maturation and experience contribute to the individual's personality type, until eventually, the individual develops a modal personality profile. Researching an integration of the theoretical concepts necessitates an investigation of the relationship among the variables of self-concept as measured by the Tennessee Self-Concept Scale, vocational maturity attitudes as measured by the Vocational Development Inventory, and vocational preference categories as determined by the Vocational Preference Inventory. Focusing on one age group leads to such questions as: Do adolescents in the six vocational categories have different levels of vocational maturity attitudes? Are there differences in the level of self-concept among adolescents in the six vocational categories? Is the relationship between self-concept and vocational maturity different within the specific vocational categories? From these questions the following research hypotheses were investigated:

1. There are significant differences in vocational maturity among subjects in the six vocational categories.
2. There are significant differences in self-concept among subjects in the six vocational categories.
3. There is a significant relationship between self-concept and vocational maturity among subjects in the six vocational categories.

Method

Subjects

The subjects were selected from four junior high schools and two senior high schools in the Niagara Falls, New York School District. A stratified random sample of 100 males and 100 females per grade were drawn independently and at random from the total population of eighth through twelfth grade students enrolled in the above schools. The original sample of 1000 consisted of 80.2 per cent white, 18.1 per cent black, and 1.7 per cent other, which reflects the ethnic population of the school district. Eighty-five (84.9) per cent of the 1000 students completed all instruments, resulting in a sample of 846 (401 males, 445 females). The number of the original 200 per grade level who completed the instruments are as follows: grade 8, 180; grade 9, 185; grade 10, 154; grade 11, 158; grade 12, 169. The majority of the students came from lower middle class and lower class families. The sample represented a broad spectrum of adolescents, ages 13 to 19, from an academically heterogeneous population.

Instruments

Personal Data Form. This form was designed by Putnam (Note 1) to obtain more specific knowledge of the subject's background and current status. By means of this questionnaire an indication of each subject's family structure, parents' educational-vocational background, and socioeconomic status can be derived. In addition, information regarding the subject's age, grade, and sex was sought in order to verify the appropriateness of his or her inclusion in the study. Finally, each subject's educational plans and occupational choice were elicited.

Tennessee Self-concept Scale. This was developed by William H. Fitts from research begun in 1955 in conjunction with the Tennessee Department of Mental Health. It contains 90 items that are equally divided between positively and negatively worded statements. The score obtained on these items is referred to as the Total *P* score and it reflects the overall level of self-esteem. Persons with high scores tend to like themselves, feel that they are persons of value and worth, have confidence in themselves, and act accordingly. People with low scores are doubtful about their own worth, see themselves as undesirable, often feel anxious, depressed, and unhappy, and have little faith or confidence in themselves.

Four kinds of validation procedures were used: (1) content validity; (2) discriminate analysis between groups; (3) correlation with other personality measures; and (4) personality conditions (Fitts, 1965). In all cases the results were statistically significant, thus supporting the use of this instrument in the present investigation.

Vocational Development Inventory. The attitude scale of the Vocational Development Inventory was constructed by Crites so that the variables represented central concepts in vocational development theory and so that the obtained scores would relate monotonically to time. The concepts used, "which assess dispositional tendencies in the individual's vocational development, were: (1) involvement in the choice process, (2) orientation toward work, (3) independence in decision-making, (4) preference for vocational choice factors, and (5) conceptions of the choice process" (Crites, 1969, p. 204).

VARIABLE	N	SEX	GRADE 8	GRADE 9	GRADE 10	GRADE 11	GRADE 12	TOTAL
Realistic	145	M	29.45	29.91	31.13	32.41	29.26	30.19
		F	40.00	34.00	32.67	33.00	39.00	35.00
		Total	30.06	30.24	31.31	32.47	29.61	30.56
Investigative	160	M	32.30	32.41	32.50	34.58	36.75	33.56
		F	33.56	37.50	33.78	36.87	38.50	36.02
		Total	32.66	33.78	32.90	35.42	37.15	34.31
Social	240	M	25.07	28.87	30.67	32.33	32.83	28.91
		F	31.94	34.16	32.58	33.69	35.44	33.64
		Total	30.36	32.63	32.22	33.49	35.15	32.71
Conventional	144	M	30.67	36.00	32.25	34.50	33.60	32.93
		F	31.87	31.48	33.22	34.45	34.79	33.10
		Total	31.67	31.62	33.12	34.45	34.59	33.08
Enterprising	83	M	30.50	33.50	35.00	33.43	32.30	30.96
		F	30.70	29.71	31.00	31.60	31.07	32.57
		Total	30.62	30.56	32.09	32.18	31.56	31.51
Artistic	74	M	33.30	34.70	31.17	33.57	34.00	31.31
		F	31.13	28.50	33.67	31.18	31.00	33.43
		Total	32.33	32.37	32.67	32.11	31.86	32.31

[a] N = 846.

A program of research involving the VDI is presented by Crites in his 1969 publication which suggests that sufficient validity exists for inclusion of this instrument in the present study.

Vocational Preference Inventory. This inventory devised by Holland (1965) was based on the assumption that an inventory can be used to assess personality types corresponding to vocational preference categories. It consists of 160 occupational titles. A person is instructed to respond yes on the answer sheet if the occupation is of interest or appeal and no if the occupation is one that is disliked or uninteresting. The third choice is that the respondent can choose not to mark yes or no for the occupation if undecided.

The inventory yields eleven scales: Realistic, Investigative, Social, Conventional, Enterprising, Artistic, Self-Control, Masculinity, Status, Infrequency, and Acquiescence. For this study, only the six personality categories of the VPI were used. The remaining scales were omitted because their content did not appear germane for assessing adolescents vocational preference categories or other study variables. The first six scales correspond to the six personality types and model environments which are the basis of Holland's theory of personality and vocational choice (Holland, 1966, 1973). The higher a person's score on a scale, the greater his resemblance to the type that scale presents. His highest score represents his preference type (Holland, 1973).

The VPI is valid based on construct and predictive validity tests. Corrected split-half (Kuder-Richardson formula 21) reliabilities based on 6,289 male subjects range from .57 to .89 with a median of .84 and for 6,134 female subjects range from .50 to .89 with a median of .77.

Analysis. Analysis of variance was used to determine the significance of differences in vocational maturity among the six student personality categories. This statistical procedure was also used to determine the significance of level of self-esteem differences among the same six groups. Correlation analysis yielded coefficients indicating the relationship between vocational maturity and level of self-esteem for subjects in each personality category. In all of the statistical analyses the .05 level of significance was utilized.

Results

Vocational Maturity and Vocational Preference Categories

An analysis of the data involved multivariate analysis of variance for the effects the differentiation in vocational preference categories may have had on the dependent variable vocational maturity. An analysis of variance yielded an F value of 7.299 ($df = 5,840$), statistically significant beyond the .0001 level. Since an F ratio of 2.21 was required to accept the hypothesis that a difference exists at the predetermined .05 level of significance, the hypothesis was accepted. There is a significant difference between mean vocational maturity scores in the six vocational categories.

To locate where specific differences occurred, an univariate analysis of variance was conducted which yielded F ratios statistically significant beyond the .05 level. Table 2 presents the obtained F ratios. These results indicated that there were significant differences in mean vocational maturity scores between (1) Realistic and Investigative, Social, Conventional, and Artistic preference categories; (2) Investigative and all others except Conventional; (3) Conventional and Enterprising preference categories.

Subjects whose preferences are in the Realistic category are less vocationally mature than are subjects whose preference are in the Investigative, Social, Conventional, and Artistic categories. Subject preferences in the Investigative category are more vocationally mature than all others except Conventional. Subjects whose vocational preference is Conventional are more vocationally mature than subjects whose preference is Enterprising.

In addition to the major hypothesis, separate analysis of variance

TABLE 2. Analysis of Variance Results Using Vocational Maturity as Criterion

| | VOCATIONAL PREFERENCE CATEGORIES | | | | | |
	R	I	S	C	E	A
Realistic	—	31.78*	12.09*	12.86*	1.29	4.26*
Investigative			7.76*	3.60	13.64*	6.73*
Social				.37	2.70	.28
Conventional					3.85*	.89
Enterprising						.38
Artistic						

* Significant at the .05 level of confidence.

were conducted according to sex and grade level for subjects within preference categories. The analysis of variance conducted for subjects classified within the six vocational preference categories on all grade levels yielded F values for Investigative (F 3.77, df = 4,150), and Social (F = 5.03, df = 4,230) vocational preference categories are statistically significant beyond the level adopted for this study. Students whose vocational preferences are in the Investigative and Social categories mature in vocational attitudes as they progress through school.

The analysis of variance results for male and female subjects classified within the six vocational preference categories yielded statistically significant F values beyond the .05 level for subjects in Realistic, (F = 6.38, df = 1.35), Investigative (F = 7.57, df = 1,150), and Social (F = 30.88, df = 1,230) categories. This indicates that female subjects whose vocational preferences are in Realistic, Investigative, and Social categories are more vocational mature in attitudes than are males in the same categories.

Self-concept and Vocational Preference

A multivariate analysis of variance for differences in level of self-esteem among subjects in the six vocational preference categories yielded an F value of 3.893 (df = 5,840), which is statistically significant beyond the .01 level. A significant difference exists in the mean self-concept scores among subjects within the six personality categories, thus supporting the second hypothesis.

Table 3 presents total mean self-concept scores for students in the six vocational preference categories. To further investigate where specific differences existed, univariate analysis of variance was conducted. These results reported in Table 4 indicate that there were significant differences in mean self-concept scores between (1) Realistic and Investigative, Social, and Conventional preference categories; and (2) Intellectual and both Enterprising and Artistic categories. Subjects

TABLE 3. Total Grade Level and Sex Mean Scores Reflecting Self-Concept for Subjects Classified in Vocational Preference Categories

VARIABLE	N	SEX	GRADE 8	GRADE 9	GRADE 10	GRADE 11	GRADE 12	TOTAL
Realistic	145	M	306.00	320.94	318.57	323.41	313.93	315.8
		F	340.00	308.67	283.00	296.50	377.00	311.4
		Total	307.90	319.90	314.50	320.60	316.20	315.42
Investigative	160	M	341.35	327.74	334.95	335.52	325.85	333.0
		F	325.78	316.30	314.22	330.80	338.83	324.9
		Total	337.00	324.60	328.50	333.60	328.80	330.50
Social	240	M	314.00	336.08	322.83	319.33	312.17	322.6
		F	324.36	325.19	332.31	329.09	335.31	329.2
		Total	322.00	328.30	330.50	327.70	332.70	327.88
Conventional	144	M	337.67	341.00	315.50	313.50	312.80	320.5
		F	330.40	318.18	332.84	330.65	329.71	327.9
		Total	331.60	318.90	331.10	329.10	326.80	327.11
Enterprising	83	M	325.40	302.71	321.38	323.40	321.87	320.4
		F	313.17	292.50	323.67	331.14	314.50	317.8
		Total	320.80	300.40	322.00	325.90	318.90	319.53
Artistic	74	M	314.63	309.00	331.11	327.27	316.80	321.4
		F	310.50	322.50	289.50	342.86	308.50	317.2
		Total	312.30	318.10	314.50	333.70	314.40	319.41

whose preferences are in the Realistic category are lower in self-esteem than are subjects whose preferences are in the Investigative, Social, and Conventional categories. Subject preferences in the Investigative category have a higher level of self esteem than subjects whose preferences are Realistic, Enterprising, and Artistic.

Further examination of the data revealed that students' mean self concept do not show clear differentiation among the five grade levels or between males and females. Analysis of variance results yielded

TABLE 4. Analysis of Variance Results Using Self-concept as Criterion

	VOCATIONAL PREFERENCE CATEGORIES					
	R	I	S	C	E	A
Realistic		12.47*	10.10*	9.30*	.70	.56
Investigative			.45	.75	4.76*	4.17*
Social				.04	3.10	3.05
Conventional					3.13	2.72
Enterprising						.01
Artistic						

* Significant at the .05 level of confidence.

VARIABLES	N	SEX	R	R^2
VM + SC	401	M	.260*	.07
VM + SC	445	F	.219	.05
VM + SC	846	T	.244*	.06

* Significant at the .05 level of confidence.

nonsignificant *F* values. No differences in levels of self esteem exist in vocational preference categories when examined by subjects grade levels or sex.

Vocational Maturity, Self-concept, and Vocational Preference

Correlation analysis was computed to determine whether vocational maturity and self-concept were significantly related within the six vocational preference categories. A simple regression analysis revealed that the relationship between vocational maturity and self-concept was weak but significantly positive in four of the six groups. Vocational maturity and self-concept are significantly correlated in the Realistic, Social, Conventional, and Artistic vocational preference categories.

Fourteen per cent of vocational maturity variance can be attributed to self-concept scores within the Realistic category, 9 per cent can be attributed within the Artistic category, and 4 per cent within the Social and Conventional categories.

For the students whose vocational preferences are in the Realistic, Social, Conventional, and Artistic categories, there is a positive relationship between their levels of self-esteem and vocational attitude maturity.

Self-concept and Vocational Maturity

Table 5 shows statistical data reflecting the relationship of vocationally mature and self-concept for the total sample and for males and females. A correlation coefficient of .244 indicates that the relationship of vocational maturity and self-concept is characterized as weak but significantly positive beyond the .05 level for the total group.

The coefficient of .260 indicates that the relationship is weak but significantly positive beyond the .05 level for males. The coefficient for females is not significant. While level of self-esteem may be viewed as a predictor of vocational maturity for the total sample, it is only a predictor for males.

Discussion

This paper investigated three questions generated from an examination of the relationship among Super's vocational theory variables of self-concept and vocational maturity and Holland's theory variables of personality and environmental-vocational categories. The results demonstrated that there were differences in vocational maturity and levels of self-esteem in six vocational preference categories. Further analysis indicated that subjects in the Investigative, Social, and Conventional categories had more mature vocational attitudes and higher levels of self-esteem. On the other hand, students of three vocational orientations (Realistic, Enterprising, and Artistic) were not as adequately prepared to make educational-vocational decisions as their peers.

It appears that students in certain vocational preference categories have more awareness and involvement with vocational choice factors than students in other categories. Is it the individual's personal characteristics which influence his choosing certain occupations which also contribute to his or her more mature vocational attitudes? This would probably be the contention of Holland's theory. Could the structure and school curriculum affect the awareness and involvement with certain areas? Schools typically offer a curriculum with more focus on vocational areas encompassed by the Investigative, Social, and Conventional categories.

In examining the vocational attitude maturity means from grades 8 through 12, it is apparent that three categories, Investigative, Social, and Conventional show a progression with the Investigative and Social categories showing statistically significant change. Although students in these three categories have the highest levels of self-esteem there is no important progression through the grades.

The relationship of vocational maturity attitudes and self-concept with the categories produced an interesting result. Even though students in the Investigative category consistently had the highest mean scores on both instruments, there was not a significant correlation between the scores. It was in the Social, Enterprising, Conventional, and Realistic categories that there was a weak but significant positive relationship between vocational attitudes and level of self-esteem. This information can probably best be used to encourage career guidance programs to be concerned with examining self as well as information about careers.

The significance of the finding of no positive relationship between vocational maturity and self-esteem within the Investigative category can probably best be understood if viewed in relation to other findings. Self-concept and vocational maturity were found to be significantly related for the total population but not for females. Females whose preferences were Investigative, Realistic, and Social had a higher level of vocational maturity than males in the same category. However, female preferences were concentrated in the Social and Artistic categories while male preferences were concentrated in the Investigative and Realistic categories. It would appear that the sex differences in preferences and relationship between vocational maturity and self-esteem for students in this sample, mainly lower class and lower middle class families, produced the lack of relationship within the Investigative category. This supports earlier findings by Putnam (1971) that controlling for self-concept, there is a positive relationship between social class and vocational maturity for females: the higher the social class, the more vocationally mature the female.

The results of this study suggests that the investigation of the inter-relationship of different theories can be fruitful. This cross-sectional exploration has shown enough variation among vocational categories to indicate a need for longitudinal studies. One such study is currently being carried out in the Niagara Falls School System. It is hoped that continued research can lead to a more comprehensive theory of vocational development.

References

CRITES, J. O. *Vocational psychology.* New York: McGraw-Hill, 1969.

FITTS, W. H. *Tennessee Self-Concept Scale: manual.* Nashville, TN: Counselor Recordings and Tests, 1965.

HOLLAND, J. L. *Vocational Preference Inventory manual.* Iowa City, Iowa: Educational Research Associates, 1965.

HOLLAND, J. L. *The psychology of vocational choice.* Waltham, MA: Blaisdell, 1966.

HOLLAND, J. L. *Making vocational choices: a theory of careers.* Englewood Cliffs, NJ: Prentice-Hall, 1973.

SUPER, D. E., STARISKEVSKY, R., MATLIN, N., and JORDAAN, J. P., *Career development: self-concept theory.* New York: College Entrance Examination Board, 1963.

Reference Note

1. PUTNAM, B. A. Relationship of self-concept and feminine role concept to vocational maturity in young women. Unpublished doctoral dissertation. State University of New York at Buffalo, 1971.

The relationship of the social structure to the value system of a society has been central to the sociological tradition. Karl Marx attempted to base the value system of any society ultimately upon the material, or technological, infrastructure. In response to late nineteenth century popularizations of Marxism which claimed that values were always the effect of antecedent technological factors, Max Weber demonstrated that values or "ideational" factors were a necessary part of any explanation of the generation of technological change. More recently, Kerr et al., (15) developed what has been termed the "convergence thesis" that "industrialization in any country displays many of the same features"; a crucial feature of which was the development of a similar value system, despite different pre-industrial cultural traditions. Kerr (42) states that, "the industrial society, as any established society, develops a distinctive consensus which relates individuals and groups to each other and provides a common body of ideas, beliefs and value judgments." Upon the basis of such a theoretical explanation, it is clear that one would expect a priori a high similarity of popular evaluations of occupational prestige rankings in societies at the same stage of industralization, despite different cultural traditions.

Since the original National Opinion Research Center study on occupational prestige in the USA, there has been an increasing number [1] of similar studies into the concept. However, before discussing these results in a cross-societal framework, it is necessary to investigate the meaning of these different studies. The operational definitions of occupational prestige cited by Hodge et al. (313–15) are "social standing," "prestige," "social status," "respect," "admiration," "social prestige," "honor or importance" and "general desirability." Such a diversity leads one to wonder if the operationalizations are interchangeable or whether they are measuring different concepts. The only possible solutions to this dilemma are either to analyze the concept of prestige (a feature generally lacking in the research material) and thereby discern the logical relevance of the various operationalizations or to discover empirically if a given set of respondents treat different

Reprinted from *Social Forces*, **54**:352–364 (Dec. 1975), by permission.

operationalizations in the same manner when they are asked questions involving different operationalizations on a questionnaire.

Prestige is a broad conception. In popular usage it refers to notions of esteem, honor, reputation, eminence, renown, admiration and acclamation. In any society, each type of social role will possess more or less prestige relative to other types of roles and it will be accorded its relative position depending on its being generally defined as superior or inferior according to the dominant value system. The basis of these societal definitions of relative superiority has been suggested by Shils in his analysis of the nature of deference behavior. He suggests that there enters into every interaction between an "ego" and an "alter," an element of appreciation or derogation of the partner towards whom the action is directed. The granting of deference in social interaction entails an attribution of worthiness. This notion of the relative worthiness of a social role would appear to signify a notion of relative goodness in terms of the operative ideals of a collectivity —those ideals that are expressed in norms and enforced by sanctions, thereby constituting the ideals by which members of a given society are actually supposed to guide their behavior.

The actual bases of deference are multiple. Shils (106) suggests occupational role and occupational accomplishment, wealth, income, style of life, education, political power, corporate power, ethnicity and the possession of "objective acknowledgements," such as titles and ranks, as all constituting "prestige entitling properties." Yet the prestige of any particular social role is based on a different combination of factors which produce its relative moral worthiness and, consequently, entitle it to the show of deference behavior. These many empirical bases of prestige as an attitude and deference behavior as action only become meaningful in a given societal context if the dominant value system erects such criteria as subjectively relevant. Wealth and power, for instance, only become meaningful symbols of worthiness and, therefore, legitimate grounds for the general allocation of prestige and deference when the dominant value system selects such criteria as acceptable. Prestige as an attitude forming the basis for deference behavior can only be similar in different societies if the accepted criteria of worthiness are similarly alike.

It is evident that all the different operationalizations appear to be related to this broad conception of prestige. Yet, in order to discover whether such an assumption was empirically justified, 120 American college students [2] were asked two different questions about the same set of thirty occupations.[3] The first question was a direct replication of the original NORC questionnaire.[4] The alternative operationalization was to ask the same students to rank the occupations "according to how much you personally esteem and honor that occupation," [5] and was based upon the question used by Brenner and Hrouda [6] (1–27) in their research on Czechoslovakia that asked "Give the order of the

3 occupations you personally esteem and honor the most." The correlation coefficient [7] of "social standing" and "esteem and honor" within the U.S. sample was .95, which indicates that the two operationalizations measure the same concept. The correlation coefficient of "social standing" in the U.S. student sample and the NORC results was .97, and this suggests strongly that students in the U.S. are typical in their attitudes of the wider population. These two summary measures indicate that the research of Brenner and Hrouda and my research can be compared on the broader basis of a general comparison between Czechoslovakia and the U.S. and that the results can be added to the other studies on occupational prestige.

The increasing number of industrial studies of occupational prestige has led sociologists to investigate the relationship of prestige hierarchies across societies. Inkeles and Rossi present rank-order correlation coefficients for the U.S., U.K., New Zealand, West Germany, Japan and the USSR, all of which are very high,[8] indicating a basic similarity cross-nationally in the respective prestige rankings. Since the six nations were all relatively industrialized, Inkeles and Rossi conclude (339) that "a great deal of weight must be given to the cross-national similarities in social structure which arise from the industrial system." By and large, they found little evidence to support any "culturalist" contention that, "within each country or culture the distinctive local value system would result in substantial—and, indeed, sometimes extreme—differences in the evaluation of particular jobs in the standardized modern occupational system," and much to support the "structuralist" position that "there is a relatively invariable hierarchy of prestige associated with the industrial system, even when it is placed in the context of larger social systems which are otherwise differentiated." Clearly, Inkeles and Rossi's interpretation suggests that Kerr et al.'s theory about convergence is empirically close to the mark and that the "logic of industrialism" produces a relatively invariant popular evaluation of occupational prestige in all industrialized societies.

The extension of the study of occupational prestige to nonindustrialized societies has produced evidence that many of these societies have prestige hierarchies very similar in profile to industrialized societies. Tiryakian, in his quota sample of Manila suburban residents and of four rural communities discovered a correlation of .96 between the U.S. and the Philippines. A study of Javanese high school students by Murray Thomas found that the correlation between Indonesia and the U.S. was .94. These results led Hodge et al. (321) to modify the interpretation of Inkeles and Rossi and state that it is "the essential structural similarity shared by all nations of any degree of complexity," rather than simply industrialized social structures, that produce these broadly similar prestige rankings. They conclude (312), "once again we are led to the same conclusion: gross similarities in occupational prestige hierarchies can be accounted for on the basis of gross uniformities in social structure across societies." These alleged uniformities have been specified by Marsh (214), who explains what he calls "one of the great empirical invariants in sociology" in terms of highly similar role attributes for a given occupation in every society and he claims (222) "a given occupation has highly similar requirements for recruitment (educational level), role functioning (authority and power), and similar relative rewards (income) across societies." The basic similarity of all these explanations is that despite occasional minor discrepancies, the role of distinctive cultural values is relatively unimportant when compared to the necessary structure of both industrialized and complex societies.

Socialist societies, most of which are complex and industrialized social structures, are assumed to fall within this general framework. The evidence for the apparent unimportance of socialist values is based on research on the USSR and Poland. The study by Inkeles of Soviet emigres forms the basis for a correlation between the U.S. and the USSR of .90. However, the study suffers from two serious methodological problems; first, emigres are not likely to produce attitudes representative of the Soviet population, and second, only 10 occupations are directly comparable—a number so low that the correlation coefficient of .90 could be very misleading as an indication of a high similarity between the two societies. A Polish study (Sarapata and Wesolowski) permitted a comparison of 19 occupations with the original NORC study and produced a correlation of .87, a figure that suggests strongly that this socialist society falls into the same "logic of industrialism" model.

However, the results in Table 1, based on the comparison of "esteem and honor" rankings between the U.S. and Czechoslovakia do not support such a contention.

The comparison between "esteem and honor" rankings in Czechoslovakia and the U.S. student sample produced a correlation of .56. When a direct comparison was made between the 1966 Czechoslovakian responses on esteem and honor and the original NORC results on the question on "social standing" the correlation was .30. The reason for the lower correlation was that only 15 occupations were directly comparable with NORC, as compared to 25 in the former correlation. The occupations that were most different in relative position were as shown in Table 2. When the esteem and honor rankings of occupational roles in Czechoslovakia and the U.S. were aggregated the results were as indicated in Table 3.

It would appear as if two distinct but interrelated processes are at work in Czechoslovakia that explain the gross dissimilarities between the Czechoslovakian prestige hierarchy and that of the U.S. The Czechoslovakian respondents seem to have a far more favorable evaluation of skilled manual workers than is the case in the U.S. Yet they seem to view the symbols of the political regime in a far less favorable

RANK	OCCUPATION	POINTS
	Czechoslovakia	
1.	Doctor	3,074
2.	Collective farmer	1,016
3.	Scientist	826
4.	Miner	782
5.	High school teacher	761
6.	Engineer	450
7.	University professor	206
8.	Architect	151
9.	Mason	141
10.	Agronomist	111
11.	Locomotive driver	94
12.	Writer	85
13.5)	Cabinet minister	71
13.5)	Actor	71
15.	Cabinet maker	63
16.	Foreman	59
17.	Nurse	54
18.	Priest	53
19.	Judge	46
20.	Army officer	31
21.	Journalist	24
22.	Policeman	16
23.	Sewage worker	14
24.	Cleaning woman	9
25.	Road construction worker	3
26.	Secretary	1

* Brenner and Hrouda report data on 42 occupations: this list contains all those occupations directly comparable with their question on "utility to society."

light. In addition, the main difference between the U.S. sample of students and the main body of the American population, as revealed in the NORC results, was that the students gave occupations like Cabinet Minister and Army Officer far less prestige than the general population. Hence, the lower position of political roles in the Czechoslovakian prestige hierarchy is even more striking. The Czechoslovakian respondents have internalized the values of socialism with its special emphasis on the dignity and worthiness of manual work which is based upon the underlying Marxist philosophical assumption that the industrial proletariat are the universal, revolutionary class that will destroy bourgeois capitalist society and build a new, liberated communist social structure. Yet, they clearly have not accepted the legitimacy of the "new class" of political bureaucrats. (See Djilas.) The political

RANK	OCCUPATION	MEAN SCORE
	USA	
1.	Doctor	4.45
2.	Scientist	4.29
3.	University professor	4.10
4.	Engineer	3.93
5.	Judge	3.92
6.	Architect	3.91
7.	Writer	3.81
8.	Cabinet minister	3.66
9.	Journalist	3.49
10.	High school teacher	3.38
11.	Nurse	3.32
12.	Actor	3.20
13.	Farmer	3.15
14.	Priest	3.08
15.	Cabinet maker	3.05
16.	Policeman	2.81
17.	Foreman	2.67
18.5)	Tailor	2.61
18.5)	Mason	2.61
20.	Civil servant	2.56
21.	Bookkeeper	2.43
22.	Secretary	2.41
23.	Army officer	2.33
24.	Locomotive driver	2.30
25.	Road construction worker	2.25
26.	Shop assistant	2.24
27.	Miner	2.16
29.	Cleaning woman	1.76
29.	Garbage collector	1.76
29.	Sewage worker	1.76

elite's lack of legitimacy helps to explain how the reform movement under Dubcek became a radical assault upon the totalitarian nature of the Czechoslovakian Communist party and precipitated the Soviet invasion of 1968.

Additional evidence to support the idea of a distinctive and socialist value system within Czechoslovakia can be seen when a comparison is made between the U.S. student sample and Czechoslovakia on the question of the utility to society of the 30 occupations [9] (see Table 4).

The responses to these questions on social utility would appear to indicate an aspect of the moral assessment of the worthiness of the occupational role. The influence of distinctively socialist values on notions of moral worth are clear and consistent with the results al-

TABLE 2. Occupations Most Different * in Rank Order of Prestige Between USA and Czechoslovakia

		CHANGE IN POSITION
U.S. Students, 1973—Czechoslovakia, 1966		
Higher in Czechoslovakia:	a. Miner	(+19)
	b. Locomotive driver	(+11)
	c. Farmer	(+11)
	d. Mason	(+ 9)
Lower in Czechoslovakia:	a. Judge	(−13)
	b. Journalist	(+11)
NORC, 1947—Czechoslovakia, 1966		
Higher in Czechoslovakia:	a. Miner	(+10)
	b. Farmer	(+10)
Lower in Czechoslovakia:	a. Judge	(−10)
	b. Cabinet minister	(− 6)

* Differences based upon the results presented in Table 1 and the original NORC results.

TABLE 3. Aggregated Rank Orders for "Esteem and Honor" in Czechoslovakia and the USA

RANK ORDER	OCCUPATIONAL GROUPING *	MEAN SCORE †
Czechoslovakia		
1.	Professionals	5.0
2.	Skilled workers	8.6
3.	Political roles	13.3
4.5	Unskilled workers	16.0
4.5	White collar	16.0
USA		
1.	Professionals	5.0
2.	Political roles	8.0
3.	White collar	11.0
4.	Skilled workers	14.4
5.	Unskilled workers	19.3

* The aggregates were Professionals—doctor, scientist, university teacher, engineer, architect, high school teacher; Political Roles—judge, policeman, cabinet minister, army officer; Skilled Workers—foreman, miner, mason, tailor, cabinet maker, locomotive driver; White Collar—nurse, journalist civil servant, secretary, bookkeeper; Unskilled—sewage worker, road construction worker, shop assistant, cleaning woman.
† Mean scores computed from Table 1 by taking the average of the individual rankings within each occupational grouping.

ready analyzed on prestige. A correlation coefficient of 0.42 was found between the U.S. and the Czechoslovakian rankings of occupational utility to society. When the gross occupational groupings were compared for social utility the results were remarkably similar to those on esteem and honor (see Table 5).

The same pattern of values reveals itself once again. The Czechoslovakian respondents evaluated the utility of skilled workers much higher and roles associated with the political regime far lower. The correlation of utility to society hierarchies with esteem and honor in Czechoslovakia was .87 and in the U.S. was .77. It would appear that popular

TABLE 4. Rank Orders for "Utility to Society" in Czechoslovakia * and the USA

RANK	OCCUPATION	MEAN SCORE
	Czechoslovakia	
1.	Doctor	9.51
2.	Professor	8.72
3.	Scientist	8.60
4.	Engineer	8.57
5.	Miner	8.32
6.	High school teacher	8.28
7.	Locomotive driver	7.90
8.	Collective farmer	7.85
9.	Nurse	7.55
10.	Architect	7.51
11.	Mason	7.47
12.	Cabinet minister	7.38
13.	Foreman	7.28
14.	Judge	6.95
15.	Cabinet maker	6.89
16.	Agronomist	6.86
17.	Writer	6.80
18.	Bookkeeper	6.27
19.	Journalist	6.16
20.	Actor	5.98
21.	Tailor	5.82
22.	Shop assistant	5.81
23.	Policeman	5.77
24.	Sewage worker	5.71
25.	Road construction worker	5.40
26.	Army officer	4.93
27.	Civil servant	4.74
28.	Cleaning woman	4.69
29.	Secretary	4.54
30.	Priest	3.47

* Brenner and Hrouda.

RANK	OCCUPATION	MEAN SCORE
	USA	
1.	Doctor	9.32
2.	Scientist	8.53
3.	Judge	8.02
4.	University professor	7.89
5.	Engineer	7.83
6.	Farmer	7.72
7.	Nurse	7.39
8.	High school teacher	7.34
9.	Policeman	6.97
10.	Architect	6.83
11.	Cabinet minister	6.80
12.	Writer	6.57
13.	Journalist	6.34
14.	Priest	6.22
15.	Garbage collector	5.75
16.	Foreman	5.25
17.	Sewage worker	5.21
18.	Civil servant	5.18
19.	Mason	5.15
20.	Miner	5.11
21.	Road construction worker	5.01
22.	Cabinet maker	4.86
23.	Secretary	4.67
24.	Locomotive driver	4.61
25.	Bookkeeper	4.50
26.	Tailor	4.41
27.	Shop assistant	4.39
28.	Actor	4.37
29.	Army officer	4.01
30.	Cleaning woman	3.60

perceptions of utility to society are very dissimilar in the two societies and that these different perceptions of social utility are legitimating factors in the differential attribution of relative moral worthiness to respective social roles. These large differences in popular perceptions are highly significant for the stratification structure in these societies since they involve systematic differences in the feelings of self-worth and self-esteem of large groups of people and, consequently, lead to different occupational roles and different patterns of deference behavior.

The major problem of interpretation is how to explain these systematic differences between Czechoslovakia and the U.S. A possible explanation might be that they are the results of indoctrination and

TABLE 5. AGGREGATED RANK ORDERS FOR "UTILITY TO SOCIETY" IN CZECHOSLOVAKIA AND THE USA

RANK ORDER	OCCUPATIONAL GROUPING *	MEAN SCORE †
1.	Professionals	4.3
2.	Skilled workers	11.8
3.	Political roles	18.25
4.	White collar	19.6
5.	Unskilled	23.75
	USA	
1.	Professionals	5.0
2.	Political roles	12.75
3.	White collar	16.6
4.	Skilledworkers	20.7
5.	Unskilled workers	22.75

* The groupings are the same as in Table 3.
† Mean scores computed from Table 3 by taking the average of the particular rankings within each occupational grouping.

propaganda by the Communist party. Such an explanation might fit the results on manual workers but it fails to account for the low relative position of political roles. If propaganda were the sole reason for the relatively high prestige of skilled workers, then it should also have been successful in prescribing very high prestige for political roles, since this is crucially necessary for the legitimacy of the regime. Another explanation might be that skilled workers are objectively better off relative to other positions in terms of material rewards and consequently they receive higher prestige. However, such an explanation, despite the correctness of its analysis of the structure of material rewards in Czechoslovakia, again fails to explain why political roles fare so badly in their relative prestige. Clearly, roles such as Cabinet Minister, Judge and Army Officer possess more power and more income than skilled jobs like Miner or Locomotive Driver. The most plausible explanation would appear to be that the general population in Czechoslovakia perceives the relative moral worth of occupational roles quite differently than is the case in the U.S. The results on popular perceptions of social utility indicate that different categories of occupations have been differentially defined as usefully contributing to the general welfare of society in the two societies. Popular perceptions of social utility legitimate the distribution of prestige since they crucially define notions of relative moral worth. The distribution of moral worth in the USA has remained almost constant between 1947 and 1963.[10] There is also evidence that the distribution of moral

TABLE 6. SOCIAL UTILITY IN CZECHOSLOVAKIA IN 1937 *

1. Farmer	7. Businessman
2. Teacher	8. Owner of an industrial plant
3. Worker	9. Soldier
4. Craftsman	10. Politician
5. Doctor	11. Priest
6. Engineer	12. Lawyer in private practice

* Obrdliks, cited in Brenner and Hrouda.

worth has remained fairly constant in Czechoslovakia between 1937 and 1966, despite the structural transformations during the period. Obrdliks in his pre-war research [11] asked a sample of Czechoslovakians [12] to "determine the rank order of the listed occupations according to their importance for the public good." The results clearly reveal a similar pattern to the results of Brenner and Hrouda's research in 1966.

The low position of the priest both in 1937 and 1966 is not surprising in view of popular traditional hostility towards the Roman Catholic Church, a fact intimately tied to the close relationship of Austrian imperial rule and the Catholic clerical hierarchy during Austrian domination of Czechoslovakia. What is surprising is the low relative position of roles associated with the capitalist economic system and the political regime and the high relative position of workers and farmers. The same distinctive socialist value system is evident and it would seem that, given the industrialization of Czechoslovakia between the two world wars, and the vast influx of peasants into the cities—many of which were dominated by capitalists of German ethnicity, these strong socialist attitudes can be explained in terms of Trotsky's notion of the "uprooted." [13] Based on his experience in Russia during the Revolutionary period, Trotsky observed that when peasants entered the industrial working class, they tended to become radical and militant. The sharp discontinuity of peasant life in the countryside and life in the city and the factory was the root of this radical socialist consciousness. The difficulties of the peasant adapting to urban existence was the basis of Durkheim's notion of "anomie." It would appear that out of this situation of initial normlessness felt by peasants entering the industrial work force, there develops socialist consciousness which elevates the worker and the farmer (symbol of a golden age prior to the feelings of uprootedness in the city) and denigrates all roles associated with the political and economic structure of capitalism. It would also appear that these attitudes, associated with the initial dislocation of city life, have persisted over a thirty-year period. This can be explained in part as a result of continued influx of peasants into the cities and also as a consequence of both objective changes in the structure of material rewards and of Communist party propaganda. Nevertheless, this socialist consciousness clearly poses a threat to the stability and legitimacy of the party.

The pattern in Czechoslovakia is very similar to that found by Sarapata and Wesolowski. The correlation of esteem and honor in Czechoslovakia and social prestige in Poland is 0.76, and when Farmer is removed from the original list of 15 comparable occupations, the correlation becomes 0.88. However, the clear similarity of Poland and Czechoslovakia is revealed when Sarapata and Wesolowski's data are aggregated into groupings of occupational roles as shown in Table 7.

This aggregated prestige hierarchy in Poland is identical to the results for Czechoslovakia presented in Table 3, despite the fact that the intercorrelation of individual occupational roles was 0.76.[14] This suggests that it is probably better to look at aggregated groupings of occupations that correspond to the class structure of a society, rather than to focus simply on individual occupational roles if one wishes to make a comparison of prestige hierarchies cross-societally. This is particularly true when the number of occupations compared is small, since the occupations upon which the comparison is made may well be untypical of the overall occupational hierarchy, and hence give very misleading correlation coefficients. The overall stratification system in Poland and Czechoslovakia looks much different than the U.S. In addition to the absence of big business in societies ruled by Communist parties, it is clear that the hierarchies of prestige are very different.

TABLE 7. Aggregated Rank Orders for Social Prestige in Poland

RANK ORDER	OCCUPATIONAL GROUPING *	MEAN SCORE †
1.	Professionals	4.57
2.	Skilled workers	12.33
3.	Political roles	17.33
4.	White collar	18.75
5.	Unskilled	28.0

* The groupings were Professionals—professor, doctor, teacher, engineer, lawyer, agronomist, journalist; Skilled Workers—skilled steel-mill worker, factory foreman; Political Roles—minister of the national government, army officer, policeman; White Collar—airplane pilot, nurse, accountant, office supervisor, railway conductor, office clerk, typist, sales clerk; Unskilled—unskilled construction worker, cleaning woman, unskilled farm laborer on a state farm.
† Mean scores determined in the same manner as Tables 3 and 5.

Notions of moral worth embodied in the attribution of prestige and legitimated on the basis of perceived social utility suggest that Czechoslovakia is a stratified society in the sense that there are clear differences in the moral evaluation of occupational roles. These notions of moral worthiness are very different from the U.S. which suggest that the theoretical analysis of Kerr et al. concerning the "logic of industrialism," and the interpretations of previous empirical comparisons of occupational prestige by Hodge et al., Inkeles and Rossi, and Marsh are all mistaken. There is no necessary structure of moral evaluation of occupational roles associated either with industrial society or with complex social systems. The fact that roles may involve similar attributes, like education, in different societies does not mean that popular evaluations of such attributes will necessarily be the same. This is especially true in the case of an attribute like power. Czechoslovakia and Poland possess political regimes that lack the legitimacy of the American political system. The Communist party, which in Leninist theory constitutes the "dictatorship of the proletariat" and the "vanguard of the revolution," lacks the possession of moral worth that is crucial to its own arrogated position. This conflict between the role of the Party as the leading force in society and the fact that, in the eyes of many people in Eastern Europe, the Party lacks the necessary moral worth to possess the moral authority to lead is a dynamic feature of societies like Poland and Czechoslovakia, and is an indication of potential transformations.

The results discussed in this research indicate that the "convergence," "structuralist" explanations of occupational prestige hierarchies are mistaken, partly because they have tended to ignore socialist societies and partly because they suffer from the serious methodological problem of trying to base an intersocial comparison upon a few similar occupational roles, rather than upon an analysis of the stratification profiles in an aggregated manner. Marsh's "great empirical invariant of sociology" (214) is merely a great empirical myth of sociologists.

Notes

1. R. HODGE et al. cite evidence from 28 studies made in 24 different societies, and provide an extensive bibliography.
2. The sample comprised 53 sophomore engineering students and 67 students from two sociology classes. In addition to this difference in academic orientation, questions were asked to determine the sex, year of college, occupational status of the mother and father (including a question asking if the father was self-employed) and the educational level of the parents. No statistically significant differences were found at either the .05 or the .001 level for any of these background variables.

3. The order of occupations was changed to increase the likelihood that the two questions would be answered on their own merits.
4. "Here is a list of 30 occupations. Please rank each occupation according to the statement that best gives your own personal opinion of the general social standing that such an occupation has. 1. Poor 2. Somewhat below average 3. Average 4. Good 5. Excellent."
5. "Here is a list of 30 occupations. Please mark for each occupation a rank according to how much you personally esteem and honor that occupation. 1. Not very much 2. Somewhat below average 3. Average 4. Good 5. Excellent."
6. "Wissenschaft und Hochschulbildung in Prestige der Berufe." The study involved a mixed quota and random sample that was proportionate to the 1965 Czech micro-census with respect to income, age, occupation, religion, place of residence and ethnicity in the form of the division between Czechs and Slovaks. The number of respondents was 1,400. Given the large size of their respondents, it was felt that the ordinal data that they had generated was directly comparable with the U.S. student sample.
7. All correlation coefficients used in this research are Spearman's rank order correlation coefficient.
8. In most cases the correlations were greater than 0.9, with the lowest being USSR—Japan which was 0.74.
9. BRENNER and HROUDA and the questionnaire administered to the 120 American students both asked the same question to determine popular perceptions of utility to society. "Here is a list of 30 occupations. Please mark for each occupation your opinion as to how useful each is for society. A "1" signifies *least* usefulness and a "10" signifies *most* usefulness."
10. HODGE et al. report an intercorrelation of 99 between the social standing in 1947 and 1963 of the 90 occupations used by NORC.
11. OBRDLIKS, cited by Brenner and Hrouda.
12. OBRDLIKS sample was 914 respondents whose compostion is very strange Nineteen per cent were lower civil servants, 9 per cent workers, 5 per cent soldiers and 5 per cent professors. No reason is given for this by Brenner and Hrouda and I cannot think of any myself.
13. LEGGETT makes use of this theory in his explanation of class militancy in Detroit.
14. 0.88 when Farmer was removed.

References

BRENNER VON V. and HROUDA, M. 1969. "Wissenschaft und Hochschulbildung in Prestige der Berufe." *Soziale Welt* 20: 1–27.
DJILAS, M. 1966. *The New Class, an Analysis of the Communist System.* London: Allen & Unwin.
DURKHEIM, E. 1897. *Suicide: A Study in Sociology.* John A. Sjpaulding (trans). New York: Free Press.
HODGE, R.W., D.S. TREIMAN, and P.H. ROSSI. 1967. "A Comparative Study of Occupational Prestige." In R. Bendix and S. M. Lipset (eds.), *Class, Status and Power.* 2d ed. London: Routledge & Kegan Paul.
HODGE, R.W., P.M. SIEGAL, and P.H. ROSSI. 1969. "Occupational Prestige in the United States: 1925–1963." In R. Bendix and S.M. Lipset (eds.), *Class, Status and Power.* 2d ed. London: Routledge & Kegan Paul.

INKELES, A., and P.H. ROSSI. 1956. "National Comparisons of Occupational Prestige." *American Journal of Sociology.* 61:229–39.

KERR, C. et al. 1960. *Industrialism and Industrial Man.* Cambridge: Harvard University Press.

LEGGETT, J.C. 1968. *Class, Race and Labor: Working Class Consciousness in Detroit.* New York: Oxford University Press.

MARSH, R.M. 1971. "The Explanation of Occupational Prestige Hierarchies." *Social Forces* 50(December), 214–22.

MARX, K. 1859. *Zur Kritik der politischen Oekonomie,* Berlin.

NORC, 1947. "Jobs and Occupations. A Popular Evaluation." In R. Bendix and S.M. Lipset (eds.), *Class, Status and Power.* London, Routledge & Kegan Paul.

OBRDLIKS, A. 1937. *Povolani a verejne blatio. Prestiz povolani a verejne blaho ve svetle postoju.* Prague, Orbis.

SARAPATA, A., and W. WESOLOWSKI, 1961. "The Evaluation of Occupations by Warsaw Inhabitants." *American Journal of Sociology* 66(May), 581–91.

SHILS, E. 1968. "Deference." In John Jackson (ed.), *Social Stratification.* Cambridge: Cambridge University Press.

THOMAS, R.M. 1962. "Reinspecting a Structural Position on Occupational Prestige." *American Journal of Sociology* 67(March) 561–5.

TIRYAKIAN, E.A. 1958. "The Prestige of Occupations in an Underdeveloped County: The Philippines." *American Journal of Sociology* 63(January) 390–99.

TROTSKY, L. 1959. *History of the Russian Revolution.* New York: Doubleday.

WEBER, M. 1904. *The Protestant Ethic and the Spirit of Capitalism.* Talcott Parsons (trans.). London: Allen & Unwin, 1931.

Self-Identification of Talents: First Step to Finding Career Directions

Henry G. Pearson

"Occupational choice is a lifelong process of decision making. . . . The individual remains the prime mover." That was the nub of Eli Ginzberg's classic restatement in 1972 of his theory of occupational choice [6, pp. 172, 175]. Currently there is increasing recognition that

Reprinted from *The Vocational Guidance Quarterly,* **24:**20–26 (Sept. 1975), by permission. Copyright 1975 American Personnel and Guidance Association. Reprinted with permission.

the counselor's role is not merely to assist clients in making particular career choices but to help them learn a method for making such choices [2]. If occupational choice is a lifelong process (from career-related choices in junior high school and earlier to retirement choices at age 65), then it seems logical to teach young people a way they can do it themselves for the rest of their lives.

Although progress is being made in teaching self-awareness and decision making [11; 5], these subjects do not necessarily focus on systematic methods of career decision making. For these methods the guidance profession is relying mainly on traditional approaches to finding skills and interests plus some newer approaches to exploring occupations.

The traditional method for determining skills and interests is, of course, testing. Yet giving youngsters tests simply signals them that the information about themselves is going to come from some other source and not from themselves. They may listen to and even agree with test results but they have learned little about how to identify their skills and interests on their own.

The newer approaches to learning about occupations are career education, explorations, and experiences. All three are vital to career decision making but they usually do not offer students the chance to learn how to spot the skills and qualifications required by an occupation or how to relate the skills they have to that occupation. It is one thing to observe, read, or be told that the airline reservation clerk writes up a ticket, but another to understand that ticket writing is a form of universal skill called record keeping. This chance to learn how to translate a specific skill into its generic equivalent is usually overlooked.

The reason for this lost opportunity is that students have not been coached first in how to identify their own skills and interests; in fact, just the opposite occurs. A test might tell Mary, "Your interests are the same as most computer programmers' interests," but it does not alert her to the daily evidence, past or future. She does not learn that her playing chess and winning debates are evidence of logical thinking, a skill that can be used in computer programming or innumerable other occupations.

Also, Mary may get the impression from the testing process that some other person or instrument is really going to be responsible for picking a career for her. Her natural dependency on parents, teachers, friends, and guidance counselors is enhanced by this conventional approach of telling her where her interest is. Someone else does the evaluating and reporting; someone else is really still in charge. So she does not see herself as the prime mover. It is not surprising that this same dependency on others for career decisions surfaces on her first job and possibly every job thereafter. She sees the boss is largely responsible for her future.

The Career Direction Workshop: First Stage

It was partly to lessen this dependency on the employer for career decision making that my colleague, Gladys M. Bishop, and I developed a method for teaching it in a business setting. She had been exposing employees at Polaroid Corporation to new career fields inside the company by arranging temporary assignments in areas that interested them [1]. But she found that employees not turned on by such career exposures rarely gained much insight into why they did not like them. Furthermore, the exposures had not necessarily helped them analyze what kinds of jobs would be more suitable. What these employees needed was not just exposures and try-out—a "shopping around" process—but an opportunity to learn how to identify their own talents systematically before shopping around.

Together we developed the Polaroid Career Direction Workshop to teach employees how to identify their talents for themselves and how to link these talents to career fields that used them best. This procedure involved group and individual sessions totaling about 10 hours. Emphasis was not on the ultimate outcome, but on learning the process.

In these workshops the participants examined their successful experiences, things they had done well and enjoyed. They described them in detail and analyzed the skills and traits that had made these experiences successful. They could find these events in any period or facet of their lives [10].

Warren, a high school graduate and truck driver, gave as an example his having climbed Mt. Washington as a youth. Describing it, he said it was his idea, he got some others interested, found a map and studied it, talked with his father about the best route, set up a time schedule, met with the others to decide what food to take and clothes to wear, started on schedule, stopped en route to chat with another party, made the top, admired the view, saw a deer, ran into a thunderstorm, and arrived home on time. Parents were worried but congratulatory.

Out of this description Warren extracted the following skills, values, capabilities, and environmental factors: coming up with ideas, persuading others, leadership, consulting with others, investigating and studying, planning, decision making, goal setting, scheduling, physical exertion, persistence, socializing, group cooperation, achieving goals, appreciation of nature, appreciation of beauty, outdoors, overcoming obstacles, and recognition. Some of these words he and others in the group suggested; some he got from a check list of the most commonly used expressions.

Then Warren described and factored a second achievement, selling the most tickets to his senior class play. He was surprised to find how many of the same talents he had displayed: persuasion, planning, goal setting, persistence, socializing, group activity, goal achieving, overcoming obstacles, and recognition. He was intrigued that two such apparently dissimilar activities as mountain climbing (a sport) and ticket selling (an extracurricular school activity) called for some of the same talents. He was beginning to get out of his own subcultures by learning another kind of language [3].

This process continued until Warren had described nine or ten achievements and uncovered the skills and characteristics involved. By logging them on a simple chart, he was able to determine which occurred most frequently and to detect a pattern of common-denominator talents. These were the talents he had actually enjoyed and used successfully in the past and could count on enjoying and using successfully in the future. As Bernard Haldane, who pioneered this concept, commented in his recent book, *Career Satisfaction and Success,* "When you have identified the strong threads of your motivated skills, you will find they weave together into a lifeline that gives job freedom as you choose your changing career paths" [8, p. 160].

This self-analysis of one's past successful experiences to discover talents is the first stage in the career decision-making process. It capitalizes on the principles that people are the products of their past experiences and that emphasizing accomplishments helps them become aware of their own worth [9].

Second Stage

Once Warren had organized his own personal talent bank he was ready to go to the second stage of the Career Direction search, that is, analyzing jobs and careers for the talents (qualifications) required and determining whether or not he had them.

He looked at once into career fields or clusters, either inside or outside the company, that held some interest for him and could use his talents. He could either browse through the 22 "Areas of work" in the *Dictionary of Occupational Titles* (Vol. II) [12] or the 13 groupings in the *Occupational Outlook Handbook* [13]. He could also get leads from the Office of Education charts of 15 occupational clusters [14]. He could have accomplished the same thing by talking to people in his areas of interest.

As he surveyed various occupations he kept his eye on the talents they required and compared them to his own. At this point he did not allow himself to be deterred by the sometimes formidable education and training requirements. The cluster he looked up first in the *Occupational Outlook Handbook* was air transportation. As he had found he had skills with people, he analyzed the air transportation job descriptions for *people* activities. Having learned the terminology as it applied to himself, he could now spot it in job descriptions. For instance, aircraft air traffic controllers *communicate* with pilots; aircraft mechanics *obtain* descriptions of problems from pilots; airline dispatchers *confer* with captains; flight attendants *help* make passengers comfortable; pilots *supervise* other crew members; reservation clerks *sell* tickets. These are all *people* skills required on the job and, thus, desirable as qualifications for the job.

The aim, though, was not to get Warren to decide whether he wanted to be an airline dispatcher or traffic controller, or even to work in that cluster, but to get practice identifying talents required by jobs in terms of his own particular skills. He could use this art repeatedly in exploring careers.

A shipper at Millipore Corporation in Bedford, Massachusetts, listed eight achievements and from these developed half a dozen key talent areas: mobility/physical, manual/mechanical, numbers, working closely with people, learning/observing/following instructions, and planning/following through/getting results. He came up with two quite different career directions: police officer and all-around maintenance mechanic. The fact that they appeared occupationally unrelated did not bother him; he could see they were linked by his six primary talent areas.

As there were no current openings for police officers in his home town or for maintenance mechanics at Millipore, he was considered for another job as an electrical helper. In his interview he produced tangible evidence of the skills that qualified him for that job even though he had no previous electrical experience. The electrical foreman was impressed and took him on.

A dramatic outcome like this is not necessarily the prime purpose of the workshop. Among working adults who participate, usually 25 per cent report that they find new career directions. Another 25 per cent say that it confirms for them that they are in the right careers. And 50 per cent feel it helps them to organize their thoughts, spot unrealized talents, enlarge their view of themselves, and gain confidence. To illustrate, a typically frustrated secretary came to realize during the workshop that she was really good at figures. Thus assured, she asked her boss for some project involving numbers and he promptly obliged. He had never dreamed she would be interested!

A Natural for Students

After teaching this process to about 300 people I have found it a natural for students. One high school senior who first claimed he had never enjoyed or done anything well finally described his favorite pastime, playing baseball. He was delighted to find that he used 15 skills playing second base: observation, following instructions, fast reactions, thinking ahead, close team work (infielding), independent activity (at bat), eye-hand-body coordination, physical energy, numbers, mobility, practice, dependability, perseverance, showmanship, and competition. By the end of our first session, when I pointed out that some of these were traits much prized by employers, his self-esteem had risen noticeably.

An English teacher/adviser used the method in class. She wrote me,

> The students and I felt the approach to be practical, effective, and fun, to say nothing of revealing about one's skills and interests. Some reasonably good resumes for summer jobs came out of the unit, but perhaps even more important was the way the students came to think about careers and about themselves as people. Afterwards they used the material for their college board applications. It helped them be specific.

A liberal arts senior at Northeastern University said she had liked parts of her college career and had done well academically, but she wondered how to relate a liberal education to a career. The group analyzed the skills it takes to be a liberal arts college student: planning, decision making, investigating, research, ideas, imagination, gathering data, consulting, reading, writing, figuring, evaluating, synthesizing, listening, following instructions, setting goals, following through, meeting deadlines, working under pressure, relating to others, independence, competition, budgeting, and self-organization.

Among these factors she saw a considerable number that were common to her other achievements. Although at the start of the workshop she was stumped about what she could do, when she finished she had begun to see several realistic possibilities. But this was not to say she had made a final decision. She did not want at this particular time to get "tracked" but she was learning how to get on or off a track. The others in the workshop also realized that their four "useless" years in liberal arts had produced a flock of employable skills [4].

The rueful testimony of these seniors included such comments as, "If I had taken this earlier it would have helped me decide my major," and, "If I had analyzed myself this way in high school I would have had some idea what I was good at." At Columbia University, where these basic concepts have been used in a workshop for five years, the students say the process "liberates them." Rarely had anyone asked them before to focus on what they liked to do. Alumni report that they use it as an aid to lifelong development of a vocational philosophy [7].

Universal Application

My impression from training fourscore school and college counselors and from coaching individuals is that the method has universal application. The process is reasonable structured: Examine only your successes. Spot the skills and traits used. Translate these factors into generic terms that are transferable to other experiences. Determine which of these links occur most frequently. Keep watching for these common-denominator talents when exploring careers. Focus on learning the process rather than expecting immediate outcomes. And yet, outcomes will result from learning the process. These methods, I believe, can apply to people of all ages, levels, and backgrounds.

The practice of this methodology is not always simple. Some people find it harder than others to conceptualize. They find it hard to see, for example, that a systematic approach to solving a mechanical problem may be related to a similarly systematic approach to solving problems with people. A high school junior had trouble seeing that the precision required for knitting and piano playing could relate to the precision required in a research lab. She could still relate piano playing only to being a musician.

The process also seems to require coaches who are both teaching and counseling oriented. These coaches need skills in teaching groups about ideas and words and in counseling individuals on a one-to-one basis.

The principle that people can learn what talents to use in the future by researching what talents they used best in the past is incontrovertible. It serves as a lifelong guideline for making career decisions and insures the individual's remaining the prime mover in making these decisions.

References

1. BISHOP, G. M. A blueprint for the future in business/education/industry. In *People development: Commonalities in business, education and industry*. Boston: Massachusetts Personnel and Guidance Association, 1974. Pp. 115–121.
2. CRITES, J. O. A reappraisal of vocational appraisal. *Vocational Guidance Quarterly*, 1974, 22(4), 272–279.
3. CRYSTAL, J. C., and BOLLES, R. N. *Where do I go from here with my life?* New York: Seabury, 1974.
4. FIGLER, H. E. PATH: Vocational exploration for liberal arts students. *Journal of College Placement*, 1973, 34(4), 40–50.
5. GELATT, H. B.; VARENHORST, B.; CAREY, R.; and MILLER, G. P. *Decisions and outcomes*. Princeton, N.J.: College Entrance Examination Board, 1973.
6. GINZBERG, E. Toward a theory of occupational choice: A restatement. *Vocational Guidance Quarterly*, 1972, 20(3), 169–176.
7. GUMMERE, R. M., JR. DIG/Columbia University's program to help students find answers. *Journal of College Placement*, 1972, 32(4), 38–45.
8. HALDANE, B. *Career satisfaction and success*. New York: Amacom, 1974.
9. HOYT. K. B. Career education: Challenges for counselors. In *People development: Commonalities in business, education and industry*. Boston: Massachusetts Personnel and Guidance Association, 1974. Pp. 103–114.
10. PEARSON, H. G. Career education in industry. In L. P. Zani (Ed.), *Youth caught in culture conflict*. Boston: New England Personnel and Guidance Conference, 1974. Pp. 95–98.
11. SIMON, S. B.; HOWE, L. W.; and KIRSCHENBAUM, H. *Values Clarification*. New York: Hart, 1972.
12. U.S. Dept. of Labor. *Dictionary of occupational titles* (Vol. II). Washington, D.C.: U.S. Government Printing Office, 1965.
13. U.S. Dept. of Labor. *Occupational outlook handbook* (1974–75 Ed.). Washington, D.C.: U.S. Government Printing Office, 1974.

14. U.S. Office of Education. Career clusters: *An organizational technique to facilitate the delivery of career education*. A working paper. Washington, D.C.: U.S. Office of Education, Division of Vocational and Technical Education, 1972.

Congruences in Personality Structure and Academic Curricula As Determinants of Occupational Careers

Gordon J. DiRenzo

Functions usually served by the selection and pursuit of an academic major in undergraduate studies are the general preparation, and, increasingly so in the majority of cases, the specific preparation for an occupational or professional career. Accordingly, to whatever extent personality may be related to occupational and professional careers, it could be expected that a similar relationship may exist between personality and one's particular field of academic pursuit. Particularly important is the question of differential associations of personality, in its dimensions, with educational and occupational systems of various structure and function. Stern, Stein, and Bloom (1956) have shown that certain educational systems, with given structural environments, tend, in terms of academic success, to select individuals of particular personality type. To what extent would the same type of differential selection be true in terms of specific academic curricula and/or disciplines? A promising attempt was made by Rosenberg (1957), who, in his studies of values among college students, found differences among undergraduates in terms of their choices for occupational and professional careers, and demonstrated that "future" natural scientists and "future" economic executives (business majors) belonged to quite op-

Reprinted with permission of author and publisher from: Di Renzo, G. J. Congruences in personality structure and academic curricula as determinants of occupational careers. *Psychological Reports,* **34:**1295–1298 (1974).

posite sets in terms of their personality typology. What needs to be explored is the nature of relationships such as these. This article reports a preliminary study relating personality to the selection and the pursuit of academic curricula by undergraduates.

Method

In much research on the relationship of personality to occupations and on personality to academic categories, the focus has been placed on personality traits, capacities, and skills. Whatever merits this approach may have, its principal weakness is that it is based on a distorted, or at least partial, conception of personality in that it ignores the fundamental properties of organization and structure. Many of the shortcomings in the prediction of academic and/or occupational success have been due to such faulty and/or inappropriate conceptions of personality. Roe pointed out some time ago that "programs in individual psychology have not gone farther than they have . . . because job allocation has been conceived in terms of aptitude rather than in terms of the whole personality who is to do the job" (1956, pp. 379–386). One promising alternative dimension for this analytical problem may be that of personality structure.

The personality measure was derived from the conceptual orientation of dogmatism offered by Rokeach (1954, 1960) as an alternative approach to that of *The Authoritarian Personality* (Adorno, et al., 1950). With the concept of dogmatism, Rokeach is concerned essentially with the organization of belief systems and more especially with what he calls the openness and closedness of belief systems. The theoretical utility of this approach is that the Dogmatism Scale concentrates on the structural properties common to authoritarian ideologies to delineate personality structure. It is not so much *what* one believes as *how* one believes that distinguishes the dogmatic personality structure. He may be described as one who has a closed or dogmatic way of thinking about any ideology regardless of its content, is rigid in regard to opinions and beliefs, and makes an uncritical acceptance of authority. Central to the dogmatic syndrome, moreover, is the intolerance of ambiguity. Intellectual ambiguity in many respects is a focal characteristic of the higher educational enterprise, especially in the Humanities and the Liberal Arts. The dogmatic personality structure in its ideal-typical form is one that prefers stereotypic thinking and black-white, categorical judgments to subjective speculation on unresolvable questions involving judgments of personal value. Such a personality structure should have crucially functional significance in the academic enterprise.

Ss were 198 male students, representing a 20 per cent random sample of the undergraduate student body of a small, private, Eastern university. Our sample is distributed uniformly in terms of class status, and the frequency distribution in terms of academic curricula, as well as the quality of academic performance, properly reflect those which existed for this student universe. Ss were classified in terms of major fields of study, which in turn were categorized into four principal types of curricula, reflecting different career preparations: Behavioral Sciences (sociology, psychology, and economics), Liberal Arts, Business Administration, and Physical Sciences (comprising physical and natural sciences, and mathematics).

Ss were administered Form E (complete version) of the Rokeach Dogmatism Scale (1960) as part of a questionnaire concerned with measuring attitudes toward student roles and academic life in general. The personality inventory was scored on a positive/negative basis along a continuum of scores polarized from -120 to $+120$. Directions for answering the Dogmatism Scale were essentially those used by Rokeach in his original research. The standard Likert response-format, with no neutral category, was used. These data were collected on the final day of the academic year. Accordingly, all Ss had at least one, complete academic year in their curricula.

Our hypothesis is that significant differences in personality structure modally characterize the major curriculum/career areas. More specifically, relatively structured fields (such as those disciplines which comprise the physical and natural sciences) are more likely to attract students with dogmatic personality structures than are the relatively nonstructured fields (such as those disciplines which comprise the humanities).

Results

Our findings, as given in Table 1, show that significant differences in personality do characterize the principal academic areas of curriculum/career choice, precisely as hypothesized (χ^2, $p = .02$).

Behavioral Sciences and Liberal Arts majors show a distribution of dogmatic and non-dogmatic scores in a 1:2 ratio respectively; Business Administration majors, despite a slight dominance of non-dogmatic scorers, are rather evenly divided between both types of scorers, but

TABLE 1. Curriculum and Dogmatism Scores

CURRICULUM	NON-DOGMATICS		DOGMATICS		TOTAL
Behavioral Sciences	34	(67%)	17	(33%)	51
Liberal Arts	57	(61%)	36	(39%)	93
Business Administration	15	(56%)	12	(44%)	27
Physical, Natural Sciences	8	(30%)	19	(70%)	27
Totals	114	(58%)	84	(43%)	198

$$\chi^2 = 10.94, df = 3, p < .02$$

for Physical and Natural Sciences majors an antithetical pattern obtains with a more than 2:1 distribution of dogmatic to non-dogmatic scorers.

There is a progressive change in personality distribution as one moves from the Liberal Arts and Behavioral Sciences (relatively unstructured disciplines) toward the Physical Sciences (highly structured disciplines). The modal personality structure for Behavioral Sciences and Liberal Arts is non-dogmatic, and for Physical Sciences dogmatic. Such a polarity of modal types in the frequency distribution of dogmatic and non-dogmatic personality structures substantiates our specific hypothesis. Further support both individually and collectively comes from the categories of Behavioral Sciences and Humanities being markedly distinguished from Business Administration and Physical-Natural Sciences, which in turn are notably distinguished from each other.

The distribution of these gross personality types by grade-point levels is not statistically significant ($\chi^2 = .06$, $df = 1$, $p > .90$). These findings are generally consistent with those of Low (1972), but not with those of Hanson (1972) who utilized much smaller samples.

One curious finding concerns the Behavioral Sciences. The results for these disciplines reflect the various directions (scientific, humanistic, activistic, empirical) which characterize these fields today, as well as the significant difference in subject matter (human behavior) when contrasted with the Physical and Natural Sciences.

Individuals seem to be attracted to particular academic pursuits, and may be recruited into specific occupations, in a differential manner such that given academic disciplines and related professional careers are characterized by modal personality types. Further delineation by major findings may prove interesting.

Personality alone, of course, does not determine an academic or career choice, but personality structure may determine the broad areas of one's choices in both respects. Our thesis is one of structural congruence between the personality system and the respective academic and work systems which is functional for both the personal and the social system. With varied options available, personality structure may help channel choice and even play a dominant role in selection of the occupational or professional career.

Crucial to this whole question of structural-functional congruence is the consequence of systemic performance. Certain dynamics of individual behavior within educational systems and processes, such as success and failure (degrees thereof) in academic performance, can be understood more thoroughly in terms of the total personality functioning, and the nature of the congruent relationship with the given processes and system, rather than as simple questions of aptitude and motivation. For example, much of the individual alteration of major fields of study (academic "job changing"), not only at the undergraduate level, but even that observed between the various levels of higher education, might be a consequence of the lack of functional congruence between the structural dimensions of the disciplines and the psychological requirements and capacities of the personalities involved.

The search for systemic congruence between personal and academic systems has a direct parallel in the occupational/professional realm. One example would be that of job changing which for young Americans occurs on an average of seven times in a lifetime (U. S. Department of Labor, 1964). Job changing involves other psychological factors, not to mention economic considerations, but the search for congruency, we suggest, operates more saliently than has been recognized. The awareness and understanding of such dynamics can have notably similar and consistent value, both practically and theoretically for work systems.

References

ADORNO, T. W., FRENKEL-BRUNSWIK, E., LEVINSON, D. J., and SANFORD, R. N. *The authoritarian personality.* New York: Harper, 1950.

HANSON, D. J. Dogmatism and the college major. *Psychological Reports,* 1972, 30, 190.

LOW, W. B. Open-closed mindedness of students in teacher education and in other college fields. *Dissertation Abstracts International,* 1972, 32(7–3), 4107.

ROE, A. *The psychology of occupations.* New York: Wiley, 1956.

ROKEACH, M. The nature and meaning of dogmatism. *Psychological Review,* 1954, 61, 194–204.

ROKEACH, M. *The open and closed mind.* Glencoe: Free Press, 1960.

ROSENBERG, M. *Occupations and values.* Glencoe: Free Press, 1957.

STERN, G. G., STEIN, M. I., and BLOOM, B. S. *Methods of personality assessment: trauma behavior in complex social situations.* Glencoe: Free Press, 1956.

U.S. DEPARTMENT OF LABOR. *Manpower Report,* June, 1964, No. 10.

UNIT BIBLIOGRAPHY

ARBUCKLE, DUGALD S. "Occupational Information in the Elementary School." *Vocational Guidance Quarterly,* **12** (Winter 1963–64), 77–84.

BAILARD, VIRGINIA. "Vocational Guidance Begins in the Elementary Grades." *Clearing House,* **26** (April 1952), 496.

BOROW, HENRY. *Vocational Planning for College Students.* Englewood Cliffs, N.J.: Prentice-Hall, Inc., 1959.

BROWN, STEPHEN J. Career Planning Inventories: "Do-It-Yourself" Won't Do. *Personnel and Guidance Journal,* **53** (March 1975), 512–519.

CALVERT, R., JR., et al. "College Courses in Occupational Adjustment." *Personnel and Guidance Journal,* **42** (March 1964), 680–682.

CHRISTENSEN, KATHLEEN C. The Career Motivation Process Program, *Catalyst for Change,* **4** (Spring 1975), 26–28.

COHEN, ELI E. "The Employment Needs of Urban Youth." *Vocational Guidance Quarterly,* **10** (Winter 1962), 85–89.

CURRIE, LAWRENCE E. "An Index of Vocational Awareness." *Vocational Guidance Quarterly,* **23** (June 1975), 347–352.

DIPBOYE, W., and W. ANDERSON. "The Ordering of Occupational Value of

High School Freshmen and Seniors." *Personnel and Guidance Journal,* **38** (October 1959), 121–124.

FLEEGE, V. H. "Motivation in Occupational Choice Among High School Students." *Journal of Educational Psychology,* **37** (February 1946), 77–86.

GALLER, ENID H. "Influence of Social Class on Children's Choice of Occupation." *Elementary School Journal,* **51** (March 1951), 439–445.

HEALY, CHARLES. "Interrelationships among Indexes of Vocational Maturity." *Vocational Guidance Quarterly,* **23** (December 1974), 146–151.

HUTSON, P. W. "Vocational Choices, 1930 and 1961." *Vocational Guidance Quarterly,* **10** (Summer 1962), 218–222.

KATZ, M. "A Critical Analysis of the Literature Concerned with the Process of Occupational Choice in High School Boys," mimeo. *Harvard Studies in Career Development,* No. 6 (August 1954).

KEHER, ANDREW. Knowledge of the World of Work: A Test of Occupational Information for Young Men. *Journal of Vocational Behavior,* **6** (February 1975), 133–144.

LEHMAN, H. C., and P. A. WITTY. "Some Factors Which Influence the Child's Choice of Occupation." *Elementary School Journal,* **31** (December 1930), 285–291.

"OCCUPATIONAL INFORMATION FOR THE JUNIOR HIGH SCHOOL YOUTH" (Symposium). *Personnel and Guidance Journal,* **39** (October 1960), 115–127.

O'HARA, ROBERT P. "Acceptance of Vocational Interest Areas by High School Students." *Vocational Guidance Quarterly,* **10** (Winter 1962), 101–105.

O'HARA, R. P. and V. D. TIEDEMAN. "Vocational Self Concept in Adolescence." *Journal of Counseling Psychology,* **6** (1959), 292–301.

SCHMIDT, J. and J. ROTHNEY. "Variability of Vocational Choices of High School Students." *Personnel and Guidance Journal,* **34** (November 1955), 142–146.

STERN, BARRY E. "The Occupational Information Systems Grants Program of the U. S. Department of Labor." *Vocational Guidance Quarterly,* **23** (March 1975), 202–209.

SUPER, D. E. "Critical Ninth Grade: Vocational Choice or Vocational Exploration." *Personnel and Guidance Journal,* **39** (October 1960), 106–109.

SUPER, D. E. and P. L. OVERSTREET. *The Vocational Maturity of Ninth Grade Boys.* New York: Teachers College, Columbia University, 1960.

TENNYSON, W. WESLEY and LAWRENCE P. MONNENS. "The World of Work Through Elementary Readers." *Vocational Guidance Quarterly,* **12** (Winter 1963–64), 85–88.

THOMPSON, ALBERT S. "Developmental State and Developmental Needs at the Junior High School Level." *Personnel and Guidance Journal,* **39** (October 1960), 116–118.

WEINSTEIN, E. A. "Children's Conceptions of Occupational Stratification." *Social Science Review,* **42** (March–April 1958), 278–284.

———. "Assessment of Career Awareness of Elementary School Children." *Journal of Career Education,* **1** (Spring 1975), 80–86.

part 9
Career Development:
Adulthood

Career development in adulthood includes establishing a career, maintaining it, and making adjustments in it during an adult's declining years. To be successful in finding a place in the occupational world may involve mobility as seriously as credentials. Adult identity is largely a function of career movements within occupations and work organizations. In the maintenance stage the individual has made his place in the occupational world. He has developed his role in the home, community, and job and will continue to follow that role. In the years of decline the individual curtails, or modifies, his activities, or he may even change the type of work. Hence, the individual's role in the occupational world changes throughout his career.

Lou Varga discusses the phenomenon of occupational floundering—that is, a time when a person is working without a commitment to an occupational goal. Three stages of floundering are described: initial entry into the job market, a shopping period, and the mid-career stage. Some positive aspects of floundering are also identified. René V. Dawis and Lloyd H. Lofquist offer a theory regarding work adjustment. They describe work personality styles and their relationship to work adjustment. Harold L. Sheppard presents some patterns of individuals moving toward second careers. He suggests a way of identifying individuals who will seek second careers and indicates some dimensions that differentiate them from noncandidates for second careers.

There also is a trend now toward retirement preparation programs; however, there is a need to increase counseling and planning in that area. Patricia L. Kasschau proposes that definitive retirement preparation programs be systematically conceived, designed, and implemented. The new concerns in vocational guidance for adulthood are second careers, changing life personality patterns as one develops on the job, and adjusting to retirement.

Occupational Floundering

Lou Varga

Career stabilization seems to follow three modes of vocational development. The first is used by those who choose an occupational goal prior to entering the labor market, prepare for that goal, seek it, attain it, and become stabilized in it. The second mode is used by those who choose an occupational goal that does not require pre-entry preparation, seek it, find it, and become stabilized in it. The third mode is to flounder.

The term *flounder* is a blend of the concepts "founder" and "blunder," and it implies an awkward expenditure of energy—a struggle to free oneself from a psychological mire. Occupational floundering occurs when an individual enters the labor market seeking full-time work without having a chosen commitment to an occupational goal or for one reason or another does not adapt to that goal once it is attained. The major affective characteristic of floundering is one of deprivation. The individual frequently experiences either one need or an accumulation of needs, including those for well-being, self-worth, self-esteem, belonging, some level of wealth beyond his or her present status, safety, meaningfulness, and social acceptance (from both peers and employers).

Floundering can occur during any period of the work life. Choosing a curriculum and preparing for an occupation does not necessarily preclude a person's having to deal with this usually uncomfortable experience. Graduates from various types of schools who do not seek the type of work they prepared for, who enter a labor market in which there is no demand for their training, or who enter the labor market without adequate training to meet the current demands of employers have a tendency to become engaged in floundering activities. Job seekers also frequently manifest the floundering syndrome if they attain their goals through the first and second modes of vocational development described at the beginning of this article but then leave that occupation before becoming stabilized in it and without having established a commitment to a subsequent goal.

Reprinted from *Personnel and Guidance Journal*, **52**:225–231 (1973), by permission of the publisher and author. Copyright 1973 American Personnel and Guidance Association. Reprinted with permission.

The Intensity of the Floundering Experience

Floundering can be either an adventure or a crisis, depending on the individual. It might also be described as a period of effort. The degree of effort may either be enhanced or restricted, depending on the sense of urgency the job seeker experiences at any one time, and it frequently waxes and wanes with the fluctuation of the individual's sense of deprivation. The intensity of the floundering period can also be affected by the types of needs the individual experiences. Hoppock (1967) has cited the example of workers during the Depression years who took any job they could get in order to meet their physiological needs. Even while they were working, however, they sought other jobs that would more adequately meet additional needs that were nagging them for gratification. Such cases indicate the possibility that physiological need deprivation might result in a more intense floundering experience than, for example, the need for self-esteem.

Several employment counselors with whom I have worked reported that they had occasion to interview heads of households who were intensely worried that their families might suffer from a lack of adequate food and shelter. The fact that these clients were not amenable to explorations of factors other than those that would gratify their more immediate or perceived physiological and safety needs might indicate that Roe's (1956) theories of occupational choice based on a hierachy of needs might also be applicable to an ordinal concept of floundering intensity.

The Floundering Process

Floundering, like other aspects of vocational development, can be subdivided into stages. The three stages of floundering are: the initial entry stage, the shopping stage, and the mid-career stage.

The Initial Entry Stage

Floundering consists primarily of a lack of commitment to an occupational goal. However, it is more than that. It is also an attitude about the labor market: Individuals assume that if they find a satisfactory job, it will happen primarily because of chance. They are frequently motivated by a sense of hope—if they are "lucky," a good job will become available to them. During this first stage of floundering, the job seeker does have some goals. In many instances the objective of a floundering career-seeker is money. My own experience documents that many clients who have adopted this goal have been willing to take any job paying a salary commensurate with the wage level they have set their hopes on achieving. And they initially define a job as "good" when it meets or surpasses this criterion. But frequently they seem not to assess themselves in monetary terms because they assume that luck will do that for them. More specifically, they tend to hope that fortune will allow them to find a training program that will pay a decent salary while teaching them a salable skill. They also assume that they will adjust to the job as long as its pay level meets or exceeds their vague financial standard.

New entrants into the labor market who are ostensibly motivated by a wage standard frequently link their concept of self-worth to that criterion. Others are motivated by monetary standards because of parental pressures, family responsibilities, or other financial demands. They do not feel that they can allow themselves the luxury of choosing jobs on the basis of interests or personal preferences. Their sense of well-being seems to be dominated by needs that—from their perspective—can only be met by monetary gain.

In other instances, new entrants into the labor market naively assume that the only ingredient necessary for successful career attainment is an interest in that career. In fact, numerous job seekers blindly denounce monetary values and enter the labor market willing to accept any salary as long as the job is something they think they will like. One example of this type of applicant is an adolescent who came to an employment counselor and asked the counselor to intervene on his behalf with an employer who was offering a gardener's job in a small community 35 miles from the youth's home. The job paid the minimum salary, and the employer had specifically requested that referrals be limited to persons who resided close to the nursery. Because of the client's sincerity and enthusiasm for this type of work, the counselor urged the employer to make an exception in his case. The employer did so, and the young man obtained the job. Two weeks later the youth reappeared, asking the counselor for further assistance. It seemed that the travel costs, combined with other work expenses, overcame the young man's initial enthusiasm for the job he had chosen primarily on the basis of interest.

Vocationally oriented educational programs may also aggravate floundering tendencies by overemphasizing the factor of interest, either through discussion groups or through the selection of occupational literature and films. In many instances such programs might be more helpful in the long run if they were broadened to take into account the monetary return, the personal and social characteritics, the basic skill requirements, and the nature of the labor market. Also, vocational education programs that implicitly encourage youth to make specific occupational choices at an early age should be approached with appropriate caution. Early career choices that are not understood by the student to be tentative might decrease the student's flexibility and enthusiasm for continued exploration of established or newly developing careers. Tentativeness adds a dimension of reality to vocational decisions, and it should be stressed to allow for choices of occupations that suddenly become overcrowded or obsolete.

Some job seekers spend only a short period of time floundering. Having appropriate work values, manifesting such observable personal characteristics as enthusiasm and neatness, and getting a chance opportunity, they obtain a satisfactory position or career and stabilize in it. Others, who have access to a socially inherited career but who want to try to find one on their own, may flounder in the labor market for a while and, after a period of dissatisfaction, take advantage of an opportunity provided by parents, friends, neighbors, or relatives who are in a position to provide a means out of their maze. In fact, this is probably one of the more frequent paths for many young people.

In some instances the floundering process is an intentional training period—so intended by parents—that provides the means by which new workers learn employer values. Some parents I have known have allowed their sons and daughters to go out and flounder before allowing them to return to a provided position in the belief that the deprivation the adolescents experienced during this period would heighten their appreciation for a better-paying job with better working conditions and other benefits. There have also been instances where former clients have returned to vocational counselors to discuss the positions in which they have become stabilized and to express their appreciation for experiences acquired during the floundering period. Examples of benefits obtained from floundering experiences have included an increased ability to work with one's hands and an increased ability to appreciate a variety of human differences in work life. Beneficial knowledge occurring as a result of floundering has also included negative reactions to some types of work.

The Shopping Stage

If, as a result of a job search, a client finds a position that continuously satisfies most of the needs that he or she expects to have gratified, there is a reasonable probability that the client will become stabilized in it. On the other hand, if the new worker's expected level of need gratification is not satisfied, chances are that this worker will not become stabilized but will continue to flounder. If a floundering job seeker enters into a position that is not the goal of an occupational commitment, the worker will in all probability begin shopping for another opportunity within a relatively short period of time. Although the intensity of this floundering experience may be mitigated by the gratification of some pressing needs, the worker will still be expending energy in varying degrees toward modifying his or her present job or toward getting a "better" one. The term *shopper*, then, refers to a flounderer who is either permanently or intermittently employed and who is either consciously or unconsciously attempting to achieve stabilization in some occupation other than the one in which she or he is presently engaged.

Occupational shopping takes a variety of forms. Employment counselors and placement interviewers with whom I have worked have described several types of floundering activity, which seem to fall into three categories.

Specific Shoppers. Flounderers in this category usually go to employment service offices asking for a specific job or training program because they have heard that it is available. They actually know very little about the nature of the work or about their own ability to adapt to it. They are primarily motivated by the assumption that it will be more satisfying than their present job.

Impulse Shoppers. This term applies to applicants who periodically go to employers and employment service offices on the basis of a whim. They are motivated by capricious impulses to gratify intermittent needs for improvement of their feeling of well-being, their feeling of self-worth, their monetary income, etc. Their purpose is to try to satisfy their particular motivating need by investigating the possibility of a chance opportunity. They are periodically dissatisfied with their current occupation, and their searching activity, though constantly reoccurring, tends to be temporary in nature.

Window Shoppers. This category of job seekers is made up of individuals who either continuously or periodically seek jobs for which they do not basically qualify. They are different from other flounderers in the sense that they have an occupational goal or at least have a good idea about the type of work they want. However, they will not or cannot take the steps that would prepare them to compete for entry into that career. These shoppers are periodically motivated to investigate the labor market by a vague hope that fortune might guide them to an opportunity that came about as the result of an unusual need by an employer, a need that forced the employer to modify the usual job requirements so that the flounderer would be able to gain a "lucky" entry into a desirable position. The window shopper's motivation is periodically refueled by "shop stories" about other individuals who attained success in this manner.

A subcategory of the window shopper includes those individuals who survive by means of casual, or temporary, labor and who seek permanent jobs without actually intending to accept them, sometimes in the belief that they do not have the characteristics necessary for occupational stabilization. This category consists largely of persons who, because of repeated job losses as well as other adverse experiences in life, do not view themselves as normal work force participants. They are frequently motivated toward casual labor or other activities, sometimes illegal, that provide more immediate gratification of perceived needs, even though such activities are frequently of a temporary nature. Alcoholics and chronic drug users might comprise a portion of this category.

A second subcategory of the window shopper includes individuals who make their living by means that are outside the law, or at least outside the socially acceptable work norms. Prostitutes, narcotics pushers, and gambling promoters are in some cases committed to follow their "careers" and do actually have their anticipated level of satisfaction achieved through them. In some of these cases the individuals would not really be classified as floundering under the present definition. Many of them, however, are discomforted by a nagging fear of legal retribution or other forms of social punishment. In order to attempt to convert their discomfort to a sense of social well-being, they periodically visit an employment office or read the classified ads in their local newspapers to see if some compelling opportunity will present itself. In a few cases what appears to be job search activity is actually a device employed to gain relief from the pressures of a parole officer or to meet the requirements for welfare or unemployment insurance benefits.

It is important to note that there is a significant difference between a person's shopping during the floundering period and a stabilized worker's shopping for a better job. Many stabilized workers who are relatively satisfied with their current jobs become exposed to new opportunities that arise, and others actively seek them. The factor that distinguishes the floundering activity from stabilized shopping is the degree to which the shopper is committed to a given occupation. Stabilized shoppers, in essence, are either shopping for an opportunity within their current occupational field or are committed to a new field.

The Mid-Career Stage

Mid-career floundering usually occurs as the result of an environmental accident; a worker who had previously committed himself or herself to an occupational goal has achieved it, has become stabilized in it, and then, due to some unforeseen event, has been forced to abandon it. Examples of this often traumatic experience have occurred in recent years among engineers, scientists, and technicians in aerospace firms throughout the country who suddenly became unemployed. Several thousand engineers, who had been lavishly recruited during the period following the launching of the Sputnik satellites, suddenly found themselves with little or no market in which to utilize their skills. Less publicized, but just as numerous, are workers who, because of the intervention of some physical or emotional disability, are forced to change occupations during what is normally considered the mid-career period of their working life. Physically debilitating circumstances occur when, for example, a butcher develops arthritis and cannot tolerate cold meat lockers, a teacher becomes severely allergic to chalk, or a skilled worker loses a vital limb.

The mid-career stage is frequently complicated by factors such as age, limited opportunity for training, and wage reductions, any of which might intensify the floundering experience. The affective characteristic of mid-career floundering is frequently described by those persons who experience it as a sense of hopelessness and depression. It is conceivable that skilled counselors could facilitate relief from these psychologically debilitating influences by appropriate intervention in the motivational processes of the client. In addition to helping the client explore alternatives to his or her current occupation, the counselor can use this intervention to focus on the client's strengths. A few of the personal characteristics that mid-career flounderers frequently lose sight of include their stability, their dependability, and their knowledge of general employer work values (getting to work on time, keeping busy on the job, being productive and efficient, etc.).

The Termination of Floundering

As indicated by its definition, floundering doesn't end with stabilization in an occupation. It ends when the job seeker becomes committed to an occupation or an occupational goal. Commitment can occur simultaneously with the attainment of a career in which the client becomes stabilized. It is possible, however, to become stabilized without being committed and vice versa.

Occupational choice prior to career entry is not a necessary prerequisite to commitment. Many job seekers, while stumbling through the floundering period, have accidentally found themselves in a career to which they either commit themselves immediately or become gradually committed. In both circumstances commitment occurs because the individual attains a relatively acceptable level of job satisfaction. The reasons for this satisfaction can vary: One employee might not like the work but might become comparatively contented with the routine, the companionship, or the salary; others might become committed to the work itself.

Commitment in everyday terms suggests a sense of perseverance, of obligation, either self-imposed or imposed by other individuals. However, Kroll and others (1970) have described commitment as a general developmental process that occurs in three stages. The initial stage is a tentative one, based on a choice. The second stage occurs when an individual experiences the effect of the choice; if the choice appears successful, the tentativeness decreases. The final stage occurs when the individual expands the commitment and remakes it with the understanding that she or he will continue to choose and modify future commitments as personal growth and adaptive tendencies dictate.

Commitment might better be described as a psychological investment in which uncertainty plays an important part. Doubt introduces a sense of reality to commitment. It acknowledges the presence of environmental power, influence, or reaction. Commitment is similar to motivation in that it embodies hope, values, a goal, and action. A major difference, however, is that motivation can be an avoidance activity, whereas commitment tends to be comprised of an approach orientation that provides the individual with a sense of meaning and purpose.

It should be kept in mind that floundering is not necessarily a destructive phenomenon. Although for some it may be a source of demoralization, excessive stress, and psychological debilitation, for others it could be an experience that facilitates personal growth and self-acceptance in other than monetary terms. At the present time vocational guidance theories tend to be oriented toward the avoidance of floundering. Eventually, however, a more comprehensive theory of vocational development will include an acceptance of the existence of floundering, an appreciation of its values, a thorough understanding of its dynamics, an awareness of its hazards, and therapeutic models of relief from its traumas.

References

HOPPOCK, R. *Occupational information.* (3rd ed.) New York: McGraw-Hill, 1967.

KROLL, A. M., DINKLAGE, L. B., LEE, L., MORELY, E. D., and WILSON, E. A. *Career development.* New York: Wiley, 1970.

ROE, A. *The psychology of occupations.* New York: Wiley, 1956.

Personality Style and the Process of Work Adjustment

René V. Dawis
and
Lloyd H. Lofquist

The theory of work adjustment (Dawis, England, and Lofquist, 1964; Dawis, Lofquist, and Weiss, 1968; Lofquist and Dawis, 1969) provides a model for conceptualizing the interaction between individuals and

Reprinted from the *Journal of Counseling Psychology,* **23:**55–59 (1976), by permission of the publisher and authors. Copyright 1976 by the American Psychological Association. Reprinted by permission.

work environments. The major sets of variables used in the theory are abilities and needs to describe work personalities, ability requirements and reinforcer systems to describe work environments, and satisfactoriness, satisfaction, and tenure to describe outcomes of the interaction. Prediction of the work adjustment outcomes utilizes the concept of correspondence between work personalities and work environments. The theory thus formalizes the matching model that psychologists have used in such applied problem areas as vocational guidance, vocational counseling, and personnel selection. The theory does place added emphasis on needs, reinforcers, and the outcomes of satisfaction. Nevertheless, these aspects of the theory, taken alone, would seem to present work adjustment as a fixed state of affairs that does not accommodate change. They deal solely with work personality structure and with work environment structure.

In the theory of work adjustment, the concept of correspondence extends beyond a simple static matching of the work personality with the work environment and incorporates the notion of corresponsiveness. That is, individuals and environments are described in terms of their mutual responsiveness to each other. The concept of work adjustment, therefore, is envisioned as the continuous and dynamic process by which the individual seeks to achieve and maintain correspondence with his or her work environment. Proposition IX of the theory also states that "work personality—work environment correspondence increases as a function of tenure" (Dawis et al., 1968, p. 11).

These concepts of corresponsiveness and change over time lead to the necessity for conceptualizing both the work personality and the work environment in terms of style dimensions that will permit description of the interaction between the work personality structure and the work environment structure. Inasmuch as corresponsiveness is reciprocal, it is reasonable to think of both work personality style and work environment style. In this article attention will be given only to work personality style. Work environment style can then be described in work personality style terms as required by the theory of work adjustment. Thus, both work personality style and work environment style are described in psychological terms. Such description is analogous to the description of work personality structure and work environment structure in terms of abilities and needs, that is, in psychological terms.

Individuals may be expected to differ in the amount of discorrespondence with the work environment they will tolerate. In other words, individuals with very similar work personality structures may differ in the amount of correspondence they will require of the work environment structure to remain in it. Tolerance of discorrespondence may be described on a personality style dimension of *flexibility*.

As an obvious example of flexibility, if two individuals prefer to work in a room with 70-degree temperature, the more flexible individual will continue to work even if the temperature rose to, say, 85 degrees, or dropped to 60 degrees. The less flexible individual would interrupt work to take some action to adjust the temperature to an effective level of 70 degrees. An example of a more psychological situation might be that of two individuals who have a strong preference for working alone. The more flexible individual would tolerate some presence and interaction with other workers, whereas the less flexible individual would do something about the situation to achieve aloneness. The description of minimal correspondence for the prediction of tenure requires knowledge of an individual's flexibility.

In addition, for an individual with minimal correspondence for tenure, according to the theory, correspondence will increase as tenure increases. This leads to the logical expectation of observable change in the work environment, in the work personality, or in both. Such observable change may result from an individual seeking to change the work environment or a work environment effecting change in the individual's manifest work personality, or both.

When an individual acts on the work environment to increase correspondence, the mode of adjustment may be described as *active*. When this kind of behavior is typical, the individual can be described as active. Individual differences in the likelihood of using this mode of adjustment may be described on a personality style dimension called *activeness*.

When an individual responds to the work environment by changing the expression or manifestation of the work personality structure to increase correspondence, the mode of adjustment may be described as *reactive*. Individuals who typically exhibit this mode of behavior may be described as reactive, and the likelihood of using such behavior can be expressed on a personality style dimension called *reactiveness*. It is not expected that individuals would limit themselves exclusively to either the active or the reactive mode of adjustment but that both modes would be used.

In the examples of flexibility cited above, the less flexible individuals, if they adopted the active mode of adjustment, might (1) readjust the thermostat, (2) open or close windows, (3) move to another room, (4) complain about the presence of other workers, (5) move to a solitary location, or (6) request transfer to another job. On the other hand, these same (less flexible) individuals, if they adopted the reactive mode of adjusting, might (1) drink hot or cold liquids, (2) remove or put on clothing, (3) endure and suffer through, (4) concentrate on the work to exclude the perception of others, (5) use daydreams and fantasies to escape from others, or (6) rationalize the situation to themselves in order to endure the presence of others. Although these examples focus on possible behaviors of the less flexible individuals, the same kinds of behaviors, indicative of active-

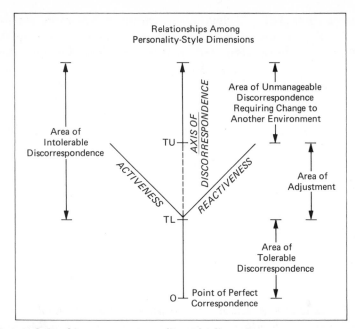

FIGURE 1. Relationships among personality style dimensions.

ness or reactiveness, might be observed for the more flexible individuals when their tolerance for discorrespondence is exceeded.

It is also expected that individuals will differ in the speed with which they move to increase correspondence. Individuals who typically move speedily may be described as *celerious*. An individual's typical rate of movement toward increased correspondence may be measured along a personality style dimension called *celerity*. In other words, celerity can be observed in terms of how quickly or slowly an individual responds (actively or reactively) to a discorrespondent situation.

It would seem that these four dimensions of flexibility, activeness, reactiveness, and celerity represent a minimal set of dimensions by which personality style can be described. Inclusion of these dimensions in the theory of work adjustment will make it possible to view work adjustment as a continuing and dynamic process.

Figure 1 illustrates the interrelationships among the three personality style dimensions designated as flexibility, activeness, and reactiveness. The fourth dimension, celerity, indicates the speed with which the individual is likely to move (in active and/or reactive modes) from an area of excessive (intolerable) discorrespondence to the *area of tolerable discorrespondence* defined by the individual's flexibility. The individual's *initial flexibility* defines the distance from point 0 to point T_L (lower threshold) on the axis of discorrespondence shown in Figure 1. When the individual is in the area of adjustment, the modes of adjustment can be described in terms of the independent dimensions of activeness and reactiveness. The length of time an individual can remain in the *area of adjustment* will depend not only on the effectiveness of these modes of adjustment but also on the celerity level of the individual. In addition to *initial flexibility* (which defines the distance from point 0 to point T_L), an individual has what may be termed an *adjustment flexibility* which defines the distance from point T_L to point T_U (the upper threshold on the axis of discorrespondence). Both an individual's initial state and his or her continuing adjustment states can be plotted on the *axis of discorrespondence*.

Since the personality style dimensions discussed above are developed and exhibited over time, appropriate sources of data for the assessment of an individual's status with regard to them would include biographical data, cumulative records, school and work history information, and psychometric data over a time period. Clinical observation of current behavior in a variety of settings may also be utilized. Ratings of specific behaviors by persons who have observed the individuals over extended periods of time may supplement recorded data and clinical observations. The literature of vocational psychology and psychometrics has not attended to the development of measures of these specific personality style dimensions. There is a need to study data from the sources mentioned to clarify the constructs themselves and to develop instruments to measure them. Illustrations of how this might be accomplished are given in the following paragraphs.

In the assessment of *flexibility* we may hypothesize that an individual who has a history that includes such things as participation in a wide range of activities, experience in a wide range of situations, a successful work history over a wide range of jobs, and a heterogeneous group of friends will have a high level of flexibility. Contrariwise, an individual with few or a very homogeneous group of friends, a narrow range of successful jobs or other activities, and exposure to a very narrow range of situations will have a low flexibility level.

We may hypothesize that the *activeness* of an individual is at a high level if there is evidence of, as examples, having held positions of leadership, having organized groups and activities, having developed new ways of doing things, and of taking the initiative in school, work, or community activities. Low-level activeness, on the other hand, should be indicated by a lack of initiative and innovativeness in an individual's history.

We may hypothesize that a high level of *reactiveness* is indicated by a history that includes abiding by the rules, carrying out assignments according to prescribed procedures, comfort or satisfaction in highly structured situations and groups, and loyal and continued participation in groups as a member rather than as a leader. Low-level reactiveness would be evidenced by inability to participate in group situations, difficulty in following rules and prescribed procedures, and other evidences of isolationist tendencies.

We would expect the highly *celerious* individual to have a history that shows prompt or early completion of assignments, almost impulsive behavior, and tendencies toward emphasizing speed of response even at the expense of accuracy. Low celerity should be indicated by deliberateness of response, seeming procrastination, and longer latencies of response.

Obviously the illustrations described above provide only a few examples of the kinds of historical data that may be useful in the assessment of these personality style dimensions. Data from such conventional psychometric instruments as interest or personality inventories and ability tests may also be useful for the assessment of personality style. As examples, a high Like score on the Strong Vocational Interest Blank (Strong, Campbell, Berdie, and Clark, 1966) may be one indicator of high flexibility; preferences for activities involving self-direction may be an indicator of high-level activeness; flat ability or need profiles may indicate high reactiveness; and rapidity in completing self-report inventories or attitude scales may be an indicator of high celerity.

If personality style can be assessed as suggested, there are a number of implications for the practice of vocational counseling and career planning: The ability of the counselor and the client to predict the likelihood of work adjustment should be enhanced. The usefulness of the correspondence (matching) model in choosing careers or jobs should be increased. The client's understanding of his or her unique style of behaving in the work setting from day to day should be improved. Finally, counselor knowledge of the client's personality style should be useful in facilitating the counseling process itself, for example, in choosing the most appropriate intervention techniques. In addition to implications for practice, information on personality style dimensions and their counterparts in work environments should enrich the vocational psychologist's conceptualization of the processes by which people relate to the world of work.

At its present stage of development, the concept of personality style obviously has its limitations and requires additional research. Research is needed to explore such questions as: Can personality style dimensions be considered as traits (that is, as generalizable across situations)? What role does measurement play in determining the apparent features of personality style dimensions (for example, is the apparent stability of measured personality style due to the conceptualization or to the techniques used in its measurement)? How amenable is personality style to change (for example, to training or to unusual experiences)? Are personality style and personality structure independent or are they correlated in some manner? Questions like these need to be explored before the concept of personality style can be considered to contribute significantly to explication of the process of work adjustment.

The present article has extended the theoretical description of work adjustment as given in the propositions of the theory of work adjustment. Hopefully, it also demonstrates the capability of a trait-and-factor matching model to address the dynamic aspects of work adjustment.

References

DAWIS, R. V., ENGLAND, G. W., and LOFQUIST, L. H. A theory of work adjustment (Minnesota Studies in Vocational Rehabilitation, Whole No. 15). Minneapolis: University of Minnesota, Industrial Relations Center, 1964.

DAWIS, R. V., LOFQUIST, L. H., and WEISS, D. J. A theory of work adjustment (a revision) (Minnesota Studies in Vocational Rehabilitation, Whole No. 23). Minneapolis: University of Minnesota, Industrial Relations Center, 1964.

LOFQUIST, L. H., and DAWIS, R. V. Adjustment to work. New York: Appleton-Century-Crofts, 1969.

STRONG, E. K., JR., CAMPBELL, D. P., BERDIE, R. F., and CLARK, K. E. Strong Vocational Interest Blank for Men (Form T399). Stanford, California: Stanford University Press, 1966.

The Emerging Pattern of Second Careers

Harold L. Sheppard

Two fundamental social conditions—changing technology and increased longevity—have created the need to overhaul radically our current and traditional work patterns. This article discusses the implications of such an overhauling. The press recently dramatized a number of case studies of individuals, mostly men in professional and business positions, who have made drastic leaps from one type of occupation to another seemingly unrelated one. Whether this phe-

Reprinted from Vocational Guidance Quarterly, 20:89–95 (Dec. 1971). Copyright 1971 American Personnel and Guidance Association. Reprinted with permission.

nomenon is called the middle-age work crisis, male menopause, or mid-career depression, more signs of it do seem to be evident. At the very least, counselors and other persons in related behavioral sciences may be integrating old problems into new bottles.

The critical point is that such a phenomenon does exist, apart from the issue of whether it is any more extensive today than in the past. Our popular mentality—perhaps even the academic literature—is dominated by the single-career concept, i.e., that an individual has or should have a single lifetime occupational role-identity. Perhaps in a more static society, it made sense from both the individual and societal points of view to stress the acquisition of a single set of skills to be used during one's working life, a span that actually was not very great to begin with.

But today the average life expectancy is higher, and the social and physical technology of the environment is constantly in flux. Longevity, the first factor encouraging this trend, increases the probability that a number of intervening experiences—environmental and subjective—will affect the individual's occupational self-identity and his continued interest in a given occupation.

As Boulding has said:

> Perhaps the biggest threat to the human race at the moment is not so much the nuclear weapon as the possibility of eliminating the aging process. If we could arrange the human genetic structure to program death at the age of 1,000 rather than at 70 . . . the human race would face the highest crisis of its existence, a crisis which I illustrate easily to an academic audience by asking who wants to be an assistant professor for 500 years[1].

The second factor, changing technology, is naturally accompanied by changes in the skills necessary to use that technology. One of the critical points here is that our sources of socialization—chiefly the family and the school—do little, if anything, to prepare members of society for more than one career *prior* to their entering the world of work. Such preparation need not be strictly devoted to actual acquisition of specific task skills of widely varying character. Perhaps it would be more relevant to prepare young people psychologically for the fact that, before they leave the labor force, they will have entered a variety of somewhat differing jobs. Another critical point is that, with perhaps the exception of the military establishment, our other institutions that touch the lives of adults are doing little to make it possible for middle-aged and older persons to enter new occupations.

One could make a case for the proposition that such institutions do everything in their power to discourage and make impossible the facilitation of occupational change. A more charitable proposition would be that in our effort to solve certain problems and to achieve other goals, we have developed solutions and mechanisms that, without malice or deliberate intent, function today as anachronistic obstacles to the encouragement and facilitation of second careers. Typical examples include provisions of pension plans, narrow-range seniority rules, and early retirement.

Thomas Green of Syracuse University's Educational Policy Research Center has argued before the House of Representatives Committee on Science and Astronautics that the post-industrial society will have to be based on the cultivation of knowledge rather than on craft skills— the idea of reshaping the education system to encourage multiple careers by individuals and even provide for occasional "moratoriums from productive work."

> Surely there is nothing more damaging to the human spirit than the knowledge—or belief—that one's capacities are unused, unwanted, or expended in something of no particular value.
>
> Who knows what human misery would be relieved and what human energies released if the possibility of multiple careers were the rule, and if there were, as a consequence, ready means of entry and exit to and from new avenues of work [3].

Another possible factor may be the emergence of concern regarding flexible or second careers, namely, the saliency among adults of a discrepancy between original aspirations and mid-life achievements. It is interesting—and at first, to some observers, paradoxical—that amount of education is positively related to the tendency among employed men to define work as an activity that is required or not enjoyed. Weiss and Kahn [7], in their study of Detroit workers, suggest their own explanations for this finding, but another may be added that is derived from a discussion by Brim in his survey of adult socialization research [2]. Brim points out that the greater the person's educational achievements, the higher his aspirations, but that higher aspirations are accompanied by a higher risk of nonachievement of those aspirations. He states further that a person "handles these discrepancies for a long period of time by successively displacing fulfillment of aspirations into the future, but the day of reckoning does come."

Second Careers Critical for Some

The point to be made here is that persons whose occupational achievements do not equal their original aspirations come to look upon their jobs as something that must be performed but not necessarily enjoyed. Such persons may constitute the group for whom second career opportunities may be the most critical.

The need for a policy of second career opportunities can be strengthened by such arguments as (1) the need for upgrading middle-level workers and professionals to "make room" for lower working-class men and women who complain about being in dead-end jobs; (2) the needs of society for more people to perform higher level functions and public service functions now in sad neglect; and (3) the need for workers today to be "loose" when it comes to over-identification with one occupation in times of high unemployment. In a study of unemployed workers done by the Upjohn Institute, it was found that workers who looked for jobs really different from what they had been doing regularly had a higher job-finding success rate [5].

Preliminary findings of my own research may shed some light on the characteristics of potential candidates for flexible careers in the adult, male working population. During July and August of 1970, interviews with approximately 300 white male workers in four selected urban areas of Pennsylvania were conducted, primarily concentrating on working conditions, job satisfaction, social and political attitudes and behavior, and related topics. The material presented below is based on a preliminary coding and tabulation of the first 210 interviews. Of the 210 respondents, 140 were 40 years of age or older. Thirty-five per cent of these older men may be considered as candidates for second careers. This group of 49 individuals are operationally defined here on the basis of their responses to two key questions:

	Response Qualifying Individual as Second-Career Candidate
Question 1	
"How often have you thought very seriously about making a real effort to *enter* a *new* and *different* type of occupation: Very often? Once in a while? Hardly ever? Never? Already did it."	"Very often, Once in a while, or Already did it."
Question 2	
Suppose your employer, the government, your union—or some *other* organization offered you a training and education program with enough money to support yourself and family, to make it possible to get a promotion with the employer you have now, *or* to get a much better job somewhere else. "Would you choose the program leading to a promotion with your present employer? Or the program leading to a better job somewhere else? Or would you just not take *any* program like that?"	"With present employer or Better job somewhere else."

Table 1 presents the preliminary results of a comparison of these 49 candidates with the 91 noncandidates for second careers, all of whom

TABLE 1. CANDIDATES AND NONCANDIDATES FOR SECOND CAREERS (IN %)

CHARACTERISTIC	CANDIDATES	NONCANDIDATES
Age: 40–54	71	57
55–59	7	29
60+	12	14
Achievement values: high [a]	67	47
If completely free, would prefer some other job to the kind they now have	41	25
Have actually tried to get into a line of work really different from any they have been in	37	18
Perceived mobility on present job: above average chance, or excellent chance	10	34
Aspiration-achievement discrepancy index: high [a]	51	36
Perceived job autonomy: low [a]	48	29
Stating job rotation a "very good idea"	57	40
Satisfied with job "most of the time"	41	60
Feeling that employers and/or unions doing "too much" in getting good training or good jobs for minority groups like Negroes and Puerto Ricans	33	16
Earning $3.50 per hour	45	42
Saying that their own take-home pay is good enough to take care of family's usual bills and expenses	67	71
Reported family income:		
Under $8,000	33	33
$10,000 plus	37	36
Education: with high school diploma	46	39

[a] See Appendix for items used to measure this variable.

were at least 40 years of age. (Three-fourths of the *younger* men also qualified as second-career candidates.)

Let us first examine the variables on which there is little or no difference between the candidates and noncandidates for second careers. Three items are especially pertinent. First, there is little difference between the two types insofar as hourly wages or their felt adequacy regarding take-home pay; second, the two groups are virtually identical regarding family income; third, there is no overwhelming contrast regarding education, although one might expect to find the average education level of the candidate group higher since they tend to be the *younger* members of the 40-plus men's sample. The critical point is that the usually considered economic variables such as income and/or adequacy of take-home pay do not appear to contribute to an identification or understanding of the second-career candidate.

It is in the social-psychological sphere where differences between the two groups appear. For example, the candidates for second careers have higher achievement values, and it may be suspected that if we had administered McClelland's projective test, they would also register higher on achievement motivation (n Ach). As a further indication of this on the behavioral level, a higher proportion of the 40-plus candidates report that they actually have tried to get into a really different kind of work.

The other variables on which the candidates for second careers stand out as different—their lower perceived mobility chances in their current jobs, their greater preference for a job different from the one they have now if they were completely free to go into any type of job they wanted, their lower job satisfaction—all point to a group of men who would benefit from a more structured opportunity program enabling them to shift to new and different kinds of work life. Their apparent job discontent (or greater aspirations for a different kind of job), as well as the wider gap between their aspirations and their actual achievements, may lead to some socially undesirable points of view. Witness the one-third among them who feel employers and/or unions have done too much to help minority groups, a proportion twice that among the noncandidates. That they are really more discontented or more ambitious or more restless is further confirmed by the finding (not shown in Table 1) that nearly one-half of the candidates (45 per cent) say that they would choose a training or education program that would lead them to a better job *away from their present employer*. In contrast, among the group of noncandidates some did say they would take a training program but only one-sixth (16 per cent) would choose a program for a better job elsewhere.

One of the most provocative findings is the high proportion of the second-career candidates who reported having a low degree of autonomy on their jobs as measured by items adapted from Turner and Lawrence's research [6]. These men feel that they have little or no freedom to do their jobs as they want to, and can use little or none of their potential ideas and skills on their current jobs. Only a small minority (10 per cent) report having an excellent chance to advance themselves or to be promoted in their present work situations, in contrast to more than one-third of the noncandidates who are by definition either not interested in changing occupations, or not willing to take an upgrading training or education program.

When we combine any two of the three variables of achievement values, aspiration-achievement discrepancy, and autonomy-on-the-job, the differences between the candidates and noncandidates become even more striking. The ratio of the proportion of candidates with high achievement values and a high aspiration-achievement discrepancy to the proportion of noncandidates with the same combination of social-psychological attributes is more than 2.5 to 1 (33 versus 13 per cent). The proportion of candidates with high discrepancy and low autonomy is in a ratio of more than 2.8 to 1 (27 versus 9.5 per cent). In the case of those with low autonomy and high values, the ratio is 4 to 1 (28 versus 7 per cent).

Appendix
Questions Used to Measure or Define
Variables Cited in Table 1

Achievement Values (from Bernard Rosen's Research [4],
Degree of Agreement or Disagreement with)

1. In his work, all a person should want is a secure, not-too-difficult job, with enough pay for a nice car and home.
2. Nowadays a person has to pretty much live for today and let *tomorrow* take care of itself.
3. When a person is born, the success he will have is in the cards, so he may as well accept it.
4. It is best to have a job as part of an organization all working together, even if you don't get individual credit.
5. Don't expect too much out of life and be content with what comes your way.
6. Planning only makes a person unhappy since your plans hardly ever work out anyway.

Discrepancy Between Aspiration and Achievement

1. How well would you say your job measures up to the kind you wanted when you *first* took it? Is it very much like the kind of job you wanted? Somewhat like the job you wanted? Or, not very much like the kind you wanted?
2. Compared with what you had hoped for when you finished school, are you better off than you hoped for at that time? Not as well off? Or just about as well as you *had* hoped for?
3. Compared with where you were 10 years ago, are you further ahead in the things you've wanted out of life? Behind? Or just about the *same* as where you were 10 years ago?

Perceived Autonomy on the Job (from Turner and Lawrence [6])

1. Which statement best describes the kind of job you have?

   I have *no* freedom at all to do my work as I want to.
   I have *little* freedom to do my work as I want to.
   I am *fairly free* to do my work as I want.
   I am *completely* free to do my work as I want.

2. Which one of the following items best describes how much of their *potential ideas and skills* are being used on the job by the people working on the same general kind of job as yours?

   Almost *none* of what they can offer.

About *one-fourth* of what they can offer.
About *half* of what they can offer.
About *three-fourths* of what they can offer.
Almost *all* of what they can offer.

In summary, one could argue that there is a malaise among a significant portion of white male workers in America—the "blue collar blues," to use a recently coined journalistic expression. Much of this relates, it appears, to a growing need for flexible or second careers among such persons. The same may be said even for the technician and professional classes in our society. Nor should we exclude the growing numbers of minority group members of our labor force. I have presented here one suggestion for identifying such persons and, in a preliminary fashion, have also indicated some of the social-psychological dimensions in which they differ substantially from the so-called noncandidates for second careers. Effective use of such data might contribute to a program that conceivably could combine improved counseling and education efforts designed to improve the work lives and social environment of the contemporary generation of men and women in our constantly changing, tense society.

References

1. BOULDING, K. Outlook section. *Washington Post,* September 6, 1970.
2. BRIM, O. In J. A. Clausen (Ed.), *Socialization and society.* Boston: Little, Brown, 1968.
3. GREEN, T. Panel examines new technology. *New York Times,* January 30, 1970.
4. ROSEN, B. C. Race, ethnicity, and the achievement syndrome. *American Sociological Review,* 1959, *24,* 47–60.
5. SHEPPARD, H. L., and BELITSKY, A. H. *The job hunt.* Baltimore, Md.: Johns Hopkins Press, 1966.
6. TURNER, A., and LAWRENCE, P. R. *Industrial jobs and the worker: An investigation of response to task attributes.* Boston: Harvard Graduate School of Business Administration, 1965.
7. WEISS, R., and KAHN, R. Definitions of work. *Journal of Social Problems,* 1960, *8,* 142–150.

Reevaluating the Need for Retirement Preparation Programs

Patricia L. Kasschau

Although many authors have hailed the increasing trend among employers to provide preretirement counseling (Tuckman and Lorge, 1952; Wermal and Beideman, 1961; Mitchell, 1969; Pyron, 1969; White House Conference on Aging, 1971; McCarthy, 1973), the empirical evidence suggests that the status of retirement preparation programs has changed little in the past decade.

The statement of the U. S. Civil Service Commission study of retirement planning (1961:6) still seems completely appropriate today: "Many employers, both public and private, have a watchful, wait-and-see attitude, accompanied by a strictly limited program or none at all, because they think that the right and wrong answers have not been found in this relatively new area of personnel management."

The burden thus fell to the social sciences in the 1960s and 1970s to prove the need for the effectiveness of such retirement preparation programs, but the results to date have been criticized as "nonconclusive" or "contradictory." As a result, business and government have persisted in their noncommittal, wait-and-see posture.

But a review of the available evidence evaluating the programs reveals it is not the evidence but the analytical framework in which the evidence has been weighed which suffers the problems of ambiguity and contradiction. There exists considerable confusion about the appropriate goals of these programs. Are they designed to develop favorable attitudes toward retirement and thereby promote good adjustment in retirement (in which case they might most properly be labeled retirement *counseling* programs) or are they, instead, meant to serve as an information-disseminating and stimulant-to-planning device (in which case retirement *planning* programs might be a more appropriate descriptive term)?

Typically, these programs are conceived and charged with the former counseling function (that is, to change attitudes and promote adjustment), but the overwhelming majority are only brief lecture series which barely fulfill the function of disseminating useful information

Reprinted from the Winter 1974 (Vol. 1, No. 1) issue of *Industrial Gerontology*, a quarterly journal published by The National Council on the Aging, Inc.

to participants. The existing programs simply are not designed in terms of format or content to focus on basic attitude change, so it is unreasonable to condemn retirement preparation programs for their failure to accomplish this goal. Yet retirement preparation programs as typically presented by today's business and government organizations can effectively fulfill a useful *planning* function. They need not be wholly condemned for the failure to adequately effect attitude change and other *counseling* functions.

Lobby for Counseling Emphasis

Proponents most frequently lobby for programs based on these same counseling notions. In a work-oriented society such as ours, they argue, although retirement precipitates a transition crisis for the individual shifting from work to nonwork activities, retirement preparation programs can help him to make the necessary adjustment.

Now that social science research has been unable to document any such pervasive crisis among retiring workers, critics are responding that there is no need for retirement preparation if there is no adjustment crisis. This line of thinking again overlooks the useful planning function performed in providing relevant information to workers approaching retirement age and stimulating them to do their own planning.

Meaningful evaluation of the effectiveness of these programs is not only handicapped by confusion over the appropriate goals and the lack of subsequent implementation of suitably designed programs, but also by the quality of the evaluation research. Many of the evaluation studies are methodologically weak; samples are small and nonrandomly selected. Operational measures of attitude changes are frequently superficially designed and inappropriately applied.

Rarely are follow-up techniques employed to evaluate the long-range effects of program participation, the best having a follow-up after only two years. The findings of these studies frequently contradict each other; it is difficult to separate out the methodological inconsistencies from the substantive ones.

Several good studies do seem to establish the foundation for a fairly reputable evaluation of program effectiveness. This paper will attempt to reassess the utility of current retirement preparation programs, drawing heavily on the results of three large-scale, well-designed studies: The longitudinal Cornell Study of Occupational Retirement (Thompson, 1958; Streib and Thompson, 1958; Streib and Schneider, 1971), the extensive University of Michigan study (Hunter, 1968a, 1968c) and that of the University of Oregon (Greene, *et al.,* 1969; Pyron, 1969; Pyron and Manion, 1970).

The definitive evaluation of retirement preparation programs must wait until such time as these programs are systematically conceived, designed and implemented, and until rigorous experimental research procedures are employed that include participant randomization and long-run follow-up techniques.

The Counseling Perspective

Retirement preparation has most frequently been urged on the basis that retirement precipitates a transition crisis in the individual's life and that such programs can help the individual adjust to retirement. This crisis rationale, endorsed by a substantial number of social scientists, postulates that America is a work-oriented society, with occupational identity pervading all other areas of an individual's life: When an individual moves into retirement and relinquishes the work role, the subsequent role loss constitutes a personal crisis. So intuitively appealing is this explanation that researchers, as well as lay people, refuse to abandon it in the face of mounting evidence recording "no crisis situation."

Sussman (1972), Taylor (1972), and Atchley (1971a) have all succinctly challenged the crisis rationale postulates. Atchley (1971b) found that, while retirees in two quite different occupational settings carried over their work-role identity into retirement, they had very low work orientations. He concluded that *identity continuity* rather than identity crisis was a more appropriate characterization of the retirement transition. Additional evidence comes from the Cornell study confirming that retirement *per se* has no negative impact on individual health, morale or psychological well-being (Streib and Schneider, 1971).

Many point to the apparently increasing older workers' acceptance of retirement as reducing the urgency for formal programs to ease adjustment, documented by studies during the 1950s (Ash, 1966). The growing trend of early retirement is often cited as evidence; some studies indicate good adjustment in early retirees (Barfield and Morgan, 1969; Streib and Schneider, 1971; Pollman, 1971b).

Data Are Inconsistent

A note of caution: The data are not fully consistent on this point. For example, Davidson (1969) found that relatively few eligibles opt for early retirement, and early retirees are not necessarily voluntary retirees. In the 1950s, poor health precipitated most early withdrawals from the labor force (Steiner and Dorfman, 1957); in the 1960s, adequate retirement income was a more important consideration (Pollman, 1971a). Nevertheless, Palmore (1971), using data from a 1963 survey of Social Security beneficiaries, found that seven in 10 still retired involuntarily.

Some workers clearly do resist retirement. Palmore (1965), Palmore (1971) and Jaffe (1970) confirm that retirement rates vary inversely with income, occupation and education. Resistance to the idea has been consistently related to a high work orientation, commitment or intrinsic work satisfaction (Chandler, 1950; Hall, 1954; Simpson, et al., 1966; Eaton, 1969; Monk, 1971; Streib and Schneider, 1971). The 30 per cent of the over-65 age group who elect to continue working are generally motivated by high work involvement rather than financial need (Fillenbaum, 1971a, 1971b; Jacobsohn, 1970; Powers and Goudy, 1971).

Those most resistant to the idea of retirement are concentrated in upper occupational status groups. At the same time, they constitute the group most likely to have the resources to plan for retirement and to have made some plans (Burgess, et al., 1958; Thompson, 1958; Thompson and Streib, 1958; Davidson and Kunze, 1965; Simpson, et al., 1966; Greene, et al., 1969; Charles, 1971; Fillenbaum, 1971c). These upper occupational groups have the greatest opportunity to continue working if they wish. If forced into retirement, even they show a good adaptation after the first few years (Stokes and Maddox, 1967). Thus, it appears retirement constitutes a psychological crisis for only a small segment of the working population, that with the greatest number of resources to cope with any crisis.

If there is, then, no real crisis, how effective are retirement preparation programs in performing this counseling function? One of the most comprehensive studies to date suggests it is difficult to change basic attitudes toward life, retirement, health or income, but that such programs have had a positive effect on stimulating workers to prepare for retirement (Hunter, 1968c). Hence, the counseling function was inadequately performed, although the planning function seemed reasonably effective.

Evaluation Prognosis Poor

Several factors, first in program designs and second in evaluation researches, militate against a more favorable evaluation of the programs to perform effectively their counseling function of promoting better retirement adjustment. Even the best company programs involve only one-and-a-half to two-hour weekly group sessions for five to 12 weeks. How can individual attitudes toward life, work and retirement change from such brief, impersonal encounters? Generally designed to feed information in only one direction, from informant to participant, they do not allow the exchange of ideas and information necessary to promote attitude changes. But any significantly new program formats for either new or existing programs do not now appear to be on the horizon.

A second counteracting influence to documented attitude changes involves a second factor in program design; namely, that all participants are volunteers. As a result, generally only individuals with initially favorable retirement attitudes are likely to enroll; people with negative or neutral attitudes subject to potential influence are simply unlikely to expose themselves to the program. More than one researcher has had to apologize for the inability to document more substantial attitude changes because initially high satisfaction levels did not allow room for much positive change (Mack, 1958; Streib and Thompson, 1958; U. S. Civil Service Commission, 1961; Hunter, 1968c; Charles, 1971). Any satisfactory evaluation of these programs would require randomly assigning individuals to a participant/nonparticipant group and then monitoring attitude changes in both groups by before-and-after program tests. But such improved sampling techniques are not likely to occur soon.

How Permanent Are Changes?

Finally, few studies have attempted anything beyond a pre-test and post-test design immediately connected with the program. At best, follow-up studies occur one or two years after participation, and the few reported results are not particularly encouraging. Hunter (1968a) observed that participants' gains recorded in the first year were attenuated somewhat in the second year follow-up. And there is always the question of whether attitudinal changes lead to behavioral changes (Charles, 1971). Only a handful of studies have been attempted to measure behavioral changes; findings are spotty and inconclusive. Charles (1971), for example, notes changes in information-seeking and behavior planning and increased involvement in social organizations after participation in a retirement preparation program. But Charles admits the important question is still unanswered: How permanent are these changes?

In summary, the weight of evidence appears to be against retirement preparation programs successfully performing the counseling function. But the findings of these evaluation studies may be so biased by the inability to apply rigorous experimental design techniques to gather data (specifically, randomization of participants and longitudinal studies of adjustment) as to make even this weighty body of evidence highly inconclusive.

A fair assessment of how these programs fulfill counseling objectives to ease retirees' adjustments waits for the day when programs are better designed and implemented—and evaluation studies can monitor their success over a long period of time using proper research design. At present, the hit-and-miss character of evaluation research seems intimately tied to the hit-and-miss fashion in which these programs are administered.

The Planning Perspective

The evidence suggests that retirement preparation programs have not been completely successful in counseling employees for better retirement adjustment by focusing on attitude change. The same body of evidence substantiates their capability for stimulating the individual to begin his own planning (Mack, 1958; Hunter, 1968c; Charles, 1971; Fillenbaum, 1971c). Most often, enrollment in a formal program is the individual's first serious consideration of his approaching retirement.

Planning for retirement can be effective in promoting satisfactory adjustment. The Cornell study concludes that good retirement adjustment is related not only to having favorable attitudes, but also an accurate preconception about it (Thompson, 1958; Streib and Thompson, 1958). Realistic planning should thus help develop reasonable expectations about retirement living, which could properly be the goal of these programs.

Recognizing the importance of this planning function, most authorities recommend that preparation for retirement should begin 15 to 20 years ahead (Ash, 1966; Mitchell, 1969; Monk, 1970; McCarthy, 1973). Monk (1970) proposes that planning be focused separately on the age ranges of 50–54, 55–59 and 60–64. The range makes sense according to Johnson's and Strother's (1962) finding that financial planning decreases with increasing age but activity planning increases. Different age groups have different planning needs. Yet, effective financial planning, development of nonwork activity patterns and adoption of proper health care habits can all be most effectively initiated during the middle years when there is time to conserve or even expand resources for the later years.

The retirement literature consistently documents that good adjustment in retirement relates most strongly to adequate health and income (Thompson, 1958; Thompson and Streib, 1958; Simpson, et al., 1966; Greene, et al., 1969; Shanas, 1970), yet the level of planning—even of the most basic financial sort—is severely retarded among middle-aged and older employees.

Many Delay Planning

According to Johnson and Strother (1962), most hourly workers do not compute their benefits until they are between 60 to 65; salaried workers check their benefits only five years earlier on the average, somewhere between 56 to 60. McEwan and Sheldon (1969) report that the middle-income group worries most about retirement finances. Greene, et al. (1969) and Ash (1966) discovered that retirement planning relates to satisfaction with present and projected income and to *not* viewing it as a potential problem.

Numerous studies confirm that upper-income employees are more likely to plan for retirement (Burgess, et al., 1958; Davidson and Kunze, 1965; Charles, 1971; Fillenbaum, 1971c), but other studies question the adequacy of such preparations (Hall, 1954; Prasad, 1964; Eaton, 1969; Monk, 1971; Rowe, 1972 and 1973). The over-all conclusion seems to be that those for whom retirement is likely to pose problems (because of low income, poor health, etc.) are least likely to plan for it and those who do attempt some planning accomplish it in desultory fashion. The majority arrive at the date of retirement without concrete, realistic plans.

Realistic Approach Best

Planning programs, therefore, should focus on helping employees achieve realistic expectations. The need is clearly demonstrated for assistance in how to anticipate and cope with the inevitable income loss. Budget planning that begins only a year or two prior to actual retirement and confrontation with reduced income realities is no solution. It takes time to bolster financial resources; most experts agree that planning should begin in the midforties when major financial commitments of the middle years have stabilized.

That long-term financial planning does ease the adjustment to income loss is unconfirmed, but the logic of the assertion is inescapable. At the very least, an early projection of retirement income would give the employee realistic expectations (already shown to be an important ingredient for adjustment) and, more importantly, he possibly would still have time to bolster his resources.

Employees Themselves Recognize the Need for Early Planning. But, too often, they do not know how to project their retirement income levels or how to build financial reserves if there are deficiencies. So the situation that Fillenbaum (1971c) describes is not uncommon: 97 per cent of her sample of workers, aged 35–64, believed in planing for retirement, but only 28 per cent had actually done so. Unfortunately, those who perceive the need to plan (but do not know how to proceed) generally spend their time worrying about money rather than establishing ameliorative actions. The bleaker the retirement picture, the *more* time the individual is likely to spend worrying and the less embarking on any real course of action. Helping employees to project retirement income levels by providing specific information on long-term financial planning to expand meager resources is of great value.

Employees Are More and More Requesting Company Assistance in Many Areas of Retirement Planning. Fillenbaum (1971c) found nearly unanimous agreement that an employer-sponsored retirement preparation program would be highly desirable. More than 47 per cent said they would participate; an additional 32 per cent said they might. Of the 24 per cent who would not, most were aged 25–44 years. Such employee response is typical. Pyron and Manion (1970) reported that 84 per cent of their sample wanted company assistance in planning retirement, but less than 40 per cent said they received it. When Pyron (1969) studied several company retirement programs in which participation was completely voluntary, he found that attendance rates varied from 30 to 100 per cent. And the U. S. Civil Service Commission Study

(1961) observed there were few dropouts among existing programs.

So the need and desire of employees for retirement preparation programs with a planning focus has been documented.

What Has Been the Employer Response? Superficially, Mitchell (1969) found most employers of 1,000 or more believe preretirement programs are desirable; not having a program generally is due to personnel and budget constraints or overriding work priorities. Pyron (1969), in a study of 100 West Coast firms, found that most had some minimal kind of program, if only to provide the employee with benefit information.

The growth and current status of retirement preparation programs offered by employers are difficult to evaluate; the definition of formal and informal programs varies widely from one study to the next. Early surveys hailed the increase of preretirement programs from 13 per cent in 1950 (Equitable Life Assurance survey), to 45 per cent in 1952 (Hewitt and Associates survey) and 65 per cent in 1955 (National Industrial Conference Board). But many "programs" consisted of little more than informing the employee about his benefits.

Few Programs Are Intensive

Wermel and Beideman (1961) tried to refine the distinction between informal and formal retirement planning programs, concluding that only 25 per cent consisted of more than benefit information. Pyron (1969), in an even more rigorous definition of "formal" programs as "intensive" and "comprehensive," found that only 12 per cent of his sample of employer-sponsored programs qualified. This figure is consistent with several other reputable studies (Riley, *et al.,* 1968; Management Survey, 1971). Also, Pyron (1969) discovered that most of the programs he examined had been in existence less than three years, underscoring the apparent new interest of employers in these programs.

What Benefits Accrue to Employers Who Offer Retirement Planning Programs to Their Employees? Wermel and Beideman (1961) and Pyron (1969) suggest several benefits: Encouraging older workers to retire; raising older workers' morale and increasing their productivity; easing acceptance of mandatory retirement provisions; augmenting effectiveness of company pension plans. Surprisingly little data has been gathered to confirm such assertions.

Thus, a company's decision to get involved in retirement planning remains a function of either management's perception that a serious adjustment problem exists for its retirees or its commitment to a philosophy of assistance deriving from some basic notion of corporate social responsibility (U. S. Civil Service Commission, 1961). Tuckman and Lorge (1952) provided data indicating that employers do not perceive aging workers as persons with serious anxieties over approaching retirement problems; most do not make any special provision for older workers. This position is hardly surprising, given the inability of social science to document conclusively the existence of any adjustment crisis.

Most companies must be motivated by some attitude of corporate responsibility to institute such programs. Indirect evidence to this effect comes from Pyron's (1969) study showing that companies with retirement preparation programs tend to have other "humane" employee benefits such as good pensions, insurance policies, etc. As might be expected, these are the larger firms able to afford the program costs (National Industrial Conference Board, 1955); Mitchell (1969) points out the costs can range from only a few hundred to several thousand dollars.

Commitment Is Prerequisite

Until employers are convinced of the real value of retirement preparation programs (in terms of concrete gains in worker productivity and morale), no longer considering them merely fringe benefits or a token expression of concerned management's "corporate responsibility," there will not be the genuine commitment prerequisite for adequate program design. Most employer-sponsored retirement preparation programs are administered by regular personnel staff counselors who take on the additional responsibility without giving up former ones; rarely is a person hired full time to administer retirement preparation programs.

Assigning the programs to the personnel rather than the training division is indicative of the employers' low-level "fringe benefit" attitude. One might posit that, if retirement preparation programs are meant to serve a *counseling* function (that is, promote good retiree adjustment) they properly belong in the personnel department. But if the main goal is *instruction* on how to plan for retirement, it might more reasonably be considered the domain of training.

Training, generally considered more basic to business operations than personnel functions, tends to be more institutionalized and available to workers as a matter of course. Counseling, in contrast, is usually based on individual situations and circumstances. The stigma felt by the individual employee in taking tests or receiving counseling/advice from personnel does not carry over to his enrollment in training programs, although both may be a form of self-renewal. A valid question is: Would moving retirement preparation programs from personnel to training departments and substituting the counseling emphasis to planning improve the programs' quality, employee acceptance of those programs and, ultimately, their effectiveness in aiding employees?

Guidelines for Ideal Program

There are, then, many guidelines for establishment of a good retirement preparation program.

The program should be *institutionalized* in much the same way that training and retraining programs are; if successful, it will reduce any shame from program participation (self-admission of aging) and increase voluntary enrollment. If the program is open to *all* employees, enrollees would probably include representatives from all age groups (Davidson and Kunze, 1965).

The program should emphasize the *planning* function rather than counseling objective; that is, its goal should be to stimulate enrollees' planning by raising appropriate questions and providing relevant information. Many who refuse counseling focused on psychological adjustment to retirement might welcome concrete, objective information and assistance in financial, legal and health planning. Even employers who resist involvement with retirement preparation programs as an intrusion into individual privacy or are, at best, paternalistic might feel comfortable enough with the more concrete and objective goals of the planning-oriented program to become involved at this level.

The program should be *flexible* to meet the differing needs of different employees. The best retirement planning often occurs in stages (Johnson and Strother, 1962; Monk, 1970). Effective long-range health and financial planning should begin by the midforties; planning for leisure, avocation or part-time employment can begin later, in the fifties. Serious planning for daily retirement living (for example, living on fixed incomes, choosing suitable housing, etc.) can best be considered in the last few years before retirement.

Few programs include sessions on family and social relationships primarily because employees don't often demonstrate the need for assistance in this area—and it comes too close to counseling on personal matters for the employer to become involved (Tuckman and Lorge, 1952; Mack, 1958; U. S. Civil Service Commission, 1961). Nevertheless, a broad program should allow the employee to seek information or any other assistance.

Most employers find some form of group presentation (seminar format or lecture-discussion style) the most efficient, convenient way to disseminate a large body of information to a large number of employees (Mack, 1958; Mitchell, 1969; Charles, 1971). But the major problem is that information will not be detailed or relevant enough to meet individual needs. Often employees are invited to ask for follow-up individual counseling, but Charles (1971) found such requests infrequent. A few researchers maintain that individual counseling, despite the employer's time and cost factors, is the only way to deal satisfactorily with the divergent needs of all employees (Tuckman and Lorge, 1952; Ash, 1966; Pyron and Manion, 1970).

Content Should Vary with Needs

Even with a group program format, content should vary to meet employee needs. Different age groups seek different kinds of information, depending on whether they are engaged in long- or short-range planning. A company's program could also be open to its own retirees. Some who resisted retirement planning because they were unrealistically optimistic might return to the program in a more receptive frame of mind. Including retirees is not a common practice; based on indirect evidence, one would have to guess it is rare. (A 1964 National Industrial Conference Board study indicated only 20 per cent of firms had *any* contact with their retirees.)

Some experts suggest that a program designed for manual or hourly workers will not satisfy the needs of management employees, so they recommend two different programs (Burgess, *et al.*, 1958). Moreover, Monk (1970) found that high-level employees in one industry did not necessarily have the same concerns as those of comparable level in another. Retirement preparation programs may, therefore, be most effective when occupations of the participants are considered.

Employers considering adoption of a retirement planning program or reevaluating an existing program should begin with the specific needs of their particular employees. It would seem obvious that if a company adopts a retirement program from feelings of social responsibility (that is, an employee benefit), it would be designed to meet employees' needs. But Pyron and Manion (1970) indicate that employer response in providing programs lags far behind employee requests for assistance; when retirement preparation programs are set up by an employer, it frequently is done without assessing employees' needs or expectations. Rather, employees are "surprised" with a completely designed program, relevant only in hit-or-miss fashion to particular needs.

Conclusions

The major purpose of this paper has been to distinguish between two previously confused functions of retirement preparation programs —*counseling* and *planning*—and to reevaluate the evidence bearing on each of these functions in program effectiveness.

The current lack of enthusiasm for retirement preparation programs traces back to the empirical evidence suggesting such programs are ineffective; that is, by failing to change employees' attitudes toward work and retirement, they fail to perform their counseling functions. Several reasons for the participants' lack of substantial attitude changes have been highlighted, including the fundamental fact that the programs themselves are neither intensive enough nor properly designed to focus on such attitude changes as the basic goal. Without well-designed programs, objective evaluations of effectiveness are impossible to obtain. Lacking outstanding results, employers are reluctant to implement new programs or to revamp the old. And so the situation of the 1960s persists into the 1970s—a wait-and-see attitude by many employers.

Fulfills Useful Function

In spite of *apparent* failures to adequately fulfill the counseling functions with which the programs have been charged, they have served a useful function in providing information to participants and encouraging them to do their own planning. Employees have overwhelmingly expressed a desire for company assistance in retirement planning. When employers have responded, it has been more in the spirit of good public relations than from any conviction that such programs are in some fundamental way important. As a result, employers tend to discharge this obligation rather perfunctorily, with superficially designed and sloppily implemented programs. Then they resist improving them because the evidence indicates small pay-off from the initial investment.

In contrast, employees seem delighted to get any kind of assistance. When programs are offered, participation is good, dropouts few and requests for additional information voluminous. The programs seem to stimulate planning. Still to be answered is the question of whether concrete planning in the middle years means entering the retirement years prepared with better resources. To date, evaluation research has virtually ignored this facet, focusing almost exclusively on the degree to which retirement preparation programs effectively change attitudes. Ironically, existing programs are better designed to cope with planning objectives than attitude changes, and yet primarily the latter function has been evaluated to the exclusion of the former. It is no wonder the results have been inconclusive and contradictory.

Evaluation research cannot be meaningful if the programs themselves are ineptly designed and implemented. The author suggests a more careful design of retirement preparation programs, including adoption of reasonable, concrete objectives and evaluation studies utilizing rigorous experimental designs. Only then will a fair assessment of the programs' effectiveness be possible, and only then will employers commit themselves fully to the idea of helping employees plan for retirement.

References

ASH, PHILIP. "Pre-retirement Counseling," *The Gerontologist*, 6(2): 97–99, 1966.

ATCHLEY, ROBERT C. "Retirement and Leisure Participation: Continuity or Crisis?" *The Gerontologist*, 11(1): 13–17, Pt. I, 1971a.

———. "Retirement and Work Orientation," *The Gerontologist*, 11(1): 29–32, Pt. I, 1971b.

BARFIELD, RICHARD and JAMES MORGAN. *Early Retirement: Time Decision and the Experience*, Ann Arbor, Institute for Social Research, 1969.

BIXBY, LENORE E. and LOLA M. IRELAN. "The Social Security Administration Program of Retirement Research," *The Gerontologist*, 9(2): 143–147, 1969.

BURGESS, ERNEST W., L. G. COREY, P. C. PINEO and R. T. THOMBURY. "Occupational Differences in Attitudes toward Aging and Retirement," *Journal of Gerontology*, 13(2): 203–206, 1958.

BUSSE, EWALD W. and JUANITA KREPS. "Criteria for Retirement: A Reexamination," *The Gerontologist*, 4(3): 115–120, Pt. I, 1964.

CHANDLER, ALBERT R. "Attitudes of Superior Groups Towards Retirement and Old Age," *Journal of Gerontology*, 5(3): 254–261, 1950.

CHARLES, DON C. "Effect of Participation in a Pre-retirement Program," *The Gerontologist*, 11(1): 24–28, Pt. I, 1971.

DAVIDSON, WAYNE R. "Some Observations about Early Retirement in Industry," *Industrial Gerontology*, No. 1, pp. 26–30, February, 1969.

———, and KARL R. KUNZE. "Psychological, Social and Economic Meanings of Work in Modern Society: Their Effects on the Worker Facing Retirement," *The Gerontologist*, 5(3): 129–133, 1965.

EATON, MERRILL T. "The Mental Health of the Older Executive," *Geriatrics*, 24(5): 126–134, 1969.

ELLISON, DAVID L. "Work, Retirement, and the Sick Role," *The Gerontologist*, 8(3): 189–192, Pt. I, 1968.

FILLENBAUM, GERDA G. "A Consideration of Some Factors Related to Work After Retirement," *The Gerontologist*, 11(1): 18–23, Pt. I, 1971a.

———. "On the Relation Between Attitude to Work and Attitude to Retirement," *Journal of Gerontology*, 26,(2): 244–248, 1971b.

———. "Retirement Planning Programs—At What Age and for Whom?" *The Gerontologist*, 11(1): 33–36, Pt. I, 1971c.

———. "The Working Retired," *Journal of Gerontology*, 26(1): 82–89, 1971d.

GREENE, MARK R., H. C. PYRON, U. V. MANION and H. WINKELVOSS. *Pre-Retirement Counseling, Retirement Adjustment and the Older Employee*, Eugene, Oregon, Graduate School of Management and Business, College of Business Administration, 1969.

HALL, HAROLD R. "Activity Programing for Retirement by Executives," *Journal of Gerontology*, 9(1): 214–217, 1954.

HAVIGHURST, ROBERT J., et al. "A Cross-national Study of Adjustment to Retirement," *The Gerontologist*, 6(3): 137–138, Pt. I, 1966.

HEWITT, EDWIN S., et al. *Company Practices Regarding Older Workers and Retirement*, Libertyville, Illinois, 1952.

HEYMAN, DOROTHY, R. "Does a Wife Retire?" *The Gerontologist*, 10(1): 54–56, Pt. II, 1970.

———, and FRANCES JEFFERS. "Wives and Retirement: A Pilot Study," *Journal of Gerontology*, 23(4): 488–496, 1968.

HIBBARD, DONALD R. and JOHN P. LEE. "Ministers and Their Widows in Retirement." *Journal of Gerontology*, 9(1): 46–55, 1954.

HUNTER, WOODROW W. *A Longitudinal Study of Pre-Retirement Education,* Ann Arbor, Division of Gerontology, 1968a.

————. *Preparation for Retirement,* Ann Arbor, Division of Gerontology, 1968b.

————. *Pre-retirement Education for Hourly-Rated Employees: Final Report,* Ann Arbor, Division of Gerontology, 1968c.

JACOBSOHN, DAN *Attitudes Toward Work and Retirement Among Older Industrial Workers in Three Firms,* Unpublished doctoral dissertation, London School of Economics, 1970.

JAFFE, A. J. "Men Prefer Not to Retire," *Industrial Gerontology,* No. 5, pp. 1–11, Spring, 1970.

JOHNSON, GEORGE E. "A Program to Prepare College Teachers for Retirement," *Journal of Gerontology,* 9(2): 218–223, 1954.

JOHNSON, LEROY and GEORGE B. STROTHER. "Job Expectations and Retirement Planning," *Journal of Gerontology,* 17(4): 418–423, 1962.

KATONA, GEORGE. *Private Pensions and Individual Savings,* Ann Arbor, Survey Research Center, Institute for Social Research, 1965.

KLEEMEIER, ROBERT W. "Leisure and Disengagement in Retirement," *The Gerontologist,* 4(4): 180–184, 1964.

LIPMAN, AARON. "Role Conceptions and Morale of Couples in Retirement," *Journal of Gerontology,* 16(3): 267–271, 1961.

MACK, MARGERY J. "An Evaluation of a Retirement Planning Program," *Journal of Gerontology,* 13(2): 198–202, 1958.

MADDOX, GEORGE L. "Adaptation to Retirement," *The Gerontologist,* 10(1): 14–18, Pt. II, 1970.

MANAGEMENT INFORMATION CENTER, INC. "Most Firms Neglect Retirement Counseling," *Administrative Management,* 32(10): 44–45, 1971.

MC CARTHY, JOSEPH M. "Management's Job in Retirement Planning Programs," *Perspective on Aging,* II(2): 8–10, 1973.

MC EWAN, PETER J. M. and ALAN P. SHELDON. "Patterns of Retirement and Related Variables," *Journal of Geriatric Psychiatry,* III(1): 35–54, 1969.

MITCHELL, WILLIAM L. *Preparation for Retirement: A New Guide to Program Development for Business and Industry,* American Association of Retired Persons, 1969.

MONK, ABRAHAM. Attitudes and *Preparation for Retirement Among Middle-Aged Executives and Professional Men,* Unpublished doctoral dissertation, Brandeis University, 1970.

————. "Factors in the Preparation for Retirement by Middle-aged Adults," *The Gerontologist,* 11(4): 348–351, Pt. I, 1971.

MOORE, ELON H. "Preparation for Retirement," *Journal of Gerontology,* 1(2): 202–212, Pt. I, 1946.

NADELSON, THEODORE. "A Survey of the Literature on the Adjustment of the Aged to Retirement," *Journal of Geriatric Psychiatry,* III(1): 3–20, 1969.

NATIONAL INDUSTRIAL CONFERENCE BOARD, INC. *Retirement of Employees,* New York, 1955.

PALMORE, ERDMAN B. "Differences in the Retirement Patterns of Men and Women," *The Gerontologist,* 5(1): 4–8, 1965.

————. "Why Do People Retire?" *Aging and Human Development,* 2(4): 269–283, 1971.

PETERSON, DAVID A. "Financial Adequacy in Retirement: Perceptions of Older Americans," *The Gerontologist,* 12(4): 379–383, 1972.

POLLMAN, A. WILLIAM. "Early Retirement: A Comparison of Poor Health to Other Retirement Factors," *Journal of Gerontology,* 26(1): 41–45, 1971a.

————. "Early Retirement: Relationship to Variation in Life Satisfaction," *The Gerontologist,* 11(1): 43–44, 1971b.

POWERS, EDWARD A. and WILLIS H. GOUDY. "Examination of the Meaning of Work to Older Workers," *Aging and Human Development,* 2(1): 38–45, 1971.

PRASAD, S. BENJAMIN. "The Retirement Postulate of the Disengagement Theory," *The Gerontologist,* 4(1): 20–23, 1964.

PYRON, H. CHARLES. "Preparing Employees for Retirement," *Personnel Journal,* (September): 722–727, 1969.

―――. and U. V. MANION. "The Company, the Individual and the Decision to Retire," *Industrial Gerontology,* No. 4, pp. 1–26, Winter, 1970.

RILEY, MATILDA W., MARILYN JOHNSON and ANNE FONER. *Aging and Society,* Volume One (An inventory of research findings), New York, Russell Sage Foundation, 1968.

ROMAN, PAUL and PHILIP TARETZ. "Organizational Structure and Disengagement: The Emeritus Professor." *The Gerontologist,* 7(3): 147–152, 1967.

ROWE, ALAN R. "The Retirement of Academic Scientists," *Journal of Gerontology,* 27(1): 113–118, 1972.

―――. "Scientists in Retirement," *Journal of Gerontology,* 28(3): 345–350, 1973.

SHANAS, ETHEL. "Health and Adjustment in Retirement," *The Gerontologist,* 10(1): 19–21, Pt. II, 1970.

SIMPSON, I. H., K. W. BACK and J. C. MC KINNEY. "Attributes of Work Involvement in Society and Self-evaluation in Retirement," *Social Aspects of Aging,* I. H. Simpson and J. C. McKinney, eds., Durham, North Carolina, Duke University Press, 1966.

STANFORD, E. PERCIL. "Retirement Anticipation in the Military." *The Gerontologist,* 11(1): 37–42, Pt. I, 1971.

STEINER, PETER O. and ROBERT DORFMAN. *The Economic Status of the Aged,* Los Angeles, University of California Press, 1957.

STERN, KARL. "Observations in An Old-age Counseling Center: Preliminary Report," *Journal of Gerontology,* 3(1): 48–60, 1948.

STOKES, RANDALL G. and GEORGE L. MADDOX. "Some Social Factors on Retirement Adaptation," *Journal of Gerontology,* 22(3): 329–333, 1967.

STREIB, GORDON F. and CLEMENT J. SCHNEIDER, JR. *Retirement in American Society,* Ithaca, New York, Cornell University Press, 1971.

SUSSMAN, MARVIN. "An Analytic Model for the Sociological Study of Retirement," *Retirement,* Frances M. Carp. ed., New York, Behavioral Publications, 1972.

TAYLOR, CHARLES. "Development Conceptions and the Retirement Process," *Retirement,* Frances M. Carp. ed., New York. Behavioral Publications, 1972.

THOMPSON, GAYLE B. "Work Versus Leisure Roles: An Investigation of Morale among Employed and Retired Men," *Journal of Gerontology,* 28(3): 339–344, 1973.

THOMPSON, WAYNE E. "Pre-retirement Anticipation and Adjustment in Retirement," *Journal of Social Issues,* XIV(2): 35–45, 1958.

―――, and GORDON F. STREIB. "Situational Determinants: Health and Economic Deprivation in Retirement," *Journal of Social Issues,* XIV(2): 18–34, 1958.

―――, GORDON F. STREIB and JOHN KOSA. "Effect of Retirement on Personal Adjustment: A Panel Analysis," *Journal of Gerontology,* 15(2): 165–169, 1960.

TUCKMAN, JACOB and IRVING LORGE. "Retirement Practices in Business and Industry," *Journal of Gerontology,* 7(1): 77–86, 1952.

UNITED STATES CIVIL SERVICE COMMISSION. *"Retirement Planning: A*

Growing Employee Relations Service," Washington, D.C., U.S. Government Printing Office, 1961.

VERWOERDT, ADRIAN. "The Physician's Role in Retirement Counseling," *The Gerontologist,* 10(1): 22–26, Pt. II, 1970.

WERMEL, MICHAEL and GERALDINE BEIDEMAN, *"Retirement Preparation Programs: A Study of Company Responsibility,"* Los Angeles, California Institute of Technology, 1961.

WHITE HOUSE CONFERENCE ON AGING. *Retirement: Background,* Washington, D.C., U.S. Government Printing Office, 1971.

WILSON, STUART and MARTIN LAKIN, "A Method of Studying Group Interaction Effects among Middle-aged and Retiring Workers," *Journal of Gerontology,* 17(1): 61–64, 1962.

UNIT BIBLIOGRAPHY

BELL, BILL D. "Cognitive Dissonance and the Life Satisfaction of Older Adults." *Journal of Gerontology,* **29** (1974), 564–571.

BROEDLING, LAURIE A. "Relationship of Internal-External Control to Work Motivation and Performance in An Expectancy Model." *Journal of Applied Psychology,* **60** (1975), 65–70.

CAMPBELL, DAVID P., and KENNETH L. KLEIN. "Job Satisfaction and Vocational Interests." *The Vocational Guidance Quarterly,* **24** (1975), 125–131.

CAPLAN, ROBERT D., and KENNETH W. JONES. "Effects of Work Load, Role Ambiguity, and Type A Personality on Anxiety, Depression, and Heart Rate." *Journal of Applied Psychology,* **60** (1975), 713–719.

CLOPTON, WILL "Personality and Career Change." *Industrial Gerontology,* **17** (1973), 9–17.

CUTLER, STEPHEN J. "An Approach to the Measurement of Prestige Loss Among the Aged." *Aging and Human Development,* **3** (1972), 285–292.

DARNLEY, FRED, JR. "Adjustment to Retirement: Integrity or Despair." *The Family Coordinator,* **24** (1975), 217–226.

DAVIDSON, WAYNE R., and KARL R. KUNZE. "Psychological, Social, and Economic Meanings of Work in Modern Society: Their Effects on the Worker Facing Retirement." *Gerontologist,* **5** (1968), 129–159.

DAWIS, RENÉ V., and LLOYD H. LOFQUIST. "Personality Style and the Process of Work Adjustment." *Journal of Counseling Psychology,* **23** (1976), 55–59.

DEUTSCHER, MAX. "Adult Work and Developmental Models." *American Journal of Orthopsychiatry,* **38** (1968), 882–892.

DIMARCO, NICHOLAS, and STEVEN NORTON. "Life Style, Organization Structure, Congruity and Job Satisfaction." *Personnel Psychology,* **27** (1974), 581–591.

DYER, LEE D. "Implications of Job Displacement at Mid-career." *Industrial Gerontology,* **17** (1973), 38–46.

DYER, LEE, and DONALD F. PARKER. "Classifying Outcomes in Work Motivation Research: An Examination of the Intrinsic-Extrinsic Dichotomy." *Journal of Applied Psychology,* **60** (1975), 455–458.

FILLENBAUM, GERDA G., and GEORGE L. MADDOX. "Work After Retirement: An Investigation into Some Psychologically Relevant Variables." *The Gerontologist,* **14** (1974), 418–424.

GECHMAN, ARTHUR S., and YOASH WIENER. "Job Involvement and Satisfaction as Related to Mental Health and Personal Time Devoted to Work." *Journal of Applied Psychology,* **60** (1975), 521–523.

HABERLANDT, KARL F. "Learning, Memory and Age." *Industrial Gerontology,* **19** (1973), 20–37.

HENRY, W. E. "The Role of Work in Structuring the Life Cycle." *Human Development,* **14** (1971), 125–131.

KELLEHER, CAROL H. "Second Careers—A Growing Trend." *Industrial Gerontology,* **17** (1973), 1–8.

KINN, JOHN M. "Unemployment and Mid-career Change: A Blueprint for Today and Tomorrow." *Industrial Gerontology,* **17** (1973), 47–59.

MC FARLAND, ROSS A. "The Need for Functional Age Measurements in Industrial Gerontology." *Industrial Gerontology,* **18** (1973), 1–19.

NORD, WALTER R., and ROBERT COSTIGAN. "Worker Adjustment to the Four-Day Week: A Longitudinal Study." *Journal of Applied Psychology,* **58** (1973), 60–66.

PALMORE, ERDMAN B. "Differences in the Retirement Patterns of Men and Women." *Gerontology,* **5** (1968), 4–8.

RUSALEM, HERBERT. "The Floundering Period in the Late Careers of Older Disabled Workers." *Rehabilitation Literature,* **24** (1963), 34–40.

SCHLOSSBERG, NANCY K. "Programs for Adults." *Personnel and Guidance Journal,* **53** (1975), 681–685.

STEVENS, NANCY D. "Job-Seeking Behavior: A Segment of Vocational Development." *Journal of Vocational Behavior,* **3** (1973), 209–219.

THOMAS, L. EUGENE. "Why Study Mid-Life Career Change?" *The Vocational Guidance Quarterly,* **24** (1975), 37–40.

TROPMAN, JOHN E. "Social Mobility and Marital Stability." *Applied Social Studies,* **3** (1971), 165–173.

TURNER, ROBERT G., and WILLIAM M. WHITAKER, III. "The Impact of Mass Layoffs on Older Workers." *Industrial Gerontology,* **16** (1973), 14–21.

part 10
Vocational Guidance and Career Development of the Disadvantaged

Guidance and counseling are concerned with the education, employment, and general welfare of all young people. However, particular emphasis must be placed on services to disadvantaged youth. Although various terms are used, the **disadvantaged** classification is determined by family income and the major problem deals with the person's estrangement from the mainstream of society and the denial to him or her of access to the rewards of life by the dominant culture. In many cases previous failures in social experiences cause these youth to feel they cannot perform academic tasks or hold jobs. They may be hesitant to enter training programs and feel reluctant to approach employment services. They may not recognize their abilities or the available opportunities.

Disadvantaged *is used as a general term that does not specify any particular race or group. It does emphasize the fact that society may place certain restrictions on lower socioeconomic class groups, thus making it difficult for them to attain economic equality. One must always remember that there is a variation between and within all ethnic and socioeconomic groups.*

Guidance for disadvantaged youth will require certain specific knowledge and a variation of traditional methods. Youth who have not learned about vocations from their parents, are not eager to read about vocations, and whose aptitudes may not be accurately appraised with formal instruments will need special assistance. To be of assistance a counselor will need to understand the individual and his environment and be able to communicate with him. Charles C. Harrington's article on ethnicity and schooling discusses the performances of ethnic groups in school. Attitudes and performance in school are related to vocational development and counselors can use this knowledge to plan vocational guidance. The background information may be helpful for counselors in understanding different ethnic groups; however, such information should not be used to construct stereotypes.

Two studies illustrate some similarities in vocational attitudes among different disadvantaged groups. Edgar M. Ansell and James C. Hansen conducted a study that found no significant difference between lower-class black and white students' vocational maturity; however, there were differences between lower-class and middle-class students' vocational development. William P. Kuvlecky et al. report a study examining the projected frames of status reference of black, Mexican-American, and Anglo youth. The findings indicated that the three groups were generally similar, except in reference to status expectations and intensity of aspiration.

A Psychological Anthropologist's View of Ethnicity and Schooling

Charles C. Harrington

Psychological anthropology is that branch of anthropology concerned with the interface between individuals and their culture. A natural concern for psychological anthropologists is how individuals are socialized, and particularly, as Henry Murray used to say, how one becomes in some ways like all persons, in some ways like some persons, and in some ways like no other person. Psychological anthropology as such is concerned mainly with the first two phenomena, leaving the last to psychology. We are here concerned with the ways in which we categorize or divide people into groups, or how they divide themselves.

The purpose of this paper is to review some significant research related to the very important social category or classification of ethnicity. I have chosen first to review the literature on some of the fundamental issues of ethnicity and schooling and then to discuss particular ethnic groups not only to provide a body of information, but also to suggest a number of unresolved theoretical and practical problems in our understanding of cultural pluralism, which I feel are best illustrated in the research on particular ethnic groups. The resolution of these problems I feel is critical: how we understand and use the concepts of ethnicity and cultural pluralism will affect our ability to educate a multi-ethnic school population.

I first review the concept of ethnicity particularly as it relates to schooling. At the outset I stress the importance of our recognizing the possibility of different educational values among various ethnic groups and how the ways in which a particular ethnic group evaluates competent performance may be in conflict with another group's view. This is especially significant if one is a minority ethnic group and the other is the dominant sociocultural group. In my subsequent discussion of Spanish speaking groups in New York City, I illustrate these value conflicts and point to the kind of further research that is needed to increase our understanding of ethnic children in the schools. I next turn to Mexican Americans and review the research on the factors

Reprinted from IRCD Bulletin, *Teachers College, Columbia and Educational Testing Service*, Vol. X, No. 4, Fall 1975.

affecting their school performance, particularly again the educational values and attitudes of students, parents, and school people, but here I point to the unfortunate educational results of our failure to recognize properly the cultural differences that exist between and among Mexican Americans and Anglos and to adequately respond to them. A discussion of blacks follows. Here, rather than reviewing the research about cultural attitudes and values, about which much is already known, I have chosen to review some of the seminal works conceptualizing black culture, which have had a profound effect on how we view black culture in its complex relationship to the larger white culture of which it is a part. This discussion is important because our perspective dictates our choices in educating not only this group but also all minority ethnic groups with a distinct culture that is variously affected by the majority culture. In the next discussion of American Indians I review some of the issues already raised showing their distinct character when looking at American Indians, particularly the acculturation difficulties unique to these peoples. Here too our conceptualization of this cultural group, possibly the most removed from the mainstream culture, will affect any future action for improving their educational opportunities. Finally, I turn to the issue of cultural pluralism, the ways in which a particular group can have a repertoire of behavior, and the kinds of educational interventions that the society must provide in order to educate a multi-ethnic school population.

Ethnicity in the Schools

Ethnicity is here viewed as a complex interaction of a variety of factors which may create important differences among groups of individuals. First, in order for a concept of ethnicity to be effective for use in the United States it must contain the factor of nationality. Extensive studies have been done by applied anthropologists from Columbia University in the past ten years concerning the various nationality groups found in New York City, studied not only in New York but also in their countries of origin before and during the process of migration. We have been able to identify critical sociological dimensions that affect the move to the United States, such as the demographic composition of the migrant group and the types of migration which occur, particularly the circulatory (or shuttle) migration practiced by Dominicans and increasingly by Puerto Ricans. It is clear that there are differences among these nationality groups and that these differences are not clearly understood by the staffs of many schools. Language is one variable that distinguishes among the nationality groups, although it can also link them. While there are more refined differences among them, Spanish speaking groups are often lumped together: many teachers—indeed many New Yorkers—assume that Spanish speaking students are all Puerto Rican. Such inference of nationality from language is not welcome by, for example, the Dominicans to whom it is applied. In addition to language differences, nationalities differ in the legal definition of their stay in the United States. Puerto Ricans are legally citizens and legally residents in the United States. Dominicans are denizens. Those who are in the country legally are still waiting to meet eligibility requirements for citizenship. Even more confounding is the fact that an unknown proportion of Dominicans reside in this country illegally, that is they may have overstayed a vistor's visa (Hendricks 1971) and they must actively seek to hide their status from authorities. Thus Dominican parents are much less able to participate in school politics or to provide the school with accurate data about family size, birth place, and so forth.

In addition to the differences by nationality, language and legal status, there are also differences on an additional set of factors which contribute to a meaningful definition of ethnicity. Differences along these variables can be found to some degree within *all* the nationality groups. These factors are important in influencing relationships among adults, among children, and between the groups and school personnel. They include skin color; educational background and attainment by parents; migration from either rural or urban backgrounds; occupation and income; religion; and dialect differences that are found within language groups.

Research I carried out at Teachers College's Center for Urban Studies and Programs in the early 1970s (now continuing at the Institute for Urban and Minority Education) has strongly suggested that each of these variables can influence how a teacher responds to a child in class. Skin color is sometimes used by teachers as the sole criterion for judging a child's ethnicity and, through ethnicity, his ability; children of lighter skin receive more positive attention (see also Rubovits and Maehr 1973). Highly educated parents have been observed entreating and receiving special favors and treatment for their children. Teachers feel that children from rural areas face adjustment problems in New York City to a greater degree than urban children ("His parents are just peasant farmers—he has a long way to go"). Since teachers bear many norms of American culture as well as norms of the city culture, they also respond to occupation and money cues of parents. Dialect differences between spoken languages of the nationality groups are also used as cues to infer inferiority. Black English is "wrong"; Puerto Rican Spanish "does not sound good," and so forth (see also Campbell 1970). Observers have also described non-verbal communication habits being used as criteria for evaluation. For example, children attending a Spanish Heritage Day in a Spanish-dominant school assembly were upbraided (by a U.S. born, middle class black school administrator) for shouting approval and clapping and haughtily told that "*here* we express approval only with our hands, *not* our mouths."

We perceive ethnicity not as a rigid category, but as a semi-fluid interaction of the variables outlined above. Indeed while these variables produce a very large number of combinations and hence an enormous potential number of ethnic categories, the actual diversity is not so great. For example, there are few Dominican immigrants from urban backgrounds; most have not been granted citizenship; and most are lower class *campesinos*. More important, in any give interaction an individual may choose to accent one variable and play down others, for example, as when a rural Puerto Rican with other Puerto Ricans emphasizes his "Puerto Ricanness" but when with Dominicans emphasizes his common Spanish language or rural origin.

Ethnicity and Performance

It is an anthropological commonplace that disparate cultural values will affect one group's evaluations of another's performance or one group's perceptions of another's competence. It would be unwise, however, to extend that commonplace and to assume we know specifically how disparate values are related to one group's evaluations or perceptions of another without testing them. This means first identifying the values held by the various ethnic groups which could affect their performance or competence as perceived by the school, and, second, demonstrating that these values in fact are reflected in the school's evaluations and perceptions.

Probably the best known account of how cultural values different from those of the school have affected performance evaluation, success, failure and perceptions of competence is work done among the Navajo and the schools run by the Bureau of Indian Affairs (see, for example, Lighton and Kluckhohn 1946). The Navajo value a democratic harmony. To be different from a norm is to be deviant and by definition to fail on this important standard. Teachers, however, judge achievement purely in terms of success on school tasks, and distribute rewards differentially on that basis. The literature describes an incident in which a student who achieved an "A" on a test in which "C" was the norm was praised in front of the class as an example to be emulated. The "successful" child, however, was filled with embarrassment and shame at being so exposed as different from his peers. He could be expected to take care not to "fail" in this way again.

The thrust of anthropological literature has been to demonstrate that different cultures allocate values differently and that these values have consequences for behavior. This literature has gone well beyond simplistic assertions that culture A is different from culture B. Anthropologists have been able to account for value differences by examining child raising practices, family, political, and economic organizations. Value systems, then, are deeply embedded within a cultural matrix and more difficult to change in an acculturation situation than knowledge or belief systems (see Whiting and Whiting 1961). Therefore, the way the values of a particular cultural group lead them to evaluate tasks expected of their children in schools may lead to serious and pervasive conflict when schools are run by and attentive to the values of a different culture.

There is evidence from research to support a lack of responsiveness on the part of schools to the values of the children they serve. Wax (1967), examining high school dropouts from the Pine Ridge Sioux schools, documents the dissimilarity between the values of the Sioux culture and that of the middle class, white oriented schools. Fuchs and Havighurst (1972) point to the insubstantial Indian influence on curriculum design and content in schools for Indians and the predominance of non-Indian personnel in these schools. Judgments of success or excellence by school personnel may be at variance with judgments produced by a particular ethnic group. Indeed, what the school values as an objective may not be so perceived by a particular group being served, and what a particular group defines as a goal may seem inappropriate to the school. For example, many schools are setting up bilingual education programs in response to the obvious perceived needs of many Spanish speaking students. However U.S. born blacks object to the diversion of funds from their children, and "middle class" Puerto Rican parents object to their children being taught to read in Spanish because this will prevent them from getting "white" (English speaking) jobs.[1]

Conversely, other Spanish parents are actively concerned with maintaining their own ethnic identities with their linguistic heritage and want their children to read and write adequately in Spanish. At the same time, in more traditional schools there are no bilingual programs; even schools having 60 per cent Spanish speaking children can have less than 1 per cent staff who even speak Spanish. These schools clearly only value learning to read and write in English, and judgments of competence are often made solely on this criterion. In such a setting a student's *ability* to learn, no matter how well he can read or write Spanish, is evaluated solely by his scores on English reading tests.

These examples emphasize the contradictions that can exist between school goals and the goals of the ethnic groups which make up the school population. While the findings from psychology consistently suggest that competence on a particular task is rewarding, the anthropological literature would suggest that competence in a task valued by one's culture is more rewarding than competence in a task not valued by one's culture, and that failure at a task valued by one's culture is more costly than failure at a task not valued by one's own culture.

[1] This is a matter of structural versus cultural pluralism; see below.

Spanish Speaking Groups in New York City

New York's Spanish speaking population is composed of several distinct ethnic groups, including Puerto Ricans, Dominicans and Cubans. Puerto Ricans constitute the single largest group in New York's Spanish population, and it is the case in fact that other large Spanish speaking groups are often confused with Puerto Ricans. The following discussion will focus on another of those large groups—the 300,000 Dominicans who live in New York—in part to correct this imbalanced view and in part because data on Dominicans usefully illustrate the disparity in values between ethnic group and school which we have described above.

Results from three major sources (Hendricks 1973, Walker 1973, and Foxworthy 1972) argue that Dominican parents tend to view education as learning how to read and write. Tasks undertaken in school other than these are said to have no place. There is some evidence that Dominican children, at least when they first enter school, share their parents' views. Dominican parents perceive the purpose of schooling as the means by which their children can acquire a proficiency in English enabling them to get good jobs. Education is said to be seen by Dominican parents as a validation of the change of status brought about by their social mobility from the life of the *campesino* in the rural Dominican Republic to urban New York. While the prime reasons for migration are said to be economic, an educated child is evidence that the migration has been successful, for had it been necessary for the child to work in order to contribute to the support of his family, he could not have attended school.

Not only are Dominican parents' attitudes toward the content of education often at odds with those of the school, but discrepant values concerning the personal characteristics of teachers have been noted. Dominican parents expect the teachers of their children to be authoritarian and to maintain strict and effective discipline. Teachers who define their role in a more informal way (for example, in an open classroom) are often interpreted by Dominicans as weak and incompetent. Further, if a child acts out Dominican parents expect the teacher to take care of the matter. A teacher who calls a parent to ask for a conference, to enlist the parents' cooperation or alert them to their child's conduct is regarded as weak and unable to handle discipline. Teachers who attend to teaching reading and mathematics are valued; those who concern themselves more personally with the child are not.[2]

It should be noted that not all ethnic groups in New York share

[2] Care should be exercised in applying these descriptions of Dominicans in New York to those in other settings. In addition, Hendricks' (1973) study, from which a number of my observations have been drawn, was of a largely stable "middle class" group, which may differ in important respects from more recently arrived Dominicans.

the attitudes toward school described above. While some Puerto Ricans and U.S. born blacks, and nearly all Dominicans and Cubans, favor successful reading instruction and more formal aspects of education as the means by which their children can aspire to the middle class, others take a different view. More politically oriented sections of the Puerto Rican and black groups value verbal and social skills and denigrate school tasks as middle class "white" skills improperly imposed on a different culture. These groups appear to emphasize political and economic maneuvering in the gaining of resources. It is interesting that Cubans and Dominicans are disenfranchised while U.S. born blacks and Puerto Ricans are citizens and potentially politically potent. It seems to be the more politically secure groups which can support cultural pluralism (not surprising in view of our discussion of cultural pluralism below).

It seems clear that if we are to truly educate the child we must consider not only the ethnicity of his family background but also the ethnicity of his comprehensive social milieu—that is, the composition of his class, his peer group, his teachers, and the placement of his ethnic group in various neighborhood-defined hierarchies.

As much as we do know, further research is required if we are to achieve adequate understanding of these groups. We must first ascertain what kinds of indigenous learning situations exist for the various populations outside of school, and what are the successes of these learning situations in achieving their goals, whether the goals are self-expressed or implicit. Identification of the impact of variables like socioeconomic status, language, cultural values, income, occupation, and religion must therefore be examined. We must analyze the kinds of rewards and sanctions used in those situations and the styles of instruction in each. Data must be collected on a sufficient number of categories of educational settings to allow descriptions of the types of settings important for each of the migrant groups and the characteristics of instruction in each setting type for each group.

We must also ascertain on the macro level the effect of migration on educational processes in whatever setting they occur. Where possible, data relevant to pre-migrational instructional patterns must be collected, allowing gross comparisons of a pre-post migrational kind. Some of these peoples have moved to new sites to stay. Others have come here to work and obtain resources so that they can return to their home country with capital to establish businesses or otherwise improve their status. Still others engage in what can only be described as circular migration, in which, for most individuals, two bases can be said to exist. It makes considerable difference to schools which pattern of migration is encountered. If children will return to their native, non-English speaking homes, there is little need for special programs to teach them English; what is needed is instruction in their native tongue. An important question is how "individuals and small groups, because of specific economic and political circumstances in their *former position* and among the assimilating group, may change their locality, their subsistence pattern, their political allegiance and form, or their household membership" (Barth 1969:24).

Then, we must discover the implicit cultural values that are relevant to schooling, specifically examining what is perceived to be important to learn and what is not. We must determine which of two variables —language or cultural values—is the most powerful predictor of school failure or success. If nationality were synonymous with ethnicity and cultural values, knowing from school records which language is spoken in the home and the birth place of the parents would allow us to easily assess which variable is more potent. But nationality and ethnicity are not the same. Only by a thorough knowledge of the family based upon ethnograhic data can one hope to identify truly cultural variables.

We must begin to understand the processes whereby children learn about their own ethnicity and the ethnicity of others. The following observations from Foxworthy's New York City field notes illustrate the kinds of phenomena we need to understand more fully.
In a sixth grade class:

> "A Cuban-Chinese boy is called 'Chino' by Dominican boys but not by Cuban boys." "Dominican boys never dance at class parties with U.S. born black girls, but dance with Dominican girls of the same skin color." "Friendship choices for girls tend to be across ethnic lines, while the choices of boys are always within ethnic lines."

In a fourth grade class:

> "The teacher starts a discussion about Dominican Independence Day and the Dominican leader Duarte. A Dominican boys ask the teacher if she is from the Dominican Republic. When she says no, Puerto Rico, he gives her a thumbs down sign and tells her that's bad . . . Santo Domingo is better." "There is a lot of talk between boys about whose hair is getting long enough to be an Afro, and whether Afros are good or bad. The children's discussions center on the trouble of combing it, however, while a similar discussion among adults, i.e. mothers, has racial considerations ('he'll look like an African') as the dominant feature."

The processes of development of such images in children, and their consequences, are important areas of study which have significance far beyond the particular setting under study.

Finally, we must shed light on the consequences of stereotyping in the process of the classroom. Rosenthal's (1971) study made an empirical argument that stereotypes, in this case of a pupil's ability, could become self-fulfilling stereotypes. Gumpert and Gumpert, while acknowledging defects in the statistical analysis of the Rosenthal book, find evidence to substantiate this point. (But see also Elashoff and Snow 1971).

To summarize, in order to arrive at an understanding of ethnicity we need to know more about the interaction among variables which determine the life patterns and values of these groups, how they view themselves and how they are viewed by others. With this knowledge, directives for educational planning should become clearer.

Mexican Americans

Recent research on Mexican Americans has investigated specifically some of the factors influencing school performance which we discussed above with particular reference to the Spanish speaking groups in New York City. Several of these studies address the issue of values and attitudes—of students, parents, and school—from which we might draw conclusions about the nature of ethnicity which may have implications for educational practice.

Schwartz (1971) emphasizes that ethnicity must be defined by variables in addition to simple nationality labels. Her study compared Mexican American and Anglo secondary school age children. She found high expectations of school attendance for both groups but a higher generalized faith in mankind and more optimistic orientation toward the future among Anglos than among Mexican Americans. These variables were also related to achievement. More important, she showed that within the Mexican American group these values were not distributed evenly, and that Mexican American pupils of higher socioeconomic status were more similar to Anglos.

Evans and Anderson (1973), while not examining variations within the Mexican American group as did Schwartz, did find that stereotypes about this group held by educators and used to explain their relation to failure are seriously in error. Mexican American students, in comparison to Anglos, did have lower self concepts of ability, experienced less democratic parental independence training, had fatalistic present time orientations, had a high striving orientation, and lower educational aspirations; however, simple minded linkages to school attitudes do not work. The Mexican Americans were also found to come from homes where education was valued and stressed. Parental encouragement of schooling was linked to values and experiences which the authors attribute to a "culture of poverty."

Madsen and Kagan (1973) report a study of experimental situations in a small Mexican town and among Anglos in Los Angeles. Mothers of both groups rewarded their children for success, but Mexican mothers more often gave rewards for failure than did Anglo mothers. Anglo mothers chose higher and more difficult achievement goals for their children. Does this matter? Yes, but again not in the simple way one might expect—high achievement goals producing better performance. Madsen's 1971 study of cooperative-competitive behavior in the same populations as those in the preceding study shows a higher level of *cooperation* among Mexican than among Anglo American children. There are also increases in *non-adaptive* competition with age for the Anglo group.

The United States Commission on Civil Rights (1971) examined "the degree to which schools in the Southwest are succeeding in educating their students, particularly minority students." Using five measures of achievement—school holding power (the ability of the school to retain students until completion of course of study), reading achievement, grade repetition, overageness, and participation in extracurricular activities—the Commission concludes that there are great discrepancies in the outcomes of students of different ethnic groups. In all measures Mexican Americans achieve at a markedly lower rate than Anglo Americans. The United States Commission on Civil Rights (1972) deals with the issue of assimilation. It sketches the conflict between the emphasis on Anglo culture (and language) in the schools and a distinct Mexican American cultural pattern. This report addresses three aspects of cultural exclusion as practiced in schools: (1) exclusion of the Spanish language; (2) exclusion of the Mexican heritage; and (3) exclusion of the Mexican American community from full participation in school affairs.

Clearly then, we are not doing an adequate job of educating Mexican American children. It may be that positive identification with one's culture or ethnicity is a powerful motivation for tested achievement. Feeling of self worth seems adaptive in the face of benign neglect of the school for one's group, but how is it acquired in the face of everyday pressures?

Blacks

If we have much to learn about the cultural attributes which contribute to the ethnic characters of the migratory Spanish groups, a different challenge altogether is illustrated by the more settled, urban, English speaking ethnic group: blacks. In point of fact, those we commonly label blacks actually constitute at least two major groups. One is the migrants and their descendents from various British West Indian islands (predominantly Trinidad, Jamaica and Barbados). These groups represent a migrant population of long history and stability, and many of our most prominent blacks are in fact British West Indian descendants. The other is the black U.S. population located in this country since its inception, the group to whom we now turn our attention.

Recent psychological anthropological studies of U.S. urban blacks have brought to the fore the problem of perspective, or how to view a relatively stable, well known ethnic population. The most psychologically oriented of these recent studies is Hannerz' (1969). His book is also interesting because it marks (with Ogbu's 1974) attempts by non-American anthropologists to come to grips with black U.S. culture. Using the tools of the anthropologist, Hannerz describes life in the ghetto, but his particular interest is given to the development of male role behavior, a subject which also concerned Elliot Liebow in *Tally's Corner* (1969). In fact, in one way or another, much of the anthropological literature about the urban black ghetto has centered on male role behavior, either of teenagers (Walter Miller, for example) or adults.

The literature about blacks can be classed according to the following three theoretical positions using male role as an example:

1. Behavior in a black ghetto is a deviant form of normal "mainstream" male role behavior. For example, black ghetto males are more aggressive because they are protesting their masculinity in terms defined as masculine by white, middle class people. That they overdo their behavior into a caricature of the white middle class male role is attributable to their coming from a subculture where matrifocal families predominate, depriving the child of male role models. Their inability to successfully carry out instrumental aspects of the male role results from their lack of training and exclusion from jobs.

2. Behavior in a black ghetto is evidence of a ghetto-specific or black culture-specific (see Young 1970) phenomenon; the ghetto is simply a different culture from white, middle class America. For example, it is a mistake to interpret male ghetto behavior as a reaction or in relation to white, middle class definitions. This is just the way ghetto males behave. Upholders of this position typically downgrade the "protest masculine" explanation as inappropriate, and also suggest it to be inaccurate since male influence in the ghetto is strong, particularly through extra-familial groups.

3. Behavior in a black ghetto is merely a local expression of a "culture of poverty" which is found worldwide. The critical dimension here is that the state of poverty, in a culture in which wealth is also present, creates certain behavioral patterns which hold, regardless of what mainstream culture is like. For example, matrifocal households and aggressive males are part of this "culture," and are therefore to be expected in our black ghetto.

So we have in anthropology a choice, and increasingly a dispute, among respectively the "subculture" (or subsociety), the "separate culture," and the "culture of poverty" schools in interpreting black ghetto behavior. Liebow upholds the first position and Valentine (1968) appears to lean toward it; Hannerz the second; and Oscar Lewis and his followers the third. Much of Hannerz' book *Soulside* is a justification of his own position. But all three schools and the dogmas which surround them may block our understanding of life in a ghetto, or anywhere. The concept of culture, instead of being an analytic tool, can *prevent* analysis by obscuring what it is we are talking about.

To pursue our argument further, Hannerz suggests that ghetto sex role behavior cannot be accounted for as protest against middle class values. Such an explanation would postulate that, for example, father absence leads to feminine identity and a subsequent exhibition of hypermasculine traits. Hannerz argues that since there *are* men in the ghetto who could serve as role models, the subculture position is fallacious; however his own argument is misdirected. Hannerz is right, if not original, in attacking a theory that fixates on father absence to explain sex role learning. Why not father salience, mother salience, sibling presence and salience, peer groups, etc., not to mention effects of street society, power positions, and so forth? But this has nothing to do with whether the black ghetto is a culture or a subculture.

There is a fair amount of psychological anthropological literature which talks about the effects of such variables regardless of a particular culture's definitions. But what we need for blacks are studies which link these influences to behavior. In our anthropological studies of the urban ghetto, we must see to what extent our *cross-cultural* findings of the last twenty years in the fields of perception, cognition and socialization can account for what we see in the ghetto. This, not polemic about what kind of culture or subculture ghetto life is (for example, Valentine 1968), is what is required. To say, as Hannerz does, that black male behavior is ghetto specific is *not* an explanation and is barely a description. But an extensive ethnographic study to account for behavior as a result of certain developmental and situational pressures which are themselves extensively treated and tested in anthropological literature is the kind of contribution I hope to see come out of psychological anthropology in the future.

Nevertheless, whether to conceptualize the black ghetto as a subculture, a culture, or a local manifestation of a culture of poverty *is* an important problem for educators. Each leads to different action and each position can find its defenders. I think all three are true to a certain extent, each perhaps helps us better understand one or another aspect of behavior. But I think none of them alone can help us very much. Further, the blacks are stratified so that for some groups one may matter more than for other groups.[3]

Educators should therefore recognize the inadequacy of any one approach. Valentine (1972) comes close to this kind of approach in his discussion of "biculturation." He states:

> The collective behavior and community life of Afro-Americans can best be understood as bicultural in the sense that people regularly draw upon both an ethnically distinctive repertoire of beliefs and customs and, at the same time, make use of behavior patterns from the European American cultural mainstream (p. 33). [4]

3 J. Milton Yinger's discussion of contraculture and subculture (1960) is also important. Yinger's discussion of contraculture is closely related to the issue of ethnicity; Yinger claims that he has found the concept of subculture used in several distinct ways a problem not unlike that surrounding the concept of ethnicity. "Contraculture" refers to the creation of a "series of inverse or counter values (opposed to those of the surrounding society) in face of serious frustration or conflict" (1960:627). It is not difficult to tie in this concept with Valentine's notion of biculturation (which Valentine in fact does).

4 Biculturation for Mexican Americans and the issue of bicognitive development is addressed in Ramirez and Castaneda, 1974.

It would be useful to educators to understand contemporary human behavior, to specify the importance of what goes on outside of school to the learning of social behavior, and to study the techniques of instruction that exist there, and the processes of learning that are involved. In some ways we know more about Samoa than about what happens six blocks east of my office.

American Indians

Studies of American Indians present a special case to the psychological anthropologist concerned with determining the factors which contribute to a definition of ethnicity of these peoples, and resultant implications for education. A great deal of anthropological research was carried out more than twenty years ago because North American Indian cultures provided an easily accessible "laboratory" for the study of acculturation (for summaries see Honigmann 1972, Barnouw 1973, Haring 1956). Some recent studies have focused on the phenomena occurring as these peoples, perhaps the most removed from mainstream culture, are brought up against urban life. However, recent studies sometimes lose sight of the differences among the groups that fall under the label American Indians. These differences, in addition to obvious tribal distinctions, involve all the variables listed in our earlier discussion of ethnicity, and the reader should not lose sight of them. Some of the problems that have been noted in our discussions of other ethnic groups—values and value conflict, ethnic identity and community, the perspective from which to view a cultural group—are demonstrated in studies of American Indians, as well as acculturation difficulties unique to these peoples.

Graves (1970) has written with eloquence about the Indians for whom urban migration is chosen as a result of inadequate economic opportunities on the reservation, and who then find the economic role of the migrant in the city to be only marginal (Sanday, 1973, has gone so far as to call them culturally marginal). To this economic insecurity he attributes, in large part, their extremely high rate of arrest in Denver for drinking and drinking related offenses. His ten year study of 259 Navajo male migrants reveals the economic, social and psychological pressures and constraints (see also Graves 1973).

Trible (1969) has compared the psycho-social characteristics of employed and unemployed western Oklahoma male Indians representing nineteen tribes. Several salient differences were found which reinforce Graves' thesis: while level of training and education were unrelated to employment status, self concept variables were clearly linked.

Robbins (1973) describes an increase in interpersonal conflict as a concomitant of economic change. He describes the drinking behaviors of the Naskapi Indians of Quebec and claims an increase in frequencies of identity struggles and the development of ritualized or formalized social interactions which serve as identity resolving forums. He concludes (Robbins 1971) that drinking behaviors provide an arena in which individuals can make status claims. Those who are successful wage earners (a status formerly achieved through hunting) make such claims by gift giving. Those who are failures make status claims through aggressive behavior. Robbins argues then that aggressive drinking behavior provides the Naskapi with a means for taking an identity he has not been able to achieve through the new economic channels. This research is a cut above the usual studies of the linkages between stress and alcoholism because of its analysis of the behaviors associated with drinking rather than drinking per se.

Savard (1969) concludes that the Navajo alcoholic seems to use alcohol not as an escape but as a means of entree into social relationships. Group fellowship among drinkers is seen as countering an inability to function in as large a variety of social groups as nonalcoholics function in. Explanations of culturally sanctioned responses for dealing with stresses of acculturation are congruent with the description in Whiting et al. (1966) of culturally sanctioned defense mechanisms for handling a failure to live up to cultural norms. A considerable promise for future research in this area can be assured.

Of course not all cultures succeed in establishing such cultural defenses, and individual expressions of stress-induced anger are possible. For example, Ackerman (1971) relates juvenile delinquency among Nez Perce Indians to marital instability, loss of communal discipline, loss of patrilocality, and sex role definition changes. Levy and Kunitz (1971), studying the Navajo, argue that feelings of anomie are not responses to acculturation but should be seen rather as persisting elements of Navajo culture. And Boag (1970) feels that the social problems faced by Arctic natives resemble those of underprivileged minorities elsewhere. While traditional patterns of psychopathology are obscured by social change, they are replaced by familiar identity and family disorganization pathologies. It is worth noting that we have heard this debate before. To make the linkage clear, for some theorists stress reactions are Indian culture-specific, for others they represent reactions to new role demands made by the larger Anglo society, and for others they represent yet another manifestation of a culture shared by poor minorities elsewhere. Again, more data are needed to adequately sort out for which areas of life these processes operate.

More directly relating cultural attributes of American Indians to education, Fuchs and Havighurst (1972) examined data on Indian residents of Chicago. In the last twenty years Chicago has experienced a surge of Indian migration. The authors claim that although approximately seven thousand Indians reside in Chicago only 237 Indian children were found in attendance at the schools located in the area of highest Indian concentration. They assert that urban life has not suppressed indigenous values of these native people and attribute the educational isolation to feelings on the part of Indian youth that schools are punitively directed against them, to their unfamiliarity with educational prerequisites to careers and socioeconomic success, to their isolation from the mainstream, and to influence of peers. (For linguistic variables, see Philips 1970.) The authors conclude:

> Indian education is an essential part of the complete process by which the Indian peoples make progress toward their own goals as individuals and as social groups. For this, they must secure a higher material standard of living, and more *real* options for themselves as individuals, families, and tribes (author's emphasis, p. 314).

However, how are Indians to achieve these options *and* change their pattern of underdevelopment? The authors suggest that the "dominant society [will] act in good faith, mainly through the Federal Government." This is hardly likely in the light of history and their own ethnographic evidence.

Cultural Pluralism

In this paper we have been building to an argument for a greater orientation in schools to the cultural pluralism of the peoples they serve. Cultural pluralism is a cultural diversity. It refers to differences brought about by group norms, resulting in different behavioral styles among various ethnic and linguistic groups. Group identity is nourished; attempts to minimize group differences and achieve melting pot models are eschewed. Sanday (1973) has recently distinguished cultural pluralism from structural pluralism. It is an important differentiation. Structural pluralism is the differential incorporation (or stratification) of various population categories into the opportunity structure of the society. It prevents some groups from achieving the social and economic status which others are able to achieve; racism is an example of structural pluralism. One can talk about maintaining cultural differences and, at the same time, providing the learning experiences required to successfully compete for resources. Presumably this prevents cultural pluralism from becoming structural pluralism. But is this in fact true or possible in a society so used to differentially incorporating race and sex and nationality populations in its opportunity structure?

Ethnic differentiation is clearly the most basic form of cultural pluralism (see Van den Berghe 1973). When ethnicity corresponds to racial divisions, however, the more structural forms of pluralism emerge. Examples are not difficult to come by to suggest that in many societies, including our own, racial identification has been important and necessary to support an exploitative, subordinating relationship (for example, slavery and colonialism). Exploitation and subordination *need not* be aspects of *cultural* pluralism, but because of its context in our own de facto economically stratified society, is a completely benign cultural pluralism really possible?

Educators must be aware that schools form only a part of a child's life. The education of American minority group children takes place within the context of the way in which our society is actually stratified. For example, Ogbu (1974) argues that black and Mexican American students reduce their efforts in school tasks to the level of rewards they expect as future adults. We must ask what differences in children we can reasonably expect through our educational innovations, given the everyday reality of growing up in an economically discriminated segment of the population. This is especially important in evaluating what we do. For example, we must not judge the effects of school integration too quickly when there is so much that remains segregated in our lives.

Yet schools must do a better job, must not turn or help turn cultural pluralism into structural pluralism. Our directives point in the following ways. We need to increase the diversity of educational environments to increase the likelihood of children finding one within which they can function. We need to increase the number and diversity of educational outcomes sought for assessment and the procedures for measuring them. We need to nurture the legitimacy of multiple educational outcomes that foster cultural pluralism without reinforcing structural pluralism. We must insist on curriculum definitions that allow the examination of what goes on in school as part of a larger context—the rest of the child's life.

Conclusions

Let me end with a warning. We have been reviewing a wide range of literature on a number of ethnic variables as they relate to processes of schooling. It would indicate a serious misunderstanding if the information we have given about the various groups were used to construct yet more stereotypes, however refined, about these groups. The reader should remember that we have been dealing with the second aspect of Murray's aphorism. The other two still operate and, however much a child may be like other children because of ethnicity, there are still ways in which he is like all other children regardless of ethnicity. That is, he is still human, able to learn, able to think and able to feel. The ethnic differences we have been describing are small compared to these.

In other ways a particular child is like no other and knowing something about the culture from which he comes or the ethnic group to which he belongs does not excuse an educator from his obligation to know the child as an individual unique from other individuals and respond to his own special needs with a personally designed plan of instruction. The information about ethnicity growing out of research described in this article is, I think, important and valuable for educators to have, but it is not the only information that they need in planning their actions.

References

ACKERMAN, LILLIAN A. Marital Instability and Juvenile Delinquency among the Nez Perces. *American Anthropologist*, 1971, 73:595.

BARNOUW, VICTOR. *Culture and Personality*. Homewood, Ill.: Dorsey Press, 1973.

BARTH, FREDRICK. *Ethnic Groups and Boundaries: The Social Organization of Cultural Difference*. Boston: Little, Brown & Co., 1969.

BOAG, THOMAS J. Mental Health of Native Peoples of the Arctic. *Canadian Psychiatric Association Journal*, 1970, 15:115.

CAMPBELL, RUSSELL N. English Curricula for Non-English Speakers. In James E. Alatis (Ed.), *Bilingualism and Language Contact*. Proceedings of the Georgetown University Round Table on Languages and Linguistics 1970. Washington: Georgetown University Press, 1970.

ELASHOFF, JANET and SNOW, RICHARD E. *Pygmalion Reconsidered*. Worthington, Ohio: Charles A. Jones, 1971.

EVANS, FRANCIS B. and ANDERSON, JAMES G. The Psychocultural Origins of Achievement and Achievement Motivation: The Mexican-American Family. *Sociology of Education*, 1973, 46:396.

FOXWORTHY, NANCY. Unpublished Field Notes: Applied Anthropology Program. New York: Teachers College, Columbia University, n.d.

FUCHS, ESTELLE and HAVIGHURST, ROBERT J. *To Live on the Earth: American Indian Education*. Garden City, N.Y.: Doubleday, 1972.

GRAVES, THEODORE D. The Personal Adjustment of Navajo Indian Migrants to Denver, Colorado. *American Anthropologist*, 1970, 72:35.

GRAVES, THEODORE D. The Navajo Urban Migrant and His Psychological Situation. *Ethos*, 1973, 3:321.

GUMPERT, PETER and GUMPERT, CAROL. The Teacher as Pygmalion: Comments on the Psychology of Expectation. *The Urban Review*, 1968, 3(1): 21–25.

HANNERZ, ULF. *Soulside*. New York: Columbia University Press, 1969.

HARING, DOUGLAS G. (Ed.). *Personal Character and Cultural Milieu*. Syracuse: Syracuse University Press, 1956.

HENDRICKS, GLENN. The Dominican Diaspora: The Case of Immigrants from the Dominican Republic in New York City. Ed.D. Dissertation, Teachers College, Columbia University, New York, 1971.

HENDRICKS, GLENN. La Raza en Nueva York: Social Pluralism and Schools. New York: *Teachers College Record*, 1973, 379–394.

HONIGMANN, JOHN J. *Personality in Culture*. New York: Harper & Row, 1967.

LEIGHTON, I. and KLUCKHOHN, C. *Children of the People*. Cambridge: Harvard University Press, 1946.

LEVY, JERROLD E. and KUNITZ, STEPHEN. Indian Reservations. Anomie and Social Pathologies. *Southwestern Journal of Anthropology*, 1971, 27:97.

LIEBOW, ELLIOT. *Tally's Corner*. Boston: Little, Brown & Co., 1969.

MADSEN, MILLARD C. Developmental and Cross-cultural Differences in the Cooperative and Competitive Behavior of Young Children. *Journal of Cross-Cultural Psychology*, 1971, 2:365.

MADSEN, MILLARD C. and KAGAN, SPENCER. Mother-directed Achievement of Children in Two Cultures. *Journal of Cross-Cultural Psychology*, 1973, 4:221.

MILLER, WALTER. Lower Class Culture as a Generating Milieu of Gang Deliquency. In M.E. Wolfgang, L. Savitz and N. Johnson (Eds.), *The Sociology of Crime and Delinquency*. New York: Wiley, 1958.

OBGU, JOHN. *The Next Generation*. New York and London: Academic Press, 1974.

PHILIPS, SUSAN U. Acquisition of Rules for Appropriate Speech Usage. In James E. Alatis (Ed.), *Bilingualism and Language Contact*. Proceedings of the Georgetown University Round Table on Languages and Linguistics 1970. Washington: Georgetown University Press, 1970.

RAMIREZ, MANUEL and CASTANEDA, ALFREDO. *Cultural Democracy, Bicognitive Development, and Education*. New York: Academic Press, 1974.

RUBOVITS, P. C. and MAEHR, M. L. Pygmalion Black and White. *Journal of Personality and Social Psychology*, 1973, 25:210–218.

RESNIK, H. L. and DIZMANG, LARRY H. Observations on Suicidal Behavior Among American Indians. *American Journal of Psychiatry*, 1971, 127: 882–887.

ROBBINS, RICHARD H. Drinking Behavior and Identity Resolution. Ph.D. Dissertation, University of North Carolina at Chapel Hill, 1970.

ROBBINS, RICHARD H. Alcohol and the Identity Struggle: Some Effects of Economic Change on Interpersonal Relations. *American Anthropologist*, 1973, 75:99.

ROSENTHAL, ROBERT. *Pygmalion in the Classroom*. Worthington Ohio: Charles A. Jones, 1971.

SANDAY, P. Cultural and Structural Pluralism in the United States. MSSB Conference on the Contribution of Anthropology to Social Policy Planning. Philadelphia, October 1973.

SAVARD, ROBERT J. Cultural Stress and Alcoholism: A Study of Their Relationship Among Navaho Alcoholic Men. Ph.D. dissertation, University of Minnesota, 1968.

SCHWARTZ, AUDREY J. A Comparative Study of Values and Achievement: Mexican-American and Anglo Youth. *Sociology of Education*, 1971, 44(4): 438–62.

TRIBLE, JOSEPH E. Psychosocial Characteristics of Employed and Unemployed Western Oklahoma Male American Indians. Ph.D. dissertation, University of Oklahoma, 1969.

UNITED STATES COMMISSION ON CIVIL RIGHTS. Report II: The Unfinished Education. 1971.

UNITED STATES COMMISSION ON CIVIL RIGHTS. Report III: The Excluded Student. 1972.

VALENTINE, CHARLES. *Culture and Poverty: Critique and Counter-proposals*. Chicago: University of Chicago Press, 1968.

VALENTINE, CHARLES. Black Studies and Anthropology: Scholarly and Political Interests in Afro-American Culture. McCaleb Module 55, pp. 1–53. Reading, Mass.: Addison Wesley, 1972.

VAN DEN BERGHE, PIERRE L. Pluralism. In John Honigmann (Ed.), *Handbook of Social and Cultural Anthropology*. Chicago: Rand McNally, 1973.

VINCENT, JOAN. The Structure of Ethnicity. *Human Organization*, 1974. 33: 375–9.

WALKER, MALCOLM T. *Politics and the Power Structure: A Rural Community in the Dominican Republic*. New York: Teachers College Press, 1973.

WAX, ROSALIE H. The Warrior Dropouts. *Transaction*, 1967, 4(6):40–46.

WHITING, JOHN W. M. and WHITING, BEATRICE B. Contributions of Anthropology to the Methods of Studying Child Rearing. In Paul H. Mussen (Ed.),

Handbook of Research Methods in Child Development. New York: John Wiley, 1960.

WHITING, JOHN W. M., et al. The Learning of Values. In E. A. Vogt and E. M. Albert (Eds.), *People of Rimrock: A Study of Values in Five Cultures.* Cambridge: Harvard University Press, 1966.

YINGER, J. MILTON. Contraculture and Subculture. *American Sociological Review,* 1960, 25:625–35.

YOUNG, VIRGINIA H. Family and Childhood in a Southern Negro Community. *American Anthropologist,* 1970, 72:269–88.

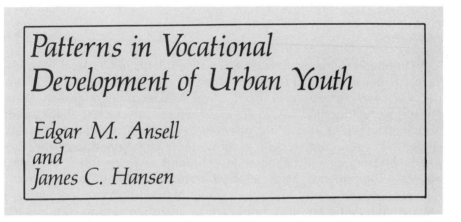

Patterns in Vocational Development of Urban Youth

Edgar M. Ansell
and
James C. Hansen

Vocational development has received considerable attention both in theory and research. A tenet of vocational development theory is that vocational decision making is an ongoing process which occurs over a number of years. As an individual matures vocationally, he proceeds through a series of developmental life stages with each stage affording him opportunities to deal with specific tasks. An individual's ability to cope successfully with the tasks reflects his level of vocational maturity. Vocational maturity focuses on both the rate and level of an individual's development with respect to career tasks. The assessment of vocational maturity in adolescence is important if we are to determine the extent the goal of integrative vocational adjustment is being attained.

Three longitudinal research projects have been devoted to the assessment of vocational maturity (Crites, 1965; Gribbons and Lohnes, 1965, 1967, 1968; Super and Overstreet, 1960). However, the Career Patterns Study, the Career Development Study, and Crites' research

Reprinted from the *Journal of Counseling Psychology,* **13**:505–508 (1971). Copyright 1971 by the American Psychological Association. Reprinted by permission.

have not been focused directly on career development among lower socioeconomic subjects. Hall (1963) has suggested that psychologists have looked at homogeneous populations and Gribbons and Lohnes (1968) note that too little vocational development research has been directed toward the less academically able students and students from lower socioeconomic groups. Some writers have been concerned that theory and research relative to vocational maturity have been based on middle-class groups (Amos and Grambs, 1968; Calia, 1966; Tyler, 1967) and call for research relevant to the lower-class individual.

The purpose of this study was to investigate the rates and levels of vocational maturity in lower- and middle-class adolescent boys. Do lower-class white and black adolescents achieve vocational maturity at a rate similar to middle-class white adolescents?

Method

A stratified random sample of 375 male students in Grades 8 through 12 participated in the study. This involved randomly selecting 25 students at each grade level from three socioeconomic groups. The groups were identified as lower-class white, lower-class black, and middle-class white. It was not possible to select 25 middle-class black students in each grade. Lower-class students were identified from the free lunch program, and middle-class students were identified by street address. The subjects were selected from two of four urban junior high schools and two of four urban senior high schools in a large northeastern city. Although all schools are in an urban setting, the lower-class students did attend different schools from the middle-class students. Curricular choice was not a criterion selection but once the sampling was complete, all programs in the curriculum were represented.

The Readiness for Vocational Planning Scale was used to assess vocational maturity. This scale consists of 22 items which were selected by factor analysis from the original 45 items of the eighth-grade interview conducted in the Career Development Study (Gribbons and Lohnes, 1968). The scale is designed to assess eight dimensions of readiness for vocational planning: Factors in Curriculum Choice, Factors in Occupational Choice, Verbalized Strengths and Weaknesses, Accuracy of Self-Appraisal, Evidence for Self-Rating, Interests, Values, and Independence of Choice. The scale is a questionnaire that is answered in an interview with a counselor. The responses are rated from 0 to 2 with the highest possible total score being 44. The score indicates the student's level of readiness for vocational planning or his vocational maturity.

The most recently reported group IQ score in the student's permanent record was used in the study. For the entire population, this involved scores from the California Test of Mental Maturity, the Primary

TABLE 1. CELL MEANS OF VOCATIONAL MATURITY SCORES FOR LOWER-CLASS BLACK, LOWER-CLASS WHITE, AND MIDDLE-CLASS WHITE MALES BY GRADE LEVEL ON THE READINESS FOR VOCATIONAL PLANNING SCALE

GROUP	GRADE 8		GRADE 9		GRADE 10		GRADE 11		GRADE 12	
	M	SD	M	SD	M	SD	M	SD	M	SD
Lower-class black	8.72	4.42	11.24	5.25	10.72	4.29	17.16	5.51	22.36	7.74
Lower-class white	11.40	3.65	13.84	5.20	13.48	6.04	18.04	5.89	21.68	7.79
Middle-class white	13.92	5.72	16.56	4.92	20.76	6.67	24.44	6.69	30.96	6.01

Note.—n = 25 in each grade.

Mental Abilities Test, and the Pintner Mental Abilities Test (Advanced). All scores were converted to T-scores.

Statistical procedures first included a univariate analysis of covariance with intelligence controlled as the covariate to determine the effect of socioeconomic groups and grade levels on vocational maturity. Scheffé's post hoc comparisons were made when permissible.

Results

Table 1 reveals mean scores reflecting the vocational maturity of the three groups when assessed by the Readiness for Vocational Planning Scale. When the means were adjusted with intelligence controlled as a covariate, the patterns of the means did not change.

Vocational maturity does increase with age for all sample groups but the samples developed at different rates. Middle-class students earned the highest scores at each grade level, generally followed by lower-class white, and then lower-class black students. Vocational maturity for the middle-class students represented a relatively steady progression from Grades 8 through 12 while the lower-class students made their largest increases during the last 2 years.

A univariate analysis of covariance tested for interaction between socioeconomic groups and grade levels. Table 2 represents the interaction effects of groups and grade levels on vocational maturity. The significant F ratio means that the differences between socioeconomic groups on the dependent variable, vocational maturity, when assessed by the Readiness for Vocational Planning Scale, is not consistent across the various grade levels. Since significant interaction occurred, analysis of main effects was omitted and comparisons by employing the Scheffé's technique were employed to detect where significant differences existed between the socioeconomic groups within grade levels.

Scheffé post hoc comparisons were computed regarding the simple effects of socioeconomic class within grade levels as shown in Table 3. When zero is included in the confidence interval, the difference is not significant. Therefore, the post hoc comparisons revealed no significant

TABLE 2. Univariate Analysis of Covariance of Socioeconomic Groups and Grade Levels Using the Readiness for Vocational Planning Scale as a Dependent Variable and Intelligence as a Covariate

VARIABLE	MS_b	MS_E	UNIVERSAL F
Readiness for Vocational Planning Scale	62.4665	31.305160	1.9954*

* $p < .0462$.

TABLE 3. Confidence Intervals Obtained for the Post hoc Comparisons of the Readiness for Vocational Planning Mean Scores Concerning Interaction between Socioeconomic Groups and Grade Levels

COM-PARISON	GRADE	GROUP		GRADE	GROUP	CONFIDENCE LEVEL
φ_1	8	LCB	$\neq$	8	MCW	$-1.74 \leqslant \varphi \leqslant 8.18$
φ_2	9	LCB	$\neq$	9	MCW	$-2.10 \leqslant \varphi \leqslant 7.82$
φ_3	10	LCB	$\neq$	10	MCW	$3.15 \leqslant \varphi \leqslant 13.07*$
φ_4	11	LCB	$\neq$	11	MCW	$.49 \leqslant \varphi \leqslant 10.41*$
φ_5	12	LCB	$\neq$	12	MCW	$.29 \leqslant \varphi \leqslant 10.21*$
φ_6	8	LCW	$\neq$	8	MCW	$-3.60 \leqslant \varphi \leqslant 6.32$
φ_7	9	LCW	$\neq$	9	MCW	$-2.65 \leqslant \varphi \leqslant 7.27$
φ_8	10	LCW	$\neq$	10	MCW	$1.04 \leqslant \varphi \leqslant 10.96*$
φ_9	11	LCW	$\neq$	11	MCW	$.39 \leqslant \varphi \leqslant 10.29*$
φ_{10}	12	LCW	$\neq$	12	MCW	$2.84 \leqslant \varphi \leqslant 12.76*$
φ_{11}	8	LCB	$\neq$	8	LCW	$-3.10 \leqslant \varphi \leqslant 6.82$
φ_{12}	9	LCB	$\neq$	9	LCW	$-4.41 \leqslant \varphi \leqslant 5.51$
φ_{13}	10	LCB	$\neq$	10	LCW	$-2.85 \leqslant \varphi \leqslant 7.07$
φ_{14}	11	LCB	$\neq$	11	LCW	$-4.82 \leqslant \varphi \leqslant 5.08$
φ_{15}	12	LCB	$\neq$	12	LCW	$-2.41 \leqslant \varphi \leqslant 7.51$

Note.—Abbreviations: LCB = lower-class black; LCW = lower-class white; MCW = middle-class white.
* p significant at .05; all others are nonsignificant.

differences between eighth and ninth grade lower-class students when compared with eighth and ninth grade middle-class students. A significant difference did exist when lower-class white and lower-class black students were separately compared with middle-class white students in Grades 10, 11, and 12. However, no significant differences occurred when lower-class black students in Grades 8 through 12 were compared to lower-class white students in those grades.

Discussion

The results of this study suggest that disadvantaged high school students are slower than their middle-class counterparts in developing the ability to select a vocation. Vocational maturity generally increases with age but the level is slightly lower for disadvantaged students; in fact, they are about 2 years behind the development of middle-class students. The middle-class students show a steady progression in scores while the lower-class students made large increases in the eleventh grade. One speculation is that some less mature lower-class students dropped out of school after the tenth grade permitting the mean for those that remained to be higher. One weakness of a cross-sectional study is that it does not follow the same students through their patterns of development.

The Readiness for Vocational Planning Scale detected differences among the vocational maturity levels of the three groups of students. The differences in Grades 10, 11, and 12 were found to lie between the middle-class students and the lower-class students without regard to race. No significant difference appeared between the lower-class black and white students in their vocational maturity throughout the five grades. Economic background and possibly the school differences played a greater part in the development of vocational maturity than did racial background.

According to vocational development theory (Super, 1957), students in the eighth grade should be in the Capacity Stage. If the middle-class students have reached the Capacity Stage, the lower-class students remain behind, probably in the Fantasy Stage. Characteristics of the Capacity Stage involve the process in which individual abilities and job requirements including training are considered while during the Fantasy Stage, vocational choice is still a matter of fantasy based on individual needs. The lower-class students will be further behind when they enter the Tentative Stage where emphasis is given to individual needs, interests, capacities, values and opportunities for employment. Commonly students make high school curricular decisions during their eighth- or ninth-grade year. Although curricular decisions are not irreversible, changes are difficult and frequently costly. For years writers (Caplow, 1954; Super and Overstreet, 1960) have been critical of forced curriculum planning at an early age because students are not sufficiently vocationally mature to make a decision of such importance. Research to support this conclusion has been derived primarily from middle-class populations. Disadvantaged students are even less ready. Counselors who are directly associated with disadvantaged students must be aware of variations in their vocational development and have at their disposal reliable information relevant to the needs of their clients. Counselors must take a more active role in developing new programs and seeking change in the school which will aid the student in his vocational maturity.

The Readiness for Vocational Planning Schedule holds a promising future in vocational counseling. Rapport can be established with clients by first seeking classification information required by the instrument. Once such information is acquired, clients generally are willing to cooperate by responding to the questions requested in the interview. The total score may not necessarily be as informative as the quality of the responses offered by the clients. An item analysis of the questions relevant to the particular variable being assessed affords an opportunity to gain insight into the client as well as the client learning about his particular strengths and weaknesses.

References

AMOS, W. E., and GRAMBS, J. (Eds.), *Counseling the disadvantaged youth.* Englewood Cliffs, N.J.: Prentice-Hall, 1968.

CALIA, V. F., Vocational guidance: After the fall. *Personnel and Guidance Journal,* 1966, **45,** 320–327.

CAPLOW, T. *The sociology of work.* Minneapolis: University of Minnesota Press, 1954.

CRITES, J. O. Measurement of vocational maturity in adolescence: Attitude test of the vocational development inventory. *Psychological Monographs,* 1965, **2** (Whole No. 595).

GRIBBONS, W. D., and LOHNES, P. R. Validation of vocational planning interview scales. *Journal of Counseling Psychology,* 1964, **11,** 20–26.

GRIBBONS, W. D., and LOHNES, P. R. Predicting five years of development in adolescents from Readiness for Vocational Planning Scales. *Journal of Educational Psychology,* 1967, **56,** 244–253.

GRIBBONS, W. D., and LOHNES, P. R. *Emerging careers.* New York: Teachers College, Columbia University, Bureau of Publications, 1968.

GRIBBONS, W. D., and LOHNES, P. R. Eighth-grade vocational maturity in relation to nine-year career patterns. *Journal of Counseling Psychology,* 1969, **16,** 557–562.

HALL, D. W. The vocational development inventory: A measure of vocational maturity in adolescents. *Personnel and Guidance Journal,* 1963, **41,** 771–775.

SUPER, D. E. *The psychology of careers.* New York: Harpers, 1957.

SUPER, D. E., and OVERSTREET, P. L. *The vocational maturity of ninth-grade boys.* New York: Teachers College, Columbia University, Bureau of Publications, 1960.

TYLER, L. E. The encounter with poverty—its effect on vocational psychology. *Rehabilitation Counseling Bulletin,* 1967, **11,** 61–70.

Status Projections and Ethnicity: A Comparison of Mexican American, Negro, and Anglo Youth

William P. Kuvlesky,
David E. Wright,
and
Rumaldo Z. Juarez

One of Max Weber's most important legacies to sociology was the development of a multifaceted theory of determinants of social honor, or as it is more commonly called today, social rank (Gerth and Mills, 1958, pp. 180–195). His conceptual distinction between rank evolving from class (economic) position and status groups (ethnicity) is still viable. In our society two of the major determinants of social rank are economic class and ethnic identity. According to Shibutani and Kwan (1965, p. 35), "the underprivileged in a system of ethnic stratification are usually referred to as minority groups." In those areas where ethnic stratification is institutionalized, membership in an ethnic minority group tends to severely restrict vertical social mobility. In the stratification systems operative in Texas, there are two large well-institutionalized ethnic minority groups—Negro in the eastern counties and Mexican American in the south and southwestern regions of the state. What is more, there is ample statistical evidence to indicate that there is a very high correlation between membership in these two ethnic minority groups and placement in low levels of socioeconomic status (Upham and Lever, 1966; Upham and Wright, 1966).

It seems reasonable to assert that an awareness of limitations or impediments to vertical mobility would influence minority youth's perception of their future prospects for social attainment, causing him to set lower level goals than their counterparts in the middle-class mainstream of our society. Hyman Rodman (1963), restructuring evidence from early youth-aspiration studies, asserts as much in the development of his thesis on the "lower-class value stretch." Also J. Milton Yinger (1960) in an earlier article, utilizing much the same evidence,

Reprinted from *Journal of Vocational Behavior*, **1**:137–151 (1971).

indicates that, "Because tensions set in motion by this blockage cannot be resolved by achievement of dominant values, such values are repressed, their importance denied, counter-values affirmed." This condition he labels a "contraculture" and specifically refers to the Southern Negro as a case in point. Others arguing significant subcultural differences have maintained that lower-class youth lack ambition or have low aspirations (Rosen, 1959; Simmons, 1961; Rodman, 1963). On the other hand, Merton (1957, pp. 131–139 and 161–170) and others (Gordon, 1961; Hughes, 1965; Broom & Glenn, 1965; Dyckman, 1966) have proposed that maintenance of a high valuation on success and high level success goals are widely shared phenomena that cut widely across all segments of our society.

The purpose of this effort is to attempt to clarify some of these apparent theoretical or conceptual contradictions through a tri-ethnic—Negro, Mexican American, and Anglo—comparison of adolescents' occupational and educational status projections, utilizing data from a recent study of Texas rural youth.

Some time ago Merton proposed that young people maintain a "frame of aspirational reference" composed of personal goals for status attainment as adults (Merton, 1957, pp. 132–133). This mental configuration provides them with a cognitive map that serves to guide anticipatory socialization into adult roles. Ralph Turner (1964) has presented firm documentation for this assertion.

Merton conceived of only one frame of status projections, that involving aspirations (desires). However, Stephenson (1957), among others, has demonstrated the utility of thinking in terms of two types of projections: in addition to aspirations, youth maintain a set of expectations (anticipations) which often differs from their desires. A conceptual scheme recently presented by Kuvlesky and Bealer (1966), begins with this analytical distinction between aspiration and expectation and provides additional distinctions. The divergence, if any, between the desired and anticipated status objects within a particular area of potential status attainment (that is, education) is labeled "anticipatory goal deflection" (Kuvlesky and Ohlendorf, 1968). While most past research has focused on projected status attainments, Kuvlesky and Bealer call attention to another analytical dimension of status projections which they call the "orientation element." This idea refers to the strength of orientation that a person maintains toward the status object involved in either aspiration or expectation. In reference to aspiration this would be the strength of desire associated with obtaining the status goal specified and is referred to as "intensity of aspiration" (Merton, 1957, p. 171). The comparable element involved in expectation is labeled "certainty of expectation." This scheme has been reported in detail in a number of publications and papers, along with empirical evidence supporting the utility of the analytical distinctions involved (Kuvlesky and Ohlendorf, 1968; Ohlendorf and Kuvlesky, 1968; Juarez and Kuvlesky, 1968; Wright and Kuvlesky, 1968). The analysis of ethnic comparisons to be described here was structured in terms of the elements of status projections differentiated in the scheme described above.

An extensive review of the relevant research literature turned up only one investigation including a tri-ethnic comparison involving adolescents' status projections. From a 1958 study, including Negro, White, and Puerto Rican youth residing in a "northern metropolis," Antonovosky (1967) reported data that indicates little difference by enthnicity for occupational and educational status projections of lower class youth. Our finding should serve as basis for testing the general validity of Antonovosky's observations.

Method

Subjects. Data for this analysis were obtained from high school sophomores attending school in two widely separated study areas that were purposively selected to be homogeneous on three criteria: (1) a proportionately high rate of ethnic minority members—either Negro or Mexican American; (2) a proportionately high rate of poverty; and (3) predominantly rural populations located in nonmetropolitan areas, (Table 1). During the Spring of 1966, Negro and Anglo youth enrolled in 23 public high schools located in three East Texas counties were interviewed; during the Spring of 1967, Mexican American youth enrolled in seven high schools located in four Texas counties either bordering on or in close proximity to the Mexican border were interviewed. No attempt was made to contact students who were absent on the day of the interviews. Usable data were available for analysis on 596 Mexican American, 197 Negro, and 287 Anglo boys and girls.

Analysis of information obtained from the respondents clearly indicates that all three ethnic groupings were generally from deprived circumstances. However, some marked ethnic differences were noted as follows:

1. Almost three-fourths of the Negro youth came from homes where the main breadwinner was either unemployed or employed as a low-skilled worker, as compared with about half the Mexican American youth and only a quarter of the Anglos.
2. Many more of the Negro and Mexican American youths' parents failed to complete high school, as compared with the Anglo youth.
3. Substantially more of the Negro youth were in families lacking a parent and having a "working" mother.

In summary, the Negro youth are the most disadvantaged and, in terms

TABLE 1. SELECTED INDICATORS OF SOCIOECONOMIC CONDITIONS IN THE SOUTH TEXAS AND EAST CENTRAL TEXAS STUDY AREAS COMPARED WITH TEXAS AND THE UNITED STATES

PLACE	TOTAL POPULATION (THOUSANDS)	ANGLO (%)	MEXICAN AMERICANS (%)	LOWINCOME FAMILIES [a] (%)	MEDIAN FAMILY INCOME	MEDIAN SCHOOL YEARS COMP.[b]
South Texas						
Dimmit	10	c	67	60	$2,480	5
Maverick	15	c	78	58	2,523	6
Starr	17	c	89	71	1,700	5
Zapata	4	c	75	66	1,766	5
East Texas						
Burleson	11	62	d	59	2,451	8
Leon	10	61	d	67	1,946	9
San Jacinto	6	47	d	69	1,737	7
Texas	9,580	73	14	29	4,884	10
United States	179,323	87	2	21	5,657	11

Source: U.S. Bureau of the Census, U.S. Census of Population: 1960, Volume 1, *Characteristics of the Population*, Part 1, United States Summary and Part 45, Texas (Washington, D.C.: U.S. Government Printing Office, 1964) and U.S. Bureau of the Census, *U.S. Census of Population: 1960, Subject Reports, Persons of Spanish Surname*, Final Report Pc (2)-1B.
[a] Annual family incomes below $3,000.
[b] By persons 25 years old and over.
[c] Almost all individuals not classified as Mexican American would be classified Anglo.
[d] Percentage of Mexican American is less than one-tenth of 1 percent. Most individuals not classified as Anglo would be classified as Negro.

of normal SES indicators, the Anglo youth are considerably better off than either ethnic minority.

Instruments. Only a brief description of the indicators and measurements used in reference to the five dimensions of occupational orientation involved in our analysis will be provided here.

Two similarly worded open-end questions were used to elicit responses that would serve as indicators of occupational goals and expectations: the aspiration stimulus elicited the job the respondent would "desire most" as compared with the job he would "really expect" in the case of expectation. The responses to both of these questions were originally coded into nine categories based on a modification of the usual census scheme. In order to simplify our analysis in terms of status levels, these original measurements were collapsed into three broader level categories as follows:

1. High—"high" and "low professional" and "glamour";
2. Intermediate—"managerial," "clerical and sales," and "skilled";
3. Low—"operatives," "unskilled," and "housewife."

The stimulus used to obtain responses indicating educational aspirations and expectations were similar to those described above in reference to critical word elements distinguishing between the two types of projections—"desired" and "really expect." However, these questions were forced choice in nature—providing six alternatives ranging from "quit school right now" to "complete additional studies after graduating from a college or university." Again, the original measurement categories were collapsed into three more inclusive level categories as follows:

1. High—college graduation or more;
2. Intermediate—more than high school graduation but less than college graduation;
3. Low—terminate at graduation from high school or less.

Anticipatory deflection was determined by simply comparing the original measures of goal and expected status for each respondent. If these were incongruent, anticipatory deflection was considered to exist. A further distinction was made on the basis of the nature of deflection: positive deflection was judged to exist if expectation had a higher rank than goal and negative deflection was assumed to exist if aspiration had the high rank order. An example of positive deflection from an occupational goal would be a youth desiring to be a carpenter but anticipating becoming a school teacher. An example of negative deflection from an educational goal would be a youth desiring to graduate from college but expecting to really terminate his formal education with graduation from high school.

The degree of certainty associated with the respondent's expected was ascertained through a question that instructed the respondent to rank order the importance of attainment of seven status goals, including his occupational and educational goal. The relative importance assigned to each goal is considered an indication of the measure of the relative intensity of desire for it. This forced-response type of instrument produced a range in scores from one to seven: the lower the score, the stronger the intensity of desire was judged to be for the occupational goal. For purposes of analysis these scores were grouped into three levels of intensity as follows: Strong (1–2); Intermediate (3–5); and Weak (6–7).

The degree of certainty associated with the respondent's expected attainments was ascertained through a forced-choice stimulus question instructing the respondent to select from five alternatives indicating how certain he felt about attaining his expectations: Very certain, Certain, Not very certain, Uncertain, and Very uncertain.

Results

Overview of Ethnic Differences. The results of chi-square evaluations on the 20 ethnic comparisons involved in our analysis and shown in Table 2, indicate that only five did not result in differences having statistical significance at the .05 level of probability. Consequently, it is obvious that differences generally existed among the three ethnic groups being considered. Of course, this does not mean that the differences observed were meaningful or significant in a sociological sense. Quite to the contrary, our judgments, as summarized in Table 2 under the column labeled "Magnitude," indicate that differences among the three ethnic groupings were substantial in only 6 of the 20 comparative evaluations made. In all other cases, it was judged that the similarity of the ethnic groups was more significant than the variations existing among them.

It is significant that five of the six comparisons judged to demonstrate marked ethnic differences occur in reference to only two elements of status projections: three involve level of expectation and two involve intensity of occupational aspiration. The remaining comparison demonstrating substantial ethnic variation was the certainty of occupational expectation demonstrated by females.

As can be seen from our shorthand description of the nature of differences observed, contained in Table 2 under the column labeled "Nature," the comparisons demonstrating marked ethnic differences were definitely patterned. In reference to expectations, Negroes had substantially higher level expectations than the other two groups in all three cases demonstrating marked differences. In reference to intensity of occupational aspiration, both for males and females, the marked variation is due largely to the fact that Mexican American youth maintained a much stronger intensity of desire for their goals than the other two groupings.

In summary, the overview demonstrates that the three ethnic groups were generally similar in reference to aspiration levels, anticipatory deflection, certainty of expectation, and intensity of educational aspiration. On the other hand, substantial ethnic differences tended to occur in reference to level of expectation and for intensity of desire for occupational goals. These differences were due largely to Negroes maintaining higher expectation levels and Mexican Americans having a stronger intensity of desire for job goals. Females accounted for most of the marked ethnic variability.

Next, ethnic differences observed in reference to each of the five status projection elements under consideration will be examined. Because of the number of detailed tabular presentations involved in our original analysis, the remainder of this section will consist of rather brief summaries of major findings.

TABLE 2. SUMMARY TABLE OF ETHNIC DIFFERENCES ON ELEMENTS OF OCCUPATIONAL AND EDUCATIONAL STATUS PROJECTIONS

ETHNIC DIFFERENCES DESCRIBED

STATUS PROJECTION ELEMENTS	MALES			FEMALES		
	p [a]	NATURE [b]	MAGNITUDE [c]	p [a]	NATURE [b]	MAGNITUDE [c]
Aspiration levels						
Occupation	.001	MA,A>N	Slight	.70	None	None
Education	.05	N>MA,A	Slight	.001	N>MA,A	Moderate
Expectation levels						
Occupation	.02	Similar	Similar	.001	N>MA,A	Marked
Education	.001	N>A>MA	Marked	.001	N>A>MA	Marked
Anticipatory deflection						
Occupation	.30	None	None	.10	MA,A>N	Slight
Education	.05	MA>N>A	Slight	.001	MA,N>A	Slight
Intensity of aspiration						
Occupation	.001	MA>A>N	Marked	.001	MA>N,A	Marked
Education	.01	MA,N>A	Slight	.01	MA>N,A	Slight
Certainty of expectation						
Occupation	.001	A,N>MA	Slight	.001	A,N>MA	Marked
Education	.10	A,N>MA	Slight	.001	A,N>MA	Slight

[a] Probability of significance based on chi-square tests.
[b] Letter symbols identify ethnic group: MA = Mexican American; A = Anglo; N = Negro.
[c] Our judgment of the magnitude of differences existing among the three ethnic groupings.

Ethnicity and Status Projection Elements

Aspiration Levels. The occupational and educational aspirations of all three ethnic groups (shown in Table 3) were generally high: a majority of all six ethnic-sex groupings held high occupational and educational goals, with the exception of Anglo females in reference to education. Generally, small proportions of any of the ethnic-sex groupings held low-level job or educational goals. However, a substantial number (25 per cent) of the Negro males held low occupational goals and in this respect differed from all other groupings. Also, Mexican American boys and girls more frequently held low educational goals than the other ethnic groups: about one-fifth of the Mexican American youth maintained low-level educational goals.

Expectation Levels. A comparison of the proportion of ethnic types having high goals and high expectations (compare Tables 3 and 4)

TABLE 3. SUMMARY COMPARISON OF PROPORTIONS OF THREE ETHNIC GROUPS HAVING "HIGH" AND "LOW" GOALS

	MALES (%)			FEMALES (%)		
	MA	ANGLO	NEGRO	MA	ANGLO	NEGRO
High goals						
Occupation	54	51	49	60	53	60
Education	53	59	64	51	38	48
Low goals						
Occupation	9	8	25	3	2	4
Education	19	14	6	21	7	3

TABLE 4. SUMMARY COMPARISON OF PROPORTIONS OF THREE ETHNIC GROUPS HAVING "HIGH" AND "LOW" EXPECTATIONS

	MALES (%)			FEMALES (%)		
	MA	ANGLO	NEGRO	MA	ANGLO	NEGRO
High expectations						
Occupation	40	38	47	36	36	49
Education	39	43	63	37	39	46
Low expectations						
Occupation	13	15	29	14	30	9
Education	31	19	7	32	13	9

clearly indicates that the respondents maintained high expectations markedly less than high aspirations.

Negroes appeared to differ markedly from the other two ethnic types in their expectations, particularly in reference to education. Markedly more Negroes (a near majority in most cases) held high-level expectations. In reference to proportions expecting low-level attainment, markedly more of all groups were classified in the low-status level as compared with what was observed in reference to aspirations (compare Tables 3 and 4). About 30 per cent of the Negro males and Anglo females anticipated low-level occupational attainments. About the same proportion of Mexican American boys and girls anticipated low-level educational attainment and, in this respect, were clearly different from the others.

Anticipatory Goal Deflection. The concept anticipatory goal deflection represents the difference observed, if any, between the individual's desired and anticipated status attainments. Our findings indicate that most youth, regardless of ethnicity, did not experience anticipatory deflection from their occupational and educational goals (Table 5). Another similarity observed was that when anticipatory goal deflection did occur, it was predominantly negative. Oddly, Anglo females experienced both the highest rate of anticipatory goal deflection (41 per cent deflected from occupational goals) and the lowest (23 per cent were deflected from educational goals).

Although the similarity of the ethnic groupings, relative to anticipatory deflection, appears to be of more importance than differences,

TABLE 5. SUMMARY COMPARISON OF PROPORTIONS OF THREE ETHNIC GROUPS EXPERIENCING ANTICIPATORY DEFLECTION FROM OCCUPATIONAL AND EDUCATIONAL GOALS

NATURE OF DEFLECTION FROM GOAL	MALES (%)			FEMALES (%)		
	MA	ANGLO	NEGRO	MA	ANGLO	NEGRO
Positive						
Occupational	9	8	14	6	4	7
Educational	9	4	11	5	1	17
Negative						
Occupational	29	21	19	32	37	20
Educational	31	23	24	32	22	25
Total deflected						
Occupational	38	29	33	38	41	27
Educational	40	27	35	37	23	42

three patterns of ethnic differences were observed: (1) Anglos generally experienced less anticipatory goal deflection than the other two ethnic groups; (2) Negroes tended to experience significantly more positive goal deflection; (3) Mexican American youth generally demonstrated more negative deflection.

Intensity of Aspiration. The three ethnic groupings differed very little in reference to the strength of desire they indicated for their educational goals: a very large majority of all groupings had strong attachments to their desired education (Table 6). Nevertheless, the little variation that existed supported the rather dramatic ethnic difference observed relative to intensity of desire for job goals. The Mexican American youth indicated a markedly stronger desire for their occupational goals and a somewhat stronger desire for their educational goals than the other two ethnic groupings. In addition, Negro males stood out among all six ethnic-sex groupings for a lack of strong attachment to their occupational goals.

A similarity cutting across all ethnic-sex groupings was the fact that the respondents maintained a much stronger attachment to educational goals than to occupational goals. This might be explained by the fact that these youth perceived educational attainment as a prerequisite means to the more distant (in time) job goals they held.

Certainty of Expectation. The Negro and Anglo youth were very similar in proportions feeling certain about their expectations: about half of both groups held high levels of certainty for their occupational goals, and about two-thirds of each group maintained similar orientations toward their educational anticipations (Table 6).

In every case, Mexican American boys and girls were less certain about attaining their occupational and educational expectations than

TABLE 6. SUMMARY COMPENSATION OF PROPORTIONS OF THREE ETHNIC GROUPS HAVING HIGH INTENSITY ASPIRATIONS AND INDICATING CERTAINTY ABOUT EXPECTATIONS

	MALES (%)			FEMALES (%)		
	MA	ANGLO	NEGRO	MA	ANGLO	NEGRO
Strong aspirations						
Occupation	69	56	34	72	45	46
Education	85	69	80	89	81	79
Certain expectations						
Occupation	36	48	44	32	52	56
Education	49	62	64	50	63	67

the other two ethnic groupings: only about one-third of Mexican American youth felt certain about attaining the occupational attainment they specified, and approximately half felt certain toward attainment of their educational expectations.

For every ethnic-sex grouping, there was a greater degree of certainty toward educational expectations than there was toward occupational expectations. Also, it is important to note that although most of the ethnic-sex groupings maintained strong intensities of aspiration in reference to both occupation and education, markedly fewer felt certain about attaining their expected jobs and educational levels, even though status levels indicated for expectation were generally lower than those indicated for goals.

Discussion

Obviously, definite restrictions are faced in attempting to generalize these findings beyond the study populations involved due to the selective homogeneity (youth from economically deprived areas of rural Texas) of these units. At the same time, by considering the findings reported here in relationship to those from other relevant studies, some rather broad empirical generalizations about the relationship of ethnicity to adolescent status projections can be drawn. The findings of this study, considered together with those of Antonovsky's (1967) triethnic study of metropolitan youth and Stephenson's (1957) biracial comparison, support several broad empirical generalizations pertaining to ethnic similarities in projected frames of reference of youth. All three studies indicate that high level success goals are widely diffused throughout the various social strata of our society. In addition, all three studies clearly indicate that expectations of lower class youth are substantially lower than their aspirations (in terms of aggregate comparisons). Unfortunately, the opportunity to draw such broad generalizations about the relationship of ethnicity to anticipatory deflection, intensity of aspiration, and certainty of expectation does not exist due to the lack of other relevant data.

Whatever the limitations in deriving broad generalizations, the results of this study are useful in evaluating the general validity of several broad theoretical propositions. In the first place, the broad generalization that adolescents of all ethnic types (from both rural and metropolitan areas) maintain high occupational and educational goal levels offers strong support for Merton's contention that high-level success goals are widely diffused among the various segments and strata of our society. Given this ethnic commonality, at a less abstract level of analysis our data indicate some patterned variations among ethnic groups: Negro youth apparently more often hold high educational goals than other youth, and Spanish-speaking minorities more often maintain low-level goals.

Merton's thesis that youth structure their goals in terms of a hierarchy of importance receives support from the finding that, among the respondents considered here, intensity of aspiration for education was stronger than that associated with occupation (Merton, 1957, p. 171). The fact that the ethnic groups demonstrated similarity in respect to this differential valuation of education and occupation, provides a basis for extending Merton's proposition to indicate that this aspect of the projected frame of reference is patterned and cuts across ethnic and class boundaries. This may prove to be a very fruitful hypothesis for future research, for it has been suggested that the intensity aspect of aspiration may be at least as important as the level of aspiration for prediction of future attainments (Kuvlesky and Bealer, 1966, p. 272).

In the same measure that these findings support Merton, they support the more specific hypothesis of Gordon (1961) that ethnic minorities in our society have become acculturated in terms of the values of the larger society and the related idea of Antonovsky (1967) that Negroes are in the process of dissociating themselves from the negative status of their ethnic identification. What is more, the results would indicate that Mexican American youth are also beginning this process. The evidence produced in this analysis may indicate that Mexican American youth have not progressed in this process of "dissociation" to the same extent as Negroes. Consistent patterns of difference indicate that Mexican American youth are consistently, although in many cases only slightly, distinguished from the other two ethnic types: Mexican Americans more often held low-level goals, experienced a greater frequency of negative anticipatory deflection, and were less certain about attaining their expectations. One possible inference that can be drawn from these data is that a somewhat larger number of Mexican American youth, as compared with Negroes, are willing to conform to their negative status position, relative to Anglos, or that more of them perceive greater restrictions to desired mobility (in accordance with Stephenson's hypothesis). On the other hand, the fact that the Mexican American youth maintained consistently stronger attachments to their goals than the other two groupings does not fit this pattern and is difficult to explain.

The results on status expectations would appear to strongly support Stephenson's hypothesis that expectations are more variable than aspirations relative to social class. However, the theoretical rationale for this proposition is that lower class youth perceive less opportunity for attainment of their aspirations than more fortunate youth and, therefore, anticipate lower levels of expectation (Stephenson, 1957, pp. 211–212). The results reported here apparently challenge this thesis! Negro respondents indicated higher level expectations than either Mexican Americans or Anglo groupings, which were similar in their expectation levels. Considering the fact that Negroes are more disadvantaged relative to SES indicators than either of the other two ethnic groups, it would appear that the difference in expectations that was observed is in direct contradiction to Stephenson's thesis. Furthermore, the results on anticipatory goal deflection indicate relatively similar rates of goal-expectation divergence for all three ethnic groups. This is interpreted to mean that both ethnic minorities experience the same degree of aspiration-expectation incongruity as the dominant Anglo group, which also conflicts with Stephenson's thesis.

As far as we know, no empirical evidence has been reported to question Rodman's thesis of the lower class value stretch (Rodman, 1963). The findings on rural Negro and Mexican American youth from the South and Southwest indicate that they maintain goal profiles similar to the dominant Anglo group. This brings into question the general validity of Rodman's thesis that greater variability exists among the goal specifications of lower class youth as compared with others. His related thesis that the "major lower class value change . . . is a stretched value system with a low degree of commitment to all the values within the range, including the dominant middle class values" is directly challenged by our findings on intensity of aspiration. Likewise, our findings bring into question Yinger's (1960) proposition pertaining to the development of contracultures among lower class groups, particularly his specific proposition that Negro youth in the South would demonstrate a contraculture. It may be that Rodman's and Yinger's related propositions regarding lower class culture may be applicable to only a certain segment of the lower class and not to low-status groups generally.

While our evidence has been interpreted to indicate a lack of substantial ethnic differentiation relative to most elements of youth's projected frames of status reference, another interpretation is possible. This relates to the selective homogeneity involved in the selection of the ethnic populations under investigation. In the context of the larger society, particularly the dominant metropolitan areas, all three ethnic groups considered here would be ethnic minorities. This could be one reason for the broad similarities observed despite the obvious differences in status and socioeconomic rank of the three ethnic groups relative to their local communities of residence. It may be that elements involved in communities of residence—in this case rurality and economic deprivation—are more significant determinants of variations in value orientations than being a Negro or of Mexican descent. In our judgment, this interpretation is questionable in that findings from other studies, including those of metropolitan youth, support those reported here (Antonovsky, 1967; Stephenson, 1957).

References

ANTONOVSKY, A. Aspirations, class and racial-ethnic membership. *The Journal of Negro Education*, 1967, **36,** 385–393.
BROOM, L., and GLENN, N. D. *Transformation of the Negro American.* New York: Harper and Row, 1965.

DYCKMAN, J. W. Some conditions of civic order in an urbanized world. *Daedalus,* 1966, **95,** 802–803.

GERTH, H. H., and MILLS, C. W. *From Max Weber: Essays in sociology.* New York: Oxford University Press, 1958.

GORDON, M. M. Assimilation in America: Theory and reality. *Daedalus,* 1961, 263–285.

HUGHES, E. C. Anomalies and projections. *Daedalus,* 1965, **94,** 1133–1147.

JUAREZ, R. Z., and KUVLESKY, W. P. Ethnic group identity and orientations toward educational attainment: A comparison of Mexican American and Anglo Boys. Paper presented at the annual meetings of the Southwestern Sociological Association, Dallas, Texas, 1968.

KUVLESKY, W. P., and BEALER, R. C. A clarification of the concept 'Occupational Choice.' *Rural Sociology,* 1966, **31,** 265–276.

KUVLESKY, W. P. and OHLENDORF, G. W. A rural-urban comparison of the occupational status orientations of Negro boys. *Rural Sociology,* 1968, **33,** 141–152.

MERTON, R. K. *Social theory and social structure* (revised and enlarged edition). Glencoe: The Free Press, 1957.

OHLENDORF, G. W., and KUVLESKY, W. P. Racial differences in educational orientations. *Social Science Quarterly,* 1968, **49,** 274–283.

RODMAN, H. The lower-class value stretch. *Social Forces,* 1963, **42,** 205–215.

ROSEN, B. C. Race, ethnicity, and the achievement syndrome. *American Sociological Review,* 1959, **26,** 47–60.

SHIBUTANI, T., and KWAN, K. M. *Ethnic stratification: A comparative approach.* New York: The Macmillan Company, 1965.

SIMMONS, O. G. The mutual images and expectations of Anglo-Americans and Mexican-Americans. *Daedalus,* 1961, 286–299.

STEPHENSON, R. M. Mobility orientations and stratification of 1,000 ninth graders. *American Sociological Review,* 1957, **22,** 204–212.

TURNER, R. H. *The Social context of ambition.* San Francisco: Chandler Publishing Company, 1964.

UPHAM, W. K., and LEVER, M. F. *Differentials in the incidence of poverty in Texas.* Texas A&M University: Department of Agricultural Economics and Sociology, Departmental Information Report 66-9, 1966.

UPHAM, W. K., and WRIGHT, D. E. *Poverty among Spanish Americans in Texas: Low-income families in a minority group.* Texas A&M University, Department of Agricultural Economics and Sociology, Departmental Information Report 66-9, 1966.

WRIGHT, D. E., and KUVLESKY, W. P. Occupational status projections of Mexican American youth residing in the Rio Grande valley. Paper presented at the annual meeting of the Southwestern Sociological Association, Dallas, Texas, 1968.

YINGER, M. J. Contraculture and subculture. *American Sociological Review,* 1960, **25,** 625–635.

Profile of the Black Individual in Vocational Literature

Elsie J. Smith

After a long period of neglect, vocational psychologists and counselors are beginning to focus their attention on the career development of Black individuals. Much of this interest is reflected in the relatively recent increase in the number of studies which have investigated the vocational aspirations, interests, choices, the maturity of Black adolescents as well as the job attitudes, job values, and work satisfaction of Black adults. The question remains, however: Has this growing body of research actually contributed to a better understanding of the vocational development of Black individuals? What do we know of their concept of work, their process of making vocational choices, their interest patterns, occupational aspirations and expectations, and their vocational maturity? Is the process of career development for Black youth similar to or different from that of their white counterparts? What are the factors that may potentially have a bearing on similarities and/or differences in the vocational development of Black and white youth? If there are marked differences in the career progress of these two groups, what are the implications for vocational theory development? Finally, what, according to the investigations that have been conducted, is the status of the Black worker—specifically, in terms of his perceptions of work and job satisfaction?

At present, research on the vocational development of Black individuals—both adolescents and adults—constitutes a disparate body of knowledge. The purposes of this article are as follows: (1) to examine the "state of the art" 'in this field; (2) to gather together the diverse strands into a meaningful unit; (3) to investigate some of the salient issues in the career development of Blacks; and (4) to present, on the basis of the research reviewed, a profile of the Black individual in vocational literature.

Family Role Models and Family Background

The influence of family role models has been cited by many authors as a potent factor in the development of a person's concept of work

Reprinted from *Journal of Vocational Behavior*, **6**:41–59 (1975).

(Super, 1957; Henderson, 1967; Smith, 1973). The general tenor of most of these writings is that family work role models provide not only a source of identification for a person but also help him to formulate feelings about the world of work. Typically, writers have emphasized that lower socioeconomic Black youth have few opportunities to associate positive meanings with the value of work—primarily because they are seen to lack positive adult role models and because the Protestant work ethic may not be a part of their upbringing.

Salient in much of the literature on family role models is the importance of the father. Although mothers are seen to have an influence on the vocational development of their children, the impact of the father has been considered paramount (Kohn and Carroll, 1960; Mink and Kaplan, 1970). Basically, Black fathers, particularly those who are categorized as lower socioeconomic, have been singled out as being at best dubious and at worst negative work role models (Moynihan, 1965; Rainwater, 1966). A variety of reasons have been given to explain and to support this position, among which are (1) Black men work in a disproportionately high number of low menial jobs, in comparison with white men of the same level of education; (2) There exists an insidious cycle of racism which predisposes Black children to view their fathers as men who have little power to affect their career development; (3) Black families are seen to suffer from a high proportion of father absent homes; and (4) Lower-socioeconomic parents, in general, lack the technical know-how needed to assist their children in the vocational decision-making process (Henderson, 1967; Neff, 1967; Rainwater, 1966; Sexton, 1971).

Blocher (1973) stresses the significance of family instability on the lower socioeconomic Black youth. He suggests that family instability may lead to lack of career commitment. In his estimation, lower class children from minority backgrounds frequently do not have the opportunity to experience or to even observe close, stable, and long-term interpersonal or work relationships. Lacking such visible models of commitment and involvement either to career or family, they are less inclined to view work as an integral part of their own development.

Supporting Blocher's ideas, Murphy (1973) proffers that lack of positive role models may incline the Black youth to not value life primarily in terms of his work status. According to him, providing a flurry of positive role work models on a short-term basis to combat family instability and lack of commitment to a career goal as a way of life is akin to giving a person two aspirins when major surgery is needed. Frequently, such efforts are much too late to make any real differences in an individual's vocational development. Murphy contends, therefore, that the crucial problem is one of absence of ego involvement and lack of a conception of life built around successful work. Valuing life primarily in terms of one's work status requires more than the presence of role models. It demands a steady indoctrination of this conception of life a long period of time and necessitates some degree of ego involvement with work.

Moulton and Stewart (1971) maintain that vocational psychologists may be overestimating the influence of family instability, and, correlatively, family work role models on the career development of Black youth. In their study of upwardly mobile and low mobile Black males from lower socioeconomic backgrounds, the authors found that the physical presence of the father did not significantly discriminate among members of these two groups. Instead, Moulton and Stewart (1971, p. 249) assert a "high proportion of a group of highly successful Black males came from families in which the father was frequently absent" or not appreciably present at all. The authors concluded that families with a fundamentally matriarchal structure are, indeed, capable of producing "highly achieving males who may acquire many of the necessary skills and values through identification with their mothers" (Moulton and Stewart, 1971, p. 251).

The research of Pallone, Rickard, and Hurley (1970) suggests that despite the low socioeconomic status of Black fathers, their sons tend to select them as significant role models. In an investigation of key influencers of occupational preferences of lower socioeconomic Black male and female students, they established that the same sex parent was a major influencer of students' occupational preferences.

Gottlieb (1967) has taken exception with the general notion that lower socioeconomic Black parents function as negative work role models for their children. Analyzing the statements of Black and white lower socioeconomic youth, he reports that both groups of adolescents saw their parents as being understanding and encouraging of their occupational aspirations. The problem seemed to revolve around parental inability to assist their children in goal clarification. Gottlieb (1967, p. 27) explains: "There are few adults in their lives who have the ability to help the youngster in both the business of goal clarification and goal attainment." Henderson (1967), for one, has taken issue with the notion that only Black people can serve as effective work role models for minority youth. He emphasizes that such an approach is unrealistic because it denies the potential positive influence of a vast reservoir of white role models in occupations wherein Blacks are either in small numbers or nonexistent. The issue herein seems to be not only a question of can whites serve effectively as work role models —the credibility gap debate—but also do conditions mandate that whites be chosen as work role models?

The influence of family role models and family stability as it relates to the minority individual's career development has been called into question. Family instability has not been demonstrated to be the great roadblock that some investigators theorize it to be. As Moulton and Stewart (1971) emphasize, some upwardly mobile black males have climbed the occupational ladder in spite of the absence of their fathers or the nuclear family unit. What is missing in most of the studies on family background and vocational development is the possible influence of surrogate fathers. Until this information is supplied, there will be continued debate as to what the real impact is of a broken home on the vocational development on minority youth.

Concept of Work—Work Values

The literature on the Black person's concept of work has been more descriptive than empirical, more based on an intuitive feeling level than upon any kind of definitive research evidence. In general, it has been stated that the lower socioeconomic Black has a negative concept of work, that there is little ego involvement in their work, and that Blacks tend to be less satisfied than whites with their jobs even when socioeconomic status is held constant (Tyler, 1967; Neff, 1967; Ash, 1972; Murphy, 1973).

Comparing the differences in job satisfaction between Black and white clerical workers at a large metropolitan state university campus, Ash (1972) found that the mean score of the Black clerical workers on each of five areas of the Job Description Index was lower than the mean score for the white workers. The following indices of job satisfaction were used: (1) type of pay; (2) work; (3) opportunity for advancement; (4) supervision; and (5) co-workers on the job. Given his findings, Ash concluded that Blacks have a noticeably less favorable attitude toward their jobs than do whites, even when workers in the same occupations are compared.

In an earlier study, Singer and Stefflre (1956) explored the area of racial differences in job values of white and Black senior high school males. After matching subjects on the factors of age, sex, grade, and socioeconomic level, the authors established that Blacks chose significantly more frequently than whites value E, "a job which you were absolutely sure of keeping" and whites chose significantly more frequently value B, "a very interesting job." From these results, the authors concluded that an individual's racial membership is related to the job value of risk taking. Singer and Stefflre affirm that race was correlated with job values independent of the occupational level of the subject's home, but compatible with the then existing relationship of race and opportunity.

Champagne and King's (1967) study of job satisfaction factors among underprivileged Black and white workers in project STEP (Special Training Program for Economic Progress) supports those of Singer and Stefflre. Given 16 factors in a paired fashion dealing with work motivation, trainees were required to select for each pair the factor which was more important to them. The subgroup analyses based on race indicated that while "duty to do one's best" was first in importance across racial groups, white workers were more concerned with liking the job than Blacks. On the other hand proving that one can do the job was a greater motivating factor for Blacks than for whites. The authors hypothesized that the greater need among Blacks to prove their capability to others may have been precipitated by their desire to disprove generalized societal notions of their racial inferiority.

Several authors have explained differences in job values—particularly those that relate to risk taking—in terms of Maslow's need hierarchy theory (Lieberson and Fugitt, 1967; Lipsman, 1967; Grier, 1963). The dominant motif herein is that lower socioeconomic Black youth respond to the major vocational decision points in their lives according to unsatisfied needs for job security rather than for self-fulfillment.

Slocum and Strawser's (1972) investigation of Black and non-Black certified public accountants lends partial support for many of the assumptions made regarding job values and need satisfaction. The authors report that although self-actualization and compensation need categories were the most important but, nevertheless, the most deficient areas for both Black and non-Black certified public accountants, the Black certified public accountants expressed greater need deficiency than their colleagues in all given categories.

Some 21 years after Singer and Stefflre's study, Lieberson and Fugitt (1967) reexamined the issue of race and occupational opportunity, ostensibly to answer the question: Have changing times, or at least the illusion of changing times, had any measurable effect on occupational value differences observed between Black and white people? Using a Markov model to project future Black-white occupational patterns, the authors concluded that even if racial discrimination were eliminated tomorrow in the job market, broad societal processes which operate at the pervasive disadvantage of Black people would not immediately eliminate racial differences in occupations. Blacks would still have a disproportionate high percentage of low status jobs.

If Lieberson and Fugitt's findings are accurate, they would seem to lend support to Singer and Stefflre's earlier observation that race is still associated with job values. That is to say, that the caste-like system in which some Black people live would not only predispose them toward work alienation but would also encourage them to search for positions which meet the lower order need of security rather than the higher order need of self-actualization.

Departing from the approaches of other researchers, Bloom and Barry (1967) used the motivation-hygiene theory to investigate possible differences and/or similarities in work attitudes between Black and white workers occupying blue and white collar positions. Their findings indicate that hygiene factors are more important than motivator variables to Blacks. Beyond this observation, however, the authors concluded that the work motivations of Blacks are too complicated to be explained by their two-factor theory. One possible explanation might lie in the reactions of Black people against jobs wherein a great deal of "dirty work" is involved. As noted, Blacks have been historically located in lower status and menial positions. Therefore, to such individuals, a job which offered them the opportunity to remain "clean" while performing their work would seem to indicate a step up the occupational ladder.

According to the research cited on the Black individual's concept of work, the following profile emerges: The average lower socioeconomic black worker is work alienated, evidences low risk-taking in job preferences, tends to value job security over self-fulfillment, and generally responds to major occupational decision points in terms of unsatisfied lower order needs.

Self-concept, Identity Foreclosure, and Work

Although educational literature is replete with references concerning the self-concept of Black people (Ausubel and Ausubel, 1963; Clark, 1967; Grambs, 1965; McGrew, 1971), few authors have systematically explored the possible relationships between the self-concepts of Black people and their outlooks on work. The same may be said for their job values and self-concepts. Some crucial questions are: Are there significant differences in job values and concepts of working according to their individual self-perceptions? Do Black people who tend to have positive self-images also tend to have more positive outlooks on work than those who do not? Do their job values change as their self-images become more positively or negatively oriented?

Throughout vocational literature theorists have generally assumed that Black youth have low self-esteem and consequently negative concepts of work. Researchers have tended to operate on the premise that if they can change the self-concepts of Black youth, they can simultaneously modify their outlooks on work and job values. The work of Leonard and Petrofesa (1969) and Youst (1967) illustrate this approach. In both instances, the authors used a variety of methods— ranging from the provision of cameras for children to take pictures of people in the world of work to deliberate curricula intervention techniques to assist the disadvantaged child in his development of a more positive picture of himself and his life chances in the occupational structure.

Along these lines, Hefland (1967) maintains that peer group support is an effective way of boosting the self-confidence of minority youth seeking employment. Relating his experiences with socially rejected youth in the Mobilization for Youth Program, Hefland asserts that group sharing of common employment problems helps such individuals to gain psychological support in their occupational endeavors. The problem, as Hefland conceptualizes it, is not so much one of disadvantaged youth not wanting to work but rather that they lack self-confidence in themselves. Hefland submits that group support for those experiencing employment difficulties makes it easier for minority youth to face their own limitations without losing status among their peers or feeling greater destructive erosion of their self-concept. The group affords a kind of dress rehearsal to help overcome employment shock.

Hauser's (1971) research on identity formation and foreclosure in the vocational development of adolescents is a landmark in the field. Using Erickson's conceptual model of identity formation, Hauser employed a combination of personal interviews and data gathered from a number of Q sorts to examine the vocational development of 14- to 16-year-old lower socioeconomic Black and white adolescents.

According to Hauser, the Q sort findings for Black adolescents indicated little structural integration of their ego or self-image. Quite the contrary, their structural integration over a 4-year period was static. In comparison, the intrayear averages of the structural integration of white youth rose steadily, so much so that there was a progressive structural integration at three different intervals.

In addition, Hauser reports that whereas the self-images of Black males were relatively fixed, whites demonstrated greater flexibility in their self-image content during the taped interviews. Black males also experienced a significantly higher degree of identity foreclosure—that is, they evidenced a rigid closing out of vocational possiblities, primarily on the basis of their fixed sense of self and direction.

Although work was a dominant theme of both groups, Black and white males also contrasted in the content of their work themes during taped interviews. Whereas Blacks talked about their current employment frustrations, their repeated disappointments and degradations, their failure to secure satisfactory work, and the absence of abundant work heroes, the discussions of whites centered around their own free will, the probability of living up to their ideal, the plethora of men and boys to emulate for their future occupational plans, favorable work experiences and promotions, and the general idea that many work opportunities were available to them after high school graduation.

In short, the sociocultural predicaments of Black males were potent factors not only in the formation of a rigid, negative self-identity but also in the sense of identity foreclosure. Translated into occupational terms, minority adolescents stopped far short of the white youth in their exploration of their own personal and vocational identity. While white youth saw themselves in the process of developing a personal and occupational identity, Black youth saw themselves as defeated before they even started. Hence, according to Hauser, the primary differentiating factor between Black and white youths' vocational development is a matter of reinforcement of a positive self-identity and continual integration rather than foreclosure of that identity.

Studies have indicated that racism and its deleterious effects should be taken into consideration when analyzing the minority person's career development. Limitations of job opportunities not only tend to perpetuate the "like father like son" syndrome but also leads toward alienation and a low self-concept. Hence, for the Black youth and the adult, two conditions may exist: (1) a global, impersonal societally imposed negative image of himself; and (2) the feeling that he has little control to affect his self-image by way of his occupational decisions.

Two things seem quite evident in the majority of the studies cited. First, in considering the black individual's concept of work, work values, or vocational self-concepts, one must understand the importance of his cultural and racial background. Secondly, one must be aware that the majority of the research cited pertains to mainly the lower socioeconomic Black and not to those who are members of the middle class. In short, there are serious questions as to the generalizability of many of the findings to other Black populations.

Vocational Aspirations and Expectations

Basically, investigators have presented antithetical points of view on the aspirations of the Black youth. While some report that he has similar aspirations as white youth, others declare just the opposite (Antonovsky and Lerner, 1959; Dreger and Miller, 1968; Lott and Lott, 1963; Antonovsky, 1967; Rosen, 1959; and Veroff et al., 1960). Most authors agree, however, that the Black adolescent has a great deal of incongruency of vocational aspirations and his occupational expectations.

Haberman (1966) explains the Black youth's incongruency of vocational aspirations and expectations by noting: "Disadvantaged youngsters often overcompensate for feelings of inadequacy by assuming superficially high aspirations." Taking a somewhat different route, Sexton (1971) suggests that recent gains of Black people have contributed to soaring and unrealistically high ambitions.

Although research on lower and middle class Black youth has been scanty, it has generally supported much of that completed on Black and white subjects of these same socioeconomic backgrounds. Studies indicated that lower class Black youth are inclined to retreat from competition and that middle class Black youth are inclined to set very high levels of academic and occupational achievement—levels even higher than those of white youth of a comparable socioeconomic background (Mussen, 1953; Boyd, 1952; Rosen, 1959; Pettigrew, 1964). Middle class Black adolescents also evidence greater expectations of reaching their occupational goals (Henderson, 1967).

Littig (1968) examined the idea of achievement motivation in terms of Black freshmen college males' aspirations to traditionally closed or traditionally open occupations for members of their racial group. He established that those males who identified with the working class tended to have a strong achievement motivation and aspired to traditionally closed occupations and that those who identified with the middle class were inclined to evidence weak achievement motivation and aspired to traditionally closed occupations.

Sprey (1962) is one of the few authors who has focused on sex differences in occupational aspirations and expectations among Black adolescents. According to Sprey's findings, ninth grade Black male students expressed significantly lower aspirational levels than Black females and white students in both sex categories. Although both white and Black females had higher measured levels of occupational aspirations than males in their respective racial groups, the differences within the black group were significantly larger than those within the white one. Black males, particularly the sons of manual workers, reflected a high degree of uncertainty about their occupations.

The issue of vocational aspirations has been related to school desegregation. Analyzing the impact of school desegregation on the goals and work values of Black students who had participated in school desegregation in Texas, Hall and Wiant (1973) found that the degree and duration of school desegregation (1–5 years) had little measurable influence on the respondents' work values and occupational aspirations.

Contrary to Hall and Wiant's findings, Wilson (1967), in an earlier study demonstrated that when parents' occupation and education were held constant, black students' academic preferences and aspirations were highest when they went to middle class white schools. Crain's (1969) study of the effects of school desegregation in the North on the occupational achievement of Blacks (aged 21–45) also revealed findings different from Hall and Wiant's. According to Crain, Blacks who attended integrated public schools had better jobs and higher incomes throughout the next three decades of their lives. The author declared that differences in incomes could not be accounted for by the higher educational attainment of graduates of integrated schools or even by their higher socioeconomic backgrounds. Instead, the most significant effect of integrated schooling was not "educational" but rather that Blacks who attended integrated schools were inclined to have more contact with whites as adults, and, accordingly more trust in them than did Blacks from segregated schools. Crain surmised that this factor partially helped them to overcome a crucial barrier to equal opportunity—that is, access to information about employment opportunities that is normally spread by the informal social contacts to which few Blacks have access.

Ducette and Wolk (1972) studied the relationship between locus of control and levels of aspiration in Black and white children. The authors concluded that those Black students who seemingly evidenced the greatest degree of internal control also stated that they realistically expected to enter lower status occupations than those who subscribed to more external control factors.

In a similar study examining the motivation and aspirations of Southern Black college students, Gurin (1969) established that students believing in external control have higher aspirations than those who adhere to the Protestant Work Ethic. In short, both findings suggest that an external rather than an internal ideology goes along with greater expectations of accomplishing one's occupational goals.

As noted, the general findings pertinent to the black adolescent's aspirations are conflicting. Conversely, research seems to indicate few differences of opinions concerning the matter of vocational expectations. Not only do black youth tend to have lower expectations of reaching their occupational aspirations but also there exists a greater discrepancy between desired goals and expected obtained goals for black males than for black females.

The issue of desegregation and vocational aspirations, expectations, and occupational attainment is still in the debate stage. However, evidence does seem to be leading toward the idea that segregation of Black students, particularly those who are lower class, has a negative, homogenizing effect upon achievement and vocational aspirations of Black youth.

Vocational Interests and Choices

Studies on the vocational interests of Black individuals have been directed toward answering mainly two questions: (1) Are the vocational interests of Black individuals similar to or different from those of white people? and (2) Do present instruments measure accurately their vocational interests?

In an early study of the interests of Black and white youth, Witty, Garfield, and Brink (1941) concluded that the vocational interests of members of these two racial groups appeared to be between the extremes of the "thing" versus the "people" dimension. Whites seemed to prefer occupations which were largely "thing-oriented," and Blacks selected occupations which were more "people-oriented." The authors hypothesized that this polarity in interests and choices suggests that racial backgrounds and subcultural values may be in operation.

Examining the relationships between interests and aptitudes and race and interests, Chansky (1965) established that the vocational interests of Black and white ninth graders were significantly different. Whereas Black youth were interested in interpersonal, business, verbal, and long training occupations, white youth were more intrigued by occupations concerned with the prestige implications of a career rather than their true interests.

Clark (1967) examined the relationship between peer perceptions of

Black and white occupational preferences. Clark's findings showed that Black males expressing a preference for professional careers were more likely to be cast in these roles by their peers than were white boys. He conjectured that the occupational image projected by Black males aspiring to professional status had a greater impact on their classmates than did the occupational image of professionally aspiring white boys.

Borgen and Harper (1973) investigated the predictive validity of the Strong Vocational Interest Inventory Blank for Black and white college men who were either winners of National Achievement or National Merit Scholarships. Three-year follow-up information involving career choices of subjects found that the Occupational and Basic scales of the Strong had a predictive accuracy for Blacks which equaled, if not surpassed that for whites. Borgen and Harper advised against generalizing the validity of the Strong Vocational Interest Blank to Blacks who come from disadvantaged economic and educational backgrounds.

The types of occupations minority individuals select have been explored by several authors (Hyte, 1936; Lawrence, 1950; Brazziel, 1961). Studying the process of vocational choice of Black students attending Virginia State College, Brazziel (1961) found that a number of students chose teaching as a career. When questioned about their choice, more than half of the total group stated that teaching was their second choice, and slightly less than half revealed that they planned to use it as a stepping-stone to another occupation. From Brazziel's work, it would appear that Black students were both aware of race and the restrictions it placed upon their occupational choices. This was most readily seen in their adoption of "second best" but realizable goals.

In reporting the recent trends of Black college freshmen, Bayer (1972) maintains that in the period from 1968–1971 conditions had not changed very much in the minority youth's occupational choices. He states that whereas black freshmen continued to choose majors in the social sciences, education, business, or health fields, non-Black freshmen continued to select majors in the physical sciences or engineering, the biological sciences, and agriculture. Differences in actual career choices followed the same pattern.

The research on interests of Black youth is marked by a great deal of lacunae. One significant finding, however, is that Black youths' interests are more geared toward people-oriented occupations than thing-oriented jobs. This fact may reflect their general dissatisfaction with the dehumanizing process which many of them have been forced to undergo.

In spite of the fact that interest inventories have proved equally as useful with Blacks as they are with whites when their education is at a high level, there still exists a question of their predictive validity with the Black population in general. The feeling seems to be that many Black children have not or probably will not have an opportunity to develop interests similar to those of whites in various populations as measured by current interest inventories.

Vocational Maturity

For the most part, research on the vocational maturity of Black adolescents has tended to be largely comparative in nature, that is, investigators have been inclined to compare the vocational development of Blacks with their white counterparts. Generally speaking, lower socioeconomic Black youth have been characterized as being less vocationally mature than middle class whites.

Using the Vocational Development Inventory for examining the vocational maturity of 450 eighth grade white suburban, white lower socioeconomic inner-city males, Black lower socioeconomic males Maynard and Hansen (1970) found that the Black youth were lowest in maturity; the white inner-city youth were next; and the white suburban youth were the highest. From their research, the authors concluded that the Black youth seemed unaware of the factors designated important for vocational planning at the eighth grade level.

A recent study by these same authors using the Readiness for Career Planning Scale as well as the Vocational Development Inventory reverses somewhat their earlier findings. Concerning the Readiness for Career Planning Scale, Hansen and Ansell (1973) report "The middle class white students earned the highest scores at each level followed by the lower class white, then the lower class Black students except at grade twelve." At the twelfth grade, Black students manifested greater vocational maturity than lower class white males.

Vriend also investigated the vocational maturity of inner-city youth from lower socioeconomic backgrounds. Although both white and Black subjects were used, no racial comparisons were made between the two groups. Using an instrument he developed himself (Vocational Maturity Rating Scale—VMR), Vriend found that second-semester seniors who had been exposed to a 2-year vocational program of structured career-related activities consistently obtained higher group VMRs in all component areas than those who were placed in control groups and not exposed to any special kind of vocational program.

The general conclusion of these studies is that lower socioeconomic Black youth are vocationally immature. However, if one accepts the results of Vriend (1969), this condition can be alleviated if long-term vocational programs are inaugurated in the schools.

A word of caution is appropriate, however, in interpreting the results of the studies cited. That is, none of the reported investigations have been able to ascertain to what extent the vocational immaturity of lower socioeconomic Black youth can be associated with their social class or racial membership group. Such research is needed if one is not to confound the issues of race and social class. Along these lines, studies comparing the vocational maturity of lower class Black youth with that of middle class Black adolescents would seem to be in order.

What research has been completed on the vocational maturity of Black youth is rather unanimous in its conclusions. That is, by and large, Black youth, in comparison with white ones, are vocationally immature. What is lacking in this entire area on vocational maturity (regardless of the race of the student) is information concerning the specific areas in which young people are vocationally mature or immature. Beyond this, however, findings that lower class Black children are fundamentally vocationally immature would seem to have serious implications for the counselor, especially if he subscribes to Super's notion that the process of vocational development can be guided. What kind of guidance, for example, offers the potentiality of facilitating vocational maturity among Black youth?

Vocational Theories: Their Failure

On the whole, vocational literature has revealed very little information about the career development of Black people. Part of the problem is that most theories are based upon the vocational development of white middle class males. From their explorations into the vocational development of this group, theorists have generalized to other populations. That there exists a limited generalizability of the present theories to minority populations and certain socioeconomic subgroups has been emphasized by many (Stefflre, 1966; Tyler, 1967; LoCasio, 1967). Yet, being able to point out that a problem exists is far easier to do than to rectify it. As Stefflre observes, vocational psychologists' zest for power in a theory has led them to all-purpose explanations which purport to elucidate the behavior of all people—men, women, lower class, middle class, Blacks, whites, Western, and non-Western. Such a quest for a monolithic, all-embracing theory may be an academician's search for the impossible dream. It would seem that the stages through which an individual passes as he prepares to take his place in the world of work would differ, both with respect to substance and time, according to the social psychological forces impinging upon his life.

As long as theorists continue to generalize vocational theories based upon white people to Black people, research on Black people will continue to have large loopholes and conflicting results. One must begin to use an internal Black frame of reference for analyzing this group's vocational behavior. Much of what has been said should not be necessarily interpreted to mean that one must have a separate theory for the vocational development of Black people. It would seem quite possible, however, to pool what collective knowledge we have on the psychology of the Black individual's career development into more coherent statements. Along this line, the unification of reference group theory with vocational theories might prove helpful. In such an instance, reference group theory should provide a microanalytic level for analyzing the subjective aspects of group life which regularize and make discernible the occupational behavior and activities within a social structure. It may potentially supply a means of analyzing how people with the same objective socioeconomic status differ in their career development.

Summary

Research on Black individual's vocational development has been examined in terms of the impact of family role models, family stability/instability, work concept and job values, Maslow's need hierarchy, the motivator-hygiene theory, self-concept, and identity foreclosure. A survey has also been taken on the vocational aspirations, interests, choices, and maturity of Black individuals. Much of the research has produced conflicting hypotheses and results. While on the one hand, Black people are seen to have a noticeably less favorable attitude toward their jobs than whites, Hauser significantly points out that according to the findings he obtained from interviewing young Black males, work is an important aspect of their lives.

The Black individual's concept of work and work values have been examined in terms of Maslow's need hierarchy. Proponents of this position maintain that the Black person's lower order needs for security preclude his needs for self-fulfillment or self-actualization in work. Although this theory provides a plausible and convenient explanation for the seemingly low risk-taking of blacks in the occupational world, it lacks the empirical research required to support it. One question, among many, that needs answering is: Are there significant differences in the need hierarchy of lower class Black individuals and Black professionals?

The state of the art in vocational literature in terms of the variables mentioned is in dire need of a powerful dosage of adrenalin. A great deal of empirical or experimental research is necessary to support certain theorists' conjectures and intuitive feelings. A number of facts are missing. First, what is the impact of family role models and family stability on one's concept of work? How can this suggested influence be assessed? What family experiences—regardless of whether or not the home is intact or broken—affect an individual's work values or occupational mobility? What are the possible relationships between self-concept and different aspects of one's vocational development? Do sex differences among Blacks influence their self-concepts, outlooks on work, or job values? The questions one could ask are endless, but are, nevertheless, ones that need answering.

The profile of the Black individual as portrayed in the research cited is a portrait of a vocationally handicapped person. According to the studies examined, the average Black, if one can speak of average individuals of any racial group, is one who may lack positive work role models; does not manifest a lifetime commitment to a career as a way of life; is work-alienated; and places a greater priority on job security rather than self-fulfillment in an occupation. Moreover, he tends to have a negative self-image which fosters identity foreclosure or a rigid closing out of self and direction. His aspirations are high, but his expectations of achieving his desired occupational goals are low. He has limitations placed upon his occupational mobility because of his racial membership; evidences interests that are more person than thing-oriented; is vocationally immature, and makes his vocational choices in the social sciences and in those careers traditionally open to Blacks.

The extent to which this profile is accurate or inaccurate is still open to debate and research verification, for there are many notable exceptions to it. Vocational stereotyping of Blacks does no one any good; neither does ignoring or dismissing summarily the findings of various investigators as racially biased. If one takes the position that vocational literature has been "culturally unfair" to Blacks, then one must be prepared to delineate carefully what, in his opinion, makes it so as well as what would help in making it less so. Only in this way can one truly begin to fill the gaps in existing knowledge concerning the career progress of Black people. In doing this, the variables of race, socioeconomic class, and family background need to be looked at both separately and conjointly.

Thus, the profile outlined represents more than what some individuals may conceive as a negative description of the career evolution of Black people. Underlying all that has been discussed is an undeniable indictment of the situational factors as well as the limited research resources available that have either potentially or in actuality contributed to the profile sketched.

Proceeding solely on the basis of what research findings have been reported in this article, the counselor must ask of himself eventually: Where do I go from here? It seems evident that counselors and those involved in adult training programs must adopt more well-thought-out approaches to the guidance of Black people. On the child and adolescent level, compensatory vocational programs have little chance for survival if the workable features of the program are not built into the entire educational experience. The school must accept the responsibility of preparing young people for work as one of its major objectives. Teaching isolated facts and skills is not enough; values and attitudes toward work as well as the occupational opportunity structure also have to be changed. One without the other is not sufficient.

The recommendations made for young people are likewise applicable to adult training programs. That is, besides the inculcation of skills, attention should also be directed toward the conditions of the job environment, the relationship of the trainee and his supervisor, and the attitudes of both toward work. The training of Black people has to be more than attempts to make them resemble greater their white counterparts. Some Black individuals have poignantly summarized this feeling in the question: How white does one have to be in order to obtain and maintain a job? In short, intervention techniques are needed to facilitate the vocational development of Black people, but they should be techniques which involve the whole individual—techniques which take into account his background, his cultural differences as well as his points of human commonalities.

References

ANSELL, E. M. and HANSEN, J. C. Patterns in vocational development of urban youth. *Journal of Counseling Psychology,* 1971, **18,** 505–508.

ANTONOVSKY, A. Aspirations, class, and racial-ethnic membership. *The Journal of Negro Education,* 1967, **36,** 385–393.

ANTONOVSKY, A. and LERNER, M. J. Occupational aspirations of lower class Negro and white youth. *Social Problems,* 1959, **7,** 132–138.

ASH, P. Job satisfaction differences among women of different ethnic groups. *Journal of Vocational Behavior,* 1972, **2,** 495–507.

AUSUBEL, D. P. and AUSUBEL, P. Ego development among segregated Negro children. In H. A. Passow (Ed)., *Education in depressed areas.* New York: Bureau of Publications, Teachers College, Columbia University, 1963.

BAYER, A. E. *The Black college freshman: Characteristics and recent trends.* American Council of Education Research Reports, Vol. 8, No. 1. Washington: ACE, 1972.

BLOCHER, D. H. Social change and the future of vocational guidance. In H. Borow (Ed.), *Career guidance for a new age.* Boston: Houghton Mifflin, 1973, 41–82.

BLOOM, R. and BARRY, J. R. Determinants of work attitudes among Negroes. *Journal of Applied Psychology,* 1967, **51,** 291–294.

BORGEN, F. H. and HARPER, G. T. Predictive validity of measured vocational interests with black and white college men. *Measurement and Evaluation in Guidance,* 1973, **6,** 19–27.

BOYD, G. F. The levels of aspiration of white and Negro children in a nonsegregated elementary school. *Journal of Social Psychology,* 1952, **36,** 191–196.

BRAZZIEL, W. F., JR. Occupational choice in the Negro college. *Personnel and Guidance Journal,* 1961, **39,** 739–742.

CHAMPAGNE, J. E. and KING, D. C. Job satisfaction factors among underprivileged workers. *The Personnel and Guidance Journal,* 1967, **45,** 420–434.

CHANSKY, N. M. Race, aptitude, and vocational interests. *The Personnel and Guidance Journal,* 1965, **43,** 780–784.

CLARK, E. T. Influence of sex and social class on occupational preference and peer perception. *The Personnel and Guidance Journal,* 1967, **45,** 440–444.

CLARK, E. T. and MISA, K. F. Peer perception of Negro and white occupational preferences. *The Personnel and Guidance Journal,* 1967, **46,** 288–291.

CRAIN, R. L. School integration and occupational achievement of Negroes. *Journal of American Sociology,* 1969–1970, **75,** 593–607.

DOLE, A. C. and PASSONS, W. R. Life goals and plan determinants reported by Black and white high school seniors. *Journal of Vocational Behavior,* 1972, **2,** 209–222.

DREGER, R. M. and MILLER, K. S. Comparative psychological studies of Negroes and whites in the United States: 1959–1965. *Psychological Bulletin Monograph Supplement,* 1968, **70.**

DUCETTE, J. and WOLK, S. Locus of control and levels of aspirations in Black and white children. *Review of Educational Research,* 1972, 493–504.

DUNCAN, O. D. Patterns of occupational mobility among Negro men. *Demography,* 1968, **5,** 11–22.

GOTTLIEB, D. Poor youth do want to be middle class but it's not easy. *Personnel and Guidance Journal,* 1967, **46,** 116–122.

GRAMBS, J. D. The self-concept of Negro youth. In W. C. Kvaraceus, et al. (Eds.), *Negro self-concept: Implications for school and citizenship.* New York: McGraw-Hill, 1965, Pp. 11–34.

GRIER, E. S. *In search for a future.* Washington, D.C.: Washington Center for Metropolitan Studies, 1963.

GURIN, P. Motivation achievement and locus of control. In I. Katz & P. Gurin, *Race and the social sciences.* New York: Basic Books, 1969.

HABERMAN, M. Guiding the educationally disadvantaged. In C. E. Beck (Ed.), *Guidelines for guidance: Readings in the philosophy of guidance.* Dubuque, Iowa: Wm. C. Brown Co., 1966. Pp. 49–60.

HALL, J. A., and WIANT, H. V., JR. Does school desegregation change occupational goals of Negro males? *Journal of Vocational Behavior,* 1973, **3,** 175–179.

HANSEN, J. C. and ANSELL, E. M. Assessment of vocational maturity. *Journal of Vocational Behavior,* 1973, **3,** 89–94.

HAUSER, S. T. *Black and white identity formation studies in the psycho-social development of lower socioeconomic class adolescent boys.* New York: Wiley-Interscience, 1971.

HEFLAND, A. Group counseling as an approach to work problems of disadvantaged youth. *Rehabilitation Counseling Bulletin,* 1967, **9,** 111–116.

HENDERSON, G. Occupational aspirations of poverty-stricken Negro students. *Vocational Quarterly Journal,* 1967, **15,** 41–45.

HYTE, C. Occupational interests of Negro high school boys. *School Review,* 1936, **44,** 34–40.

KOHN, M. L. and CARROLL, E. E. Social class and the allocation of parental responsibilities. *Sociometry,* 1960, **23,** 372–392.

LAWRENCE, P. F. Vocational aspirations of Negro youth in California. *Journal of Negro education,* 1950, **19,** 47–56.

LEONARD, G. E., PIETROFESA, J. J., and BANKS, I. M. A workshop for the improvement of the self-concepts of inner-city youngsters. *The School Counselor,* 1969, **16,** 375–379.

LIEBERSON, S. and FUGITT, G. V. Negro-white occupational differences in the absence of discrimination. *American Journal of Sociology,* 1967–1968, **73,** 188–200.

LIPSMAN, C. K. Maslow's theory of needs in relation to vocational choice by students for lower socio-economic levels. *Vocational Guidance Quarterly,* 1967, **15,** 283–288.

LITTIG, L. Negro personality correlates of aspiration to traditionally open and closed occupations. *The Journal of Negro Education,* 1968, **37,** 31–36.

LO CASIO, R. Continuity and discontinuity in vocational development theory. *Personnel and Guidance Journal,* 1967, **46,** 32–46.

LOTT, A. J. and LOTT, B. E. *Negro and white youth: A psychological study in a border-state community.* New York: Holt, Rinehart, and Winston, 1963.

MASLOW, A. H. *Motivation and personality.* New York: Harper and Brothers, 1954.

MAYNARD, P. E. and HANSEN, J. C. Vocational maturity among inner-city youths. *Journal of Counseling Psychology,* 1970, **17,** 400–404.

MC GREW, J. M. Counseling the disadvantaged child: A practice in search of a rationale. *School Counselor,* 1971, **18,** 165–176.

MINK, O. G. and KAPLAN, B. A. *America's problem youth: Education and guidance of the disadvantaged.* Scranton, Pa.: International Textbook Co., 1970.

MOULTON, R. W. and STEWART, R. H. Parents as models for mobile and low mobile Black males. *Vocational Guidance Quarterly,* 1971, **45,** 247–253.

MOYNIHAN, D. P. *The Negro family: The case for nation action.* Washington, D.C.: Office of Policy Planning and Research, U.S. Dept. of Labor, 1965.

MURPHY, G. Work and the productive personality. In H. Borow (Ed.), *Career guidance for a new age.* Boston: Houghton Mifflin Co., 1973. Pp. 151–176.

MUSSEN, P. H. Differences between the TAT responses of Negro and white boys. *Journal of Consulting Psychology,* 1953, **17,** 373–376.

NEFF, W. S. The meaning of work to the poor. *Rehabilitation Counseling Bulletin,* 1976, **9,** 71–77.

PALLONE, N. J., RICKARD, L. S., and HURLEY, R. B. Key influencers of occupational preference among Black youth. *Journal of Counseling Psychology,* 1970, **17,** 498–501.

PETTIGREW, T. F. *A profile of the Negro American.* Princeton, N.J.: D. Van Nostrand Co., 1964.

PHILLIPS, B. N. School-related aspirations of children with different socio-cultural backgrounds. *Journal of Negro Education,* 1972, **41,** 48–52.

RAINWATER, L. Crucible of identity: The Negro lower-class family. In T. Parsons and K. B. Clard (Eds.), *The Negro American.* Boston: Houghton Mifflin and the American Academy of Arts and Sciences, 1966. Pp. 160–204.

ROSEN, B. C. Race, ethnicity, and the achievement syndrome. *American Sociological Review,* 1959, **24,** 47–60.

SEXTON, P. Negro career expectation. In H. J. Peters and J. C. Hansen (Eds.), *Vocational guidance and career development.* New York: The Macmillan Co., 1971. Pp. 353–363.

SINGER, S. L. and STEFFLRE, B. A note on racial differences in job values and desires. *The Journal of Social Psychology,* 1956, **43,** 333–337.

SLOCUM, J. W., JR. and STRAWSER, R. H. Racial differences in job attitudes. *Journal of Applied Psychology,* 1972, **56,** 28–32.

SMITH, E. J. *Counseling the culturally different black youth.* Ohio: Charles E. Merrill Co., 1973.

SPREY, J. Sex differences in occupational choice patterns among Negro adolescents. *Social Problems,* 1962, **10,** 11–22.

STEFFLRE, B. Vocational development: Ten propositions in a search of a theory. *Personnel and Guidance Journal,* 1966, **44,** 611–616.

SUPER, D. E. *The psychology of careers.* New York: Harper and Row, 1957.

TYLER, L. E. The encounter with poverty: Its effect on vocational psychology. *Rehabilitation Counseling Bulletin* (Fall special), 1967, 61–70.

VEROFF, J., ATKINSON, J. W., FELD, S. C., and GURIN, G. The use of thematic apperception to assess motivation in a nationwide interview study. *Psychological Monographs,* 1960, **74,** Whole No. 499.

VRIEND, J. Vocational maturity ratings of inner-city high school seniors. *Journal of Counseling Psychology,* 1969, **5,** 377–384.

WILSON, A. B. Residential segregation of social classes and aspirations of high school boys. In A. H. Passow, M. Goldberg, and A. J. Tannebaum (Eds.),

Education of the Disadvantaged. New York: Holt, Rinehart and Winston, 1967. Pp. 268–283.

WITTY, P., GARFIELD, S., and BRINK, W. A comparison of the vocational interests of Negro and white high-school students. *Journal of Educational Psychology,* 1941, **32,** 124–132.

YOUST, R. *Beacon lights: Rochester career guidance project.* Rochester Board of Education, 1967.

UNIT BIBLIOGRAPHY

AQUILAR, LINDA. "Unequal Opportunity and the Chicana." *Civil Rights Digest,* **5** (1973), 31–33.

BAKER, SALLY HILLSMAN, and BERNARD LEVENSON. "Job Opportunities of Black and White Working-Class Women." *Social Problems,* **22** (1975), 510–532.

CASAVANTES, EDWARD. "Pride and Prejudice: A Mexican American Dilemma." *Civil Rights Digest,* **3** (1970), 22–27.

COSBY, ARTHUR. "Black-White Differences in Aspirations Among Deep South High School Students." *Journal of Negro Education,* **40** (1971), 17–21.

CRAIN, ROBERT L. "School Integration and Occupational Achievement of Negroes." *American Journal of Sociology,* **75** (1970), 593–603.

CROWELL, SUZANNE. "Life on the Largest Reservation." *Civil Rights Digest,* **6** (1973), 3–9.

DOLE, ARTHUR A., and WILLIAM R. PASSONS. "Life Goals and Plan Determinants Reported by Black and White High School Seniors." *Journal of Vocational Behavior,* **2** (1972), 209–222.

DOLE, ARTHUR A. "Aspirations of Blacks and Whites for Their Children." *Vocational Guidance Quarterly,* **22** (1973), 24–31.

"EMPLOYMENT: Southwest Indian Report." A Report of the U. S. Commission on Civil Rights, 1973, 5–22, U. S. Government Printing Office.

GORDON, EDMUND W. "New Perspectives on Old Issues in Education for the Minority Poor." *IRCD Bulletin,* **10** (1975), 5–17.

HAGER, PAUL C., and CHARLES F. ELTON. "The Vocational Interests of Black Males." *Journal of Vocational Behavior,* **1** (1971), 153–158.

HALL, JOHN A., and HARRY V. WIANT, JR. "Does School Desegregation Change Occupational Goals of Negro Males?" *Journal of Vocational Behavior,* **3** (1973), 175–179.

HINDELANG, MICHAEL JAMES. "Educational and Occupational Aspirations Among Working Class Negro, Mexican-American and White Elementary School Children." *The Journal of Negro Education,* **39** (1970), 351–353.

KUVLESKY, WILLIAM P., and VICTORIA M. PATELLA. "Degree of Ethnicity and Aspirations for Upward Social Mobility Among Mexican American Youth." *Journal of Vocational Behavior,* **1** (1971), 231–244.

KUVLESKY WILLIAM P., and KATHERYN A. THOMAS. "Social Ambitions of Negro Boys and Girls from a Metropolitan Ghetto. "*Journal of Vocational Behavior,* **1** (1971), 177–187.

LEVINE, IRVING M., and JUDITH HERMAN. "Search for Identity in Blue-Collar America," *Civil Rights Digest,* **5** (1972), 3–10.

MANPOWER. "Indians Weave a New Image." **2** (1970), 9–13.

MONTEZ, PHILIP. "Will the Real MexAmerican Please Stand Up?" *Civil Rights Digest,* **3** (1970), 28–31.

MUSKRAT, JOSEPH. "Thoughts on the Indian Dilemma: Backgrounding the 'Indian Problem.' " *Civil Rights Digest,* **6** (1973), 46–50.

PALLONE, NATHANIEL J., FRED S. RICKARD, and ROBERT B. HURLEY. "Key

Influencers of Occupational Preference Among Black Youth." *Journal of Counseling Psychology,* **17** (1970), 498–501.

PHILLIPS, BEEMAN N. "School-Related Aspirations of Children with Different Sociocultural Backgrounds." *Journal of Negro Education,* **41** (1972), 48–52.

PICOU, J. STEVEN. "Black-White Variations in a Model of the Occupational Aspiration Process." *Journal of Negro Education,* **42** (1973), 117–122.

REUL, MYRTLE R. "The Many Faces of the Migrant." *Manpower,* **2** (1970), 13–17.

RICHMOND, CHARLOTTE. "If You Were Counseling Tom Begay." *Occupational Outlook Quarterly,* **13** (1969), 12–17.

SHAPPELL, DEAN L., LACY G. HAKK, and RANDOLPH B. TARRIER. "Perceptions of the World of Work: Inner-City Versus Suburbia." *Journal of Counseling Psychology,* **18** (1971), 55–59.

SCHMIEDING, O. A., and SHIRLEY F. JENSEN. "American Indian Students: Vocational Development and Vocational Tenacity." *Vocational Guidance Quarterly,* **17** *(*1968), 120–123.

STILWELL, WILLIAM E., and CARL E. THORESEN. "Social Modeling and Vocational Behaviors of Mexican-American and Non-Mexican-American Adolescents." *Vocational Guidance Quarterly,* **20** (1972), 279–286.

STIVALA, ANNA MAY. "Career Guidance in the Urban Setting." *American Vocational Journal,* **49** (1974), 32–34.

WITTMER, JOE. "Effective Counseling of Children of Several American Subcultures." *The School Counselor,* **19** (1971), 49–52.

part 11
Vocational Guidance and Career Development of Women

There is a growing body of literature regarding the role of women in our society. Writers are concerned about women's self-concepts, women as a minority group, the untapped labor potential, the traditional stereotype, and the homemaker-career conflict. The primary concern is with the attitudes of society generally and women specifically. Women have been stereotyped in the homemaker role, and when they entered the labor market it was in selected occupations. The attitudes of society are changing through the initiative of women. Homemaker and career roles are frequently contrasted in the literature, but many women combine them. Women are being encouraged to take advantage of the changing tenor in our society. This presents a challenge to those who assist women in their educational and vocational development. The articles in this section examine the changing concepts of women's lives, examine some of their aspirations, look at the special considerations in women's vocational development, all with different impact than on men, and discuss the role of a counselor in working with girls.

The life-cycle perspective of women has a variety of changes. Roxann A. Van Dusen and Eleanor Bernert Sheldon examine changes in several key aspects of women's lives—that is, education, marriage and the establishment of a separate household, childbearing, and entering the labor force. All changes in these variables

423

affect different stages in the life cycle. Chrysee Kline concentrates on the socialization process of women; she discusses their various roles throughout their career development.

Two articles focus on counseling with women. L. Sunny Hansen discusses trends and patterns in women's career development and then specifically deals with the obstacles to it. She concludes with counselor interventions and strategies to facilitate female career development. Lewis E. Patterson suggests reasons why vocational counseling has had little impact on girls and makes proposals to overcome the obstacles.

The Changing Status of American Women
A Life Cycle Perspective

Roxann A. VanDusen
and
Eleanor Bernert Sheldon

The "life cycle," a familiar concept to the public and to the media, has recently been receiving substantial attention from social scientists (Riley, Johnson, and Foner, 1972). The life cycle (or "life course") is a way of conceptualizing the aging process: a sequence of statuses and roles, expectations and relationships, constituting, in the broadest meaning of the word, an individual's "career." While the life cycle is universal, it is also infinitely varied. It is shaped by the variety of roles and opportunities available to an individual, as well as by the resources that individual can marshal at various stages of his or her "career."

In the past decade or so, sociologists and other social scientists have borrowed from demographers the concepts and techniques of cohort analysis for studying the process of social change. To state it simply: Social change has been viewed as the succession of cohorts through various stages of the life cycle. This cohort-analytic perspective highlights three important components of social change: (1) change associated with the aging process; (2) change associated with changes in the "external" environment; and (3) change associated with the replacement of one group of people (usually the succession of age groups) by the next.

Consider, first, the aging process: An individual's life is patterned by a variety of role sequences, probably the most important of which is the family life cycle, but also including sequences of student, career, and community roles. The combination and juxtaposition of various role sequences provide texture to an individual life cycle. Certain roles are traditionally associated with certain ages: student roles with the young; parental roles with the middle years; life alone (whether as a result of divorce, widowhood, or lifelong singleness) with the middle aged and elderly.

Reprinted from *American Psychologist,* **31**:106–116 (1976), by permission of the publisher and authors. Copyright 1976 by the American Psychological Association. Reprinted by permission.

Second, the historical times during which an individual matures also affect expectations and behavior: the 1930s Depression, World War II, the Vietnam War—all have an impact on patterns of marriage, fertility, and employment.

Finally, each birth cohort has a unique pattern of experiences as it progresses through the life cycle, experiences that may be seen as the interaction of the aging process and the period during which it occurs. The cohort that grew up and reached maturity during the 1930s bears the mark of the Depression. The baby-boom cohort faces (and will continue to face) sharp competition for education, for jobs, and for a variety of social services—the consequences of belonging to a group that is larger than both the group it follows and the one that will follow it.

The combination of the notion of the life cycle (and subcycles within it) and the notion of cohort succession provides a powerful tool for characterizing and understanding some of the recent changes in the roles and status of American women. Some of these changes have resulted from changes in the perception of appropriate role sequences for women; some are the result of the interaction of social, political, and economic events of the 1960s and 1970s; and some of the changes (and certainly the speed of the changes) may be attributed to the fact that the cohort that reached maturity in the past few years is not an ordinary cohort but rather the baby-boom generation.

Let us examine, briefly, some of these changes. It was noted at the outset that the *family* life cycle constitutes perhaps the most important subcurrent of an individual's life cycle. It is certainly the most important subcycle if that individual happens to be a woman. In fact, the tendency until recently has been to equate the family life cycle with the female life cycle. After all, most women marry at some point in their life, and most married women have children. In 1974, for instance, 95 per cent of all women 35 and older had been married at least once, and all but about 10 per cent of them had had at least one child (U.S. Department of Commerce, 1974d, 1975a). Most women's lives have been regulated by the family life cycle, their "career" choices to one extent or another circumscribed by the responsibilities attending their family roles—the bearing and rearing of children.

From this presumed identity of female and family life cycles, there developed well-defined notions of what activities and roles are appropriate for women of different ages, corresponding to different stages of the family life cycle. These expectations were, to some extent, suspended for women who did not fit the mold: the 5 per cent or 10 per cent who never married, and the ever-increasing number of divorced, separated, and widowed women. Thus there developed the notion that there are two categories of women: those who are married and those with careers.

In fact, of course, such a dichotomy never existed. In 1950, one quarter of all married women who were living with their husbands were in the labor force, and more than one quarter of all women in intact marriages who had school-age children were employed: more than 10 per cent of married women with husband present and pre-school children were in the labor force. And the number of women who combine career and family roles has risen steadily since then. Nevertheless, it has only been in the last decade or so that notions about what activities and roles are appropriate for women at each stage of the family/female life cycle have become somewhat less rigid. Slowly, social definitions of women's roles are catching up with reality.

Many have seen this trend as the increasing overlap and similarity of men's and women's life cycles. An alternative is to view this trend as the decreasing salience of marriage and the family in the life choices of women. In a recent article, Presser (1973) examined some of the consequences for women and for the family of perfect fertility control. Many of the changes she envisioned are becoming evident in the trends to be highlighted in this article: continuing education for women, an orientation toward lifelong careers, smaller families, and child-free marriages. This is not to suggest that all of these changes may be directly attributed to greater contraceptive efficiency. But what it does suggest is that the distinction (in terms of roles and expectations) between child-free women and those with children (whether by choice or through contraceptive failure) is gradually disappearing. Or, to phrase it differently, the family life cycle is becoming but one of a number of sub-currents in the lives of American women.

In documenting some of the facets of this general trend, it is important not only to examine changes in several key aspects of women's (and men's) lives—education, marriage and the establishment of a separate household, childbearing, and labor force participation—but also to examine these changes with a view to the variable effects on different age groups at different stages in the life cycle.

Education

It is appropriate to begin the discussion of changes in the status of American women with some information on changes in their educational attainment. Education has traditionally been regarded as an early stage of the life cycle—a stage that is completed before a career (be it job, marriage, family or whatever) is launched. Furthermore, the educational system plays a major role in influencing the goals and expectations of individuals; it also is a major source of the contacts and training that will enable the individual to pursue those goals. Thus, the education system plays both a formal and an informal role in channeling individuals into certain lifework and life-styles.

That there has been a steady rise in the educational attainment of the U.S. population over the past 35 years is well known: the proportion of Americans between the ages of 25 and 34 with at least 4 years of high school has risen from 35 per cent in 1940 to 80 per cent in 1974. The percentage of female high school graduates 20 and 21 years old who have completed at least some college has risen from 24 per cent in 1940 to 46 per cent in 1974; the comparable figures for men are 30 per cent in 1940 and 49 per cent in 1974 (U.S. Department of Commerce, 1974a).

Yet important differences exist between men and women both in the level of educational attainment of each group and in the types of educational training each pursues. For instance, though women are somewhat more likely to finish high school than are men, women are less likely to continue on to college. And if they do go on to college, women are less likely to complete all 4 years. In 1974, 47 per cent of all white women between 25 and 34 years old had completed high school but had no college training, and an additional 33 per cent had completed some college. The comparable figures for white males are 38 per cent with only a high school degree, and 44 per cent with at least some college (U.S. Department of Commerce, 1974a).

There are several stereotypic explanations for these sex differences in educational attainment. First, it is argued, a family is more likely to invest in a son's education than in a daughter's, in the belief that the son *must* be able to find a job, but the daughter may not have to. Second, even if the daughter intends to work, most jobs open to her do not require a college degree: skills necessary for secretarial, clerical, and operative positions can be learned on the job. And third, so the argument goes, the daughter will undoubtedly get married and have children, and will in any case stop her education at that point.

Indeed, marriage and childbearing have traditionally been considered sufficient reasons for women to terminate their schooling, though the parallel roles for men (husband and father) did not, in general, preclude a man from continuing to be a student as well. In discussing the results of a recent national survey, Campbell, Converse, and Rodgers (Note 1) state:

> The proportion of unmarried young women who report attending school of some kind (61 per cent) is twice as high as that of their married age cohort [18–29] (29 per cent), but the proportion of unmarried men of this age [who report attending school] (47 per cent) is virtually identical to that of married men (48 per cent). When asked why they had terminated their formal education when they had, almost half of the married women referred to their marriage; this response was far less common among young married men.

These explanations for sex differences in educational attainment have taken a rather severe beating in the past decade. First, the argument that women need not support themselves: Increasing numbers of women are the sole wage earners for their families or are economically independent. In March 1973, 42 per cent of all women in the labor force were single, widowed, divorced, or separated, and thus (to a greater or lesser extent) economically on their own; another 19 per cent of the female labor force were married to men with less than $7,000 annual income (U.S. Department of Labor, 1975). Increasingly, women must face the likelihood that at some point in their lifetime they will have to support themselves or contribute to the family income.

Second, the argument that women's work does not require extensive training or educational degrees fails on two counts: (1) women are bringing more education to their traditional jobs and thus making that training a requirement of the position (most secretaries, for instance, are now expected to have some college training); and (2) women are beginning to challenge the rigidity with which "women's work" has been defined, and in seeking entrance to "male jobs," they have had to acquire the prerequisite educational background.

And third, the argument that women will give up their schooling for marriage and family: Increasingly numbers of women, in examining their prospects for entering or reentering the labor force, are not abandoning their educational careers upon marriage and the advent of children. The composition of the student population of the United States—in terms of both age and sex—is rapidly changing. Between 1970 and 1974, the number of women in college increased by 30 per cent, while the number of men only increased by 12 per cent. Furthermore, although overall graduate school enrollment has dropped 9 per cent since 1969, the proportion of women in graduate school continues to rise. In 1971, women earned 42 per cent of all BAs and 40 per cent of all MAs. Although women constituted only 14 per cent of all Ph.D.s awarded in 1971, that number is likely to rise quickly in the next few years, for the pool of candidates from which they are drawn is growing rapidly (both in actual numbers and compared with men) (U.S. Department of Labor, 1975).

Not only is the proportion of women seeking education beyond the high school diploma fast approaching that of men, women are also beginning to compete with men to gain entry to the high-prestige occupations that were traditionally closed to them. The proportion of women enrolled in professional schools for such fields as law, medicine, architecture, and engineering, although still low, has risen steadily since 1960. For instance, of the total enrollment in law schools, women accounted for 4 per cent in 1960, 12 per cent in 1972, and 19 per cent in 1974. The same trend may be seen in total enrollments in medical schools, in which women represented 6 per cent of the total in 1960, 13 per cent in 1972, and 18 per cent in 1974. The increasing proportion of women in the first-year class of these programs suggests that these trends will continue (McCarthy and Wolfle, 1975; Parrish, 1974).

Finally, evidence exists that fewer women are abandoning their educational plans upon marriage and childbearing, or they are setting aside these plans only temporarily. This trend may be seen in the number of women 25 years and older who are in school. Between 1970 and 1974, for instance, the college enrollment of women between the ages of 25 and 34 rose from 409,000 to 831,000—an increase of 102 per cent. The comparable increase for men between 25 and 34 was 46 per cent: from 940,000 to 1,371,000 in 1974. Of women in college between the ages of 16 and 34, those 25 years and older rose from 14 per cent in 1970 to 21 per cent in 1974 (U.S. Department of Commerce, 1975c).

During the period 1970–1974, part-time enrollment in college increased 50 per cent, compared with a 10 per cent increase in the number of full-time students. The role that the older college students play in this trend toward part-time continuing education is evident: 63 per cent of the 25–34-year-olds were enrolled on a part-time basis in 1974, compared with only 17 per cent of those in the traditional college cohort (18–24-year-olds) (U.S. Department of Commerce, 1975c).

These changes have had two important effects on the lives of American women. First, the young women in the age cohort that traditionally constituted the student population (those under age 25) are facing much less resistance—social and institutional—in their efforts to gain access to the training that is a prerequisite for career mobility. Second, and perhaps more important, those women *not* in the traditional student cohort—those who are older, who are married, or who have children—are no longer deemed to have "missed the boat" by having taken on familly roles before completing their schooling. "Student" is no longer synonymous with "pre-adult."

In the following sections, some of the push and pull factors associated with the return of older women to school will be discussed: changes in the marital and childbearing patterns that have made continuing education more easy to arrange and changes in the labor market that have made that education more desirable to acquire— at least for women.

Marriage and Childbearing

Three of the most remarkable trends in the past two decades have all had a direct effect on the phasing of what was traditionally considered the main portion of a woman's life cycle—namely, marriage and childbearing. Specifically, women are postponing marriage, postponing childbearing within marriage, and reducing their family size expectations.

Take marital patterns, for instance. The median age at first marriage for women has risen from 20.3 in 1950 to 21.1 in 1974. Furthermore, in the age group in which most men and women traditionally marry

(20–24), the percentage of women remaining single has risen from 28 per cent in 1960 to 39 per cent in 1974—an increase of one third. In general, while the percentage remaining single is up sharply for persons under 35, it continues to decline for persons 35 and over (U.S. Department of Commerce, 1974d). The long-term effect of the trend among the 20–24 cohort to remain single may be a later marriage age, or it may be a growing commitment to lifelong singleness: it is too early to say.

There are many explanations for this dramatic change in marriage patterns in the last 25 years. First, the expansion of educational opportunities for women has provided them with alternatives to their traditional life choices, and they are postponing (sometimes indefinitely) parental roles in favor of occupational careers. Second, there is increasing acceptance of nontraditional living arrangements; couples who might have bowed to social pressure to marry no longer feel compelled to do so. Third, the 1960s saw a dramatic rise in the number of young marriage-age men inducted into the armed forces, and thus made relatively inaccessible to the marriage market. But, in addition to these and other explanations for delayed marriage, demographers have given us one other: *the marriage squeeze.* Since women tend to marry men two or three years older than themselves, the women of the baby boom reached marriage age before the comparably large male marriage cohort. Or, to put it another way, there were not enough men in the appropriate age groups for the marriage-age women. For some women, then, the postponement of marriage may have been involuntary—the demographic fallout of the baby boom (Glick and Parke, 1965; Parke and Glick, 1967).

In part as a consequence of postponed marriage, in part for other reasons, women are postponing childbearing. For instance, 70 per cent of white women married between 1955 and 1959 had their first child in the first 24 months of marriage; 10 years later (that is, among women married between 1965 and 1969), only 60 per cent had had their first child within 2 years of marriage. The same trend is seen for later-order births as well. It should be noted, however, that in the same 10-year comparison for black women, the trend is reversed (U.S. Department of Commerce, 1974c).

Not only are women having their children later, they are also having, and planning to have, fewer children. This phenomenon has given us another term in the popular lexicon on the changing life cycle: *the birth dearth.* Between 1960 and 1974, the percentage of ever-married women between the ages of 15 and 19 who were child free increased by 25 per cent (from 44 per cent to 56 per cent); for ever-married women 20–24, those child free rose by two thirds (from 24 per cent to 41 per cent); and for ever-married women 25–29, the rise was close to 60 per cent (from 13 per cent to 20 per cent) (U.S. Department of Commerce, 1975a). It is interesting to note that this drop in births since

1960 will produce a reverse marriage squeeze in the next five years or so: young men will be locating mates from a *smaller* cohort of women.

In 1974, the birth rate in the United States reached a point lower even than the level reached during the 1930s Depression: 14.8 per 1,000 population. Not only the birth rate but the fertility expectations of women have dropped dramatically and quickly. In 1955, 38 per cent of women aged 18–24 expected to have four or more children (U.S. Department of Labor, 1973); between 1967 and 1974, the proportion of women in this age group who expected to have four or more children dropped by more than two thirds: from 26 per cent in 1967 to 8 per cent in 1974. At the same time, the number of women anticipating *two* children rose dramatically: from 37 per cent of the women 18–24 in 1967 to 56 per cent in 1974—an increase of 50 per cent. For women in the 25–29 age range, the increase in the number expecting only two children was even more dramatic: from 29 per cent in 1967 to 52 per cent in 1974 (U.S. Department of Commerce, 1975a).

At the same time that family size expectations are decreasing, there is an increasing proportion of childless women who expect to *remain* childless: in 1974, 11 per cent of childless women 14–24 and 27 per cent of childless married women 25–29 did not expect to have any children. These figures represent an increase of 23 per cent in just 3 years in wives under 30 who do not plan to have children (U.S. Department of Commerce, 1975a).

In short, then, women have been entering the traditional family cycle more slowly, and because of their smaller families, they have been spending less time in that phase of their life.

Female Heads of Households [1]

One way to examine some of the changes that have taken place in family living arrangements in the past two decades is to look at changes in female-headed households. Between 1954 and 1969, the number of female heads of families increased by about 40 per cent; this number grew another 22 per cent between 1970 and 1974, so that by 1974 female-headed households represented 10 per cent of all households in the United States, and approximately 15 per cent of all families with children. Much of this change reflects the increase in the number of black female family heads. Since 1960 there has been a 10 per cent increase in the number of white female family heads, and a 35 per cent

[1] Any woman 14 years old or older may head a family if she is not married and living with her husband. She may or may not live alone, and if she lives with others, they may or may not be related to her. If she lives alone or with nonrelatives, she is called a primary individual. If she lives with others who are related to her by blood, marriage, or adoption, she is the head of a primary family. For a detailed discussion of households headed by women, see Ross and MacIntosh (Note 2).

increase in the number of black female family heads. In 1973, black women represented 28 per cent of all female family heads (U.S. Department of Commerce, 1975b).

Female heads of households are younger (on average) than previously, and more apt to be divorced, separated, or single, rather than widowed. Between 1960 and 1973, the median age of women who headed families declined by about 5 years, from 50.5 in 1960 to 45.1 in 1973, with black female family heads about 9 years younger than their white counterparts (U.S. Department of Commerce 1974b). The shift toward younger, divorced, or separated female family heads (from older, widowed family heads) will no doubt continue as a result of the continuing and rising rate of divorces and separations. In 1973, 37 per cent of female family heads were widowed, 13 per cent unmarried, and 50 per cent divorced or separated. This is in contrast with 1960, when 50 per cent of them were widowed and 36 per cent divorced or separated (U.S. Department of Commerce, 1974b).

There are two fundamental reasons for interest in and concern for increases in the number of households headed by women. First, as a group, these households are particularly disadvantaged. Two thirds of all female household heads have less than a high school education. In 1972, more than half of them had incomes below the poverty threshold ($4,254), compared with less than 10 per cent of male heads of households. In 1973, a higher proportion of children under 18 years of age lived in fatherless families than ever before: about 10 per cent of white children and 38 per cent of black children. Nearly one half of all female family heads between the ages of 25 and 44 have three or more children. In short, increasing numbers of children are experiencing the economic disadvantages which attend households headed by women (U.S. Department of Commerce, 1974b; U.S. Department of Labor, 1975; Waldman and Whitmore, 1974).

The second major reason for interest in the growth of female-headed households is that increasing numbers of women have experienced or will experience this status at some point in their lives. The shift toward later marriage age, when combined with the ability and inclination of young single women to leave their parent's home and set up their own household, has been a major element in the increase in households of "primary individuals" who are female. The rise in the number of children born to unmarried women, coupled with the tendency for these women to set up their own household rather than move in with relatives, has also contributed to the trend.

But the major factor in the rise in the number of households headed by women is the increasing likelihood that a marriage will end in divorce or separation. The number and rate of divorces increased in 1974 for the 12th straight year. The ratio of divorced people to those in intact marriages has risen from a level of 35 per 1,000 in 1960 to 63 per 1,000 in 1974, with approximately 50 per cent more divorced women than divorced men in 1974—an indication of the greater like-lihood that divorced men will remarry. Perhaps the most important element in this trend has been the shift in the age patterns of divorce in recent years. In 1974, the ratio of divorced persons to persons in intact marriages was higher for those under 45 years old (66 per 1,000) than for those 45 years and over (59 per 1,000), representing a reversal of the situation a decade earlier (U.S. Department of Commerce, 1974d).

It has been argued that the rise in the number of families headed by women represents not a preference for single-parent families but rather a transitional status which increasing proportions of women will enter (and leave) at some point in their lives (Ross and MacIntosh, Note 2). The vast majority of the individuals who are postponing mar-riage today are likely to marry at some point; a growing proportion of them will experience separation and divorce; and an increasing proportion of those divorced will experience remarriage. Between 1960 and 1969, the rate of remarriage of divorced women rose by almost 11 per cent (from 122.1 per 1,000 divorced women to 135.4). In con-trast, the remarriage rate for widows has remained fairly constant: 36.1 per 1,000 widows in 1960 to 39.3 per 1,000 in 1969. Thus, the major group of women who are likely to remain in female-headed households are widows. But, as noted earlier, widows represent a shrinking proportion of the total female household heads (NCHS, 1973).

If, in fact, there has been a decrease in the importance of marital status in predicting or determining the sorts of activities and roles a woman adopts, part of the reason is that marriage is not eternal. More and more women are spending more and more time in roles that lie outside the traditional family life cycle. The length of time after child-hood and before marriage is growing, as is the number of women spending time between marriages.

It is not really surprising that the social perception of appropriate female roles is catching up with the reality of post-World-War-II America. It is rather more surprising that it has taken so long to rec-ognize that the "career woman" and the mother may be one and the same person. But then, as Keller (1972) has noted, the working woman is "one of America's best kept secrets."

Labor Force Participation [2]

The contrast between the female labor force of 1920 and that of the 1970s is striking. In 1920, the typical working woman was single, under 30 years old, and from the "working class." Today, most working

---

[2] For a discussion of trends in female labor force participation in the United States in the 20th century, see Oppenheimer (1970). For additional information, see the annual publication of the U.S. Department of Labor, *Manpower Report of the President*.

women are married; over two thirds of them have child-rearing responsibilities in addition to their jobs; they represent the entire socioeconomic spectrum; and more than half of them are 40 or over.

Between 1950 and 1973, overall labor force participation of women rose by one third. Although women who have never married have been and continue to be much more likely to work, the distinction between never married and other categories of women in terms of their labor market activity is rapidly disappearing. While the labor force participation of never-married women rose 13 per cent between 1950 and 1974 (from 50.5 per cent to 57.2 per cent), it rose over 80 per cent for married women who were living with their husbands (from 23.8 per cent to 43.0 per cent).

Since the mid-1960s, the greatest increase in labor force participation of women has been among those in the 25–34 age range—the ages during which women are most intensively involved in child-rearing, and the ages at which female labor force participation has traditionally been lowest. Among women 25–34, the proportion in the labor force has risen from 36 per cent in 1960 to 50 per cent in 1973 —an increase of close to 40 per cent in 13 years (U.S. Department of Labor, 1975).

Several reasons can be given for the changing composition of the female labor force over the past several decades, some of which have already been highlighted. The rise in the educational attainment of young women in the past several decades has given women access to jobs that were previously inaccessible to them because they lacked the requisite training. Demographic trends have also played a role in encouraging increasing numbers of women to enter the labor force, and to stay there. Because young women have been postponing marriage, and postponing childbearing within marriage, they experience a relatively long period of time after completing high school or college during which they may advance in their careers. And increasingly, women are finding it difficult to give up the economic independence, as well as the challenge, recognition, and satisfaction they derive from their jobs. Over a third of married women with preschool children were in the labor force in 1974, as contrasted with only 12 per cent in 1950.

In a study of female labor market activity using data from the 1960 U.S. Census, Sweet (1973) found that women with more education were more likely to be in the labor force while their children were preschoolers than were those women with less than a high school education. Sweet suggests two reasons for these findings: differences in child-spacing patterns and differences in previous labor market experience. If women with less education are likely to have the second child relatively quickly, they will be pregnant again while the first child is still a preschooler, and thus less interested in returning to the job. And with good reason: The jobs less educated women perform tend to be more hazardous than the jobs open to women with a college education.

Well-educated women are more likely to have worked both before marriage and before childbearing, and for a longer period of time. This fact has two consequences: (1) the family's consumption patterns have become adapted to two incomes, a level of living difficult to abandon; and (2) these women, with their relatively recent work experience, have greater contact with the labor market and knowledge of job opportunities and are more likely to find employment when they want it.

In addition to affecting the number of women in the labor force, demographic trends have also affected the composition of the female labor force, more particularly the shift from a young, unmarried female labor force to a middle-aged, married one. This shift has been explained, in part, by the concept of a *life cycle squeeze* (Gove, Grimm, Motz, and Thompson, 1973; Oppenheimer, 1974). Expenses are particularly high two times during the typical family life cycle: the first occurs soon after the couple is married, when the acquisition of home and other accoutrements of married life usually takes place; the second occurs when children reach adolescence. Both are times when the husband's income alone is not likely to be sufficient to cover these expenses: the first because he is at the beginning of his career at the time that he is beginning his marriage; the second because the time when the costs of maintaining the family are highest (adolescence of children) may not coincide with the time when his income reaches it peak. Oppenheimer (1974) finds that men in occupations where the peak median earnings in 1959 were $7,000 or more were much more likely to have their incomes rise roughly in proportion to increases in the cost of maintaining their families. However, men in occupations with peak median incomes under $7,000 in 1959 were likely to experience peak child-care costs at a time when they were not earning much more, and sometimes less on average, than were younger men with younger and therefore less expensive children. These situations create strong economic pressures for an additional income, and are undoubtedly one reason why young brides continue to work after marriage, and why women in their forties and fifties have entered or reentered the labor market in record numbers in recent years.[3]

Changes in the U.S. economy in the 20th century have also encouraged women to enter and remain in the labor force. The industries and occupations that have expanded most rapidly (particularly during the period after 1940) are those that were the major employers of women.

---

[3] Comments by A. J. Jaffe and Murray Gendell on Oppenheimer's article appear in *Demography* (1975, *12*, 331–336). Gendell notes that it may be the financial squeeze that propels middle-age women into the labor force (as Oppenheimer suggests), or it may be the decreased child-care responsibilities associated with adolescent children which *enables* women to seek outside employment.

This trend has been characterized as a shift from the goods-producing economy prior to World War II to the service-producing economy of the 1970s (Waldman and Whitmore, 1974). The post-World-War-II baby boom created the need for an expansion of a wide variety of services—educational, medical, governmental, and recreational among them—services in which most women workers were concentrated.

But while the demand for female labor was rising, the women who traditionally filled these jobs—the young and the single—constituted a stable or declining population, at least until the late 1960s. The dramatic expansion and changing composition of the female labor force in post-World-War-II America, then, are seen in part as the response of older married women to the growing demand for female labor (Oppenheimer, 1970).

Let us consider for a moment the notion of a demand for female labor and the question of the sex labeling of jobs and professions. It is well known that women are highly concentrated in a few occupations in which they constitute an overwhelming majority of all workers. For instance, in 1960, elementary school teachers and registered nurses accounted for almost 54 per cent of all female professional employment; in 1970, they were still just over 46 per cent of all female professionals (Fuchs, 1975). Oppenheimer (1970) has argued that the U.S. labor market is actually two markets—male and female—and that men and women in most cases do not really compete for the same jobs. The expansion of "women's" occupations after World War II led not to a demand for additional labor but to a demand for additional *female* labor.

The principal employer of women today, as it was in 1940, is the service industries and, more particularly, professional services (medical) and health, education, and legal) (Waldman and McEaddy, 1974). As Oppenheimer (1970) has suggested, a number of reasons can be given for the persistence of sex labels on certain jobs:

1. Such "women's jobs" as teaching, nursing, and secretarial work depend on skilled but cheap labor in fairly large quantities—and women who are entering the labor force for the first time, or reentering after a long absence, are willing to accept pay that is not commensurate with their skills or training.

2. Most of the training for these occupations is acquired *before* employment. Thus the employer does not bear the risk of investing time and money training women, with the attendant possibility that they will soon leave.[4]

3. These "women's jobs" do not require a long-term commit-

---

[4] A recent study examines patterns of quitting for men and women, and finds that quitting to exit the labor force is larger for women, and quitting to move to another job is larger for men. Barnes and Jones (1974) also find that total female quitting is usually greater than male quitting, but male quitting is more variable from year to year.

ment, or extensive sacrifice of time, and thus women, who have traditionally been seen as secondary earners who lack high career aspirations, are attracted to them.[5]

4. These jobs exist all over the country, and thus women are not usually handicapped by their mobility (if their husbands must move frequently in their jobs) *or* their immobility (if their husbands must stay in one place).

5. Finally, these jobs have traditionally been held by women. The jobs are thought to call on skills that are innately female (the greater manual dexterity often attributed to women) or on skills that are acquired in the home (the patience to work with children!). Furthermore, these traditional female jobs rarely put women in a supervisory position over men—a situation that is thought to create rebellion among male underlings.

Considerable debate continues as to whether there has been any change in the sex labeling or sex segregation of occupations in recent years (Fuchs, 1975; Gross, 1968; Hedges and Bemis, 1974; Knudsen, 1969). Gross (1968) has argued, for instance, that what small decrease there may be in occupational segregation is due not to the entrance of women into traditionally male occupations but the reverse: a "decreased resistance by female occupations to the entry of males" (p. 198). Fuchs (1975) has argued that the trend is much more complex. A drop in an index of occupational segregation could occur either as a result of a change in the average amount of segregation within occupations or as a result of differential rates of growth of occupations. Using a simple index of sex segregation, which may be interpreted as the proportion of people who would have to shift to occupations dominated by the opposite sex in order to eliminate sex segregation, Fuchs finds a drop of 7 percentage points between 1960 (66.2 per cent) and 1970 (59.2 per cent). Fuchs notes that between 1960 and 1970 some occupations became less segregated: the greatest changes were among elementary school teachers and registered nurses (in female-dominated professions) and among engineers, accountants, and science technicians (in male-dominated professions). At the same time, the less sex segregated occupations (for example, college and secondary school teachers, computer specialists, health technologists) were growing more rapidly.

If there is today less resistance to female employment in traditionally male-dominated occupations, it has not been without its adverse consequences. In the present recession, women workers have accounted for significantly larger proportions of the unemployed—a fact that underscores their recent entry and consequent low status in a range of

[5] For a discussion of the assumptions about female career aspirations, see Crowley, Levitin, and Quinn (Note 3).

occupations (U.S. Department of Labor, 1975). And among women who have been able to keep their jobs, there seems to be no decrease in the income differentials between men and women. The grim news in the 1975 *Manpower Report of the President* was that "nearly two-thirds of all full-time, year-round female workers earned *less* than $7,000 in 1972" while "over three-quarters of fulltime, year-round male workers earned *over* $7,000" (p. 55). Even when earnings are adjusted for hours worked and level of education of the worker, the large differentials in earnings between male and female workers persist. For instance, Suter and Miller (1973) found, in working with income data from 1966, that "if women had the same occupational status as men, had worked all their lives, had the same education and year-round full-time employment in 1966, their income would be . . . 62 per cent of that received by men" (p. 962).

The sex labeling of jobs, the occupational segregation of women, and the consequent income differentials between men and women have been remarkably persistent in the face of dramatic demographic and socioeconomic changes. But it is precisely these changes that will inevitably restructure the career experiences and labor market activity of women in the next several decades. The present female occupational distribution, as is noted in the 1975 *Manpower Report,* is the result of myriad influences, some in early childhood: "Role differentiation in early life later affects educational and occupational choices, hours and location of work, and other factors which relegate women to lower level positions in the lower paying industries" (U.S. Department of Labor, 1975, p. 63).

The change that is coming can already be seen in the choices young women have been making in their educational and their family "careers." Because marriage is no longer an end in itself; because so many women spend time outside of marriage or in between marriages; because family/parental roles occupy a relatively short portion of a woman's total life in today's two-child society; because women are receiving the education and training (and with it the career aspirations) to cause them to plan for and expect employment opportunities parallel to those of men; and finally, because all of these conditions represent changes from the recent past, to note that the pattern of female labor force participation is likely to change is anticlimactic.

However, despite all these changes, nowhere is it suggested that the pattern of female occupational choices, earnings, or job mobility will approximate that of men, and certainly not in the near future. The reasons have nothing to do with women's skills or aspirations, and surprisingly little to do with the prospects for economic recovery in the United States in the next few years. The reasons have everything to do with the life cycle concerns discussed above. Although marital status and parental responsibilities are likely to become less salient in women's career choices, women will continue to bear the major responsibility for children, and it is their career that will continue to be marked by the need to accommodate both parental and occupational roles.

Whether female labor force participation will approximate that of males, or even whether it should—given that the distribution of mothers, and most of the responsibilities that accompany that role, is 100 per cent female—is not a particularly fruitful line of inquiry. More productive of insight will be some close attention to the social and economic lags created by these recent social and demographic trends. Two examples come readily to mind: the "two-career family" and the "dual career" woman.

The two-career family is one in which both the husband and the wife are employed; it characterizes a growing portion of all U.S. families. Traditionally, career mobility has involved some geographic mobility. A family with school-age children and headed by one wage earner is not particularly mobile; the two-career family is even less so. What will be the effects on the labor market of the increased reluctance or inability of talented young people to move to further their careers? Or, alternatively, what will be the effect on marriage and divorce patterns on the continued importance of a certain amount of geographic mobility in furthering one's career?

Second, "dual careers": Dual careers refer to the combination and juxtaposition of parental and occupational responsibilities which confront increasing numbers of women. As more and more women with family responsibilities enter the labor force, certain institutional changes may be necessary—among them, the improvement of child-care facilities, increased flexibility of work schedules, and better provisions for job training. At what cost will these changes to accommodate the dual career woman be made? Or, alternatively, what will be the costs (social and otherwise) of *not* making the necessary institutional changes?

Conclusion

At the outset it was suggested that one way of summarizing these various trends was in terms of the declining importance of the family life cycle in the woman's total life cycle—the diminishing social importance of the distinction between married women and those who are unmarried (never married, no longer married, not yet married). In examining this general proposition, recent changes in a number of areas which have a direct impact on a woman's life choices were highlighted: education, marriage, childbearing, and employment.

The essential message has been: The traditional family life cycle for women has been slowly disappearing for the past quarter century; the rapid-paced changes of the past decade have released the secret, and another sacred myth is being dispelled. With the death of the myth, little doubt now exists that during the last decades of the century these trends will exert a profound effect on family, economy, social values— and, of course, the changing bases of self-identification and of sex roles.

Reference Notes

1. CAMPBELL, A., CONVERSE, P. E., and RODGERS, W. *The perceived quality of life*. Ann Arbor: University of Michigan, 1975. (Prepublication draft)
2. ROSS, H. L., and MACINTOSH, A. *The emergence of households headed by women*. Washington, D.C.: Urban Institute, June 1973. (Unpublished paper)
3. CROWLEY, J. E., LEVITIN, T. E., and QUINN, R. P. *Facts and fictions about the American working woman*. Ann Arbor: University of Michigan, Institute for Social Research, January 1973. (Mimeo)

References

BARNES, W. F., and JONES, E. B. Differences in male and female quitting. *Journal of Human Resources*, 1974, 9, 439–451.

FUCHS, V. R. A note on sex segregation in professional occupations. *Explorations in Economic Research*, 1975, 2, 105–111.

GENDELL, M. Further comment on V. K. Oppenheimer's "The life-cycle squeeze: The interaction of men's occupational and family life cycles." *Demography*, 1975, 12, 333–336.

GLICK, P. C., and PARKE, R., JR. New approaches in studying the life cycle of the family. *Demography*, 1965, 2, 187–202.

GOVE, W. R., GRIMM, J. W., MOTZ, S. C., and THOMPSON, J. D. The family life cycle: Internal dynamics and social consequences. *Sociology and Social Research*, 1973, 57, 182–195.

GROSS, E. Plus ça change . . . ? The sexual structure of occupations over time. *Social Problems*, 1968, 16, 198–208.

HEDGES, J. N., and BEMIS, S. E. Sex stereotyping: Its decline in skilled trades. *Monthly Labor Review*, 1974, 97 (May), 14–22.

JAFFE, A. J. Comment on V. K. Oppenheimer's "The life-cycle squeeze: The interaction of men's occupational and family life cycles." *Demography*, 1975, 12, 331–332.

KELLER, S. The future status of women in America. In C. F. Westoff and R. Parke, Jr. (Eds.), *Demographic and social aspects of population growth* (Research Reports of the Commission on Population Growth and the American Future, Vol. 1). Washington, D.C.: U.S. Government Printing Office, 1972.

KNUDSEN, D. D. The declining status of women: Popular myths and the failure of functionalist thought. *Social Forces*, 1969, 48, 183–193.

MC CARTHY, J. L., and WOLFLE, D. Doctorates granted to women and minority group members. *Science*, 1975, 189, 856–859.

NATIONAL CENTER FOR HEALTH STATISTICS. *Remarriages, United States* (Series 21, No. 25, Vital and Health Statistics). Rockville, Md.: Author, December 1973.

OPPENHEIMER, V. K. *The female labor force in the United States: Demographic and economic factors governing its growth and changing com-*

position (Population Monograph Series, No. 5). Berkeley: University of California, 1970.

OPPENHEIMER, V. K. The life-cycle squeeze: The interaction of men's occupational and family life cycles. *Demography,* 1974, *11,* 227–245.

PARKE, R., JR., and GLICK, P. C. Prospective changes in marriage and the family. *Journal of Marriage and the Family,* 1967, *29,* 249–256.

PARRISH, J. B. Women in professional training. *Monthly Labor Review,* 1974, *97*(May), 40–43.

PRESSER, H. Perfect fertility control: Consequences for women and the family. In C. F. Westoff et al. (Eds.), *Toward the end of growth.* Englewood Cliffs, N.J.: Prentice-Hall, 1973.

RILEY, M. W., JOHNSON, M., and FONER, A. (Eds.). *Aging and society.* New York: Russell Sage Foundation, 1972.

SUTER, L.E., and MILLER, H. P. Components of differences between the incomes of men and career women. *American Journal of Sociology,* 1973, *79,* 962–974.

SWEET, J. A. *Women in the labor force.* New York: Seminar Press, 1973.

U.S. DEPARTMENT OF COMMERCE, BUREAU OF THE CENSUS. Educational attainment in the United States: March 1973 and 1974 (P-20, No. 274). *Current Population Reports.* Washington, D.C.: Author, December 1974. (a)

U.S. DEPARTMENT OF COMMERCE, BUREAU OF THE CENSUS. Female family heads (P-23, No. 50). *Current Population Reports.* Washington, D.C.: Author, July 1974. (b)

U.S. DEPARTMENT OF COMMERCE, BUREAU OF THE CENSUS. Fertility histories and birth expectations of American women: June 1971 (P-20, No. 263). *Current Population Reports.* Washington, D.C.: Author, April 1974. (c)

U.S. DEPARTMENT OF COMMERCE, BUREAU OF THE CENSUS. Marital status and living arrangements: March 1974 (P-20, No. 271). *Current Population Reports.* Washington, D.C.: Author, October 1974. (d)

U.S. DEPARTMENT OF COMMERCE, BUREAU OF THE CENSUS. Fertility expectations of American women: June 1974 (P-20, No. 277). *Current Population Reports.* Washington, D.C.: Author, February 1975. (a)

U.S. DEPARTMENT OF COMMERCE, BUREAU OF THE CENSUS. Population profile of the United States: 1974 (P-20, No. 279). *Current Population Reports.* Washington, D.C.: Author, March 1975. (b)

U.S. DEPARTMENT OF COMMERCE, BUREAU OF THE CENSUS. School enrollment—Social and economic characteristics of students: October 1974 (P-20, No. 278). *Current Population Reports.* Washington, D.C.: Author, February 1975. (c)

U.S. DEPARTMENT OF LABOR. *Manpower report of the President.* Washington, D.C.: U.S. Government Printing Office, annual.

WALDMAN, E., and MC EADDY, B. J. Where women work—An analysis by industry and occupation. *Monthly Labor Review,* 1974, *97*(May), 3–13.

WALDMAN, E., and WHITMORE, R. Children of working mothers. *Monthly Labor Review,* 1974, *97*(May), 50–58.

The Socialization Process of Women

Chrysee Kline

Literature dealing with the occupational involvement of Americans has for the most part been based on male work history, and, except for very recent working generations, neglects the substantially different pattern of women (see, for example, Hughes, 1958; de Grazia, 1964; Kreps, 1971). Jackson has commented that this reflects "an implicit assumption that the working roles of women are relatively unimportant and that retirement is not a significant stage for women" (Jackson, 1971).

With few exceptions, some of which are noted below, retirement studies that include women do so only in relation to their reactions as wives toward the retirement of their husbands (Heyman and Jeffers, 1968).

Career Development

Cumming's (1974) position, too, is that women's basic difference from men lies in having experienced a much "smoother" life cycle:

> Disengagement from central life roles is basically different for women than for men, perhaps because women's roles are essentially unchanged from girlhood to death. In the course of their lives, women are asked to give up only pieces of their core socioemotional roles or to change their details. Their transitions are therefore easier. . . .

Others have reported on informative studies concerning work roles of women. Lopata and Steinhart (1971) studied work experiences of metropolitan Chicago widows aged 50 or over and succeeded in demonstrating the marginality of older women vis-à-vis the occupational structure of the society. Most typical of the respondents was an "inflexible work history involving routinized and directed jobs handled passively." The average subject had a very uneven employment history and had dropped out of the labor market several times during her life, withdrawing to the home to perform the roles of wife, mother, and housewife. In general, however, the work histories of these older

Reprinted from *The Gerontologist*, December, 1975, pp. 486–492.

women reflect frequent engagement in the work world. Most of those respondents who had continuous or almost continuous work histories shared several characteristics: they spent relatively few years in marriage, entering late in life and/or being widowed or separated; they had no children or only one offspring; and they moved around frequently. The jobs they took were the ones available conveniently at the time they were looking, with no program of career-type succession. Part-time work was common after retirement.

Despite the heavy use of the working world during their life cycle, the older women interviewed in Chicago did not place much value on the role of worker in the list of social roles most often performed by women. The role of worker is not assigned major importance by widows, women who never married, and those who never performed the role of mother. The American culture, locating women in the home as wives and mothers, has had so strong an influence on housewives (Lopata, 1971a) and widows (Lopata, 1972) as to prevent the roles of worker, citizen, and even friend from reaching the top three positions in a six-rank scale of importance.

While Williams and Wirths (1965) do not discuss the differential career development of men and women, they do consider differences between their career patterns. Although they give attention to homemaking as the primary career role of women, they fail to specify career patterns in terms of an acceptance of work as a primary or secondary mode of validating identity. This distinction seems crucial, because many who work are unable and/or unwilling to work full-time consistently throughout the year.

Roles

The basic notion of the concept of role, as employed in this paper, is focused on descriptive real life roles such as parent, spouse, worker, retiree, widow. Involved in these roles and many others which older persons enact are three basic conceptual distinctions: the normative, the behavioral, the interactional. A role is always associated with a position in a social structure, organization, or group. These positions are normatively defined, and these norms establish expectations for what is appropriate behavior to the role. A second major dimension is the behavioral or performance aspect. This component is what a person does in enacting a certain role or set of roles. Almost all roles are interactional, encompassing "both the behaving organism and the expectancies which the perceiving organism has regarding his behavior" (Steinmann, 1963)—that is, they involve some kind of social exchange with other persons who are, i.e., parent, child, spouse, worker, supervisor.

Each person normally has several roles to enact because of the various positions occupied in the different institutional aspects of the social structure. In the context of role theory, the enactment of these multiple roles is considered to be the primary basis for most of a person's behavior, attitudes, values, prestige, and personal integration. The "role theory perspective," as defined by Biddle and Thomas (1966) is:

> a limited social determinism that ascribes much but rarely all of the variance of real-life behavior to the operation of immediate or past external influences. Such influences include prescriptive framework of demands and rules, the behavior of others as it facilitates or hinders and rewards or punishes the person, the positions of which the person is a member, and the individual's own understanding of, and reactions to these factors.

The problem of analyzing roles at any stage of the life cycle is complicated by the fact that the person has a number of intersecting and overlapping roles which must be undertaken—sometimes simultaneously and sometimes sequentially, according to the expectations of that particular situation. This problem is accentuated for the female who, according to Atchley (1972), is under greater pressure to assume a number of conflicting roles throughout the life cycle than is the male. For the female, the various roles of worker, housewife, and mother occupy different priority positions at different points throughout the life cycle. Although the male's "role set," or "complement of role specializations" (Biddle and Thomas, 1966) throughout the life cycle also typically consists of a number of roles, the role of worker consistently occupies the greatest area of "role space."

The reasons for the predominance of the role of workers are twofold: (1) it is the one role which most frequently takes precedence over other roles, and (2) the one which derives greater societal rewards relative to rewards from other male roles (Palmore, 1965).

Work Role

Historical tables of United States labor force participation rates (Gallaway, 1965) suggest a much greater degree of fluctuation in importance of the work role for today's aged woman. A female born in 1900, for example, probably entered the labor force during or immediately after finishing high school, then retired to her home to bear and rear children, perhaps re-entered employment outside the home during World War II, and then exited again. The Women's Bureau reported that about 9 out of 10 women work outside the home sometime during their lives, whether they marry or not. Marriage and the presence of children tend to curtail employment, while widowhood, divorce, and the decrease of family responsibilities tend to attract into the work force (Women's Bureau, 1969). During 1973, the highest proportion of women in the labor force was between 20–24 years of age (61 per cent). After this there is a sudden drop in the proportion of women who are working, followed by an upswing until the high of

53.4 per cent between the ages of 45 and 54 years. (U.S. Dept. of Commerce, 1974, Table 543).

Other recent trends show that among married women aged 25 to 44 living with their husbands, the proportion in the labor force increased by 41 per cent between 1960 and 1973, from 33.1 per cent to 46.4 per cent, and among wives between the ages of 45 and 64 years, the proportion of workers increased similarly (U.S. Dept. of Commerce, 1974, Table 545). One important consideration, however, is that the employment figures of women in the labor force often camouflage a minimal level of involvement. Only 42 per cent of those women who worked some time in 1967 did so full time the year round (Women's Bureau, 1969). Thus, despite strong indication that women will continue to increase their number of years of work involvement over the life cycle, and despite a seeming gradual change in attitude of the traditional culture toward women's roles, the intermittent nature of the female work career will most likely continue, and the work cycles of women will remain clearly distinguishable from those of men.

Lopata (1966) maintains the social role of housewife has a unique cycle compared to other roles, involving relatively little anticipatory socialization, very brief time devoted to the "becoming" stage, and a rather compressed and early peak. It can be performed during the major part of the life cycle of a woman, yet "its entrance, modifications, and cessation are usually not a consequence of its own characteristics or rhythm but of those of other roles." She goes on to explain that some women never become "inside-located," so that the return to work or other community involvement (of married women) after the birth of the children is rapid and complete. Women who have placed themselves in the home and for whom the housewife role became important may be attracted to the outside or forced out of the inside by a feeling of obligation to help in the financial support of the family, or through crises such as widowhood. Those who do not go out completely, but do so part time, include women who have never cut off ties with the outside, or who develop new lines of connection. They most frequently combine both orientations through the addition of some outside role, such as part-time worker, without letting such identification grow into a total commitment. Most of the aforementioned Chicago interviewees, even those who had full time employment outside of the home, expressed an "inside" identity.

Housewife Role

The "shrinking circle" stage in the social role of housewife starts when the first child is married or has left home and is very difficult for women who have invested their lives in that role and who do not have alternative sources for the focusing of identity. According to Lopata (1966), the "shrinking" of the "circle" removes many of the sources of prestige without any choice or control on the part of the woman whose identity is bound with it. No matter how well she performs it, how many and how important are the persons for whom it is performed, or how significant is the role in the lives of recipients, modern society automatically decreases the ability of the role of housewife to serve as a center of relations. Thus, "the housewife ceases to perform the role at a high plateau level, long before capacity to carry out its duties decreases, providing a reason or excuse for its cessation." Changes in the role come basically and primarily from changes in characteristics of the circle prior to any changes in her which could provide justification for decreasing functionality. Furthermore, the shrinking of the role importance of housewife and mother cannot always lead to a shift of self and of role-focus to a concentration on the role of wife, if such an emphasis was absent, since the husband tends still to be highly involved in the role of worker.

Also, according to Lopata (1966), for those aging women who have survived the "shrinking circle" stage, fewer decision-making problems, a lack of pressure from demanding and often conflicting roles, satisfaction with past performance of the role of housewife and with the products of the role of mother, and prior adjustment to the lack of centrality in the lives of children can all contribute to a relatively high degree of satisfaction in the later years. For those who are not widows, the focal nature of the role of wife may be increased with the retirement, or "fade out," from occupational roles on the part of the spouse. Widowhood is more likely to occur for females than for males (Lopata, 1972); at any point during the life cycle, death of a spouse could cause a major transformation in the social role of housewife and could demand a role realignment.

Thus, the life cycle of a human being can be seen as involving shifts in the components of his or her role cluster, when new ones are added and old ones dropped, and when shifts occur in the location of each role in the cluster. The general attitude which seems to pervade the gerontological literature is that while circumstances and family composition may vary over time, the female's identification with the roles of wife, mother, homemaker, and worker remains unchanged throughout her adult life.

Retirement Role

The facts *are*, however, that the female is constantly undergoing modifications in the characteristics of each assigned role as she enters different stages of the life cycle or changes her definition of the role, in response to events external to the person. Heyman (1970) remarks that while some wives may retire as many as three different times during a lifetime, these retirements obviously differ from the "retirement" of a man who at a relatively advanced age and with declining physical health is facing a single, final separation from his central life role as a wage-earner and principal provider for his family. The male is faced with loss of what has heretofore been conceived as a permanent work role, reduced economic resources, and necessity for role realignment and the need for new role opportunities. For today's elderly women, on the other hand, retirement may have begun quite early in her lifetime and have recurred periodically.

There currently exists considerable disagreement as to the impact of retirement upon the male. Miller's (1965) identity crisis theory suggests that retirement in and of itself negatively influences the quality of one's life, while Atchley's (1971) identity continuity theory posits that work is not necessarily at the top of several roles on which one's identity rests and that its removal is not regarded negatively by most retired people. However, there is a general consensus in the literature that retirement rarely poses any problems for women because "she is merely giving up a secondary role in favor of the primary roles of housewife, mother, and grandmother" (Palmore, 1965).

Role Continuity and Discontinuity

The writer would agree with Lowenthal and Berkman (1967) that "adjustment to the later stages of life may be more gradual for women than for men," and with McEwan and Sheldon (1969) that "women tend to be more satisfied at retirement than men," but would not attribute the positive adjustment to the static nature of women's roles from girlhood to grave. Rather, it appears that the impact of socialization on American women creates *impermanence* in the form of role loss and repeated adjustment to change in the life situation—and that this socialization process facilitates adjustment of women to old age.

Our society defines "permanence" as having a long-lasting, viable social and economic role. While it appears that this "permanence" is relatively accessible to at least middle-majority males, for women it is tenuous and thwarted. Women of all educational, geographical, and economic positions have been subjected to changes produced by our modern industrial society. Increasing mobility, for example, has changed the complexion cf American society in the diminution of the extended family structure in its varied form as well as its demands upon individuals. The striving of women for permanence is dead-ended numerous times during the life cycle, resulting in role *discontinuity* or change in life situation. This striving for permanence is periodically redirected until old age when societal roles for the aged, both male and female, are further withdrawn.

Failure to attain permanence is exhibited throughout the entire social life cycle of women. Role losses impede attaining permanence before facing the impermanence impact of old age. Symbols of permanence that are thwarted, resulting in role discontinuity and changes in life situation, are numerous.

As stated by Steinmann (1963), the feminine role is "not only ill-defined, but full of contradictions, ambiguities, and inconsistencies. Education, for instance, prepared women for membership in the labor force; yet many parents still raise their daughters with a view of marriage rather than furthering their personal development through employment. The women who are processed through the educational system and then marry experience a strong role discontinuity, as described by Decter (1971). For the woman who disbands her work role to give priority to roles of mother and housewife, there is discontinuity when the children leave home or become increasingly independent of home and parents. Another role discontinuity to consider is the disrupted marital status such as widowhood. In 1968, the wife was the surviving spouse in 70 per cent of all marriages broken by the death of one partner (Lopata, 1971b). Although men also suffer the loss of husband role through widowhood, the loss is experienced by fewer numbers of men and is not coupled with financial loss due to widowhood.

Thus, role discontinuity and change in life situation are more likely suffered by women than men. Adjustments to the discontinuities are imposed on women by society through the socialization process.

It is suggested here, then, that precisely because women *are* subjected to repeated role discontinuities and changes in life situation to which they adjust, the final adjustment to old age is made more easily by them.

Readjustment Theory

Cottrell (1942) maintains that an individual will make a facile adjustment to a role change to the extent that he has undergone anticipatory preparation for that role situation. Women have had considerable experience in adjusting to age-linked changes (children leaving home, menopause) and have therefore become accustomed to change and impermanence. Thus, women are not as devastated as men are likely to be when old age, another impermanence, separates them from the productive, involved, financially independent world of middle age; and the adoption of new roles and the giving up of middle-age roles should be relatively more facile for women than for men. If this theory of repeated readjustment fosters adjustment to old age for women more readily than for men is valid, one should be able to demonstrate that the process of adjustment to aging, especially as it reflects a response to impermanence or discontinuity, is different for men than for women.

Mulvey (1963) organized what data she had found on characteristics of women's vocational behavior into seven career patterns, defined in terms of a career with and without marriage, and with and without work. Her study of women between the ages of 50 and 60 years concludes that high life satisfaction is associated with career patterns marked by: (1) return to career after children entered school ("inter-rupted-work primary"), (2) entry upon deferred career ("delayed-work secondary"), (3) contribution of talent and time to volunteer activities when children were young ("stable homemaking-work secondary"), (4) continuous and simultaneous homemaking and working. The vocational behavior of women who displayed the least degree of life satisfaction was characterized by a single, continuous role of either homemaker or worker over the adult life-span. The woman with a greater degree of life satisfaction has experienced more discontinuity and change of primary roles over the lifetime.

Dunkle (1972) reanalyzed data from Schooler's (1969) study of non-institutionalized elderly to investigate the relationship of length of time at residential location, distance moved, change in marital status, and change in position within the labor force to morale in old age. The value of her work in application to this paper's hypothesis is greatly enhanced by the inclusion of sex differentiation in her sample. Her results show that 47.1 per cent of the men experiencing only a small degree of change in residence, marital status, and work involve-ment have high morale, while 51.8 per cent of those men who have experienced a considerable amount of change over the life cycle dis-play high morale, a difference of 4.3 percentage points; 6.3 per cent more women who display a large amount of change over their lives have higher morale than the women characterized by stability in resi-dence, marital status, and work involvement. Furthermore, Dunkle's data show that almost twice as many women as men experience change with relation to the tested variables.

With admittedly weak measures in the sense that the data were not originally intended for this purpose, Dunkle's study suggests that women are socialized differently from men such that they were in the past more likely to experience discontinuity and impermanence, and that women, in fact, are better able to adjust in old age as a result of this past impermanence in life situations. It seems, therefore, that if discontinuity could be shown to be positively associated with adjust-ment to old age as measured by morale, there would be important implications for a theory of successful aging, based on discontinuity and impermanence over the life cycle.

Work and Leisure Patterns

Probably the most feasible method of building an option for discon-tinuity into our societal structure would be to revamp our current work and leisure patterns. Kreps (1971) points out:

> The individual's choice seems to have little to do with how much he works. At any point in time, institutional arrangements largely dictate the terms of nonworking time, i.e., when it occurs and who receives it.

Compulsory retirement at age 65 is one example; the statutory 40-hour week, as well as negotiated vacation plans, help to standardize the length of the workyear. It is important to raise the question of worker preference: preference as to how much free time one would elect, under any given income status; and preference as to when that free time would be taken. "For there may be ways to bend the institutions to the workers' wishes, once they are known" (Kreps, 1971).

Little is known about people's perceptions of the worth of free time; certainly, there is no evidence on the price that will be paid for time off. Most important, there is the question of whether leisure becomes more or less valuable as one grows older. Research might indicate that retirement in the optional years has the effect of conferring leisure on man when he least wants it—a curious inversion of the notion that youth is wasted on the young. The total number of workers involved in career changes during middle age or later worklife might increase, moreover, if such changes were made to be viable alternatives to present continuous cycles of employment.

Senator Mondale (Special Committee on Aging, 1969), a member of the Senate Special Committee on Aging, called for the altering of traditional work lifetime patterns, including institution of sabbaticals, phased retirement, trial retirement, and part-time work arrangements for those near retirement years. Such experiments, however, have been limited. For most elderly males, retirement, whether compulsory or voluntary, has provided the first opportunity for considerable amounts of leisure time throughout all of the adult years. It is no wonder then that renouncing the primary work role and substituting new roles for which there has been little change for "rehearsal" presents difficulty for the male.

Lopata and Steinhart (1971) suggest it might be valuable for our society to assume that few persons actually benefit from working in one occupation for more than perhaps 10 years, and that, with some exceptions, those who do produce diminishing returns for the organization. More efficient methods of education could then be introduced to retrain people at the end of each "natural cycle" of involvement in a particular occupation. We still lack adequate re-engagement procedures in the work world, because of a myth that modern workers work continuously and have steady careers from education to retirement. This fiction does not reflect lives of men, let alone women.

Career Flexibility

Recently, important strides are beginning to be made in liberating women to engage in meaningful employment and in liberating society at large to make positions of power available to women. Perhaps the seeming goal to attain the same rigid, life-long role to which most males in our society are now subjected should be reconsidered by women's activist groups. If the theory that impermanence and discontinuity over the adult life cycle exert a direct effect upon positive adjustment to old age is valid, then a new system of career flexibility should be adopted as the new battle cry by men and women alike.

References

ATCHLEY, R. C. Retirement and leisure participation: Continuity or crisis? *Gerontologist*, 1971, 11 (1:1), 13–17.

ATCHLEY, R. C. Role changes in later life. In R. C. Atchley (Ed.), *The social forces in later life*. Wadsworth, Belmont, CA, 1972.

BIDDLE, B. J. and THOMAS, E. J. (Eds.) *Role theory: Concepts and research*. Wiley & Sons, New York, 1966.

COTTRELL, L. S., Jr. The adjustment of the individual to his age and sex roles. *American Sociological Review*, 1942, 7, 617–622.

CUMMING, M. E. New thoughts on the theory of disengagement. In R. Kastenbaum (Ed.), *New thoughts on old age*. Springer, New York, 1964.

DECTER, M. *The liberated woman and other Americans*. Coward, McCann, & Geoghegan, New York, 1971.

DEGRAZIA, S. *Of time, work and leisure*. Anchor Books, Garden City, NY, 1964

DUNKEL, R. E. Life experiences of women and old age. Paper presented at 25th annual meeting of Gerontological Society, San Juan, Dec. 17–21, 1972.

GALLAWAY, L. E. *The retirement decision: An exploratory essay*. Report No. 9. USDHEW, Washington, 1965.

HEYMAN, D. K. Does a wife retire? *Gerontologist*, 1970, *10*, 54–56.

HEYMAN, D. K., and JEFFERS, F. C. Wives and retirement: A pilot study. *Journal of Gerontology*, 1968, *23*, 488–496.

HUGHES, E. C. *Men and their work*. Free Press, Glencoe, IL, 1958.

JACKSON, J. J. Negro aged: Toward needed research in social gerontology. *Gerontologist*, 1971, *11*, 52–57.

KREPS, J. M. Career options after fifty: Suggested research. *Gerontologist*, 1971, *11* (1:2), 4–8.

LOPATA, H. Z. The life cycle of the social role of the housewife. *Sociology & Social Research*, 1966, *51*, 5–22.

LOPATA, H. Z. *Occupation: Housewife.* Oxford Press, New York, 1971. (a)

LOPATA, H. Z. Widows as a minority group. *Gerontologist*, 1971, *11* (1:2), 22–27. (b)

LAPATA, H. Z. *Widowhood in an American city*. Schenkman, Boston, 1972.

LAPATA, H. Z. and STEINHART, F. Work histories of American urban women. *Gerontologist*, 1971, *11*, (4:2), 27–36.

LOWENTHAL, M. F., and BERKMAN, P. *Aging and mental disorder in San Francisco*. Jossey-Bass, San Francisco, 1967.

MCEWAN, P. J. M., and SHELDON, A. P. Patterns of retirement. *Journal of Geriatric Psychiatry*, 1969, *3*, 35–54.

MILLER, S. J. The social dilemma of the aging leisure participant. In A. M. Rose and W. A. Peterson (Eds.), *Older people and their social world*. Davis, Philadelphia, 1965.

MULVEY, M. C. Psychological and sociological factors in prediction of career patterns of women. *Genetic Psychological Monographs*, No. 68, 1963.

PALMORE, E. B. Differences in the retirement patterns of men and women. *Gerontologist*, 1965, *5*, 4–8.

SCHOOLER, K. K. The relationship between social interaction and morale of the elderly as a function of environmental characteristics. *Gerontologist,* 1969, *9,* 25–29.

SPECIAL COMMITTEE ON AGING. The federal role in encouraging preretirement counselling and new work lifetime patterns. Hearing before the Subcommittee on Retirement and the Individual of the Special Committee on Aging, U. S. Senate, 91st Congress, 1st Session, July 25, 1969.

STEINMANN, A. A study of the concept of the feminine role of 51 middle class American families. *Genetic Psychological Monographs,* No. 67, 1963.

U. S. DEPT. OF COMMERCE, Bureau of the Census. *Statistical abstracts of the U. S.* Washington, 1974.

WILLIAMS, R. H., and WIRTHS, C. G. *Lives through the years.* Atherton Press, New York, 1965.

WOMEN'S BUREAU. *1969 Handbook on women workers,* Bull. No. 294, U. S. Dept. of Labor, Washington, 1969.

Counseling and Career (Self) Development of Women

L. Sunny Hansen

Counselors today need to be concerned about the career development of women as well as the career development of men. For, as we are well aware, women do not exist in a vacuum or make decisions in a vacuum; what women do and can do affects and is affected by the perceptions and actions of men. By the same token, the limitations put on female development also create obstacles and prescriptions for the way men act, behave, and grow. Yet, it seems appropriate that special focus on the career planning and counseling process for women is justified at this point in time, though perhaps it will not be necessary in another 12 or 15 years. And perhaps, as human liberationists have pointed out, both men and women eventually will have more options open to them as a result of the current attention to the concerns and development of girls and women.

It is an underlying assumption of this article that both men and women can have greater control over their lives and development if both males and females, counselors and teachers all accept some re-

Reprinted from *Focus on Guidance,* December 1974, pp. 1–15.

sponsibility for doing something about women's untapped resources, talents, and potentials. It would seem logical that counselors, who are supposed to be facilitators of human growth and development, should be key persons in bringing about changes in this area, in public school, college, and vocational school settings, not only through counseling but also through curriculum interventions and consultation with teachers. This article attempts to make a case for such interventions by (1) reviewing some of the literature on female self-concepts, career patterns, and aspirations; (2) summarizing the facts about women in the work force and obstacles to women's career development; (3) suggesting practical approaches to facilitate female development through counseling and curriculum; and (4) offering a few multimedia resources to assist in the above task.

Societal Trends and Changing Life Patterns

A number of societal trends and changing work and family patterns have contributed to the changing roles of women and particularly to their increased participation in work and community. While it is difficult to assess the rate and strength of movements, it seems reasonable to say that these trends (Hansen, 1974b) are having an impact on women's career development and the roles of men as well. A few of them are cited below:

1. Technology, labor-saving devices, and the "decline of motherhood" as a full-time occupation.
2. The population explosion and birth control with its powerful effects on norms and decisions regarding number of children.
3. Legislation and federal regulations providing a legal context for improving the status of women in education and work.
4. The Women's Movement which has highlighted issues and concerns about equal rights in a variety of sectors and the concomitant movement for men's liberation.
5. New life styles and female sense of identity—the movement toward a more androgynous society in which roles in work and family are shared, diverse family patterns are acknowledged, and women are risking different kinds of patterns and self-definitions based on their own needs.
6. Increasing numbers of part-time jobs and day-care centers making part-time work and more humanized day-care facilities more available.
7. Continuing education with its opportunities for women to enter and re-enter education and/or work and to update or retrain for new fields.
8. Breakdown of occupational and career stereotypes so that continuous career patterns and dual or equal partnership marriage

patterns are becoming more common and both male and female occupational stereotypes are being reduced.

Female Career Patterns

There is no full-blown theory of female career development. While most of the career development literature has dealt with male populations, Super (1957) postulated a "Logical Scheme" of women's career patterns. He identified seven kinds of female patterns, including what he labels the stable homemaking, the conventional, the stable working pattern, a double-track pattern, the interrupted pattern, the unstable pattern, and multiple trial pattern. The first attempt of any major theorist to direct his attention toward female participation in the world of work, Super's descriptive schema was prefaced with the somewhat prescriptive statement, "Woman's role as childbearer makes her the keystone of the home and, therefore, gives homemaking a central place in her career."

Others also have offered descriptions of women's patterns by socioeconomic divisions. In 1968, for example, Psathas suggested the importance of cultural and situational factors and chance elements in the environment which limit women's freedom of vocational choice. Anastasi (1969) identified the blue-collar pattern, the active volunteer, the interim job, the late-blooming career, and the double-life pattern. Zytowski (1969), like Super, began his "contribution toward a theory" with the assumption that the modal role of woman is homemaker. He then identified three factors which affect female vocational development: (1) age of entry into an occupation, (2) span of participation, and (3) degree of participation. Combinations of these elements yield three different vocational patterns which he labeled the mild vocational, the moderate vocational, and the "unusual" (the latter being the career-oriented woman).

These theories are important not because they provide the last word on women's career development but because they open the doors to research and provide some beginning attempts to understand women in other than traditional stereotypic roles. They also offer support for the thesis that women's life patterns are not uniform and that a variety of life styles and multiple roles are possible, desirable, and feasible for women as well as for men.

Sex Role Socialization

There is another growing body of literature on women's growth and development that offers startling evidence of the limits on that growth. Although space does not allow detailed summary here, the studies of early sex role socialization present convincing evidence of the programming of girls and boys for prescribed roles (Hochschild, 1973; Hartley, 1960; Maccoby, 1966; Weitzman et al., 1972). The textbook messages are clear: boys are active, outdoor, strong, and breadwinners; girls are passive, dependent, weak, and homemakers; boys need to be able to be smart, to take care of themselves, boss, do a variety of jobs; girls are to stay behind, watch, wait, work puzzles, help boys, and stay home (New Jersey Commission on Women, 1972). In one book of phonics, the 21 consonants are boys, the 5 vowels are girls. The girls all have something wrong with them; when put with the consonants, the girls lose their names and their identities. One book about girls shows a defected little girl sitting on the steps asking, almost plaintively, "What can I do?" The parallel book about boys shows a standing, active, happy boy saying, What I *can* do. Girls group up narcissistic, asking "How will I look? What will I wear?" Boys learn early that they can be, as one pre-school book for four- to six-year-olds suggests,

A pirate, a sailor, a gypsy, a knight,
An actor, a cowboy, a king.
I'll be strong, it shouldn't take long,
I'll be five by spring.

That this programming is reinforced in early childhood became evident recently at my daughter's sixth birthday party. Having bought a variety of inexpensive role-free gifts for the children to fish out of an imaginary pond, I let the children fish randomly for such toys as police set, doctor set, binoculars, jump ropes, dental set, nurse set, etc. While the game was in progress, I was surprised to find one of the girls in tears. When asked what was the matter, she replied that she had gotten a dental set and that was for boys; she wanted jewelry instead. It was interesting, however, that one of the other girls, whose father was a dentist, also had randomly fished out a dental set; she was pleased because her father wanted her to become a dentist (she was one of three daughters).

Obviously, we are not trying to force children to make choices regarding what they want to be at the tender age of six; we *do* want them to fantasize and develop their sexual identity (as different from traditional sex roles). However, such examples are significant because as studies such as those by Goodman and Schlossberg (1972) have shown children link occupations with sexes and begin the premature occupational foreclosure process early in life.

Female Self-concepts and Aspirations

What does this early conditioning do to female self-concepts and aspirations? Matthews and Tiedeman (1964) found that girls who had expressed strong vocational goals in junior high had shifted to marriage goals in senior high, although the more recent study by Rand and Miller (1972) suggested that a new cultural imperative for women was being expressed in the options perceived by girls in junior high, senior high, and college—that of the dual role of career and marriage. Other studies have cited women's lack of vocational goals and realistic planning (Lewis, 1965; Zytowski, 1969) though more recent studies, such as the follow-up study on Project Talent population, reveal girls as showing more concern for career planning and wanting more control over their own lives (Flanagan and Jung, 1971).

Horner's widely quoted study of female career motivation (1968), though recently replicated with different results (Hoffman, 1974), does give cause for reflection. Academically talented college females, asked to complete a story about "Anne, who was graduating at the top of her medical class," revealed all kinds of "fear of success" themes, fantasies that it couldn't be true—having Anne drop to eighth in the class and marrying the boy at the top; seeing her as an acne-faced bookworm experiencing feelings of rejection, loneliness, and doubts about her femininity; having her see a counselor who suggests that she try nursing, and the like. The young women simply could not cope with the image of Anne as a competent, feminine person who might be able to have a successful career and marriage. In another oft-quoted study of Broverman et al. (1970), mental health practitioners were asked to describe a mature, well-adjusted man, woman, and person. The descriptions for the well-adjusted person and well-adjusted man coincided. However, the well-adjusted woman was described as more submissive, less independent, less adventurous, more easily influenced, less aggressive, less competitive, more emotional, exictable, and vain, and less interested in science and mathematics. While the results of self-concept studies are conflicting, some of the investigations of female self-concepts have found that girls tend to devalue themselves and other girls and that both boys and girls value males more than females. These studies seem to indicate a number of factors which mitigate against women feeling very good about themselves as achieving, motivated, participating human beings.

Women in the Work Force

What happens when we move from the theoretical descriptions of women's lives and the sociological and psychological studies of their self-perceptions and aspirations to the realities of their participation in the work world? Even here the data can be somewhat shocking, especially to the high school boy or girl who may find it difficult to internalize the information. While there are numerous myths about working women, there is an abundance of data available on the nature and extent of women's participation in education and work—data gathered by occupational analysts in the U. S. Department of Labor.

Women and Employment

It is well-known, for example, that there are some 32 million working women, comprising one third of the labor force; that 42 per cent of all women are working, over half of them married; that most women work for economic reasons; that the number of employed mothers, even those with small children, has increased; and that there is an increasing proportion of female heads of households.

We are told that the average woman marries at 20 (although some women appear to be marrying later and having fewer children), has her last child at age 26, her last child in school by 32. The average age of women in the labor force is now 42. With a life expectancy of 74 or 75, the average woman can expect to have 30-35 years after children (if she has them) are in school to develop new meaning and interests in the second half of her life. A chart prepared by the California Advisory Commission on the Status of Women presents very vividly a typical married woman's life (Figure 1). Of course there is considerable variation in work force figures, dependent on whether the woman is from a minority or poverty family, her marital status, the number of children she has, the amount of education she has, and her work motivation. But the long-range Labor Department projections are that 9 of 10 girls will marry; 8 of 10 will have children; 9 of 10 will be employed outside the home for some period of time; 6 of 10 will work full-time outside their homes for up to 30 years; 1 of 10 will be widowed before age 50; 1 of 10 will be heads of families; probably 3 of 10 will be divorced; and 1 of 5 will obtain a college degree (Impact, 1972).

Occupational Distribution

One of the hard realities is that women who are working are concentrated in a few occupations; many of them low-paying, low-level and dead-end. Although the *Dictionary of Occupational Titles* has classified approximately 23,000 different occupations in the United States, one-third of all working women are concentrated in only seven of them: retail sales clerk, secretary, household worker, elementary school teacher, bookkeeper, waitress, and nurse. An additional one-third are found in 20 occupations: for example, typist, cashier, cook, telephone operator, babysitter, assembler, hairdresser, stenographer, high school teacher, practical nurse, receptionist, maid, and file clerk (Bem and Bem, 1971). Only four million women—15 per cent of all women workers—are professional or technical workers: women comprise only 7 per cent of the physicians, 3 per cent of the lawyers, 1 per cent of the engineers. The proportion of women in professional jobs has declined over the past 30 years, from 45 per cent in 1940 to 37 per cent in 1969. Three of four clerical workers are women. The average full-time female worker makes three-fifths of the earnings of the full-time male worker in all occupational levels and fields. A

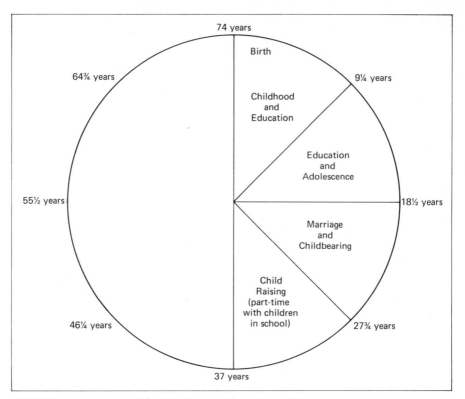

FIGURE 1. A Woman's Life. The blank half could be filled in with "vegetation," employment, political activity, community work, church or club work, etc., but should it not be filled with productivity and the utilization of talents, abilities, and interests? Do people stagnate if they don't continue to grow? What happens to a woman who hasn't worked in 20 years if she is suddenly widowed or divorced at age 43? Shouldn't the full-time homemaker's child-raising years be devoted part-time to continued education and preparation for the last half of her life? Prepared by California Advisory Commission on the Status of Women, 1972

more detailed presentation of these statistics appears in Kreps' (1971) *Sex in the Marketplace: American Women at Work* and Kievit et al. (1972) *Women in the World of Work* as well as in numerous pamphlets published by the Labor Department. Such are the realities of women and work.

Obstacles to the Career Development of Women

It must be apparent that the obstacles to the development of women are real and pervasive. While they have been alluded to, the most common ones are summarized below:

1. *Sex-Role Conditioning and Socialization.* If it is true, as appears increasingly to be so, that on many of the major variables in human development (self-concept, moral development, career aspirations,

peer evaluation) female development levels off in early adolescence, counselors need to be justly concerned. The image females get of themselves through our curriculum and child-rearing practices seems to have taken hold, the self-fulfilling prophesy comes true, and 78 per cent of women end up in the same role despite their individual differences.

2. *Role Conflicts About Fulfilling Multiple Roles in Marriage and Work.* While there is a natural expectation that men will be able to fill multiple roles of employee, husband, and father, we do not have that same expectation for women. Thus the woman who is considering both career and family may experience role conflict. Besides the fear of success and concern about femininity which Horner (1968) found, the woman may be caught between trying to vie with men in jobs, career, and business and at the same time trying to find an identity as wife, mother, and woman. She may face the problem of meeting the multiple demands on her once she has accepted multiple roles and may find she has to be a superwoman to meet those demands—to organize her time, to manage the household, to attend to her children, to have an abundance of energy—unless she has a partner who recognizes that such roles and household tasks can be shared. If she has small children, she may be criticized for not spending enough time with them—although the literature on the employed mother suggests that her children are no less well-adjusted than other children, that they are more independent, that they have more career aspirations and, when asked to name the person they would most like to be like, most frequently mention their mother (Bem and Bem, 1971).

Counselors increasingly must recognize that women's development is both a male and female concern, for when women increase their participation in work and community the lives of men and families will be affected. The problems of the re-entry woman with children, for example, may include the way in which her husband and children cope with her transition from a traditional to a contemporary woman. Problems associated with the changing roles and status of women require not only (1) the resocialization of men's attitudes towards women's roles, as Farrell suggests, but (2) the resocialization of women's attitudes towards men's roles and (3) of women's attitudes towards women's roles. As we move toward an androgynous society, we may see a greater variety of life patterns—the equal partnership marriage, in which both partners have professional careers and share that part of their career that is in the home; the two-person career, in which one job or appointment is shared by two partners who want to work 20 hours or so and have more time for other parts of their lives; the extended family, in which members develop alternative life patterns for work and family and leisure; or the single parent, who prefers not to marry but adopts a child. One of the ways we can reduce the role conflicts is to be more accepting of a variety of life patterns and life styles.

3. *Focus on Marriage or Its Prospect.* We know that the modal role is still marriage, in spite of increasing choices of the single life. But we as educators and parents need to make our young men and women aware of the fact that life does not end at 40 and that Prince Charming is not going to take care of his Princess forever. The modern fairy tale of "Atalanta" in *Free to Be You and Me* provides an excellent antidote to this myth. Young people need to be made aware of those last 25 to 35 years of a woman's life and to do some conscious planning for their preferred life style. Consistently studies have shown that girls lack planfulness, that they tend not to seek occupational information, that they lack realistic educational-occupational plans. If it is true that both boys and girls "do not know what information they need, do not have what they want, and cannot use what they have," we as counselors have a responsibility to help them get this information, to use it, and to internalize it in terms of their own goals, plans, abilities, preferred life styles, and self-images.

4. *Lack of Work Orientation.* While junior high girls and upward are beginning to see themselves in multiple roles, especially dual roles of career and marriage, women simply are not as work oriented as men, nor are they expected to be. Working outside the home in the past has not been as central to women as to men, and those who have career motives at the head of their motivational hierarchy are labeled "unusual" as Zytowski (1969) suggests. Concern for women's career development is not a movement to get every woman into the labor force but, rather, a concern for her uniqueness and individuality as a person and for her right to have some freedom of choice in both her personal and work life. It is concern about the overwhelmingly subordinate nature of women's roles—as nurses rather than doctors, teachers rather than principals, assembly workers rather than supervisors, secretaries rather than bosses, bank tellers rather than lending officers, administrative assistants rather than deans. It is concern about the ancillary nature of women's careers, with only small numbers in banking, engineering, medicine, and management. It is concern about the passivity and dependence that keep her from finding room at the top even if she has ability. It is concern about fear of competency that keeps her from maximizing her potentials and from making what Tyler (1972) has called first-class rather than second-class contributions to society. It is concern about the complexity of demands, pressures, and conflicts facing women at different life stages and the limited reward system which denies them the range of options and rewards available to men. What counselors need to do here has to do with changing self-concepts and expectations, opening up opportunities, and upgrading aspirations so that more talented women will be able to say not "What can I *do?*" but "What I *can* do."

5. *Sexism and Sex Discrimination.* While it is true that some of the barriers between women's work and men's work are being broken down, the discrimination in hiring, wages, and promotion is still very

real, affirmative action programs notwithstanding. The problems of conscious and nonconscious sexism (Bem and Bem, 1971) are as prevalent in education as in other parts of society. The Minnesota Board of Education passed a position paper offering nine suggestions for what school systems could do in "Eliminating Sex Bias in Education." There was little action in implementation until the Human Rights Division hired a person to coordinate implementation efforts around the state. Areas of concern include athletic budgets, promotion to administrative positions, curriculum texts and materials, counseling, career education, and the like. As educators, we need to look at ways in which we perpetuate discrimination and sexism through our actions, inactions, and even denials that a problem exists.

Practical Approaches to Facilitate Female Career Development

One of the things we know from organizational change literature is that it is futile to offer solutions before people recognize there is a problem. Unfortunately, to many parents and educators in higher education as well as K-12 settings, concern about women's career development is still considered a "ha-ha." It is an assumption of this paper that counselors view it as more than a "ha-ha."

Counselor Attitudes

Counselors have been indicted in the professional literature as being sexist. While we need much more data on this (and I do not assume that counselors are any more or less sexist than people in general), several studies have supported these charges. Thomas and Stewart (1971) found that secondary school counselors responded more positively to female clients with traditional (feminine) goals than to female clients with deviant (masculine) goals. Pietrofesa and Schlossberg (1973) found differences in counselor attitudes toward women entering "masculine" occupations. Fridersdorf (1973) examined attitudes of male and female secondary counselors toward college-bound and noncollege-bound girls and found males with more traditional expectations about female occupational choices. Bingham and House (1973a) found counselors to be misinformed on women's occupational status (on such issues as women in the work force, discrimination against women, income discrepancies, and the probability of women getting leadership jobs). Male counselors were found to be less well informed than female counselors (on such issues as the occupational alternatives needed by women, their general ability, women's ability to fill both worker and mother roles, and length of time in labor force). In a follow-up study on counselor attitudes toward women and work, the investigators (1973b) found that substantial numbers of male counselors had negative attitudes and agreed with such statements as "training women for high-level jobs is wasteful," "married men should receive more pay than single women doing the same work," and "boys should be better educated than girls." They also felt that motherhood is the primary function of woman. Hawley's study (1972), in contrast, suggested that female counselors hold a wider view of the roles of women. Such studies point up the need for counselors to become aware of their own attitudes and practices and ways in which these limit options for female clients.

Counseling Interventions

While the role of the counselor in school and college is changing in certain ways, it is likely that one-to-one counseling and group counseling procedures will still persist. Counselors can play a critical part (but not the only part) in counseling both boys and girls and men and women for changing roles in society. Matthews et al. (1972) have addressed themselves to the importance of counseling girls and women over the life span, from infancy through mature adulthood and old age. Tyler (1972) stressed the need for all individuals at various life stages to have counseling available regarding their multi-potentialities. Below are suggested a few counseling strategies that might help make a positive difference in the lives of females.

1. We need to become aware of our own conscious and nonconscious attitudes, expectations, and practices in the counseling interview.

There are a number of subtle and not-so-subtle things we do both verbally and nonverbally in our counseling that communicate to boys and girls what is acceptable or appropriate and what is not. In our interviews, how do we react when a girl says she wants to become a pilot, an engineer, or an auto mechanic? How do we help girls plan and choose their school courses and programs with open options? By the same token, how do we react when a boy says he wants to be a nurse? How much do our own sex-role stereotypes and expectations affect our counseling behavior? Among the things we might do to counteract our biases is to help females think of themselves as persons, to affirm their sense of personal worth, to face and work through their identity and role conflicts, to learn to say "I can." We need to be aware of the development stage the woman is at in her life span and "where she is coming from" as a person and as a woman.

2. We need to become increasingly aware of sex bias in guidance materials, tests and inventories, and our own bias in interpreting and using those materials.

Schlossberg and Goodman (1972) have called attention to the channeling that can occur through use of biased interest inventories. The

National Institute of Education (NIE) sponsored a national conference on this topic, resulting in a manual of "Guidelines for Assessment of Sex Bias and Sex Fairness in Career Interest Inventories" (NIE, 1974). It seems to me counselors have to be equally sensitive to other kinds of instruments, especially in career planning and exploration. A recent study by Birk, Cooper, and Tanney (1973) of illustrations in an array of career literature—including the *Occupational Outlook Handbook,* the *Encyclopedia of Careers and Vocational Guidance,* Volumes I and II, 1972, and the Science Research Associates Occupational Briefs, 1973 —revealed the same kinds of racial and sexual stereotypes that have been found in the children's textbooks and picture books: women and minorities appeared only infrequently in comparison with white males and often were in passive, helping, subordinate roles. If there is one major area in which counselors have been criticized, it is in our selection, use, and interpretation of tests, earlier with minorities and more recently with women; we would be well advised to examine our own test interpretation practices and to help eliminate from use those that are clearly biased in the way they present opportunities for men and women in the world of work.

3. We need to know and help clients obtain accurate information about trends both in the world of work and in the larger society.

We have to do a better job not only of getting accurate information ourselves but of helping boys and girls get the information they need and to use it. They need information about themselves, the labor force (present and projected), work environments, alternatives, and decision processes. Because of this expectation of marriage and the Prince Charming myth, many girls do not seek education-occupational information. Presumably if one is seeking a job merely as a stopgap until marriage, one does not need much information. When examining the human life cycle of women today and the second half of her life, ask what kind of information does she need? When, how, and under what circumstances do we get across the reality of what is happening to the woman in American society—that she may be working 25–35 years out of her life even if she marries and takes time out for childbearing? And how do boys obtain and react to that same kind of information? How do we help him and her to internalize the information? One way might be to provide group guidance and group counseling experiences in which boys and girls can talk together about these trends and what they mean in relation to both male and female goals and roles and family patterns and the possible androgynous society of the future.

4. We need to help young men and women become increasingly aware of the options available to them in a pluralistic society— in education, occupation, life styles, and career patterns.

We may have to help both boys and girls think through and plan for the multiple roles they may have as workers and parents. They need to be aware of the variety of life styles and family and work patterns from which they can choose and of potential conflicts involved in choosing one pattern over another (for example, single life, multiple children, two-person career, dual career without children, etc.). Particularly, we need to help female clients consider a wide range of educational and occupational options in addition to the traditional stereotypic ones. This becomes extremely important at a time when the traditional options, such as teaching, for example, are becoming less available. Society is beginning to realize that college is not the only road to success and that other excellent opportunities exist in such institutions as vocational-technical schools. With the small percentages of women in the skilled trades, we should encourage adolescent girls to explore new and emerging training programs and occupations and expose them to contact with women in atypical fields. While we need competent secretaries, teachers, and nurses (of both sexes), we do not want women programmed into limited types, numbers, or levels of occupations; we want to help female clients choose from that larger pool of alternatives those appropriate to their abilities, goals, interests, and motivations.

5. **We need to help young men and women learn the processes involved in decision making.**

If counselors really are concerned about human development, they have to help each individual, regardless of race, sex, or age, to know that s/he can choose in accord with his or her values, abilities, motivations, and preferences from a variety of life options. Clients need to be helped to explore the alternatives, the probability and possibility of achieving the alternatives, and the consequences of choices they make for both themselves and the significant others in their lives. They need to be able to examine themselves as risk takers, to critically evaluate the information about self and options, and to synthesize or integrate it as they think about themselves in relation to society. They need to be encouraged to challenge traditional assumptions and expectancies about roles and to realize that changing women's opportunities for different life patterns also have implications for work, family, and leisure patterns of men.

The problems of decision making for women have been cited often in the professional literature—the lack of planning orientation; the fear of loss of femininity if she chooses a career; the shift from vocational goals to marriage goals from junior to senior high; the assumption of marriage as the modal role and not perceiving the dual roles of marriage and work (or other patterns) as viable options. All of these contribute to the view that females do not have choices or decisions to make, that they do not have alternatives to choose from since they are programmed from early childhood for the one option of marriage and motherhood. If females are to develop their potentials to reduce the gap between what they do and what they can do, counselors must help them know and be able to choose and decide from diverse life patterns, from traditional nuclear family to single parent to single person to dichotomous or multiple roles; they need to be helped to know that they can have goals of their own and an identity of their own.

6. **We need to provide female clients with a variety of role models with whom they can identify and from whom they can learn that multiple roles are possible, desirable, and real.**

The importance of putting females in touch with women who are in nontraditional roles cannot be over-emphasized. Many of the early and late adolescents we counsel today are familiar only with the female image to which they have been exposed at home, in their school books, and in the media. Counselors can help broaden their views and expose them to wider options by helping identify women in the school and community who have chosen all kinds of career and family patterns.

7. **We need to involve parents more systematically and developmentally in the career development process of boys and girls.**

Since parents still have the greatest impact on their children's self-concepts, goals, attitudes, and aspirations, it is exceedingly important they be oriented to the facts about the life span of women, changes in the labor force, the need for career planning for girls, and the trends in work and family. Orientation and information groups for parents regarding the development of women's potentials might be one vehicle; perhaps what we need is a career development counterpart to parent effectiveness training called CDTP, Career Development Training for Parents.

These are just a few strategies we might use as counselors to become facilitators not only of female career development but of the development of all human beings for a variety of life roles.

Curriculum Interventions

The foregoing suggest modifications of traditional counselor roles in interviewing, in test interpretation, in career information, and in parent counseling. The other major thrust toward which counselors are moving today is a more central and direct involvement with curriculum, particularly through working with teachers in new ways. There seems to be a lot of support at every level of the educational process for counselors to move in the direction of outreach programs, to become a part of the mainstream of the teaching-learning process, and to take active leadership in changing the school system to more effectively promote the positive growth and development of students.

Career development or guidance-based career education offers an excellent vehicle for counselors to have some significant inputs. Since women, like minorities, by and large have been outside the educational and opportunity structure, special attention of counselors needs to be directed at this point in time to helping to eliminate the barriers and open up more opportunities. In a recent non-yet-finalized APGA Position Paper on "Counselor Role in Career Education," Hoyt (1974) recommends leadership in eliminating sexism and racism in career opportunity as one of six major counselor roles.

Elsewhere I have presented a career development conceptual framework for facilitating female growth (Hansen, 1974a). I would like to summarize it here. Such a framework is totally appropriate if one accepts the broad definition of career development as self-development over the life span. In our work on the Career Development Curriculum (CDC) at the University of Minnesota, Wes Tennyson, Mary Klaurens, and I have built on the concept of career development as a lifelong process of self-clarification, as a consequence of positions one holds in a lifetime, as the various choices and decisions one makes to implement a life style, and the ways work and leisure fit in with the kind of person one perceives herself or himself to be. This definition assumes that consideration of work is intimately related to family roles and patterns and to matters of career-marriage conflict and commitment. Drawing from career development theorists and development psychology, the definition includes such career management tasks as developing positive self-concepts, gaining control over one's life, and maximizing vocational possibilities; such as goals as awareness of self, awareness of preferred life styles, formulation of tentative career goals, clarification of the decision process, obtaining employability skills, interpersonal skills, a sense of planfulness, and commitment with tentativeness within a changing world (Tennyson, Hansen, Klaurens, in press).

A Conceptual Framework

The CDC is a comprehensive unified curriculum model, presently K-12, to be used by counselors and teachers in implementing career education programs. An interdisciplinary staff refined a set of career management tasks for the primary, intermediate, junior high, and senior high years, developed performance objectives appropriate for the various life stages, and suggested enabling objectives to reach them. A number of supplementary objectives relating to emerging life patterns of women were incorporated into the curriculum model, many of them relating to men as well. The objectives provide a framework for sequential, developmental experiences for boys and girls, a guide from which resourceful teachers and counselors can create their own lesson plans and learning activities. Although there are many innovative women's programs, units, and courses emerging throughout the country at various levels of school systems, few have attempted to build their efforts around a theoretical framework of career development. Since the CDC is only a conceptual model (intended for students in general), the intervention strategies have yet to be developed. A few resource guides for teachers and counselors are available under such titles as "Life Styles and Work," "Self-Concept Exploration," "Women and the World of Work," "Significant Others," "Value Identification," and "The Social Contribution of Work" (Minnesota Department of Education, 1972).

Intervention Strategies

Several educators have suggested a variety of curriculum interventions which could be tied to developmental goals. In a recent article (1972) I urged that counselors work with teachers in creating, planning, and teaching units aimed at the career development of females in the elementary, junior high, and senior high. Among suggestions for the elementary years were positive reinforcement and hands-on experiences with tools, auto mechanics, home maintenance, and political leadership; putting girls and boys in contact with atypical role models to help females gain the political savvy they need to assure equal opportunity; equal assignment of chores and leadership tasks; and utilization of both male and female community resource persons and media to show the work that humans do.

At the junior high we can use such strategies as helping teachers provide broad exploratory action-oriented experiences to introduce both sexes to the vocational and avocational implications of subjects; continued exposure to atypical role models both directly and through resource directories and multimedia; strength groups in which both boys and girls focus on potentials and develop action plans to become the kinds of persons they would like to be. Elimination of sex-linked courses in home economics and industrial arts is essential to keeping educational paths open to all kinds of occupations. Values clarification experiences, cross-age teaching, and tryout experiences tutoring young children can increase awareness of work opportunities and satisfactions.

At the senior high we need to help girls and boys continue their values clarification and examine their needs, drives, goals, interests, and abilities as they face real decisions about life style preferences and life patterns. They need information about the reality of discrimination, trends in the work force, stereotypes, and sexism. Apprentice or shadowing experiences with a variety of role models in preferred occupations and tryout tasks will help them reality test their preferences and tentative decisions. They need more specific information about educational paths and exposure to vocational specialties or college majors related to subjects in which they have a continuing interest and success. Direct courses in Psychology of Self, Psychology of Interpersonal Relations, and Psychology of Careers as well as Women's Studies can facilitate such development. Life Planning Labs in which students have an intensive opportunity to examine values, potentials, goals, and priorities can also be helpful, as could a variety of well planned consciousness raising and role reversal exercises. Strategies summarized by the author include infusion through curriculum, exploratory work experience (paid and unpaid), career resource centers and multimedia approaches, hands-on experiences, role models, counseling, cross-age teaching, and staff development.

Mitchell (1972) recommended that the miseducation of girls might be redressed through a variety of curriculum strategies not unlike those already mentioned. She also recommends special training for counselors to eliminate sexism in career counseling. Simpson (1972) offered 11 specific steps in "Career Education—Feminine Version," including efforts by elementary educators to enlarge girls' vocational self-concepts; a variety of single and married role models; new curriculum materials portraying women in a variety of constructive life styles and occupational roles; teacher orientation to vocational preparation of women; women's history courses in social studies; training programs including opportunity to prepare for dual roles; and alternatives and supplements to in-school instruction related to vocational preparation.

Practitioner Examples

A number of creative teachers and counselors have moved beyond the conceptual level and have developed units, courses, and strategies for promoting female development. A few examples are presented here.

Ann Schmid, a fourth grade teacher, uses "the teachable moment" to help her children become sensitive to sexism and sex-role stereotyping in their readers and other curriculum materials. They wrote letters of protest to Hallmark regarding ways in which boys and girls were portrayed on greeting cards; they examined their illustrated *ABC of Occupations* book and rewrote it when they found sterotypic presentations of occupations (A as in Astronaut, B as in Beautician) with new illustrations. Both boys and girls work at the tool bench, bake cakes, rewrite stereotyped materials, and interview workers in nontraditional occupations.

Suzanne Laurich, a first grade teacher, in a series of career development lessons has boys and girls look at such topics as "Who Am I?" "Workers Who Come to Our Home," "Our Parents' Jobs," "Day Workers and Night Workers," and "What I Can Do" in nonstereotypic ways.

Ronnie Tallen and Claire Allyn helped boys and girls get more in touch with their own feelings, values, and self-concepts through a three-week unit on Male and Female Images. Students learned to analyze sex-role images on TV, in newspapers, and on radio; read fact and fiction, biographies and autobiographies; did independent study on women's issues (including the school's athletic policies); studied women in nontraditional occupations; interviewed workers in sex-typed occupations; and even analyzed their teachers' and parents' sexist language. Anne Saxenmeyer taught a Women's Liberation Unit directly in her ninth grade civics class. A counselor and a teacher, Georgia Loughren and Helen Olson, teamed to develop a three-week group counseling course on Women in the '70s. Students built a support system and looked at their own attitudes and expectations through a variety of awareness exercises, did some values voting regarding their attitudes about women's roles, and were exposed to a variety of role models through class visitors and field interviews—for example, the traditional homemaker, the dual career, the two-career family, the single adoptive parent, the single career woman.

Two senior high social studies teachers teamed to create a unit on Women in History under the Minnesota Council on Quality Education. Students investigate several facets of the role and status of women and look at the issues critically. A senior high counselor created a questionnaire for faculty to look at their own attitudes toward women's roles; another created a model for a faculty workshop on sexism in education; a group of counselors and teachers developed an interdisciplinary program called Women's Seminar in which senior women (and later senior men by their own request) spent 10 three-hour weekly sessions looking at women's changing roles and human sexuality. Another senior high counselor developed a Women in Literature course intended to facilitate female development by studying the lives of women who had functioned at higher levels of development based on the Kohlberg Scales of Moral Development and Loevinger Scales of Ego Strength. Erickson (1973) through a curriculum intervention found that it was possible to promote female growth through a positive program designed for that purpose.

Besides the K-12 efforts there has been a burgeoning of activity to promote female development at the post-high level, particularly on college and university campuses. Besides the traditional counseling, these interventions have taken such forms as women's resource centers; courses on assertive training, career planning, and women's search for identity; personal assessment and career planning groups; courses for the mature or adult student, women's support groups (counseling groups, job-seeking groups, feminist groups, human sexuality groups), and special seminars and conferences, women's study programs, creation of alternate study options, and the like; research topics related to women's development; units on sexism in human relations courses; creation of multimedia presentations and video cassettes for training of counselors; and creating and evaluating intervention models.

The Task for Counselors

It is probably safe to say that we have just begun to chip away at the top of the iceberg of the enormous problems and implications of counseling and career development of girls and women. The topic, like the larger career development area itself, is still unfinished business; there is much we need to know about female career patterns, self-concepts, aspirations, and decisions. And yet we know enough to chart some humanistic paths which will lead to greater options and genuine freedom of choice for both men and women. The following poems express the essence of my concern—the first a negative example, the second a positive one.

Following is a song students are asked to learn in a career education program in a junior high school, sung to the tune "Jingle Bells":

> *Styling hair, styling hair*
> *To make you gals look neat,*
> *So that hubbys when at home*
> *Will see their wives look neat.*
> *Fixing twirls, fixing swirls,*
> *Maybe a French bob,*
> *Don't let feminine society*
> *Look like crumby slobs.*

Besides being bad poetry, this is not career education but career miseducation. This is not what we are about as teachers and counselors involved in career development programs. In contrast, the following poem appeared a few years ago in an elementary level career development project which offered a variety of methods to help children gain more positive self-concepts, to upgrade their aspirations, to feel good about themselves. The poem appeared on the cover of the project booklet.

> *DISCOVERY: A CHILD'S FIRST AWARENESS OF HERSELF*
>
> *She looks into the mirror with eager eyes,*
> *And all the world is bells, and she is wise.*
> *The wonder of herself she sees therein.*
> *And longs to play the world's violin.*
>
> *Her name is written and no turning tide*
> *Will wash it from the sand or oceans wide.*
> *She feeds on knowledge and her mind is stirred,*
> *Fed on the beauty of a thought, a word.*
>
> *Where she must walk, a slant of light has shown,*
> *Knowledge is the lamp her heart has known.*
> *And when she thinks of all her eyes might find,*
> *She says, "Quickly, pull the cord and lift the blind."*
> *Adapted from Kaleen Sherman*

This poem, adapted from Kaleen Sherman, is a beautiful expression of the openness to life, to knowledge, to growth that a child feels. And yet we do something to females in our society as they grow up, something that keeps the blinds drawn on many of their possibilities and potentialities.

When I say "adapted," I should hasten to explain that the poem originally was written using "he." But isn't it equally beautiful and equally meaningful with "she"? It is exciting to think what we as counselors could do, even with some slight changes, a few facts, some innovative approaches, and a commitment to open the blinds of the school and eliminate our own biases to promote the positive growth and career development of our female clients along with our male clients.

References

ANASTASI, A. "Sex Differences in Vocational Choices." *National Catholic Conference Journal, 13* (4), 1969 (63–76).

BEM, S. J. and BEM, D. J. "Training the Woman to Know Her Place: The Social Antecedents of Women in the World of Work." Palo Alto, California: Stanford University, 1971 (mimeo).

BINGHAM, W. C. and HOUSE, E. "Counselors View Women and Work: Accuracy of Information." *The Vocational Guidance Quarterly*, 1973a (262–268).

BINGHAM, W. C. and HOUSE, E. "Counselors' Attitudes toward Women and Work." *Vocational Guidance Quarterly, 22*, 1973b (16–23).

BIRK, J., COOPER, J. and TANNEY, F. "Racial and Sex Role Stereotyping." In "Career Information Illustration." College Park: University of Maryland, 1973 (mimeo).

BROVERMAN, I. K. et al. "Sex-Role Stereotypes and Clinical Judgments of Mental Health." *Journal of Consulting and Clinical Psychology, 34*, 1970 (1–7).

ERICKSON, L. V. "Personal Growth for Women: A Cognitive-Developmental Curriculum." University of Minnesota, March, 1973 (mimeo).

FLANAGAN, JOHN D. and JUNG, STEVEN M. *Progress in Education: A Sample Survey* (1960–1970). Palo Alto: American Institutes for Research, December, 1971.

FRIEDERSDORF, N. "A Comparative Study of Counselor Attitudes toward the Further Educational and Vocational Plans of High School Girls." Paper delivered at American Personnel and Guidance Convention, San Diego, February, 1973.

GOODMAN, J. and SCHLOSSBERG, N. K. "A Woman's Place: Children's Sex Stereotyping of Occupations." *Vocational Guidance Quarterly, 20*, 1972 (226–270).

HANSEN, L. SUNNY. "We Are Furious (Female) But We Can Shape Our Own Development." *Personnel and Guidance Journal, 51*, October, 1972 (87–93).

HANSEN, L. S. "A Career Development Curriculum Framework to Promote Female Growth." In M. A. Guttman and P. Donn (Eds.), *Women and ACES— Perspective and Issues*. Washington, D.C.: Association for Counselor Education and Supervision, 1974a.

HANSEN, L. S. "The Career Development Process for Women: Current Views and Programs." In T. Hoshenshil (Ed.) *Career Development of Women.* Conference Proceedings, Virginia Polytechnic Institute, Blacksburg, Va., March 7–8, 1974b.

HARTLEY, R. E. "Children's Concepts of Male and Female Roles." *Merrill-Palmer Quarterly, 6,* 1960 (83–91).

HAWLEY, P. Perceptions of Male Models of Femininity Related to Career Choice. *Journal of Counseling Psychology, 19,* 1972 (308–313).

HOCHSCHILD, A. R. "A Review of Sex Role Research." In J. Huber (Ed.), *Changing Women in a Changing Society. American Journal of Sociology, 4,* 1973 (1011–1029).

HOFFMAN, L. "Replication of the Matina Horner Study." In D. McGuigan (Ed.), *New Research on Women.* Ann Arbor, Michigan: University of Michigan, 1974.

HORNER, M. S. "Women's Will to Fail." *Psychology Today,* 1968 (36–38).

HOYT, KENNETH B. "The Counselor's Role in Career Education." APGA Position Paper presented at National APGA Convention, New Orleans, Louisiana, March 11, 1974 (mimeo).

IMPACT. When I Grow Up I Want to Be Married. California Commission on the Status of Women, 1972 (simulation game).

KIEVIT, MARY BACH. *Review and Synthesis of Research on Women in the World of Work.* Columbus, Ohio: The Center for Vocational and Technical Education, The Ohio State University, 1972.

KREPS, JUANITA. *Sex in the Marketplace: American Women at Work.* Baltimore: Johns Hopkins Press, 1971.

LEWIS, E. C. "Counselors and Girls." *Journal of Counseling Psychology, 12,* 1965 (159–166).

MACCOBY, E. E. "Sex Differences in Intellectual Functioning." In E. E. Maccoby (Ed.), *The Development of Sex Differences.* Stanford, California: Stanford University Press, 1966.

MATTHEWS, E. E. and TIEDEMAN, D. "Attitudes toward Careers and Marriage and the Development of Life Style in Young Women." *Journal of Counseling Psychology, 11,* 1964 (375–384).

MATTHEWS, E. E. et al. *Counseling Girls and Women over the Life Span.* Washington, D.C.: National Vocational Guidance Association, 1972 (375–384).

MINNESOTA DEPARTMENT OF EDUCATION. *Career Education Resource Guides.* Seven Learning Packages, 1972.

MITCHELL, E. "What About Career Education for Girls?" *Educational Leadership,* December, 1972 (233–236).

NATIONAL INSTITUTE OF EDUCATION. *Guidelines for Assessment of Sex Bias and Sex Fairness in Career Interest Inventories.* Washington, D.C.: Department of Health, Education, and Welfare, 1974.

NEW JERSEY COMMISSION ON STATUS OF WOMEN. *Dick and Jane as Victims.* Princeton, New Jersey, 1972.

PIETROFESA, J. J. and SCHLOSSBERG, N. K. "Perspectives on Counseling Bias: Implications for Counselor Education." *The Counseling Psychologist, 4,* No. 1, 1973 (44–54). (Special Issue on Counseling Women)

PSATHAS, G. "Toward a Theory of Occupational Choice for Women." *Sociology and Social Research, 52,* 1968 (253–268).

RAND, LORRAINE and MILLER, ANNA. A Developmental Sectioning of Women's Careers and Marriage Attitudes and Life Plans. *Journal of Vocational Behavior, 2,* 1972 (317–331).

SCHLOSSBERG, N. K. and GOODMAN, J. "Imperative for Change: Counselor Use of the Strong Vocational Interest Blanks." *Impact, 2,* 1972 (26–29).

SIMPSON, E. J. "Career Education—Feminine Version." Paper presented at

Regional Seminar/Workshop on *Women in the World of Work,* Technical Education Research Centers, Chicago, Illinois, October, 1972.

SUPER, DONALD E. *The Psychology of Careers.* New York: Harper Brothers, 1957.

TENNYSON, W. WESLEY; HANSEN, L. S.; KLAURENS, M. K. and ANTHOLZ, M. B. *Teaching and Counseling for Career Development.* St. Paul: Minnesota Department of Education, in press.

THOMAS, H. and STEWART, N. R. Counselor Response to Female Clients with Deviate and Conforming Career Goals. *Journal of Counseling Psychology, 18,* 1971 (352–357).

TYLER, L. E. "Counseling Girls and Women in the Year 2000." In E. Matthews (Ed.), *Counseling Girls and Women over the Life Span.* Washington, D.C.: National Vocational Guidance Association, 1972 (89–96).

WEITZMAN, L. J. et al. "Sex-Role Socialization in Picture Books for Pre-School Children." *American Journal of Sociology, 77,* 1972 (1125–1150).

ZYTOWSKI, D. G. "Toward a Theory of Career Development for Women." *Personnel and Guidance Journal, 47,* 1969 (660–664).

Girls' Careers—
Expression of Identity

Lewis E. Patterson

Few girls today leave school at any level with clear and realistic career plans. This continues to be true, even though the guidance and counseling profession has focused on educational and vocational choice since its beginnings at the turn of the century. This is true even when women are an ever-increasing portion of the American labor force.

It is necessary to consider what it is about girls—or about counselors —that has contributed to this constant deficiency in planning. It is important for counselors to develop programs and practices that can assist girls in making plans consistent with today's (and tomorrow's) world.

Evidence supporting the limited vocational planning of girls has long been available. The early [5] pioneer work in vocational development theory showed that girls do not choose college majors with voca-

Reprinted from *Vocational Guidance Quarterly,* **21:**269–275 (1973), by permission of the publisher and author. Copyright 1973 American Personnel and Guidance Association. Reprinted with permission.

tional implications. Douvan and Kaye [3] showed that girls typically do not engage in reality planning and do not understand the vocational-instrumental functions of their education.

The dearth of recent research on women's career development makes it difficult to discover significant shifts toward more effective planning. Astin and Myint [1] studied Project TALENT data bank information and found that the women's career choices showed great instability between the 12th grade and the five-year period after high school. Nearly half of the studied female population had changed career plans during that period.

There are six significant reasons why vocational counseling seems to have so little impact on girls:

1. By the time girls reach secondary schools, where most vocational counseling begins, they have usually become predisposed by enculturation to express the "feminine core" of personality, at the expense of effective planning encompassing both the sex role and the competitive achievement role [8].
2. Some counselors, unfortunately, are as unaware as their clients of the societal changes that have made career planning for girls more necessary. They still operate within the old stereotype of the girl having a career "to fall back on." Some counselors do not know that 40 per cent of all married women are currently employed and that a girl who marries and has two children can still anticipate a 22-year period of employment during her life [15, p. 18].
3. Counselors generally do not directly confront the issues of sex identity and vocational identity as an interrelated package. Therefore they fail to deal with the intrapsychic conflict experienced by the adolescent girl client.
4. Vocational counselors rarely use the full power of the vocational development theories in their work. Instead of concentrating on the life style, life space, and life stage of the client, they focus on those client attributes that can more easily be codified for trait-factor matching.
5. Counselors often do not face job discrimination and do not prepare female clients to meet the challenge of finding career satisfaction in spite of discrimination.
6. Time limitations on contact between counselor and client often reduce the likelihood of significant impact.

The Reluctant Client

The most important limitation on effective counseling is the adolescent girl herself—the uninterested vocational counseling client. In a sense, such girls are victims of a cultural lag, where home and school have conditioned them to accept a role definition that is no longer valid. They have been encouraged to see the homemaker and mother role as the primary female role, while boys know from an early age that they will be expected to seek employment.

The Women's Liberation Movement has made a contribution by highlighting this lag and discounting outdated stereotypes regarding sex-determined roles. It is significant that in a study of achieving women [4], three-fourths had mothers who had worked at some time, and 84 per cent reported that their parents had expressed attitudes supporting career planning.

Stefflre [11] suggests that career is most "psychologically central" for the masculine sex, the middle class, and Western culture. Thus, being female seems automatically to delete one impetus for career centrality, and being female and a member of either the disadvantaged or the advantaged social class would relegate career to a comparatively insignificant part of the psyche.

Douvan and Kaye [3] reported that much of what appears to be reality planning in girls masks their real interest in marriage. This apparent reality planning does not initiate a long-term investment of psychic energy necessary to effective career development. Without such investment, it is the chance factors in life that determine whether or not a girl will work and what work she will do. Unfortunately, vocational counselors rarely spend much time talking with girls about marriage, despite the finding that sex-role fantasy and planning marriage are important factors in limiting girls' other reality planning.

Two Identity Issues

To assist girls ably in developing career plans, counselors must understand the typical girl's priorities in the expenditure of psychic energies. There are elements of intrapsychic conflict in the vocational development of a girl, derived from two aspects of her identity which are often contradictory in her mind and in the collective mind of society. The two identity issues are:

1. The acceptance of her sex role, including selecting a partner and probably establishing a home and caring for children. Accepting this role provides substantial outlets for nurturance.
2. The acceptance of her assets and liabilities as they pertain to vocational and economic patterns of the society in which he lives. Accepting the vocational role provides substantial outlets for competitive achievement [9, p. 14].

The demands of home and family are often in conflict with the demands of employment for men as well as for women. In the case of women, however, the cultural expectations of the domestic role, as well as the physiological fact of childbearing, impose far greater limitations on the vocational role.

Girls can resolve the conflict imposed by the two potential identities and can seek fulfillment in several ways:

Accept the sex role, being exclusively a wife and mother.
Accept the sex role, perhaps also taking employment but with no career implications.
Accept the competitive achievement role (career) without marriage.
Accept the competitive achievement role (career) with marriage but with little expenditure of psychic energy on the nurturant aspects of marriage.
Attempt to balance both roles so as to gain fulfillment through both nurturant and competitive achievement activities.

Some girls face both identity crises simultaneously in adolescence, whereas others choose one or the other role with permanence. Some seek fulfillment in the sex role and face the career crisis only when they pass what they think is a marriageable age without a husband. Others choose the sex role at adolescence and face the career crisis later in life. It is likely that the career crisis is qualitatively different when faced at different life stages.

It is only the girl who accepts the sex role exclusively and with permanence who does not face choices about employment, and even she may experience intrapsychic conflict in the choice making process and in living with her choice.

At the time vocational counseling becomes available (usually in junior high school) girls are deeply involved in realizing their sexuality and related sex role, which in American culture has not typically included vocation as an integral element. Their thoughts about career remain indefinite and unrealistic. The evidence [3, 5] suggests that it is difficult for the adolescent girl to relate to typical vocational counseling approaches. Steinmann [12] says:

> Counselors must now be able to grasp the nature of intrapsychic conflicts of students. . . . This task is particularly urgent in counseling young women, and since role conflicts are so prevalent, the need for early counseling in school is especially urgent [p. 28].

Using Vocational Development Theories

It has become commonplace to suggest that a separate theory of vocational development should be created to account for the development of women. In the wake of theory making, it also has been common to ignore what is already known about vocational development. The broadly recognized theories of vocational development do provide concepts useful in vocational counseling with female clients. Girls in a pioneer [5] study moved through fantasy, tentative choice, and realistic stages, as did boys. But for girls, choices included the alternative of marriage. Deutsch [2] stated that the girl's intellectual development, social adjustment, and professional activity are all subject to disturbance if marriage fantasies become excessive.

Tiedeman's [14] decision making paradigm also is as applicable to decisions of girls as to decisions of boys. Tiedeman describes how an individual sets goals relevant to the environment in which those goals may be achieved, how one absorbs information from the environments in which he places himself, and how he ultimately influences those environments and maintains himself in those environments. The data that girls must process in making decisions undoubtedly differs from boys' data, but the process is the same.

Hershenson [6], in organizing vocational development theories around the concept of energy expenditure, proposes five developmental stages. The stage-relevant vocational questions indicating how energy is spent are: Am I? Who am I? What can I do? What will I do? What meaning does what I do have for me? This sequence of questions is useful in counseling girls with respect to both the sex role and the competitive achievement role they wish to develop. Hershenson states that a common fault in vocational counseling comes from asking questions about will and value (those late in the sequence) before identity questions have been asked and processed.

Other theorists, notably Super [13], Roe [10], and Holland [7], have contributed concepts useful in thinking about girls' vocations, even though their study groups have been predominantly male. Super's major contribution relates career choice to the expression of self-concept. For women, it would seem that self-concept is the pervasive variable that determines not only what career, but also whether a career. Roe's work ties the satisfaction of childhood needs within the family context to ultimate vocational motivation. Holland proposes a career typology system, organizing careers according to the personality attributes required for success and satisfaction.

The vocational development theorists have contributed germinal ideas that are useful in vocational counseling with women. More research with these ideas using female study groups is needed, but in the interim, some counselor perspective for counseling girls emerges from an understanding of available literature.

Beginnings for More Effective Counseling for Girls

Counselors who can use the knowledge that exists about the psychology of women and vocational development can go a long way in developing vocational interests in the adolescent girl. It is appropriate for counselors who have this depth of understanding to take the lead in establishing activities and practices that contribute to realistic career planning by girls.

A kindergarten-to-college program for vocational development could lead to greater fulfillment for women by encouraging planning.

Counselors and teachers should begin in the early grades of school to predispose girls to thinking in career terms. By attitude and action it should be made clear to young girls that it is acceptable for them to plan to work, and that girls—as surely as boys—can be respected for their work contributions. Women who have resolved the marriage and career conflict in all varieties of ways should be invited to participate in elementary school programs, either as staff or as guests. While there may be some usefulness to field trips where girls see women working, it is more important that girls have an opportunity to learn the meaning of work to those women. Women coming into the schools for that purpose can make an impact.

Westervelt [16] has also pointed to the elementary school's capacity for extinguishing "prosocial aggression" in young girls. She defines prosocial aggression as an initiative in organizing people to get things done. The little girl organizer in our schools often finds herself rejected by peer and teacher alike as "bossy" and unfeminine. Thus, by the end of elementary school, boys, who initially exhibit less prosocial aggression than girls, have taken the lead.

It is perhaps useful to help boys develop prosocial aggression, but it is doubtful that in the process girls must learn to give it up. The counselor, in his role as a human development specialist, can help set a tone more favorable to developing girls' potential through consultation with staff and through inservice training programs.

As girls begin to mature, group guidance activities focused directly on the psychology of women should be initiated in junior high school. These groups might follow the now common sessions explaining physiological maturation. With a background of exposure to achieving and nurturing women during the elementary years, pubescent girls would be interested in a fairly cognitive picture of how women may resolve role conflict related to sex identity and career identity. Material similar to that presented here as two identity issues could serve as a starting point. This kind of activity would expand a girl's awareness of the options open to her well beyond her family experience and would emphasize the fact that she has a choice about what she will do. Timing this activity to precede the dating years would reduce the danger of planning activity becoming lost in marriage fantasy. Parent and teacher groups focused on the same content would also be useful.

At the high school level, counselors must be prepared to deal with the conflict that is now personal and real. Counselors cannot afford the insulation of saying, by word or action, "I'm interested in your career, but your dating behavior and sex life are your own private business." For women, vocation and sexuality are so closely bound together that to treat one without the other in counseling can only lead to irrelevance. Individual and small group counseling would be the appropriate forum. Opportunity should exist for counseling with couples and heterosexual groups. Provision should also be made for work with parents as needed and desired by students.

Better counselor education and more realistic counselor load would resolve most of the remaining problems in counseling for girls. Counselors must avoid giving outdated and irrelevant information. If counselors have the training and time to enter meaningful counseling collaboration with their clients, outdated advice will subside in favor of informed leadership and understanding.

The outcome of such a program should be greater fulfillment of women, through the vehicle of effective and honest recognition during the developmental years of the intrapsychic conflict associated with sex-role and career-role attainment.

References

1. ASTIN, H. S., and MYINT, T. Career development of young women during the post-high school years. *Journal of Counseling Psychology,* 1971, *18,* 369–393.
2. DEUTSCH, H. *The psychology of women: A psychoanalytic interpretation.* Vol. I. New York: Grune & Stratton, 1944.
3. DOUVAN, E., and KAYE, C. Motivational factors in college entrance. In N. Sanford (Ed.), *The American college.* New York: Wiley, 1962. Pp. 199–224.
4. GINZBERG, E., BERG, I. E., BROWN, C. A., HERMA, J. L., YOHALEM, A. M., and GORELICK, S. *Life styles of educated women.* New York: Columbia University Press, 1966.
5. GINZBERG, E., GINSBURG, S. W., AXELROD, S., and HERMA, J. L. *Occupational choice.* New York: Columbia University Press, 1951.
6. HERSHENSON, D. B. Life-stage vocational development system. *Journal of Counseling Psychology,* 1968, *15,* 23–30.
7. HOLLAND, J. L. A theory of vocational choice. *Journal of Counseling Psychology,* 1959, *6,* 35–45.
8. MATTHEWS, E. Elements of a theory of career development for girls. Unpublished paper, Harvard Graduate School of Education, 1957.
9. MATTHEWS, E. Counseling girls and women over the life span. Washington, D.C.: National Vocational Guidance Association, 1972. (Monograph)
10. ROE, A. Early determinants of vocational choice. *Journal of Counseling Psychology,* 1957, *4,* 212–217.
11. STEFFLRE, B. Vocational development: Ten propositions in search of a theory. *Personnel and Guidance Journal,* 1966, *44,* 611–616.
12. STEINMANN, A. Female-role perception as a factor in counseling. *Journal of the National Association of Women Deans and Counselors,* 1970, *34,* 27–33.
13. SUPER, D. E. A theory of vocational development. *American Psychologist,* 1953, *8,* 185–190.
14. TIEDEMAN, D. V. Decision and vocational development: A paradigm and its implication. *Personnel and Guidance Journal,* 1961, *40,* 15–20.
15. WALDMAN, E. Women at work: Changes in the labor force activity of women. *Monthly Labor Review,* 1970, *93,* 10–18.
16. WESTERVELT, E. The feminine agenda: Influences of biology, society, and culture on the lives of women. Paper presented at workshop: Counseling Girls and Women over the Life Span, University of Oregon, July 6–17, 1970.

UNIT BIBLIOGRAPHY

EPSTEIN, CYNTHIA F. "Encountering the Male Establishment: Sex-Status Limits on Women's Careers in the Professions." *American Journal of Sociology,* **75** (1970), 965–982.

FARMER, HELEN S. "Helping Women to Resolve the Home-Career Conflict." *Personnel and Guidance Journal,* **49** (1971), 795–801.

FARMER, HELEN S., and MARTIN J. BOHN, JR. "Home-Career Conflict Reduction and the Level of Career Interest in Women." *Journal of Counseling Psychology,* **17** (1970), 228–232.

HARMON, LENORE W. "The Childhood and Adolescent Career Plans of College Women." *Journal of Vocational Behavior,* **1** (1971), 45–56.

JACOBSON, DAN. "Rejection of the Retiree Role: A Study of Female Industrial Workers in Their 50's." *Human Relations,* **27** (1974), 477–492.

KALEY, MAUREEN M. "Attitudes Toward the Dual Role of the Married Professional Woman." *American Psychologist,* **22** (1967), 301–306.

KING, LOURDES MIRANDA. "Puertorriquenas in the United States." *Civil Rights Digest,* **6** (1974), 20–28.

KOMISAR, LUCY. "Where Feminism Will Lead: An Impetus for Social Change." *Civil Rights Digest,* **6** (1974), 2–9.

LEWIS, JUDITH. Guest Ed. "Women and Counselors." *The Personnel and Guidance Journal* (1972), Special Issue, 51.

LOOFT, WILLIAM R. "Sex Differences in the Expression of Vocational Aspirations by Elementary School Children." *Developmental Psychology,* **5** (1971), 366.

MOSTOW, E., and P. NEWBERRY. "Work Role and Depression in Women: A Comparison of Workers and Housewives in Treatment." *American Journal of Orthopsychiatry,* **45** (1975) 538–548.

NIETO, CONSUELO. "Chicanas and the Women's Rights Movement: A Perspective." *Civil Rights Digest,* **6** (1974), 36–42.

ORDEN, SUSAN R., and NORMAN M. BRADBURN. "Working Wives and Marriage Happiness." *American Journal of Sociology,* **74** (1969), 392–407.

PENN, J. ROGER, and MARY E. GABRIEL. "Role Constraints Influencing the Lives of Women." *The School Counselor,* **23** (1976), 252–256.

QUERY, JOY M. N., and THOMAS C. KURUVILLA. "Male and Female Adolescent Achievement and Maternal Employment." *Adolescence,* **10** (1975), 353–356.

SAARIO, TERRY N., CAROL NAGY JACKLIN, and CAROL KEHR TITTLE. "Sex Role Stereotyping in the Public Schools." *Harvard Educational Review,* **43** (1973), 386–416.

SIEGEL, CLAIRE LYNN FLEET, "Sex Differences in the Occupational Choices of Second Graders." *Journal of Vocational Behavior,* **3** (1973), 15–19.

THOMAS, ARTHUR H., and NORMAN R. STEWART. "Counselor Response to Female Clients with Deviate and Conforming Career Goals." *Journal of Counseling Psychology,* **18** (1971), 352–357.

VANEK, JOANN. "Variations in a Sixty Hour Week: Trends in Women's Time in Work in the USA." *Ekistics,* **39** (1975), 37–39.

WITT, SHIRLEY HILL. "Native Women Today: Sexism and the Indian Woman," *Civil Rights Digest,* **6** (1974), 43–45.

YOSHIOKA, ROBERT B. "Asian American Women: Stereotyping Asian Women." *Civil Rights Digest,* **6** (1974), 43–45.

ZATLIN, CAROLE E., MARTHA STORANDT, and JACK BOTWINICK. "Personality and Values of Women Continuing Their Education After Thirty-Five Years of Age." *Journal of Gerontology,* **28** (1973), 216–221.